In *The Origins of Industrial Capitalism in India*, Rajnarayan Chandavarkar presents the first major study of the relationship between labour and capital in early twentieth-century India. The author examines not only how a labour force formed in Bombay, but more generally how working-class responses to industrialization shaped capitalist strategies. He follows workers as they migrated from their villages to the city and investigates the social linkages which conditioned their opportunities in the labour market, their experience of the workplace and the patterns of their daily and long-term resistance.

Chandavarkar finds the rigid distinctions – between factory workers and casual labour, peasant migrants and urban proletarians, neighbourhood and workplace – which have dominated thinking about the subject untenable. The social organization of the neighbourhood significantly influenced both workers' bargaining power and the structure of authority at the workplace. He also demonstrates that large-scale factory production, far from increasing their homogeneity, accentuated the differences between workers. Thus the sectionalism of the working class was not simply the result of their caste, religious, village or other traditional ties, but was actively produced by the process of industrialization.

Finally Chandavarkar analyses the emergence of Bombay's capitalists, the development of the cotton-textile industry, the business strategies of the mill-owners, the crises of the 1920s and 1930s and the discourse of rationalization which it stimulated.

This study of industrialization and class formation in colonial India illuminates the working of similar processes not only in 'developing' societies but also in what are described as 'advanced' capitalist societies. It will therefore be of interest to students and specialists of Indian and comparative history, labour movements and colonial and 'developing' societies.

Cambridge South Asian Studies

The Origins of Industrial Capitalism in India

The Origins of Industrial Capitalism in India

Business strategies and the working classes in Bombay, 1900–1940

Rajnarayan Chandavarkar

*Assistant Director of Research, History,
University of Cambridge and
Fellow of Trinity College*

CAMBRIDGE
UNIVERSITY PRESS

UNIVERSITY COLLEGE OF THE FRASER VALLEY LIBRARY

PUBLISHED BY THE PRESS SYNDICATE OF THE UNIVERSITY OF CAMBRIDGE
The Pitt Building, Trumpington Street, Cambridge, United Kingdom

CAMBRIDGE UNIVERSITY PRESS
The Edinburgh Building, Cambridge CB2 2RU, UK
40 West 20th Street, New York NY 10011–4211, USA
477 Williamstown Road, Port Melbourne, VIC 3207, Australia
Ruiz de Alarcón 13, 28014 Madrid, Spain
Dock House, The Waterfront, Cape Town 8001, South Africa

http://www.cambridge.org

First published 1994
First paperback edition 2002

A catalogue record for this book is available from the British Library

Library of Congress Cataloguing in Publication data
Chandavarkar, Rajnarayan.
The origins of industrial capitalism in India: business
strategies and the working classes in Bombay, 1900–1940 / Rajnarayan
Chandavarkar.
   p. cm. – (Cambridge South Asian studies)
Includes bibliographical references and index.
ISBN 0 521 41496 2
1. Working class – India – Bombay – History – 20th century. 2. Cotton
textile industry – India – Bombay – History – 20th century. 3. Bombay
(India) – Industries – History – 20th century. 4. Capitalism – India –
Bombay – History – 20th century. I. Title. II. Series.
HD8690.B6C43 1992
305.5′62′09547923–dc20 91-4276 CIP

ISBN 0 521 41496 2 hardback
ISBN 0 521 52595 0 paperback

To my mother and the memory of my father

Contents

Acknowledgements

In the writing of this book, I have benefited from the support of institutions and the generosity of friends.

For their help I would like to thank the custodians and staff of the Maharashtra State Archives and the Mumbai Marathi Grantha Sangrahalaya in Bombay; of the record rooms of the Bombay Millowners' Association, the Commissioner of Police, Bombay and the Deputy Inspector-General, Criminal Investigation Department, Maharashtra; the Gokhale Institute of Politics and Economics, Pune; the National Archives of India and the Nehru Memorial Museum and Library in New Delhi; the India Office Library and the British Library in London; the University Library and the Centre of South Asian Studies, Cambridge.

I am grateful to Shri N.M. Wagle who made many useful suggestions, helped me to gain access to valuable material and arranged for me to make repeated visits to cotton mills, and to Shri H.R. Thanawalla of the Bombay Dyeing and Manufacturing Company who also facilitated several visits to their mills, allowed me to look at the minute books of their Board of Directors and enabled me to gain access to the records of the Bombay Millowners' Association. Shri R.G. Gokhale, Labour Officer of the Bombay Millowners' Association for about three decades from the 1930s, patiently answered numerous questions and lent me some of his own papers. I learnt a great deal from conversations and more or less formal interviews with a number of millworkers, trade-union leaders and political activists; some of these are acknowledged in the bibliography and cited in the footnotes. But I would in particular like to record my gratitude to Shri P.G. Sawant and Shri S.G. Sardesai, who spent many hours talking to me and pointed me in fruitful directions. For granting me access to material in his care, I would like to thank Shri R.L.N. Vijayanagar, Secretary of the Bombay Millowners' Association.

For their generous support, I am grateful to the Master and Fellows of Trinity College, Cambridge, and the Managers of the Smuts Memorial Fund. Lionel Carter, Secretary–Librarian of the Centre of South Asian Studies, has been unstinting in his help. At various stages of this work, I have profited from the comments and suggestions of Professor John Saville and Dr Tapan Raychaudhuri. I have enjoyed the help and support of numerous friends and colleagues: Chris Baker, Arup Banerji, Chris Bayly, Ruchira Chatterji, David Feldman, Cynthia Holton, Joanna Innes, Julian Jackson, Gordon Johnson, Polly O'Hanlon, Eve Rosenhaft, Gareth Stedman Jones, Faraz Tyebjee, Hari Vasudevan and David Washbrook – and especially Anil Seal, who first brought me to the study of Indian history and has always been a source of friendship and encouragement. I owe a special debt, for her perception and support, to Jennifer Davis whose influence and perspectives are to be found throughout the book.

Abbreviations

AICC	All-India Congress Committee
AIMO	All-India Manufacturers' Organisation
AITUC	All-India Trade Union Congress
BB&CI Railway	Bombay, Baroda & Central Indian Railway
BDEC	Bombay Disturbances Enquiry Committee
BIT	City of Bombay Improvement Trust
BMOA	Bombay Millowners' Association
BPBEC	Bombay Provincial Banking Enquiry Committee
BPP, SAI	Bombay Presidency Police, Secret Abstracts of Intelligence
BPTUC	Bombay Provincial Trade Union Congress
BRIC	Bombay Riots Inquiry Committee
BSEC	Bombay Strike Enquiry Committee
BTLU	Bombay Textile Labour Union
CEHI	The Cambridge Economic History of India
Census, 1864	Census of the Island of Bombay taken on 2nd February 1864
Census, 1872	Census of the City of Bombay taken on 21st February 1872
Census, 1901	Census of India, 1901
Census, 1921	Census of India, 1921
Census, 1931	Census of India, 1931
EcHR	Economic History Review
Gazetteer	The Gazetteer of Bombay City and Island (Bombay, 1909)
GIP Railway	Great Indian Peninsular Railway
GOB	Government of Bombay
GOI	Government of India
HJE	Hitotsubashi Journal of Economics
Home (Poll.)	Home Department, Political
Home (Sp.)	Home Department, Special

ICBEC	Indian Central Banking Enquiry Committee
IESHR	Indian Economic and Social History Review
IFC	Indian Factory Commission, 1890
IFLC	Indian Factory Labour Commission
IIC	Indian Industrial Commission
IOR	India Office Library and Records
ITB	Indian Tariff Board
JAS	Journal of Asian Studies
MAS	Modern Asian Studies
MSA	Maharashtra State Archives
NAI	National Archives of India
NMML	Nehru Memorial Museum and Library
PP	Parliamentary Papers
Presidency Gazetteer	Gazetteer of the Bombay Presidency
PWD	Public Works Department
RCAI	Royal Commission on Agriculture in India
RCL	Royal Commission on Labour, 1892
RCLI	Royal Commission on Labour in India
RNNP	Report on the Native Newspapers Published in the Bombay Presidency
TLIC	Textile Labour Inquiry Committee
TOI	Times of India

Glossary

akhada:	gymnasium; meeting place; residence of religious mendicants
badli:	substitute, temporary or casual labourer
badliwallah:	substitute labourer
badmash:	'hooligan'
bania:	trader, money-lender, grain-dealer; also a caste name
bardan:	cotton waste
baroot:	dock labourers who specialized in stacking case cargo
bhaiya:	literally, 'brother'; used derisively in Bombay to describe migrants from the United Provinces
bidi:	a 'country' cigarette
cadjan:	coconut-palm leaves matted to form a thatch
chawl:	tenement
crores:	a unit of ten million
dada:	literally, 'elder brother'; used to describe a neighbourhood tough
dasturi:	a customary fee, perquisite, commission
dhoti:	a garment worn by men, wrapped around the waist
doffer:	occupation in cotton mills of workers who placed bobbins on or removed them from the spinning frame
dubash:	an intermediary, in the European trading companies and business houses
fazendari:	a type of land tenure prevalent in Bombay City
gali:	an alley or back-lane
gaon bhai:	literally, a 'village brother', a co-villager
ghat:	a mountain pass, landing place (e.g. for a ferry); a slope; the name of the mountain ranges along the east and west coasts of India
godown:	warehouse
halalkhores:	sweepers who removed refuse and excreta from houses and streets

hali:	agricultural bondsman; a form of labour servitude for debt
hamal:	porter, labourer
hartal:	a strike, cessation of work or trade in a dispute
hissa:	a share
hundi:	a bill of exchange
huqqah:	a pipe for smoking opium
huqqah-pani:	(slang) association; camaraderie, sociability
inam:	land held rent free as a gift from the state
inamdar:	holder of an inam
jagir:	a land grant from the state, usually free of revenue, associated with the power to collect revenues in the pre-colonial period
jaitha:	here, market
jamat:	council of a caste, neighbourhood or sect
jati:	endogamous unit of caste; a sub-caste
karkhana:	workshop
khadi:	coarse, homespun cloth, made famous by Gandhi as a nationalist symbol
khanavali:	an inn, boarding-house
khot, khoti:	land-revenue farming rights; later, superior proprietary rights in the Konkan. Khot: holder of these rights
Kshatriya:	the second of the four varnas or orders of the Hindu caste system, consisting in theory of warriors and kings
lathi:	stick, bludgeon
mahagai:	here, the dearness of the cost of living
maistry:	foreman, master-workman, artisan
mandali:	assembly, association, gathering
matadi:	dock labourers, especially those who moved heavy bags
maulvi:	scholar of Muslim law, a learned person
mela:	festival
maund:	a unit of about 82 lbs.
mochi:	cobbler
mofussil:	the provinces or hinterland
moholla:	neighbourhood, a quarter of a town
mowali:	a rough, thug, hooligan
mukadam:	foreman, labour contractor
nowghani:	labourer who moved bales of cotton in the cotton mills
panchayat:	council or tribunal, typically consisting of five people

pice:	small copper coin, 1/4 anna; slang for money in general
pugdee:	a deposit paid as security on the rental of a house or land
ryot:	tenant or cultivator
ryotwari:	the form of land-revenue settlement in southern and western India by which government sought to settle directly with the individual cultivator
sabha:	assembly, association
sarraf:	money-changer, banker
satyagraha:	truth-force; the term used by Gandhi for his technique of passive resistance
serang:	foreman who recruited and supervised labour among stevedores and ships' workers; frequently worked on contract
sowkar:	money-lender, banker
tabut:	shrine; a model of the tomb of Husain at Kerbala which is carried in procession during the Mohurram festival
taluk:	an administrative unit below the level of the district
tamasha:	a show or entertainment; folk theatre
tarwalla:	occupation in the preparatory departments of a cotton mill
tazia:	representation of Husain's tomb at Kerbala
tindal:	leader of a gang of labourers among stevedores and ships' workers
toli:	gang of men who levied contributions from shopkeepers for Mohurram and other festivals
toliwalla:	contractor and supervisor of shore labourers in the docks
ugarani:	the collection of money which is considered to be due
vakil:	pleader, attorney, authorized representative
vania:	*see* bania
vatan:	literally, 'native country'; hereditary rights to office, property, patrimony, privilege or means of subsistence
waaz:	sermon or discourse preached in a mosque
wadi:	a quarter or neighbourhood of a town

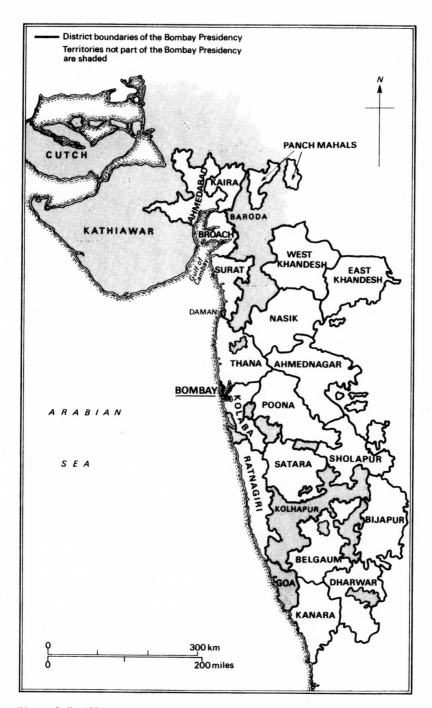

N

PANCH MAHALS

CUTCH

KAIRA

AHMEDABAD

KATHIAWAR

BARODA

BROACH

WEST
KHANDESH

EAST
KHANDESH

SURAT

Gulf of Cambay

DAMAN

NASIK

THANA

AHMEDNAGAR

BOMBAY

KOLABA

POONA

ARABIAN

SEA

RATNAGIRI

SATARA

SHOLAPUR

KOLHAPUR

BIJAPUR

BELGAUM

GOA

DHARWAR

KANARA

0   300 km
0   200 miles

Western India, 1931

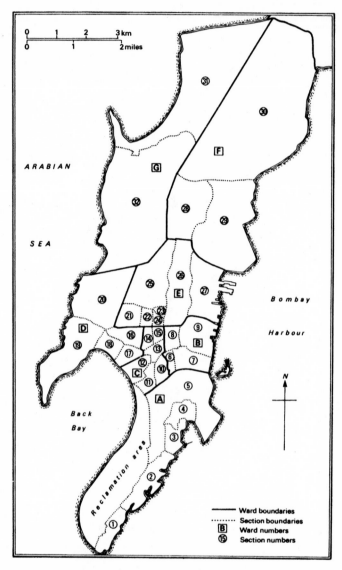

Municipal wards and districts of Bombay City, 1931 (section listed below)
A Ward: 1 Upper Colaba, 2 Lower Colaba, 3 Fort South, 4 Fort North,
5 Esplanade; *B Ward*: 6 Chakla, 7 Mandvi, 8 Umarkhadi, 9 Dongri;
C Ward: 10 Market, 11 Dhobi Talao, 12 Fanaswadi, 13 Bhuleshwar,
14 Kumbharwada, 15 Khara Talao; *D Ward*: 16 Khetwadi, 17 Girgaum,
18 Chaupati, 19 Walkeshwar, 20 Mahalaxmi; *E Ward*: 21 Tardeo,
22 Kamathipura, 23 First Nagpada, 24 Second Nagpada, 25 Byculla,
26 Tarwadi, 27 Mazagaon; *F Ward*: 28 Parel, 29 Sewri, 30 Sion; *G Ward*:
31 Mahim, 32 Worli.

1 Problems and perspectives

Among the dominant themes of modern history has been the social organization and political action of peasants and workers in the Third World. The changing relationship between the West and the Third World has been vitally affected by perceptions of their political attitudes and social aspirations. At the same time, assumptions about their social character and expectations about their political behaviour have informed the strategies of political leaders, activists and parties in the Third World. Yet these perceptions of the working classes and their political threat have been frequently generalized from a particular under-standing of the historical experience of the West, either by contrasting it with Third World societies taken as a whole, suggesting thereby that they need their own culturally specific explanatory frameworks, or by positing it as a model towards which other societies are assumed to be moving.

The study of Indian society, conceptualized in these ways, has posed intract-able problems. On the one hand, it is often treated as an exception in the discourse of social theory. Yet rules which require such gigantic exceptions to sustain themselves can only have the most limited power to explain. On the other hand, thus excluded from the dominant discourse of social theory, it is placed and examined with the category of 'developing' or 'Third World' societies. This has depended upon lumping together, within the general category of the Third World, societies which are as fundamentally different from each other as they may bear broad similarities with the West.[1] In addition, generali-zations arising out of the empirical investigations of Indian society have fitted awkwardly within the comparative frameworks offered by 'the sociology of development'. The aim of this book is to examine the social formation of the working classes, both as it was influenced by and as it shaped the nature and development of industrial capitalism in colonial India. The issues it considers are familiar and recurrent in the analysis of industrialization and its social consequences everywhere.

---

[1] For an interesting critque of the category of the Third World, see Carl E. Pletsch, 'The Three Worlds, or the Division of Social Scientific Labour, circa 1950–1975', *Comparative Studies in Society and History*, XXIII, 4 (1981), 519–38.

2   The origins of industrial capitalism in India

Problems

If the 1970s witnessed 'the return of the peasant to South Asian history',[2] the urban poor and the working classes have remained largely in exile. The character of the Indian economy has been widely perceived as essentially 'agrarian' and historiographical concerns have largely reflected this perception. Historians have continued to be predominantly concerned with land revenue systems, agrarian production and the rural social order and, more recently, with capturing the authentic experience, specifying the consciousness and distilling the 'popular culture' of the Indian peasant.[3] Indeed, this concentration upon the agrarian economy has often excluded its interplay with the urban and industrial economy. Its serious and often restrictive effect on the discussion of Indian society and politics has been to build into the analysis of its economy, especially in the colonial period, an implicit and natural dualism. By focussing upon the economy of labour in Bombay City, this book seeks to redress the resulting imbalance in the subject. It also attempts to cross the town–country divide and examine, among other questions, the interplay between the rural base and urban context, between the nature and experience of work in large-scale industry and of the casual-labour market, between the social relationships of the workplace and the urban neighbourhoods. The purpose of this study is to investigate the social processes underlying the economy of labour and its social formation in Bombay City in the early twentieth century.

The vast open spaces of the Indian countryside have often appeared to dominate its economy, the nature of its society and the style and character of its politics. Although large-scale industrialization was substantially under way in the late nineteenth century, it was still the case in the 1920s and 1930s that less than 10 per cent of the country's workforce was employed in manufacturing industry, and this proportion had barely increased by the 1960s.[4] Those who expected large-scale industry to form the lead sector of the economy soon

[2] E. Stokes, 'The Return of the Peasant to South Asian History', in his *The Peasant and the Raj: Studies in Agrarian Society and Peasant Rebellion in Colonial India* (Cambridge, 1978), pp. 265–89.

[3] For instance, in many of the essays in R. Guha (ed.), *Subaltern Studies*, 6 vols. (Delhi, 1982–9). An exception among the 'subaltern' historians is the attempt to address the question of working-class culture by D. Chakrabarty, *Rethinking Working-Class History: Bengal, 1890–1940* (Delhi, 1989).

[4] In fact, between 1901 and 1931, it fell from nearly 11 per cent to below 9 per cent, before rising marginally to over 9 per cent by 1961. See J. Krishnamurty, 'Secular Changes in Occupational Structure of the Indian Union, 1901–61', in *IESHR*, II, 1 (1965), 42–51. J. Krishnamurty, 'The Distribution of the Indian Working Force, 1901–1951', in K. N. Chaudhuri and C. J. Dewey (eds.), *Economy and Society: Essays in Indian Economic and Social History* (Delhi, 1979), pp. 258–76; J. Krishnamurty, 'The Occupational Structure', in D. Kumar (ed.), *The Cambridge Economic History of India* (henceforth *CEHI*), 2 vols., vol. II, *c. 1757–c. 1970* (Cambridge, 1982), 533–50.

discovered, although sometimes painfully, that it simply failed to lead. Yet the 'industrial sector' had acquired, by the early twentieth century, a significance out of proportion to its weak and indecisive effect on the Indian economy as a whole. In 1931, over four million workers were employed in the perennial and seasonal factories, the mines and railways in India.[5] The strength of this labour force was overshadowed by the number of workers employed in unregulated and, therefore, uncounted factories, which either used no mechanical power or else employed less than twenty workers. Between 1901 and 1951, the urban population expanded from 11 per cent to 17 per cent.[6] Moreover, thirty-six Indian towns had a population in excess of 100,000 in 1931.[7] Numerous workshops producing a wide range of goods and services mushroomed across the back streets and pavements of every town. Between 1914 and 1947, large-scale manufacturing formed the fastest-growing constituent of the secondary sector.[8] Moreover, this industrial economy impinged increasingly upon its rural hinterlands. Towns and cities provided a ready demand for its produce. Cash crops provided the raw material for industrial production. Migration to seasonal or permanent wage employment in the towns became a necessary recourse for rural smallholders in the Konkan and the Deccan, in the United Provinces and Bihar.

The political and social significance of the industrial sector was considerably greater than these stark figures suggest. In the immediate aftermath of the First World War, the British were only too aware of the value of developing a substantial industrial infrastructure in India. It could transform India, in keeping with changing strategic imperatives, from simply an oriental barrack into an ordnance base as well. It might help to restrict the dumping of foreign manufactures even as Britain's industrial decline was becoming increasingly apparent. It could assuage Indian capitalists who might otherwise turn their minds and their pockets to Congress. It would provide employment and ostensibly inject some dynamism into the Indian economy.

But here surfaced an inherent contradiction in colonial rule. In one sense, the British were concerned to develop the Indian economy, for great empires cannot prosper on bankrupt colonies. It would be impossible to continue pulling resources out of India unless they were also nurtured and replenished. On the other hand, industrial development, as in the case of cotton textiles, created

---

[5] *Report of the Royal Commission on Labour in India* (henceforth *RCLI*) (London, 1931), pp. 6, 75–6, 106, 136.
[6] A. Bose, 'Six Decades of Urbanization in India', *IESHR*, II, 1 (1965), 39.
[7] *Census of India, 1931* (henceforth *Census, 1931*), IX, *The Cities of the Bombay Presidency*, part I, *Report*, by H.T. Sorley (Bombay, 1933), p. 3.
[8] S. Sivasubramoniam, 'Income from the Secondary Sector in India, 1900–1947', *IESHR*, XIV, 4 (1977), 427–92; R.K. Ray, *Industrialization in India: Growth and Conflict in the Private Corporate Sector, 1914–47* (Delhi, 1979), pp. 14–21.

sources of competition, within limited and increasingly impoverished markets, for metropolitan capitalists whose fortunes were on the wane even if their political influence remained intact. Furthermore, it was one thing to encourage the development of Indian resources but quite another to field the consequences of rapid social change. The rapid advance of capitalism might erode the basis of the agrarian social order and kick away the props upon which the panoplies of imperial rule rested. The performance of the industrial economy and the effects of imperial rule upon it became a cornerstone of nationalist criticism. The aggregation of large masses of workers in the cities gave rise to anxieties about social conditions and their political consequences. Until 1918, industrial disputes 'when they occurred, were regarded with almost complete apathy by those not immediately concerned with them'.[9] The two decades which followed witnessed widespread, prolonged and sustained industrial action, in Bombay and Calcutta, in Sholapur and Ahmedabad, in Kanpur, Madras and Coimbatore.[10]

Bombay City provides an obvious site for the investigation of the industrial economy and its social context in India. By the late nineteenth century, it had become India's major port, a leading commercial and financial centre, the largest cotton market in Asia and a nodal point for the cotton piecegoods trade. The first cotton mills were built in the city in the 1850s. Significantly, the industry was pioneered and developed largely by Indian enterprise. As the industry developed, so its location grew more dispersed; nonetheless, Bombay City remained, until the end of the period, the largest centre of India's most important industry, which alone employed over a quarter of the labour force working in perennial factories. The hinterland of this bastion of Indian capital extended beyond its neighbouring districts across the Indian sub-continent. Inevitably, the issues and conflicts that concerned the city readily acquired a national significance. The sectional interests of its businessmen, its millowners and merchants, expressed, for instance, in their campaigns for higher tariffs, lower exchange rates or more generous budgets, quickly appeared as national

---

[9] B. Shiva Rao, *The Industrial Worker in India* (London, 1939), p. 13.

[10] V.B. Karnik, *Strikes in India* (Bombay, 1967); R. Newman, *Workers and Unions in Bombay, 1918–29: A Study of Organisation in the Cotton Mills* (Canberra, 1981); E.D. Murphy, *Unions in Conflict: A Comparative Study of Four South Indian Textile Centres 1918–39* (New Delhi, 1981); Chakrabarty, *Rethinking Working-Class History*; C. Revri, *The Indian Trade Union Movement* (New Delhi, 1972); V.B. Karnik, *Indian Trade Unions: A Survey* (Bombay, 1966); S.M. Pandey, *As Labour Organises: A Study of Unionism in the Kanpur Cotton Textile Industry* (New Delhi, 1970); P. Saha, *History of the Working Class Movement in Bengal* (New Delhi, 1978); S.D. Punekar, *Trade Unionism in India* (Bombay, 1948); D. Kooiman, 'Jobbers and the Emergence of Trade Unions in Bombay City', *International Review of Social History*, XXII, 3 (1977), 313–28; E.A. Ramaswamy, *The Worker and His Union: A Study in South India* (New Delhi, 1977).

concerns and became nationalist shibboleths. Labour disputes in the city could scarcely be contained within its mill districts and swiftly gained a national prominence. Bombay, as Lord Willingdon, the Governor, explained in 1917,

is the nerve-centre of India, both [*sic*] from a political, social and economic aspect. I say this knowing fully well that Calcutta will not agree! but it is a fact and will become more of a fact year by year. It is the metropolis to which princes, chiefs and citizens from all other parts are perpetually coming, and we have therefore opportunities which no one else has got of getting to know the general feeling on important political questions.[11]

Furthermore, in the 1920s and 1930s, Bombay became the most dramatic centre of working-class political action. Until 1914, strikes in the cotton mills were largely confined to individual departments and mills; at times, they affected groups of mills and even neighbourhoods. After the First World War, however, they were increasingly coordinated across the entire industry. Between 1919 and 1940, the industry witnessed eight general strikes, all of which lasted for at least a month; some continued for considerably longer periods. The general strike of 1928 began officially in April, after several mills had experienced extended strikes over the previous six months, and ended favourably for the workers in October. Between October 1928 and April 1929, more than seventy strikes occurred in the industry. Another general strike which began in April 1929 lasted nearly as long, although it was never as complete as the general strike of the previous year. The general strike of 1934 was not broken for three months. The general strikes of 1919 and 1920 were launched in the absence of an effective trade union. In 1924 and 1928, the prominent trade-union organizations and their leaders opposed industrial action and indeed attempted to prevent it. During the 1928 strike, a group of communists emerged as the dominant force on the strike committee. They formed the Girni Kamgar Union which, despite continued repression, dominated the labour movement in Bombay throughout the period. As Bombay became the scene of militant industrial action, its labour movement, under communist direction, acquired an explicitly political direction.[12]

Moreover, if the millworkers formed the most active and militant section of

[11] Willingdon to Montagu, 25 September 1917, Montagu Papers, MSS. EUR. D 523/18, pp. 31–5. IOR.

[12] R. Chandavarkar, 'Workers' Politics and the Mill Districts in Bombay between the Wars', *MAS*, XV, 3 (1981), Special Issue, *Power, Profit and Politics: Essays on Imperialism, Nationalism and Change in the Twentieth Century*, ed. C. J. Baker, G. Johnson and A. Seal, pp. 603–47; Newman, *Workers and Unions*; S. Bhattacharya, 'Capital and Labour in Bombay City, 1928–29', *Economic and Political Weekly, Review of Political Economy*, XVI, 42 & 43 (17–24 October 1981), pp. PE36–PE44; D. Kooiman, 'Bombay Communists and the 1924 Textile Strike', *Economic and Political Weekly, Review of Political Economy*, XV, 29 (19 July 1980), 1223–36; G.K. Leiten, *Colonialism, Class and Nation: The Confrontation in Bombay Around 1930* (Calcutta, 1984).

the working class, industrial action was not confined to them. The railway workshops went on strike in 1917 and again in the early 1920s. In 1930, the workshop men came together with the workers on the line of the Great Indian Peninsular Railway to offer determined resistance against wage cuts, retrenchment and increased workloads. Transport workers struck in 1922; the dock workers organized a major strike in 1932; the leather workers followed suit in 1937. Around these bitter and often protracted disputes, trade unions formed, fractured and collapsed.

In the 1920s and 1930s, Bombay witnessed a wide range of social and political conflicts. These conflicts informed and often developed the contradictions at the base of Britain's Indian Empire. 'The second city of the Empire' was the centre of India's largest industry in Britain's most important, if turbulent, colony. Colonial rulers ranked the city's millowners among their best and most loyal collaborators. Yet the growth of the textile industry posed a major threat to the decreasingly competitive cotton mills of Lancashire, the mainstay of British imperialism, in its most important foreign market. As the Bombay industry encountered a slump in its fortunes in the 1920s and 1930s, the millowners campaigned for tariff protection. But keeping the Indian market open for Lancashire goods had ranked among the oldest and most abiding imperatives of colonial rule.[13]

The relationship between the colonial state and Indian capital came under growing pressure in the 1920s and 1930s. On the one hand, Indian capital was invested in import-substitution industries; on the other, the shifting fiscal base of the colonial state necessitated its dependence on revenues derived from the taxation of trade and industry. Significantly, the fiscal, monetary and tariff policies of the colonial state continued to be determined by Britain's imperial needs rather than India's industrial interests. The Fiscal Autonomy Convention remained no more than an adornment of the statute books. Budgets were framed with the aim of ensuring that the Indian Empire cost the British taxpayer nothing. Monetary policies were driven by the concern to manage the Government of India's sterling obligations rather than India's foreign trade.[14] If nationalism had been, at least partially, the product of bourgeois frustration, it

---

[13] B. Chatterji, 'Business and Politics in the 1930s: Lancashire and the Making of the Indo-British Trade Agreement', *MAS*, XV, 3 (1981), 527–73, Special Issue, *Power, Profit and Politics*, ed. Baker, Johnson and Seal; C. Dewey, 'The End of the Imperialism of Free Trade: The Eclipse of the Lancashire Lobby and the Concession of Fiscal Autonomy to India', in C. Dewey and A.G. Hopkins (eds.), *The Imperial Impact: Studies in the Economic History of Africa and India* (London, 1978), pp. 35–68; I.M. Drummond, *British Economic Policy and the Empire, 1919–39* (London, 1972); B.R. Tomlinson, *The Political Economy of the Raj: The Economics of Decolonization in India* (London, 1979).

[14] Tomlinson, *Political Economy of the Raj*, especially pp. 57–152; A.K. Bagchi, *Private Investment in India 1900–39* (Cambridge, 1972), especially pp. 34–67.

was also the case that as nationalist opposition mounted, the colonial state became increasingly concerned not to alienate the millowners and merchant princes whose collaboration it so highly valued. In the 1920s and 1930s, Bombay City came to be regarded as 'the Keep of Gandhism',[15] a seething base of nationalist agitation and anti-colonial politics, as well as the epicentre of working-class political action.

The social formation of the working classes in Bombay and their interaction with the development of industrial capitalism is investigated against the background of these broad themes. Studies of capitalist development and industrialization have often tended to focus upon entrepreneurs and by subordinating workers to production, industry or the economy have sometimes relegated them to the margins of history. The history of the working classes is studied in terms of the intentions and objectives of the entrepreneurs and the processes of labour-force formation become simply a function of 'how the early entrepreneurs solved the problem of recruiting, organizing, and administering the labour force'.[16] It is implied that employers were able to conjure up the kind of labour force they sought. The choices and actions of workers and their effect upon the forms of recruitment, the nature of discipline and the patterns of labour use fade into a dimly illuminated background. The focus of this book rests upon labour and its conflicts with capital which shaped the patterns of capitalist development. Business strategies and the organization of production influenced the workings of the labour market as much as the dynamics of the latter fashioned work practices. The interaction between them shaped the policies of the employers and determined the nature and possibilities of the solidarities forged

[15] Sir Frederick Sykes, Governor of Bombay, MSS. EUR. F 150 (4), 6 March 1932, quoted by A.D. Gordon, 'Businessmen and Politics in Developing Colonial Economy: Bombay City, 1918–33', in Dewey and Hopkins (eds.), *The Imperial Impact*, p. 194.

[16] M.D. Morris, *The Emergence of an Industrial Labour Force in India: A Study of the Bombay Cotton Mills, 1854–1947* (Berkeley and Los Angeles, 1965), p. 1; C.A. Myers, *Labour Problems in the Industrialization of India* (Cambridge, Mass., 1958); R. Newman, 'Social Factors in the Recruitment of the Bombay Millhands', in K.N. Chaudhuri and C.J. Dewey (eds.), *Economy and Society: Essays in Indian Economic and Social History* (Delhi, 1979), pp. 277–95; R. Das Gupta, 'Factory Labour in Eastern India: Sources of Supply, 1855–1946: Some Preliminary Findings', *IESHR*, XIII, 3 (1976), 277–328; C.P. Simmons, 'Recruiting and Organizing an Industrial Labour Force in Colonial India: The Case of the Coal Mining Industry, c. 1880–1939', *IESHR*, XIII, 4 (1976), 455–85; B. Misra, 'Factory Labour During the Early Years of Industrialization: An Appraisal in the Light of the Indian Factory Labour Commission, 1890', *IESHR*, XII, 3 (1975), 203–28; C. Joshi, 'Kanpur Textile Labour: Some Structural Features of Formative Years', *Economic and Political Weekly*, XVI, 44–6, Special Number (November 1981), 1823–38; Sir Percival Griffiths, *The History of the Indian Tea Industry* (London, 1967), pp. 267–420. It is not intended to suggest that all these historians are agreed on how these problems were solved or that they share the same conception of the economy. But the widespread assumption of the centrality of this problem has led to an inordinate emphasis upon recruitment systems and methods of organizing a labour supply in the 'early stages' of industrialization.

between workers. Although the following chapters will not deal specifically with the patterns of industrial action, the emergence of trade unions or the nature of popular movements, the sphere of politics is brought consistently to bear upon an understanding of the social nexus of the working classes. Indeed, it is taken for granted that this social nexus and its economy can scarcely be comprehended outside a political dimension.

If the history of work and workers has been too readily subordinated to the economy, it has also sometimes been made interchangeable with the history of their leaders, trade unions and political parties. The emergence of modern trade-union organization depended, it is often argued, upon how effectively its leaders could make inroads into the traditional loyalties of the working class. For some historians, the motive force of labour politics lay in the struggle between politicians, attempting to mobilize workers and form trade unions, and the jobbers, the traditional leaders of the working class.[17] As the forces of modernity and tradition clashed, workers, in this view, constituted a passive and inert mass, mere spectators in the struggle being waged to decide their fate.

For the most part, the working class remains silent in Indian history. We have to rely upon those who spoke on their behalf: trade unionists and political leaders, journalists and social workers, civil servants and lawyers. Their protests can sometimes only be studied through the distorting lens of police intelligence reports, the hastily scribbled notes of newspaper reporters or the files of rulers and employers. The motives and ideologies of ordinary people are often only glimpsed either through the prism of dramatic moments of collective action or in the echo chambers populated by their spokesmen. It has often rendered historians vulnerable to the stereotypes of workers gravely professed by the dominant classes: the perceptions of contemporaries become the historians' dogma; their social prejudices are taken for social reality. Historians have frequently built arguments about popular politics upon assumptions about the nature of the social formation which constituted them. By examining these processes of social formation, this book seeks to interrogate some of these assumptions as well as the implications and expectations which have often been extrapolated from them. The investigation of the social formation of Bombay's workers may help, by clarifying the range of options before them, to explain more accurately the nature of their political perceptions and political action.

The second chapter sets the scene against which the main themes of the following pages are played out. It describes the transformation of Bombay from a penurious trading base of the East India Company into a leading metropolitan centre of Asia, the demographic characteristics of the city and the nature of its

[17] Newman, *Workers and Unions*; Kooiman, 'Jobbers and the Emergence of Trade Unions in Bombay City'.

rapidly changing urban environment. It attempts to locate the emergence of Bombay as the cradle of industrial development in the sub-continent within the context of the development of mercantile capitalism in the wider region and tries to analyse the structural constraints within which capital was mobilized in the early twentieth century. The pattern of mobilization and deployment of capital for industrial enterprises shaped the workings of the labour market and, more generally, influenced the changing relationship between capital and labour.

The next three chapters examine factors which shaped the formation of Bombay's labour force as a whole: the mechanisms of the labour market, patterns of labour migration and the nature of the rural connections of the city's workers, and the social organization of the working-class neighbourhoods which formed in the city.

Historians of industry and labour in India have invariably focussed upon large-scale industry, as the 'lead sector' of the economy, while relegating the others to the margins, thus obscuring our understanding of the role of the non-industrial sectors in determining the shape of the industrial economy itself. Chapter 3 locates the industry within the context of the city's economy and in particular its labour market. The casual and uncertain conditions of work have been explained primarily in terms of the character of labour supply. Workers in the early stages of industrialization, usually rural migrants, it is supposed, sought casual and temporary work because they had not sufficiently adapted to the demands of factory discipline. This chapter attempts to restore the balance by examining the conditions in which the demand for labour was generated.

Migrant workers to the city continued to maintain close connections with their village base over several generations. This has commonly been interpreted as the consequence of their rural mentalities. Lacking any commitment to the industrial setting, it is said, migrant workers were simply concerned to earn cash quickly and return to the land at the first opportunity. Yet underlying, indeed undermining, these characterizations lay the fact that the low wages and uncertain conditions of work forced most migrants to retain their rural connections as a second base of material provision in the city. Indeed, the purpose of migration was frequently to enable the peasant household to retain its village holding. For this reason, migrant workers were often strongly committed to the urban setting and struggled to defend their position within it. The rural connections of the working classes should not be seen as merely an effect of the early stages of industrialization, not least because workers in Bombay would appear to have been passing through them for over a century. Migration has often been portrayed as a process of acculturation in which peasants were initiated into new (modern) ways of life represented by the city and the factory. That the history of peasant migrants consists of their gradual, progressive initiation into the modern world is a self-regarding notion which has misconceived their behaviour and flattened their history. Chapter 4 investigates the causes of migration and the nature of these rural connections. It also examines the role of urban employment and the village base in workers' strategies for subsistence and in the operation of their household economy.

The dominant image of Indian workers has been cast in terms of their peasant character. Migration occurred within the framework of caste, kinship and village connections. Migrants to the city lived with their co-villagers, caste-fellows and relatives and sought work with their assistance. In times of distress, it was within these social connections that they found relief. Caste and kinship appeared to form indivisible social units in the city's working-class neighbourhoods. Similarly, 'the jobber's gang' has recently been described as 'a unit of urban society' and the jobber himself was frequently portrayed as a kind of village headman.[18] The nature of this so-called traditional social organization is examined in chapter 5. It investigates the nature of power and authority which flowed from the social organization of the neighbourhoods. It looks at the patterns of association which formed within them. These collectivities often informed the development of the political perceptions, organization and action of Bombay's workers. Fundamentally, this chapter investigates how the social organization of the working class came to be constituted. It was inflected by the fluctuations of the labour market and the uncertain conditions of work. The interplay between the spheres of the workplace and the neighbourhood was crucial to the social organization of Bombay's workers.

From the sphere of the neighbourhood, this book turns to the workplace in a case study of the cotton-textile industry in the final three chapters. Chapter 6 examines the origins and development of the cotton-textile industry in Bombay. The nature of its development shaped the business strategies of the millowners and the formation of the industrial labour force. The difficulties which engulfed the industry in the 1920s and 1930s emerged out of its earlier pattern of growth. The industry's history informed the millowners' perception of and response to their seemingly perpetual crisis. It also influenced the workers' response, indeed often trenchant resistance, to the policies of their employers. The following chapter investigates the economics of the textile industry in Bombay and its effects upon the organization of production: the structure of authority at work, the nature of skill, the hierarchies and differentials which marked the workforce and the patterns of labour deployment. Whereas the social organization of the workforce is supposed to have fragmented the working class, industrialization is assumed to have united it. As workers are concentrated into larger masses, it is believed, their interests become more uniform and their social consciousness

---

[18] Newman, *Workers and Unions*, pp. 28, 54; *RCLI, Evidence taken in the Bombay Presidency (including Sind)* (London, 1931), Government of Bombay (henceforth GOB), 'Memorandum on the Conditions of Labour in the Bombay Presidency', I, i, 10.

is unified. On the contrary, as chapter 7 shows, the process of industrial development heightened the sectionalism of the working class. This sectionalism was not simply a function of the traditional divisions of caste and kinship; it was also generated by the processes of economic development.

The millowners were no more able than their employees to take a single, or even steady, view of their industry and its future. Chapter 8 examines the discourse of 'rationalization', the fashionable remedy of the day offered by the colonial state and a wide range of interests for the industry's problems in the late 1920s and 1930s. But the diversity of interests within the industry made it impossible for the millowners to combine for a concerted assault upon their structural problems. At the same time, the sectionalism of the workforce was accentuated by the piecemeal introduction of rationalization schemes. Changes in employers' policies affected different groups of workers variously. As their markets slumped, the millowners, unable to embark upon the reconstruction of the industry, attempted to manipulate and exploit their labour force. Yet this only served to heighten the resistance which their policies encountered. While the millowners also sometimes perceived rationalization as a means of, or an opportunity for, breaking labour resistance, the intractability and truculence of their workers often narrowed their options and deterred them from adopting measures of fundamental reform. Significantly, although rationalization was extensively discussed, and some steps taken in its name, largely to allow the millowners to tighten their grip on labour, no comprehensive programme of reform and reconstruction was undertaken by the millowners. Nonetheless, the formulation of these schemes, and the play of competing views about them, revealed not only the complexities which marked the formation of an industrial labour force in Bombay and the nature of the business strategies in the industry, but also the ways in which working-class action shaped and limited the options of the capitalists.

Perspectives

In recent times, the conceptualization of class and social consciousness, culture and poverty, colonialism and industrialization has been in a state of flux. This enquiry into the processes which conditioned the formation of the working class in Bombay City seeks to address these broader questions and is offered as a contribution to a more general, comparative or 'theoretical' discussion of industrialization, class and labour movements. To a large extent, this discussion has thus far proceeded by generalizing from limited cases. The sociological and historical evidence of an 'Indian case' is not conventionally expected to provide material for thinking more generally about industrialization and its social consequences. Indeed, it is not often presented as if it might be. The interest of Indian society is assumed to lie in its 'agrarian' or 'pre-industrial' character, whose inwardness can only be properly comprehended in terms of its own particularisms. Alternatively, 'industrial development in India' is portrayed as 'part of the very broad movement which had its orgins in Western Europe'.[19] According to this evolutionary schemata, the patterns of social change and economic development in India were moving broadly along tramlines towards 'industrialism', or modern capitalism, familiar in the 'Western' experience. Thus, one historian of Indian labour was led to assure us that,

group tensions and conflicts in Indian industry take on the characteristics of Western industrialization and do not require any analysis specifically developed to suit the requirements of a distinctively Indian situation ... The group tensions which will confront Indian industry will not be strange to the scholar. They will remind him very much of those which affected other regions in early periods of economic development.[20]

In this way, the historical experience of the West becomes the source of the conceptual frameworks and social theories by which the Indian working classes may be comprehended.

The assumption that Indian social history was essentially particularistic or that it simply followed patterns laid down by the West in earlier centuries has effectively withdrawn its study from an active role in the comparative discussion of social change and the wider discourse of social theory. The cost has often been either to attribute a cultural specificity to fairly general phenomena or to perceive as a general effect of a broader evolutionary development towards industrialism what is produced by a particular historical context and its contingencies. The cultural specificity of the jobber system or the characterization of indigenous patterns of entrepreneurship, averse to risk, prone to speculation, slow in its response to technology, is an example of the former. So perhaps is the readiness with which urban neighbourhoods are conceived primarily in oxymorons like 'urban villages'.[21] Conversely, historians have sometimes taken for granted that 'early industrial workers' or insufficiently industrialized or non-industrial urban labour were marked by their rural origins and peasant character.[22] Their attitudes to work and politics have often been read in the light of the perceptions of similar groups at what is deemed a comparable stage of industrialization in Britain or elsewhere in the West.

---

[19] M.D. Morris, 'The Growth of Large-Scale Industry to 1947', in Kumar (ed.), *CEHI*, II, 553.

[20] M.D. Morris, 'The Effects of Industrialization on "Race Relations" in India, in G. Hunter (ed.), *Industrialization and Race Relations: A Symposium* (London, 1965), p. 160.

[21] See, for example, O.M. Lynch, 'Rural Cities in India: Continuities and Discontinuities', in P. Mason (ed.), *India and Ceylon: Unity and Diversity* (Oxford, 1967), pp. 142–58; D.F. Pocock, 'Sociologies: Urban and Rural', *Contributions to Indian Sociology*, IV (1960), 63–81; W.D. Rowe, 'Caste, Kinship and Association in Urban India', in A. Southall (ed.), *Urban Anthropology: Cross Cultural Studies of Urbanization* (New York, 1973), pp. 211–49.

[22] Chakrabarty, *Rethinking Working-Class History*; D. Arnold, 'Industrial Violence in Colonial India', *Comparative Studies in Society and History*, XIII, 2 (1980), 234–55.

The term 'class' is used frequently in this book largely as a descriptive category. It was once taken for granted that since class and class consciousness presupposed the maturity of industrial capitalism, they could not be fruitfully applied to the study of the labour force in India. Indeed, it was argued, more generally, that the development of industrial capitalism would tend towards the increasing homogeneity and polarization of classes. From their concentration into factories, it was supposed, flowed the political solidarities of the working classes. On the other hand, peasants were in this view characterized by their 'low classness' – 'often lacking the discipline and leadership that would encourage opposition of a more organized sort'. This was why, as James Scott has recently argued, affirming an old orthodoxy, 'everyday forms of peasant resistance', individual and anonymous action, are 'eminently suited to the sociology of the class from which it arises'.[23] Factory workers by contrast are expected to manifest an inherent propensity to collective action. Yet the natural solidarities of the working class should not be taken for granted. The Indian working classes were highly fragmented. Their sectionalism has usually been perceived as a symptom of its pre-industrial economy. But their differentiation did not simply derive from the village and the neighbourhood, caste and kinship; rather, it was accentuated by the development of industry. At the same time, an increasing sensitivity among historians of the Western working classes to the competing and conflicting identities of ethnicity and gender, religion and nation, kinship and neighbourhood, has focussed attention upon the very issues which had in this perspective rendered Indian society exceptional in the first place and sometimes even demanded a culturally specific sociology for its proper analysis. It is one purpose of this book to investigate how far the factors which are deemed to make up the common experiences of the working class in the process of its formation have registered differences between them.

The notion that social groups have 'real' or objectively defined interests in common derived from theoretical assumptions about the effects of production and distribution. Class consciousness became the process by which classes recognized and realized the interests which they shared in common and in opposition to others. Yet the concepts of class and class consciousness were articulated by Marx and Engels before the emergence of the type of 'modern' working class in Europe to which they have been most frequently considered applicable. Significantly, these concepts were based upon philosophical, not sociological, assumptions about the ontological role of the working class in the

---

[23] J.C. Scott, 'Everyday Forms of Peasant Resistance', in J.C. Scott and B.J.T. Kerkvliet (eds.), *Everyday Forms of Peasant Resistance in South-East Asia* (London, 1986), p. 28; J.C. Scott, *Weapons of the Weak: Everyday Forms of Peasant Resistance* (New Haven, 1985).

transition to socialism.[24] They were fashioned from an already prevalent vocabulary of class in early-nineteenth-century England.[25] Moreover, they have never been easily transposed to the analysis of social conflict and political change within any other context in the West or the Third World. Yet, paradoxically, where the vocabulary of class reflected daily social reality less directly than in nineteenth-century England, it has more frequently and overtly informed an explicitly revolutionary ideology and inspired more sustained and effective radical political movements.

The assumption that social groups have common interests which derive from their broadly similar relationships to the means of production has led to the quest for its manifest consequences in the development of class consciousness: the processes by which classes recognized and realized the interests which they shared in common and in opposition to others. Not surprisingly, in some forms of social and cultural history, sociology and anthropology, an important, sometimes hidden, occasionally explicit, concern has been to explain the gulf between political expectations based upon class and their real shortcomings in practice: not only why revolutionary movements failed but also why they failed to occur. Recent attempts to direct attention away from revolutionary movements to 'the quiet, unremitting guerilla warfare that took place day-in and day-out' have nonetheless conceived social relations in terms of the distinction between 'exploiters' and 'resisters'.[26] Similarly, some have depicted Indian society in terms of the fundamental divide between the subaltern classes and elites.[27] In these accounts, the working classes rather than peasants seemingly retain their status, attributed to them by Marx, as the most appropriate vehicle for the transition to socialism.

This book proceeds on a different set of assumptions about the conceptualization of class. It remains sceptical of the notion that exploiters and resisters were characterized by simply adversarial or consistently oppositional relationships. It would be misleading to suppose that 'resistance' flows naturally from the social situation of the subaltern classes. Moreover, the lines of exploitation, as we shall see, moved in diffuse and complex ways through society. The subordinate classes were drawn into competitive and exploitative relationships with each other; rivalries and factions within dominant classes limited their ability to exploit and weakened possibilities of hegemony or social control. Between subordinate and dominant groups were complex layers of intermedi-

[24] G. Stedman Jones, *Languages of Class: Studies in English Working Class History, 1832–1982* (Cambridge, 1983), pp. 1–24.

[25] A. Briggs, 'The Language of "Class" in Early Nineteenth Century England', in A. Briggs and J. Saville (eds.), *Essays in Labour History* (London, 1960), pp. 43–73.

[26] Scott, 'Everyday Forms of Peasant Resistance', p. 5.

[27] Guha (ed.) *Subaltern Studies*. For an early manifesto, see R. Guha, 'Introduction', in *Subaltern Studies*, vol. I, pp. 1–8.

aries who, in changing situations, could be identified in either category and who, in any case, facilitated the processes of both exploitation and resistance. Their relationship was mediated by institutions which were driven by their own logic and subject to pressures not simply reflective of the prevailing sets of production relations and their attendant effects.

Furthermore, abstractions of apparently common interests based upon theoretical assumptions about the character and consequences of production relations will not necessarily match individual or even collective perceptions and calculations of self-interest. Perceptions of mutuality and indeed their notations, the language for their description, were produced by the specificities of a particular political and intellectual context. Moreover, the interests of social groups were shaped by and contingent upon specific historical circumstances, which were themselves constantly in flux. In turn, changing circumstances could serve to redefine the interests of the diverse elements which made up the working classes and reconstitute social identities. From this perspective, it would seem likely that the very processes which help to form and constitute social classes could also serve to fragment them. Our concern, therefore, should be not so much why the working classes have failed to realize the expectations theoretically imputed to them but how and why at times they came together at all.

Finally, the attempt to trace the subjective realization and expression through 'class consciousness' or 'culture' of objective and real interests based upon relations of production has tended to give class consciousness an essentialist meaning, as an expression and manifestation of a latent, concealed, perhaps even immanent reality within the working classes. In this light, scholars ask not only whether or how far a working class had achieved 'consciousness' but also seek to assess whether it matched qualitatively a given stage of social development: whether it constituted the 'consciousness' of a 'pre-industrial', 'early industrial' or 'fully mature' proletariat. There is an inherent tautology in such reductive reasoning. For social consciousness is first defined as the property of a given state of social being and then, in any particular case, described and measured according to its standard. As the unease among historians about the handling of 'consciousness' has increased, so the number of surrogates for the term have proliferated: culture, identity, mentality, in some usages, even ideology, ranking among the more common to have been wheeled in to do service. The theoretical vagueness of their conceptualization conceals the assumption of essentialism upon which they are constructed, whereby a single, essential way of thinking can be attributed to social groups or even whole societies.

Mounting scepticism about the definition of culture as an autonomous sphere of social action has cast into doubt the viability of attempts to recapture the mind and world of the common man and woman, and in particular, their prior assumption of the existence of a single popular mind or a homogeneous common world. Historians who set out to investigate 'popular culture' or delineate 'working-class culture' have sometimes either written its economic and social context out of the account or simply taken it for granted. Thus, Foucault's assumptions about and emphasis upon the 'industrial revolution' as a causative moment allowed him to structure around it his meditations on discursive practices in the cultural sphere. Conversely, assumptions about the cultural characteristics of the working classes at various stages of development have often informed the analysis of their attitudes to work and politics. It is often taken for granted that casual workers primarily sought temporary employment, rural migrants were unsuited to factory discipline and early industrial workers were inherently volatile: as passive as peasants and, like peasants, prone to spasmodic bouts of violence.[28] These characterizations constituted the ideology of capitalists seeking a more firmly subordinated labour force and historians have often adopted them unwittingly.

There has been a similar propensity to attribute cultural characteristics to social groups defined by their relation to the means of production or to assume a simple and direct correspondence between social and economic status and behavioural traits and attitudes beyond the 'cultural' realm of the factory system. Casual labour is often distinctively set apart from 'industrial' or more permanent workers. They are assumed to display specific behavioural characteristics, marked especially by an aversion to work and political organization and a propensity to crime and violence, and to adopt lifestyles peculiar to themselves. Historians have frequently perceived 'peasant' mentalities characterizing the social action of proletarians, as if the rural and the urban formed generic social entities defined by the specificity, distinctiveness and coherence of their own particular cultures. Similarly, the quest for the culture of working-class 'communities' has been marked by a similar tendency to read cultural characteristics from class position. Thus, village characteristics are firmly etched into the foreground in portrayals of urban neighbourhoods while the romantic notion of 'community' has lent itself naturally to the exaggeration of homogeneity.

The relationship between social being and social consciousness is not overlooked in the following chapters but the issues are addressed from a somewhat different perspective. The emphasis rests not on the essential properties or generic character of migrant or casual workers, the neighbourhood or the workplace but upon the changing historical circumstances which shaped their formation and conditioned their development. The distinction between casual

---

[28] Arnold, 'Industrial Violence'; Chakrabarty, *Rethinking Working-Class History,* chs. 5 and 6; C. Joshi, 'Bonds of Community, Ties of Religion: Kanpur Textile Workers in the Early Twentieth Century', *IESHR,* XXII, 3 (1985), 251–80. But it should not be supposed that these lines of reasoning are confined to Indian social history.

and permanent workers was not a function of individual choice but the result of business strategies, the mechanisms of the labour market and employer policies. More crucially, there was no permanent gulf between them. Indeed, the divide between the formal and informal sectors was entrenched and formalized only by changes effected in the legal framework and conditions of employment beginning in the late 1930s and gathering momentum after the Second World War. But this should not lead to the conclusion that because the divide between them was blurred and because they formed, in a sense, ideological constructs, the working classes were united and homogenous. Similarly, rural migrants were not the carriers and purveyors of a putative peasant culture. Indeed, they were deeply committed to the urban and the industrial, and often acted after the fashion or stereotype of urbanized and industrialized workers, more so than those who had no connection with the countryside. The urban working-class neighbourhoods neither formed rural cities nor urban villages; but, conversely, the experience of living together did not necessarily forge homogeneous bonds of community between residents. Moreover, the social organization of the working-class neighbourhood was constituted largely by its relationship to the workplace. Although it contributed in significant ways to shaping the political struggles of the working class, the neighbourhood also formed an arena of competition and conflict. The sectionalism of the working class did not arise from its ascriptive divisions, traditional roots or rural origins; even at the point of production, Bombay's workers entered into relationships which did not develop solidarities among them but often entailed divisions. By assuming that social groups, variously defined, possessed (or developed) a specific culture and a consciousness ascribed to their role, however ambiguous, in production relations, historians have perhaps played down the significance or ironed out the awkwardness of this sectionalism. The study of the social organization of Bombay's working class suggested that its cultural affinities, common interests and political solidarities formed within and were closely related to changing social and political contexts. Their presence at one moment did not necessarily ensure their persistence at the next.

The agenda of social history, as a specialism within the discipline, originally set in the 1960s, was characterized by a populist ambition to reconstruct the authentic social experience of ordinary men and women and their everyday lives and struggles.[29] Social historians tended to focus ever more closely upon the local community, yet their ambition was to grasp the 'total experience' of their subjects and they retained an increasingly tenacious determination not to leave the politics out. Slowly and unevenly, as research in social history developed,

---

[29] For a programmatic statement, see E.J. Hobsbawm, 'From Social History to the History of Society', in M.W. Flinn and T.C. Smout (eds.), *Essays in Social History* (Oxford, 1974), pp. 1–22.

the contradictions inherent in these programmatic intentions rose more clearly to the surface. Totality was often found only in the eye of the beholder. Close attention to the local community made it difficult to grasp the larger play of political forces or to define the role of the state. Not only did the totality appear circumscribed but the 'social' seemed to lose its sanctity. Political conflicts and movements could not be explained adequately in terms of their social character or referred back to their roots in the local community. They also called to be located in their widest or most general political and ideological context. To explain political conflicts, it was necessary to look at politics and this search could not be satisfactorily confined to the local community.[30]

One response to this problem was to shift the focus of investigation towards politics and its role in determining social forms and social relationships. Another was to eschew social and economic explanation as unduly deterministic, reject implicit or explicit notions of its prior role in daily life and condemn its failure to grasp the symbolic forms, popular beliefs and cultural practices through which 'ordinary people' construed their experiences. This perspective had the merit of returning the study of popular experience to the wider currents of ideological discourse.[31] It also appeared to offer an alternative approach, running from the same direction as the social history of the 1960s and 1970s but by a different route towards the understanding of popular politics and its relationship with the dominant classes and the state. Along this route, historians were able to draw upon the insights of ethnography and cultural anthropology. Perhaps, to a greater degree than the sources of their inspiration, historians appreciated that this level of popular culture was defined in relation to its parts as well as to elite culture and by the participation of the masses in and their responses to wider social and political struggles. Nonetheless, the scope of this approach has been limited by the assumption that objective conditions inscribed a mutuality into particular social groups, whether defined by production relations, ascriptive or primordial categories, ethnicity or gender. By a different, often scenic and pleasurable route, it returns to a familiar destination. It adopts and projects the simplistic distinction between exploiters and resisters, the dominant and the subordinate, the elite and the subaltern. It assumes away the

---

[30] G. Stedman Jones, 'From Historical Sociology to Theoretical History', *British Journal of Sociology*, XXVII, 3 (1976), 295–306; E.F. and E.D. Genovese, 'The Political Crisis of Social History', *Journal of Social History*, X, 2 (1976), 205–21; T. Judt, 'A Clown in Regal Purple: Social History and the Historians', *History Workshop Journal*, VII (1979), 66–94.

[31] For interesting examples, see W.H. Sewell, Jr., *Work and Revolution in France: The Language of Labour from the Old Regime to 1848* (Cambridge, 1980); S. Kaplan (ed.), *Understanding Popular Culture: Europe from the Middle Ages to the Nineteenth Century* (Berlin and New York, 1984); S. Kaplan and C. Koepp (eds.), *Work in France: Representations, Meaning, Organization and Practice* (Ithaca, 1986); R. Chartier, *Cultural History: Between Practices and Representation* (Cambridge, 1988).

problem of explaining how social groups formed, whether in a material or ideational sense. Conversely, it assumes the existence of given social groups and categories and seeks to examine through their discursive practices how their preconceptions, beliefs and symbolic forms ultimately coincided with the prior definition of their objective status.

This book leans towards the 'political' rather than the 'cultural' interpretation of social history. The significance of Bombay City within India's political economy necessarily gave local events an immediate national importance. The formation of its labour force, conceived as a continuous process of social production, had inescapably political characteristics as well as consequences. It is scarcely possible to investigate Indian society in the twentieth century without reference to the state, whether in its colonial or national phase. The examination of the economy of labour, itself shaped and conditioned by political initiatives and conflicts, suggests that production relations, village, caste and kinship connections, the linkages of rural and urban communities, the social organization of the workplace and the neighbourhood, did not progressively increase the homogeneity of the working class; it often accentuated the divisions and heightened the conflicts between them. The scale and momentum of industrial action in the cotton-textile industry and more generally in the city as a whole cannot be explained in terms of the structure or material conditions of the working class, even as the latter could scarcely be grasped outside the context of the political struggles waged around them.

In the 1960s and 1970s, the significance of nationalism, the colonial state and the relationship between India and the world (or metropolitan) economy blunted in the case of the sub-continent the preoccupations of the old social history with recovering the total experience of local communities. Yet it is curious that the ambition to recapture the genuine experience of ordinary people, when it manifested itself in Indian history in the 1980s,[32] focussed at first upon the local community and local struggles before taking the form of investigating the mental and cultural universe of the populace and seeking to grasp the 'mind' of already given or assumed social groups.

To a large extent, the explanatory and conceptual frameworks for analysing industrialization and class have been upon the historical experience of the West, and especially the exceptional, even unique, case of Britain. Recent research, however, has suggested that these conceptual frameworks or models do not readily comprehend the particular cases upon which they were based.[33] It is

---

[32] For instance in the work of the 'subaltern' historians. See Guha (ed.), *Subaltern Studies*.

[33] D. Cannadine, 'The Present and the Past in the English Industrial Revolution, 1880–1980', *Past and Present*, CIII, (1984), 131–71; C. Sabel and J. Zeitlin, 'Historical Alternatives to Mass Production: Politics, Markets and Technology in Nineteenth Century Industrialization', *Past and Present*, CVIII, (1985), 133–76.

time, therefore, to turn to the cases they regarded as exceptional, not only for their intrinsic interest, but also for the challenge they pose to the general arguments and received expectations. In particular, it is easy to see why evolutionary and developmental, almost Whiggish, conceptions of industrialization and class acquired such plausible meaning in British and European history. Industrialization, especially given the apparent disappearance of the peasantry in England, could signify the evolution from artisanal and domestic production to the factory and the production line. The development of the working class could be perceived in a trajectory from small peasant or rural pauper to factory proletarian and an increasingly homogenized (if at a very 'advanced' state, once again segmented) labour force. Class consciousness could be perceived in its early and developed manifestation and following its dissipation in the mid nineteenth century to receive expression once more in growing labour movements and political parties of the working class, gathered beneath the banner of socialism. In India, these trajectories of development were far less clear and far more complex. The differentiation of the peasantry, the expansion, decline and stabilization of artisanal industry and the emergence of large-scale factory production ran concurrently. Most factory workers, after a century of industrialization, remained rural migrants who retained their village base. Casual labour could scarcely be taken for the residue of the past or the social discipline of the factory as the signpost of the future. Trade unions were ruthlessly repressed in the workplace, often on the streets and sometimes by the state; yet working-class militancy exceeded the wildest expectations of a significantly casual, predominantly rural labour force, divided by caste, community and religion and in apparently an 'early' phase of industrialization. Yet this militancy received limited, indeed halting expression at the level of party politics and the state. Many of these developments will be familiar in the social history of industrialization elsewhere; some make it difficult to proceed on the assumptions and expectations of labour and social history. It is not intended to suggest that the burden of rethinking and re-casting social theory and the assumptions of social history could rest entirely upon the empirical investigation of Indian society. But it is probable that the scope and intellectual reach of the former has been significantly diminished by its neglect of the latter.

2   The setting: Bombay City and
its hinterland

In 1661, Britain acquired Bombay from the Portuguese as part of Charles II's dowry on his marriage with Catherine of Braganza. Eight years later, it was transferred as a worthless possession to the East India Company by the Crown. In 1788, it was almost abandoned by Cornwallis, the defeated hero of Yorktown. For nearly a century and a half, this sparsely populated cluster of islands off the west coast of India was more notable for its pestilential swamps than its commercial value. Fortune hunters were better advised to rely upon their winnings from whist rather than risk the slim pickings of trade. Arrack alone, it was said, could 'keep the soldiers from the pariah houses'.[1] Alcoholic fevers and venereal diseases made up the white man's burden.

At the close of the seventeenth century, it appeared impossible 'that Bombay from its situation could ever become a place of trade notwithstanding the great attention paid to it by the Government'.[2] By 1872, however, this inhospitable fishing hamlet, where Englishmen did not expect to survive two monsoons, had become the second city of the Empire.[3]

It was only in the 1780s that Bombay began to replace Surat as the largest trading port and major commercial centre of the region. But the rise of Bombay was scarcely inexorable and the eclipse of Surat was far from complete in the late eighteenth century.[4] Political uncertainties at Surat in the early eighteenth century had induced the Company to retain its humble settlement at Bombay as a refuge from the turmoil of the west coast. To develop its marine force, the

---

[1] Quoted by T.G.P. Spear, *The Nabobs: A Study in the Social Life of the English in Eighteenth Century India* (Oxford, 1963), p. 71.

[2] *Gazetteer of Bombay City and Island*, compiled by S.M. Edwardes (henceforth *Gazetteer*), 3 vols. (Bombay, 1909), I, 403. On the early history of Bombay, see P.B.M. Malabari, *Bombay in the Making* (London, 1910); and M.D. David, *History of Bombay, 1661–1708* (Bombay, 1973).

[3] *Census of the City of Bombay Taken on 21st February 1872*, (henceforth *Census, 1872*) (Bombay, 1872), pp. 9–10.

[4] A. Das Gupta, *Indian Merchants and the Decline of Surat, c. 1700–50* (Weisbaden, 1979); P. Nightingale, *Trade and Empire in Western India, 1784–1806* (Cambridge, 1970); M. Torri, 'In the Deep Blue Sea: Surat and the Merchant Class during the Dyarchic Era, 1759–1800', *IESHR*, XIX, 3 & 4 (1982), 267–99.

21

Company built its own shipyard at Bombay and from the 1730s encouraged the emigration of Parsi shipwrights and artisans from Surat.[5] By the mid eighteenth century, the Bombay Marine was able to run the most effective protection racket in the Arabian Sea,[6] and with the opening of the China trade, more substantial profits began to flow in the direction of the Company's settlement and its merchants.

The expansion of British power on the sub-continent now began to act upon the growth of Bombay. The Company's economic and political expansion in the east and south registered it as the rising power in the sub-continent, and for indigenous bankers and creditors, a power worth backing, even in its far more modest enterprises in the west. The response of indigenous credit networks to the Company's potential served in turn to strengthen its hand in competition with rival state powers along the west coast.[7] Between 1802 and 1818, the British asserted political control over Western India. The defeat of the Marathas opened the way to the development of Bombay as an administrative centre and political capital. At the same time, Bombay's commercial growth came to be centred on its role as the major port for the export of raw cotton and, from the 1820s onwards, opium to China, which enabled the Company to pay for its purchases of tea and thus facilitated the only profitable part of the Company's operations.[8] Bombay's growing commercial and political importance combined to facilitate its tightening grip on an expanding hinterland.

Throughout the nineteenth century, economic and political changes in the structure of internal and foreign trade appeared to act in Bombay's favour as an expanding commercial and trading centre. In the mid nineteenth century, the value of India's foreign trade multiplied rapidly, and an increasing proportion of it was diverted from Calcutta to Bombay.[9] The American Civil War boom

---

[5] R.A. Wadia, *The Bombay Dockyard and the Wadia Master Builders* (Bombay, 1955); R.A. Wadia, *Scions of Lowjee Wadia* (Bombay, 1964); R.P. Masani, *N.M. Wadia and His Foundation* (Bombay, 1961).

[6] H. Furber, *Bombay Presidency in the Mid Eighteenth Century* (London, 1965); D.R. Banaji, *Bombay and the Sidis* (Bombay, 1932); L. Subramaniam, 'Bombay and the West Coast in the 1740s', *IESHR*, XVIII, 2 (1981), 189–216.

[7] Subramaniam, 'Bombay and the West Coast'; L. Subramaniam, 'Capital and Crowd in a Declining Asian Port City; The Anglo-Bania Order and the Surat Riots of 1795', *MAS*, XIX, 2 (1985), 205–37; M. Torri, 'Surat During the Second Half of the Eighteenth Century: What Kind of Social Order? – A Rejoinder to Lakshmi Subramaniam', *MAS*, XXI, 4 (1987), 679–710.

[8] P.J. Marshall, *Problems of Empire: Britain and India, 1757–1813* (London, 1968), p. 90; V. Harlow, *The Founding of the Second British Empire, 1763–93*, vol. II, *New Continents and Changing Values* (London, 1964), pp. 482–544; Nightingale, *Trade and Empire*; M. Greenberg, *British Trade and the Opening of China, 1800–1842* (Cambridge, 1951), pp. 124–31.

[9] *Imperial Gazetteer of India, The Indian Empire*, vol. III, *Economic* (Oxford, 1908), p. 268. C.A. Bayly, 'The Age of Hiatus: The North Indian Economy and Society, 1830–50', in C.H. Philips and M.D. Wainwright (eds.), *Indian Society and the Beginnings of Modernization* (London, 1976), pp. 83–105.

of the 1860s provided another powerful, if short-lived, stimulus to Bombay's commerce. As its supplies of American cotton dried up, the British textile industry turned increasingly to the Indian crop. Bombay handled 92 per cent of Indian raw-cotton exports in 1860, and although this proportion declined during the boom, the value of cotton exports from Bombay increased exponentially.[10] Since most of this cotton was paid for in bullion, the resulting inflow of capital created new opportunities for investment: credit was almost frantically extended, share prices rose steeply, money poured into construction projects and, literally and most famously, into the sea at Back Bay.[11] The end of the American Civil War and the collapse of cotton prices resulted in the inevitable panic, and the withdrawal of credit brought down over-extended financial and trading empires. Although contemporary writers fulminated against reckless speculators, it was soon apparent that the city's commerce had 'suffered no permanent injury from the wild excesses of these five years'.[12]

The crises of the mid 1860s appeared to have interrupted Bombay's commercial growth, but in fact recovery from its shock was rapid. Several factors now combined to accelerate Bombay's growth. The opening of the Suez Canal benefited Bombay more than any other single port, reducing its distance from London by more than three-quarters.[13] The cotton famine had enabled Bombay's export traders to break into continental markets, while the depreciation of silver after the 1870s and improvements in communications helped to boost Indian exports of primary produce. These exports to Europe and the USA contributed substantially to the settlement of Britain's balance of payments deficits with those areas.[14] By 1900, Bombay was the most important port for India's foreign trade and the major centre for the distribution of imports to internal markets.

From the 1850s, the gradual extension of road, rail and telegraph links also facilitated Bombay's rapid commercial growth and, indeed, enabled the port to

---

[10] M.L. Dantwalla, *A Hundred Years of Indian Cotton* (Bombay, 1948), p. 20; A.M. Vicziany, 'The Cotton Trade and the Commercial Development of Bombay, 1853–1875', PhD thesis, University of London, 1975, pp. 72–134.

[11] S.M. Edwardes, *The Rise of Bombay – A Retrospect* (Bombay, 1902), p. 275; *Gazetteer*, II 161–80; R.J.F. Sullivan, *One Hundred Years of Bombay: History of the Bombay Chamber of Commerce* (Bombay, 1937), pp. 64–85.

[12] Edwardes, *The Rise of Bombay*, p. 278. For a detailed examination of the boom and its consequences, see Vicziany, 'The Cotton Trade'.

[13] D.A. Farnie, *East and West of Suez* (Oxford, 1969), pp. 161, 101, 157–9 and *passim*. See also J. Adams, 'A Statistical Test of the Impact of Suez Canal on the Growth of India's Trade', *IESHR*, VIII, 3 (1971), 229–40.

[14] S.B. Saul, *Studies in British Overseas Trade* (Liverpool, 1960), pp. 188–207; B.R. Tomlinson, 'India and the British Empire, 1880–1935', *IESHR*, XII, 4 (1975), 339–80; B.R. Tomlinson, *The Political Economy of the Raj, 1914–47: The Economics of Decolonization in India* (Cambridge, 1979), ch. 1.

command a larger proportion of a diversifying export trade. Railway lines built to stimulate the export trade linked Bombay most securely to the more commercialized tracts of a widening hinterland. The first railway line, built in 1853, stretched twenty-one miles northwards from Bombay to Thana, but it was not until the following decade that it cut a path through the Western Ghats into the Deccan. By 1870, the railway connected Bombay to Jabalpur providing a link to Calcutta and offering access to the cotton- and wheat-growing regions of Central India. At the same time, the railway linked the port to the rich agrarian hinterlands of Gujarat, Rajputana and Malwa.[15] By the early twentieth century, direct connections were made with Delhi and Agra providing access to the fertile tracts of the Punjab and the Gangetic Valley.

The railways did not, however, create a regional economy around Bombay; sometimes, they followed trade routes which had long been established. Nor did the development of a railway network substantially alter the nature and composition of this trade. The bulk of the rail-borne trade in the 1870s and 1880s continued to be in cotton and grain from the Deccan and the Central Provinces and from Gujarat.[16] From the earliest days of the Company settlement, the inhabitants of this offshore island had to buy essential commodities, like grain, from the mainland and, having little else to sell, returned consignments of salt.[17] From the late eighteenth century onwards, the promise of the China trade brought cotton and opium in larger quantities to Bombay from Gujarat and Central India, Rajputana and Malwa; and from the 1820s onwards, there was a growing trade in the distribution of manufactured imports, especially cotton piecegoods.[18]

But it cannot be supposed that the extension of the railway network left Bombay's relationship with its hinterland unaffected. It enabled goods to be moved in larger quantities more easily, quickly and cheaply. It improved the condition of the cotton exported and reduced its cost. The pressure of demand generated within this rapidly growing town as well as the gains offered by a flourishing export trade ensured that the flow of goods into Bombay was far greater than the reverse.[19] The siting of the railway lines could boost the trade of one district at the expense of another. People, like goods, had always moved readily across the sub-continent, but the

---

[15] *Gazetteer*, I, 342–50, 350–1, 353; Somerset Playne, assisted by J.W. Bond, ed. Arnold Wright, *The Bombay Presidency, the United Provinces, the Punjab, etc.: Their History, People, Commerce and Natural Resources* (London, 1917–20), pp. 502–13; Sullivan, *One Hundred Years of Bombay*, p. 128 and *passim*.

[16] *Gazetteer*, I, 446.

[17] *Ibid.*, I, 450.

[18] *Ibid.*, I, 518–21.

[19] In 1913–14, the rail-borne trade brought 3,230,000 tons of 'country produce of all kinds' into Bombay and carried away about 1,642,000 tons for distribution to internal markets. *Report of the Indian Industrial Commission, 1916–18* (henceforth *IIC*) (Calcutta, 1918), p. 14; J.M. Hurd, 'Railways', in Kumar (ed.), *CEHI*, II, 737–61.

railways provided new and more flexible choices and opportunities for labour migration across longer distances and in all seasons.

By the early twentieth century, Bombay was firmly established as the pre-eminent commercial centre in India. In the 1920s, Bombay handled about two-fifths of the total value of India's foreign trade,[20] 70 per cent of the value of the coastal trade[21] and the bulk of the re-export trade to the Persian Gulf and to the Arab and East African ports.[22] The foreign trade of the Presidency was 'almost entirely confined to the port of Bombay'.[23] By 1860, Bombay had become, next to New York and Liverpool, the largest cotton market in the world.[24] In the 1920s, it was still the largest cotton market in Asia. 'In several years during the last decade', it was reported in 1927, Bombay had handled a larger volume of cotton than Liverpool.[25] It was also a major centre of the cotton piecegoods trade, located primarily in its three major markets: the Mulji Jetha, the largest, the Lakhmidas Khimji market in Sheikh Memon Street and the Morarji Goculdas market in Kalbadevi Road.[26] The merchants of Dana Bunder handled a valuable export trade in groundnuts and oilseeds, serving an extensive hinterland, from Kanpur and Allahabad in the north to Raichur and Hyderabad in the south, from Gujarat to Central India and the Nagpur region.[27] And there were, of course, a number of grain, vegetable and meat markets in the city. Rice was imported from Burma, wheat from the Punjab and cattle for the meat trade were obtained from various parts of the Presidency while fruit and vegetables were 'drawn from a wide area', largely from the Presidency, but a 'considerable quantity' came from 'more distant places'.[28]

---

[20] *Bombay, 1921–22: A Review of the Administration of the Presidency* (Bombay, 1923), pp. 89–104. This foreign trade based upon Bombay reflected the pattern for India as a whole; manufactured goods accounted for 70 per cent of the imports while raw materials and non-manufactured goods made up 74 per cent of the produce which passed through the port. *Ibid.*, pp. 91–2; see also Tomlinson, *Political Economy of the Raj*, pp. 1–6, 30–56; H. Venkatasubbiah, *The Foreign Trade of India, 1900–1940: A Statistical Analysis* (New Delhi, 1946); A.K. Banerji, *India's Balance of Payments, 1921–22 to 1938–39* (London, 1963).

[21] *Report of the Bombay Provincial Banking Enquiry Committee* (henceforth, *BPBEC*) (Bombay, 1931), I, 20. The smaller ports of the west coast – Karanja, Honawar, Vengurla, Broach, Uran, Bankot, Ratnagiri, Malwan – had an annual coastal trade, not only with Bombay and each other, but also with other Indian ports on both coasts, estimated at Rs. 40 lakhs.

[22] *Bombay, 1921–22*, pp. 97–8.

[23] *Ibid.*, p. 92.

[24] Vicziany, 'The Cotton Trade', chs. 2 and 3.

[25] S.M. Rutnagur (ed.), *Bombay Industries: The Cotton Mills – A Review of the Progress of the Textile Industry in Bombay from 1850 to 1926 and the Present Constitution, Management and Financial Position of Spinning and Weaving Factories* (Bombay, 1927), p. 464.

[26] For an account of the piecegoods market in Bombay, see Gordon, *Businessmen and Politics*, pp. 77–9; on the ruling body, the Bombay Native Piecegoods Merchants' Association, see *Gazetteer*, I, 457. For a biographical account of various trading firms, including piecegoods merchants, see Playne, and Bond, *The Bombay Presidency*, pp. 104–374.

[27] J.C. Bahl, *The Oilseeds Trade of India* (Bombay, 1938).

[28] *Gazetteer*, III, 53–62.

By the late nineteenth century, the bullion market at Jhaveri Bazar and Sheikh Memon Street was the largest in the country.[29] The city's banking business was conducted largely by about one hundred Hindu sarrafs, whose hundis and bills of exchange were 'accepted and honoured all over India'.[30] Although 'indigenous bankers' were sometimes thought to operate within a separate informal sector, they were in fact 'engaged in almost every line of industry, trade and commerce', and it is possible that the extent to which millowners turned to them to raise some of their working costs has been underestimated.[31]

Furthermore, in the later nineteenth century, Bombay emerged as the most important base of India's largest industry: cotton textiles. The first cotton mills were built in the 1850s and in 1875 the industry still consisted of 'a small cluster of pioneer factories at the foot of Cumballa Hill and about a dozen more that were scattered over the Parel district'.[32] By the early 1890s, however, the industry's spinning capacity had increased two-and-a-half times, its looms had doubled in number and its labour force expanded by a factor of five.[33] Despite the expansion of the industry at a number of up-country centres in the early twentieth century, it was still reported in the mid 1920s that the industry in Bombay 'not only exceeds the combined output of the 126 factories in other parts of the Bombay Presidency, but also exceeds the total production of the 125 factories working ... in all other parts of the country'.[34] Moreover, the inception and development of the industry, at its two most important centres in Bombay and Ahmedabad, was largely the achievement of Indian capital. Indian industrial investment was concentrated almost exclusively in Bombay Presidency and especially on its capital city. In 1914, Bombay received over 87 per cent of the total value of Indian capital investment while Indian capital accounted for nearly half the total value of private industrial investment centred in the city.[35] In the late nineteenth and twentieth centuries, Bombay remained the bastion of Indian capital.

---

[29] Gordon, *Businessmen and Politics*, pp. 79–80.
[30] *Gazetteer*, I, 288–9.
[31] L.C. Jain, *Indigenous Banking in India* (London, 1929), pp. 43, 42–9; Gordon, *Businessmen and Politics*, pp. 81–2; R.K. Ray, 'The Bazaar: Changing Structural Characteristics in the Indigenous Section of the Indian Economy Before and After the Great Depression', *IESHR*, XXV, 3 (1988), 263–318; R.K. Ray, 'Pedhis and Mills: The Historical Integration of the Formal and Informal Sectors in the Economy of Ahmedabad', *IESHR*, XIX, 3 & 4 (1982), 387–96.
[32] Rutnagur (ed.), *Bombay Industries*, p. 2.
[33] M.C. Rutnagur, *The Indian Textile Journal Directory of Indian Manufactories, 1894* (Bombay, 1894); *Annual Reports of the Bombay Millowners' Association, passim*.
[34] Rutnagur (ed.), *Bombay Industries*, p. 2.
[35] R.K. Ray, *Industrialization in India: Growth and Conflict in the Private Corporate Sector, 1914–47* (Delhi, 1979), pp. 49–53.

The emergence of Bombay as a major commercial and industrial metropolis was paralleled by its growing importance as an administrative and political capital. Just as the city's growth diverted the region's commercial centre from Surat to Bombay, so the focus of political activity and influence shifted increasingly in the nineteenth century from Pune to the new capital. Bombay became not only the seat of the provincial government but also the major educational and judicial centre of the Presidency: its university, one of the earliest in India, was founded in 1857[36] and its High Court, the highest tribunal for the region, was established in 1862.[37]

The Bombay Presidency had one of the most centralized administrations in colonial India. This was not simply the fruits of its administrative inheritance from the Maratha Empire or even the necessary consequence of collecting into a single administration such a culturally and socially diverse set of regions. Rather it reflected the nature and form of the land-revenue settlement in Bombay. The ryotwari system had in general facilitated the deeper penetration of government into rural society than permanent settlements allowed. But in Bombay it was carried a step further. The revenue demand was fixed here according to each field, calling for the detailed scrutiny and classification of the natural quality of the soil of each block of arable land. Thus, as Sir William Hunter observed, the District Officer in Bengal 'is seldom in tents for more than sixty days in the cold weather, and spends the remaining ten months of the year under the shelter of a good roof', and in the Punjab and the North-West Provinces he might spend ninety days on tour.

But in Bombay the period under canvas, and in defiance of the more vertical sun, is nearer 180 or 200 days ... The good Assistant Collector of the Bombay Presidency is the young man who is driven into the station from his tent-life among the villagers by the deluge of the monsoon. To an officer from Bengal the Bombay Civil Service seemed a small but exceedingly active body with a very big head.[38]

As the tasks of administration became more complex, and the body grew larger, the head appeared to become relentlessly stronger. Changes in the administrative structure, witnessed throughout the country, prompted more not less centralization. As greater powers came to be lodged at the level of the provincial government, so the workings of local government were probed further, their

---

[36] *Gazetteer*, III, 99–138; A. Seal, *The Emergence of Indian Nationalism: Competition and Collaboration in the Later Nineteenth Century* (Cambridge, 1968), pp. 84–93, 114–30; C. Dobbin, *Urban Leadership in Western India: Politics and Communities in Bombay City, 1840–85* (London, 1972), pp. 27–52, 154–72; S.R. Dongerkery, *A History of the University of Bombay, 1857–1957* (Bombay, 1957).

[37] *Gazetteer*, II, 204–37; anon., *The Bombay High Court, 1862–1962* (Bombay, 1962).

[38] Sir W.W. Hunter, *Bombay, 1885 to 1890: A Study in Indian Administration* (London and Bombay, n.d. [1892?]), pp. 10–11.

functions divided and their efficiency more closely supervised. Moreover, the changing political structure accentuated the processes already at work. For as the rudimentary outlines of representative government were developed and expanded, they increasingly converged upon the provincial capital, in Bombay as elsewhere in India.[39]

No significant interest in the Presidency could afford to ignore the growing economic and political resources of Bombay City. At the same time, from the early nineteenth century onwards Bombay's magnates gained an increasing degree of control over the administration of the city.[40] This in turn, as they discovered, compounded the measure of power over provincial affairs to be gained from the domination of the city's politics. Between 1893 and 1899, twenty-two out of the thirty-nine non-official members of the legislature lived habitually in Bombay but several among them represented mofussil constituencies by virtue of owning property in the districts. The Government of Bombay was aware of the inequity of this arrangement. But the contemplation of a remedy generated its own dilemmas:

> while a stricter interpretation might ensure a more exact representation of the local interests ... it would entail a lower standard of intelligence and education among the candidates for election by bodies outside the city of Bombay.[41]

However circumscribed its practical scope, the logic of representative government could, as British governments were beginning to learn, force upon them representatives they would not necessarily have chosen.

Although the city's magnates did not dominate the politics of the mofussil, their position in Bombay gave them considerable influence in its extensive hinterland. This hinterland was by no means confined to the boundaries of the Presidency. The quest for capital and raw materials, labour and food supplies, took Bombay's entrepreneurs further afield. Competition for raw materials and

---

[39] For an account of the changing structure of colonial administration in an Indian province, see D.A. Washbrook, *The Emergence of Provincial Politics: The Madras Presidency, 1880–1920* (Cambridge, 1976), especially ch. 2.

[40] By 1834, the city's most favoured magnates were appointed Justices of the Peace and thus gained access to municipal government. From 1862, they could be nominated to the Governor's Executive Council. Municipal reform in 1872 and 1888 vastly extended the control which Indians could exercise in the administration of their city. See R.P. Masani, *Evolution of Local Self-Government in Bombay* (Oxford, 1929); C. Dobbin, 'Competing Elites in Bombay City Politics in the Mid-Nineteenth Century (1852–83)', in E.R. Leach and S.N. Mukherjee (eds.), *Elites in South Asia* (Cambridge, 1970), pp. 79–94 and Dobbin, *Urban Leadership*, pp. 24–5, 131–85; J.C. Masselos, *Towards Nationalism: Group Affiliations and the Politics of Public Associations in Nineteenth Century Western India* (Bombay, 1974).

[41] Secretary, General Department, GOB to Secretary of State for India, 12 April 1899, Bombay Legislative Proceedings, 1899, vol. 5777, IOR. Cited by G. Johnson, *Provincial Politics and Indian Nationalism: Bombay and the Indian National Congress, 1880–1915* (Cambridge, 1973), p. 9, n. 1.

markets was determined more by transport costs or credit mechanisms than by administrative divisions. The city's hinterland extended beyond its neighbouring districts across far-flung areas of the sub-continent. By the late nineteenth century, Bombay's economic and political influence was unmistakably national in scope.

The transformation of Bombay from a fishing hamlet into a major industrial metropolis was in part the product of its imperial connection. It has, not surprisingly, become a commonplace to regard the city as the principal agent of westernization and the harbinger of the modern world to the sub-continent. Some have found it useful to fit Bombay into the typology of 'colonial port cities';[42] others have seen the Presidency capitals as enclaves of foreign trade and foreign ways.[43] But this is a narrow and superficial view. Bombay may have owed its origins and early growth to the Company settlement but its commercial and industrial development was shaped increasingly and in important ways by its place within the internal economy and not simply by the 'modernizing' forces of the West. Its commodity markets were linked to wider relations of production and exchange in the hinterland. Its mills depended increasingly upon the penetration of the domestic market. Labour for the city's commercial enterprises not only migrated from distant regions, but retained close ties with the village and through the remittance of cash earnings contributed to the reproduction of the rural economy. The nature and pattern of capitalist development in India were shaped by the position of these major centres of commerce and industry within the entire economy, as well as by the global relationships of profit and power into which India was drawn.

[42] The concept was defined by Rhoads Murphey, 'Traditionalism and Colonialism: Changing Urban Roles in Asia', *JAS*, XXIX, 1 (1969), 67–84. For its application to Bombay, see F.F. Conlon, 'Caste, Community and Colonialism: Elements of Population Recruitment and Urban Rule in British Bombay, 1665–1830', *Journal of Urban History*, XI, 2 (1985), 181–208; M. Kosambi, 'Commerce, Conquest and the Colonial City: The Role of Locational Factors and the Rise of Bombay', *Economic and Political Weekly*, XX, 1 (5 January 1985), 32–7; M. Kosambi, *Bombay in Transition: The Growth and Ecology of a Colonial City, 1880–1980* (Stockholm, 1986); D. Kooiman, 'Bombay From Fishing Village to Colonial Port City (1661–1947)', in R. Ross and G. Telkamp (eds.), *Colonial Cities: Essays on Urbanism in a Colonial Context* (Dordrecht, 1985), pp. 207–30. For an indication of the pervasiveness of this concept in the South Asian literature, see H. Spodek, 'Studying the History of Urbanization in India', *Journal of Urban History*, VI, 3 (1980), 251–95. See also D.K. Basu (ed.), *The Rise and Growth of the Colonial Port Cities in Asia* (Santa Cruz, 1979) and S. Lewandowski, 'Changing Form and Function in the Ceremonial and the Colonial Port City in India: An Historical Analysis of Madurai and Madras', in K.N. Chaudhuri and C.J. Dewey (eds.), *Economy and Society: Essays in Indian Economic and Social History* (Delhi, 1979), pp. 299–329.

[43] R.K. Ray, 'The Crisis of Bengal Agriculture, 1870–1927 – The Dynamics of Immobility', *IESHR*, X, 3 (1973), 252–3.

Table 1. *Population of Bombay City*

1661	10,000
1780	113,726
1814	180,000
1830	229,000
1846	566,119
1864	816,562
1872	644,405
1881	773,196
1891	821,764
1901	776,006
1911	979,445
1921	1,175,914
1931	1,161,383
1941	1,489,883

Sources: Gazetteer, I, 150–63, for estimates for 1661–1846; Census reports for post-1864 figures.

A social and demographic profile

The prodigious growth of Bombay in the nineteenth century was most directly reflected in the rate of its population increase and indeed its demographic characteristics (see table 1). In the 1780s, the island's population was estimated at little more than 100,000. From this modest base, it grew rapidly in the wake of the China trade[44] and in the midst of the American Civil War boom at least 816,562 people inhabited the town.[45] Although the collapse of the boom reversed the flow of migrants into the town, Bombay had become by the 1870s the largest city in the Empire after London.[46] The expansion of the textile industry led to a further spurt of growth, heightened by the rural scarcities of the 1890s, until the outbreak of plague at the end of the decade led to a large number of deaths and a mass exodus from the city.

There was another massive influx of migrants into the city during and immediately after the First World War, when unparalleled prosperity in the city coincided with famine and the influenza epidemic of 1918. This spurt of growth was checked by the problems which afflicted the textile industry and the depression of the 1930s, but the city's population once again began to increase

[44] *Gazetteer*, I, 150–66.
[45] *Census of the Island of Bombay taken on 2nd February 1864* (henceforth *Census, 1864*) (Bombay, 1864), i–vi. Of course, these figures need to be treated with caution. The British were concerned to show the largest possible increase as evidence of the popularity of their rule. At the same time, the population of Bombay was far from stable and its strength varied according to the seasonal ebb and flow of migrants. Counts made at different times of the year distorted the extent of growth and placed census figures beyond comparison.
[46] *Census, 1872*, pp. 9–10.

Table 2. *Distribution of population by religion, Bombay City, 1881–1931*
(percentages)

Religion	1881	1891	1901	1911	1921	1931
Hindu	65.2	66.1	65.5	67.8	71.2	68.0
Muslim	20.5	18.9	20.1	18.3	15.7	18.0
Zoroastrian	6.2	5.8	6.0	5.2	4.5	5.0
Christian	5.5	5.5	5.8	5.8	5.8	7.0
Jew	0.4	0.6	0.8	0.7	0.6	0.8
Other	—	—	—	0.1	0.2	0.2

Source: Census, 1931, IX, Part I, 12.

during the Second World War. The general movements of people which followed the partition of India brought another wave of migrants to the city and after a further influx in the wake of agrarian scarcities in the 1970s the city's inhabitants numbered over 8 million by 1981. The growth of the urban population was neither a function of natural increase nor the gradual agglomeration of neighbouring settlements but almost predominantly the result of immigration from a widening hinterland. Increasingly, and especially after the depression of the 1930s, the growth of the largest cities did not signify economic development so much as agrarian crisis.

The social and demographic structure of Bombay bore the marks of its pattern of growth. Its profile registered the effects of rapid and dramatic expansion. Its social composition testified to the fact that Bombay transcended its hinterland. The city housed people of every faith (see table 2); its streets echoed with every tongue spoken in the sub-continent; its residents migrated from all over India.

Hindus, divided by caste and language, class and sectarian belief, made up about two-thirds of the city's population. But their strength of numbers did not ensure their social dominance. Other religious groups constituted substantial and powerful minorities. Parsis contributed no more than about 5 per cent of the population but their prominence in commerce and industry gave them an economic and political influence highly disproportionate to their numbers. Even this relatively small religious group cannot be assumed to have formed a homogeneous community. There were doctrinal differences between the Shahamshahi and Kadmi sects,[47] social tensions between rich and poor and political conflicts between the sometimes Anglophilic merchant princes and the more nationalist-minded humbler professional groups, who were liable to

[47] R.E. Enthoven, *Tribes and Castes of Bombay*, 3 vols. (Bombay, 1920–2), vol. III, pp. 177–221.

challenge the authority of the Parsi Panchayat[48] or intone against the 'Biryani-wallahs of Willingdon [Club] fame'.[49] Similarly, Jains and Jews formed small communities but they contained within their ranks many who were prominent in the business and public life of the city and could not readily be reduced to the margins of local society.

The most substantial religious minority in the city was composed of Muslims who made up roughly one-fifth of the city's population. Like the Parsis and Hindus, they were not a homogeneous social grouping, but were deeply divided socially as well as theologically. The 1901 Census helpfully classified the city's Muslims into fourteen different communities, leaving some for an 'unspecified' category.[50] They were also divided across all the major language groups to be found in the city. The doctrinal differences between Sunnis and Shias led regularly to broken heads but their conflicts were perhaps most acutely manifested in the communal riots of the first decade of the twentieth century.[51] The major Islamic communities in the city, Memons, Bohras and Khojas, often converts from Hinduism or the descendants of Arab traders, had emigrated to the city from Gujarat; others came to the city from the Deccan as well as the Konkan. In Bombay, as elsewhere in India, many of the Muslim communities, often converted from Hinduism, retained affinities with and adopted the ritual practices of their former caste-fellows. 'If a Hindu Kshatriya is converted to Islam', it was reported in 1909, 'he is at once received into the Rangari Jamat, just as a Bhattia who turns Mussalman is received by the Khoja community and a Lohana by the Memon community'.[52] Most of these so-called communities were further subdivided. The Sheikhs, it was said, 'comprise three main divisions'. Bohras were divided between the Sunni, Aliya, Sulemani and Daudi sects while there were at least three large sects among the Khojas.[53] Urban society was also divided as, if not more, deeply and consistently by the

[48] C. Dobbin, 'The Parsi Panchayat in Bombay City in the Nineteenth Century', *MAS*, IV, 2 (1970), 149–64; *Dobbin, Urban Leadership*, pp. 1–26, 98–112, 217–19; Gordon, *Businessmen and Politics*, pp. 49–50; E. Kulke, *The Parsees in India: A Minority as Agent of Social Change* (New Delhi, 1978).

[49] Letter to the Editor, *Bombay Chronicle*, 1 November 1921, cited by Gordon, *Businessmen and Politics*, p. 49.

[50] *Census, 1901*, XI, *Bombay (Town and Island)*, part v, *Report* by S.M. Edwardes (Bombay, 1901), 52; *Census, 1901*, XIA, vi, *Tables* (Bombay, 1901), table XIII, 128–9.

[51] S.M. Edwardes, *The Bombay City Police: A Historical Sketch, 1672–1916* (Bombay, 1923), chs. 8, 9 and appendix; J. Masselos, 'Power in the Bombay "Moholla", 1904–15: An Initial Exploration into the World of the Indian Urban Muslim', *South Asia*, VI (1976), 75–95; J. Masselos, 'Change and Custom in the Format of the Bombay Mohurram During the Nineteenth and Twentieth Centuries', *South Asia*, N.S. V, 2 (1982), 47–67.

[52] *Gazetteer*, I, 180.

[53] *Ibid.*, I, 180–2; *Bombay Chronicle*, 28 April 1917; J.C. Masselos, 'The Khojas of Bombay: the Defining of Formal Membership Criteria During the Nineteenth Century', in I. Ahmad (ed.), *Caste and Social Stratification Among the Muslims* (Delhi, 1973), pp. 1–20.

Table 3. *Distribution of population by main language, 1911–31 (percentages)*

Language	1911	1921	1931
Marathi	50.9	51.4	47.6
Gujarati	20.9	20.1	20.9
Western Hindi	14.8	14.8	17.0
Konkani	2.8	2.8	3.5
Sindhi	4.2	0.2	2.2
English	2.0	2.1	1.8
Telegu	—	1.7	1.5

Source: Census, 1931, IX, Part I, 37.

distribution of wealth and power, which tended to cut across ascriptive social categories, as by caste hierarchies and religious communities alone.

Although about half the city's inhabitants spoke Marathi as their main language, no single linguistic group exercised an untrammelled dominance in the city's affairs (see table 3). Marathi, as it was spoken in Bombay, the *Gazetteer* discovered, 'varies appreciably according to the caste which speaks it', while the dialect spoken by immigrants from the Konkan 'is classed by many as a separate language'.[54] Gujarati, spoken by a fifth of the urban population, was the lingua franca of the business world. In the twentieth century, the census took increasing note of Hindi-speakers, reflecting the influx of North Indians into the cotton mills and railway workshops of the city. By 1931, nearly one-fifth of the city recorded it as their main language. Others learnt to speak it. As languages spoken in the city grew more numerous, and migrants came from every corner of the sub-continent, a hybrid 'Bombay Hindi', later immortalized by the cinema of the 1950s and 1960s, evolved as a means of communication for those who lacked a common tongue, borrowing freely from the various languages spoken in this metropolitan Babel. While about 2 per cent returned English as their main language, many others had some command of it, and of the 9 per cent in 1931 who were bilingual, another one-third named it as their second language.[55] Similarly, levels of literacy and, especially, in English, were relatively high in the city.[56]

The rapid growth of Bombay in the nineteenth and early twentieth century,

---

[54] *Gazetteer*, I, 203.
[55] *Census, 1931*, VIII, part i, *Bombay Presidency, General Report*, by A.H. Drac., and H.T. Sorley (Bombay, 1933), 324–5; *Census, 1931*, IX, *Cities of the Bombay Presidency*, Part i, *Report* by H.T. Sorley (Bombay, 1933), pp. 37–8.
[56] *Ibid.*, IX, i, 36.

Table 4. *Number of females per 1,000 males: Bombay City, 1872–1931*

Year	Number of females per 1,000 males	Year	Number of females per 1,000 males
1872	612	1911	530
1881	664	1921	525
1891	586	1931	554
1901	617		

Source: *Census, 1931*, IX, Part I, 31.

Table 5. *Distribution of population per 1,000 by age group*

Age group	1881	1891	1901	1911	1921	1931
0–15	306	256	245	212	211	244
15–25	266	246	232	259	235	231
25–50	362	406	438	459	487	474
15–50	628	652	670	718	722	705
50+	66	92	85	70	67	51

Source: *Census, 1931*, IX, Part I, 27.

no less than its rhythm of expansion, characterized by stops and starts, ensured that it remained a city of migrants. The vast majority of its residents, even at the end of the period, retained close ties outside the city. Bombay's growing commercial, industrial and financial activities propelled some streams of migration. Others were driven to the city by scarcity and distress in the countryside. Labour as well as capital was attracted by the wide range of opportunities which the rise of Bombay created. Poorer migrants, in search of work, could calculate that the contraction of work in one sector of the urban economy might be offset by expansion in another. For merchants and traders, vakils and scribes, the attraction of the city lay in the fact that the structure of opportunities in the region had been gradually shifting from Surat and Pune to Bombay. Migrants who had once come to the island from its contiguous districts increasingly arrived in the twentieth century from all over India.

Another legacy of Bombay's rapid growth in the nineteenth century, in part the consequence of the fact that most of its inhabitants were migrants, and compounded by its vulnerability to economic fluctuations, was manifested in the age structure and gender composition of its population (see tables 4 and 5). Bombay was predominantly a city of adult male migrants. As the city's population grew in the later nineteenth century, and the flow of migrants quickened, so the ratio of males to females increased further. By the early twentieth century, there were only half as many females as males in the city. Similarly, the proportion of the population between the ages of fifteen and forty-five years rose slowly and exceeded two-thirds in the 1920s and 1930s.[57] These demographic features of the city were not only shaped by the nature of its growth but they also fundamentally affected the shape of social relations, economic development and political action in Bombay in the 1920s and 1930s: the nature of the labour market and the social organization of the neighbourhood; the perceptions and policing of the working classes as well as the styles and patterns of working-class politics. They affected the relationship between the sexes. They informed the development of the relationship between capital and labour.

Putting the city together

The dramatic transformation of Bombay from a fishing hamlet and penurious trading settlement into a modern industrial metropolis occurred in a matter of generations. Far more impressive than the rate of change was its extent. Industrial cities have often grown rapidly, but few have developed from such a modest economic and infrastructural base. Although the rise of Bombay can be dated to the dying years of the eighteenth century, its growth was accelerated in the second quarter of the nineteenth century and only reached really massive proportions between 1840 and 1900.

That its urban and economic growth outstripped the sophistication of its infrastructure has been an old and recurring theme in the city's history. Bombay's natural harbour and island setting may have adequately served modest seafaring interests, but as the expansion of trade drew it into the hinterland and locked it firmly into the wider imperial economy, the limitations of its urban setting were increasingly exposed. It was not until 1838 that the seven islands of Bombay were finally linked.[58] By 1914 the most congested parts of the city had barely a century earlier been lying beneath the sea.[59] A closer examination of the development of Bombay provides an insight into the standards and conditions of life in the city and the social context within which its labour force formed. In addition, the response to these conditions of the city's rulers and indigenous elites reflected their attitudes towards the urban poor and illuminates the development of the relations between the classes in the city.

---

[57] Calculated from *ibid.*, IX, i, 27.
[58] Edwardes, *The Rise of Bombay*, p. 249.
[59] J.P. Orr, *Density of Population in Bombay: Lecture Delivered to the Bombay Co-operative Housing Association* (Bombay, 1914), p. 1.

In the mid nineteenth century, when Bombay's commercial expansion had begun to accelerate, the conditions of hygiene and sanitation were rudimentary. From the earliest days of its growth, land was scarce and the town was overcrowded. As early as 1753, the Company's government in Bombay reported to London that 'the town is so overcrowded, that the people are murmuring for to have it enlarged'.[60] Town planning, first attempted in the 1760s,[61] and more seriously pursued by the Town Repair Committee after fire had destroyed much of the existing bazaar in 1803,[62] was never to be brought to a satisfactory conclusion.[63] Housing conditions, especially for the poor, were characterized by extreme overcrowding, long before the influx of migrants in the boom of the 1860s imposed unprecedented pressures on the urban fabric. As early as 1852, it was observed that 'a large proportion of our labouring population inhabit lodging houses too densely crowded to admit of private [lavatory] accommodation to the requisite extent'.[64] It was scarcely surprising, therefore, that a visitor to Bombay at the height of the boom was 'to see in the foreshore the latrine of the whole population of the Native Town'.[65] By the mid 1860s, the *Bombay Builder* attributed to 'the wretched rows of cadjan huts' hastily assembled by migrants to the city close to their places of work, the primary reason for the fact that 'two out of three coolies that come to Bombay for employment do not return to their homes, but are carried off by fever or other diseases'.[66]

The sanitary state of the town intensified the threat of disease and death for its poorer inhabitants. 'Open drains or rather receptacles of filth' which formed 'continuous open cesspools', extended 'along (on both sides) the whole length of nearly every street in the Native Town' in the 1850s and soaked 'into the foundations of the whole street-frontage of each house'.[67] The drainage of these streets, an official estimated, 'would of itself and irrespective of all other sanitary improvements' save at least 3,000 lives per year, while fully 'one-half (or about 8,000) of the deaths that annually occur in Bombay are due to

[60] Government of the East India Company, Bombay, to Directors, East India Company, London, 1 December 1753. Quoted in F. Warden, *Report on the Landed Tenures of Bombay, dated 20 August 1814. Selections from the Records of the Bombay Government* (henceforth *Selections*), no. 64, N. S. (Bombay, 1861), p. 77.

[61] Anon., 'The Town and Fort of Bombay', *Alexander's East India and Colonial Magazine*, IX (Jan.–June 1835), 244.

[62] Edwardes, *The Rise of Bombay*, pp. 228–31.

[63] N. Harris, *Economic Development, Planning and Cities: The Case of Bombay* (Bombay, 1978).

[64] H. Conybeare, 'A Comparison between Different Methods of Conveyancing and Ultimately Disposing of Night Soil', in H. Conybeare, *Report on the Sanitary State and Requirements of Bombay. Selections*, n.s., no. XI (Bombay, 1855), appendix H, p. 28.

[65] Quoted in Edwardes, *The Rise of Bombay*, pp. 279–80.

[66] *The Bombay Builder*, September 1866, quoted in Edwardes, *The Rise of Bombay*, p. 293.

[67] Conybeare, *The Sanitary State*, pp. 16–17.

removable causes'.[68] In the absence of adequate sewers, human excreta had to be carried away in straw baskets by workers who were called 'scavengers' or halalkhores, and emptied into the sea at designated points, often a mile or more away. Sensibly, in these circumstances, the halalkhores 'frequently emptied their baskets in the first dark corner they could find'.[69] Those who got as far as the sea, it was said, 'were in the habit of flinging down the filth barely within the line of the water, to be scattered in all directions, along the shore, thereby occasioning a most horrible nuisance'.[70] In the late 1840s, conditions of work were marginally improved by the introduction of carts for halalkhores to clear away the 'night-soil' and receiving stations were built to collect the refuse. The construction of sewers in some parts of the city substantially modified these conveyancing practices over the following decades. But as late as the 1920s, when halalkhores could still be expected to carry 'the baskets of excreta through public thoroughfares to the nearest depot', Burnett-Hurst observed that they often 'shirk their duties and empty the contents of the baskets into the open drain'.[71]

Nor could the city's residents be sure of an adequate, let alone hygienic supply of water. At times of scarcity, for instance in 1854, water had to be brought to the town by rail and country boats.[72] If the supply was irregular, its distribution was uneven. The city's Health Officer recorded the 'pitiable sight' in the 1870s 'of men, women and children awaiting around a pipe eagerly and quarrelling for the miserable dribble from it'.[73] In some parts of the city, the poor only had access to water which 'ought to be pronounced unfit for drinking purposes' and if the rains failed, they were 'compelled to drink the water of these filth-sodden wells and tanks'.[74] More than half a century later, it was still observed that when water supplies began to dry up, 'the poor quarters of the city suffer the most'.[75]

The disposal of the dead, like the disposal of sewage, posed apparently insuperable problems. Mid-nineteenth-century observers described how 'low caste Hindus, cattle etc.' were sometimes buried on the beach at Back Bay.[76]

---

[68] *Ibid.*, p. 2.

[69] Conybeare, 'Different Methods of Conveyancing', pp. 8–10; Masani, *Local Self-Government*, pp. 151–2, 191–3.

[70] *Ibid.*, p. 10.

[71] A.R. Burnett-Hurst, *Labour and Housing in Bombay: A Study in the Economic Condition of the Wage-Earning Classes of Bombay* (London, 1925), pp. 21–2.

[72] *Gazetteer*, III, 33–4.

[73] *Report of the Bombay Health Officer, for the 3rd Quarter of 1871* (Bombay, 1872), p. 24.

[74] *Ibid.*

[75] Burnett-Hurst, *Labour and Housing*, p. 24, n. 1.

[76] G. Hancock, Clerk to the Board of Conservancy to J.G. Lumsden, Secretary to Government, Letter No. 134 of 1852, 15 June 1852, in *Correspondence Relating to the Prohibition of Burials in the Back Bay Sands, and to Dr Leith's Mortuary Report for 1854* (Bombay, 1855), p. 1.

The scarcity of space in the designated burial ground[77] was mitigated, we are told, by 'the rapidity with which the bodies decompose' so that after only eight days an old grave could be re-opened for another corpse.[78] At high tide, during the monsoons, it was possible to observe the effects of the 'surf washing the newly interred from their graves'.[79] Since Back Bay lay to the windward side of the Native Town, the graveyards produced a 'stench which is most disgusting and overpoweringly offensive'.[80]

The colonial state, concerned to take resources out of India, was not about to invest in the refinement of Bombay's urban environment. On the other hand, the full commercial potential of Bombay could scarcely be realized under these conditions. Government and municipal expenditure was directed more readily towards the development of its commercial infrastructure than the improvement of its social conditions, towards roads rather than houses or drains.[81] However, the British and Indian magnates could neglect the state of the urban environment only at their own peril: insanitary conditions generated disease. Epidemics which were bred in the hovels of the poor could not always be stopped at the gates of the rich. Just how far the state would be drawn into ameliorating these conditions, however, was determined by and indeed reflected ruling-class notions of the habits and customs of the poor and their perceptions of the necessary minimum at which the poor could be expected to live. These perceptions combined with political and ideological constraints upon municipal and government expenditure, and its objects, to foster selective improvement. Thus the Girgaum and Kalbadevi Roads, 'the two principal thoroughfares of the Native Town, and those most frequented by Europeans' were the first to have their drains covered as early as 1848. 'Owing to the deficiency of funds', however, 'very little progress' had been made 'in the back streets of the Native Town'.[82] As late as 1925, when Bombay had more sewers than any other city in the East, the city's 'poorer quarters' still had none.[83]

---

[77] It was calculated in 1854 that if the number of corpses buried each year was 'laid at the same time, without intervening space, they would not only cover the whole area, but they would have to be laid in two tiers, the second equally closely packed as the first and there would still be more to form part of a third tier of corpses'. *Mortuary Report for 1854* by Dr A. Leith, para. 10, quoted by W. Hart, Secretary to Government, to the Acting Clerk of the Peace, 7 July 1855, *Correspondence Relating to the Prohibition of Burials*, p. 10.

[78] *Mortuary Report for 1854* in *ibid.*

[79] W. Hart, Secretary to Government, to the Acting Clerk of the Peace, 7 July 1855, in *ibid.*, pp. 10–11.

[80] *Mortuary Report for 1854*, para. 11, quoted in *ibid.*, p. 11.

[81] *Annual Administration Reports of the City of Bombay Improvement Trust* (Bombay, 1899–); K.T. Shah and G.J. Bahadurji, *Constitution, Functions and Finance of Indian Municipalities* (Bombay, 1925); Burnett-Hurst, *Labour and Housing*, pp. 31–4; Gordon, *Business and Politics*, pp. 119–31.

[82] Conybeare, 'Different Methods of Conveyancing', p. 17.

[83] Burnett-Hurst, *Labour and Housing*, p. 21.

Piecemeal social engineering and selective improvement led inevitably to catastrophe. The outbreak of bubonic plague in 1896 was perceived as the most dramatic and destructive manifestation of municipal failure. Municipal health officials had long feared that as a consequence of their sanitary neglect, some disease, perhaps as yet unknown, would 'arise and sweep away the most effete of the population'.[84] In 1892, the Health Officer, considering the inadequacy of the city's drainage system, had predicted that 'there will surely come a time when the population of each district will not be able to live in health'.[85] The plague represented the apocalypse which officials had long feared. As mortality rose, the city was consumed by a widespread moral panic, which was reflected in the frenzied measures adopted to combat the disease.[86] As late as the 1920s, it was said, the plague 'still retains its hold on the city'.[87]

Necessarily, the epidemic and its attendant panic had serious social and political consequences. It combined as a social moment the disruption of the city's commerce with the subversion of its political order. The plague, which was interpreted as a consequence of the state's resolute neglect, became the site of its most ferocious intervention into the lives of its subjects. During the epidemic, the working classes, perhaps for the first time, experienced the colonial state, acting on a massive scale, as a relentlessly intrusive and oppressive force. Officials grew increasingly apprehensive that the social and political fabric of the city was on the verge of disintegration.[88] As half of the city's population fled, there was 'open bidding for labour at the street corner and the shattering of the tie hitherto binding the employer and the employed'.[89] In the plague riots of 1898, Europeans, in particular, became a target of popular violence.[90] Although it should not be supposed that the working classes consistently opposed the plague measures while elites, by contrast, collaborated with

[84] Tenth Annual Report of the Health Officer, in *Annual Report of the Municipal Commissioner of Bombay for 1875* (Bombay, 1876), pp. 148–9.

[85] Report of the Health Officer in *Annual Report of the Municipal Commissioner for Bombay, 1892* (Bombay, 1893), p. 383.

[86] R. Chandavarkar, 'Plague Panic and Epidemic Politics in India, 1896–1914', in P. Slack and T. Ranger (eds.), *Epidemics and Ideas: Essays on the Historical Perception of Pestilence* (Cambridge, 1992). There is a growing literature on the plague epidemic in India: see, especially, I.J. Catanach, 'Plague and the Tensions of Empire, 1896–1918', in D. Arnold (ed.), *Imperial Medicine and Indigenous Societies* (Manchester, 1988), pp. 149–71; I. Klein, 'Urban Development and Death: Bombay City 1870–1914', *MAS*, XX, 4 (1986), 725–54; I. Klein, 'Plague, Policy and Popular Unrest in British India' *MAS*, XXII, 4 (1988), 723–55; D. Arnold, 'Touching the Body: Perspectives on the Indian Plague, 1896–1900', in Guha (ed.), *Subaltern Studies*, vol. V, pp. 55–90.

[87] Burnett-Hurst, *Labour and Housing*, p. 5.

[88] P.C.H. Snow, *Report on the Outbreak of Bubonic Plague in Bombay, 1896–97* (Bombay, 1897); Capt. J.K. Condon, *The Bombay Plague, Being A History of the Progress of Plague in the Bombay Presidency from September 1896 to June 1899* (Bombay, 1900).

[89] Edwardes, *The Rise of Bombay*, p. 330.

[90] GOB, Judicial, 1898, vol. 217, Compilation no. 669, part I, MSA.

the state, the epidemic did help to crystallize social antagonisms and class identities. It was a symptom of the plague panic, and the guilt which decades of sanitary neglect evoked among officials, that an Improvement Trust, established in 1898, launched itself frenetically into the demolition of slums and the provision of housing and drainage, until, as the panic passed, its constructive energies were quickly spent.[91] While the experience of the plague stimulated urban planning, it also served to strengthen an older tradition which envisaged, more clearly than it ever successfully effected, the social segregation of Bombay's residents.

The social geography of the city was steadily transformed in the nineteenth and twentieth centuries, but three phases may conveniently be identified. First, in the early nineteenth century, a native town was separated out from the Fort. The major geographical division in eighteenth-century Bombay was, as Burnell put it, between 'its two distinct limits, the English and the Black'.[92] One early description of the Fort identified the area between the Church and Apollo Gates (which led into the Esplanade) as the European residential quarter, and the north-east corner of the town as the business quarter of 'Parsees, Borahs and Banians'.[93] Nevertheless, there was 'strong evidence of the unequal distribution of wealth throughout the Native community'.[94] The turn of the century witnessed the first attempts to exclude Indian merchants from the Fort. The fire of 1803 had destroyed a large part of the town and razed the Customs House to the ground. The rebuilding of both provided the best opportunity for relocating the Indian merchant community. The new Customs House was built outside the Fort, on the site of an old Koli fishing hamlet near Masjid Bunder. The merchants were

allotted a space in the oarts adjoining the Fort and Esplanade for the erection of a Black Town such as Madras; or gradually to effect such a separation between the town and fortifications, as exists in Calcutta.[95]

Since the fortifications were to be renewed, it was decreed that the space between them should be determined by the range of the Company's cannons.[96] Apartheid was to characterize the social layout of Calcutta and Madras in this period as well. But there racial segregation was considerably sharper and cruder than in Bombay, where collaboration in business and politics could legitimize social fraternity.

The later nineteenth century witnessed further shifts in the social geography

[91] This shift is particularly evident in the *Annual Administration Reports of the Bombay Improvement Trust*, especially from the mid 1900s onwards.
[92] J. Burnell, *Bombay in the Days of Queen Anne*, edited by S.T. Sheppard (London, 1933), p. 20.
[93] Anon., 'The Town and Fort of Bombay', pp. 244–5.
[94] *Ibid.*
[95] Masani, *Local Self-Government in Bombay*, p. 89.
[96] Orr, *Density of Population*, p. 1.

of the city. From the mid nineteenth century onwards, Indian magnates began to move out of their wadis and mohallas to Malabar and Cumballa Hills, Breach Candy and Mahalaxmi, occupied mostly by European officials and merchants.[97] At the same time, trades which 'caused danger or offence to the public' were removed from the Fort to the areas north of the native town: tanners were pushed out to Bandra and Mahim; catgut makers to Worli; fat-boilers to Naigaum and the Sewri Cross Road and even the indigo dyers of Suparibagh were moved further north and east to Sewri.[98] In 1887, one official committee recommended sternly that 'all trades and manufactures that create an offensive smell, or cause a nuisance, should be located only in the neighbourhood of Sion'.[99]

With the expansion of Bombay's population in the mid nineteenth century, the native town itself crept northwards to Byculla and Kamathipura, and west through Khetwadi and Girgaum up to the sea at Chaupati. Within the native town, the divisions between its richer and poorer areas, however blurred, became more apparent. Areas like Girgaum, Khetwadi and Fanaswadi became primarily the suburbs of 'respectable' and rising Maharashtrian middle classes of the city. The wealthy merchants lived in the neighbourhood of their markets, especially in the south-western sections of the town. The triangle formed by the Esplanade Cross Road, Kalbadevi Road and Sheikh Memon Street was 'said to contain the greater part of the accumulated riches of Bombay'.[100] On the other hand, the poorer parts of the native town were insanitary and overcrowded. Gogari in Bhuleshwar, on the whole a relatively rich district of Hindu merchants, was an 'indescribably filthy quarter of milk sellers'. Chakla was notorious for its cattle-stables and its human 'warehouses'. Kumbharwada was 'a shamefully neglected district' where the people were 'generally poor and the house-owners portion off the floors of their house into as many rooms as possible'. In the 'dirty, irregular labyrinth' of Cavel, the principal thoroughfare was through a liquor shop which opened into the Girgaum Road.[101] By contrast, the Fort, which had been characterized in the 1850s by its 'extraordinary salubrity (as compared with our other districts)'[102] was still in 1864 splendidly 'isolated from the urban portion by its recently levelled ramparts and its esplanade'.[103] The characteristic feature of the period was the extent to which

[97] Proceedings of the Committee on the Future Extension of the City of Bombay, 1887, Appendix: Written and Oral Evidence, Mr J. Fleming, p. 30, in GOB, Public Works Department (henceforth PWD) (General), vol. 1162; Compilation no. 4133 W, 1868–89, MSA.
[98] Masani, Local Self-Government in Bombay, p. 176.
[99] Report of the Committee on the Future Extension of the City of Bombay, 1887, p. 12, in GOB, PWD (General), vol. 1162, Compilation no. 4133 W, 1868–89, MSA.
[100] Maclean, Guide, p. 197.
[101] Edwardes, The Rise of Bombay, p. 295.
[102] Conybeare, 'Different Methods of Conveyancing', p. 21.
[103] Census, 1864, p. xiii.

wealth, rather than race, religion or caste alone had begun to define residential patterns. However, social segregation was always more fervently imagined, perhaps by planners and residents alike, than it was consistently effected in practice. Thus, as Mr D. Gostling, an architect, told the Extension Committee in the 1880s, 'A good many middle-class Europeans live in Tarwadi and Byculla. Poor Europeans live in the same class of houses as poor natives'. Moreover, he added, 'the rich and the poor have always lived together – the former in the principal, the latter in the back streets – and always will'.[104]

In a third phase, following the outbreak of the plague epidemic, and in the two or three decades which followed, the social geography of the city crystallized more sharply along class lines. The cotton mills which were being built in the 1870s and 1880s were located to the north of the native town. As the native town grew more congested and land values rose and rents followed them in their spiral, some workers, especially the older residents who were better established in the city, began to move to Parel and Byculla, and to the vicinity of the docks at Mazagaon and Sewri. At the same time, improvements in communications also facilitated the greater dispersal of the population. The eastern and western parts of the island were linked by the construction of major thoroughfares: Grant Road in the late 1830s, Princess Street and Sandhurst Road in the 1850s and 1860s. Hornby Road linked the native town to the Fort while the completion of Mahim Causeway and reconstruction of the old road through Sion which linked the island to Salsette improved communications to the north. In the 1870s, roads constructed across the Byculla and Tardeo flats brought the new mill areas to the north into closer contact with the commercial sections of the Fort.

In the same decade, tramways began to operate along these thoroughfares.[105] From the 1890s, the Great Indian Peninsular Railway as well as the Bombay, Baroda and Central Indian Railway started local passenger services which were widely used.[106] By 1909, the Great Indian Peninsular Railway had nine stations within the city limits and the Bombay Baroda and Central India another ten.[107] These improvements in transport encouraged the growth of new suburbs. If the growth of middle-class suburbs eased the overcrowding of the old native town, it also delineated more sharply its plebeian profile. At the same time, the area north of Tardeo towards Parel, Byculla and beyond began to constitute the mill district of the city: Girangaon or the mill village as it came to be known to the

[104] Proceedings of the Committee on the Future Extension of the City of Bombay, 1887, Appendix, Evidence, Mr D. Gostling, p. 2, in GOB, PWD (General), vol. 1162, Compilation no. 4133 W, 1868–89, MSA.
[105] Edwardes, The Rise of Bombay, pp. 268–9, 280–2, 290–1, 308–9; Gazetteer, I, 358–67.
[106] Statements received by Mr G.H.B. Radcliffe, Secretary to the Agent, BB&CI Railway, 1 December 1913, giving figures to show the growth of suburban traffic, Report of the Bombay Development Committee (Bombay, 1914), pp. 177–81.
[107] Gazetteer, I, 348, 356.

mill-workers and, indeed, the city's residents more generally. As the factory proletariat employed in the cotton industry grew, it was in this area that it became increasingly concentrated.

The plague epidemic accentuated the tendency of officials to perceive social segregation as the solution to Bombay's urban problems.[108] In 1898, the Government of Bombay created an Improvement Trust for the city, with autonomy from the Municipal Corporation. Its brief was both to improve the sanitary state of the city and the standard of housing for the poor as well as to build and widen roads, reclaim land and generally improve transport facilities and communications. It acted to enshrine the separation of social classes as the orthodoxy of town planning for Bombay. The Back Bay reclamations, the planners imagined, would be reserved for wealthier classes while it was supposed that 'the whole of the foreshore from the Hornby Vellard northward up to Bandra Creek affords suitable sites for residence of the best class'. On the other hand the area south of Mahim Bay was 'useless for such a purpose so long as the nuisance due to the defective nature of the arrangements for sewage discharge continues'. Should this condition be ameliorated, however, 'the natural tendency of the wealthy classes will be to take up their residence there'. Similarly, the upper middle classes were expected to live in Salsette or at Matunga, in the better blocks planned by the Trust for that neighbourhood; the lower middle classes would go to Matunga and the area inland from Mahim woods; while the still poorer classes were expected 'to spread out from the more crowded areas in the city' to the areas vacated by the lower middle classes. The poorer classes would be accommodated largely 'in the east, north-east and central portions of the island, in the vicinity of the docks, factories and workshops'. Factories were to continue to be located in the north-east of the island. Since 'mill employees follow the mills in which they are employed, such restriction will automatically prevent increased congestion in the south as a consequence of the development of industrial enterprise'.[109] In these ways, the slums of the poor were to be sealed off from the citadels of the rich.

But these well-laid plans amounted to little. For all the breathless energy and radical purpose with which the Trust embarked on its voyage of improvement, its achievements were remarkably modest. As the threat of the plague receded, so its efforts were diverted from sanitation and housing to the traditional objective of strengthening and improving the commercial infrastructure of the

---

[108] GOB, PWD, 1868–89, vol. 1163, Comp. no. W 4133, MSA. F.F. Conlon, 'Industrialization and the Housing Problem in Bombay, 1850–1940', in K. Ballhatchet and D. Taylor (eds.), *Changing South Asia: Economy and Society* (School of Oriental and African Studies, London, 1984), pp. 153–68.
[109] *Report of the Bombay Development Committee*, p. 1; *Annual Report of the City of Bombay Improvement Trust, 1907–08* (Bombay, 1908), appendix A, pp. xix-xxxiv.

city. It succeeded in demolishing more houses than it constructed. Sometimes
it demolished slums because it considered them uninhabitable but often the
older consideration weighed as well: demolition cleared a convenient path for
a necessary carriageway.[110] By 1917–18, it had acquired 11 per cent of the land
area of the island in pursuit of its schemes of improvement, but more than
two-thirds of this property was simply left undeveloped.[111] The causes of its
failure are as complex as they are numerous, but among them must surely lie
the limits within which strategies for improvement were conceived. To the
extent that it developed a strategy at all, its implications served to accentuate
the tendencies already at work by which class and ethnic divisions more
markedly overlaid patterns of residence.

The evolution of capitalism in western India

Until the late nineteenth century, Bombay's urban economy was dominated by
its commerce and in particular its export trade. Despite the Company's attempt
to recruit skilled workers and artisanal castes to the island since the early days
of the settlement,[112] Bombay did not become a major centre of artisanal
production. The export trade in piecegoods which it handled at the turn of the
nineteenth century was substantially the output of Gujarat's handloom weavers.[113] The shipyards built in the mid eighteenth century had begun to decline
with the advent of steam and their functions were reduced progressively from
building to repair and maintenance after the 1850s.[114] It was, on the other hand,
the opium and more enduringly the cotton trade, at first to China, later to
Liverpool and Western Europe, and by the end of the century to Japan, which
provided the drive and dynamism behind the city's growth and commercial
prosperity.[115]

The political weakness of the Company in this region until the early nineteenth century allowed Indian merchants in Bombay to participate in and
appropriate a significant share of this commercial expansion. Company merchants and private traders relied upon Indian brokers not only to interpret the
languages and the currencies of the region but also through their local connections and influence to obtain necessary supplies, discipline labour and ensure

---

[110] Burnett-Hurst, *Labour and Housing*, p. 32; *Annual Report of the City of Bombay Improvement Trust, 1912–13* (Bombay, 1913), appendix M-6, pp. 122–39.

[111] *Annual Administration Report for the Bombay Presidency, 1917–18* (Bombay, 1918), p. vi.

[112] Conlon, 'Caste, Community and Colonialism'; Kosambi, 'Commerce, Conquest and the Colonial City'; Kooiman, 'Bombay from Fishing Village to Colonial Port City'.

[113] The exports of piecegoods from Bombay amounted to nearly 17 per cent of the total value of
exports in 1801–2 and fell below this level only after the 1840s. Calculated from the *Gazetteer*,
I, 514–15.

[114] Wadia, *The Bombay Dockyard; Gazetteer*, III, 258–78, especially 266–70.

[115] Dantwalla, *A Hundred Years of Indian Cotton*; Vicziany, 'The Cotton Trade'.

the delivery of contracts. The dependence of the Company as well as private traders in the late eighteenth century upon their credit also left them strongly placed to take a cut in the growing accumulations of the China trade. Although their position was gradually whittled away in the early nineteenth century, it was not until the 1870s that the great merchant princes were properly subordinated within the structure of the export trade.[116] The most portentous effect of this subordination was the drift of mercantile capital into the cotton-spinning mills floated in this period.

The development of capitalist enterprise and the strategies which its protagonists adopted must be situated within the context of the options available to the capitalist classes as a whole. It is frequently assumed that, because industrialization did not transform the economy, capitalism could have no part in the history of India. Indian society in this view remained static, unchanging and traditional, except when its movement or development was fashioned by the 'impact' of the West. Conversely, historians who have put together considerable evidence of a vigorous pre-colonial capitalism in India have tended to downplay its significance because the 'potentialities' for factory industrialization are perceived to be weak.[117]

Once large-scale industries begin to appear, an almost unchallenged convention examines the history of the Indian capitalist class in terms of the emergence of industrial entrepreneurs. Following this convention, historians trace the evolution of the capitalist classes 'from traders to industrialists'. The most significant division in Bombay's mercantile community in the nineteenth century is found in their proximity to and participation in the export trade while in the early twentieth century this is superseded by the distinction between 'industrialists' and 'marketeers'.[118] This distinction, too neatly effected and perhaps too firmly maintained, obscures a broader view of the general influences upon the development of the capitalist classes as a whole. Bombay City is thus portrayed as a capitalist enclave, pulled out of its regional moorings, by its development within an international economy. Industrialization is taken as a process of technological diffusion spreading slowly if unsteadily outwards from Western Europe; it is taken for granted that its dynamic was external, working ceaselessly upon a passive, traditional indigenous economy.[119] This

---

[116] Marika Vicziany, 'Bombay Merchants and Structural Changes in the Export Community, 1850 to 1880', in Chaudhuri and Dewey (eds.), *Economy and Society*, pp. 163–96.

[117] For instance, the classic and masterly analysis by I. Habib, 'The Potentialities of Capitalistic Development in Mughal India', *Journal of Economic History*, XXXIX, 1 (1969), 32–78.

[118] Dobbin, *Urban Leadership*, ch.1; Gordon, *Businessmen and Politics;* Ray, *Industrialization in India*, ch. 6.

[119] These arguments are examined more closely in R. Chandavarkar, 'Industrialization in India before 1947: Conventional Approaches and Alternative Perspectives', *MAS*, XIX, 3 (1985), 623–68.

view of the development of the capitalist classes has often tended to mistake the tip of the iceberg for the solid mass beneath the water-line. If the choices made by industrial capital were shaped by the options before the capitalist classes as a whole, their development must be situated within the regional economy. Necessarily, the treatment will be schematic rather than detailed or exhaustive. The emphasis rests on the suggestion that industrialization was the outcome of the narrowing options before the capitalist classes. It did not signify their transcendence of the inescapable constraints within which they operated.

Western India, and in particular the Gujarat region, was the scene of an active mercantile capitalism before the advent of colonial rule. The ports of Gujarat had traded for at least three millennia with the Red Sea and the Persian Gulf.[120] Cambay was the only part of the Estado da India which did not simply process the circular trading economy of the Portuguese Empire but exported its own produce so that its overseas trade provided a major stimulus to the internal economy of its hinterland. This flourishing commercial economy was founded on a firm industrial base.[121] Gujarat was one of the most important industrial regions in South Asia which between the sixteenth and eighteenth century, it is estimated, commanded over a quarter of the world's total manufacturing capacity.[122] The inflow of bullion which paid for the region's exports provided the foundation for prodigious money-markets and extensive banking networks which served far-flung parts of the sub-continent. The Deccan and even the coastal strip of Konkan, by contrast, were marginal to the trading world of the Indian Ocean and did not match Gujarat's level of economic development; but even here there were in the sixteenth and seventeenth centuries 'mercantile surpluses and opportunities available in the region'.[123] Moreover, agrarian elites and revenue farmers, governors and captains of the leading ports and not simply merchants and traders, played a major role in the accumulation and deployment of capital.

[120] M.N. Pearson, *Merchants and Rulers in Gujarat: The Response to the Portuguese in the Sixteenth Century* (Berkeley and Los Angeles, 1976), ch. 1.
[121] *Ibid.*; S. Gopal, *Commerce and Crafts in Gujarat in the Seventeenth Century: A Study in the Impact of European Expansion in Pre-Capitalist Economy* (New Delhi, 1975); K. Gillion, *Ahmedabad: A Study in Indian Urban History* (Berkeley and Los Angeles, 1968), ch. 1; B.G. Gokhale, 'Ahmedabad in the XVIIth Century', *Journal of the Economic and Social History of the Orient*, XII, 2 (1969), 187–97; B.G. Gokhale, *Surat in the Seventeenth Century: A Study in Urban History of Pre-Modern India* (London, 1978); A. Das Gupta, *Indian Merchants and the Decline of Surat* (Weisbaden, 1979); K.N. Chaudhuri, 'The Structure of the Indian Textile Industry in the Seventeenth and Eighteenth Centuries', *IESHR*, XI, 2–3 (1974), 127–82.
[122] Chaudhuri, 'Structure of the Indian Textile Industry'; P. Bairoch, 'International Industrialization Levels from 1750 to 1980', *Journal of European Economic History*, XI, 2 (1982), 269–333; D.A. Washbrook, 'Progress and Problems: South Asian Economic and Social History, 1720–1860', *MAS*, XXI, 1 (1988), 57–96.
[123] B.G. Gokhale, 'Some Urban Commercial Centres of the Western Deccan in the XVIIth Century', in N.K. Wagle (ed.), *Images of Maharashtra: A Regional Profile of India* (London, 1980), p. 66.

The political and economic developments of the later eighteenth century, in particular, processes of state formation associated with increasing military activity and the steady extension of revenue farming, worked strongly to the advantage of these agrarian and mercantile elites.[124] They gained from the commercial and political expansion of the Company, which created conditions favouring the development of capital, and profited in particular from the growth of the China trade, especially after 1784. The rapid commercial expansion of Bombay, which was sustained through the agrarian depression of the 1830s, continued to generate opportunities for merchants, creditors and artisans. Indeed, the buoyancy and dynamism of this mercantile capitalism facilitated and financed the Company's territorial expansion in the late eighteenth and early nineteenth centuries.[125]

But as the Company became the paramount power in the land, so the European private traders came increasingly to dominate the commercial economy of the Presidency capitals, Bombay included. The capital which they accumulated in the China trade loosened their dependence upon and radically altered their relationship with their Indian agents and brokers, and even the Gujarati banking houses. Increasingly, they replaced Indian merchants as the preferred bankers to the Company state and assumed the dominant role in Bombay's growing export trade.[126] While the abolition of revenue farming, the advance of bureaucracy and the resumption of alienated lands weakened the position of local elites, the rapid decline of the textile industry in the face of manufactured imports from Britain, the replacement of bullion imports as the primary engine of commercial expansion by the notoriously over-assessed land-revenue demand and the effects of the long depression of the second quarter of the nineteenth century, served to undermine mercantile and agrarian capital.[127] The subordination of Indian capital in Bombay occurred gradually, taking over half a century to manifest itself, and affecting different levels and functions of capital variously.[128]

Since the eighteenth century, the expansion of British power had not only

[124] S. Gordon, 'The Slow Conquest: Administrative Integration of Malwa into the Maratha Empire, 1720–1760', *MAS*, XI, 1 (1977), 1–40; C.A. Bayly, *Rulers, Townsmen and Bazaars: North Indian Society in the Age of British Expansion, 1770–1870* (Cambridge, 1983), pp. 110–228; Washbrook, 'Progress and Problems', 68–72; F. Perlin, 'Proto-Industrialization and Pre-Colonial South Asia', *Past and Present*, XCVII (1983), 30–95.
[125] L. Subramaniam, 'Banias and the British: The Role of Indigenous Credit in the Process of Imperial Expansion in Western India in the Second Half of the Eighteenth Century', *MAS*, XXI, 3 (1987), 473–510.
[126] Nightingale, *Trade and Empire*, pp. 23–7, 219–22.
[127] Washbrook, 'Progress and Problems', 79–84.
[128] A.K. Bagchi, 'Reflections of Patterns of Regional Growth in India During the Period of British Rule', *Bengal Past and Present*, XCV, 1 (1976), 247–89.

appeared to facilitate the accumulation of capital but also enabled its owners to tighten their control over labour and increase their share of its product.[129] The very processes by which indigenous capital was now subordinated to expatriate and metropolitan capital also served to increase its domination of labour. For instance, the prevailing form of the putting-out system in Gujarat placed weavers under no obligation to deliver their contracts as long as they returned the capital advanced to them.[130] Already by the 1730s, the English were seeking to restrict the remarkable degree of control which weavers enjoyed over their own labour and, in particular, began 'coercing their weavers to honour their agreements'.[131] But not until the late eighteenth century when the Company became a territorial power was it able to breach these customary conventions which so strongly protected weavers. By 1800, the Company had promulgated new regulations to prevent 'Manufacturers or other persons in their Employ from embezzling the Money advanced to them or disposing of the Goods, otherwise than in the due pursuance of their engagement'. Weavers whom they engaged could neither accept contracts from nor sell their cloth to anyone else. Not only were they fined for what was deemed unsatisfactory work, but they were required to pay up to 35 per cent of the value of any orders which they failed to deliver on time. In addition, the Company threatened to indemnify merchants who attempted to procure cloth from its weavers or otherwise prevented them from meeting their commitments.[132] If the land-revenue ad- ministration of early British rule had acted adversely upon rural capital, the burden of its assessments also contributed strongly to the subordination of labour by rendering cultivators increasingly dependent upon credit.[133] More- over, the statecraft and legal framework of the early colonial state, by securing and sanctifying private property rights, considerably strengthened the position of mercantile and agrarian capital in relation to labour.[134]

Coincidentally, other factors which acted to increase the supply of labour

[129] Washbrook, 'Progress and Problems', 79–95; Perlin, 'Proto-Industrialization', 85–8.
[130] Das Gupta, *Indian Merchants*, pp. 36–7.
[131] *Ibid.*, p. 36, n. 4; Habib, 'Potentialities', 67.
[132] Bombay Secret and Political Proceedings, range 381, XIV, 4435–48, 20 May 1800, cited by Nightingale, *Trade and Empire*, pp. 172–3.
[133] A.M. Shah, 'The Political System of Gujarat', *Enquiry*, N. S., I, 1 (1964), 83–95; N. Rabitoy, 'Administrative Modernization and the Bhats of British Gujarat, 1800–1820', *IESHR*, IX, 1 (1974), 46–73; N. Rabitoy, 'System vs. Expediency: The Reality of Land Revenue Administra- tion in Bombay Presidency, 1812–20', *MAS*, IX, 4 (1975), 529–46; C.N. Bates, 'The Nature of Social Change in Rural Gujarat: the Kheda District, 1818–1918', *MAS*, XV, 4 (1981), 771–821; S. Prakash, 'The Evolution of the Agrarian Economy in Gujarat (India), 1850–1930', unpub- lished PhD thesis, University of Cambridge, 1983, ch. 1.
[134] E. Stokes, *The English Utilitarians and India* (Cambridge, 1965); B.S. Cohn, 'From Indian Status to British Contract', *Journal of Economic History*, XXI, 4 (1961), 613–28; D.A. Washbrook, 'Law, State and Agrarian Society in Colonial India', *MAS*, XV, 3 (1981), 649–721.

served at the same time to erode its bargaining power. The effects of de-indus-
tralization and the contraction of some of the great urban centres, the disbanding
of armies and the closer policing and taxation of forest-dwellers and tribals
forced growing numbers back to the land.[135] The subordination of indigenous
capital was accompanied, indeed facilitated, by its increasing control over
labour. While indigenous capital was increasingly confined to usury and petty
trading in the nineteenth century, its development came to depend upon the more
intensive exploitation of labour.

The structural constraints within which capitalism in nineteenth-century
Western India would develop were in these ways already being more clearly
defined during the agrarian depression of the 1830s and 1840s. For the 1850s
onwards, however, the depression began to lift and the following decades up to
the First World War have often been portrayed as a period of steady expansion
and rising prosperity.[136] As the revenue settlements were revised downwards in
the 1850s and prices began to rise, cultivated acreage expanded and the
population began gradually to increase. As railway construction and better
communications made wider markets accessible, the intensity of price fluctuations was ironed out and the risks attached to growing crops for sale were
reduced. Indeed, rising prices provided the incentive for capital to strengthen
its claims on the agrarian produce.[137]

In the 1850s, Alexander Mackay observed that even in Broach, where cotton
cultivation had expanded during the early-nineteenth-century depression, 'the

---

[135] Perlin, 'Proto-Industrialization'; on the decline of the towns, see Das Gupta, *Indian Merchants*;
Gillion, *Ahmedabad*; V. Divekar, 'Pune', in J.S. Grewal and I. Banga (eds.), *Indian Urban
History* (n.d., n.p.), pp. 91–106; on forest-dwellers, pastoralists and tribals, see S. Gordon, 'Bhils
and the Idea of a Criminal Tribe in Nineteenth Century India', in A. Yang (ed.), *Crime and
Criminality in British India* (Tucson, Ariz., 1985), pp. 128–39; J. Breman, *Patronage and
Exploitation: Changing Agrarian Relations in South Gujarat, India* (Berkeley and Los Angeles,
1974); D. Hardiman, 'From Custom to Crime: The Politics of Drinking in Colonial South
Gujarat', in Guha (ed.), *Subaltern Studies*, vol. III, pp. 165–228 and Ramchandra Guha,
'Forestry and Social Protest in British Kumaun, c. 1893–1921', in Guha (ed.), *Subaltern Studies*,
vol. III, pp. 54–100.

[136] M.B. McAlpin, *Subject to Famine: Food Crises and Economic Change in Western India,
1860–1920* (Princeton, 1983); M.B. McAlpin, 'The Effects of Expansion of Markets on Rural
Income Distribution in Nineteenth Century India', *Explorations in Economic History*, XII
(1975), 289–302; N. Charlesworth, *Peasants and Imperial Rule: Agriculture and Agrarian
Society in the Bombay Presidency, 1850–1935* (Cambridge, 1985), pp. 125–225; N. Charlesworth, 'Rich Peasants and Poor Peasants in Late Nineteenth Century Maharashtra', in Dewey
and Hopkins (eds.), *The Imperial Impact*, pp. 97–113; N. Charlesworth, 'Trends in the Agricultural Performance of an Indian Province: the Bombay Presidency, 1900–1920', in Chaudhuri
and Dewey (eds.), *Economy and Society*, pp. 113–40; R. Kumar, *Western India in the Nineteenth
Century: A Study in the Social History of Maharashtra* (London, 1968); Prakash, 'Agrarian
Economy in Gujarat'; A. Heston, 'National Income', in D. Kumar (ed.), *CEHI*, II, 376–462. But
see also S.C. Mishra, 'Agricultural Trends in Bombay Presidency, 1900–1920: The Illusion of
Growth', *MAS*, XIX, 4 (1985), 733–59.

[137] Charlesworth, *Peasants and Imperial Rule*, especially ch. 6.

class who would be most likely to improve the land, the monied class, is kept wholly disconnected from it'.[138] But with the recovery, capital showed a renewed willingness to seize its opportunities in the countryside. During the American Civil War boom, as the supply of credit to the countryside swelled, Bombay witnessed a proliferation of small money-lenders.[139] When the boom burst and prices began to fall in the 1870s, the credit market tightened. The Deccan Riots of 1875, it would now appear, were the consequence of the tensions and conflicts caused by the withdrawal and contraction of credit rather than the inexorable advance of capital at the expense of the small peasant.[140] From the 1880s onwards, substantial peasants increasingly picked up the slack in the rural credit market left by retreating townsmen.[141] But theirs represented a strategic retreat rather than an absolute withdrawal and both stood to gain from this rough specialization of function. The agriculturist sowkar not only borrowed from urban traders and money-lenders to effect his own loans, but he was obviously more creditworthy than the insolvent peasant household. The sowkar could borrow cheaply in the towns and lend at monopsonist rates in the village. He was better placed to assess the risks of lending and to wield his influence to recover the debts. His own interests as a cultivator made land or produce a more acceptable, even realistic collateral for his capital. The professional money-lender, on the other hand, lacked the advantages of local knowledge, influence and agricultural skills which the wealthy peasant enjoyed.[142] The withdrawal of credit by the professional money-lender was in these conditions a response to the low returns offered by an essentially stagnant agriculture rather than the capture of rural banking by a rising entrepreneurial peasant elite.[143] Urban merchants could thereby diversify their operations from the risk-laden and low returns business of subsistence lending and share in the growing profits of expanding trade.

It is not surprising that the first sign of stabilizing produce markets and rising prices brought capital into a closer engagement with agriculture. Yet if this suggested that sections of mercantile capital had done well in the depression of

[138] A. Mackay, *Western India: Reports Addressed to the Chambers of Commerce of Manchester, Liverpool, Blackburn and Glasgow* (London, 1853), p. 134.
[139] S. Guha, *The Agrarian Economy of the Deccan, 1818–1941* (Delhi, 1986), pp. 70–8; J. Banaji, Capitalist Domination and the Small Peasantry: Deccan Districts in the Late Nineteenth Century', *Economic and Political Weekly*, XII, 33–4 (1977), 1383–4; Charlesworth, *Peasants and Imperial Rule*, p. 87.
[140] Charlesworth, *Peasants and Imperial Rule*, pp. 95–115.
[141] *Ibid.*, pp. 169–72; Guha, *Agrarian Economy of the Deccan*, pp. 147–9; Banaji, 'Capitalist Domination and the Small Peasantry', 1384–7.
[142] D.A. Washbrook, 'Country Politics: Madras, 1870–1930', in J. Gallagher, G. Johnson and A. Seal (eds.), *Locality, Province and Nation: Essays on Imperialism and Nationalism in India, 1870–1940* (Cambridge, 1973), pp. 155–211.
[143] Guha, *The Agrarian Economy of the Deccan*, pp. 148–9.

the 1830s and 1840s, it also demonstrated the paucity of alternative investment opportunities open to capital in general and their narrowing options with the advent of colonialism. Moreover, our immediate concern must lie not simply with the fact but with the particular character of its engagement. Although capital was increasingly attracted to the land, it does not appear to have been invested on any significant scale in agricultural improvement. Even in Gujarat, the level of investment in agriculture scarcely increased between the 1820s and the 1870s.[144] Significantly, while the economic recovery of the mid nineteenth century was marked by the virtual absence of capital investment in agriculture, it created conditions both more secure and more attractive for its employment in usury and petty trade. As commodity prices rose and their fluctuations were lessened, it became increasingly attractive for capital to obtain and tighten its grip on agricultural produce. Thus, during the boom of the 1860s, up-country merchants in the cotton tracts appear to have withdrawn the credit they had earlier offered the agency houses and export firms on their cotton purchases and diverted their capital to local trade and money-lending.[145] For the most part, small pools of capital appear to have been invested in the domination and expropriation, the control and cheapening of labour power. In its extreme form, the terms of repayment effectively transformed the smallholding peasant from simply a debtor into a wage labourer, who in return for an advance parted with the bulk of his produce and was, in turn, allowed to retain a subsistence share.[146]

This pattern of capitalist engagement with agricultural production was scarcely conducive to its structural transformation. Underlying its limited role in this area were the considerable risks of investment in fragile small-scale agriculture, subject to the vagaries of the weather and international price fluctuations. The returns on agricultural production were too low to justify the costs of long-term borrowing,[147] while the famines which periodically devastated this region in the late nineteenth and early twentieth centuries only heightened the perception of risk.[148] Under these conditions, smallholders who often had to give up a share of their produce in payment of rent or interest had

---

[144] Prakash, 'The Agrarian Economy in Gujarat', p. 43.

[145] Guha, *The Agrarian Economy of the Deccan*, pp. 76–8; Banaji, 'Capitalist Domination and the Small Peasantry'.

[146] Mackay, *Western India*, p. 135; *Gazetteer of the Bombay Presidency* (henceforth *Presidency Gazetteer*), II, *Surat and Broach* (Bombay, 1877), 452, and *ibid., Ahmedabad* (Bombay, 1879), IV, 69–70; Banaji, 'Capitalist Domination and the Small Peasantry', 1389.

[147] *Royal Commission on Agriculture in India* (henceforth *RCAI*), II, part 1, *Evidence taken in the Bombay Presidency* (London, 1928), Dr H.H. Mann, Director of Agriculture, Bombay Presidency, q. 2854, p. 25.

[148] Guha, *The Agrarian Economy of the Bombay Deccan*, pp. 184–94; McAlpin, *Subject to Famine*; M.B. McAlpin 'Death, Famine and Risk: The Changing Impact of Crop Failures in Western India, 1870–1920', *Journal of Economic History*, XXIX, 1 (1979), 143–57.

little incentive, even if they had the means, to plough their occasional surplus back into the land. Money-lending provided a safer and more lucrative outlet for surplus cash. On the other hand, for money-lenders and wealthy peasants, who sometimes commanded a larger surplus, investment in agricultural improvement was no more appealing. The returns it yielded were lower than the profits of usury.[149] It was preferable, therefore, to invest in the subordination and reproduction of the peasant household and seek thereby to exercise a firmer control over its produce than to invest in wells, implements or cattle and risk a large outlay on variable seasons, uncertain output or unpredictable price fluctuations. The failure to invest in agricultural production placed serious constraints on the accumulation of capital.

The apparent risks of investment in agrarian production were fortified by the policies of the colonial state. Anxious that fundamental social change might kick away the props on which British rule so gingerly rested and mindful of the social conflict which might accompany it, the colonial state often acted to shore up the fragile smallholding base of the agrarian economy while its rhetoric advertised its rather more progressive and modernizing intentions.[150] The Deccan Agriculturists' Relief Act, whose eventual measures had for decades received close attention and prompted considerable discussion, was founded firmly on Wingate's private nightmare in which 'the whole of this country will rapidly pass into the hands of the Marwarees'.[151] When it finally received the Viceroy's assent in 1879, the Act limited the sale of land for debt unless specifically pledged, restrained urban money-lenders from acquiring land in case of default and invited the courts to scrutinize all debt transactions brought before them.[152] Stripped of the security which the seizure of the debtor's lands offered them, mercantile capital was accordingly deprived of the incentive to invest in agrarian production or to assume a controlling interest in it.[153]

Similarly, tenants in Bombay were not protected by the definition of their occupancy rights as they had been in Bengal and the United Provinces in the later nineteenth century.[154] However, government policies did enough to disturb

[149] Guha, *Agrarian Economy of the Deccan*, pp. 141–7.
[150] Washbrook, 'Law, State and Agrarian Society', 670–94.
[151] Wingate Diary, 1 April 1852, Wingate Papers, Box 293/4, quoted by Charlesworth, *Peasants and Imperial Rule*, p. 123.
[152] Charlesworth, *Peasants and Imperial Rule*, p. 123.
[153] The wider implications of this point are discussed by Washbrook, 'Law, State and Agrarian Society', 674–81.
[154] E. Stokes, 'The Structure of Landholding in Uttar Pradesh, 1860–1948', in E. Stokes, *The Peasant and the Raj: Studies in Agrarian Society and Peasant Rebellion in Colonial India* (Cambridge, 1978), pp. 205–27; B.B. Chaudhuri, 'The Land Market in Eastern India (1793–1940)', *IESHR*, XII, 1 (1975), 1–42 and XII, 2 (1975), 133–68; B.B. Chaudhuri, 'Agrarian Relations: Eastern India', in Kumar (ed.), *CEHI*, II, 86–177.

the landlords' security. The Khoti Settlement Act of 1904 gave tenants in Ratnagiri the right to commute their crop shares into cash rents according to a stipulated and officially guided procedure which may have had the initial effect of scaling them down.[155] In the alienated tracts of predominantly ryotwari areas, landlords, frequently absentee and often Brahmin, were relatively weaker in relation to their tenants than the dominant peasant castes who paid the revenue under ryotwari tenure.[156] Nonetheless, government policies served to narrow the landlord's freedom of manoeuvre. From 1907, inamdars were required to follow the general ryotwari practice with regard to revenue remissions. Even under the ryotwari tenure, landlords consistently encountered 'some official attitudes resentful of the dispossession of traditional tenants'.[157] This may have sufficed, in combination with prevailing production conditions, to deter landlords from investing capital in the improvement of lands.

As capital showed a willingness to take a firmer grip on agricultural production, its power and penetration was thus blunted. The emergence of a land market in the later nineteenth century offered substantial peasants effective collateral for their loans at the very moment when they began increasingly to enter the credit market as usurers. But it is not surprising, given the legal and social encumbrances upon land, that wealthy peasants showed little enthusiasm for relentlessly extending their holdings and they were no less averse to acquiring land than the professional money-lenders. For one thing, the land which they received through default might be highly dispersed and difficult to consolidate. In addition, accumulating land holdings might swiftly take the wealthy peasant household beyond the threshold at which it would have to employ wage labour. When agricultural prices rose, wage levels were liable to follow, squeezing their surplus; when crops failed or prices fell, excessively large holdings swiftly appeared an onerous burden. In any case, land represented and remained at best no more than a safe investment offering modest returns.[158] The optimal use of additional land was often to rent it and take half its produce rather than to work it with hired labour.

Merchant money-lenders also remained reluctant to take up the land of their debtors because the returns on landownership were considerably lower than the profits of usury.[159] They knew too little about cultivation and as outsiders frequently encountered the hostility of the local community if they attempted to eject insolvent cultivators indiscriminately. The most common forms of transaction by which money-lenders dispossessed peasants not only left the

[155] Charlesworth, *Peasants and Imperial Rule*, pp. 188–9.
[156] *Ibid.*, pp. 174–92.
[157] *Ibid.*, p. 186.
[158] Guha, *Agrarian Economy of the Deccan*, pp. 141–7, 149–58.
[159] *Ibid.*, pp. 141–7.

incumbents on the land to continue to cultivate it but also gave them the right to buy back their land at a future date on specified terms.[160] Furthermore, as rentals declined in relation to land prices in the late nineteenth and early twentieth centuries, so their reluctance to acquire land increased correspondingly.[161] Merchant money-lenders able to command produce could use their trading and kinship connections to diversify their operations away from usury. Wealthy peasants could not compete with these trading and banking networks. For the merchant money-lender and the wealthy peasant alike, the priority was to tighten their control over the agrarian produce rather than necessarily to acquire the land itself. These priorities were entirely compatible with the tendency to invest capital not in improving agricultural productivity but in the subsistence and reproduction of the small peasant household economy. The returns on the former were uncertain; the latter yielded extra dividends in terms of local influence. But this strategy of securing a closer grip on agrarian produce served only to expose the structural constraints within which capital would develop. The form of capital's engagement with agrarian production came largely to focus upon usury and petty trade; much of this was limited to subsistence lending to largely insolvent peasant households which entailed high risks and yielded low returns.[162] In this way, capital was confined to a narrow range of activities, its impact upon production relations was limited and the agrarian base of the economy was eased into structural stagnation.

The terms on which capital engaged with agriculture and the social relations to which it gave rise varied according to local production conditions. Over most of the Deccan, usury meant little more than lending for subsistence and the usurer might try to convert a relationship of debt into the bonds of labour.[163] Near the margin of subsistence the very notion of collateral melted away. Moreover, this impoverished agrarian base could scarcely be regarded as promising material for significant capital accumulation. In Gujarat and Khandesh, rising prices, the profits of cotton cultivation and competition among dealers eager to secure the crop enabled a large section of the peasantry to loosen the grip of the money-lended and assert its independence of his control from as early as the 1870s and 1880s.[164] From these areas, especially from Gujarat,

---

[160] Charlesworth, *Peasants and Imperial Rule*, p. 177.

[161] Guha, *Agrarian Economy of the Deccan*, pp. 141–7.

[162] Banaji, 'Capitalist Domination and the Small Peasantry'; Guha, *Agrarian Economy of the Deccan*, pp. 125–60, especially pp. 147–9; S.C. Mishra, 'Commercialization, Peasant Differentiation and Merchant Capital in Late Nineteenth Century Bombay and Punjab', *Journal of Peasant Studies*, X, 1 (1982), 3–51; H.H. Mann, *Land and Labour in a Deccan Village* (Bombay, 1917).

[163] Banaji, 'Capitalist Domination and the Small Peasantry', 1387–91; Guha, *Agrarian Economy of the Deccan*, pp. 125–60.

[164] Prakash, 'Agrarian Economy in Gujarat', chs. 3 and 4, Banaji, 'Capitalist Domination and the Small Peasantry', 1394–7; Guha, *Agrarian Economy of the Deccan*, especially pp. 129–32.

where the dynamism and the sophistication of the early development of capitalism had enabled it to withstand more effectively the economic and political pressures of colonialism, merchants and bankers were able to diversify their activities to long-distance and export trades and industry[165] and some successfully extended their operations to Bombay and Ahmedabad. Not only was mercantile capital more firmly established in this region, but it was also constructed on a more prosperous productive base and it was able to appropriate and deploy a sizeable share of a growing agrarian surplus. It is not surprising, therefore, that Gujarati capital was to play so vital a role in the commercial development of Bombay.

It is within this context of the subordination of indigenous capital that the commercial and industrial growth of Bombay should be viewed. The commercial expansion of Bombay from the 1780s created fresh opportunities for merchant capital and, even in the midst of the depression of the late 1820s and 1830s, its export trade was characterized by growth and buoyancy.[166] Nevertheless, the growth of Bombay was not the gift of a benevolent and progressive colonialism. Its industrialization and its entrepreneurial class did not evolve naturally out of the export trade. We will not find here a heroic story of entrepreneurial genius, of great men of business who power their way through frontiers demarcated by custom and resources. Rather, the innovations in business method and commercial style often occurred as defensive measures taken by relatively disadvantaged or subordinate groups with less to risk and fewer alternatives to hand.

Significantly, the mercantile groups who played a leading role in the early economic history of Bombay were not the dominant elements in Gujarat's trading economy. The Parsis who boasted the richest and most powerful merchant princes of nineteenth-century Bombay scarcely registered their presence in the extensive trading and banking networks of sixteenth- and seventeenth-century Gujarat.[167] The Muslim dominance of the overseas trade in the sixteenth and seventeenth centuries[168] was gradually whittled away by the eighteenth.[169] But even at the height of this dominance, the most prominent Muslim merchants were settlers from Persia, Arabia, Turkey and Egypt. Yet

---

[165] Gillion, *Ahmedabad*, pp. 11–104; M.J. Mehta, *The Ahmedabad Cotton Textile Industry: Genesis and Growth* (Ahmedabad, 1982).

[166] The value of exports from Bombay increased from Rs. 79 lakhs in 1810–11 to Rs. 5,71 lakhs in 1850–1 to Rs. 15,47 lakhs in 1860–1. *Gazetteer*, I, 514–17, appendix IV.

[167] Pearson, *Merchants and Rulers in Gujarat*; Gillion, *Ahmedabad*, pp. 11–36; Gokhale, 'Ahmedabad'; Gokhale, *Surat*; Das Gupta, *Indian Merchants*.

[168] Pearson, *Merchants and Rulers in Gujarat*.

[169] Furber, *Bombay Presidency*, pp. 64–5.

those Muslim merchants who prospered most handsomely from Bombay's commercial expansion were not the superior breeds who claimed exotic descent but the indigenous Khoja and Bohra traders of the Ismaili community, who had long been looked down upon as mere converts and sometimes persecuted as heretics. These Ismaili communities often followed social practices and customary laws which bore close relation to the Hindu communities from which they had converted.[170] The most revered book of the Khojas thus took Ali to be the tenth incarnation of Vishnu.[171] More crucially, local usages regarding usury and inheritance laws allowed them to accumulate and retain capital within the family beyond the constraints which orthodox Islamic law may have imposed. Khojas had 'raised themselves from obscurity, poverty and illiteracy to prominence, wealth and intelligence'[172] in the course of the nineteenth century while Bohras, it was reported, in the early twentieth century were 'excellent businessmen and are engaged in every branch of trade and commerce'.[173] Memons, converts from the Lohana and Cutch Bania castes, moved to Bombay in large numbers after the famine of 1813. They first set up as tailors in the thieves' bazaar 'but their status steadily progressed as Bombay advanced in material prosperity' until by the 1900s they were said to 'indulge in every class of trade ... and include among their number some of the richest individuals in Bombay native society'.[174] Similarly, Bhatia merchants, followers of the Vallabhcharya sect, were relatively humble in the trading world of early modern Gujarat and Cutch but played a large part in Bombay's export trade and later its mill industry. They crossed the seas to trade in the Persian Gulf, East Africa and the Far East but were 'forbidden by religion to journey to Europe and America', which entailed a higher capital outlay as well as greater risk.[175] 'As a class', it was said in the early twentieth century, 'they are extremely diligent, and placing very little faith in ordinary school education as a means towards gaining a livelihood, they usually introduce their male children to commerce at an early age'.[176]

It was not the case that the dominant Hindu vania merchants and great Jain bankers abjured the opportunities created by the expansion of the Company's trade. But they were too firmly established within the Gujarat economy to seek

[170] Pearson, *Merchants and Rulers in Gujarat*, pp. 26–8, 136–8; S.T. Lokhandawalla, 'Islamic Law and Ismaili Communities (Khojas and Bohras)', *IESHR*, IV, 2 (1967), 155–76; *Gazetteer*, I, 180–2; Masselos, 'The Khojas of Bombay'.
[171] Lokhandawalla, 'Islamic Law and Ismaili Communities'; Pearson, *Merchants and Rulers*, p. 27.
[172] *Gazetteer*, I, 181.
[173] *Ibid.*, I, 181.
[174] *Ibid.*, I, 178.
[175] *Ibid.*, I, 169.
[176] *Ibid.*, I, 226.

dependence upon or patronage from the European companies or to abandon the centre of their highly successful operations. Accordingly, they preferred to send their agents to Bombay and maintain their base in Surat. Bombay seemed remote to these dominant mercantile elites. To follow the Company to their pestilential island might also require them to submit to unfavourable terms or entail the risk that English merchants might be favoured at their expense. The Company's commercial and military expansion had only increased the demand for their financial services.[177] Their loans and venture capital were indispensable to the growth of the China trade. In any case, the raw cotton which was exported in larger quantities from the 1770s onwards to China was predominantly the produce of Gujarat and Kathiawar, while Bombay's piecegoods trade was driven by the looms of the weavers of Ahmedabad and Surat.[178] Moreover, Hindu vania and Jain merchants whose commercial success had enabled them to develop substantial interests in local structures of power could not simply discard them and move to Bombay. Their commercial orientation was towards the internal economy. They left the risks of seafaring to lesser trading communities who had no option but to seize them and they even sometimes invested in their goods and made loans available to these groups. By the 1820s and 1830s, the leading Gujarati merchants, seeking fresh outlets for their capital following the decline of the local textile industry, invested on a larger scale in the increasingly profitable opium trade, and especially in the consignments of Jamsetjee Jejeebhoy.[179]

The major risk-takers in the overseas trade were therefore the more marginal mercantile communities. Armenian traders were initially the most active in the China trade until they were replaced by Parsi merchants by the end of the first decade of the nineteenth century.[180] Similarly, Khoja and to a lesser extent Bohra merchants profited from the revival of the Arabian trade in the 1790s and then began to look increasingly towards the East in the early 1800s.[181] The Konkani Muslim shipbuilding families, like the Roghays and Ghattays, also became prominent in the China trade by the 1820s.[182] Similarly, Bhatia merchants showed no great inhibition for crossing the *kalapani* at least in the Indian

[177] Das Gupta, *Indian Merchants*; Subramaniam, 'Banias and the British'; Torri, 'In the Deep Blue Sea'.
[178] Chaudhuri, 'Structure of the Indian Textile Industries'; Nightingale, *Trade and Empire*, chs. 2, 5–7; Dobbin, *Urban Leadership*, ch. 1; Gillion, *Ahmedabad*, pp. 11–73.
[179] A. Siddiqi, 'The Business World of Jamsetjee Jejeebhoy', *IESHR*, XIX, 3 & 4 (1982), 311–12.
[180] A. Guha, 'More About Parsi Seths: Their Roots, Entrepreneurship and Comprador Role, 1650–1918', *Economic and Political Weekly*, 21 January 1984, 117–32.
[181] Subramaniam, 'Capital and the Crowd'; Subramaniam, 'Banias and the British'; Torri, 'In the Deep Blue Sea'; Torri, 'Surat During the Second Half of the Eighteenth Century'; *Gazetteer*, I, 181–2.
[182] *Gazetteer*, I, 255–6.

Ocean as the export trade in cotton and opium proved increasingly lucrative.[183] These merchants were able to knit together several lines of interrelated commercial activity. They traded on their own account but also acted as guarantee brokers, dubashes and commission agents for the Company and the English private traders. The Company's brokers often obtained favourable terms for transporting their goods in ships and received help in recovering their loans to private traders. Moreover, some merchants, especially Parsis and Konkani Muslim families, had developed interests in shipbuilding and shipping since the eighteenth century and these could now be deployed in the profitable China trade.

Caste and kinship connections provided the basis for mobilizing capital and organizing trading and banking activity. But it would be misleading to assume that entrepreneurial behaviour can be understood exclusively in terms of community. Business in Bombay often cut across these primordial lines. Vanias invested in the carrying trade of Parsis and Khojas.[184] Indeed, they had even helped to finance not only the Company's commercial activities but also its territorial expansion in India. They provided the capital for the ventures of the European private traders which in turn was guaranteed by Parsi, Bhatia or Ismaili brokers. When Nusserwanji Tata came to Bombay, he was apprenticed to a Hindu merchant and banker. He took as partner for his firm of general merchants a Hindu vania called Kaliandas and later their expansion and diversification into cotton and opium exports was driven by the model Jain ascetic and speculator, Premchand Roychand.[185] Similarly, Jamsetjee Jeejeebhoy 'developed intimate business connections with persons belonging to almost every community and religious group' and in the 1830s became a close associate of Jardine and Mathieson.[186]

Although communal categories are by no means the most appropriate for the history of entrepreneurship, the success of Parsi merchants helps to illustrate some of the major themes in Bombay's commercial expansion. Their entrepreneurial achievements have usually been ascribed to their specific communal characteristics and, in particular, their religious values,[187] but it was more consistently shaped by historical contingencies. Moreover, the example of the Parsis is sometimes taken to demonstrate that Indian entrepreneurs, by imitating the British example, could adopt the attitudes, strategies and institutions which

---

[183] *Ibid.*, I, 168–9.

[184] Siddiqi, 'Jamsetjee Jeejeebhoy', 304–6, 309–11.

[185] F.R. Harris, *Jamsetji Nusserwanji Tata: A Chronicle of His Life* (London, 1925, 2nd edn, Bombay, 1958), pp. 2–10.

[186] Siddiqi, 'Jamsetjee Jeejeebhoy', 307 and *passim*.

[187] R.E. Kennedy, 'The Protestant Ethic and Parsis', *American Journal of Sociology*, LXVIII, 1 (1962), 11–20. For a critique, see A.V. Desai, 'The Origins of Parsi Enterprise', *IESHR*, V, 4 (1968), 307–17; Bagchi, *Private Investment in India*, pp. 199–203.

would facilitate their development from traders to industrialists. Yet the development of Parsi enterprise demonstrates rather more clearly that their acceptance of greater risks in the export trade or factory industry was largely a function of their narrowing options elsewhere.

In Navsari and Surat, Parsis had occupied a fairly humble social and economic position. Ovington's most generous claim on their behalf was that they were 'the principal Men at the Loom in all the country'.[188] They constituted a nation of toddy tappers and liquor distillers, tobacco farmers and cattle breeders, artisans and shopkeepers.[189] Parsi retailers in Surat and the port cities of Gujarat began to act as ship's chandlers, supplying food and liquor to merchant vessels. In addition, their role in the weaving trade and in particular their close connections with artisan communities made them highly attractive allies for European trading companies. From the late seventeenth century, Parsi traders and brokers placed themselves increasingly under the protection of the Dutch and the English East India Companies, and with the eclipse of the former they turned increasingly to the latter after the 1750s.[190] Their readiness, indeed their eagerness, to acquire European protection arose from their own weakness both in the region's commerce and within its structures of power.[191] Similar reasons underlay the readiness of Parsi traders, brokers and artisans to respond to the incentive of a secure refuge and follow the Company to Bombay.

Historical contingencies shaped both their commercial success as well as their changing business interests. The first Parsi immigrants to Bombay followed broadly the same range of occupations which they had practised in Gujarat.[192] Parsi merchants as a whole gained considerably from the appointment of men like Rustomji Manock in Surat and Byramji Jijbhai in Cambay as chief brokers to the Company. The chief broker enjoyed enormous powers of patronage from which smaller Parsi traders were often able to profit. He was privy to scarce but vital market information and enjoyed access to and influence with Company officials; he could transport his goods on Company ships, borrow money at favourable rates, obtain special discounts on the purchase of English

[188] J. Ovington, *A Voyage to the East* (ed. H.G. Rawlinson, London, 1928), p. 219; Guha, 'More About Parsi Seths', 119; D.L. White, 'Parsis in the Commercial World of Western India, 1700–1750', *IESHR*, XXIV, 2 (1987), 183–203.

[189] D.F. Karaka, *History of the Parsis, Including their Manners, Customs, Religion, and Present Position*, 2 vols. (London, 1884), vol. II, pp. 244–5; Guha, 'More About Parsi Seths', 118–19; E. Kulke, *The Parsis in India: A Minority as Agent of Social Change* (New Delhi, 1978), pp. 23–34, 48–50.

[190] Karaka, *History of the Parsis*, vol. II, pp. 1–46; White, 'Parsis', 183–203; Guha, 'More About Parsi Seths', 119.

[191] Karaka, *History of the Parsis*, vol. II, pp. 8–10, 242–4. In the mid eighteenth century, Parsis accounted for no more than one-tenth of the non-European trading capital in Surat. Furber, *Bombay Presidency*, pp. 64–5.

[192] Guha, 'More About Parsi Seths', 122–3.

cloth and, most crucially, secure assistance in the recovery of loans made to English traders. Cheap money for the most prominent Parsis became the basis for lending to their more humble kinsmen and caste fellows, no doubt on terms of mutual gain. Significantly, Manock's tenure as chief broker enabled his kinsmen and co-religionists to consolidate their community's close relationship with the Company, from which several Parsi merchants were able to profit in the following decades.[193] Parsi traders sought to preserve, nourish and develop these connections, and indeed profit from them, long after the Rustomji Manock family fell out of favour with the Company.[194]

Parsi merchants acted as guarantors for the credit the shore-based merchants extended to the English private traders as well as to the Company. Not only did they consolidate their connections with the Company, but, in these ways, they also offered mercantile capital, stripped of its revenue farming and collecting function and squeezed by the decline of the local textile industry, an outlet for the investment of their surplus wealth. Using their connections with the Company to obtain cheaper freight or remit their profits through the Company's treasury at Canton, and deploying their foothold in shipbuilding, Parsi merchants became increasingly prominent in the China trade. In 1756, Jivaji Readymoney, a Parsi merchant, was able to embark on a voyage to China to explore its trading opportunities. By 1803, Jamsetjee Jejeebhoy had undertaken four such odysseys of investigation and profit.[195] In 1812–13, it was said, twelve out of twenty-nine large ships trading with China were owned by Parsi merchants. Between 1809 and 1833, there were more Parsi merchants in the China trade than European private traders.[196] However, their domination of vital ancillary sources, like cotton pressing and marine insurance, enabled the private traders to operate at cheaper margins and secure a larger share of the profits of the China trade than the more numerous Parsi merchants.[197]

In the early nineteenth century, Bombay's merchants, and especially the leading Parsis among them, began to ship cotton to England on their own account, whereas previously they had been limited to seeking a share in the consignments of British ships.[198] Exporting cotton to England brought Jamsetjee Jejeebhoy a profit estimated at Rs. 2 crores during the Napoleonic Wars.[199] By 1830s, Jejeebhoy combined with Jardine Mathieson to corner

[193] Karaka, *History of the Parsis*, vol. II, pp. 9–18; White, 'Parsis'.
[194] White, 'Parsis'; Das Gupta, *India Merchants*.
[195] *Gazetteer*, I, 194–5; Karaka, *History of the Parsis*, II, 78–111; Siddiqi, 'Jamsetjee Jejeebhoy'.
[196] A. Guha, 'Parsi Seths as Entrepreneurs, 1750–1850', *Economic and Political Weekly, Review of Management*, August 1970, M-107.
[197] Guha, 'More About Parsi Seths', p. 125.
[198] *Ibid.*, 124–5; Guha, 'Parsi Seths as Entrepreneurs', M-109.
[199] J.R.P. Mody, *The First Parsee Baronet* (Bombay, 1966), p. 32; Siddiqi, 'Jamsetjee Jejeebhoy', 307–8.

the rapidly growing and increasingly valuable trade in Malwa opium.[200] When the Company's monopoly was finally abolished under the Charter Act of 1833, Parsi merchants were among the busiest and most enthusiastic buyers of its ships. By 1838, Parsis owned eighteen of the forty-nine country ships sailing out of Bombay.[201] When Commander Lin forced the private traders to surrender their stock of opium in 1839, and generally sought to crack down on the drug traffic, a number of Parsi merchants were caught flat footed. In the 1840s, Parsi capital gradually withdrew from the opium trade and indeed lost its lead in the drug traffic.[202]

Although it was still possible for Indian merchants to make substantial profits in the China trade, the big exporters were also gradually subordinated to the wider international credit and trading networks of metropolitan capital. Not only were British agency houses able to obtain bills of exchange at rates which Indian merchants, operating with high interest and short-term credit, could not afford, but they were able to undercut the freight charged by Indian shippers. Moreover, as the balance between Indian merchants and their agents in China shifted in favour of the latter, especially as they became decreasingly reliant on the former's capital and supplies, the consignment system appeared increasingly a means for feeding Indian commodities and capital cheaply into the business activities of the European agency houses.[203] As the subordination of Indian capital became increasingly evident in the China trade, the larger traders, who felt the brunt of the disturbances of the Opium Wars in the early 1840s and again in the 1850s, began to explore alternative possibilities.

The withdrawal of Parsi capital from the China trade was by no means complete. Nusserwanji Tata opened a branch of their family firm in Hong Kong as late as 1859.[204] When the opium trade was banned in 1912, a number of Parsi firms were still found among its leading operators and the Tatas, now firmly established in the ranks of the largest industrialists, remained one of the most prominent firms in the China trade.[205] However, Parsi merchants had begun to lose their lead in the China trade to Khoja and Baghdadi Jewish traders, who, less entrenched in the China trade and less damaged by the disruptions of

---

[200] Siddiqi, 'Jamesetjee Jejeebhoy', 310–11; A. Guha, 'The Comprador Role of Parsi Seths', *Economic and Political Weekly*, V, 48 (28 November 1970), 1933.

[201] Guha, 'Parsi Seths as Entrepreneurs', M-111; N. Benjamin, 'Bombay's "Country Trade" with China (1766–1865)', *Indian Historical Review*, I, 2 (1974), 295–303.

[202] Greenberg, *British Trade and the Opening of the China*, pp. 196–215, especially 206–7; Benjamin, 'Bombay's "Country Trade"', 301; Guha, 'The Comprador Role of Parsi Seths', 1933.

[203] Siddiqi, 'Jamsetjee Jejeebhoy', 317–24.

[204] Harris, *Tata*, p. 5.

[205] *Ibid.*, pp. 12–13, 92–4; Siddiqi, 'Jamsetjee Jejeebhoy', 323–4; R. Newman, 'Bombay and the China Trade', Seminar paper, Centre of South Asian Studies, Cambridge, 1987; R. Newman, 'India and the Anglo-Chinese Opium Agreements, 1907–14', *MAS*, XXIII, 3 (1989), 525–60.

1839–42, had begun to displace them in the mid nineteenth century.[206] Clearly, the China trade still retained sufficient promise of dividends to attract fresh and rising entrepreneurial groups. These new men, however, tended to establish branches of their own family firms or appoint their own agents in China, rather than follow the older method of working through the good offices of European private traders.[207] Their branches in Shanghai and Hong Kong did not simply or even predominantly sell opium, but by the late nineteenth century were facilitating the export of yarn to the Chinese market and raw cotton to China as well to Japan.[208] By the early twentieth century, a number of leading millowners, like Fazulbhoy Currimbhoy and the Sassoons, had acquired major interests in the opium trade with China.[209] It should not be entirely surprising, therefore, that the 'communal' riots of 1851 and 1874 in Bombay occurred primarily between Paris and Khojas and similar tensions governed by rivalries in trade were present in 'the Prince of Wales riots' of November 1921.[210]

As Parsi capital withdrew from the China trade, it sought a variety of outlets. Even before the crisis of 1839, this capital was by no means exclusively concentrated in the opium trade with China. Shipping cotton and opium to China had been only the most lucrative and rewarding of a wide range of business activities. While trading on their own account, many had also served as contractors and suppliers to the East India Company and as guarantee brokers, money-changers and creditors for private traders as well.[211] Some, like Jijabhai Dadabhai, invested in coffee, rubber and coconut plantations on the Malabar coast, in Ceylon and even south-east Asia. Others invested extensively in real estate: Dadabhai Pestonji Wadia, it was estimated, owned about a quarter of the island of Bombay in the early nineteenth century.[212] Those who served the Company as brokers, suppliers and shipbuilders received sizeable properties as inami lands in Bombay and Salsette: Framji Cowasji Banaji acquired a vast

---

[206] Siddiqi, 'Jamsetjee Jejeebhoy'; Benjamin, 'Bombay's "Country Trade"'; Newman, 'Bombay and the China Trade'.

[207] Harris, *Tata*, pp. 93–4; S. Jackson, *The Sassoons* (London, 1968).

[208] Dantwalla, *A Hundred Years of Indian Cotton*.

[209] Newman, 'Bombay and the China Trade'.

[210] *The Bombay Riots of February 1874: Reprinted from the Times of India* (Bombay, 1874); *The Bombay Riots* (reprinted from the *Bombay Gazette*) (Bombay, 1874); Bombay Confidential Proceedings, Home Department, December 1921, vol. 62, pp. 771–81, IOR.

[211] Prosopographical information on Parsi merchants may be found in Guha, 'More About Parsi Seths'; Siddiqi, 'Jamsetjee Jejeebhoy'; Karaka, *History of the Parsees*, especially, vol. II, pp. 1–145, 242–95; H.D. Darukhanawalla, *Parsi Lustre on Indian Soil* (Bombay, 1939); Wadia, *Scions of Lowjee Wadia*; K.N. Banaji, *Memoirs of the Late Framji Cowasji Banaji* (Bombay, 1892); R.P. Masani, *Dadabhai Naoroji: The Grand Old Man of India* (London, 1939); Harris, *Tata*.

[212] F. Warden, *Report on the Landed Tenures of Bombay, 1814, Selections from the Records of the Bombay Government* (Bombay, 1862), pp. 96–7.

estate at Powai where he experimented with the growing of cash crops and particularly with silk; the Lowji Wadia family received properties in Parel, where they built their castle in the neighbourhood of the Governor's residence; others like Dadabhai Naoroji and Naoroji Furdunji inherited jagirs in south Gujarat. By the mid nineteenth century, the leading Parsi merchants were involved in a wide range of business activities from shipping to joint-stock banking. This range is exemplified by the business interests of the Banajis. In addition to their role as the leading merchants and shipowners of the China trade, they had invested in the *Times of India* newspaper, in banking, coastal shipping lines, paper and silk manufacture, cotton screws, horticultural farms, salt pans, shipbuilding docks and insurance agencies in Calcutta as well as Bombay.[213]

Perhaps the most important trading activity of Parsi merchants diversifying out of the China trade in the middle of the nineteenth century, and the obvious successor to the opium trade, was the export of raw cotton to England. In 1849, for the first time, more Indian cotton was bought in Lancashire than in China.[214] By then, the Lancashire millowners had virtually abandoned their cherished dream of turning India into their own cotton field. Indian cotton remained resolutely shortstapled and it could only be used by English millowners in a variety of mixings with the long-stapled American supply. But the ring frames with which French and Italian mills were equipped created a ready demand for Indian cotton from the 1860s and 1870s onwards.[215]

The pickings of the cotton export trade were by no means confined to the Parsis alone. By the mid nineteenth century, Parsi merchants were strongly established as the dominant commercial community in Bombay and their prominent role in the overseas trade enabled them to gain substantially from the revival of cotton exports. However, merchants of most communities were able to participate in and profit from its expansion. The merchant princes of the export trade were already sufficiently acquainted with the cotton trade to seize the fresh opportunities which these new sources of demand offered.

The export trade in raw cotton was subject to severe fluctuations of supply and demand. Since the Indian crop was used to supplement the American cotton in Lancashire, the demand and price levels of the former were determined largely by the supply of the latter.[216] Moreover, the cultivation of cotton presented difficulties: because it was extremely demanding on the soil and on

213 Guha, 'More About Parsi Seths', 125; Karaka, *History of the Parsis*, vol. II, pp. 111–24; Banaji, *Memoirs*.
214 D.A. Farnie, *The English Cotton Industry and the World Market, 1815–1896* (Oxford, 1979), p. 108.
215 Vicziany, 'The Cotton Trade,' chs. 2, 5; D.A. Farnie, *East and West of Suez* (Oxford, 1969), pp. 100–2, 140–4, 161–3, 360–3.
216 Vicziany, 'The Cotton Trade', pp. 55–9.

labour and cultivators were willing to grow the crop only when they were assured of an adequate food supply, the supply of cotton and the extent of its cultivation were also subject to considerable fluctuation.[217] To transport the crop cleanly and effectively was an arduous and demanding task. Necessarily, the export of raw cotton to Europe entailed higher risks and lower returns than the opium trade to China.[218] It is not surprising, therefore, that most exporters operated on a relatively small scale. In 1851, 195 out of 228 exporters in Bombay shipped less than 500 bales and accounted for less than 30 per cent of the total volume of cotton.[219] On the other hand, the flexibility and sophistication of the cotton trade was reflected in its swift response to the Lancashire cotton famine in the 1860s which rapidly overcame these supply constraints. The volume of cotton shipped to Britain in 1861 increased by 80 per cent over the preceding year;[220] cotton cultivation not only increased rapidly but became for the first time widely diffused throughout the Presidency, and indeed beyond;[221] credit became more readily available and the countryside witnessed a proliferation of small money-lenders.[222] Nonetheless, the real structural constraints on the cotton trade were sufficient to limit cotton exporters to small-scale operations. Between 1851 and 1875, the share of the export trade in the hands of the small merchants declined from 30 per cent to a mere 8.5 per cent.[223]

By the 1870s, Indian merchants in the cotton trade found that the changing character of its organization affected them adversely and that they were subject to increasingly severe competition from the European agency houses. As railway construction gathered momentum in the 1860s and extended from Bombay into the cotton tracts of Gujarat and the Deccan and then north, the agency houses became less reliant on their Indian dealers up country. They began to establish their own steam presses in the cotton-growing districts and sent out their own agents to buy the crop in its primary markets or at the source.[224] Moreover, a series of innovations in the organization of the cotton trade favoured its specialization and concentration in the hands of large-scale

---

[217] *Presidency Gazetteer, Poona* (Bombay, 1885), vol. XVIII, part 2, pp. 47–8; Charlesworth, *Peasants and Imperial Rule*, p. 79.

[218] Siddiqi, 'Jamsetjee Jejeebhoy', 311–13. In the 1850s, the export of cotton to Lancashire fluctuated by 60–70 per cent: 'Statistical Papers Relating to India, Section on Cotton', *PP*, LXIX (1852–53), 53, cited by Charlesworth, *Peasants and Imperial Rule*, p. 81; Vicziany, 'The Cotton Trade', pp. 135–84.

[219] Vicziany, 'Bombay Merchants', Table 1, p. 166.

[220] Charlesworth, *Peasants and Imperial Rule*, p. 135.

[221] P. Harnetty, 'Cotton Exports and Indian Agriculture, 1861–1870', *EcHR*, XXIV, 3 (1971), 414–29.

[222] Banaji, 'Capitalist Domination and the Small Peasantry', 1383–84; Charlesworth, *Peasants and Imperial Rule*, p. 87.

[223] Vicziany, 'Bombay Merchants', Table 1, p. 166.

[224] *Presidency Gazetteer, Khandesh* (Bombay, 1880), vol. XII, pp. 220–2; *Presidency Gazetteer, Surat and Broach* (Bombay, 1877), vol. II, p. 429.

exports. Access to capital enabled larger exporters to gain better market information by taking advantage of improved communications, especially the telegraph, or by opening branches in Liverpool or Manchester. They employed vital auxiliary services like insurance, now available on a larger scale, and improved facilities for storage so that they could spread their shipments throughout the year and time their sales in accordance with the fluctuations of the American supply and of the demand in Liverpool. They could also invest more heavily in up-country pressing, which improved the quality of the raw cotton and made its processing both more efficient and more economical. As the cotton trade was increasingly concentrated in the hands of the large exporters, it was not simply the merchants operating on a relatively small scale who suffered, but the relative share of Indian merchants among the large exporters also declined steeply. This decline was the outcome of the structural changes in the organization of the trade, but they were concealed by the boom of the 1860s. By the 1870s, however, its effects were clearly manifested. In 1861, 7 out of 12 merchants exporting over 10,000 bales of cotton and 102 out of 134 exporting over 1,000 bales of cotton were Indians; by 1875, there was only one Indian merchant in the highest class and only 37 out of 74 who exported more than 1,000 bales.[225] The innovations in the cotton trade combined with the growing importance of the Liverpool and European markets to work strongly in favour of the large European agency houses and to facilitate the subordination of Indian capital in the export trade.

Indian merchants thus subordinated to expatriate capital in the export trade responded by diversifying into the spinning of raw cotton and began to invest in the building of mills. In this sense, the development of the cotton-textile industry was a response to the subordination of the Indian capital and not a function of its linear progression from trade to industry. The Petit family, which promoted one of the first cotton mills in Bombay in the 1850s and then another couple by 1870,[226] had boasted the only Indian merchant to ship over 10,000 bales of cotton in 1875.[227] Moreover, the early promoters of the cotton mills were almost exclusively Parsis and Bhatias, communities which had gained substantially from the early growth of Bombay and participated actively in the China trade. Certainly nine out of the thirteen mills floated by 1870, fifteen years after Cowasji Davar launched his Bombay Spinning and Weaving Company, were Parsis.[228]

By investing in mill production, the large cotton traders gained considerable

[225] Vicziany, 'Bombay Merchants', pp. 163–97.
[226] Rutnagur, *Bombay Industries*, pp. 10–16, 25–34.
[227] Vicziany, 'Bombay Merchants', p. 170.
[228] Rutnagur, *Bombay Industries*, p. 10.

flexibility.[229] They could buy raw cotton when prices were low and sell when prices rose. If the cotton trade was depressed, they could switch stocks intended for export to the manufacture of yarn. Rather than build warehouses to store their cotton and await the next failure of the American crop or increased demand from Chinese spinners, they could deploy their stock of cotton according to its optimal short-term use, adjust their operations of the uncertainties of the market and adapt to the severe competition in both trade and industry. Cotton brokers and piecegoods dealers, indeed traders and entrepreneurs of all kinds, seeking to diversify their commercial interests provided the thrust behind the expansion of the number of entrepreneurs in the industry.

The industry expanded in fits and starts; periods of prosperity precipitated frantic mill building only to be followed by slumps in which capital was swiftly diverted to more profitable uses. The first mills were composite units, capable of spinning as well as weaving. But by the 1870s, in response to the growth of the Chinese demand for low count yarn, investment was concentrated in spinning and processing for the export trade. The saturation of the Chinese demand led to the revival of cloth production, this time on a much larger scale, and by the 1920s directed the attention of the millowners rather abruptly to the domestic market. Moreover, as the industry's weaving capacity grew, so too did the mills diversify into dyeing, bleaching and finishing processes. These characteristics of the industry's growth and their consequences will be examined in detail in the following chapters. Taken together they signified the difficulties of mobilizing capital. To attract capital and remedy the difficulties created by its scarcity, entrepreneurs had to maintain a rapid turnover, show quick profits and pay handsome dividends.

Yet even a cursory glance at the economic development of Bombay suggests the perennial constraints upon the mobilization of capital and a closer examination suggests that these constraints arose less from an inherent aversion to risk than to the effects of the subordination of indigenous capital under the impact of colonialism. From the early nineteenth century, the merchant princes of Bombay had found it difficult to draw capital for their high-risk ventures out of the stronger claims and safer returns of the internal economy. These merchant princes were themselves recruited from groups which were relatively marginal to its most powerful trading and banking networks. The constraints of expensive and short-term credit had narrowed the options of merchants exporting cotton and opium to China in competition with the European private traders in the 1830s, who in turn had better access to the international shipping and banking facilities centred on Britain.[230] Undermined in the China trade, these merchants

---

[229] See ch. 6 below.
[230] Siddiqi, 'Jamsetjee Jejeebhoy'; Vicziany, 'The Cotton Trade', pp. 135–84.

tried to take advantage of the rising demand for Indian cotton in Europe. By the 1870s, however, those who had diversified into shipping cotton to Europe failed to keep pace with the innovations in the organization of the export trade which put large demands upon capital and favoured the largest operators. By diversifying into textile production, Bombay's capitalists had not escaped these structural constraints; rather the pattern of their diversification into and subsequently within the industry was a response to them. Moreover, these structural constraints were rooted in a more fundamental development: the subordination of indigenous mercantile capital and the narrowing of its function in the agrarian economy, with the advent of colonialism, to usury and petty trade.

The strategies of capital

These structural constraints upon the development of capital also shaped the ways in which it was mobilized. In turn, the pattern and character of capital investment inscribed itself on the industrial structure of Bombay. Capital moved more readily into the safer outlets of usury and petty trade, mortgages and property than into industry. Capital for investment in the long-distance and overseas trade and for large-scale industry was generated from an increasingly narrow social base. Characteristically, it was mobilized in small pools. Although Bombay's entrepreneurs had easier access to public subscription than their counterparts elsewhere in the country, [231] yet here too, they complained, investors were 'few, nervous and suspicious'.[232] Investors placed their money with firms whose risks were known, whose profitability was proven or whose directors they trusted. As Manmohandas Ramji, leading millowner, merchant and magnate in Bombay, observed,

I find that industrial enterprises if backed by good names or by those who have influence attract capital while many a scheme without such a backing up, though good in other respects, languishes because of want of capital.[233]

Similarly, N.B. Saklatvala, a partner of Tata Sons and Company, pointed out,

The public in India, especially in Bombay are ever ready to put their money in mill concerns started by individuals or firms who have a reputation for honesty and efficiency, and who have a good deal of mill experience.[234]

[231] This was 'the largest rupee paper market in India', *Gazetteer*, I, 295, 293–7; on the history and functions of the share bazaar, see *Report of the Bombay Stock Exchange Enquiry Committee, 1936–37* (Bombay, 1937); for a recent account of the money market in Bombay in the 1920s, see Gordon, *Businessmen and Politics*, pp. 76–8, 81–2, 97–101.
[232] *IIC*, Evidence, C.N. Wadia, Agent, Century Spinning and Manufacturing Company Limited, and Representative Witness nominated by the Bombay Millowners' Association (henceforth BMOA), IV, 1.
[233] *Ibid.*, Mr. Manmohandas Ramji, IV, 58.
[234] *Ibid.*, N.B. Saklatvala, Partner, Tata Sons and Company, IV, 25.

The suspicion of investors was not a function of the uniform shyness of capital but a reflection of the magnitude of risk. The unevenness of economic development left most trades liable to seasonal and arbitrary fluctuations. Even the cotton-textile industry experienced spasmodic patterns of growth and fitful periods of prosperity. Thus, the reluctance of investors to subscribe freely to new projects was attributed by one observer to the fact that they 'knew that it would take nearly three years before a mill would begin to earn, and by the time the new mill was in a position to work fully the conditions might change and prosperous times disappear'.[235] To raise capital, entrepreneurs turned to their friends, kinsmen and caste fellows and in the absence of an adequate capital market or banking system to suit the needs of industry, they also developed institutions of their own. The managing-agency system may have originated in the Company trade,[236] but in the twentieth century it was symptomatic of this personalized system of finance, which called for skilled and specialized handling and sometimes entailed highly complex management. The purpose of the managing-agency system was primarily to raise capital and co-ordinate its supply for the enterprises which it managed.[237] Although the managing-agency system was repeatedly pilloried for its speculative tendencies and potential for malpractice, the importance of its financial and promotional role prompted one of the first official historians of the industry to claim that 'the expansion of the mill industry in Bombay has been due in great measure to the enterprise and financial resources of the Managing Agents'.[238]

Firms which operated through the Stock Exchange functioned, in this respect, along similar lines. In the early 1930s, only four out of forty-eight mills whose shares were quoted on the Stock Exchange sold them in units of less than Rs. 500, while twenty-eight quoted theirs at Rs. 1,000 and above.[239] Shareholdings tended to be concentrated in fewer hands in Bombay than elsewhere in India and the subscribers were often limited to a relatively intimate circle of the promoter's relatives and friends. Frequently, the managing agents were themselves the major shareholders.[240] Managing agents secured and retained a controlling stake in the business they had promoted and then contracted to manage for lengthy tenures extending to three or four decades.[241] They

---

[235] *Ibid.*, Mr J.A. Wadia, Merchant, IV, 135.

[236] B. Kling, 'The Origin of the Managing Agency System', *JAS*, XXVI, 1 (1966), 37–48; Rutnagur, *Bombay Industries*, pp. 49–65; R.S. Rungta, *The Rise of Business Corporations in India, 1851–1900* (Cambridge, 1970), pp. 219–55.

[237] *Royal Commission on Indian Currency and Finance*, vol. IV, *Minutes of Evidence taken in India* (London, 1926), Sir Victor Sassoon, representing the BMOA, p. 266.

[238] Rutnagur, *Bombay Industries*, p. 49.

[239] P.S. Lokanathan, *Industrial Organization in India* (London, 1935), p. 149, n. 3.

[240] *Report of the Indian Tariff Board Regarding the Grant of Protection to the Cotton Textile Industry* (Calcutta 1932) (henceforth *Report of the ITB, 1932*), pp. 85–6.

[241] *Report of the ITB, 1932*, p. 79.

nominated themselves or their relatives and friends as directors and appointed their own auditors. They were not restricted in the range of their financial or commercial undertakings and the notion that their interests might conflict was simply not entertained.[242] If the role of the directors in the affairs of the firm was minimal, shareholders were allowed 'very little voice in the management of the factories'.[243] Public limited-liability companies, thus, bore the characteristics of private concerns.

On the stock exchange investors were 'led more by names than by the actual contents of the prospectus of the new concern', and when both were favourable, it was said, 'its shares are sure to be oversubscribed in a short time'.[244] Share quotations on the stock exchange were taken as an index of the value and security of the enterprise and as a reflection of 'the opinion of leading businessmen'. Investors cannily waited to see whether the entrepreneurs invested in their own schemes; but they were often outwitted. For their part, entrepreneurs who found it difficult to raise initial capital, it was said, 'usually subscribe in large amounts to create confidence in the minds of prospective purchasers. Later on when the demand increases, they slowly unload their savings usually with great profit'.[245] They could then deploy these accumulations in other apparently profitable lines of production.

The fact that capital was mobilized in small pools was to shape the structure of the industry in numerous ways. It often confined businessmen to small industrial units and a low ratio of fixed to working costs. Capital was more readily invested in consumer durables, since the market was either already known or easily assessed. But this also meant that capital was attracted by a specific range of enterprises which at a particular moment were expected to yield returns. 'If a certain industry is found to be profitable', one survey of industrial finance pointed out in the 1930s, 'we go on investing in it to such an extent that at last it becomes over-financed and unprofitable'. Once the confidence of investors was secured in a particular industry or trade, capital would flood into it until the market was saturated; then, 'again there will be a halt, which may continue till similarly favourable conditions are created for investment in some other industry'.[246] The punctuation of investment by failure did not steel the investor's nerve. On the other hand, the intensity of competition,

---

[242] Rutnagur, *Bombay Industries*, pp. 49–65, 245–51.

[243] *Ibid.*, p. 49; *Report of the Bombay Stock Exchange Enquiry Committee* (Bombay, 1924), Official Representation of the Bombay Native Stock and Share Brokers' Association, Appendix 5, p. 53; *Report of the Indian Tariff Board (Cotton Textile Industry Enquiry, 1927* [henceforth, *Report of the ITB, 1927*] (Calcutta, 1927), *Evidence of Individual Witnesses*, IV, C.I. Parekh, 292–3; J.V. Desai, 408.

[244] D.R. Samant and M.A. Mulky, *Organisation and Finance of Industries in India* (Bombay, 1937), p. 19.

[245] *Ibid.*, pp. 20, 38–40.

[246] *Ibid.*, p. 8.

the swings of investment, the low ratio of fixed capital and, in the case of consumer goods, their vulnerability to changes in fashion, encouraged the diversification of commercial enterprise. Furthermore, because capital was difficult to mobilize, entrepreneurs were not only limited to minimal fixed investments, but they were frequently forced to resort to short-term borrowing to finance a proportion of their fixed assets, and usually the whole of their working costs. Even the Bombay millowners, believed to command public confidence more readily than their fellow capitalists, and in spite of their access to the Presidency banks and the stock exchange, depended at times upon the changeable money-market to pay for a part of their block capital and frequently the whole of their working costs.[247]

These factors played upon each other. The imitative character of investment accentuated industrial instability. The fluctuations and volatility of each trade encouraged entrepreneurs to spread their risks and diversify their business interests as rapidly as they could. At different levels, businessmen who invested their capital in one line of production might switch to another when it began to yield returns and attract investment.[248] This tendency towards under-capitalization and rapid diversification made the reputation of the entrepreneurs and the reliability of the industry an important consideration for investors. 'Considering the manner in which capital is mismanaged both by industrialists and the banks', wrote P.S. Lokanathan, 'it is surprising how optimistic the investor continues to be in India'.[249] The emphasis which contemporaries and later historians often placed on the reluctance of investors to bear risks and pioneer industrialization was to confuse the causes of the problem with its symptoms.

---

[247] *Indian Central Banking Enquiry Committee (henceforth ICBEC), 1931, Evidence, BMOA*, II, 593–97; *Report of the ITB, 1927*, I, 90–2.

[248] For instance, the two major chemical works in Bombay were launched by the mill agents, E.D. Sassoon and Company and Dharamsi Morarji. See Labour Office, Bombay, *General Wages Census, Part I – Perennial Factories, Fourth Report, Report on Wages, Hours of Work, and Conditions of Employement in the Oils, Paints and Soap, Match Manufacturing and Other Miscellaneous Industries in the Province of Bombay, May 1934* (Bombay, 1939), Wages Hours of Work and Conditions of Work in the Chemical and Pharmaceutical Industry, pp. 73–80. Adamji Peerbhoy, the Bohra businessman and magnate owned the Western India Tanneries and had large interests in cotton mills and a range of other commercial activities. See *Gazetteer*, I, 481; J.R. Martin, *A Monograph on Tanning and Working in Leather in the Bombay Presidency* (Bombay, 1903). The Wadias diversified from dyeing to spinning and weaving. See Bombay Dyeing and Manufacturing Company Limited, Directors' Minute Book, 1879–1907, Office of the Bombay Dyeing and Manufacturing Company, Bombay. The Tatas expanded from the cotton trade into the cotton industry, hydroelectric power and then into steel in Jamshedpur. Harris, *Tata*; D.E. Wacha, *The Life and Work of J.N. Tata* (Madras, 1915); S.K. Sen, *The House of Tata 1839–1939* (Calcutta, 1975). Such examples may be multiplied, but not only at these exalted levels. Cotton brokers might become piecegood merchants, invest in spinning and weaving mills and develop interests in insurance and other supporting services. See Playne and Bond, *Bombay Presidency*; see also the 'Biographical Notes' in Gordon, *Businessmen and Politics*, pp. 243–9.

[249] Lokanathan, *Industrial Organisation*, p. 145.

The risks of industrial investment contributed to its imitative character, its caution and its attraction to proven lines of production. Each of these tendencies was intricately intertwined. The low ratio of fixed capital, the intensity of competition and especially, when it occurred, the tendency to under-capitalization, required a rapid turnover to finance debts or adapt to an unpredictable market. Business strategies, based upon a rapid turnover, were likely to be associated with the regulation of production and, therefore, levels of employment according to short-term market fluctuations. This, as we shall see, was to have serious implications for the structure of the labour market. But its ramifications were wider still. In particular, most workers in Bombay experienced uncertain conditions of employment. This in turn heightened the importance of their caste and kinship ties and their village connections which provided the social means by which the urban poor struggled for survival in the city. Similarly, it imparted an enormous importance in the lives of the poor to the social organization of the neighbourhood. It would be simplistic to perceive in the patterns of entrepreneurial choice and capital investment the single determining factor in the constitution of working-class life. But it would be difficult to grasp their social economy without reference to the strategies of capital.

3 The structure and development of the labour market

The structure of the labour force is widely conceived in terms of the distinction between industrial workers and the urban poor, permanent and casual workers and, particularly, in the rather diffuse and over-extended 'case' of the Third World, the organized and unorganized, or the formal and informal sector. The narrow front of industrialization, on the one hand, and the substantial inflow of rural migrants to the city who cannot be contained within it, on the other, has appeared to lend considerable force to this description.

Conventionally, the formal sector is defined in terms of economic activities which are governed by state regulation, usually associated with large-scale factory production and operated generally on the basis of power-driven machinery. They are predominantly capital intensive and often monopolistic. Their markets are protected either by tariffs or by the size, concentration and dominance of the industry and their workforce by labour laws. Organized sector workers are believed to enjoy a greater degree of unionization and command higher levels of skill and wages than the unorganized labour force. The labour process is supposedly more sophisticated; the division of labour more developed. The informal sector, by contrast, is characterized by small producers, labour-intensive methods and highly competitive product markets. Labour is employed, if at all, on a casual basis; self-employment or the use of family labour may be widespread; the workforce is not unionized; labour is often unstable, unproductive and unprotected.

In practice, this distinction has been difficult to sustain. Economic activities grouped within the unorganized sector often bear significant characteristics of the organized sector. Not only are they often as different from each other as they are from large-scale factory industry but some of them frequently have more in common with similar activities in the organized sector than they do with each other. Significantly, a study of surplus labour in Bombay elaborated the distinction between the organized and the unorganized sectors, only to conclude that its 'family of criteria [could not] easily be used for empirical investigation' and resorted instead to 'the size of the establishment', a highly arbitrary factor, as 'the best workable criterion'.[1] The unorganized sector thus becomes a self-

[1] H. Joshi and V. Joshi, *Surplus Labour and the City: A Study of Bombay* (Delhi, 1976), pp. 46–7.

72

referential, even tautological, category or, at best, a residual one, accommodating whatever is left out of the organized sector. The problem, however, is not simply the weakness of definition but also relates to the conceptualization of social processes.

At one level, the distinction between the organized and unorganized sectors has become most sharply evident in the shadows of mounting legislation governing industrial activity and labour organization. The growing volume of legislation initiated in India in the 1930s and gathering pace after 1947 has led employers to resort to stratagems which might enable them to remain outside its purview, whether by fragmenting their operations between smaller units or by effecting a distinction between 'permanent' and 'temporary' labour and restricting entry to the former, as its rights, privileges and security of tenure came to be entrenched and protected.[2] In this light, the dualism of the labour market seems less to be constituted by factors inherent to the economic logic of its operation than by contingencies like the effects of government policy and the intimately related criterion of the 'size of the establishment'. Indeed, as D.M. Gordon observed, 'the distinction between the two sectors is not so much technologically as historically determined'.[3] But if the distinction is historically determined, it loses some of its sanctity and our emphasis needs to shift from its acceptance as a social and economic fact to its ideological and political construction. We need to ask why the structure of the labour market came to be defined along these lines and why the essential characteristics of the two sectors were perceived and delineated in this way.

In some accounts, the unorganized sector has been portrayed as passive, traditional and marginal, and its formation is explained largely as a function of dependent industrialization.[4] In another line of argument, the unorganized sector is understood as part of an evolutionary process of modernization. It corresponds to the traditional sphere of the economy as yet lagging in the process of modernization. This perspective would, for instance, juxtapose free wage labour in the organized sector with household labour in the unorganized, 'capital-intensive, imported technology in contrast to... a labour-intensive indigenous technology', the dependence upon 'modern banking' in the case of the former and the reliance upon traditional money-lenders in the latter. In brief,

---

[2] For a convenient summary, see M. Holmström, *Industry and Inequality: Towards a Social Anthropology of Indian Labour* (Cambridge, 1984), pp. 110–80.

[3] D.M. Gordon, *Theories of Poverty and Underemployment: Orthodox, Radical and Dual Labour Market Perspectives* (Lexington, Mass., 1972), p. 47.

[4] R. Bromley and C. Gerry (eds.), *Casual Work and Poverty in Third World Cities* (Chichester, 1979); J. Perlman, *The Myth of Marginality: Urban Politics and Poverty in Rio de Janeiro* (Berkeley, 1977); R. Bromley (ed.), *The Urban Informal Sector: Critical Perspectives, World Development*, Special Issue, vol. VI, parts 9 and 10 (1978); M. Santos, *The Shared Space: The Two Circuits of the Urban Economy in Developing Countries* (London, 1979).

the essential dichotomy is between ' "modern" entrepreneurs' and ' "traditional" producers'.[5] To conceive of the unorganized sector simply as an anachronistic survival of traditional society is to miss, perhaps, its essential role in the constitution of the social economy as a whole.

Moreover, these distinctions would have been difficult to sustain in early-twentieth-century Bombay City. Here, there was little that was modern about the organized sector and not very much that was traditional about the unorganized. Indeed, the nature of their integration and the extent to which economic activities overlapped and shared striking similarities across the boundaries which were supposed to divide them eroded the distinction between the formal and informal sectors to the point of obliteration. Some evidence suggests that there is no necessary relationship between capital intensity and large-scale production in the organized sector; indeed, smaller enterprises in some industries were more capital intensive.[6] Indeed, the cotton-textile industry between the wars displayed a strong preference for labour-using investment. Unorganized sector activities often appear to have been dynamic and innovative. If the unorganized economy was integral to the formation and success of large-scale factory production, the linkages between them did not always condemn the former irreversibly to poverty and stagnation. The period between the wars probably witnessed the steady expansion of small industrial units and the most rapidly growing part of the city's economy in the 1940s in the post-colonial decades was the engineering industry which might earlier have been located almost entirely within the unorganized sector and has continued to operate successfully on a relatively small scale in more recent times.

The apparent incoherence of these categories has not, however, prevented scholars from deploying them or attributing specific social and cultural characteristics to workers within each sector. The characterization of two different types of labour supply to each sector forms an important element in distinguishing between them. For some, the informal sector, a marginalized sphere of economic activity, is necessarily inhabited by marginal social groups who develop a distinctive culture of their own. Similarly, dual labour market theories focus upon job stability, labour turnover and worker commitment as the source of and guide to the division between the primary and secondary markets. Indeed, dual labour market theories have often depended upon the characterization of 'the attitudes, personality traits and behavioural rules' of each sector.[7] Workers in the 'unorganized sector' are supposed to develop a 'life style [which] is accommodated to that type of

---

[5] Joshi and Joshi, *Surplus Labour and the City*, pp. 44–6.
[6] Holmström, *Industry and Inequality*, pp. 156–61. See also A.K. Bagchi and N. Banerjee (eds.), *Change and Choice in Indian Industry* (Calcutta, 1984).
[7] Gordon, *Theories of Poverty*, p. 51.

employment'.[8] It is assumed that some workers seek casual or temporary employment wherever it may be found.

In the case of Bombay, such aspiration has sometimes been portrayed as characteristic of the single male migrant with strong village attachments.[9] By relating the mechanisms of the labour market to the nature of the rural connections of workers and the social organization of the urban neighbourhood, it is possible to see that this characterization is misplaced. Historians of the urban working classes in India have frequently assumed that rural migrants or casual labourers, not as yet assimilated into the disciplined culture of industrial society, had a special disposition towards crime, roughness and violence[10] and displayed a generic immunity to regular work and factory discipline. However, these characterizations more accurately reflected ruling-class perceptions of the casual poor than they described real patterns of behaviour among them. Similar assumptions about the casual poor have been, and continue to be, made repeatedly in a wide variety of social contexts. The power and force of their imagery is reflected in the fact that writers who dig beneath these assumptions and proclaim that the 'culture of poverty' is dead continue to work within its framework and frequently retrieve and revive many of its essential and determining characteristics.[11]

Until recently, the concept of the 'culture of poverty', first conceived in relation to Latin America, had increasingly drawn the scepticism of writers on the Third World; but it has found increasing acceptance among social historians and sociologists of the West[12] and through their influence has manifested a revival in the recent work of social historians of India.[13] Curiously, however, in contemporary discourse, late-nineteenth- and early-twentieth-century observers in India saw many of the behavioural characteristics, which since

---

[8] P.B. Doeringer and M.J. Piore, *Internal Labour Markets and Manpower Analysis* (Lexington, Mass., 1971) cited by Gordon, *Theories of Poverty and Underdevelopment*, p. 47.

[9] Mazumdar, 'Labour Supply'.

[10] D. Arnold, 'Industrial Violence in Colonial India', *Comparative Studies in Society and History*, XXII, 2 (1980), 234–55.

[11] For instance, in an excellent recent study of Coimbatore workers, John Harriss declared that the 'culture of poverty' was 'no longer ... a live [issue]' but insisted on the existence of 'the culture ... of the working poor', to be distinguished from the 'labour aristocracy', found evidence which 'shows up the lack of political organization which appears to be common amongst the poorest people in cities in many parts of the Third World, apathy in the face of violence used against them and reliance upon contacts with outside political leaders' and contrasted their 'conditions of work ... as well as their social relationships' which place particular 'emphasis upon ... individual survival' with the political strategies and solidarities of class. See J. Harriss, 'The Working Poor and the Labour Aristocracy in a South Indian City: A Descriptive and Analytical Account', *MAS*, XX, 2 (1986), 231–83.

[12] For a recent critique, see J. Davis, 'Jennings' Buildings and the Royal Borough: The Construction of the Underclass in Mid-Victorian England', in D. Feldman and G. Stedman Jones, *Metropolis London: Histories and Representations since 1800* (London, 1989), pp. 11–39.

[13] An assumption frequently made, for instance, in Guha (ed.), *Subaltern Studies*.

mid-Victorian times in Britain have been identified exclusively with the 'casual poor', as specific not to their Indian counterparts but to millworkers.[14]

This chapter will set out the salient features of the occupational and industrial structure in Bombay. It will investigate how fundamentally the characteristics of business strategies and the organization of production in what appears to constitute the informal sector differed from the formal sector. It will then proceed to analyse the mechanisms of the labour market. The nature of the demand for labour and the conditions of its supply were important determinants of the social organization of Bombay's workers. It will try to place the nature of the labour supply in the context of the pattern of demand for labour. We will have to postpone the conclusion that casual workers specially and exclusively sought out casual employment, at least until we can establish how far the strategies of capital engendered a fluctuating demand for labour, hastening its turnover and its instability, and committed and exposed large numbers of job seekers involuntarily to the uncertainties of the casual labour market.

The occupational structure

From the late nineteenth century onwards, the cotton-textile industry formed the mainstay of Bombay's economy. Its development shaped the growth and character of numerous other economic activities. Upon its prosperity depended the economic vitality of the city as well as large parts of the hinterland. Moreover, a wide range of trades and occupations were directly affected by its fortunes. The state of the cotton trade as a whole determined levels of employment in the docks and on the railways. The cotton and cloth markets, the most important in the city, were intimately connected with the industry. The city's workshops serviced or supplied the cotton mills. Many engineering workshops and factories developed in response to the textile industry's need for structures of various kinds and for the repair and maintenance of its machinery.[15] The leather industry supplied the mills with bands and belts for pulleys and machines.[16] As the mills diversified from spinning to the weaving, dyeing and printing of cloth, the demand for sizing powder and heavy chemicals began to be supplied by chemical works now being set up in the city.[17] Saw mills and

[14] *Gazetteer*, I, 207–13, 223–6; H.A. Talcherkar, 'Raghu: The Model Millhand. A Sketch', *Indian Social Reformer*, 7 March 1908, pp. 315–16 and *ibid.*, 14 March 1908, pp. 327–8.

[15] Bagchi, *Private Investment*, p. 332.

[16] J.R. Martin, *A Monograph on Tanning and Working in Leather in the Bombay Presidency* (Bombay, 1903); *Report on the Leather Industries of the Bombay Presidency* (Bombay, 1910).

[17] *Report of the Indian Tariff Board Regarding the Grant of Protection to the Magnesium Chloride Industry (including the Evidence Recorded during the Enquiry)* (Calcutta, 1925); Ray, *Industrialization*, pp. 161–76.

wood-working factories manufactured spindles and bobbins. The handloom-weaving workshops bought their yarn from the textile mills, and in periods of very brisk trading or of industrial action it is possible that the latter sub-contracted orders to the former.[18] Establishments for dyeing and printing also worked in harness with industry.[19] Many specialized trades of skilled artisans – carpenters, electricians, mechanics, blacksmiths, mochis – were employed in the mills. There were also several economic activities which were indirectly dependent upon the textile industry. For example, cotton seed was vital to the oil industry. Similarly, tailoring and dressmaking, and the retailers of cloth, tailored and ready-made clothes – perhaps the most dynamic sector of the retail trade – were affected by the textile industry.[20] In other words, the demand for the output of large sections of the city's small-industrial economy was generated directly by the cotton-textile industry.

The cotton-textile industry alone employed 16.2 per cent of the male population and 9.5 per cent of the female in 1921.[21] In addition, many millworkers were probably returned as general labour or slipped into various specialized occupational categories. 'Save for its textile manufacture', wrote the Census Commissioner in 1931, 'Bombay has really little claim to be called an industrial city. It is textile manufacturing alone that puts it into the industrial class'.[22] Indeed while eighty-four cotton-spinning and weaving mills in 1921 employed an average of slightly over 1,800 workers each (excluding the 'direction, supervision and clerical staff'), the remaining 552 units with a labour force of more than ten people, employed eighty-seven workers apiece.[23] In 1921, the cotton-textile industry accounted for about three-quarters of the workforce engaged in factories employing more than twenty workers and maintained this ratio throughout the period.[24] Over the same period, however, the cotton mills made up a decreasing proportion of the number of such factories. In part, this

[18] R.E. Enthoven, *The Cotton Fabrics of the Bombay Presidency* (Bombay, 1897); S.M. Edwardes, *A Monograph upon the Silk Fabrics of the Bombay Presidency* (Bombay, 1900); *Gazetteer*, I, 461–3; Labour Office, Bombay, *Report on Wages, Hours of Work and Conditions of Employment in the Textile Industries (Cotton, Silk, Wool and Hosiery) in the Bombay Presidency (excluding Sind), May 1934. General Wage Census, Part I – Perennial Factories, Third Report* (Bombay, 1937), pp. 193–206; Interviews, February 1979 and December 1981.
[19] C.G.H. Fawcett, *A Monograph on Dyes and Dyeing in the Bombay Presidency* (Bombay, 1896); Enthoven, *Cotton Fabrics*; Edwardes, *Silk Fabrics*; *Gazetteer*, I, 463–6.
[20] *Report on an Enquiry into Wages, Hours of Work and Conditions of Employment in the Retail Trade of Some Towns in the Bombay Presidency* (Bombay, 1936), p. 1.
[21] *Census of India, 1921*, vol. IX, *Cities of the Bombay Presidency*, part i, *Report*, by H.S. Sedgwick (Bombay, 1922), p. 37.
[22] *Census of India, 1931*, vol. IX, *The Cities of the Bombay Presidency*, part i, *Report*, by H.T. Sorley (Bombay, 1933), p. 53.
[23] Calculated from *Census, 1921*, IX, ii, City Table IX.
[24] Calculated from *Annual Factory Reports for the Presidency of Bombay*. See table 6.

Table 6. *Cotton-spinning and weaving mills and millworkers as a proportion of the total number of industrial units and workers*

Year	Number of units	Percentage of total number of units for city	Number of workers	Percentage of total number of workers
1912	80	44.19	109,806	75.07
1917	83	48.54	122,727	71.57
1922	85	32.08	151,241	73.51
1927	80	22.47	145,005	73.46
1932	74	19.79	139,963	77.32
1936	70	14.70	126,328	71.24

Source: Annual Factory Reports for the Presidency of Bombay.

reflected changes in the legal definition of a factory.[25] To some extent, it was produced by better reporting. 'Special efforts made to comb out a number of unregistered perennial and seasonal factories' resulted, according to the Chief Inspector of Factories, as late as 1937 'in a number being registered and ten prosecuted'.[26] It was, in addition, the consequence of improved methods of classification.[27] But it also reflected real changes in the industrial structure of the city.

The expansion of industry in inter-war Bombay – the growth of engineering workshops, motor works, printing presses, metal works, dyeing and bleaching factories – consisted largely of the proliferation of small units of production. As a rule they produced consumer or intermediate goods, were subject to seasonal and arbitrary fluctuations of demand and were characterized by a relatively low ratio of fixed capital. Typically, the findings of the industrial census of 1921 showed that there were nearly three times as many factories which employed more than ten workers as those which employed more than twenty.[28] Yet this section of the city's workforce constituted a small proportion of the total.

[25] Under the Factory Act of 1891 a factory was place of work which used mechanical power and employed more than fifty workers. In 1921 the Act was amended to cover factories which employed twenty workers and could be extended by notification of local government to units which employed ten workers. In 1948, it was further extended to cover establishments which employed ten or more workers; see R.K. Das, *History of Indian Labour Legislation* (Calcutta, 1941).
[26] *Annual Report on the Factories in the Bombay Presidency, 1937* (Bombay, 1938), p. 13.
[27] For instance, the enumeration of engineering workshops was taken much more seriously from the mid 1920s onwards. Until then many of these were probably returned as 'iron works' or under sundry other categories.
[28] *Census, 1921*, IX, ii, City Table IX. The industrial census enumerated factories employing more than ten persons, after the Factory Act had been amended to cover units employing more than

Significantly, only 17 per cent of the entire population and about 23.5 per cent of those between the ages of fifteen and fifty years were engaged in industrial units employing more than ten people.[29] But this proportion probably underestimated the number employed in factories of this size. There were, for instance, 'a fair number of cases of combines of relatives' with four or five working partners and six or seven employees who were excluded from the census compilations.[30] No doubt there were others who escaped the notice of the census enumerators altogether. As Mr P.B. Advani, Director of Industries, told the Whitley Commission, only one-eighth of the workforce engaged in industry in the Presidency as a whole were employed in factories covered by the Factories Act. 'Not an inconsiderable number of people', he said, 'work in factories which either because they employ under 20 persons or have no machinery, do not come under the Factories Act. Accurate information about such persons will probably not be readily available'.[31]

A wide range of operations, producing consumer goods for the local market, were to be found in the back streets and wadis of the city:[32] furniture factories turning out carved blackwood couches, screens, writing desks and chairs; innumerable small bakeries, tobacco shops and bidi manufacturers; sugar-refining factories[33] and sweetmeat makers; tailoring shops; lime-kilns, potteries and tile makers; glass manufacturers;[34] match factories,[35] especially in the suburban district; a power laundry[36] and a paper mill which made packing and coarse writing paper.[37] There was also a host of 'craft' industries and artisanal workshops: handloom-weaving workshops in Duncan Road and Madanpura; silk weavers, and dyers and printers who worked in cotton and silk; wire, tinsel and kincob workers in Bhuleshwar and Bhendi Bazar; brassworkers, blacksmiths and potters; goldsmiths and jewellers, notably in Jhaveri Bazar.[38]

The vast majority of the city's population was to be found in a wide variety

twenty. While it returned more than 400 additional units, it enumerated less than 1,500 extra workers. Allowing for errors of enumeration, the trend is clear: the growth of a large number of units employing very few workers.

[29] Calculated from *Census, 1921*, IX, ii, City Table IX.

[30] *Ibid.*, IX, i, 34.

[31] *RCLI, Evidence, Bombay Presidency (including Sind)* (London, 1931), Mr P.B. Advani, Director of Industries, Bombay, I, i, 207.

[32] For a general picture of these trades, see *Gazetteer*, I, 461–505; *Census, 1921*, IX, ii, City Table IX.

[33] Labour Office, Bombay, *General Wage Census Part I. Perennial Factories, Fourth Report, Wages, Hours of Work and Conditions of Employment in the Refined Sugar Manufacturing Industry*, pp. 64–72.

[34] *Ibid.*, Wages ... the Glass Manufacturing Industry, pp. 89–98.

[35] *Ibid.*, Wages ... the Match Manufacturing Industry, pp. 29–46.

[36] *Ibid.*, Wages ... Power Laundries, pp. 147–52.

[37] *Ibid.*, Wages ... the Paper Manufacturing Industry, pp. 117–26.

[38] Cecil L. Burns, *A Monograph on Gold and Silver Work in the Bombay Presidency* (Bombay, 1904), p. 15.

of casual occupations. There is, of course, no precise guide to their numbers and occupations. The most accessible reckoner remains the census. Yet occupation was 'the most difficult Census head' complicated by the highly intricate problem of matching people's descriptions of their work with the census categories.[39] It was in part a function of these arithmetical complexities that 'insufficiently described occupations' accounted for about 28.4 per cent of the city's population in 1921.[40] But incompetent enumeration was not the only explanation for their preponderance. By 1931, their numbers had declined from 128,123 males and 27,749 females in 1921 to 54,568 males and 7,388 females. This decline could partly be attributed to improved methods of classification; 'but there is no doubt', wrote the Census Commissioners, 'that there has been a considerable fall in this occupation due to the business and trade depression which the Census figures truly reflect'.[41] Their occupations were insufficiently described because, as with most groups of casual workers, their occupations were insufficiently defined.

General labouring jobs were to be found in the docks, the building trade, the cotton godowns, markets and warehouses, and the various public agencies such as the railways,[42] the municipality,[43] the Port Trust[44] and the Bombay Electric Supply and Tramways Company.[45] The extent of casual labouring employment in the municipality, for instance, only became apparent in 1931 when labourers, placed in the category of 'unspecified occupations' in the previous census and returned under the head of 'municipal and other local services' in 1931, inflated this group from 8,932 to 26,848.[46]

Bombay's rapid growth generated an extensive demand for a wide range of services. Domestic service was a major source of employment. The retail trades also employed a sizeable labour force. The retailing and provision of foodstuffs was the main source of livelihood for about 70,000 people.[47]

---

[39] *Census, 1921*, IX, i, 33. Indeed, a list of terms used by workers to describe their occupations – in a sense their language of work – might suggest a great deal about occupational culture, differentiations of status and the texture of social consciousness.

[40] *Census, 1921*, IX, i, 44; *ibid.*, IX, ii, City Table VII, Part I.

[41] *Census, 1931*, IX, i, 51.

[42] See *Census, 1921*, IX, ii, City Table VII, Part I.

[43] *RCLI, Evidence, Bombay Presidency*, The Bombay Municipal Corporation, I, i, 567.

[44] *Ibid.*, The Bombay Port Trust, I, i, 461–4; R.P. Cholia, *Dock Labourers in Bombay* (Bombay 1941); Burnett–Hurst, *Labour and Housing*, pp. 73–84, 92–7.

[45] *RCLI, Evidence, Bombay Presidency*, The Bombay Electric Supply and Tramways Company, I, i, 531–3.

[46] *Census, 1931*, IX, i, 51. In 1939, the Municipal Corporation employed nearly 8,000 workers, in assorted occupations from watchmen to dog-catchers and grave-diggers, who earned less than Rs.25 per month. Municipal Commissioner, Bombay to Secretary, Textile Labour Inquiry: Committee, No. SR/1092L, 21 November 1939, Proceedings of the Textile Labour Inquiry Committee (henceforth *TLIC*), File XIII of 1937–40, MSA.

[47] Including both workers and dependants, see *Census, 1921*, IX, ii, City Table VII, Part I.

Moreover, a large number of workers were occupied in various forms of petty trading and production, hawking and peddling. Everything could be bought and sold on the streets of Bombay. Anything that might be bought was made. Any service which might be sought was offered. Most people were engaged in trades which were neither regular nor secure; some had to find their livelihood however they could. Many simply failed. One observer intoned against 'the most wretched beggars' and then doused them with pity:

They are not satisfied with what they get by begging but they also rake up the spots where the dinner plates and fragments of food are thrown and lick the plates along with the dogs and cats; the dogs barking at the beggar and the beggar driving away the dog with one hand and eating with other. This is a most pitiful sight to look at.[48]

The structure of the labour market

Conventionally, the historical understanding of the labour market in Bombay (and elsewhere in India) has revolved around the supply of labour. Historians debate whether there was a scarcity of labour.[49] They investigate the stability of the labour force and its commitment to the industrial environment. The questions they address relate primarily to the 'adaptation' of a rural labour force to the industrial setting and focus almost exclusively upon the cotton-textile industry, pulled out of the economic context in which it was embedded. Whatever their differences, these accounts neglect the conditions in which the demand for labour was generated. It will be useful, therefore, to investigate the nature of the demand in the consumer goods industries, the intermediate goods sector and the casual trades. Despite important differences between them, the industries which operated in Bombay shared conditions of volatile demand and a liability to sharp and arbitrary trade fluctuations. There were also striking similarities in the organization of production across the perceived divide between the formal and informal sectors. Small-scale enterprises in the informal sector often bore the characteristics of factory production. Industrialization in

---

[48] K. Raghunathji, *Bombay Beggars and Criers* (n.d., n.p.), pp. 7–8.
[49] S.D. Mehta, *The Indian Cotton Textile Industry: An Economic Analysis* (Bombay, 1953); S.D. Mehta, *The Cotton Mills of India 1854–1954* (Bombay, 1954); M.D. Morris, 'Some Comments on the Supply of Labour to the Bombay Cotton Textile Industry, 1854–1951', *Indian Economic Journal*, I, 2 (October, 1953), 138–52; S.D. Mehta, 'Professor Morris on Textile Labour Supply', *Indian Economic Journal*, I, 3 (January, 1954), 333–40; M.D. Morris, 'The Labour Market in India', in W.E. Moore and A.S. Feldman (eds.), *Labour Commitment and Social Change in Developing Areas* (New York, 1960); Morris, *Emergence of an Industrial Labour Force*, pp. 39–177. Newman, 'Social Factors in the Recruitment of the Bombay Millhands', pp. 277–95; Mazumdar, 'Labour Supply', 477–96.

the form of factory production did not necessarily reflect a relentless commitment to progressive mechanization and its development often came to depend
upon the intensive use of manual labour. On the other hand, some 'informal'
sector enterprises at times displayed a greater readiness to adopt more sophisticated technology. Business strategies which aimed at maintaining a rapid
turnover in the face of volatile and shifting demand were shared in common
across the city's economy.

The use of casual labour is not generally associated with the manufacturing
industries, both because of the nature of the skill required and because of the
advantages of maintaining a steady level of production to reap the full advantage
of machinery, which would tend to give rise to a more even rhythm of demand
for labour. However, about one-third of the labour force in the cotton-textile
industry was hired on a daily and casual basis.[50] The key to this conundrum lies,
of course, in the economics of the cotton-textile industry.[51] The price of raw
cotton, itself subject to seasonal variation, formed a major proportion of the cost
of production. This was particularly true in the case of spinning: the more the
raw material was processed and value added to it, the less the entrepreneur
depended upon the favourable movement of cotton prices. Nevertheless, the
purchase of a good mixing at optimum prices for the particular varieties of yarn
and cloth to be produced entailed considerable expertise and determined in large
measure the profits of the enterprise.[52] Similarly, the demand for yarn and cloth
were subject to short-term fluctuations. Necessarily, it was best for a mill to
retain as much flexibility as possible in the composition of its output. The
demand for labour varied, then, with the price of raw cotton, the shifting
demand for varieties of yarn and cloth and the accumulation of stocks in the
mill itself.

Under these conditions of volatile demand, manufacturers could choose
between two strategies: they could attempt to maintain production as evenly as
possible in order to maximize returns on their fixed investment or, alternatively,
they could tailor production more closely to demand. By maintaining a steady

---

[50] *Royal Commission on Labour, Foreign Report*, vol. II, *The Colonies and the Indian Empire*,
Memorandum on the Labour Question in India. Letter from the Collector of Land Revenue,
Customs and Opium, Bombay, to the Chief Secretary, *PP*, 1892, XXXVI, 129; Labour Office
Bombay, *Report on the Wages, Hours of Work and Conditions of Employment in the Textile
Industries (Cotton, Silk, Wool and Hosiery) in the Bombay Presidency (including Sind), May
1934, General Wage Census, Part I – Perennial Factories, Third Report* (Bombay, 1937), p. 20.
[51] These issues are examined in relation to the cotton-textile industry at greater length in chapters
6 and 7 below.
[52] A Retired Mill Manager, *The Bombay Cotton Mills: the Spinning of 10's, 20's and 30's Counts*
(Bombay, 1907); Proceedings of the TLIC, Main Inquiry, Oral Evidence, Confidential Examination of the BMOA, File 78-C, pp. 5338–59, MSA.

level of production in the face of seasonal and other variations of demand, they would begin to accumulate stocks and have to meet the cost of storage and production, while exposing themselves to the risk of falling prices or a change in demand. In addition, they would have to bear the burden of their investment for a longer period. On the other hand, the regulation of production according to short-term fluctuations in demand would entail laying off workers and thus risk the loss of skilled workers and trade secrets to rival producers while also impeding the realization of the full value of machinery costs and other fixed investments. Hence it was when the ratio of fixed capital was low that employers might conveniently attempt to adjust production to short-term market fluctuations.

It was a characteristic of most consumer-durable industries that even if they could maintain a regular supply of raw materials, they were subject to considerable variations of demand. The effect of market fluctuations was felt even more incisively by the smaller industries unable to benefit from the economies of large-scale production. They operated with a low ratio of fixed to working costs, minimized their expenditure on overheads and sought to maintain a rapid turnover. Some industries, like the aerated water factories, could predict fluctuations in demand for their products, since these were primarily seasonal. In the case of other industries, such fluctuations were simply unpredictable. Flexible production strategies were essential to their general situation.

The consequences of efforts to maintain this flexibility imprinted themselves firmly upon the organization and character of Bombay's industries. They operated predominantly on a small scale. Although there were 'over a score of small tanneries in the Dharavi area', none of them, except the Western India Tanneries, was large enough to be notified under the Factories Act.[53] Out of the seventy-nine workshops outside Dharavi investigated by N.M. Joshi in 1937, fifty-nine employed less than five workers while only one employed more than fifteen workers.[54] Sonars, brought from all over India, worked in the back rooms of the large jewellery makers, mass-producing goods for the European winter excursionists.[55] Since entrepreneurs minimized their overheads, factories remained ramshackle structures, cheaply put together or hastily adapted. Some tanneries were housed in dwelling houses, their 'rooms arranged according to various occupations'.[56] Dyeing was carried out in long sheds which housed

---

[53] Martin, *Tanning and Working in Leather*; *Annual Factory Reports, passim*.

[54] 'List of the Leather Workshops in Bombay and their Addresses', N.M. Joshi Papers, File 87, pp. 17–21, NMML. This single workshop, Gaikwad's, situated at Kennedy Bridge operated judiciously with nineteen workers, to be beyond the purview of the Factories Act.

[55] Burns, *Gold and Silver Work*, p. 15.

[56] Martin, *Tanning and Working in Leather*, p. 14.

large indigo vats while adjacent structures were put up for calendering, sizing and other ancillary processes.[57]

Few factories of any kind used mechanical sources of power and frequently mechanization entailed no more than simple, hand-driven machinery.[58] The advance of mechanization often took eccentric routes. In calico printing, electro-plating processes were in many small workshops replacing the wood block, which tended to lose its sharpness and the effects of depth and light with use. Conversely, in the city's silk mills printed goods were exposed to steam but the designs were 'stamped by hand with engraved wooden blocks'. The reason for this was the apprehension that 'the inevitable change of fashion in printed goods would necessitate the constant replacing of the costly brass cylinders for newer designs and their introduction would not, therefore, pay'.[59]

The advance of mechanization and factory production did not reduce the long hours and heavy workloads for most workers. Rather, the low ratio of fixed investment was associated with the more intensive use of labour.[60] Moreover, it was symptomatic of the intensive use of labour that production was often minutely subdivided in small workshops as well as in large factories.[61]

Some trades combined a form of factory production with features of the putting-out system. Tailoring was said to be 'almost entirely in the hands of the small home worker',[62] but for many tailors this involved working at the premises of the master for wages paid on the basis of production.[63] The master supplied the cloth as well as necessary instruments, such as scissors and irons, but tailors rented their sewing machines from their employer. Tailors worked extremely irregular hours; depending upon the flow of orders, they were sometimes required to work round the clock.[64] Employers attempted to minimize their capital costs by investing in as few irons and sewing machines as possible and in periods of peak production often helped each other out. At the same time,

---

[57] Fawcett, *Dyes and Dyeing*.
[58] For examples of handloom weaving, see Enthoven, *Cotton Fabrics*; Edwardes, *Silk Fabrics*. On leather work, see *Report on the Leather Industries*, p. 19. On gold- and silver-thread production, see J. Nissim, *Wire and Tinsel in the Bombay Presidency* (Bombay, 1909), especially pp. 5–7.
[59] Fawcett, *Dyes and Dyeing*, p. 38.
[60] On dyeing, see *ibid.*; on the tanneries, see Handbill, Bombay Leather Workers' Union, N.M. Joshi Papers File 87, p. 91, NMML; *RCLI*, *Evidence, Bombay Presidency*, The Workers Employed in Tanneries and Factories in Dharavi, I, i, 573; and *Report on the Leather Industries*, p. 20.
[61] Martin, *Tanning and Working in Leather*; Edwardes, *Silk Fabrics*, pp. 40–1.
[62] *Census, 1921*, IX, i, 39.
[63] The conditions of the trade may be gleaned from a list of demands issued by the Bombay Tailors' Union when various shops in Girgaum went on strike in August 1938. AITUC Papers, File 61, pp. 158–61, NMML.
[64] Thus, one of their demands was for a fixed working day of ten hours, between 9 a.m. and 7 p.m. and the payment of overtime of an extra 8 annas for work done between 8 p.m. and 2 a.m.

they could control production through the deployment of these necessary instruments, cutting back or slowing it down, thus reducing working costs and wages without laying off skilled workers who might carry their trade secrets and even customers to their rivals and who in any case might not so easily be replaced.[65] It was perfectly compatible with these conditions that the tailors complained that their wages were paid neither punctually nor regularly nor even accurately. The withholding of wages in such a trade probably restricted the mobility of workers, provided security against damage to the sewing machines or default on their rent and served as a form of insurance against indiscipline, bad work or industrial action. Furthermore, it was also necessitated by the financial exigencies of the trade. For, operating on narrow margins, the master tailor relied upon the quick turnover of his goods and prompt payment by his customers to be able to meet the charges of his suppliers, his workers and his creditors.

Bidi making was another industry to combine features of subcontracting and the forms of factory production. These sweat shops employed mainly women and children, and pared down their overheads to an absolute minimum, rent constituting a major portion of the cost of production. While the merchant provided thread and tobacco, the workers were expected to bring their own leaves. Each woman, it was expected, could make 1,000 bidis per day for which she was paid 10 annas; if she was 'expert enough', she might make 2,000.[66] In 1922, bidi workers worked from 9 a.m. to 9 p.m., according to an official source, 'under the most trying conditions'. An enquiry into the conditions of female employment described the scene in a bidi factory:

Women and young girls were either sent to duties where the sitting posture only could be maintained or they sat on a plank hung from the roof of the room, some three feet below the roof and there in an atmosphere laden with tobacco dust these women and children sat making the Indian cigarette or Beedi. Every available space was employed for workers and in several factories I found women workers sitting in the entrance wall, perhaps 2 1/2 feet away from a drain which emptied its contents of all the latrines on the upper floor into the main drain which ran by the entrance where they sat. They are inadequately paid, and this is the only industry, this and pottery workers, where women as well as men drank.[67]

---

[65] Hence, another 'demand' made by the tailors' union was that each shopowner should ensure that an iron and a sewing machine were available for every five workers.

[66] *Gazetteer*, I, 470–2. According to the *Gazetteer*, the cost of production rose considerably in the nineteenth century. Rents had risen from Rs. 2 per month in 1836 to Rs. 75 in 1909; other monthly expenditure from Rs. 20 to Rs. 150; wages from 2.5 annas per 1,000 bidis to 8 or 12 annas, *ibid.*, p. 472.

[67] Supplementary Report by Dr (Mrs) Barnes, 23 July 1922 in Government of India (henceforth GOI) Industries 1922, Labour, File L-920 (3), pp. 20–1, National Archives of India (henceforth NAI).

In a wide range of consumer goods, employers regulated production to short-term fluctuations of demand. But there is no reason to assume that methods of financial and labour management were uniform. In some cases, demand was subject to more or less predictable seasonal variations, in others, market fluctuations were somewhat more arbitrary. Large firms did not abjure flexible business strategies altogether, but they were better able to mediate their impact. They could, for instance, maintain a permanent core of workers around which they hired labour according to need, carry a larger volume of stocks and attempt to diversify their products and markets in response to trade fluctuations. The policies of employers in relation to their workforce could also vary according to whether their workers were paid by piece or by time. Ostensibly the wage bill could be pared down in the former case by adopting short-time working or reducing output; but workers paid according to time sometimes appeared more vulnerable to retrenchment. It would be misleading, however, to exaggerate the difference between piece-rated and time-rated workers. For there was necessarily an important time element in the calculation of piece-rates while productivity was hardly ignored in the fixing of time wages and in any case, these could always be adjusted for periods when workers were temporarily laid off.[68]

These flexible patterns of labour use had important consequences for the mechanisms of the labour market. It was a general characteristic of casual labour markets of this kind that they tended to produce in the longer term and excess supply of labour in order to meet the peak demand of buoyant times.[69] The high level of employment (or for piece workers, high earnings) achieved when the market was buoyant and there was a rush of work could hold within the city, or within particular trades, workers who might otherwise have been driven into other occupations. Clearly, the uneven and imbalanced development of the economy as a whole impinged upon this: for it shaped the choice of the alternative industrial or rural livelihoods available to most workers. As mounting pressures on the land drove peasants into the towns, they encountered a volatile labour market whose fluctuations left them stranded within a growing casual labour force, buffeted between town and country by their low earnings and periodic and uncertain employment.[70] As long as this labour force was held on the fringes of the city's economy, it redefined the options before entrepreneurs. When labour was scarce, employers might be hard pressed to effect short-term adjustments of production. On the other hand, if labour was abundant, they had little incentive to maintain steady levels of employment in the face of volatile markets.

[68] D. Schloss, *Methods of Industrial Remuneration* (London, 1892), pp. 11–47.
[69] See the classic analysis by G. Stedman Jones, *Outcast London: A Study in the Relationship Between Classes in Victorian Society* (Oxford, 1971), pp. 42, 33–126.
[70] See chapter 4.

It has already been shown that a number of industries developed to supply intermediate goods and services, primarily to the cotton-textile industry. Of course, no rigid distinction between consumer and intermediate industries can be sustained. Consumer-goods industries, like leather, supplied the cotton mills with belts and bands for their machinery, while industries, like chemicals and engineering, produced both consumer durables and intermediate goods and services. The risks and uncertainties faced by these intermediate goods industries stemmed from the narrow industrial base which generated the demand for their goods. Fluctuations in the demand for their output were determined by conditions in other areas of economic activity, notably in the cotton-textile industry, over which they had little control. In addition, some of these industries, particularly in the case of engineering, were concerned with the repair and maintenance of machinery, and necessarily the demand for their services was subject to arbitrary fluctuations. It is not surprising, therefore, that the characteristic pattern of investment in these industries, as in the case of the consumer durables, took the form of small pools of fixed capital, and that production occurred in small units, relying upon a rapid turnover and a largely unskilled labour force organized around a skilled nucleus.

The engineering industry expanded steadily in the inter-war period and then more dramatically in the 1940s. Characteristically, its expansion was registered in a more dramatic increase in the number of factories than in the level of employment.[71] Using a very generous definition of the engineering industry – including the railway workshops, shipbuilding and repair units at the port, the electric transformer stations and extending to iron and steel re-rolling mills and foundries, steel-furniture factories and structural-steel-sections manufacturing works, large-scale mechanical workshops, the manufacturing of parts and tools, nuts and bolts, and assembly shops – a survey conducted by the All-India Manufacturers' Organization counted 404 factories employing 40,000 workers in 1942.[72] While most engineering workshops were small back-street operations, often concentrating upon the provision of repairs and specialized services, the major firms dealt in a wide range of goods. The manufacture of steel furniture is most closely associated with the entrepreneur A.B. Godrej whose efforts to make and sell cupboards, locks, safes, and later, consumer durables like soap and boot polish as well as printing ink developed into one of the largest

[71] In 1917, when only units employing more than fifty workers were included, three general engineering works were returned, employing 1,397 workers; by 1922 when the limit was lowered to twenty workers, there were six workshops employing 1,433. In 1936, there were twenty-five workshops which employed 2,290 workers. In the case of metal works, their numbers increased from six units with 791 workers in 1922 to twenty-seven units with 2,567 workers. *Annual Factory Reports for the Presidency of Bombay.*
[72] All-India Manufacturers' Organization, *Industries in Bombay City* (Bombay, 1944), p. 7.

manufacturing enterprises in the city.[73] The largest engineering firms were owned by Europeans. Alcock, Ashdown and Co., for example, were boilermakers and shipwrights and built launches, tugs and barges. In addition, they also acted as automobile and marine engine dealers and repairers and undertook various construction projects. Similarly, Richardson and Cruddas acted as general constructional and sanitary engineers, iron and brass founders as well as metal and hardware merchants. They were also the proprietors of the Byculla Iron Works, the Nesbit Road Iron Works and the Bombay Metal Mart. Garlik and Co. were the sole agents for various British and American engineering exporters as well as boilermakers and producers of various kinds of heavy machinery.[74] By diversifying, they were able to hedge against the sharpest fluctuations of demand, but in order to adjust to these at all, they had to remain flexible in their patterns of production.

The railway workshops ranked among the largest employers in Bombay. The Great Indian Peninsular Railway employed about 5,000 workers in the locomotive works, and another 6,000 in their carriage and wagon department, while the Bombay, Baroda and Central India Railway had a labour force of about 5,000 workers in their locomotive and carriage shop.[75] These workshops were principally concerned with repair, maintenance and the assembly of imported parts. By the 1920s, they manufactured a few parts themselves, particularly boilers and cylinders, while both workshops constructed carriages on their own premises. Their market was limited to the supply of the railways' fluctuating needs for repairs, spare parts and structures.[76] Similarly, many of the civic agencies in Bombay – the Municipal Corporation, the Port Trust and the privately owned Bombay Electric Supply and Tramways Company – had their own engineering workshops. Since their main function was repair and maintenance, they too employed a fluctuating number of workers.[77] Only about 40 per cent of the Port Trust's employees in the engineering department were given permanent status and formed the core around which its casual workforce was built. In conditions representative of the engineering industry as a whole, the Port Trust reported that 'in the workshops the number of men employed varies according to the amount of work in hand'.[78]

Necessarily, when employers varied their levels of production and employment, they risked losing their skilled labour force to their rivals, or to other trades

[73] Guha, 'More About Parsi Seths', 129.
[74] *Thacker's Directory of the Chief Industries of India, Burma and Ceylon, 1926* (n.d., n.p.), pp. 41–2.
[75] Burnett-Hurst, *Labour and Housing*, p. 92.
[76] *Ibid.*, p. 97.
[77] *RCLI, Evidence, Bombay Presidency*, The Bombay Municipal Corporation, I, i, 567; *ibid.*, The Bombay Electric Supply and Tramways Company, I, i, 531–3.
[78] *Ibid.*, The Bombay Port Trust, I, i, 462.

and industries. The stratagems which employers sometimes adopted to minimize these risks were exemplified in the case of dock labour. The demand for
skilled labourers in the dry docks was intermittent, determined by when the
ships came in, and once on the job they were required to work quickly, for the
daily charges for the dry dock were high.[79] Similarly, there was rarely enough
work to keep crane drivers employed every day. However, the Port Trust had
to maintain a sufficient force of crane drivers to meet their needs whenever there
was a rush of work.[80] In these cases, the Port Trust attempted to lay off
temporarily a proportion of workers by rotation for a specific period of compulsory leave each month, for the duration of which, however, no wages were
paid. Its object, according to the Port Trust, was 'to mitigate the hardship of
unemployment among the regular workers'. But behind benevolent sentiment
nestled a shrewd economic sense.[81] The Port Trust, as Cholia noted, 'is not in
a position to dismiss some of these skilled workers and simply keep the rest
employed each day'. For 'whenever there is a rush of work, ... additional
labourers are required to meet such an extra demand, which cannot be met by
engaging novices'.[82] In addition, the loss of wages for slack periods was made
up by overtime in busier periods, while in any case the wages paid when work
was available combined with its unpredictable rhythms to prevent workers from
moving into more permanent jobs elsewhere.[83] The system of compulsory leave
dispensed with the need for employers to dismiss skilled workers and thus
neutralized both the risk of losing them to rivals and the expense of retaining
them in slack periods.

By the later 1920s and 1930s, there had developed an excess supply of some
kinds of skilled labour, generated in part by considerable variations in the
demand for labour. Of course, the level of skill cannot be taken as an absolute
factor. Nevertheless, most employers of relatively skilled workers reported no
difficulties over recruitment by the late 1920s.[84] Thus, when General Motors
established a workshop in Bombay, it was able to recruit largely local labour,
for the number of fitters and metal-workers,

trained yearly in the various workshops of the railways and engineering firms, dockyards,
etc., creates a supply which is in excess of the demand. Apart from a few very highly
skilled positions, e.g., armature winders, high grade mechanics and coach and body
strippers, boiler makers (first class), etc., the greater portion of the other sections viz.,

---

[79] Cholia, *Dock Labourers*, pp. 93–4.
[80] *Ibid.*, pp. 93–7.
[81] *RCLI, Evidence, Bombay Presidency*, The Bombay Port Trust, I, i, 462.
[82] Cholia, *Dock Labourers*, p. 97.
[83] *Ibid.*, pp. 97, 106.
[84] GIP Railway, *Report for the Royal Commission*, pp. 1–4; *RCLI, Evidence, Bombay Presidency*,
   Bombay Electric Supply and Tramways Company, I, i, 531–3; *ibid.*, The Bombay Port Trust, I,
   i, 461–2.

fitters, painters, tailors and less skilled mechanics can be obtained any day at the factory premises.[85]

General labour was, of course, the classic site of casual employment. There was a constant and considerable demand for labour in the city: in the cotton godowns and the major wholesale and retail markets; in the docks and on building sites, with the Municipality to tar the roads or the Bombay Electric Supply and Tramways Company to lay electric cables or even in the cotton mills to carry bales of cotton. In most cases, such employers of casual labour stood to gain little from maintaining a regular and permanent labour force and these occupations were subject to sudden fluctuations in the demand for labour. There were no specialized skills required for these jobs except youth, strength and considerable powers of endurance.[86] Yet this kind of endurance presupposed enormous skill. As Cholia observed, referring to Matadi shore labourers, 'To carry bags weighing five or six maunds each, easily on the back all day long, requires an experienced labour'.[87] But experience was by the nature of the work difficult to come by. Significantly, 82 per cent of all dock labourers were aged between twenty-five and forty-five years. The Port Trust itself estimated that the average working life of a dock labourer was ten years. After this period, 'age prohibits heavy manual labour' and 'the majority retire to their village holdings giving way to younger men who take their places' – no doubt to grow old swiftly.[88] The awesome physical strain of manual labour was compounded by its inherent danger and vulnerability to accident. There were few effective safety precautions in most trades; but there were almost none in casual labour. Stevedores in the docks encountered working conditions which were hazardous in the extreme:

The Foreman stands near the opening of the hatch, and the Hatchman works at the bottom. Every few minutes some cargo swiftly passes over the head of the Foremen, and down it goes into the hatch swinging and dashing against the sides of the hatch. The Hatchman at the bottom is not sure where exactly the goods will fall, so he has often to go below the deck of the hatch to protect himself. Breakage of the chain of the crane at any moment, or even a slight mistake on the part of either the Foreman or the Craneman, would mean certain death for the Hatchman. Even the Foreman has to take care of the swings and jerks of the crane, else he would be thrown overboard. This danger is greatly enhanced when both the crane and the winch are working at the same hatch, for then it appears as if the work is being carried on at maddening speed. Though lighting arrangements are made for night-work, light is hardly sufficient inside a hatch. Night-work thus adds to the danger.[89]

---

[85] *RCLI, Evidence, Bombay Presidency*, Mr G.C. Seers, Managing Dirctor, General Motors India Ltd., Bombay, I, i, 573.
[86] Cholia, *Dock Labourers*, p. 127.
[87] *Ibid.*, p. 47.
[88] *RCLI, Evidence, Bombay Presidency*, The Bombay Port Trust, I, i, 462.
[89] Cholia, *Dock Labourers*, pp. 32–3.

The volume of demand for dock labour was subject to seasonal fluctuations.[90] It might be influenced by the harvest, the general economic situation and the volume and value of goods passing through the port. It was at times hamstrung by the monsoon which might bring the movement of cargo to a standstill, affect shipping arrangements or, over time, determine the amount of produce available for export. The patterns of employment were shaped by the arrival and departure of vessels which in turn were influenced by the tides and the weather, and the urgency with which goods had to be moved. Labour was not employed by the stevedore firms on a weekly or monthly basis, but according to need. Some stevedore firms maintained a nucleus of permanent workers and recruited the rest as they became necessary. The Port Trust engaged about 20 per cent of its dock workers on a permanent basis. They were paid monthly, albeit at daily rates, and were allowed to contribute to the Provident Fund and granted annual leave.[91] According to another source, only 70 per cent of those workers who appeared at the gates every morning received work. The rest had to 'pick up stray work from individual consignees or merchants or take up day labour in the cities'.[92] When the cloth and cotton markets were busy, many dock workers sought work in the godowns and warehouses, where at such times wages were in any case higher than in the docks.

Markets of every kind, numerous trades and factories and the docks and warehouses relied upon cartmen to transport their goods in the city. These carts were sometimes pulled by bullocks but frequently smaller hand carts, precarious to balance, difficult to manoeuvre, weighed down with bulk, were pushed manually through the city's traffic. In 1911, the census enumerated 13,576 cartmen in Bombay, more than half of them from Poona and Satara.[93] Their employment was liable to be subject to considerable fluctuations, but to secure a cart, indeed to be hired at all, workers necessarily depended upon their connections of caste and kinship, village and neighbourhood. Two-thirds of them were estimated to be periodic migrants to the city, but it is doubtful whether they could have plied their trade without firmly established urban ties.[94]

Seasonal and trade fluctuations particularly affected the building trade. The building boom of the early 1920s created a relative scarcity of labour and, until the depression dampened activity, employers, maistries and mukadams found their options with regard to the retrenchment or expansion of their labour force

---

[90] *Ibid.*, pp. 1–25; Burnett-Hurst, *Labour and Housing*, pp. 73–84.
[91] *RCLI, Evidence, Bombay Presidency*, The Bombay Port Trust, I, i, 461–2; Cholia, *Dock Labourers*.
[92] Burnett-Hurst, *Labour and Housing*, p. 76.
[93] Calculated from *Census, 1911*, VIII, *Bombay Town and Island*, Part II, 48–61.
[94] *Census, 1911*, VII, *Bombay*, Part I, *Report* by P. J. Mead and Claud MacGregor (Bombay, 1912), 45.

somewhat circumscribed. Nevertheless, even in periods of relatively regular employment, the conditions of work and forms of recruitment were predominantly casual. 'Labour generally drifts where there is work', Burnett-Hurst observed, 'or collects at one of the two markets for builders' labour – at Pydhoni and at Two Tanks – where workers assemble at 6 a.m. and take up their position on the roadside ... awaiting those in search of labour'.[95]

In the face of these exacting conditions dominated by arbitrary and sudden changes, irregular employment and arduous and debilitating physical labour, some workers attempted to escape from the perils of the labour market into 'self-employment'. This occurred particularly where capital requirements were small and credit relatively accessible. But it was not simply from the ranks of casual labour – and it is doubtful whether a homogeneous class of perennially casual workers existed – that such entrepreneurs emerged. Indeed, those who were employed in moderately stable and better-paid occupations were often the most able to acquire credit and to afford the initial outlay which the shift into self-employment entailed. At the same time, of course, the most securely employed workers were not likely to seek to emancipate themselves from the rigours of irregular employment. Moreover, it is not intended to suggest that such self-employment was without its own lurking risks, for those who attempted to set themselves up independently were more often than not engulfed by competition, meagre incomes and inescapable poverty.

Such commercial enterprises had to be, above all, those which required little capital, or perhaps none at all, and which could yield immediate returns. The retailing of foodstuffs fitted these requirements admirably. Retail grocers could operate with relatively little capital to back them. In 1909, it was said, a retail grocery business could be started with an initial outlay of between Rs. 100 and Rs. 500. Grocers bought small stocks from the wholesale merchants at Masjid Bunder and relying upon a rapid turnover 'reckon upon making a net profit of Rs. 1 to Rs. 2 per diem'.[96] Frequently, they diversified into money-lending on a small scale and some were gradually able to acquire for themselves positions of considerable influence in the neighbourhood.[97]

A sizeable contingent of itinerant traders, pedlars and hawkers was returned by each census, and their numbers were rising, an indication of how many workers were already being thrown on to the casual labour market by the early 1930s.[98] Hawkers, according to one observer, could earn between 4 annas and

---

[95] Burnett-Hurst, *Labour and Housing*, p. 87.
[96] *Gazetteer* I, 545.
[97] See chapter 5.
[98] Between 1921 and 1932, their numbers increased from 5,549 to 7, 603. Moreover, most of the 'other traders' returned each year were also probably hawkers and pedlars. *Census, 1921*, IX, ii, City Table VII, Part I; *Census, 1931*, IX, i, 54–5.

Rs. 2 per day in 1909.[99] It was indeed by no means uncommon for millworkers who were either unemployed or on strike to buy fruit and vegetables and hawk them in the mill districts or elsewhere in the city.[100]

It was possible to embark upon the manufacture of snuff without any capital, as snuff merchants sold tobacco on credit in return for weekly repayments.[101] The import of kerosene oil gave rise to a number of kerosene tinning and packing factories; but it also led to other forms of domestic industry. 'Bohras buy empty tins for about 2 annas each', the *Gazetteer* reported, and 'fashion them into lanterns, boxes, trunks, oil-pots and other cheap articles'.[102]

Tailors, barbers, cobblers and other similar traders required little capital to start their shops. They frequently set themselves up on a stretch of pavement or under the awning of another's premises and, when necessary, employed the unpaid labour of their wives, children and other relatives.[103] Similarly, in trades which involved out-working, their practitioners were already drawn into small-scale entrepreneurship. They might aspire to establish themselves as master craftsmen and free themselves from the irregularity and uncertainty of work. However, many others sought the same route to survival, often only to be faced by rising debts, microscopic returns and increasingly stiff competition. 'No single instance exists', declared S.M. Edwards in 1900, 'of a Bombay weaver having become a capitalist'.[104] But the same could probably be paid of a wide range of other artisanal occupations.

At the same time, a considerable variety of services were on offer. For instance, Pathan watchmen were often hired to guard the shops of the city's markets. Frequently, a 'head Pathan' with ten or fifteen others would go around the shops offering to keep watch for about Rs. 2 apiece. Shopkeepers, too, found this convenient, preferring to have in their employ men who they feared might otherwise pose a threat to their property. Each gang was able in this way to keep watch for seventy or seventy-five shops, yielding them a monthly income of about Rs. 150. Although this system was attributed to Pathans, it was clearly a more widespread practice. Indeed those who were 'displaced by these people as watchmen had a grudge against them' and expressed their antagonism in the communal riots of February 1929.[105]

---

[99] *Gazetteer* I, 454; Raghunathji, *Bombay Beggars and Criers*.

[100] For example, Proceedings of the Court of Enquiry, 1929, Examination, Jilloo Bhuva, 30 July 1929, File 1, MSA.

[101] *Gazetteer* I, 473.

[102] *Ibid.*, I, 474.

[103] *Report on ... Wages, Hours of Work and Conditions of Employment in the Retail Trade*, p. 4. Of course, entry into such occupations as tailor, barber, cobbler, was often inhibited by caste restrictions.

[104] Edwardes, *Silk Fabrics*, p. 40.

[105] *Proceedings of the Bombay Riots Inquiry Committee* (henceforth BRIC), 1929, Oral evidence, Sir M.M. Ramji, File 2, p. 337, MSA.

Physical strength was a requisite for most forms of manual labour; but it could also provide the means of emancipation from the uncertainty and toil of such occupations. In the mill districts of Bombay, landlords needed rent collectors; creditors required agents to recover debts; lawyers needed touts; factory managers required jobbers and sometimes broad-shouldered lieutenants able to combat pickets or squash attempts at trade-union organization.

Women's work and the labour market

Thus far this chapter has attempted to delineate the structure and processes of the labour market as it affected the entire workforce. But it impinged upon the employment of women and their general situation within the labour market in specific ways. The pattern of female employment was by no means representative of the entire workforce. Few women were returned in the census as workers. Although about two-thirds of the city's women were aged between fifteen to fifty years in the inter-war period, only about 26.12 per cent of the total female workforce in 1921 and 13.2 per cent in 1931 claimed to be employed.[106] Women workers were concentrated in non-industrial occupations beyond the jurisdiction of the Factory Acts, and within industry they were confined almost exclusively to cotton textiles.[107] Elsewhere a staple employer of female labour, the cotton-textile industry in Bombay employed only a modest proportion of women. In the 1890s, women formed about a quarter of the industry's workforce; by the 1920s, they comprised only a fifth and by the late 1930s, they made up no more than 15 per cent.[108] The structure of women's work shaped their bargaining position within the labour market.

Bombay was predominantly a city of male migrants. In 1864, only 539 women to every 1,000 males lived in the city; in 1921, the figure remained at 525.[109] This ratio between the sexes, not uncommon to Indian cities,[110] was intimately connected with the pattern and permanence of migration.

For most of the nineteenth century, the demand for labour and, therefore, rural migration was primarily seasonal, and in consequence predominantly male.[111] Workers left their families behind in the village, migrated after the

[106] *Census, 1931*, IX, i, 46–7. The figures produced by the two censuses were not strictly comparable. See *ibid.*, 48; *ibid.*, VIII, i, 218–27.
[107] *Census, 1921*, IX, ii, City Table IX.
[108] Calculated from *Annual Factory Reports for the Presidency of Bombay, passim*; Morris, *Industrial Labour Force*, Appendix II, pp. 217–18.
[109] *Census of the Island of Bombay, taken on 2nd February 1864* (Bombay, 1864), p. vi; *Census, 1921*, IX, i, 16–21, 26–27; *RCLI Evidence, Bombay Presidency*, GOB, 'Conditions of Industrial Labour in the Bombay Presidency'. See table 4, above, ch. 2.
[110] K. Davis, *The Population of India and Pakistan* (Princeton, 1951), p. 136.
[111] See chapter 4.

harvest to earn cash, and returned when their labour was needed in the fields or when the demand for labour in Bombay slackened. This pattern of seasonal male migration enhanced the importance of female field labour. If it was imperative to remit cash, it was not always possible for seasonal migrants to move between town and country according to the rhythms of the agricultural season; it might sometimes be necessary to remain in Bombay to keep a job or obtain a better one. As early as 1872, therefore, it was observed in Ratnagiri district, the largest supplier of labour to Bombay, that 'much of the field work falls upon women'.[112] This division of labour within the family came to be perpetuated even as industrial development and the proliferation of cotton mills created a greater demand for labour throughout the year.

In part, this was because the demand for labour remained liable to sudden and arbitrary changes even if its predominantly seasonal character was modified. The irregularities of employment made it crucial for migrant workers to Bombay to retain their rural connections. As the demand for labour in Bombay expanded, it was met largely from the supplies of male labour. The apparent dearth of employment opportunities for women only increased the risks of their abandoning the village for the uncertainties of the urban labour market. Whole families migrated only in periods of exceptional distress.

The expansion of the cotton industry in the 1880s was accompanied by a dramatic increase in the employment of women. Between 1884 and 1892, the number of women employed in the mills doubled from 8,816 to 16,000. While total employment expanded by 63.23 per cent, female employment increased by 81.14 per cent in the same period.[113] Of course, the famines of the late 1870s had resulted in precisely the type of distress migration which brought large numbers of women to Bombay.[114] However, the continued expansion of their numbers within the industry over a period of fifteen years does not support the view, frequently advanced, that culturally specific factors inhibited women from industrial employment.[115] Rather, it was factory legislation, passed in 1891, specifically limiting the working hours of women and children, which

---

[112] *Census of the Bombay Presidency, 1872, Part II* (Bombay, 1875), p. 171.
[113] Calculated from Morris, *Industrial Labour Force*, Appendix II, pp. 217–18.
[114] *Census, 1921*, IX, i, 25.
[115] M.D. Morris, 'The Recruitment of an Industrial Labour Force in India with British and American Comparisons', *Comparative Studies in Society and History*, II, 3 (1960), 320–4; Morris, *Industrial Labour Force*, pp. 65–69. For another view, see G. Omvedt, 'Migration in Colonial India: The Articulation of Feudalism and Capitalism by the Colonial State', *Journal of Peasant Studies*, VII, 2 (1980), 185–212. For a recent of anthropological study of male migration and its effects upon women, see H.C. Dandekar, *Men to Bombay, Women at Home: Urban Influence on Sugao Village, Deccan Maharashtra, India, 1942–1982* (Ann Arbor, Michigan, 1986).

served to check this initial expansion of female employment. Between 1892 and
1899, the textile workforce as a whole expanded by the relatively modest
proportion of 24.16 per cent and the number of women workers by only 13.68
per cent.[116] Outside the textile industry, it deterred their employment in
establishments notified under the Factory Act. Most employers, small or large,
but especially marginal entrepreneurs, relying upon a rapid turnover and
intensive use of labour, were unlikely to countenance the increase in their
transactional costs which the employment of protected categories of workers
would entail. In the twentieth century, welfare legislation, introducing the
principle of employers' responsibility for maternity benefits and the prohibition
of night shift work for women, further inhibited their employment in industries
affected by these measures.[117] Notably, the proportion of women in the
textile workforce declined from about a fifth in the 1920s to about a tenth
in the 1940s.[118]

Women who entered the Bombay labour market found employment in
out-working, retail and service occupations: in other words, they were concentrated in low-paid and sweated jobs, where they worked in appalling conditions,
from which legislation was intended to protect them. If their employment
opportunities in Bombay were increasingly restricted to low-paid and casual
work, this served as a further deterrent to female and family migration. In the
twentieth century, women who remained in their village tried to sustain the rural
base of the family. They worked in the fields and in seasonal industries, which
processed raw materials, in neighbouring districts. The role of women in the
family economy of the working class came to be reconstituted in old ways by
the effects of industrialization. In turn, this determined the terms on which
women entered the urban labour market.

Women found work most readily in assorted, casual occupations, generally
those which fell beyond the purview of the Factory Acts. Significantly, the
largest single census category for female employment was 'unspecified occupations', which accounted in 1921 for more than 26 per cent of working
women.[119] Although problems of enumeration probably inflated this proportion
in 1921, and there was almost certainly a considerable under-reporting of

[116] Morris, *Industrial Labour Force*, pp. 217–18; *Annual Factory Reports, passim*.
[117] GOI, Industries and Labour, File L-920 (3), p. 20–1, NAI; Proceedings of the TLIC, Main
Inquiry, Oral Evidence, BMOA, File 57-A, p. 172, MSA.
[118] Their numbers too went into gradual decline. *Annual Factory Reports, passim*; Morris, *Industrial Labour Force*, Appendix II, p. 217–18 and Table IX, p. 66.
[119] *Census, 1921*, IX, ii, City Table VII, Part I. Their numbers declined from nearly 28,000 in 1921
to about 7,400 in 1931; *ibid., Census, 1931*, IX, ii, City Table VII, Part I. This considerable
decline, which probably accounts for a large proportion of the total fall in female employment
is partly to be explained by improved census enumeration, and partly by the general economic
contraction.

women's participation in the labour force, its strength reflected the extent to which women were forced to pick up work wherever they could. The bidi industry was a major employer of women.[120] Nine thousand women were engaged in domestic service in 1921.[121] Outside these occupations, women were most commonly employed as sweepers and scavengers, in the 'industries of the dress and toilet' and in municipal service, in petty trading and in the running of general stores, hotels and cookshops.

Nearly 3,000 women were returned as prostitutes in 1921.[122] But the census only dealt with 'women who are so patently prostitutes as not to desire to conceal their profession' and the Police Commissioner estimated in the same year that there were twice as many prostitutes as enumerated by the census living in brothels alone.[123] In 1871, the Health Officer enumerated the occupations of women registered as prostitutes under the Contagious Diseases Act, or of their fathers or family breadwinners. His sample showed that they represented a cross-section of the city's labouring population as a whole: 'Gardener, Agriculturist, Labourer, Military-man or Pensioner, Policeman, Domestic Servant, Artizan and Grocer'.[124] Every caste was represented among them, including four Brahmins, as well as most districts from which Bombay drew its inhabitants, although they were not necessarily distributed in the right proportion. Significantly, about half the number of registered prostitutes were long-term residents and two-fifths had lived in the city for over five years. On the other hand, less than 10 per cent had come to the city in the previous year and this at a time when the influx of migrants was beginning to increase substantially.[125] The age and marital status of the prostitutes also illuminate their social and economic position. Although about 16 per cent were below twenty years of age, more than four-fifths were between twenty and forty years old.[126] Similarly, 15 per cent were married and nearly 51 per cent were widowed. Asked by the Health Officer 'why they have taken to this kind of life', the most common answer was, 'What can I do? When my husband died I was left without any means of support. I must have food'.[127] Of course, such evidence can be interpreted variously. It probably reflected male perceptions of the threat of widows, often active participants in the labour force and apparently free of family ties. It was perhaps an expression of the stigma of widowhood. It may also support the claim of another social investigator in the 1930s who concluded

---

[120] See *Report of the RCLI*, pp. 94–8.
[121] *Census, 1921*, IX, ii, City Table VII, Part I. By 1931, their numbers had fallen by a third.
[122] *Census, 1921*, IX, ii, City Table VII, Part I; also *ibid*., IX, i, 56–8.
[123] *Report of the Prostitution Committee* (Bombay, 1921), pp. 2, 7.
[124] *Report of the Health Officer, Bombay, for the Third Quarter, 1871* (Bombay, 1871), pp. 8–13.
[125] *Ibid*., p. 11.
[126] *Ibid*., p. 12.
[127] *Ibid*., p. 12.

that 'the main reason on account of which women from the Depressed Classes can be easily seduced into prostitution is their poverty.'[128]

Similarly, another investigator, M.J. Antia, found in 1917 that the number of 'clandestine or part-time prostitutes is so large that it eludes any possibility of investigation'. Servant girls, he felt, were 'beset with temptations' (some no doubt were coerced by their employers) and 'many of them supplement their wages by occasionally going out'. Among other occupations which Antia enumerated in this context were typists, telephone-operatives, shop assistants, dress makers, millhands, governesses and teachers. Thus, 'the painted beauties [of] ... Foras Road, Kamathipura ... form only a small proportion of the army of women' who offered sexual favours in return for subsistence.[129] Similarly, the Prostitution Committee, estimating the number of 'clandestine prostitutes' at between 30,000 and 40,000 in 1921, as against the 6,000 who lived in brothels, believed they were 'recruited largely from the ranks of the under-paid women worker, the hereditary prostitute, the discarded mistress, the widow and the pauper', categories which must have exluded every few women.[130] Prosti-tution was probably less the profession of a small, well-defined coterie of women than a part-time practice for many who needed to supplement their earnings.

Underlying the widespread incidence of prostitution, Antia argued, was the practice of giving 'much less remuneration to women for valuable work done than to men. Employers take it for granted that a woman wants less than a man, and that she can always obtain money from other sources',[131] and so presumably it should have come as no surprise that they did. The notion of a 'family wage', later deployed in argument by employers and the state to depress women's wages, ironically formalized this assumption and then proceeded on its basis. Since a significant proportion of women workers in Bombay were either widows or the major breadwinners, the assumption that women's wages could be determined in the light of their husband's earnings was in practice badly misplaced.[132] The exploitation of women's labour was thus closely related to the exploitation of their bodies.

The dearth of staple employers of female labour tended to create a glut and depress wage rates for women. In addition, the role of women within the family economy meant that they entered the labour market often when they had exhausted other alternatives: for instance, when the village base of the family

[128] G.R. Pradhan, 'The Untouchable Workers of Bombay City', unpublished MA thesis, University of Bombay, 1936, p. 71.

[129] TOI, 20 July 1917, p. 8.

[130] Report of the Prostitution Committee, p. 7.

[131] TOI, 20 July 1917, p. 8.

[132] K. Dwarkadas, Forty Five Years With Labour (Bombay, 1962), pp. 91–143; Radha Kumar, 'Family and Factory: Women in the Bombay Cotton Textile Industry, 1919–1939', IESHR, XX, 1 (1983), 81–110.

economy had crumbled, or when they were widowed or deserted by their husbands.[133] Women who sought work in Bombay were often forced to do so because their husbands were either unemployed or so under-employed that their earnings were too irregular for subsistence. For married women, their need for work was often determined more by the fluctuations in the demand for their husbands' labour than their own, or by the absolute pressure of poverty. As a result, they might withdraw their labour in the fortuitous circumstances of an improved harvest or the employment of their husbands, even if, sometimes, precisely when, the demand for their own labour was rising. In general, of course, this fundamentally weakened their bargaining position: they often entered the labour market when there was a glut and often withdrew as demand recovered.

These circumstances were not simply generated by the mechanisms of the labour market but also signified the nature and perceptions of gender relations. Their effect was to associate women's work with poverty and low status. Women often sought to conceal their occupations, 'which though perfectly honest and lawful in themselves, indicated stunted means or impoverished circumstances on the part of those who carried them on'.[134] If only the poorest families migrated to Bombay together, the wives of skilled workers prided themselves on the fact that they neither had to work in the city nor remain behind in the village.[135] Maratha women who went to work during a strike in 1938 were taunted by Mahar workers with: 'If you Marathas cannot maintain your womenfolk ... hand over your womenfolk to the Mahar'.[136] Moreover, by swelling the ranks of casual labour intermittently, this pattern of female employment helped to perpetuate an industrial structure dependent upon the availability of a fluctuating supply of labour and thereby reproduced the conditions which had driven them into the labour market on those terms in the first place.[137]

The recruitment of labour

It has already been shown that the labour needs of industry, whether factory or small scale, were determined by the short-term fluctuations of the market,

---

[133] Proceedings of the TLIC, Main Inquiry, Oral Evidence, BMOA, File 57-A, p. 23, MSA; Dwarkadas, *Forty Five Years with Labour*, pp. 91–143.

[134] *Census of the City and Island of Bombay taken on 17th of February 1881* by T.S. Weir (Bombay, 1883), p. 22.

[135] Proceedings of the TLIC, Main Inquiry, Oral Evidence, BMOA, File 57-A, p. 193, MSA.

[136] Bombay Disturbances Enquiry Committee (henceforth BDEC), Oral Evidence, Arjun A. Parab, GOB, Home (Sp.), File 550 (25) IIIB of 1938, p. 43, MSA.

[137] The conditions of women's work and their general situation within the labour market in Bombay bears comparison to that which obtained in the radically different context of nineteenth-century London. See especially Stedman Jones, *Outcast London*, pp. 83–7.

changes in the cost or availability of raw materials and the price of and demand for their products. The demand for labour was, therefore, subject to frequent, sometimes sudden and arbitrary variations. Employers had to devise methods of recruitment which would enable them to employ additional men at short notice or lay them off as the market required. It thus became the common practice among employers, in a wide range of occupations, to delegate responsibility for the hiring and the firing of workers to intermediaries who came to be known variously as jobber or mukadam, maistry or serang. The multiplicity of recruiting agents was liable to exaggerate the tendency of business strategies, which tailored output to short-term market fluctuations, to produce a labour supply in excess of the peak requirements of the city's employers.

Since the jobber or his equivalent was a ubiquitous figure in Indian industry and labour organization, he has been commonly portrayed as a social archetype and a cultural artefact, a pre-industrial survival or an institution peculiarly suited to the specificities of Indian culture and conditions. But the term jobber derived from Lancashire where it entailed an essentially technical, repair and maintenance function.[138] In any case, foremen in British industry also played a major role in the recruitment of labour and their involvement in the social organization of urban neighbourhoods has not perhaps been sufficiently acknowledged by historians.[139] Similar agents are to be found as commonly in the recruitment and organization of labour in Africa[140] as in China[141] or Japan.[142] Moreover, in setting out the jobber's 'functions' and registering their apparent similarities in diverse trades in India, it would be easy, and misleading, to overlook the fact that there were many kinds of jobbers and their functions varied considerably.

---

[138] P. Joyce, *Work, Society and Politics: The Culture of the Factory in Late Victorian England* (London, 1980).

[139] *Ibid.*; J. Melling, 'Non-Commissioned Officers: British Employers and their Supervisory Workers, 1880–1920,' *Social History*, V, 2 (1980), 183–221; R. Gray, *The Aristocracy of Labour in Nineteenth Century Britain, c. 1850–1900* (London, 1981).

[140] R. Sandbrook and R. Cohen (eds.), *The Development of an African Working Class: Studies in Class Formation and Action* (London, 1975); C. Katzellenbogen, 'Labour Recruitment in Central Africa: The Case of Katanga', in Dewey and Hopkins (eds.), *The Imperial Impact*, pp. 270–9; C. van Onselen, *Chibaro: African Mine Labour in Southern Rhodesia* (London, 1976); S. Stichter, *Migrant Labour in Kenya: Capitalism and African Response, 1895–1975* (London, 1892); S. Marks and R. Rathbone (eds.), *Industrialization and Social Conflict in South Africa: African Class Formation, Culture and Consciousness* (London, 1982).

[141] J. Chesneaux, *The Chinese Labour Movement, 1919–1927* (Stanford, 1974).

[142] K. Taira, *Economic Development and the Labour Market in Japan* (New York, 1970); K. Taira 'Factory Labour and the Industrial Revolution in Japan', in P. Mathias and M.M. Postans, *The Cambridge Economic History of Europe*, vol. VII, *The Industrial Economies: Capital, Labour and Enterprise*, Part 2 (Cambridge, 1978), pp. 166–214; E.P. Tsurimi, 'Female Textile Workers and the Failure of Early Trade Unionism in Japan', *History Workshop Journal*, XVIII (Autumn 1984), 3–27; T.C. Smith, 'Peasant Time and Factory Time in Japan', *Past and Present*, CXI (1987), 165–97.

In some trades, the jobber was the foreman; in others he functioned as a labour contractor; occasionally, he combined the role of paymaster and pacemaker. Necessarily, then, beneath the similarity of form, the jobber's role and the nature of his relationship with his employers and the workforce varied substantially between trades and occupations. Furthermore, these differences in recruitment patterns and disciplinary practices did not simply coincide with the division between the organized and the unorganized sectors.

The role of the jobber in the cotton-textile industry will be examined in greater detail in chapter 7. Here it is necessary to emphasize that in the cotton-textile industry the jobber's power in the workplace depended to a large extent upon his role within the labour process.[143] For instance, the jobbers in the preparatory departments of the cotton mills were men of lesser status and influence within the structure of mill management than the prestigious head jobbers of the weaving sheds. Yet they often exercised a tighter control over their subordinates. This paradox is largely to be explained by the weak bargaining position of the unskilled workers in the preparatory departments, both in the workplace, where they could not effectively resist the jobber's authority, and outside, where their uncertain conditions of employment meant that they needed his influence most. On the other hand, skilled weavers, who commanded greater bargaining strength, were able to impinge upon what was in unskilled occupations uncontested as the jobbers' domain. Moreover, in the cotton mills, as elsewhere, there were several grades of supervisory personnel who also exercised a considerable measure of influence and control over the workforce.

This would suggest that within the structure of authority at work, power was in practice diffused, although by enumerating the functions of the jobber we might be led to believe that it was largely concentrated in his hands. To add to this diffusion of power, which stemmed from the nature of supervision and its organization, recruitment often occurred on the recommendation of other workers.[144] In what was supposedly the major function of the jobber, his selections were influenced by workers and had to meet with their approval. In addition, the jobber's functions at work drew him into the wider social connections of the working-class neighbourhoods. To lay off workers and recruit them when needed, the jobber had to maintain contacts with potential recruits in the urban neighbourhoods.[145]

[143] Proceedings of the Bombay Strike Enquiry Committee (henceforth, BSEC), 1928, I, 660–93; II, 694–830, MAS; *Report of the Textile Labour Inquiry Committee*, II, 44–7, 337–47.

[144] *RCLI, Evidence*, Life Histories of twelve typical immigrant workers to Bombay City collected by the Lady Investigators of the Labour Office in June–July, 1929, XI, ii, 312–20; R.G. Gokhale, *The Bombay Cotton Mill Worker* (Bombay, 1957), pp. 55–76.

[145] *RCLI, Evidence*, Bombay Seth Ambalal Sarabhai, Ahmedabad Manufacturing & Calico Printing Company Ltd, I, i, 277. See chapter 5 below.

In certain industries, like leather or dyeing, where caste organization was strong and could be used as a closed shop to exclude rivals,[146] a similar pattern manifested itself. Unskilled workers, without much bargaining power, acquiesced in the jobber's authority both within and without the workplace.[147] But this did not mean that in these trades relationships of power flowed uniformly in one direction. Rather, where caste organization was strong, the jobber himself was vulnerable to the sanctions of the elders and of the neighbourhood. He might seek to entrench himself within these institutions, but the further he extended the range of his influence the more he would have to accommodate rival locations of power and the greater was the pressure to which his increasingly diverse clients could subject him.

In industries like printing, where the workforce as well as the plant was relatively small, the jobber or foreman was subjected to closer supervision by the management. The jobber exercised less control over recruitment, little over dismissal or leave, or the allocation of materials and machines. In the printing industry, for instance, employees were either recruited directly by the manager or proprietor, through advertisements or on the recommendation of other workers and foremen.[148] It would be wrong to assume, however, that small employers invariably recruited their own workers.[149] Although the encroachments of proprietors and managers were both more possible and more effective in smaller concerns, the relationship between jobbers and workers, if thereby sometimes modified, was not of a markedly different order in establishments of different size. In small units, too, the variety of managerial practices, the level of skill and the nature of the particular inter-relationship between workplace and neighbourhood impinged upon the jobber and served to determine the extent and character of his power.

The nature of work as well as recruitment practices varied considerably in the railways, between their mechanical workshops, their printing presses and

[146] Martin, *Tanning and Working in Leather; Report on the Leather Industries*; Fawcett, *Dyes and Dyeing.*

[147] Caste and neighbourhood ties played a crucial role in the unionization and politics of leather workers. In the 1937 strike, caste rivalries and family feuds which stretched back to Tinnevelly district opened up divisions within the workforce. See GOB, Home (Sp.) File 550 (23) A of 1937, MSA.

[148] *Report on Wages, Hours of Work and Conditions of Employment in the Printing Industry in the Bombay Presidency (excluding Sind) May 1934. General Wage Census Part I – Perennial Factories, Second Report* (Bombay, 1936), p. 7.

[149] For recruitment practices based predominantly upon the jobber in various industries, which were relatively small, although they employed over twenty workers each, see *Report on Wages, Hours of Work and Conditions of Employment in the Oils, Paints and Soap, Match Manufacturing and other Miscellaneous Industries in the Province of Bombay, May 1934, General Wage Census Part I – Perennial Factories, Fourth Report* (Bombay, 1931).

their transportation and commercial departments. Here, the various superior grades pressed heavily upon the chargemen and maistries. Workers who presented themselves and were selected were sometimes given a skill test and subjected to a medical examination. Of course, maistries and chargemen may well have helped their clients through these initial hurdles; but such tests necessarily served to check their power, especially since 'applicants invariably outnumber vacancies'.[150] In other departments, minimum educational qualifications, examinations and periods of training fulfilled a similar function. Although the Great Indian Peninsular Railway organized four staff committees on which employees were represented, discipline remained 'a reserved matter' in their business.[151] Moreover, they probably represented 'low-paid staff' least effectively. It was in relation to these predominantly unskilled workers that the conventional picture of the foreman's tyranny acquired special meaning on the railways. Here the foreman, or chargeman or maistry beneath him in the managerial hierarchy, was probably the dominant influence in recruitment and the administration of leave. 'As regards the lower-paid staff', the railway authorities complained, 'these employees, being nearly all of the illiterate class, lack practically any sense of discipline and stay away from work for trivial reasons.' It was in their ranks that the management perceived absenteeism as a major problem; and among them the majority of dismissals for unauthorized absence were registered.[152] Moreover, the attitude of the railway authorities in matters of discipline was unequivocal. Labour relations, they said, were 'on the whole harmonious'. Of course, they admitted, 'complaints of unfairness and hardship must arise'; however, they declared briskly, 'most of such complaints prove unfounded or grossly exaggerated'.[153]

The authority and role of the foreman and other subordinate supervisory positions was attenuated by other social factors. Managers and supervisory subordinates were largely recruited in England; the 'low-paid staff' entirely in India. The foremen were usually British and the chargemen were generally Anglo-Indians, Parsis and Goanese, while the employees were Hindus and Muslims.[154] There was believed to be considerable racial discrimination on the railways in relation to appointments, pay, promotion and the allocation of housing.[155] Certainly, the Indian and European workers were segregated in the housing and recreational facilities provided by the railways. In 1916, an attempt

---

[150] Great Indian Peninsular Railway (henceforth GIP), *Report for the Royal Commission*, p. 2.
[151] *Ibid.*, pp. 8–10.
[152] *Ibid.*, p. 6.
[153] *Ibid.*, p. 7.
[154] Burnett-Hurst, *Labour and Housing*, p. 98.
[155] For an account of the conditions of work among railwaymen see *Proceedings of Meerut Conspiracy Case, Defence Statement, K.N. Joglekar*, pp. 1766–965.

was made by Hindu and Muslim railway workers in Bombay to obtain the same terms of service as the Parsi and European employees.[156] But it was only in the 1920s that a larger number of Indians began to be admitted to the supervisory ranks. Moreover, the European and Eurasian railway workers, organized in the National Union of Railwaymen of India and Burma,[157] held aloof from their colleagues in industrial action as well.[158] A further inflammatory factor was the perhaps exceptional degree of violence used by European and Eurasian foremen towards their Indian subordinates.[159]

Clearly, the railway foremen operated at a level removed from the jobber. The isolation of the foreman from the rest of the workforce did not simply enable him to act as a tyrant but in some ways remained a point of weakness. If the European foremen encroached upon the maistry's preserve, constrained his freedom, and checked his power, they were also resented by the workforce for their high-handedness and their violence. Provoked by racial antagonism, their resistance perhaps legitimized by the nationalist cause, workers might sometimes group around the maistry to resist the discipline of the railway supervisors.[160]

The Bombay Electric Supply and Tramways Company recruited skilled workers to its engineering department, for instance, on the basis of testimonials or recommendations by 'a trusty employee'; recruits were subjected to trade tests or a period of probation; some vacancies were filled by the promotion of unskilled workmen who had learnt their trade on the job. The recruitment of unskilled workers, however, was left almost entirely to mukadams and the recommendation of other employees.[161] The operation of an apprenticeship scheme, however modest, also acted as a check on the power of the lesser

---

[156] *Bombay Presidency Police* (henceforth *BPP*), Secret Abstracts of Intelligence (henceforth *SAI*), 1916, no. 29, 22 July, para. 958. They launched this agitation with the assistance of a 'Jhenu Barrister' whom the police discovered was 'very probably Mohammed Ali Jinnah, Bar-at-Law'.

[157] This union, it was noted in 1929, 'displays very little activity at present', GIP Railway, *Report for the Royal Commission*, p. 52.

[158] *Proceedings of the Meerut Conspiracy Case, Defence Statement, K.N. Joglekar*, p. 1903; on the GIP Railway strike of 1930, see GOB, Home (Sp.) Files 543 (10) DC, 534 (10) DC Pt. A, 543 (10) DC Pt, II–IV of 1930, MSA.

[159] For an account of the use of violence by supervisory personnel on the railways, but with particular reference to the South India Railway, see Arnold, 'Industrial Violence', especially 249–54.

[160] In this particular case, the Superintendent of Locomotive Shop of the BB&CI Railway attempted to prevent the maistries from taking dasturi, or a commission, from the newly engaged workers. As a result, it was reported, the maistries sought to 'foment' trouble in the workshop in the hope that the authorities would be compelled to transfer the Superintendent.

[161] *RCLI, Evidence, Bombay Presidency*, Bombay Electric Supply and Tramways Company, vol. I, part i, p. 532.

supervisory ranks.[162] Similarly, the Bombay Port Trust instituted a system of compulsory leave apportioned by rotation as equitably as possible in order to deal with the problem of reserve supplies of labour in their engineering departments and maintenance workshops, and thus neutralized an important area of the jobber's power.[163] The administration of the Bombay Municipal Corporation also pressed heavily upon the mukadam's function. The sub-engineer at the various ward offices was responsible for the recruitment of unskilled labour while the mechanical engineer engaged employees taken on at the municipal workshops and pumping stations.[164] Nevertheless, certain mukadams acquired and maintained an impressive degree of control over their subordinates. In the mid nineteenth century, halalkhores who carried away the night soil grouped around jobbers who accepted contracts for particular streets. According to R.P. Masani, in time, some streets came to be regarded as the family property of the jobber and his halalkhore gang.[165] Subsequently, it would appear, mukadams were pulled into the administrative substructure of the municipality, the hierarchy of inspectors and health officers to whom they reported, and came to be distanced from the workforce. The caste composition of mukadams, for instance, became increasingly diffuse. Nevertheless, their control and exactions continued to be felt severely by the labour force. Disputes were, in this case, as in other occupations, largely settled within the jobber gang; but when sweepers did strike, their grievances were often formulated against the mukadam and communicated in appeal to the Municipal Commissioner.[166]

The recruitment of seamen became a focus of public attention. Their conditions of work were frequently discussed and resolutions repeatedly passed at the International Labour Conferences at Geneva.[167] The seamen's unions, gimcrack as they were, demanded the official regulation of recruitment.[168] In 1922, the Government of India appointed a committee to inquire into the methods of recruitment.[169] In July 1929, an assistant to the Government Shipping Master was appointed to supervise the hiring of seamen. In practice,

[162] For details of the apprenticeship scheme, see Purshottamdas Thakurdas Papers File 112/I (1931), NMML.
[163] RCLI, Evidence, Bombay Presidency, The Bombay Port Trust, I, i, 462.
[164] Ibid., The Bombay Municipal Corporation, I, i, 567.
[165] Masani, Local Self-Government, pp. 191–3.
[166] Masselos, 'Jobs and Jobbery: The Sweeper in Bombay under the Raj'.
[167] See James L. Mowat, Seafarers' Conditions in India and Pakistan (ILO, Geneva, 1949); D. Desai, Maritime Labour in India (Bombay, 1940); F.J.A. Broeze, 'The Muscles of Empire: Indian Seamen and the Raj, 1919–1929', IESHR, XIII, 1 (1981), 43–67.
[168] RCLI, Evidence, Bombay Presidency, The Indian Seamen's Union, I, i, 289–93, and The Bombay Seamen's Union, I, i, 293–94. On industrial action in the aftermath of the First World War, see Desai, Maritime Labour, pp. 183–200, especially, pp. 183–4, 187; and Broeze, 'Muscles of Empire'.
[169] A.G. Clow, Report on the Recruitment of Indian Seamen (Calcutta, 1922).

however, this tinkering had not 'in any material way improved the condition of engagement and recruitment'.[170] The serang still held the key to recruitment and jobs often went to the highest briber.[171] The serang's dominance was based on his role as a labour contractor. He was assigned a ship and informed of the number of men required. With the help of ghat serangs and tindals, he collected the men, supervised their work and was responsible for their payment.

Similar subcontracting practices were to be found in general labouring jobs where a sizeable workforce was intermittently required. Cargo was moved on the docks by stevedore firms employed for the task by the steamship companies. These stevedore firms organized their labour through an elaborate network of subcontractors. A serang was paid by the stevedore firm to organize the necessary number of workers. The serang, in turn, came to terms with tindals who supervised gangs of labourers. Wage rates were usually fixed between the tindal and his men, who then tried to come to terms with the serang.[172] Once placed on shore, the cargo was the responsibility of the Port Trust. Its Hamallage Department entered into contracts with toliwallas at a piece rate based on tonnage. The toliwalla in turn employed labourers and settled their wages.[173] Head mukadams subcontracted from the stevedore firms to load and unload coal, but in order to get the job done they had to deal with gang mukadams who worked with a team of twenty or thirty workers.[174] Under these conditions, where wages were filtered through the jobbers his control appeared overwhelming. However, in an overstocked labour market and within a framework of recruitment marked by several layers of subcontracting, the tindal, the toliwalla, the serang and the mukadam, if he sought the loyalty and adherence of his workers, had to keep his clients satisfied. Jobbers might seek to extend their control over the workers by offering them credit, providing them with housing and supplying them with patronage and protection. Yet jobbers who were unable to construct harmonious working relationships within their team or ensure an adequate supply of labour were bound to suffer in the race for subcontracts. Moreover, it cannot be assumed that dock labourers, however limited their choices, were the passive victims of serang dominance. Occasionally, they went as far as resorting to the police or the law courts to recover unpaid wages.[175] Indeed, Cholia, who suggested that the loans of the gang mukadam

[170] *RCLI*, *Evidence, Bombay Presidency*, The Indian Seamen's Union, I, i, 292; Broeze, 'Muscles of Empire', p. 54.
[171] *RCLI*, *Evidence, Bombay Presidency*, The Bombay Seamen's Union, I, i, 293–4; Desai, *Maritime, Labour*, pp. 18–64; Mowat, *Seafarers' Conditions*, pp. 16–22.
[172] Cholia, *Dock Labourers*, pp. 30–1, 34.
[173] *Ibid.*, p. 49.
[174] *Ibid.*, pp. 58–60, 67; for a general picture of recruitment of dock labour, see Burnett-Hurst, *Labour and Housing*, pp. 74–6; see also *RCLI*, *Evidence, Bombay Presidency*, The Bombay Port Trust, I, i, 461–2.
[175] *Times of India*, 2 August 1905.

bound coal labourers to him until the debt was discharged, also noted that the foremen's objective in extending credit was to resist 'the tendency amongst labourers to migrate from one Gang Muccadam to another when there is a rise in the daily rates of wages due to a sudden rush of work'.[176] The provision of credit perhaps applied the brake on such mobility, but is unlikely to have prevented it. A gang mukadam who could not provide work at favourable rates at such times would probably have been hard pressed to hold his team together and would at least have laid himself open to the default of his loans. The organization and use of labour was too labile to support the picture of the jobber as the owner and dispenser of the labour services of debt slaves. Within this institution of recruitment and supervision at work, we need to locate the dialectic of power, which created an interdependence between jobbers and men, preventing the total domination of the latter and circumscribing the options of the former.

This element of reciprocity in the relationship between jobbers and workers was manifested in another trade which depended upon a fluctuating, indeed, seasonal supply of labour: building. Workers sometimes presented themselves at construction sites in search of work. Alternatively they collected at certain points in the city such as Pydhoni or Two Tanks where the 'jobbing painters, masons, carpenters went to find men in search of work'. The large employers, however, organized their men through maistries and mukadams. But these did not necessarily consist of three autonomous labour markets. The mukadams of the large building contractors, like their counterparts in every other trade, preferred 'to secure the necessary labour from amongst his friends. He finds this course preferable as the men in the market are not only inferior workmen, but also resort to bargaining, particularly if special rates have to be fixed or a large number of workers secured'.[177] Although employers often made the hopeful and convenient assumption that their maistries and mukadams, their jobber and serangs enjoyed complete mastery over their men, there was a hidden layer of complexity in matters of labour control. In addition, to make certain of his control, the jobber had to lean on social connections outside the workplace such as his kinship and neighbourhood connections. The more diffuse the basis of his control the more difficult it would be to maintain. This reinforced the jobber or the maistry in his preference for employing his 'friends' – those who could be pulled in to his wider connections outside the workplace, based upon village, kinship and neighbourhood.

The jobber system had important consequences for the mechanisms of the labour market. Contemporaries often suggested that since jobbers were known to take a commission from each worker they employed, their interest lay in

[176] Cholia, *Dock Labourers*, p. 59.
[177] Burnett-Hurst, *Labour and Housing*, p. 87.

accentuating the rate of labour turnover.[178] These claims, sometimes too readily adopted, sometimes too briskly rejected by later historians, were exaggerated. If jobbers were to retain the goodwill of their men, they could not always afford to manipulate their jobs so ruthlessly. The power of the jobber, at times, appeared awesome but he was by no means completely free to exercise it.

Certainly, the jobber system contributed to the uncertainties of the labour market experienced by most workers. To attract the best workers, to maintain a steady and continuous supply of labour, and to obtain a regular flow of job-seekers, jobbers employed a proportion of new men and applied the sanction of refusing to hire those who did not offer themselves for work with sufficient regularity. In this way, they created a surplus pool of casual workers around each trade. The jobber's art was to distribute enough employment between his recruits to prevent them taking their labour elsewhere, without necessarily ensuring regular work for each, or indeed any of them. It was in this sense, therefore, that labour turnover came to be intimately related to methods of recruitment. On the other hand, for many workers, especially those who were casually employed, their dependence upon particular jobbers heightened the uncertainties of the labour market. The disfavour, dismissal or, most arbitrarily, the death of a jobber could result in loss of employment or at least a change of status under new management.[179]

The institution of the jobber is often considered to have had largely adverse effects upon the development of the economy.[180] Jobbers, it is said, accentuated the high rate of labour turnover and thus undermined discipline, orchestrated a supply of casual labour which was inefficient and obstructed the emergence of a perfectly responsive labour market. Perhaps, this was so. However, it is also necessary to acknowledge how the jobber system served the needs of employers. For it enabled them to reconcile the strategy of regulating production to demand with the need to minimize their operational costs: in other words, jobbers performed the indispensable function of co-ordinating the supply of labour in the face of considerable, and even arbitrary, fluctuations of demand. Moreover, if the jobber operated along lines of personal connection, ties of caste, kinship, village and neighbour-hood, his patronage created vertical loyalties and brought them into the workplace. The result was to accentuate the divisions within the workforce. Ostensibly, then, the jobber system served as a bulwark against industrial action by the workforce.[181]

[178] *Labour Gazette*, XII, 2 (October 1933), 111–12.
[179] *Report of the ITB, 1927, Evidence of Local Governments, Official Witnesses, Chambers of Commerce, Girni Labour Organizations and Other Associations*, The Girni Kamgar Mahaman-dal, III, 570.
[180] Morris, *Industrial Labour Force*, pp. 129–33; Mazumdar, 'Labour Supply'.
[181] See chapter 7 below.

It is misleading, therefore, to suggest that the operation of the jobber system was detrimental to the interests of industry. By ensuring a steady supply of labour in the face of fluctuating demand and by acting at least ostensibly, and at times effectively, to neutralize the threat of combination, the jobber system fulfilled a vital function in co-ordinating and deploying the labour force. At the same time, it was precisely because casual labour was supposed in principle to be unreliable and inefficient that the jobbers constructed a casual fringe around a nucleus of 'permanent' workers whom they knew and trusted. In the context of Bombay's labour market, the jobbers' contribution to the creation of a labour surplus was integral to their attempt to maintain the efficiency and discipline of the workforce.

In some accounts, labour turnover, stability and commitment are understood largely as a function of the adaptation of rural migrants to the urban setting.[182] Indeed, this vocabulary itself reflects the extent to which the problem of patterns of labour use within a particular economic context have been conceptualized in terms of workers' attitudes. Yet the policies of employers decisively influenced the turnover, stability and commitment of their workers. To focus upon 'instability' in the context of business strategies which depend upon the use of varying proportions of casual labour is to confuse the symptoms for the disease. The jobber system, schemes for 'compulsory leave' by rotation, the practice in some sections of giving a special 'permanent' status to a fraction of the workforce, provided the institutional form for widely prevalent policies towards the employment and use of labour. Even in the most obviously 'organized' sector – the textile industry – musters were poorly maintained, absenteeism records scarcely systematized and leave procedures rarely followed.[183] Inefficient administrative practices served to enhance managerial control. Under these circumstances, whether a worker's absence constituted temporary leave or absenteeism came to rest upon the discretion of his managers. Labile disciplinary codes were particularly useful to managers when truculent workers and union activists had to be dismissed without apparent victimization.[184]

Since the records relating to attendance and leave were poorly maintained, the available data on labour turnover or the length of service are generally

[182] C.A. Myers, *Labour Problems in the Industrialization of India* (Cambridge, Mass., 1958); Newman, 'Social Factors'; Newman, *Workers and Unions*, pp. 12–17; Mazumdar, 'Labour Supply'.

[183] M.M. Shah, 'Labour Recruitment and Turnover in the Textile Industry of Bombay Presidency', unpublished PhD thesis, University of Bombay, 1941, pp. 11–12.

[184] This charge was repeatedly made by workers in evidence before the Court of Enquiry. See Proceedings of the Court of Enquiry, Examination of Ramchandra Devji Shinde, 31 July 1929, File 1, MSA.

unreliable. This evidence, however, suggests that the duration of service in the textile industry was increasing in the twentieth century.[185] However, it is significant that while the proportion of workers who stayed at the same mill for less than five years fell between the late 1920s and 1955, the Labour Office survey, conducted as early as 1927–8, showed that nearly a quarter of the workforce had persisted in the industry as a whole for over fifteen years and this proportion endured through the following decade.[186] Until workers were able to demonstrate their loyalty, their tenure was clearly insecure.

Yet the conditions of work were not conducive to bringing forth faithful servants or indeed retaining them. Khandubhai Desai, a member of the Textile Labour Inquiry Committee, said that he had rarely seen a spinner over the age of forty-five at work in a mill.[187] Illness and infirmity might enforce the retirement of some; the tedium and exhaustion, the noise and dust, the heat and humidity probably drove others to return to their villages as soon as their family circumstances permitted. At the same time, those who had remained in the industry for more than five years and gained a relatively secure position in the city were most strongly drawn into trade-union organization and industrial action[188] and were therefore highly vulnerable to dismissal. If there was a high rate of turnover after short periods of service, a substantial proportion appears to have remained with their mills for a considerable length of time. In addition, many who left one mill went to work at another. The rate of labour turnover can only be properly assessed if the persistence of workers not with the same employer but within the industry and within the urban labour market is taken into account. It is significant that the most frequent periods of service among workers at the Meyer Sassoon mill in 1929 were one year and less and between five and ten years, 28.1 per cent and 22.38 per cent respectively falling into these two categories.[189] This pattern of employment, marked by the high initial turnover of labour, followed by a period of stabilization, culminating after about ten or fifteen years in their withdrawal from the workforce, would appear to reflect the consequences of employers' policies.

[185] The Indian Factory Commission, 1890, Evidence, pp. 22–50; Labour Gazette, IX, 5 (January 1930), 457–61. RCLI, Evidence, Bombay Presidency, GOB, 'Condition of Industrial Workers', I, i, 14; ibid., F. Stones, Director, E.D. Sassoon and Co., I, i, 484; Gokhale, The Bombay Cotton Mill Worker, pp. 101, 124; Shah, 'Labour Recruitment and Turnover'; Morris, Industrial Labour Force, pp. 85–91.
[186] R.G. Gokhale put this figure at only $9\frac{1}{2}$ per cent in 1955 as against the Labour Office estimate of $37\frac{1}{2}$ per cent in 1927–8; Labour Gazette, IX, 5 (1930), 457–61, Gokhale, The Bombay Cotton Mill Workers, pp. 24–8.
[187] Proceedings of the TLIC, Main Inquiry, Oral Evidence, BMOA, File 57-A, 278–79, MSA.
[188] RCLI, Evidence, Bombay Presidency, The Bombay Textile Labour Union, I, i, 296.
[189] Ibid., Mr F. Stones, Director, E.D. Sassoon and Co., I, i, 484.

The sources of labour supply

The nature of industrial development in Bombay, shaped by prevailing patterns of investment, gave rise to a fluctuating demand for labour. To varying degrees, as we have seen, most industries attempted to regulate their output to short-term fluctuations of demand. But this strategy assumed the existence of an excess supply of labour to meet the needs of peak periods of production. Where labour was scarce, employers might be hard pressed to effect short-term adjustments of production. In an overstocked labour market, however, employers could vary their workforce to suit changing patterns of production and demand, and dispense with the need to adopt a more regular rhythm of production. As long as labour was abundant, there was little incentive for employers to maintain steady levels of output and employment in the face of volatile markets.

How far was this assumption of over-supply borne out? The fact that employers did attempt to tailor their output and levels of employment to fit the fluctuations of the market would tend to suggest that the supply of labour did not render these flexible production strategies inoperative. However, the copious complaints of employers and their friends about the scarcity of labour makes clear that these conditions of over-supply were neither created nor maintained with ease. It was by no means unproblematic for employers to conjure up the kind of labour force they wanted or to effect the modes of labour control they chose.

The problem of labour supply has, perhaps, been approached too simplistically and scarcity has at times been understood simply as a function of numbers. To dismiss contemporary complaints about labour shortages in view of the general stability of wages is perhaps to miss the point. The extent of wage competition in the Bombay mills suggests that labour was not always readily mobilized. Moreover, the extent of absenteeism, the rate of turnover and the difficulties of keeping workers at their machines suggests that the recruitment and discipline of a labour force was not as unproblematic as it has sometimes been assumed. It is scarcely satisfactory to distinguish too neatly between the economic and political problems encountered by employers seeking to mobilize an adequate supply of stable, pliable and efficient workers.

By examining the mechanisms of the labour market and taking account of the nature of the demand for labour, it is possible to place the long and inconclusive debate about its supply in a different perspective. The supply of labour need not be evaluated in terms of the number of 'hands'. It certainly could not be measured adequately in percentages of unemployment. Its fluctuations were unlikely to be captured by the general movement of wage rates. Rather, the supply of labour became problematic at the threshold at which it became too scarce to support the flexible production strategies integral to Bombay's industrial structure. When this supply diminished so that employers could no longer manipulate the size of their casual labour force, their working costs would rise, their profits be squeezed and their control over the workforce weaken. The problems of labour supply are best understood in the context of the fluctuating demand for it. If the structure of Bombay's economy was predicated upon a particular pattern of labour use, it was not simply chosen by the employers; rather, it constituted an arena of conflict in which workers, too, contested and modified the modes of labour control.

As long as the pattern of ownership in industry was diffuse, marked by numerous and scattered units operating on a small scale, fluctuations of production would tend to be greater and more rapid. At the same time, the reserves of labour required would be inflated and a stronger tendency towards its accumulation would manifest itself. The size of the surplus labour force drawn into a particular trade in a labour market organized around numerous small employers would probably be greater than the maximum it would have required if its ownership had been more concentrated. Smaller firms operating in an intensely competitive situation were likely to experience greater and more rapid fluctuations and as a corollary would require larger reserves of labour. Furthermore, since most employers recruited their workforce through jobbers, the number of recruiting agents multiplied and the tendency to accumulate an excessive labour surplus was accentuated. The conditions of labour supply cannot, however, simply be ascribed to the activities of small employers and jobbers. Large industrial units and millowners, too, attempted to minimize their risks as well as their costs by manipulating their levels of employment dispensing with the pressure which would otherwise have existed to iron out the fluctuations of production. For many workers, this general situation held out few chances of regular employment, yet as long as they obtained sufficient work, however intermittently, to afford a subsistence, they might be held within a particular trade or occupation. It was at this point that the rural connections of the workforce became integral to the organization of work in Bombay. On the one hand, the cash needs and inadequate economic opportunities of the countryside forced workers into this unstable labour market; on the other hand, its irregularities could only be faced by recourse to the village base.

By the 1920s, employers' complaints about labour shortages had diminished. By the mid 1930s, most industries reported that the supply of labour regularly exceeded demand and that its recruitment posed no problems. The Whitley Commission claimed in 1931 that

The turning point came during the last five years. Up to that stage, labour tended to have the upper hand in that there was competition for its services; since then, the tendency has been for workers to compete for jobs.[190]

[190] *Report of the RCLI*, p. 21.

Although the problems of labour control were undiminished between the two world wars – indeed, the scale and intensity of industrial action had expanded and achieved greater momentum – it is probable that for much of the period there was a glut of labour in Bombay. We have so far been concerned with the structure of the labour market; but it would be instructive also to examine its development in the 1920s and 1930s, and in particular its sources of supply.

The development of the labour market must be set in its larger economic context. Two main forces moulded its development: short-term fluctuations and long-term changes in various occupations in Bombay, and as the next chapter will show, the interplay between the city's economy and its rural hinterland. Of course, these were not autonomous forces; they frequently interlocked. The impact of economic fluctuations was refracted most sharply upon the condition of casual labour. As long as reserve supplies of labour were thus generated, they perpetuated the conditions which created them by removing the need for employers to maintain steady levels of employment. Economic fluctuations in industry which were met by adjustments to the volume of employment served to intensify the conditions of over-supply in the casual labour market. While the prospect of employment in Bombay, where the range of jobs available was relatively large, held some workers within its labour market, those who were thrown out of work as a result of trade fluctuations frequently turned to general labouring jobs in the city. On the other hand, general labourers, often lacking skill, training or connections, could scarcely move into specialized trades and better-paid occupations.

There were other identifiable groups which fell back upon casual labour and inflated its supply. Workers who entered petty trading or set themselves up as independent artisans were, if ruined or unable to maintain themselves, thrown back into casual labour. Women and children, who were protected by factory legislation, found work most easily in casual trades which fell beyond its jurisdiction. The old and the infirm, in search of a living, had few options but to turn to 'boy labour'.[191]

Seasonal fluctuations further induced some measure of circulation around casual and general labouring jobs. The monsoon interrupted most trades, but its effect was uneven and unpredictable. For instance, two trades most immediately affected were dock labour and the building trade. Although the monsoons constituted the 'slack' season for the docks, a large workforce was required to move goods – coal, manganese ore and some 'case cargo' – which were not affected by rain, while their workload was increased by the fact that the cargo had to be moved under cover.[192] While there was usually a slackening of

[191] Burnett-Hurst, *Labour and Housing*, p. 77.
[192] *Ibid.*, p. 74.

activity in the building trade during the monsoon, it was not brought to a complete halt. Nonetheless, it was liable to several prolonged and unpredictable interruptions, depending upon the rains, resulting intermittently in a complete loss of earnings.[193] These variations of both supply and demand were registered with exaggerated effect upon casual labour. For the rush of job-seekers at the first sign of buoyancy in a particular trade invariably reduced the likelihood of regular employment for workers who normally grouped around it. Workers who retained their rural ties, in itself partly a function of the uncertainties of the urban labour market, returned to their villages each year to help with the harvest or the sowing. But the timing of their return varied according to the seasonal variations of agriculture, their urban occupations and indeed the availability of transport. In the absence of rail links and any developed system of road transport, workers from Ratnagiri relied primarily upon coastal steamers to return to their villages, but these ceased to ply with the onset of the monsoon. The major exodus of millworkers occurred in April and May;[194] dock workers migrated in September and October.[195] This seasonal exodus compounded the already complex conditions of supply and demand in the labour market.

In periods of boom, workers were attracted into particular trades in large numbers; when a slump followed, many small firms found themselves over-extended and cut back on their workforce. This process, too, might occur across the divide between town and country. Poor harvests and increased hardship in the countryside tended to increase the flow of migrants to the city. But the contraction of the rural economy would soon be reflected in the tightening of demand in the domestic economy. If agrarian crisis inflated the labour supply in the short term, falling domestic demand could leave stranded within the urban economy a pool of surplus labour which in its period of buoyancy it had helped to create.

Of course, all the processes did not necessarily channel fresh supplies of labour into the city. Seasonal variations of supply and demand sometimes simply took up and laid off the existing labour surplus. Fresh sources of labour supply were injected into the labour market by changes in the structure of employment in Bombay City and by rural migration. The latter will be the subject of the next chapter.

The changing structure of employment in Bombay contributed to the supply of labour, as particular trades contracted or withered in the wake of general economic change. Agriculture, for instance, was not simply a rural occupation.

---

[193] *Ibid.*, p. 87.
[194] *RCLI, Evidence, Bombay*, GOB, 'Conditions of Industrial Labour', I, i, 7.
[195] Burnett-Hurst, *Labour and Housing*, p. 74.

Table 7. *Average number of hands daily
employed in the textile industry*

1914	109,860
1915	111,924
1916	118,303
1917	125,713
1918	124,199
1919	126,368
1920	140,208
1921	147,740
1922	149,224

Source: BMOA, Annual Reports, 1914–1922.

In 1911, the census returned more than 10,000 agriculturists, occupied on the island, principally coconut growers in Mahim and dairy farmers. By 1921, their numbers had fallen to 6,600.[196] The expansion of economic activity during the war and the contraction which followed the peace also helped to inflate the labour supply. During the war, Bombay had been 'the main base of our supplies'[197] and 'the centre of all war work in India'.[198] The Bombay textile industry, protected from foreign competition and provided with a ready market in the form of war supplies, beat 'all records in the matter ... of prosperity'.[199] Between 1914 and 1922, its workforce expanded by about 40 per cent (see table 7).

By 1919, famine combined with the influenza epidemic to create a desperate situation in the Bombay countryside. As the Governor of Bombay reported:

Cattle are beginning to die in considerable quantities in the Deccan and we can't get fodder enough to alleviate the trouble. Large quantities of valuable fodder are being exported from here to Mesopotamia by the Army .... Luckily the Horniman press have not tumbled to the fact that fodder is being exported while the Deccan starves: if they ever do they will raise a howl and point out that Government exploit India even in famine times for their own Imperial purposes.[200]

[196] *Census, 1921*, IX, i, 35; *Census, 1911*, vol. VIII, *Bombay Town and Island, Parts I & II, Report and Tables*, by P.J. Mead and G. Laird McGregor (Bombay, 1911), p. 37. The census enumerators also located one person in 1911 who claimed to live by hunting. 'He must have been a stranger', the Census Commissioners explained, 'caught unawares in the enumeration as the days of Bombay as a game preserve are long past.' Nevertheless, in 1921 they returned six such 'strangers'.
[197] Willingdon to Montagu, 28 May 1918, Montagu Papers MSS. EUR. D 523/18, IOR.
[198] Willingdon to Montagu, 8 June 1918, *ibid.*, IOR.
[199] *BMOA, Annual Report, 1917*, p. 8.
[200] Sir George Lloyd to Montagu, 10 January 1919, Montagu Papers, MSS. EUR. D 523/24, IOR.

Table 8. *Dock labourers employed by the Port Trust, 1917–18 to 1921–2*

Year	Average daily number	Average supplied to Government	Largest number on any day
1917–18	8,542	5,153	13,153
1918–19	8,570	4,585	14,735
1919–20	7,079	2,307	9,974
1920–1	6,670	1,882	9,758
1921–2	4,906	1,134	6,777

Source: Burnett-Hurst, *Labour and Housing*, p. 74.

Food control, he reported soon afterwards, 'works badly and presses so much more hardly ... on Bombay than any other province'.[201] These conditions brought a growing influx of migrants into the city. The expanded labour requirements of wartime probably absorbed them initially. But by 1923 the boom had collapsed. The textile industry slithered into a slump. The reverberations of this crisis in the textile industry were felt sharply throughout the city's economy, partly because the period of expansion and prosperity had itself been exceptional.

The war had also witnessed 'an enormous increase in the labour requirements at the docks owing to the immense amount of stores required ... for the troops'.[202] The port had now to handle large quantities of military supplies for shipment to Mesopotamia and East Africa; its activities created a large number of jobs. When the war ended, many dock labourers were thrown out of work (see table 8). Between 1918–19 and 1921–2, the number of dock labourers employed by the Bombay Port Trust fell by 54 per cent and by a further 38 per cent by 1934.[203] Furthermore, the general decline of the export trade to Europe and the falling prices of primary products adversely affected the values as well as the volume of goods handled by the port.[204] Its impact was to be registered in the further growth of unemployment in the docks.[205]

The rapid and considerable expansion of the city since the later nineteenth

[201] Sir George Lloyd to Montagu, 12 February 1919, Montagu Papers, MSS. EUR. D 523/24, IOR.
[202] Willingdon to Montagu, 28 May 1918, Montagu Papers, MSS. EUR. D 523/18, pp. 58–9, IOR.
[203] Burnett-Hurst, *Labour and Housing*, p. 74; Cholia, *Dock Labourers*, p. 5. According to Cholia's figures the Port Trust employed 4,200 workers, excluding those employed in the mechanical workshops and the railway. However, the exact number of dock labourers, as Cholia pointed out, was impossible to calculate with any accuracy, *ibid.*, p. 6. Moreover the estimates of Burnett-Hurst and Cholia were not necessarily comparable.
[204] Cholia, *Dock Labourers*, p. 3.
[205] Indeed, workers returned as engaged in 'transport by water' in the census declined from 31,048 men in 1921 to 20,996 in 1931, and from 1,042 women to 223. *Census, 1931*, IX, i, 50; *Census, 1921*, IX, Part II, City Table VII, Part II.

century gave rise to a large and flourishing building industry. Despite the problems of supply, the high cost of raw material and rising wages during the First World War, the demand for building remained buoyant. Several public bodies proceeded with building programmes which they had embarked upon before the war. The profits of war sought outlets for investment while the provision of housing offered relatively steady returns and brought political influence. The demolition and construction programmes of the Improvement Trust since 1900, the various reclamation projects and the ambitious 'development scheme' of the provincial government further stimulated the building trade.[206] 'The Bombay building trade', Burnett-Hurst observed in 1925, 'had been experiencing a period of exceptional prosperity'; its consequence was the creation of 'unusual demands for labour'. Indeed, 'a well-known authority on builders' labour', Burnett-Hurst added, 'expressed the opinion that "no man or woman in Bombay need starve at the present movement. Anyone who wanted work in the city during the last ten or fifteen years could get it." '[207] Of course, large numbers of workers who sought work and failed to find a regular livelihood were unlikely to share this enthusiasm. By the end of the decade, it had been belied. The building industry, which employed 9,000 workers in 1921, returned slightly more than a third of that number in 1931.[208] The changing condition of the industry was reflected in the rising unemployment among wood-workers who were largely employed in construction; their increase in the 1910s had been sharp, their decline in the 1920s similarly precipitous, falling from 20,034 in 1921 to 5,863 in 1931.[209] Yet building activity reflecting the general contraction of the economy was to become even more sluggish in the 1930s.[210]

Changes in the conditions and organization of work in the 1920s and 1930s also affected the nature of both the supply and demand for labour. For instance, in the later 1920s, the turnover of the municipal workshops was reported to be 'rapidly declining resulting in a proportionate increase in the overhead charges' while attempts were being made to retain 'an almost irreducible minimum' of workers as well as to effect other retrenchments.[211] Moreover, the municipal workshops were also faced with 'increased work in the motor repair section of the workshop, whilst a corresponding decrease in the amount of work has taken

---

[206] Annual Administration Reports of the City of Bombay Improvement Trust; Report of the Bombay Development Committee (Bombay, 1914); Report of the Committee Appointed by the Government of India to Inquire into the Bombay Back Bay Reclamation Scheme, 1926 (London, 1926).

[207] Burnett-Hurst, Labour and Housing, p. 86.

[208] Census, 1921, IX, ii, City Table VII, Part I; Census, 1931, IX, ii, 196.

[209] Census, 1921, IX, i, 37; Census, 1931, IX, i, 51.

[210] Report of the Rent Enquiry Committee (Bombay, 1939), I, 26.

[211] Annual Administration Report of the Municipal Commissioner, for the City of Bombay, 1930–31, p. 181.

place in the repair of carts etc.', creating a demand for new skills and calling for changes in the composition of the workforce.[212] At the same time, 'some men in the health department', the Municipal Corporation reported, 'are being thrown out of employment owing to the adaptation of a system of removal of refuse by mechanical power and the conversion of basket privies into water closets'.[213] But it would be rash to conclude that the halalkhore, who carried the 'night-soil' baskets on his head through the city streets to refuse depots,[214] had been entirely replaced by a dramatic increase in the construction of sewers. Certainly, there does not appear to have been any remarkable decline in the number of sweepers and scavengers in the 1920s and early 1930s.[215] Similarly, unemployment among seamen owed something to the absolute decline in the number of ships plied by some of the major companies, such as Messrs Mackinnon and Mackenzie, but their conversion to oil left more serangs, and thus more workers, on their rotas than they could possibly employ.[216]

The considerable decline of domestic service may have in part reflected the general impoverishment of Bombay's economy. The sharpest decline occurred between 1911 and 1921 but the trend continued into the 1930s. Domestic service ranked among the most casual occupations and as such reflected larger tendencies operating in the labour market (see table 9).[217] It is probable that the expansion of employment opportunities during the First World War enabled some domestic servants to take up better-paid or otherwise more desirable work elsewhere; when the slump set in, many of them may have been unwilling, some perhaps unable, to return to their former occupations and found themselves trapped in the casual labour market.

Significantly, as unemployment increased, growing numbers of people took up petty trading of various kinds. 'Trade', including petty shopkeeping and peddling, was the only major occupational category to show a considerable increase in 1931, rising by a third over the decade.[218] Small-scale entrepreneurship was becoming a necessary strategy for survival.

By the end of the 1920s, retrenchment was 'the order of the day'.[219] The

[212] *Ibid.*, p. 181.
[213] *RCLI, Evidence, Bombay Presidency*, The Bombay Municipal Corporation, I, i, 567.
[214] Masani, *Local Self-Government*, pp. 191–3; Masselos, 'Jobs and Jobbery'.
[215] *Census, 1921*, IX, ii, City Table VII, Part I; *Census, 1931*, IX, ii, 196.
[216] *RCLI, Evidence, Bombay Presidency*, Messrs Mackinnon and Mackenzie, I, i, 544–5. The Indian Seamen's Union reported that there were 70,000 seamen seeking work in Bombay, *ibid.* The Indian Seamen's Union I, i, 290.
[217] Indeed, the returns may have most easily identified those who were employed, more or less permanently or professionally, as full-time domestic servants by higher-income households, and concealed the extent to which the poor, and especially women, tried to, sometimes had to, live on earnings from low-wage, part-time household work.
[218] *Census, 1931*, IX, i, 51.
[219] Proceedings of the BSEC, II, 11, MSA.

Table 9. *Numbers employed in domestic service, 1901–31*

Year	Number of men	Number of women	Total
1901	45,014	8,563	53,577
1911	45,130	9,763	54,893
1921	33,695	8,860	42,555
1931	34,117	6,180	40,297

Source: *Census, 1921* and *Census, 1931* IX, ii, City Table VII, Part I.

Census commissioners estimated that, by 1931, 200,000 unemployed workers had returned to their villages.[220] Since their rural base was equally fragile, it is more likely that many of these workers returned only temporarily. The post-war boom and the intensification of demographic and economic pressures on the land had prompted a considerable influx of migrants into Bombay; some of these migrants remained behind after the economic expansion of 1918–22 was checked.[221] The depression in the textile industry, which first emerged in 1922, began to affect other related and dependent economic activities in the city. As a consequence, the rhythms of production became even more irregular. While on the one hand variations in the demand for labour were thus accentuated, on the other hand, these variations encouraged the development of a yet larger supply of casual labour, which in some cases, was forced by the combination of slump and agrarian crisis to shuffle persistently between field and factory. The railway workshops effected sizeable cuts immediately before and after the GIP workers struck in 1930.[222] Similarly, the haphazard introduction of 'efficiency' schemes combined with the fact that seventeen mills had gone into liquidation while 'many others ... worked at below full capacity' to swell the ranks of the unemployed in the textile industry.[223] By 1934, the number of unemployed workers in the textile industry alone was estimated variously as between 40,000 and 60,000.[224]

Although there were some signs of recovery in 1937, the demand for labour did not increase significantly until the Second World War. Between 1940 and 1942, the number of factories in Bombay increased by a fifth. In 1942, there was a 13 per cent increase in electricity consumption over the previous year.[225]

---

[220] *Census, 1931*, IX, i, 9.
[221] *Ibid.*, p. 17.
[222] GOB, Home (Sp.), Files 543 (10) DC of 1930; 543 (10) DC Part A; 543 (10) DC Parts II–IV MSA; N.M. Joshi, Papers, File 61, NMML.
[223] *RCLI, Evidence, Bombay Presidency*, The Bombay Millowners' Association I, i, 386.
[224] Labour Office, Bombay, *Wages and Unemployment in The Bombay Cotton Textile Industry* (Bombay, 1934), pp. 56–9.
[225] All-India Manufacturers' Organisation, *Industries in Bombay City*, (Bombay, 1944), pp. 13–14.

The engineering industry in particular was stimulated by war requirements and the impediments to the import of machinery. Small engineering works proliferated in Byculla and Mazagaon, Reay Road and Golpitha, Khetwadi and along the Sandhurst and Grant Roads, to supply larger trades with necessary equipment. Similarly, the growing demand for uniforms and tents, mosquito nets, camouflage material and khaki set the city's looms working faster; and, in addition, a few factories were established especially to supply war needs. The mills and weaving karkhanas required new accessories like bobbins and shuttles, pickers and beltings, which provided business for wood-working factories and the leather trade. Supplying troops offered fresh opportunities for bidi makers. 'A large number of bidi workers have grown up during the last two years', reported the All-India Manufacturers' Organization, 'and are concentrated in Byculla area'.[226] Similarly, shoe and leather manufacturers also found themselves in considerable demand. The trade and manufacture of precious metals was affected by 'the phenomenal rise in the price of silver and gold' which diverted 'the smiths of Jhaweri Bazar, Sheikh Memon Street and Kalbadevi to deal in Bullion in addition to their work'.[227] Some industries, like chemicals, and those like soap and glass which were dependent on them, were seriously hampered by the disruption of trade and necessary imports. 'The chemical industry', as the AIMO noted, 'is a key industry and it is much to be regretted that Bombay has not been able to develop it in a manner worthy of its needs and enterprise'.[228] If the demand for labour increased substantially in the 1940s, the shortages and dislocations of war upon the agrarian economy, and then the bloodshed and upheavals of partition, prompted another heavy wave of migration into the city.

The patterns of investment and business strategies which tailored production to the short-term fluctuations of the market necessarily registered their effects on the nature of the demand for labour. The interplay between them provided the underpinnings of the social economy of labour in Bombay City. It would be possible to portray this economy and the organization of its labour force in terms of the distinction between the formal and informal sectors, between the primary, hegemonic or modern sector and the dependent, marginal and traditional sector. But many of the complexities of the labour market and the social organization of the workforce would simply elude these categories. Moreover, since these categories derived from and reflected the perceptions of the urban poor in the dominant discourse, they have tended to vitiate the analysis of the labour force mounted in these terms.

[226] *Ibid.*, p. 9.
[227] *Ibid.*, p. 10.
[228] *Ibid.*, p. 10–11.

Nowhere, perhaps, are these perceptions more clearly registered than in the assumption that the organized and unorganized sectors received two different types of labour supply. Workers in the unorganized sector, it is supposed, constituted a discrete social group, incapable of regular work, generally immune to the rigours of factory discipline and seeking casual employment wherever it was to be found. Casual workers, in this view, possessed a distinctive culture of their own, characterized by specific behavioural traits, habits and lifestyles peculiar to the unorganized sector: often condemned as deviant, feckless, criminal and violent, and sometimes celebrated as staunchly and immutably oppositional.

The experience of casual labour, however, was shared in common by workers who might be placed in both sectors and engendered by business strategies which relied upon a rapid turnover, a low ratio of fixed capital and operated on narrow margins. Not only were a significant proportion of cotton-mill workers hired at the factory gates, but those who were more permanently employed could easily lose their jobs and find themselves forced then to take up casual employ-ment, whether as badlis in the mills, petty traders or general labourers in the city. Alternatively, there was a considerable need for manual labour in the organized sector and migrant workers in casual employment in the unorganized sector could, with the assistance of friends and relatives or through the connec-tions of jobbers, move into the cotton mills. The mobility of labour was shaped not only by the policies of employers but also by the social connections of the working classes. Bankoti migrants from the Konkan, it was said, 'are employed as menials in Hindu households and are somewhat highly paid ... In spite of this fact, however, they evince a tendency to relinquish domestic service in favour of employment in mills and factories'.[229] Skilled workers in the dock-yards, railway workshops, the engineering and textile industries enjoyed a similar mobility. Moreover, organized and unorganized sector activities often shared not only similar business strategies but they also manifested similar attitudes to technology and mechanization, took recourse to similar financial practices and often organized production and deployed labour along similar lines.

Whatever the weakness of dual-labour-market theories, it is not intended to suggest that wages were determined in a single, homogeneous, smoothly functioning and perfectly competitive labour market. This chapter has sug-gested, and the following pages will offer evidence to show, that the labour market was indeed segmented in numerous ways, although its fractions were scarcely insulated from each other. It will be argued that no simple or single distinction between a 'labour aristocracy' in permanent wage work in the

[229] *Gazetteer*, I, 214.

organized sector and the 'casual' or 'working poor' outside can be easily sustained.[230] Certainly contemporary observers did not perceive this stark distinction which the labour force in early-twentieth-century Bombay. Indeed, it is now becoming increasingly apparent that the concept of a labour aristocracy, floated by Engels, hardened into conceptual dogma by Lenin, has perhaps hindered more often than it has helped to describe the processes of class formation even in nineteenth-century Britain, which it was originally intended to explain.[231] Far from a sharp distinction between a 'labour aristocracy' of factory workers and the rest of the working classes, there were numerous gradations of skill, status and income between them. Wage levels in one sector of the labour force were not determined in a market entirely divorced from every other. The structure of wages in the cotton-textile industry was at specific points related to the price of agrarian or urban casual labour. The broad unities, and interrelationships, of the labour market did not prevent its segmentation along particular lines.

Caste, regional and religious clusters formed within particular trades and occupations; similar clusters characterized residential patterns. Some neighbourhoods were inhabited predominantly by particular social groups. Caste, kinship and village ties played a major role in the recruitment of labour. Jobbers had every reason to hire the workers they knew or with whom they were connected outside the workplace. Once a particular group, whether defined by caste, kinship or village origins established themselves in a particular trade or line of work, they often struggled to strengthen their claims upon it and tended thereby to perpetuate their position. Similarly, the labour market could be segmented by neighbourhood. The cost and difficulty of transport in Bombay combined with the irregularity of employment induced most workers to live near their place of work. Since their social connections were vital to finding housing as well as work, housing and labour markets intersected and the tendency for occupational and residential clusters to form mirrored each other. Workers of a particular caste (or religion) or migrants from particular districts came to be attributed with a special aptitude for specific trades. Employers compared the skill and productivity of their workers with those of neighbouring, and not necessarily competitive, establishments. Workers measured their earnings against the wages received in related or similar occupations in the same neighbourhood. These factors could exercise special pressures on wage bargaining or social expectations in different neighbourhoods. In these ways, the

---

[230] Harriss, 'The Working Poor and the Labour Aristocracy'.
[231] G. Stedman Jones, 'Class Struggle and the Industrial Revolution', in G. Stedman Jones, *Languages of Class: Studies in English Working Class History, 1832–1982* (Cambridge, 1983), pp. 25–75; see also E.J. Hobsbawm, 'Artisan or Labour Aristocrat?', *EcHR*, second series, XXXVII, 3 (1984), 355–72.

workplace, the neighbourhood and the village connection were integrated within the social nexus of the working classes. But it should not be supposed that such segmentation was always rigidly maintained within neighbourhoods, caste or religious ties or networks based on kinship or village. Developments within the wider society registered their effects upon the determination of each of these spheres. Moreover, the social connections which shaped them were diffuse and varied in origin and substance. It would be simplistic, therefore, to assume that either caste or religion, either rural origins or neighbourhood association alone and separately determined the social economy of the working classes or held the key to its inwardness.

4   Migration and the rural connections of Bombay's workers

Rural migration formed the most important source of labour supply to Bombay. The fluctuations of the labour market have commonly been attributed to the migrant character of the workforce and their lack of commitment to the industrial setting. But as the previous chapter demonstrated, this is to confuse the symptoms with the problem itself. The patterns of labour use were conditioned by the structure of the city's economy; they were not simply a function of the attitudes, mentalities or culture of the workforce. Rather, the irregular and uncertain conditions of work in Bombay made it essential for most workers to retain their rural connections. The village remained integral to their social nexus in the city. But the maintenance of their rural connections cannot be understood simply as a transitional phase in the formation of the labour force in the early stages of industrialization. A recent study of the Bombay labour market in the 1970s still found that the city's working population 'consists overwhelmingly of migrants'.[1] Industrial development in India appears to have strengthened what are normatively described as the pre-industrial characteristics of the workforce. This chapter will investigate the rural connections of Bombay's workers and the interplay of town and country in shaping their social organization.

The implications of migration were innumerable and ambiguous. Scarcity and distress were the primary factors which propelled migration to the towns, yet migrant workers maintained their rural links. While a large proportion of Bombay's workers retained strong rural connections, they were also becoming increasingly dependent upon their urban and industrial livelihoods. Workers with land in the village could be expected to return in periods of unemployment. But casual unemployment was one of the most significant experiences which the city's working class was forced to confront in common. In the face of unemployment, workers often revealed considerable persistence, remaining in the city or moving to other cities in search of work rather than returning to the

---

[1] Joshi and Joshi, *Surplus Labour,* p. 122. See also K. Patel, *Rural Labour in Industrial Bombay* (Bombay, 1963); K.C. Zachariah, *Migrants in Greater Bombay* (Bombay, 1968).

land.[2] Migrant workers were assumed to be acquiescent, yet those with the strongest rural connections were often able to use them as an effective basis for sustained industrial action.[3]

Although 84 per cent of the entire population of Bombay in 1921 had been born outside the city,[4] contemporary comment focussed almost exclusively upon the migrant character of the workforce. It was considered sufficient to explain why workers were volatile and riotous,[5] as well as why they were submissive and incapable of effective organization. 'The Indian operatives', reported the Indian Factory Labour Commission in 1908, 'are capable of remaining quiescent under conditions which would probably not be tolerated by a class of similar standing in any other country'.[6] Their migrant character made them, it was said, casual and careless in their attitude to work, but it was also supposed to motivate them to earn as much as possible in order to return quickly to the land.[7] Migration was, on these premises, the defining characteristic of working-class life. As a formula it could seemingly explain anything. Thus, in 1931, the Whitley Commission poured scorn upon the notion that 'the main industries of India are manned by a mass of agricultural workers temporarily forsaking the mattock and the plough to add to their income by a brief spell in industry' as something which existed only in 'the minds of employers' anxious about the problems of labour control. Yet only a few pages later, it declared it to be 'a truth of primary importance' that 'the great majority of those employed are at heart villagers'.[8]

Problems of definition, as much as of conceptualization, have complicated the assessment of the nature and consequences of the rural connections of Bombay's workers. In public discourse, the term 'migrant' could apply equally

[2] *RCLI, Evidence, Bombay Presidency*, Mr Jamshed, N.R. Mehta, I, i, 226; Colonel Sir George Willis, 1, i, 218; The Indian Seamen's Union, 1, i, 290; see also Labour Office, Bombay, *Wages and Unemployment in the Bombay Cotton Textile Industry* (Bombay, 1934), pp. 57–8; R.G. Gokhale, *The Bombay Cotton Mill Worker* (Bombay, 1957), pp. 55–76.

[3] *RCLI, Evidence, Bombay Presidency*, M.S. Bhumgara, 1, i, 499.

[4] *Census, 1921*, IX, i, 16.

[5] This was the conventional understanding of a wide range of opinion: millowners, officials, committees of inquiry and journalists. See *Report of the IFLC*, I, 18–20; *Report of the Industrial Disputes Committee* (Bombay, 1922); *BMOA, Annual Report, 1935*, p. 34. For a recent statement of their argument articulating tacit assumptions held by contemporaries as well as later historians, see Arnold, 'Industrial Violence', 234–55.

[6] *Report of the IFLC*, I, 19; see also *Report of the RCLI*, pp. 12–17. Similarly, Newman wrote: 'However remote and impractical it was for him [the millworker] to return to his village he seldom felt it necessary to fight for reforms in his urban environment.' Newman, *Workers and Unions*, p. 67. This is notwithstanding the militancy of the millworkers, in repeated general strikes as well as numerous individual disputes, in this period.

[7] *Report of the IFLC*, I, 18; Burnett-Hurst, *Labour and Housing*, p. 61; P.P. Pillai, *Economic Conditions in India* (London, 1928), pp. 233–66; and sundry other contemporary works.

[8] *Report of the RCLI*, pp. 12–17.

to workers who were entirely dependent upon the city for their livelihood but who retained some rural connections as to workers who migrated seasonally. 'Local' labour could indicate as little as the worker's place of birth, and this in any case was an unreliable guide to residence since women often preferred to return to their villages for the birth of their children. The census reports frequently tried to distinguish not only between permanent and periodic migration, but also between semi-permanent and temporary migration, and generally failed to sustain the coherence of their categories. On such accounting, workers who could count among the second and third generations of factory workers – in the sense that their ancestors before them had spent their entire working lives in Bombay – would, by virtue of having been born or having retired outside the city, still be considered migrants. The Bombay Textile Labour Union, asserting that the 'vast majority' of millworkers were 'more or less permanent and cannot be called migratory', argued forcefully that 'if by occasional visits to their villages Bombay labour becomes migratory, practically the whole of the population in this city will have to be brought under the category'.[9] The term 'migrant' thus signified within the dominant discourse an ideological conception of the nature of the working class, the processes of its formation and its implications for the social order.

To penetrate the surface of these ambiguities, it will be necessary first to examine the pressures which came to bear upon the agrarian economy of the major regions of emigration. If shrinking rural resources made migrant workers increasingly dependent upon their urban livelihoods, they maintained close and enduring connections with the land. At times, migration appeared to be directed at the maintenance of their rural base; in turn, this impinged upon their options and strategies within the labour market and shaped their social organizations in the city. The fluctuations of the urban economy made the rural base indispensable to their survival in the city. While their rural base contracted, the importance of their village ties increased. How workers attempted to resolve these contradictory pressures will be examined in terms of their family economy. The family economy of the Bombay working class integrated both its rural and its urban interests. It may have impelled but it also facilitated migration. The social networks which were centred upon it shaped the social organization of the city's workers.

---

[9] *RCLI, Evidence, Bombay Presidency*, The Bombay Textile Labour Union, I, i, 296.

Migration: the agrarian background

Long-distance migration to industrial and urban work involved a very small proportion of the total population.[10] In Bombay Presidency, 86.35 per cent of the population was enumerated in the district of their birth, while a further 7.88 per cent was born within the Presidency.[11] Of course, there had always been movements of population across the Indian sub-continent, in search of trade or work, pilgrimage or warfare. The migration of labour to the large industrial cities was merely the tip of a sizeable iceberg. Moreover, among the large towns of the Presidency, Bombay alone attracted so substantial a proportion of rural migrants from so far-flung a hinterland.[12] Some cities like Ahmedabad and Sholapur drew the bulk of their labour from the town and its rural district; others like Karachi, Poona and Surat expanded around a solid core of local, permanent inhabitants.

The migration of labour was not the outcome of structural changes in rural society. Historians have increasingly undermined the notion that a labour force was churned up from the dead-weight of the traditional rural order by the omnipotent engines of colonial rule.[13] There was no 'mass conversion of cultivators and artisans into agricultural labourers' after 1870. While the proportion of workers engaged in manufacturing industry declined from 10.63 per cent in 1901 to 8.72 per cent in 1931 and then rose to 9.23 per cent in 1961, the proportion of agricultural labourers rose and fell, but narrowly, around about a fifth of the workforce.[14] Agricultural labourers had existed before the inception of colonial rule; forms of tied, bonded and serf labour continued well beyond its demise.[15] It was less the fundamental transformation of agrarian society than

[10] For a useful general survey of migration on the basis of demographic data, see K.C. Zachariah, *A Historical Study of Internal Migration in the Indian Sub-Continent* (New York, 1964). See also John Connell, Biplab Dasgupta, Roy Laishley, Michael Lipton, *Migration from Rural Areas: The Evidence from Village Studies* (Delhi, 1979).

[11] *Census, 1931*, VIII, ii, 51–91.

[12] *RCLI, Evidence, Bombay Presidency*, GOB, 'Conditions of Industrial Labour', 1, i, 3–9.

[13] D. Kumar, *Land and Caste in South India* (Cambridge, 1969). See also Breman, *Patronage and Exploitation*. The classic statement of this orthodoxy is to be found in S.J. Patel, *Agricultural Labourers in Modern India and Pakistan* (Bombay, 1952).

[14] J. Krishnamurty, 'The Growth of Agricultural Labour in India – a Note', *IESHR*, IX, 3 (1972), 332; Krishnamurty, 'Secular Changes', pp. 42–51; and Krishnamurty, 'Distribution of the Indian Working Force', in Chaudhuri and Dewey (eds.), *Economy and Society*, pp. 258–76.

[15] On the inequalities of Maharashtrian society before the British conquest, see H. Fukuzawa, 'Land and Peasants in the Eighteenth Century Maratha Kingdom', *HJE*, VI, 2 (1965), 32–61; H. Fukuzawa, 'Rural Servants in the Eighteenth Century Maharashtrian Village – Demiurgic or Jajmani System', *HJE*, XII, 2 (1972), 14–40 and H. Fukuzawa, 'Agrarian Relations and Land Revenue: The Medieval Deccan and Maharashtra', in T. Raychaudhuri and I. Habib (eds.), *CEHI*, vol. I, *c. 1250–1700* (Cambridge, 1982), pp. 249–60; see also Kumar, *Western India*, pp. 1–42. For evidence on the practice of slavery, see T. Coats, 'Account of the Present State of the Township of Lony', *Transactions of the Literary Society of Bombay* (London, 1823), III, 183–250. See also G. Prakash, *Bonded Histories: Genealogies of Labour Servitude in Colonial India* (Cambridge, 1990).

Table 10. *Important districts of migration to Bombay City 1881–1931*

	1881	1891	1901	1911	1921	1931
Ahmedabad	7,004	9,439	9,594	16,298	17,557	20,470
Broach	1,763	1,537	1,226	1,660	2,272	4,497
Kaira	133	1,651	2,132	2,976	3,879	4,017
Surat	35,803	29,940	25,097	35,072	39,682	58,275
Thana *a*	17,051	15,281	10,557	15,705	14,797	12,355
Kolaba	11,506	28,851	21,100	37,119	43,180	32,666
Ratnagiri	126,190	162,586	145,835	216,060	235,566	237,256
Nasik	7,142	6,352	7,939	9,863	24,451	17,347
Ahmednagar	8,274	9,543	15,100	14,611	48,501	17,467
Poona	69,004	54,543	64,791	71,185	89,231	66,999
Sholapur	8,749	4,420	8,812	8,528	11,816	7,367
Satara	45,404	37,864	60,387	56,754	65,953	53,211
Cutch	45,333	38,000	28,179	36,470	37,480	20,029
Kathiawar	32,568	39,050	45,531	58,775	72,435	53,288
Kolhapur	4,220	4,248	5,993	9,309	—	5,391
Baroda	3,906	8,857	5,625	4,501	6,349	6,027
Hyderabad State	8,525	9,518	7,431	9,302	19,602	15,914
Madras	6,075	8,276	6,005	8,278	15,156	21,415
Rajputana	9,381	12,907	10,461	12,453	19,722	8,389
Punjab (including Delhi)	2,429	6,572	6,116	8,616	10,425	11,837
United Provinces				50,682	70,911	83,323
Oudh	8,722	8,831	6,043	—	—	—
Upper India	—	15,393	—	—	—	—
North-West Frontier Province	2,227	16,653	29,881	1,101	2,273	3,091
C.P. and Berar	2,391	1,950	4,330	3,843	5,046	4,814
Central India Agency	2,088	2,966	2,407	4,005	3,360	3,330
Portuguese and French possessions in India	21,938	21,399	18,794	32,106	34,111	38,702
Population of Bombay city	773,196	821,764	776,006	979,445	1,175,914	1,161,383

a Including Bombay Suburban District.
Source: Census, 1931, IX, i, 16.

the slow accumulation of commercial and demographic pressures upon already
modest resources which pushed labour from the field to the factory and the slum.
As the Government of Bombay declared,

emigration on a large scale takes place from such places as have either a population which
they are unable to support owing to the limited amount of land available for cultivation,
absence of any industrial towns close by or constant failure of the rains.[16]

[16] *RCLI, Evidence, Bombay Presidency,* GOB, 'Conditions of Industrial Labour', I, i, 5–6.

Table 11. *Index of changes in streams of migration: 1881 = 100*

	1881	1891	1901	1911	1921	1931
Ahmedabad	100	135	137	233	251	292
Broach	100	87	70	94	129	255
Kaira	100	1,241	1,603	1,937	2,917	3,020
Surat	100	84	70	98	111	163
Thana [a]	100	84	59	87	82	72
Kolaba	100	225	184	323	375	284
Ratnagiri	100	129	116	172	187	188
Nasik	100	89	111	138	344	243
Ahmednagar	100	115	183	177	586	211
Poona	100	79	94	103	129	97
Sholapur	100	51	101	98	135	84
Satara	100	83	133	125	145	117
Cutch	100	84	62	81	83	44
Kathiawar	100	120	140	180	221	164
Kolhapur	100	100	142	221	220	128
Baroda	100	224	144	115	162	155
Hyderabad State	100	112	87	109	230	187
Madras	100	136	99	136	250	353
Rajputana	100	138	112	133	210	89
Punjab and Delhi	100	270	257	355	429	487
North India	100	375	329	475	671	789
C.P. and Berar	100	82	182	161	211	201
Central India Agency	100	142	115	194	161	159
Portuguese and French possessions in India	100	98	86	147	156	176

[a] Including Bombay Suburban District.
Source: Census, 1931, IX, i, 18.

Tables 10 and 11 set out the patterns of migration to Bombay city between 1881 and 1931.[17] The Bombay labour force was recruited predominantly from the Deccan and the Konkan, especially the Ratnagiri district. Their ranks were reinforced by migrants from the eastern districts of the United Provinces, whose numbers began to rise in the 1880s and then accelerated in the early twentieth

[17] These figures relate to the entire spectrum of the city's population and not the working class alone. Moreover, based on the birth place of the city's residents, they do not distinguish between seasonal and permanent migration or between different types of migration. Moreover, this data cannot adequately capture the changing proportions of short- and long-term migration which is crucial to an understanding of the impact of economic fluctuations upon the Bombay labour market. For a discussion of the use of census data for the study of migration, see Zachariah, *Internal Migration*, ch. 2, especially pp. 42–3; A. Bose, *Urbanization in India: an Inventory of Source Materials* (Delhi, 1970); Anand A. Yang, 'Peasants on the Move: A Study of Internal Migration in India', *Journal of Interdisciplinary History*, X, 1 (Summer, 1979), 40.

Table 12. *Land and population in Bombay Presidency, 1922–3*

Province	Area (sq. miles)	Population Total	Population Density (per sq. mile)	Land details, 1922–3 (%) Cultivated	Land details, 1922–3 (%) Cultivable	Land details, 1922–3 (%) Uncultivable
Sind	46,506	3,279,377	71	30.9	20.3	48.8
Gujarat	10,145	2,958,849	292	73.5	4.5	22.0
Konkan	13,680	3,031,669	222	45.7	1.4	52.9
Deccan	38,262	6,059,114	158	70.2	1.7	28.1
Karnatak	14,924	2,786,796	187	82.2	1.6	16.2
Total		18,115,805	147	54.3	8.9	36.8

Source: H.H. Mann, *Statistical Atlas of the Bombay Presidency* (Bombay, 1925), p. 4.

century. Migration from Goa increased significantly after 1901 and from Madras after 1911. Surat, Ahmedabad, Cutch and Kathiawar sent large numbers of migrants to Bombay as early as 1881; but these comprised large groups of traders as well as labourers and were never strongly represented in the textile workforce.[18]

The agrarian structure of the districts of the Deccan, Gujarat and the United Provinces has been studied by numerous historians. But, largely because of their close connections with Bombay, Ratnagiri and the Konkan are often treated as exceptional and neglected as a consequence. Since it was the most important and consistent supplier of labour to Bombay, this section will focus upon the pressures which propelled migration from Ratnagiri.

Ratnagiri

The landscape of Ratnagiri, marked by steep, rugged hills in its central portions, descending dramatically to the coast, made it one of the most beautiful regions of the Bombay Presidency. But it was also one of the poorest. 'The interest of the country' as the official history put it, 'must depend, therefore, on the beauty of its scenery' and 'in these respects it need not fear comparison with the more favoured and celebrated provinces in India'.[19] The proportion of uncultivable land in Ratnagiri was higher than in the desert wastes of Sind (see table 12), and

[18] See *RCLI, Evidence, Bombay Presidency*, Mrs K. Wagh, Senior Lady Investigator, The Labour Office, Bombay, I, i, 191.
[19] *Presidency Gazetteer*, I, part 2: *History of the Konkan, Dakhan and Southern Maratha Country* (Bombay, 1896), xiii.

it was the sea alone which provided 'ample protection against famine'.[20] Migration from the district was a well-established tradition. Shivaji's armies and Angre's pirates recruited sizeable contingents from Ratnagiri. In the nineteenth century, before the development of industry, it had been 'the nursery of the Bombay army, and to a large extent its police'.[21] The soldiers and constables brought back in pay and pensions amounts believed to be 'nearly as large as the whole district revenue'.[22] Moreover, the service classes of this district were to be found in 'large numbers ... in places of power all over the Maratha dominions'. Their remittances were indispensable to the local economy:

In Suvarndarg, Anjanvel and Ratnagiri were several families who, rising to high office at the Peshwa's Court, put together large estates, and spending money freely in improvements had prosperous villagers and very rich rice and garden lands.[23]

The nineteenth century witnessed a period of economic contraction and decline in Ratnagiri. The inception of British rule interrupted the flow of resources into the district. Instead of the treasure imported into the district by the Peshwa to pay for the garrison, revenues were not remitted to Bombay. The service classes, whose savings had played an increasingly vital role in the local economy in the mid eighteenth century, lost their jobs and did not retrieve their positions within the bureaucracy of the Raj until the later nineteenth century.[24] The valuable timber trade, which had once supplied the Zanzibar and East African markets, as well as the Bombay dockyard, was by the mid nineteenth century in irreversible decline.[25]

The decline of the iron-ore mines of Malwan indicates the increasing dependence of the rural economy upon agriculture. From the iron-ore mines of Malwan, it used to be said, 'one man and a boy, with a pickaxe and crowbar, could in one day raise 400 pounds of good ore from the surface veins'. Small smelting works were dotted across the district at Masura, Varangaon and several smaller villages. In the absence of a cheap and substantial supply of coal, these mines could only produce low-grade ore for a limited local market. In the 1840s, their prices began to fall while the cost of fuel necessary for smelting rose. These

---

[20] H.S. Lawrence, *Statistical Atlas of the Bombay Presidency* (Bombay, 1906), p. 91; A.C. Staples, 'Indian Maritime Transport in 1840', *IESHR*, VII, i (1970), 61–90.

[21] *Presidency Gazetteer, Ratnagiri and Sawantwadi* (Bombay, 1880), X, 143.

[22] *Ibid.*, X, 240.

[23] *Ibid.*, X, 218–19.

[24] G. Johnson, 'Chitpavan Brahmins and Politics in Western India in the Late Nineteenth and Early Twentieth Centuries', in E.R. Leach and S.N. Mukherjee (eds.), *Elites in South Asia* (Cambridge, 1970), pp. 95–118; A. Seal, *The Emergence of Indian Nationalism: Competition and Collaboration in the Later Nineteenth Century* (Cambridge, 1968), pp. 70–1, 84–93, 114–30; M.L.P. Patterson 'Changing Patterns of Occupation among Chitpavan Brahmins', *IESHR*, VII (1970), 375–96.

[25] *Presidency Gazetteer*, X, 32.

village furnaces became increasingly uncompetitive. By the 1880s, local manufacture had completely ceased.[26]

In the same period, when railway construction had begun to impinge upon the rural economy of Bombay's hinterland, it bypassed Ratnagiri. Before the coming of the railways, its natural harbours and the bullock tracks across the Ghats had made Ratnagiri an important entrepot for the Deccan trade.[27] But country craft and bullocks could scarcely compete with the railway which linked the Deccan directly to Bombay. Between 1894–5 and 1906–7, the value of the district's trade fell by more than one-half.[28]

Increasingly, therefore, as their employment opportunities narrowed, the growing population of Ratnagiri was forced to cultivate its barren and diminishing lands more intensively. By 1925, 'industry', a category which included such occupational groups as washermen, barbers and toddy drawers, accounted for no more than 6 per cent of the district's population.[29] If, historically, there had been little economic diversification in the district, it was to become even less.

It is against the background of this shrinking resource base that the mounting demographic pressures of the later nineteenth and twentieth centuries must be understood. Between 1820 and 1872, the population of Ratnagiri increased from 462,561 to over a million. By 1851, the district was already overcrowded, 'tillage had spread to the very hill tops' and 'every available spot was worked by the plough or the hoe'.[30] Between 1872 and 1921, the population of Ratnagiri expanded by a further 13 per cent, a tribute 'to the importance of its connection with Bombay'.[31] On the other hand, the possibilities for agricultural expansion were limited. In the Konkan as a whole, no more than 1.4 per cent of the cultivable waste was still available in 1923.[32]

As population pressed upon scarce resources, holdings were increasingly fragmented and subdivided. The number of holdings more than doubled between 1903–4 and 1921–2. Moreover, the 1921–2, 73.5 per cent of these holdings were less than five acres in size and almost 95 per cent less than twenty-five acres.[33] An official inquiry, in the early 1920s, citing several examples of 'the

---

[26] *Ibid.*, X, 29–30.

[27] Nevertheless, in the mid 1920s, some of the Konkan ports, including Vengurla, Bankot, Ratnagiri and Malwan, handled an annual trade of Rs. 40 lakhs. *Report of the Bombay Provincial Banking Enquiry Committee* (Bombay, 1930), vol. I, p. 20.

[28] *Papers Relating to the Second Revision Settlement of the Ratnagiri Taluka of the Ratnagiri Collectorate*, by J.A. Madan, 11 September 1914. *Selections*, new series, no. DLXXIV (Bombay, 1920), paras. 31–2; Charlesworth, *Peasants and Imperial Rule*, pp. 146–7.

[29] Mann, *Statistical Atlas, 1925*, p. 144.

[30] *Presidency Gazetteer*, X, 105–6.

[31] Mann, *Statistical Atlas, 1925*, p. 144.

[32] *Ibid.*, p. 4.

[33] Note by Deputy Secretary, GOB, Revenue, 'Proposals to check excessive subdivision and fragmentation of holdings', Bombay Revenue Proceedings, vol. 11330, February 1923, p. 71, IOR.

absurd extent of fragmentation as well as subdivision' in the Presidency as a whole, emphasized that its most serious manifestations were to be found in Ratnagiri:

The instances are by no means to be regarded as exceptional ... I am in a position to say that they are fairly common. I have myself seen cases in the coast talukas of Ratnagiri and Kanara where a single cocoanut tree is a hissa and is moreover jointly owned by several persons who divide the produce according to annevari shares.[34]

Fragmentation did not necessarily signify rural distress. It could also be a sign of buoyancy: the consequence of intense competition for a share, however small, of the best land or the desire of each cultivator to hedge his bets by obtaining a diverse mix of lands in his holding.[35] But in Ratnagiri it was primarily a function of growing demographic pressure upon largely barren land. By 1930, 'some of the cultivators', reported the collector of Ratnagiri,

are very small landholders and the rest are landless. The bulk of them therefore serve as field labourers on daily wages either in kind or cash and cultivate the lands of others.[36]

The migration of labour from Ratnagiri was not simply a function of population increase alone; its patterns were also drawn by the production relations which stemmed from the consolidation of the khoti tenure in the nineteenth century.[37] The power and influence of the khots varied throughout the district. In Malwan, where they were at their weakest, even the most powerful khots were believed to be no more than 'pure farmers'.[38] Their grip was strongest and their exactions reputed to be the most oppressive in the Chitpavan Brahmin strongholds of Dapoli, Chiplun and Khed.[39] Significantly, there was an inverse

---

[34] *Ibid.*, p. 71, IOR.
[35] See N. Charlesworth, 'Trends in Agricultural Performance in an Indian Province: The Bombay Presidency 1900–1920', in Chaudhuri and Dewey (eds.), *Economy and Society*, pp. 130–1. Moreover, the problems inherent to the reporting of fragmentation and subdivision has complicated the interpretation of the evidence relating to it. These were distinct processes which were frequently confused and sometimes conflated. Plots in different villages for instance were liable to double-counting, to being recorded as separate holdings rather than as a part of a single, larger, but more dispersed holding. The result would be the inflation of the number of cultivators, the diminishing of the size of holdings, and the exaggeration of their numbers: see E.T. Stokes, 'The Structure of Landholding in Uttar Pradesh', in E.T. Stokes, *The Peasant and the Raj: Studies in Agrarian Society and Peasant Rebellion in Colonial India* (Cambridge, 1978), pp. 221–3; Charlesworth, 'Trends in Agricultural Performance', p. 131; D. Pandit, 'The Myths around Subdivision and Fragmentation of Holdings: A Few Case Histories', *IESHR*, VI, 2 (June, 1969), 151–63.
[36] *RCLI, Evidence, Bombay Presidency*, Mr W.B. Gilligan, ICS, Collector of Ratnagiri, I, i, 217.
[37] On the history of the khoti tenure and the vicissitudes of British policy, see E.T. Candy, *Selections with Notes from the Records of Government Regarding the Khoti Tenure: Selections*, new series, no. 134; *Presidency Gazetteer*, X, 213–55; Charlesworth, *Peasants and Imperial Rule*, pp. 30–4, 56–60; R.D. Choksey, *Economic Life in the Bombay Konkan* (Bombay, 1960).
[38] Candy, *Selections ... Regarding the Khoti Tenure*, p. 8: *Selections*, new series, no. 134.
[39] *Presidency Gazetteer*, X, 213.

correlation between the areas of khoti domination and the propensity of labour to emigrate to Bombay: Malwan and Devgad sent the largest number of millworkers, Khed and Dapoli, the fewest.[40] This was because the domination of the khot was directed primarily towards the control of labour. The maintenance of the social and indeed ritual position of the khots, especially in the case of the Brahmin families who had entrenched themselves in the last days of Maratha rule, came to depend upon their command over men: it was not for them to touch the plough. But ideological and political forms of control were also grounded upon an economic logic: rice, the predominant crop of the Konkan coast, was labour intensive.

It should be clear, therefore, that the khoti tenure seriously affected the possibilities of migration. In Ratnagiri, the basis of the khot's power lay not only in his command of the means of production but also his ability to influence the relations of exchange.[41] His dominant position in any one market, whether for produce or credit, land or labour, sometimes gave him a commanding influence in others. By receiving rent as a share of the crop – generally one-half in the case of rice and garden land – the khot was able to use his tenurial position to extend his interests in the produce market. There was little to prevent the khot from exacting a higher proportion of the crop. Credit offered one useful instrument for such appropriation. 'It was very hard for tenants to combine against a khot', for, it was said, 'they were generally deep in his debt and wholly at his mercy'.[42] Although, of course, many khots were themselves deeply in debt and in any case indebtedness could mean many different things, there was no doubt that 'when his circumstances allow, the khot secures the monopoly of the village money-lending and grain-dealing business'.[43] Under these circumstances, khots were able to force their tenants to 'agree to terms worse than those of any blood-sucking money-lender'.[44] Furthermore, by letting his land at high rents and then ensuring that his tenants borrowed from him, on harsh terms, the khot could weld together his interests in the rental, produce and credit markets.

But the khot's dominance was generally directed towards the extension of his control over labour. Exchange sometimes took the form of payment in labour or other personalized services, rather than money alone. Thus, khots claimed the right to extract from all tenants one day's labour in eight as well as the service

[40] Patel, *Rural Labour*, p. 17.
[41] I have drawn here upon the model developed by Krishna Bharadwaj, 'Towards a Macro-Economic Framework for a Developing Economy: The Indian Case', *Manchester School of Economic and Social Studies*, III (September 1979), 270–302.
[42] *Presidency Gazetteer*, X, 229; Candy, *The Khoti Tenure*, p. 10: *Selections*, new series, no. 134.
[43] *Presidency Gazetteer*, X, 138–9.
[44] Weekly Report, District Magistrate, Ratnagiri District, 1 March 1933, GOB, Home (Sp.), File 800 (74) (21) of 1932–34, p. 119, MSA.

of ploughing their fields – not to mention the right of 'pressing them to carry their palanquins'.[45] Such labour services were used extensively in the clearance and preparation of rice lands and the reclamations of salt marshes and swamps which in turn contributed to the khot's interests in the grain trade. Moreover, it was by no means uncommon for cultivators to mortgage their own and some-times their descendants' labour: in the mid nineteenth century, an able-bodied labourer was valued at ten rupees per annum in liquidation of a debt. In one particular case, a loan of Rs. 16 had amounted at the death of the debtor to Rs. 20. The debtor's son had then to repay the loan by serving the creditor in satisfaction of his father's debt. After five years he executed a bond to serve a further seven years to settle his liabilities. 'I will serve you without making objections and will behave well' read the bond, adding the claim that 'we have executed this deed willingly'. The bond had to be guaranteed by a third person who undertook to repay the loan whether in cash or labour on the same terms, if the debtor should break his contract. The alternative was to repay the debt at 12 per cent interest. In this particular case, the eight-year-old boy served his father's creditor for twelve years instead of repaying Rs. 20 on these terms. While he contracted to repay his debt in this way, the debtor received food, clothing and a pair of sandals once a year and no interest was charged during the period of labour. However, he had to devote himself exclusively to the service of his creditor (although the latter had no claim on his wife's or children's services), was neither allowed to work on his own account nor given any money and was entirely dependent upon his creditor, who could not, however, transfer his services to any other person.[46] In the 1920s and 1930s, khoti oppression came to be personified by such figures as Narsi Pethe of Devrukh, who, it is reported,

has been notorious for many years past as a troublesome landlord, exacting fines and penalties for every trifling incident in his village, for instance – so many annas for his permission to go to Bombay, etc.[47]

In various ways, therefore, the khots were able to influence the forms of exchange to enhance their command over labour. As the Ratnagiri khots were forced to compete for labour with urban and industrial employers, they at-tempted to tighten their grip upon it and restrict its mobility. In certain parts of the district, they were able to effect this more easily than in others. If the

---

[45] *Presidency Gazetteer*, X, 206. The practice of taking a day's labour each week was formally abolished in 1818, but in the late nineteenth century it was still 'doubted whether the system is entirely dead', see *ibid.*, X, 140, 206.

[46] *Ibid.*, X, 162–3.

[47] Daily Letter, District Magistrate, Ratnagiri District, 17 January 1932, in GOB, Home (Sp.) File 800 (73) (21) of 1932, MSA.

remittances of some migrant workers enabled their families to challenge the dominance of their creditors, the khots for their part were able to take advantage of larger remittances from service and professional employment to defend their position.[48] Where the khots were already powerful, remittances probably enabled them to consolidate further their dominant position within the political economy of the village. Workers from the same district migrated under different sets of pressures and constraints, which shaped their strategies in the city, whether at the workplace or in the neighbourhood, and sometimes registered differences between them.

It should not be supposed, however, that the khot's power passed entirely uncontested. The definition and consolidation of their rights was the product of several decades of negotiations and acrimonious conflicts with the colonial state. The khots had consolidated their power in the early years of British rule as revenue farmers,[49] and that the term was defined by Molesworth as a 'tribe' of Brahmins reflected the preponderance of that caste in their ranks.[50] In the 1820s, and again in 1860s and 1870s, the khots effectively resisted and indeed subverted attempts to survey their district and to extend the revenue settlements within them.[51] Faced with the threat of increasing state intervention, the khots resisted the revenue settlement with sufficient force to reduce the revenue collection substantially, and fearing a closer definition of their occupancy rights, they began to evict their tenants. By the 1880s, the khots had proved themselves indispensable to the revenue administration in Ratnagiri. They had also demonstrated their ability to mobilize allies within the Government of Bombay, orchestrate a wider political campaign in defence of their rights and enlist such prominent spokesmen as Vishvanath Narayan Mandlik. It was a measure of the success of their campaign that their rights were to a large extent safeguarded by the Khoti Act of 1880.[52]

Yet by the end of the decade, colonial officials were becoming increasingly convinced that they had been duped into transforming the khots, as the Collector of Ratnagiri put it in 1873, 'from the position of heavily assessed farmers of the land revenue to that of landlords'.[53] The official mind did not easily overcome its resentment at having been out-manoeuvred by clever Brahmins of dubious

---

[48] Johnson, 'Chitpavan Brahmins'; Seal, *Indian Nationalism*, pp. 84–92, 114–30; Patterson, 'Chitpavan Brahmins'.
[49] *Presidency Gazetteer*, X, 224.
[50] Candy, *Khoti Tenures*, p. 1.
[51] *Presidency Gazetteer*, X, 203–13; Charlesworth, *Peasants and Imperial Rule*, pp. 30–4, 56–60.
[52] Charlesworth, *Peasants and Imperial Rule*, pp. 56–60; N.V. Mandlik (ed.), *Writings and Speeches of the Late Honourable Rao Saheb Vishvanath Narayan Mandlik* (Bombay, 1896).
[53] Collector of Ratnagiri to Revenue Commissioner, Southern Division, No. A421, 10 March 1873, para. 13, GOB, Revenue, vol. 61 of 1875, No. 526, quoted by Charlesworth, *Peasants and Imperial Rule*, p. 60.

loyalty. Although, after 1880, the khots could not effectively be reduced to the status of village officials, they were subjected intermittently to considerable pressure by the Government of Bombay. Increasingly, in the late nineteenth century, it felt obliged to protect tenants on alienated lands and under overlord tenures. Accordingly, in 1904, the Khoti Settlement Act enabled tenants to commute their rents from kind into cash at rates to be fixed under official supervision.[54] Its effect was believed by officials to be largely beneficial to the tenants and to lower the burden of rent which they carried. By the 1920s, the settlement report on Khed taluka claimed that the prices of primary products had risen faster than rents, which had been fixed in 1904 in a period of relatively depressed prices.[55] It is unlikely, however, that the khots consistently suffered in the early twentieth century at the expense of their tenants. For the demographic pressure on land probably enabled khots to raise their rent demands and increase their exactions, particularly in the coastal regions.[56]

If the colonial state challenged the pretensions of khoti landlords, their tenants also offered significant resistance. Acute social tensions were observed in the district in the late nineteenth century and by 1890 the Govenor of Bombay believed that Ratnagiri was 'ripe for a serious agitation, which may need the employment of troops'.[57] At first, the commutation to cash rents under the Khoti Settlement Act of 1904 was held by officials to have lessened the tensions. But tenants' movements did not wither away. In the late 1920s, it was found that,

owing to the tension between the tenants and the khots in Northern Division of this district, the khots in places find it difficult to secure an adequate number of labourers to work on their fields.[58]

In fact, the Government of Bombay, always more receptive to complaints against khots than many other dominant groups, were induced by tenants' agitation to institute an inquiry into their conditions and found reason to sympathize with their plight.[59] The means by which tenants might resist their landlord's tyrannies are suggested by a meeting convened in Guhagar Mahal in September, 1993, attended by the kunbis of the surrounding areas, to consider

---

[54] Charlesworth, *Peasants and Imperial Rule*, p. 188.
[55] *Papers Relating to the Second Revision Settlement of the Khed Taluka of the Ratnagiri District*, by R.G. Gordon, *Selections*, N.S., no. 627 (Bombay, 1929), para. 16.
[56] Charlesworth, *Peasants and Imperial Rule*, pp. 273–4.
[57] Lord Harris to Lord Cross, 25 May 1890, Harris Papers, IOR. Cited by Charlesworth, *Peasants and Imperial Rule*, p. 273.
[58] *RCLI, Evidence, Bombay Presidency*, Mr W.B. Gilligan, ICS, Collector of Ratnagiri, I, i, 217.
[59] Report on an Enquiry into the Alleged Grievances of Tenants in the Districts of Ratnagiri and Kolaba by L.J. Mountford, Resolution no. L.C. 2083, 21 July 1926, GOB, Revenue Department Proceedings, July 1926, vol. 11540, 405–20, IOR.

'how the Brahmin Khots could be suitably troubled'. It was resolved that the
women would refuse to grind and husk for the khots, while 'none of the men
should do any field work for them'. Finally, the convenors, two Muslim
cultivators, Jaffar Shaikh Daud Rumane and Isak Muhammad Abbas Rumane,
'advised the tenants not to pay khoti dues without their permission'.[60] But
tenants' resistance could sometimes take a more vengeful and violent form.
The notorious Narsi Pethe of Devrukh, for instance, was beaten to death by
a mob of kunbis in 1932. The District Magistrate had warned him of 'the
probable consequences of his tyranny'. But Pethe had 'even then ... continued his oppression', although he had also taken the precaution of engaging
'a number of Gurkha protectors'. Eventually, in 1932, 'a plot was hatched
in Bombay to do away with this village bully and rack-renting landlord'.
About twenty kunbis, helped by three or four 'stranger Muslims', stormed
his house. Pethe fired a shot, but 'his wife prevented him from firing further'.
She was 'severely beaten' and their young daughter received a blow 'as she
was following them dragging away the body of her father'. Some property
was taken away, perhaps to compensate his attackers for previous exactions,
but more crucially, 'all papers and documents were burnt'. The District
Magistrate did not grieve for Pethe: 'very little sympathy can be felt for him',
he noted sternly.[61] In the following weeks, the murder of Narsi Pethe
unleashed widespread panic among local landlords so that, the District
Magistrate complained, 'the khoti element in the District have been pestering
me for protection'.[62]

In Ratnagiri, the 'non-Brahmin movement' most readily took the form of an
anti-khot agitation. This did not, however, dissolve the divisions between
non-Brahmins or forge solidarities across them. The temple entry campaigns in
this district demonstrated that

The bulk of the population, consisting of kunbis and Mahrattas, have no intention of
mixing with untouchables, and they can boycott the Mahars at any time in their villages,
if entry were sought by them. Dr Ambedkar has already estranged the feelings between
the two parties by advising the Mahars not to skin carcasses, not to eat dead meat etc.,
and the others have retaliated by refusing to pay Baluta in cash or kind.[63]

In the late 1930s, Ambedkar's bill, introduced to the provincial legislature, for
the abolition of the khoti system exacerbated prevailing tensions. Kunbis and

[60] Weekly Letter, District Magistrate, Ratnagiri, 21 September 1933, GOB, Home (Sp.) File 800
(74) (21) of 1932–34, 176, MSA.
[61] Daily Letter, District Magistrate, Ratnagiri, 17 January 1932, in GOB, Home (Sp.) File 800 (73)
(21) of 1932, MSA.
[62] Daily Letter, District Magistrate, Ratnagiri, 16 February 1932, in *ibid.*, MSA.
[63] Weekly Letter, District Magistrate, Ratnagiri, 4 October 1932, in GOB, Home (Sp.), File 800
(74) (21) of 1932–34, p. 79, MSA.

Mahars seemed willing to accept 'any advice that would go to absolve them from their liabilities to khots, land-lords and Sawkars'.[64] From Guhagar Peta came reports that 'tenants are not paying the dues of khots under the impression that Dr Ambedkar's bill would exempt them from payment'.[65] By May, 1938, it appeared in Ratnagiri that,

the agrarian problem in this district is assuming increasing importance owing to the continuous anti-khot agitation carried on by the members of the Independent Labour Party, particularly in the North Sub-Division of the District.[66]

The Government of Bombay was prepared to let the anti-khot agitation take its course, with a Congress ministry in power in the province. 'It is generally agreed', noted the Secretary to the Home Department, 'that the Khoti System is an anachronism and the sooner it can be got rid of the better for the District.' The Government planned to institute another committee to inquire into the grievances of khoti tenants and concluded, therefore, that it would be 'more politic to obtain the co-operation of those who are working for the same ends instead of antagonizing them'.[67] In 1938 and 1939, there were frequent reports of 'intense feelings' between landlords and tenants, vociferous and angry meetings and assaults by Mahars on Brahmin or bania khots.[68] Occasional evidence suggests participation in these events by millworkers from Bombay, some while on leave and intending to return to the city.[69]

The consequence just as in part the cause of the deepening agrarian crisis in Ratnagiri was its growing dependence upon Bombay. The *Gazetteer* claimed in 1880 that 'the teeming population of Ratnagiri has been one of the chief factors in the development of Bombay city'.[70] But it would have been more accurate to say that it was the growth of Bombay City which had enabled its survival. About 40 per cent of Ratnagiri's population sought work in Bombay and about two-thirds of its emigrant population in the city was aged between fifteen and forty years.[71] This pattern of migration revealed remarkable continuities. A later study of the district reported,[72]

It is very difficult to find a young a male who is between 18 and 25 years in the village.

[64] District Magistrate, Ratnagiri to Secretary GOB, Home (Sp.), 12 January 1938, GOB Home (Sp.) File 927-A of 1938, p. 3, MSA.
[65] Weekly Confidential Report, District Magistrate, Ratnagiri, 14 January 1938, *ibid.*, p. 8, MSA.
[66] District Magistrate, Ratnagiri to Secretary, GOB, Home (Sp.), 30 May 1938, *ibid.*, p. 193, MSA.
[67] Note by Secretary, GOB, Home (Sp.), 21 June 1938, *ibid.*, p. 275, MSA.
[68] GOB, Home (Sp.) File 927-A Part I of 1939, MSA.
[69] Report by District Superintendent of Police, Ratnagiri, Report no. 75, 25 May 1938, GOB Home (Sp.) File 927-A Part I of 1939, p. 41, MSA.
[70] *Presidency Gazetteer*, X, 106.
[71] *RCAI, Evidence, Bombay Presidency*, II, 2, 425; *Census, 1921*, IX, i, 19–20.
[72] Patel, *Rural Labour*, pp. 15–16.

A young man says there [in the village] if he has not yet got a job in the city ... Most of those remaining in the villages are either retired or unfit for industrial employment in the city.

The bulk of Ratnagiri's population was becoming increasingly dependent upon the remittance of cash earnings outside the district for their subsistence.

The Deccan

The agrarian structure, tenurial forms and social relations in Ratnagiri were not by any means representative of the Presidency as a whole. Unlike the khots of the Konkan, the pretensions of inam and jagir holders in the Deccan were knocked flat by the early British administrators and, despite their caution, they effectively circumscribed the powers of the village officers as well.[73] But whatever the specificities of social, economic and institutional change in the Deccan, the later nineteenth and twentieth centuries witnessed a growing number of smallholders being forced on to the labour market. The impoverishment of the Deccan smallholder was perhaps less the outcome of any sudden or dramatic process of capital accumulation than the long-term stagnation of the agrarian economy.

Rising prices, wider markets and reduced revenue assessments were believed to have increased rural stratification and facilitated the emergence of a rich peasantry. Recent research has, however, severely qualified this view. Although the cotton boom in the 1860s stimulated the widespread cultivation of the crop, the following decade witnessed its contraction into the tracts where it had been grown most successfully two decades earlier. The 1880s and 1890s witnessed a substantial expansion of commodity production. Compared to South Gujarat[74] or the Karnataka districts of Belgaum and Dharwar,[75] its advance in the Deccan was modest and largely confined to particular areas: Khandesh, reclaimed from jungle and waste, and converted into a flourishing cotton belt; the rich soils of the Krishna Valley and the canal zones of Satara, Ahmednagar and Poona. Specialization in the production of cash crops stimulated exchange and increased the demand for foodgrains, which in earlier times would have been grown almost exclusively for subsistence, while better and cheaper transport

[73] Charlesworth, *Peasants and Imperial Rule*, ch. 2; K. Ballhatchet, *Social Policy and Social Change in Western India 1817–1830* (Oxford, 1957); Kumar, *Western India*; G.G. Kotovsky, 'Agrarian Relations in Maharashtra in Late 19th and Early 20th Centuries', in I.M. Reisner and N.M. Goldberg (eds.), *Tilak and the Struggle for Indian Freedom* (New Delhi, 1966), pp. 99–119; Stokes, 'Privileged Land Tenure', in Stokes, *The Peasant and the Raj*, 51–4.
[74] M.B. Desai, *The Rural Economy of Gujarat* (Oxford, 1948); J.B. Shukla, *Life and Labour in a South Gujarat Village* (Calcutta, 1937); Breman, *Patronage and Exploitation*.
[75] W. Walter, *History of the Culture and Manufacture of Cotton in Dharwar District* (London, 1877); R.D. Choksey, *Economy Life in the Bombay Karnataka 1818–1939* (Bombay, 1963).

made them more profitable to sell.[76] Outside the more prosperous districts, and these were few in the Deccan, commercialization appears to have proceeded rather sluggishly in the Bombay Presidency.[77] Recent calculations suggest that the cultivated area stagnated in the last three decades of the nineteenth century while, contrary to an earlier view favouring rising output, the early twentieth century now appears as a period of '*exceptional stagnation*' or even decline in the gross cultivated area in the Bombay Presidency as a whole.[78] In the Deccan alone, population increased by 27.5 per cent between 1891 and 1941 while the cropped area expanded by a mere 6.6 per cent.[79] Whereas population continued to rise, 'the great increase in the area of cultivation ... had taken place before 1885'.[80] In the 1920s, the population increased almost twice as rapidly as the gross cultivated acreage.[81] At the same time, the quality of agriculture was probably deteriorating. The expansion of commodity production occurred when cultivation had reached its land frontier in the Deccan. The loss of plough cattle in the famines of 1876–8 and the late 1890s was considerable and it was only slowly replaced, while the quality of the stock almost certainly deteriorated. The ratio of cattle power to cultivated area remained stagnant between the 1870s and the 1940s.[82] The evidence for yields has been notoriously shaky and its interpretation fraught with controversy; but the recent consensus suggests stagnation and possible decline.[83] Moreover, the growth of acreage was taking cultivation on to marginal lands and in some areas, there is evidence of significant soil deterioration.[84] Not surprisingly, this stagnant smallholding subsistence agriculture did not attract substantial capital investment. Whatever the absolute increase in the number of carts or wells, per capita ownership of these resources was meagre.[85] The growth of cash-crop cultivation and the

[76] Guha, *Agrarian Economy of the Bombay Deccan*, p. 189.
[77] S.C. Mishra, 'Commercialization, Peasant Differentiation and Merchant Capital in Late Nineteenth Century Bombay and Punjab', *Journal of Peasant Studies*, X, 1 (1982), 10–21; Guha, *Agrarian Economy of the Bombay Deccan*, pp. 125–60.
[78] Mishra, 'Agricultural Trends', 737. See also Guha, *Agrarian Economy of the Deccan*, ch. 4, especially pp. 86–7 and footnote 4. S. Krishnamurty, 'Agriculture in the Bombay Deccan, 1880–1922: Trends in Area and Output', in *Oxford University Papers on India*, edited by N.J. Allen, R.F. Gombrich, T. Raychaudhuri and G. Rizvi (Delhi, 1987), vol. I, part 2, p. 126–51. The optimistic case was made by N. Charlesworth, 'Trends in the Agricultural Performance of an Indian Province: The Bombay Presidency, 1900–1920', in Chaudhuri and Dewey (eds.), *Economy and Society*, pp. 113–40 and Charlesworth, *Peasants and Imperial Rule*, pp. 142–55, 162–225.
[79] Guha, *Agrarian Economy of the Bombay Deccan*, p. 87.
[80] G. Keatinge, *Agricultural Progress in Western India* (London, 1921), p. 44.
[81] Charlesworth, 'Agricultural Performance', pp. 134–5.
[82] *Ibid.*, p. 87; Mishra, 'Commercialization, Peasant Differentiation and Merchant Capital', 25.
[83] Mishra, 'Agricultural Trends', 744–51; Guha, *Agrarian Economy of the Bombay Deccan*, pp. 85–119; Krishnamurty, 'Agriculture in the Bombay Deccan'; Prakash, 'Agrarian Economy of Gujarat'.
[84] Guha, *Agrarian Economy of the Bombay Deccan*, pp. 121–4.
[85] Charlesworth, *Peasants and Imperial Rule*, pp. 165–74.

expansion of trade in agrarian produce under these conditions was likely to facilitate the increasing subordination of the small peasantry to capital. For capital, buoyant prices and demand stimulated the market for land and made control over its produce more attractive. On the other hand, as Harold Mann told the Linlithgow Commission,[86]

I do not think that the conditions of living in the Deccan have materially improved ... I do not think that the standard of life is materially higher than it was 20 years ago.

Demographic pressures thus acted upon the Deccan within this context of stagnation, and by the early twentieth century the fragmentation and subdivision of holdings were markedly increasing. In Pimpla Soudagar, in the vicinity of Poona, the average holdings had shrunk from about fourteen acres in the mid nineteenth century to less than five acres by 1914–15, while 156 holdings were broken up into 718 plots, some no larger than 0.05 acres.[87] In the Central Division, as a whole, which covered the Deccan, the proportion of holdings less than five acres in size increased from 12.73 per cent in 1904–5 to 37.44 per cent in 1916–17 and those less than twenty-five acres from 59.40 per cent to 82.5 per cent over the same period.[88] By the mid 1920s, as Harold Mann informed the Linlithgow Commission, 48 per cent of the holdings in the Presidency were smaller than five acres and another 40 per cent were between five and twenty-five acres. These holdings, 88 per cent of the total, covered 13.8 per cent of the total cultivated area, while the remaining 12 per cent commanded 86.2 per cent of the land.[89] Yet very few holdings in the Presidency below twenty-five acres, it was thought, 'can be said to be "economic" '. In 1916–17, one and a half million holdings were believed to be 'uneconomic'. But this estimate was probably modest. In the Central Division alone, more than seven and a half million holdings were smaller than twenty-five acres. The economic stagnation of the Deccan had bitten so deeply into its agrarian structure that 'the unchecked working of the process for thirty or forty years longer would make land in this Presidency the heritage of a pauper peasantry'.[90]

[86] *RCAI, Evidence*, Bombay, H.H. Mann, Director of Agriculture, Bombay Presidency, II, i, paras. 3171–2. Similarly Charlesworth who has made the case for increased agricultural output in early-twentieth-century Bombay noted that 'the poorer peasants, especially in the central and east Deccan, had hardly increased their living standards'. N. Charlesworth, 'Rich Peasants and Poor Peasants in Late Nineteenth Century Maharashtra', in Dewey and Hopkins (eds.), *The Imperial Impact*, p. 111.

[87] H.H. Mann, *Land and Labour in a Deccan Village*, no. 1 (London, 1917), pp. 45–7.

[88] Note by Deputy Secretary, GOB, Revenue, 'Proposals to check excessive sub-division and fragmentation of holdings', Bombay Revenue Proceedings, vol. 11330, February 1923, 70, IOR. See table 13.

[89] *RCAI, Evidence, Bombay*, H.H. Mann, Director of Agriculture, Bombay Presidency, II, i, paras. 3504–11.

[90] Note by Deputy Secretary, GOB, Revenue, 'Proposals to check excessive sub-division and fragmentation of holdings', Bombay Revenue Proceedings, vol. 11330, February 1923, p. 71, IOR.

Table 13. *Size of holdings in the Central Division*

Holdings	1904–5	1916–7
Under and up to 5 acres	62,129	342,089
Over 5 and up to 25 acres	232,592	411,795
Over 25 and up to 100 acres	173,775	146,551
Over 100 and up to 500 acres	19,148	12,946
Over 500 acres	250	428
Total	487,894	913,809

Source: Bombay Revenue Proceedings, Vol. 11330, February 1923, p. 70, IOR.

Underlying the shrinking size of holdings was an even more fundamental problem:

Leaving aside all questions of the economic holding capable of supporting a family, it will readily be conceded that land held on these absurd lines cannot be profitably cultivated. In some cases, it can hardly be cultivated at all.[91]

For a sizeable proportion of Deccan smallholders, therefore, the increased pressure of population coincided with the weakening of their own control over the land and its produce. The amelioration of these pressures demanded policies which the colonial state could scarcely contemplate on political grounds alone. The only means by which these holdings could be made economically stable, officials believed, was by 'the driving away of a large mass of population into the ranks of labour'. When allowances were made for natural increase, this would mean that 'a very large proportion of the population would have to be converted from landholders into casual labourers. It is needless to point out the social, economic and political evils of a large landless proletariat suddenly called into being whom industry cannot absorb'. In any case, it would prove impossible to devise the legislative measures to effect these changes which would also 'be accepted by the people'. Another alternative, the Revenue Department pointed out, was to consolidate scattered fragments into compact, larger and economic blocks. But this would mean 'wholesale "restripping" and a complete redistribution of most of the land in the Presidency. Such a measure is outside the range of practical politics'.[92]

Migration, whether seasonal or long-term, became essential for the subsistence of a growing number of tenants and smallholders. In the Man taluka of

[91] *Ibid.*, p. 71, IOR.
[92] *Ibid.*, pp. 72–3.

Satara district, more 'a grazing ground rather than a tract for tillage' and in the Dongri village, where 'the people are proverbially poor and always look more or less emaciated',[93] many of them forced to live 'for two or three months in the year on roots and other forest produce',[94] it was again not that migration to Bombay transformed their condition but that it enabled them to survive.

Gujarat

The close historical connections between the flourishing Gujarat hinterland and the commercial development of Bombay ensured that its districts were strongly represented among the city's population. The relatively barren tracts of Cutch and Kathiawar accounted for the predominant share of migrants from the region, but significant numbers also came from the prosperous districts of South Gujarat. Like the Khandesh districts of the Deccan, South Gujarat provided the typical conditions for the emergence of an independent peasantry out of the general mass of smallholding households. Although population grew rapidly in the second half of the nineteenth century, the gross cropped area increased even faster and the cultivation of cash crops expanded marginally at the expense of foodgrains. The favourable land–man ratio combined with the strength of the customary rights of tenants and restrictions on sales in co-parcenary villages to depress rentals. Smallholding households working with fragmented strips could consolidate their holdings by leasing-in land and participate to some extent in the general prosperity. Low rentals, fertile soils and buoyant markets allowed smallholders, accepting lower returns on family labour, to survive and prosper, whereas their counterparts in the Deccan would have needed large holdings, often beyond the resources of a household to manage, in order to remain solvent or even largely independent of their creditor.[95]

In the early 1850s, Alexander Mackay had found that in general the cultivator, even in the favoured district of Broach, 'makes little, if anything, *beyond the wages of a labourer*' and in bad years 'the cultivating population' as a whole '*lived upon remissions*'.[96] After the revenues and 'the interest due by him to the money-lender were paid, Mackay observed, 'the cultivator has nothing left him beyond the wages of a labourer'.[97] By 1900, a substantial number of peasants were able to assert their independence of the moneylender.[98] But the rise of an

[93] Mann, *Statistical Atlas*, p. 111.
[94] Lawrence, *Statistical Atlas*, p. 27.
[95] Prakash, 'Agrarian Economy in Gujarat'.
[96] Mackay, *Western India*, pp. 132–3.
[97] *Ibid.*, p. 135.
[98] Prakash, 'Agrarian Economy in Gujarat'. On Khandesh, see Banaji, 'Capitalist Domination and the Small Peasantry', pp. 1377–9 and Guha, *Agrarian Economy of the Deccan*, pp. 129–32.

independent peasantry did not dissolve the dependencies of labour. The poor cultivators continued to part with their produce as repayment for their loans and received from the bania the means of their subsistence.[99] In Broach, it was estimated, about 20 per cent of the population cultivated on these terms, which turned the ties of debt into the bonds of labour.[100] The disintegration of the hali system, by which labour was formally tied, swelled the supply of labour. Inflation had raised the costs for landlords of engaging their halis on a permanent basis and they found the labour force increasingly difficult to manage. At the same time, the decline of sugar-cane cultivation rapidly diminished the need for permanent agricultural labour. The cultivation of cotton and garden crops, especially mangoes, required a large seasonal labour force which was more economically hired according to need. The emergence of a 'free' market was integral to a wider strategy for cheapening labour and for reducing its customary claims on the employer. In the long run, it probably served to reduce the bargaining power of Dublas and agrarian labourers in general and thereby facilitated their increasing subjection to capital and its disciplines.[101]

Such groups in rural Gujarat necessarily sought wage employment, sometimes in the towns, in order to survive, repay their debts or retain their dwarf-holdings. In the late nineteenth century, the revival of urban growth in Gujarat, after a period of contraction, and the development of the textile industry, primarily, though not exclusively located in Ahmedabad, created significant alternative employment opportunities.[102] Some Dublas migrated to Bombay City in the late nineteenth and early twentieth century. But, for most migrants, the towns of Gujarat must have offered cheaper and more accessible destinations. It is probable that Gujarati migration to Bombay was somewhat different in character to the 'streams' from Ratnagiri, the Deccan and the eastern United Provinces. Some migrated to the city within the firmly established and extensive networks of trade which had long connected Gujarat and Bombay. On the other hand, family, kinship and caste connections probably enabled Gujarati migrants particularly to find work, once they had arrived in Bombay, in the city's markets, warehouses and commercial offices dominated by Gujarati merchants. There were significant groups of skilled artisans, like wood-workers and carpenters from Kathiawar and Cutch, who were drawn to Bombay. Untouchable workers from the Dhed and Bhangi castes were employed in large numbers, mainly by the Bombay Municipal Corporation, as sweepers and scavengers. Many of them were regarded by the 1920s as 'permanent' residents in Bombay. As their contacts in the city spread, some were able to find work in

---

[99] *Presidency Gazetteer, Ahmedabad*, IV, 69–70; *ibid., Surat and Broach*, II, 452.
[100] *Ibid., Surat and Broach*, II, 452.
[101] Breman, *Patronage and Exploitation*, esp. pp. 68–79.
[102] *Ibid.*, p. 76.

the mills.[103] On the other hand, migrants with the strongest rural base and perhaps weaker social connections in Bombay probably preferred to work nearer home.

North India

The eastern districts of the United Provinces and west Bihar constituted the largest and most important region of labour migration in India,[104] but it remained of relatively little consequence in the composition of the Bombay labour force until the early twentieth century. The handloom-weaving industry, which had begun to decline as Lancashire goods flooded the Indian market in the early nineteenth century, was subjected to increasingly fierce competition from domestic mill manufactures in the last quarter of the century.[105] The decline of handloom weaving and artisanal production in general narrowed the range of employment opportunities available in the countryside. To a large extent, the flow of migration from these regions had been directed towards Calcutta, while indentured labour for plantations overseas constituted another important destination. Similarly, the demand for labour in the cotton mills of Kanpur and other North Indian towns drew an increasing number of migrants.[106] The increased volume of migration to Bombay coincided with and was stimulated by legislation to control and finally to abolish indentured labour.[107]

---

[103] RCLI, Evidence, Bombay Presidency, Mrs K. Wagh, Senior Lady Investigator, The Labour Office, Bombay, I, i, 191.

[104] L. Chakravarthy, 'Emergence of an Industrial Labour Force in a Dual Economy – British India 1880–1920', IESHR, XV, 3 (1978), 249–327; for a detailed district-level study, Yang, 'Peasants on the Move', 37–58.

[105] W. Hoey, A Monograph on Trade and Manufactures in North India (Lucknow, 1880); C.A. Silberrad, A Monograph on Cotton Fabrics Produced in the North-Western Provinces and Oudh (Allahabad, 1898); A.K. Bagchi, 'De-Industrialization in Gangetic Bihar, 1809–1901', in B. De (ed.), Essays in Honour of Professor S.C. Sarkar (Delhi, 1976), pp. 499–522; A.K. Bagchi, 'De-industrialization in India in the Nineteenth Century: Some Theoretical Implications', Journal of Development Studies, XII, 2 (1976), 135–64; for an alternative view, see A.M. Vicziany, 'The De-industrialization in India in the Nineteenth Century: A Methodological Critique of Amiya Kumar Bagchi', IESHR, XVI, 2 (1979), 105–46; A.K. Bagchi, 'A Reply' IESHR, XVI, 2 (1979), 147–61; J. Krishnamurty, 'De-Industrialization in Gangetic Bihar during the Nineteenth Century: Another Look at the Evidence', IESHR, XXII, 4 (1985), 399–416; P.C. Joshi, 'The Decline of Indigenous Handicrafts in Uttar Pradesh', IESHR, I, 1 (1963), 24–35; G. Pandey, 'Economic Dislocation in Nineteenth-Century Eastern Uttar Pradesh: Some Implications of the Decline of Artisanal Industry in Colonial India', in P. Robb (ed.), Rural South Asia: Linkages, Change and Development (London, 1983), pp. 89–129; M. Twomey, 'Employment in Nineteenth Century Indian Textiles', Explorations in Economic History, XX, 1 (1983), 37–57.

[106] Joshi, 'Kanpur Textile Labour', 1823–38; Bayly, Rulers, Townsmen and Bazaars, pp. 440–9.

[107] Tinker, A New System of Slavery; Chakravarthy, 'Industrial Labour Force in Dual Economy', 249–327.

In the Deccan, legislation to govern the operation of rural credit resulted in lenders converting their customers' burden of debt into the obligations of rent, while the law neither recognized nor protected tenants. In the United Provinces, legislative intervention took the form of rent control and tenants' rights rather than debtors' wrongs. Rising prices, the switch from produce to cash rents and the general expansion of cash crops from the later nineteenth century worked in favour of occupancy tenants. But the gains of the occupancy tenants were by no means evenly distributed. The combination of expanding population and a stagnant economy had also begun to manifest itself in the eastern United Provinces from the 1860s.[108] Thus, while those who depended upon agricultural profits made some gains at the expense of those who lived by rent-receiving, 'the strongest influence at work', wrote Stokes,

was the increase in the rural proletariat. The myth of the rise of the landless labourer has helped to obscure the fact that only a very small minority of the rural population was without cultivating rights of some kind, even though such plots were hopelessly inadequate without another source of livelihood.[109]

Although the Ahirs and Kurmis of the United Provinces had travelled a different route, they arrived at the same destination and by the same means as their Kunbi counterparts of the Deccan.

These regions from which Bombay drew the bulk of its labour force shared characteristics which were widely manifested in the Indian countryside in the late nineteenth and early twentieth centuries. Rising prices, improved communications and expanding markets in the context of structural stagnation enabled mercantile capital to appropriate a larger share of the surplus. For many peasant households, outside the most successful areas of commercial agriculture, or within them, lacking the means or the luck to exploit the widening market opportunities, these conditions entailed an increasing reliance upon credit to meet their revenue obligations, the cost of seed or even the price of their own subsistence. Some households were further indebted beyond their ability to repay their loans. They depended upon borrowing for a part of their means of subsistence and production yet essentially retained in good times some measure of control over their own labour and its product. In times of famine or following a succession of poor harvests, these households could become wholly dependent for their subsistence as well as for the means of production upon the creditor. In effect, peasants in these circumstances became less the debtors than the wage labourers of the money-lender. Their decisions about cropping patterns would

---

[108] Stokes, 'Landholding' and 'Dynamism and Enervation in North Indian Agriculture: The Historical Dimension', in *The Peasant and The Raj*, pp. 205–7, 228–42; Bayly, *Rulers, Townsmen and Bazaars*, pp. 431–2.

[109] Stokes, 'Landholdings', p. 221.

often be determined by the money-lender. They were frequently committed to disposing of their produce in repayment of debt and dependent upon allowances of grain for subsistence. Their loans were little different from advances for their produce. Many peasant households in this predicament sent members away to earn cash through wage labour in agriculture or cash cropping tracts or even in the towns. The fact that many of these smallholding peasants held onto their plots disguises the real extent of their subordination to capital.

Thus the *Satara Gazetteer* distinguished between four categories of cultivators: those who were 'well-off' and 'occasionally led small sums to the poor husbandmen of their village'; those who 'are generally in need of no loans for food or seed, but they often borrow to pay the Government assessment and to meet the extraordinary expenses of marriage and other family events'; those who have to 'borrow for food as well as to pay the Government assessment' and were particularly vulnerable to poor seasons; and the rest who were 'badly off during the greater part of the year. Besides tilling small plots of land, they work as field labourers.'[110] Although the apparent buoyancy and 'commercialization' of the late nineteenth century enabled mercantile capital to increase its domination over the small peasant household, it is significant that it did not transform its labour process or the nature of production relations. The weakness of capital and the reduction of its functions to usury and petty trade in the nineteenth century blunted the thrust of accumulation and set firm limits to the expropriation of small peasant households. Migration to wage employment in Bombay constituted one of the strategies by which the latter struggled to maintain their holdings even as they shrank below the level which yielded a minimal standard of subsistence.

The rural connection

It would be misleading to assume that the Bombay labour force was recruited from a single composite class of rural proletarians. For the poorest sections of rural society, the risks of migration could appear overwhelming. Moreover, their mobility was sometimes restricted by debts or labour mortgages. For those who lacked contacts in Bombay, migration was expensive and it could prove ruinous. Those who had no friends or relatives already established in the city found it difficult to obtain work, credit to tide them over until they did so or a place to live. In addition, they paid higher interest rates and rents as well as larger commissions to the jobber.[111] If the irregularity and uncertainty of work

[110] *Presidency Gazetteer, Satara*, XIX, 185. Also cited by Banaji, 'Capitalist Domination and the Small Peasantry', 1395.
[111] Proceedings of the TLIC, Main Inquiry, Oral Evidence, Cotton Mill Workers, Bombay, Spinning Side, File 60-A, pp. 992, 985, MSA.

Table 14. *Percentage of the population of Bombay City and of millworkers born in the city*

Year	Percentage of persons born in Bombay to total population	Percentage of millworkers born in Bombay to total population
1872	31.1	—
1901	23.4	—
1911	19.6	10.92
1921	16.0	18.87
1931	24.6	26.33

Source: RCLI, Evidence, Bombay, GOB 'Conditions of Industrial Labour', I, i, 3; Morris, *Industrial Labour Force*, p. 65, Table VIII.

in Bombay made it essential to establish and develop contacts in the city, it also rendered the village base indispensable. Most urban workers held on to their ancestral plot, village rights and family connections when they migrated to the city and remitted their cash earnings to defend, maintain and occasionally enhance their rural base.

On the other hand, rural smallholders and the village resources of Bombay's workers came under increasing pressure in the twentieth century. The available evidence appears to suggest that the proportion of workers in Bombay who possessed lands in their villages was declining over the same period. As early as 1911, the Census Commissioners estimated that 75 per cent of the 'coolies', 66 per cent of the cartmen and 30 per cent of the millhands were periodic migrants to the city. They also enumerated a wide range of occupational groups, associated closely with migrants from particular districts: clerks and domestic servants from Kathiawar and Surat, millhands from Satara, Kolaba and Pune, artisans from Kathiawar and Pune, leather workers from Satara and Pune, scavengers from Kathiawar, among whom many 'have completely lost touch with their homes and it is only a question of time before they sever their connection altogether with the district of their birth'.[112] Whereas the proportion of millworkers who were born in Bombay rose substantially between 1911 and 1931, the same ratio for the entire population declined steadily between 1872 and 1921 and, although it rose once again in the following decade, it remained below that calculated for the millworkers (see table 14). Millworkers, it appeared, were relatively more urbanized than other occupational groups in Bombay. In 1929, a former mill manager estimated that about 40 per cent of the city's millworkers had no interest in agriculture, while of the rest, a substantial number, 'have made Bombay their home had though they retained their

[112] *Census, 1911*, VII, i, 45.

connections with their native towns, most of them have ceased to be agricultur-ists themselves'.[113] In 1946, one inquiry reported, only 45 per cent of its sample of workers possessed some land in the village, and most of those men reported that their land was being worked by relatives or others.[114]

Few of these estimates, however, are unproblematic or indeed comparable. Their methods of investigation, as well as their categories and their definitions varied. Their accuracy cannot be taken for granted. To some extent, the ambiguity was inherent in the situation itself. To be 'landless' was perfectly compatible with holding rights to a share of the crop; to have nothing to do with agriculture did not mean that their relatives did not cultivate the land or that they had no stake in the village at all. Such evidence need not, therefore, lead us to conclude that Bombay's workers progressively shed their rural connec-tions. The loss of the village base was more the outcome of rural distress than a function of its rejection by firmly rooted urban proletarians. On the contrary, Bombay's workers struggled actively to preserve their rural base and to resist its dissolution.

By examining the formation of a labour force in Bombay as if it was part of a serial process of 'urbanization', through which every society supposedly passes, historians and sociologists have ignored the choices which workers exercised in the pursuit of their own interests. Indeed, Harold Mann even emphasized 'the tendency ... for people to cultivate their own land, even if it means that their income is reduced', rather than subject themselves to the uncertainties of the labour market, whether rural or urban.[115] The intensity of this struggle to retain their rural base was reflected by the intensity of the fragmentation and subdivision of holdings in the twentieth century. In the early 1920s, revenue officials explained this phenomenon in terms

of the extreme attachment of the ryot to the land and the sentiment attached to the status of a landholder which makes him hold on to his minute patch of earth and pay assessment on it though its cultivation may not yield him any profit or even though he may not cultivate it at all.[116]

Behind such sentiment lay hard material imperatives. By holding on to the land, the ryot might emancipate himself from the vagaries of the labour market or at the very least retain his foothold in the village. For those who migrated to Bombay, the reasons to maintain this base were even greater.

[113] *RCLI, Evidence, Bombay Presidency*, Mr M.S. Bhumgara, I, i, 499.
[114] *Main Report of the Labour Investigation Committee* (Bombay, 1946), p. 70, cited by Morris, *Industrial Labour Force*, pp. 85–6, n. 6.
[115] *RCAI, Evidence, Bombay*, H.H. Mann, Director of Agriculture, Bombay Presidency, II, i, para. 3173.
[116] Note by Deputy Secretary, GOB, Revenue, 'Proposals to check excessive fragmentation...', Bombay Revenue Proceedings, vol. 11330, February 1923, p. 65, IOR.

As Patel observed in her study of Ratnagiri in the 1960s, village property was 'an invaluable security in times of unemployment, severe economic distress, old age and the like'. A small plot or even simply a house 'becomes the last resort for him [the migrant worker] and his family in difficult times. He comes to Bombay to earn but keeps his sheet-anchor in the village.'[117] Even if its direct economic utility was diminishing, a village base could form the hub of wider contacts, associations and networks of moral support and material provision, which were invaluable in the urban and industrial setting.

In addition, considerations of status also influenced the migrant worker's ambition to retain a foothold in the village. 'The man who has land in the village', the Collector of West Khandesh noted, 'is in every way more respected than a mere tenant. If a man gets into trouble and he wants to prove he is respectable, the first thing he tells you is that he has land of his own in the village.'[118] Among low-caste groups, this factor assumed considerable importance. For Mahars in the Deccan, for example, it was imperative to secure their base in village society, even if this was sometimes only facilitated by their migration to wage employment and by the remittance of their cash earnings. Thus, the Mahar labourers of the Deccan, wrote Mann,

will rarely, if even, think of sacrificing their connections with the village where they hold vatan rights. To do this would make them landless outcasts and hence they return – many of them very frequently, but almost all at intervals – to the old home of the family.[119]

The maintenance of the village connection remained an enduring characteristic in the patterns of migration to Bombay City.

The gradual but perceptible shift within working-class families towards a growing dependence upon their urban sources of income was also accompanied by a long-term change from predominantly seasonal to relatively permanent migration. But this change is not easily discerned, for the terms 'seasonal' and 'permanent' were used rather ambiguously by contemporary observers. They did not distinguish too carefully between seasonal out-migration from the district for a few months each year and the return of workers to help with the harvest. Estimates of population movements often failed to separate those who were returning to Bombay after a brief visit to the village from those who went specifically in search of short-term or seasonal wage employment. Often they did not specify the destination of the migrant and, of course, never his purpose. What urban commentators called the 'annual exodus' from Bombay was often what was understood by rural observers as seasonal migration.

---

[117] Patel, *Rural Labour*, p. 37.
[118] *RCAI, Evidence, Bombay*, H.F. Knight, ICS, Collector of West Khandesh, II, i, para. 630.
[119] H.H. Mann, *The Social Framework of Agriculture: India, Middle East, England*, edited by D. Thorner (Bombay, 1967), p. 74.

Moreover, the pattern of migration varied not only between villages and districts but often between workers from the same district. The size of their holdings as well as their families influenced the timing and pattern of migration. Indeed, the relationship between the size of their holdings and their families determined not only the pressures upon their rural resources but also the availability of labour to cultivate their land. The nature and conditions of their employment in Bombay – whether they could leave their jobs and expect to regain them on their return from the village – affected their mobility between town and country. The cost and availability of transport also impinged upon their movements. For much of the period, the best form of transport from Ratnagiri was the steamer. Workers who went to their villages in the Konkan in April and May had to return before the monsoon broke and the steamer services were suspended. Railway construction greatly increased the mobility of workers from the Deccan and made Bombay more accessible to migrants from North India. The cost of transport made it uneconomical for workers to move frequently between their villages and Bombay and was an inducement, once they had returned, to stay for longer periods.[120] Similarly migrants from North India went back less often to their villages and were less able to lean upon the material resources of their rural base in periods of unemployment or industrial action than workers from Ratnagiri or the Deccan.[121]

By investigating the process of migration from the viewpoint of the rural district, outside the context of the urban labour market, it would be easy to suppose that migration was exclusively a seasonal phenomenon.[122] But it would also be misleading. Impressionistic evidence from the countryside tends to suggest that the overwhelming pattern of migration was seasonal. For instance, the *Gazetteer* estimated in the 1880s that about 100,000 people left Ratnagiri for Bombay in the fair season and returned to sow rice in time for the monsoon.[123] This figure was subsequently repeated by most official sources down to the 1930s.[124] It had obviously become the rough working estimate of officialdom and had long ceased to be, if it ever was, an accurate computation.

[120] D.R. Gadgil, *Regulation of Wages and Other Problems of Industrial Labour in India* (Poona, 1954), p. 75.

[121] *RCLI, Evidence, Bombay Presidency*, GOB, 'Conditions of Industrial Labour', I, i, 7.

[122] For a rural-based study which comes precisely to this conclusion, in the case of migration from Saran district in Bihar to Calcutta, see Yang, 'Peasants on the Move'. In fact, Yang adduces some evidence which would suggest 'recurring' or more 'permanent' patterns underlying the migration to Calcutta. Certainly, the Whitley Commission found that it was by no means usual for Calcutta workers to return to their villages in eastern United Provinces to help with the harvest. See *Report of the RCLI*, p. 14.

[123] *Presidency Gazetteer*, X, 106.

[124] Mann, *Statistical Atlas, 1925*, p. 143; *RCLI, Evidence, Bombay Presidency*, Mr W.B. Gilligan, ICS, Collector of Ratnagiri, I, i, 217.

The volume of seasonal migration to Bombay is very difficult to estimate; it is equally thankless to specify how far and in what ways it changed. Of course, there had been an annual influx of migrants from the surrounding countryside into Bombay since the seventeenth century. The floating population of the island, 'a mixture of most of the neighbouring countries, most of them fugitives and vagabonds' as Fryer described them,[125] was still estimated at 60,000 in the early nineteenth century.[126] In 1905, it was estimated that more than half a million seasonal migrants came to Bombay by coastal steamer alone.[127] On the eve of the First World War, the Settlement Commissioner estimated that 70,000 people left for Bombay from the ports of Ratnagiri taluka between October 1913 and May 1914.[128] The seasonal migration from Satara was estimated by the Divisional Commissioner of Poona at between 15 and 20 per cent of its population. Indeed, 'in any labour centre', he said in 1929,

a sprinkling of labour from Satara district would be found in almost any sphere of labour. As far as I know the conditions in this district, the people have got the peculiar knack of picking up any kind of ordinary labour and of adapting themselves to different surroundings and circumstances.[129]

Migration from the countryside to Bombay was not purely seasonal in character; on the other hand, patterns of seasonal migration were not simply dissolved by industrial development.

Moreover, throughout the inter-war period, the streams of migration remained highly sensitive to changes in the demand, and more slowly, and to a lesser extent, the supply conditions in the Bombay labour market. When, in 1909, the trade was brisk and even unskilled labour scarce, wages doubled in Bombay to a rupee per day. 'Such a [wage] rate can, however, remain only for a few days', it was said,

as it serves to swell rapidly the available supply from the almost limitless reserves of the Ghat villages, whence cultivators proceed in large numbers to Bombay to work for a few months and return with their savings to their villages, either at the Holi festival or at the commencement of the south-west monsoon.[130]

---

[125] Quoted in *Gazetteer*, I, 150–1.
[126] *Census, 1864*, p. ii.
[127] GOB, General, 1905, vol. XXIII, p. 195, MSA. These migrants probably came predominantly from Ratnagiri and Goa.
[128] *Papers ... Second Revision Settlement of the Ratnagiri Taluka* by J.A. Madan, *Selections*, N.S., no. 574, para. 39.
[129] *RCLI, Evidence, Bombay Presidency*, Mr J. Ghosal, ICS, Divisional Commissioner, Poona Division, I, i, 205. According to Mr Ghosal's estimate, this would have involved about 165,000 people; another estimate put the figure more modestly at 35,000. See Mann, *Statistical Atlas, 1925*, p. 111.
[130] *Imperial Gazetteer of India, Provincial Series, Bombay Presidency*, vol. I (Calcutta, 1908), p. 62.

Rural workers were alert to the fluctuations in the demand for labour not only in casual and unskilled occupations, but also in the cotton-textile industry. The pattern of boom and slump which characterized the history of the textile industry tended to create an excess supply of labour with some training and experience of work in the mills.[131] In the 1930s, mills intermittently employed night shifts for short spells to deal with a rush of orders in particular lines of production. This practice accentuated the volatility of the labour market. But as Maloney, the Secretary of the Millowners' Association, albeit exaggerating for once the smooth functioning of the labour market, explained:

Bombay is in a peculiar position. There is a very large supply of labour available in the Konkan and other various areas along the Coast ... When night shift is wanted, we draw additional men from these areas, and when night shifts are stopped, they go back to these areas ... They are regular [workers], but they seem to have dual occupations. They come to Bombay when work is put forward, otherwise go back and work with the agriculturists or other labourers in the villages in their own district.[132]

'Regular workers' with 'dual occupations', urban labourers dependent upon the countryside for a part of their livelihood, the oxymorons used to describe their movements, reflected the real ambiguity in the social economy of Bombay's workers who straddled the divide between town and country. At times when labour was scarce, in the early twentieth century, it had to be attracted by higher wages. By the 1930s, mounting demographic and economic pressures on the land combined with retrenchment in Bombay to tilt the balance against the workforce: now they came to the city when work was available but on increasingly unfavourable terms.

It was widely believed the rural migrants revealed a preference for casual, 'unskilled out-door labour'. This preference, it was held, stemmed from the fact that casual and seasonal wage employment was most readily adapted to the demands of cultivation. Peasants, it was said, preferred to work in construction, public works, the maintenance and working of the great irrigation and transport systems, building, quarrying, forest exploitation and mining. Industrial employment, on the country, 'necessitates their [the workers] remaining long enough in it to acquire a certain skill'.[133] It might be supposed, therefore, that employers who sought a regular supply of semi-skilled labour were forced to buy it out of the countryside. Of course, many migrant workers in these occupations worked in the countryside, and not in Bombay city at all. In addition, large numbers

---

[131] See chapters 3 and 7.
[132] Proceedings of the TLIC, Main Inquiry, Oral Evidence, The Bombay Millowners' Association, File 58-A, 328, MSA.
[133] Indian Revenue Proceedings, GOI, Commerce and Industry, 'Memorandum on Labour Conditions in India', enclosure in Dispatch no. 21, GOI to Secretary of State for India, 6 August 1919, L/E/3/150, IOR.

migrated from the Deccan to Khandesh and Berar for the cotton-picking season. The leading cash crops of the Deccan, cotton and sugar cane, were both labour intensive. Several mofussil industries processed these crops, notably the cotton-ginning and pressing mills and sugar refineries. These were seasonal industries, best suited to such a work preference. In the 1930s, the expansion of the cotton industry to Khandesh and the development of the sugar industry in Ahmednagar, Nasik and Poona also offered employment for rural labour. But it would be misleading to conclude that a distinct class of casual, seasonal workers, often associated with rural-based industries, could be clearly demarcated from a permanent industrial labour force or that some types of labour exclusively sought out casual employment.

First, casual and seasonal employment was poorly paid and often entailed appalling conditions of work, in trades which were usually not governed by the Factory Acts.[134] In Bombay, most worked in the casual trades because they could not avoid them. The low wages, intermittent employment and arduous toil which characterized these occupations did not enable workers to supplement the rural resources of their family economy. Second, if industrialists had to buy out their workforce, there is some evidence to support the view that wages for agricultural labour had been rising in the first three decades of the twentieth century, especially in districts directly affected by migration to Bombay.[135] Third, it is necessary to recall that the demand for labour itself was by no means permanent. It fluctuated substantially as employers took workers on and laid

---

[134] See *Report of the Commission Appointed to Consider the Working of Factories in the Bombay Presidency, 1888* (Bombay, 1888), p. 7. The Commissioners noted that in the ginning and pressing factories of Khandesh, men and women worked about $80\frac{1}{2}$ hours per week in the cold weather and 98 hours in the hot, and 'if artificial light is used, they may be worked day and night for days consecutively'. See also *ibid.*, evidence of Mr Rustamji Framji Wadia, p. 13, and Mr Thomas Drewett, pp. 14–15. See also *Report of the IFLC*. As late as 1939, the TLIC found, even in the protected cotton-textile industry, 'the employment of a considerable number of juveniles as adults in several Cotton Textile Mills in various centres in the province of Bombay, especially in Barsi and Gadag'. Not only were these workers not adults, but 'in many cases they should not have passed even as adolescents'. N.A. Mehrban, Secretary, TLIC, Town Hall, Bombay to the Commissioner of Labour, Bombay, no. 4967, 27 March 1939, Proceedings of the TLIC, 1938–40, File IX, MSA; see also Labour Office, Bombay, *General Wage Census, Part II, Seasonal Factories* (Bombay, 1935).

[135] *Papers Relating to the Second Revision Settlement of the Alibag Taluka of the Kolaba District*, by J.R. Hood, 30 April 1924, *Selections*, N.S., no. 632 (Bombay, 1929), para. 21; *Papers ... Settlement of the Panvel Taluka, including Uran Mahal of the Kolaba District* by J.R. Hood, 31 July 1922, *Selections*, N.S., no. 609 (Bombay, 1925), para. 22; *Papers ... Settlement of the Kalyan Taluka of the Thana District*, by M.J. Dikshit, 5 September 1923, *Selections*, N.S., no. 613 (Bombay, 1927), para. 48; *Papers ... Settlement of the Satara Taluka of the Satara District*, by H.D. Baskerville, 30 July 1923; *Selections*, N.S., no. 635 (Bombay, 1929), para. 68; *Papers ... Settlement of the Man Taluka of the Satara District*, by M. Webb, 2 March 1923, *Selections*, N.S., no. 634 (Bombay, 1929), para. 98; *Papers ... Settlement of the Patan Taluka of the Satara District*, by C.H. Bristow, 27 February 1925, *Selections*, N.S., no. 623 (Bombay,

them off as the market for their products required. These conditions helped to generate an excess supply of labour, even as agrarian scarcity pushed larger numbers to seek wage employment.

It became increasingly difficult in the early twentieth century for workers to balance their rural and their urban interests simply through seasonal migration to wage employment in Bombay. To obtain work in the face of a fluctuating demand for labour required a considerable commitment to the urban and industrial setting. Migrant workers had to entrench themselves within the social nexus of the workplace and the neighbourhood. They had to become known to jobbers, creditors and landlords. In these respects, the seasonal and the short-stay migrant remained at a disadvantage compared with relatively more perma-nent residents of the city. This did not apply to factory workers or the formal sector alone; it also affected the casual trades. Seasonal migration was becoming increasingly incompatible with the need to find work which would be suffi-ciently remunerative to facilitate adequate remittances to support the rural base. At the same time, the pattern of demand for labour was itself slowly changing, as industrial development called for a supply of labour more evenly distributed throughout the year.

The previous chapter showed how, by withdrawing their patronage, jobbers disciplined casual workers who failed to appear sufficiently regular at the mill gates.[136] This served to restrict the mobility of labour and narrow the options confronting migrant workers in Bombay. In 1935, the jobber's practice was formalized in the cotton-texttile industry by the decasualization or badli control scheme introduced by the Bombay Millowners' Association.[137] According to the scheme, each mill was to maintain a register of its own badli workers, who would have first claim on temporary employment. Ostensibly each badli was attached to and registered with one particular mill. Casual workers were

1928), paras 84–6; Papers … Settlement of the Mandangad Petha of the Ratnagiri District by R.G. Gordon, 4 July 1924, Selections, N.S., no. 619 (Bombay, 1928), para. 19; H.H. Mann, The Economic Progress of the Rural Areas in the Bombay Presidency (Bombay, 1924), p. 17; RCAI, Appendix to the Report (London, 1928), vol. XIV, p. 122. For recent works which draw different conclusions, see S. Krishnamurty, 'Real Wages of Agricultural Labourers in the Bombay Deccan, 1874–1922', IESHR, XXIV, 1 (1987), 81–98; Brahma Nand, 'Agricultural Labourers in Western India: A Study of the Central Division Districts of the Bombay Presidency During the Late Nineteenth and Early Twentieth Centuries', Studies in History, N.S., I, 2 (1985), 221–46. See also Guha, The Agrarian Economy of the Bombay Deccan, pp. 132–41.
136 See chapter 3 above.
137 BMOA, Annual Report, 1935, pp. 29, 150–1. R.C. James, 'Labour Mobility, Unemployment and Political Change: An Indian Case', Journal of Political Economy, LXVII, 6 (December, 1959), 545–57; R.C. James, 'The Casual Labour Problem in Indian Manufacturing', The Quarterly Journal of Economics, LXXIV, 1 (February, 1960), 100–16; Morris, Industrial Labour Force, pp. 138–41; C.A. Myers, Labour Problems in the Industrialization of India (Cambridge, Mass., 1958); Mazumdar, 'Labour Supply; pp. 477–96; Holmström, Industry and Inequality, pp. 181–309.

required to come to the mill every day, although they were by no means guaranteed employment. The attendance of the badli worker was recorded on his registration card. Badlis who did not appear at the mill gates every day were liable to be penalized in the distribution of work and only the most regular among them were promoted, when vacancies arose, to the permanent workforce. The pool of registered badlis was linked in 1936 to estimates of absenteeism on the day following the payment of wages. It was intended thereby to reduce the size of the casual labour force in the industry as well as the extent of labour mobility into the textile workforce. By limiting the pool of badlis, the scheme attempted to solve the problem of unemployment by the simple expedient of transferring it out of the industry.

The badli control scheme impinged upon the jobber's domain which rested on the deployment of casual labour. While it did not destroy the influence of the jobber, it may have modified the more arbitrary features of the prevailing system of labour recruitment.[138] By formally distinguishing between casual and permanent labour, the millowners were able to limit their liabilities and the workers' rights under an expanding legal framework, which incidentally offered labour greater security of tenure, some welfare entitlements from the employers and a measure of protection against unfair dismissal.[139]

But the problem of casual labour was scarcely resolved. Casual workers were retained as badlis for longer periods, not because fewer vacancies now arose but because employers were reluctant to confirm their employees in permanent posts.[140] The enforced dependence of casual labour upon its rural links persisted, but with one major difference: their movement between town and country was no longer negotiable. Since their elevation to permanent status depended upon the regularity with which they appeared at the mill gates, the badli control scheme complicated the casual labourer's option of returning to the village in periods of unemployment; yet by extending his spell as a 'substitute' worker, it increased his dependence upon his village connections.

---

[138] *Report of the TLIC*, II, *Final Report* (Bombay, 1953), 337–47, especially 338–40.
[139] *Ibid.*, II, 355–9; on the Payment of Wages Act, see GOB, General, 5773-D, Part I of 1924–38; File 5773-D, Part II of 1924–28 and File 5773-D, Part II of 1927, MSA; and *Labour Gazette*, XVI, 10 (June 1937), 760–3; *Labour Gazette*, XVI, 11 (July 1937), 846–50 and XVI, 12 (August 1937), 926–7; on the Bombay Industrial Disputes Act of 1938 which introduced some safeguards against unfair dismissal, but in general constituted anti-union legislation, which provoked a general strike in November 1938, see GOB Home (Sp.) Files 550 (25) III-A, 550 (24), 550 (25)-B, 550 (25)-III. See also Proceedings of the Bombay Disturbances Enquiry Committee, File 550 (25) III-B of 1938, MSA.
[140] On the development of a semi-permanent casual workforce in the 1940s and 1950s, see James, 'Labour Mobility, Unemployment and Political Change'. On the effect of the Port Trust's policies which created a privileged, permanent status, and in practice slowed down the rate of promotion from the casual workforce, see *RCLI, Evidence, Bombay Presidency*, the Bombay Port Trust, I, i, 461–4.

Employers in most trades effected through their policies a distinction between 'permanent' and 'temporary' labour. Some employers formalized the distinction between their permanent and temporary workers by granting some security of tenure and welfare benefits to the former. In the case of the Bombay Port Trust, for instance, permanent workers were granted paid leave and allowed to participate in the Provident Fund after three years' continuous service. But many workers returned to their village 'during or before the monsoon to attend to the cultivation of their fields or repairs to their homes in their native villages and rejoin afresh on their return to Bombay after an absence of two or three months'.[141] This period of absence could be taken to constitute a break in the continuity of service necessary to qualify for 'permanent' status. Thus, only those who could break their village ties, or those who had none which required their absence for more than the fourteen days' leave allowed each year, stood any chance of being admitted to the corps of permanent employees. Moreover, this was a useful means for the employers both to control entry into the permanent workforce and to enforce regular attendance and discipline upon casual labour. The Social Service League made the same point even more explicitly about the prevailing practices in the cotton-textile industry. When a worker

returns from his native village, he seeks employment of the same kind as he had before, and if possible, in the same mill or factory. Although in the absence of the system of granting long leave of absence to employees in mills the man is treated as a new hand when he returns to work.[142]

Having created these categories, employers often referred to the casual workforce as if their temporary status reflected not so much their insecurity of employment as their attitude of mind and their lack of commitment to the factory. 'Speaking generally' the Bombay Millowners' Association reported, 'the labour force may be said to be more or less permanent, allowing, of course, for badlis'.[143] Yet the category of badli or substitute worker was the product of their own pattern of labour use.

Certainly, casual workers in the city had to pay the most careful attention to their rural connections. The Bombay Electric Supply and Tramways Company reported that their casual, unskilled employees

usually take some leave, prior to, or at the beginning of the monsoon, chiefly to repair their houses in their native country, or to make agricultural preparations.[144]

---

[141] RCLI, Evidence, Bombay Presidency, The Bombay Port Trust, I, i, 461.
[142] Ibid., The Social Service League, I, i, 429.
[143] Ibid., BMOA, I, i, 386.
[144] Ibid., The Bombay Electric Supply and Tramways Company, I, i, 533.

While the Bombay Municipal Corporation claimed that there was no labour turnover among their permanent staff, they also reported that

the men on the temporary staff do not always continue in employment throughout the year. They generally go to their native places before the rains for tilling the fields and return at the end of the monsoon after gathering the harvest.[145]

The timing of the return of casual workers to their village was crucial. In some occupations, it was determined by the seasonal fluctuations of their trade, which might become impossible to ply during the monsoons. For many workers, it was dictated by the needs of agriculture. They returned to their village when their labour was most urgently required for the harvest or for the sowing and tilling of the fields. Yet this often coincided with the 'annual exodus' of Bombay's workers, which was the period when casual workers could most easily find 'permanent' work in the city. That they could be drawn away to the village when their chances of entrenching themselves within the urban labour market and capturing a permanent place in the workforce were greatest reveals the importance of their rural connections. Not only did this deprive them of their best opportunity to achieve more secure conditions of work, it also weakened their bargaining position within the labour market. For they withdrew from the market when the demand for their labour was at its peak and offered their services again when the market was once more overstocked. Cumulatively, these factors served to accentuate the uncertainties of work and to reinforce the volatility of the labour market.

The importance of these rural connections stemmed partly from the instability inscribed into the conditions of the labour market in Bombay. On the one hand, it was becoming increasingly important for even the casually employed to remain in the city. They had to appear at the mill or the dock gates regularly and could be penalized for failing to do so. As the number of competitors for their jobs increased, a prolonged absence could entail a loss of favour and of their place within the patronage networks of the neighbourhood. On the other hand, since the conditions of employment were far from secure, they had to build up and maintain their rural connections. Yet seasonal flows of migration tended to accentuate the conditions of over-supply in the labour market and further intensify the uncertainties of employment.

The family economy of Bombay's workers

Although workers may have migrated without their families, they did so within the structure of their kinship connections. If migration was meant to boost the rural resources of their family, urban workers also sought its support in num-

---

[145] *Ibid.*, The Bombay Municipal Corporation, I, i, 567.

berless ways. When they moved to the city, they lodged with relatives and found work with their assistance. In sickness and retirement, they returned to the village. They were not merely providers for the village economy; they were also dependent upon its use as the basis of their system of welfare provision and material protection. Since migration occurred within this family economy, its operation provides some insight into the strength, meaning and significance of the rural connection within the urban context.

The family economy provided the basis for the symbiosis between the urban interests and rural connections of Bombay's working class. The official memorandum to the Whitley Commission described the manner in which this family economy operated:

Only a few members of a family migrate to the towns. The family itself remains domiciled in the mofussil and the centre of the family life is there, so that the women folk return to it to bear their children; the men folk when age or disability comes to them, or when death causes a vacancy in the agricultural workers of the family.[146]

If wage employment in Bombay was necessary to supplement the rural resources of the family, the village was an essential source of support for workers in the city. It is this integrative operation of the family economy which explains why workers could be both permanent in their dependence upon the city and yet maintain a close attachment to the village.

Necessarily, in this context, kinship was very generously interpreted. It could indeed extend beyond the extended family to include caste fellows, co-villagers or even those who were known to or recommended by relatives. To be materially effective, in conditions of considerable poverty, both rural and urban, the joint family had to be extensive rather than exclusive in its operation. This explains why workers whose stake in the village had long since ceased to be based in land or whose share in the crop was little more than a part of a coconut tree would be able to maintain and utilize these village connections. It explains why they, too, would return periodically to attend village ceremonies, arrange marriages or celebrate festivals. Above all, it demonstrates how in the context of this integrative family economy the rural connection could endure the 'proletarianization' of the working class.

Indeed, only those for whom 'conditions were so bad in their villages that they had no option'[147] migrated as whole families to settle permanently in Bombay, and consequently weakened their connections with the village. In particular the famines of 1918–19 brought streams of family migrations from Nasik and Ahmednagar.[184] Even millworkers, with relatively permanent jobs,

---

[146] *Ibid.*, GOB, 'Conditions of Industrial Workers', I, i, 8.
[147] *Ibid.*, GOB, 'Conditions of Industrial Workers', I, i, 8.
[148] L.S. Sedgwick, 'The Composition of Bombay City Population in Relation to Birth Place', *Labour Gazette*, I, 7 (March 1922), 15–19.

if able to support their immediate family in the city, nevertheless retained close ties with their villages. Thus, as the Government of Bombay noted,

So far as the Bombay textile workers are concerned it may be said that although they maintain a very close and living contact with their villages, the bulk of them are permanent in the sense that they are not merely birds of passage but continue to work in the industry for a considerable period of time once they join it.[149]

The severing of village ties was more often the product of hopeless distress than abnormal success.

The very factors which made the maintenance of their rural base indispensable – low wages, casual employment and high costs – also forced Bombay's workers to leave their families behind in their villages. These factors reinforced each other. If inadequate wages enforced a dependence on the village base, some members of the family had to remain behind to maintain the rural connection. At the same time, if social conditions in Bombay made it impossible and imprudent for whole families to migrate, then for its working class, strong connections outside the city became inevitable. 'The most important reason' for the separation of working-class families, according to the Social Service League, was 'the inadequacy of wages in the case of a large number of workers'. But there were others: the League listed

the bad effect of continued residence in Bombay on health, periods of unemployment when a man is unable to support his family but has to stay in Bombay in search of employment, and the necessity of there being someone from the family to look after the property in the village, or to look after an old person in the family staying there. In the case of joint families all the brothers working in Bombay do not bring their families in [sic] Bombay, as it is found more economical and convenient for one or two brothers only to have their families here and to keep the wives of others at the village by turns.[150]

Of course, the separation of working-class families between town and country was most marked in the casual trades or those particularly vulnerable to arbitrary fluctuations. 'Indian seamen', reported their union, 'are so poorly paid that they cannot afford to live with their families.'[151] Similarly, Cholia found in the case of dock workers that while 'many skilled labourers prefer staying with a family in Bombay', most unskilled manual labourers left them in the village because 'their income hardly permits them to maintain a family in the city. At times when a little saving is made they invite their families to Bombay.'[152] Only the most affluent workers could afford to be urban proletarians.

On the other hand, the rural base fulfilled a range of vital functions for the

---

[149] *RCLI, Evidence, Bombay Presidency*, GOB, 'Conditions of Industrial Workers', I, i, 8.
[150] *Ibid.*,The Social Service League, I, i, 429–30.
[151] *Ibid.*, The Indian Seamen's Union, I, i, 291.
[152] Cholia, *Dock Labourers*, p. 108.

organization of workers' lives in the city. The rural connections of Bombay's workers were essential to their attempts to find work, housing and credit in the city. Among the migrants from Satara, one official observed, 'a considerable number ... have practically established themselves in different labour centres. The annual migrants go to these men who form a sort of nuclei around which the others congregate'.[153] More immediately the new migrants might lodge with their relatives in the city, supplementing the latter's income while enabling the former to find their foothold in Bombay.[154]

Workers also returned to the village when they fell ill. The mortality rate in the working-class districts was the highest in the city.[155] 'Respiratory diseases constitute the determining factor', wrote the Bombay Medical Officer in 1921, 'in rendering the death rate of a working-class districts notably higher than that of a good class residential district and in rendering that of a poor slum higher still.'[156] At the same time, medical attention was expensive, sometimes unattainable. Those who survived these conditions returned to their villages to recuperate. Similarly, the scarcity of maternity hospitals and the inadequacy of cheap, accessible medical care prompted working-class families to return to their villages to have their children. 'The reason for not sending women to the maternity homes', wrote one observer, was that 'they believe that either the mother or the child dies.'[157] This belief was based on sound reason and tragic experience.

Similarly, workers also returned to their villages sometimes in periods of unemployment and more usually in retirement. The Bombay Port Trust, commenting that ten years of labouring in the docks made men too old and infirm to work, reported sanguinely: 'When age prohibits heavy manual labour, the majority retire to their village holdings giving way to younger men who take their places. Their old age is therefore automatically provided for by the custom of the country.'[158] This was just as well. Since neither employers nor the state made these provisions, the retention of village connections was imperative.

On the whole, the remittance of cash earnings probably contributed significantly to rural subsistence. In the early 1920s, 26.2 per cent of average industrial earnings were estimated to have been remitted.[159] This average is deceptive since it was skewed in favour of those who earned the most and who were also

[153] *RCLI, Evidence, Bombay Presidency*, Mr J. Ghosal, I, i, 205.
[154] *Ibid.*, Social Service League, I, i, 429; *Labour Gazette*, 4, 2 (October 1924), 159–68.
[155] *Gazetteer*, III, 179.
[156] Dr J. Sandilands, 'The Health of the Bombay Worker', *Labour Gazette*, I, 2 (October 1921), 16.
[157] Pradhan, 'The Untouchable Workers of Bombay City', p. 20.
[158] *RCLI, Evidence, Bombay Presidency*, The Bombay Port Trust, I, i, 462.
[159] Labour Office, Bombay, *Report on an Enquiry into Working Class Family Budgets in Bombay* by G.F. Shirras (Bombay, 1923), p. 35.

likely to remit the most. Another estimate for the same period calculated that 306,000 money orders to the value of Rs. 71 lakhs were dispatched from thirteen post offices located in the mill district in 1921 or an average of Rs. 23.02 per money-order.[160] By the early 1930s, the practice of sending money orders had proved so disruptive to the discipline and functioning of the mills, that the Bombay Millowners' Association attempted to come to an arrangement with the postal authorities to enable workers to send their remittances directly from the mill premises.[161] Between July 1937 and July 1939, nearly 100,000 money orders worth sixteen million rupees were remitted from the post offices of the working-class districts of Bombay.[162]

However, these figures are very crude. They neither tell us where these money-orders went nor who sent them. It is probable that the working classes sent their cash home with friends or carried it back themselves in preference to using the postal system,[163] which forced them to rely upon more literate intermediaries. It is not only that statistics derived from postal records do not serve as a reliable guide to the amount of money sent back by the working class, they probably also form a singularly inappropriate source of evidence on the subject of working-class remittances. Moreover, it would be safe to assume that those money-orders that were sent by workers emanated disproportionately from the better-paid among them, thus skewing the average in their favour. Since they do not inform us about the sender, we cannot know how far remittances accentuated existing social inequalities.

Nevertheless, the problems of obtaining credit and the monumental difficulties of repaying debts made remittances indispensable to the family economy in its rural base. However modest, the remittance of cash could play a major role in a predominantly subsistence economy, enabling their kin to purchase seed or, however, temporarily, freedom from debt. The life histories of various workers collected by the Labour Office in 1929 reveal the varieties of remittance practices.[164] Thus, Pandurang Gunaji, a weaving jobber, who earned between Rs. 80 and Rs. 110 per month said in 1929 that he used to remit Rs. 50 per year to his mother; after she died, he maintained his village links by sending his sister

---

[160] Burnett-Hurst, *Labour and Housing*, p. 10; see also *Labour Gazette*, III, 6 (February 1924), 25. Not all these money-orders were sent by the city's workers and among them there must have been some sent by clerks, jobbers and the better-paid workers. Some senders were probably not labourers at all, but residents of the neighbourhood, and some may have sent more than one money order. However, assuming that each money order was issued by a separate person, that they were all workers and that they were equally distributed throughout the workforce, the average remittance amounted to Rs. 23.02 per year.

[161] *BMOA, Annual Report*, 1930, p. 376.

[162] Proceedings of the TLIC, File 13, MSA.

[163] *Imperial Gazetteer, Bombay Presidency*, I, 62.

[164] *RCLI*, 'Life Histories of 12 typical immigrant workers to Bombay City', collected by the Lady Investigators of the Labour Office in June–July 1929, XI, ii, 312–20.

Rs. 25 'for paying land taxes'. Several workers reported they were unable to save any money to send home; one that he used to remit all his savings when he was single, but after his marriage had sent his father Rs. 100 each year; another 'handed over the village property and his house to his uncle's son on condition that he should send him a part of the income of the property'. Similarly, Anaji Shinde had 'given his share of the land [divided between four brothers] to another person for purposes of cultivation and gets in return four or five maunds of rice per year'; Dagdoo Hari remitted a part of his savings to his maternal uncle; another worker stopped remittances when he had children, and his wife gave up her job, for he could no longer 'defray his expenses'. In an exceptional case, Narayan, 'a good weaver', who came to Bombay to earn cash when his father died and debts mounted, worked in a mill for eight months each year and returned to cultivate his land for four months during the monsoon. Perhaps only the most skilled workers could work regularly on such flexible terms. The variety of these practices reflects the differences registered between workers in the operation of this family economy which integrated their rural and urban interests.

For most working-class or smallholding families, migration to wage employment enhanced their access to cash, not only in terms of their earnings, but also in the relatively more competitive credit market in the city. Their remittances, sometimes dependent upon borrowing, probably enabled their families to resist the complete erosion of their position within the agrarian social structure. The decisive advantage of a relative in Bombay was not so much his often mythically sizeable savings but his easier access to credit. By facilitating borrowing, migration thus locked some families into a circuit of credit, which when enabled them to stand still. Beneath the old recurring patterns of migration lay deeper layers of stagnation.

This circle of immobility has exemplified in the case of Bhaga Ganga,[165] who worked for nineteen years in a mill, first as half-timer from the age of nine, and later as an inter-tenter in the roving department. His family plot had always been too small to support them without supplementary earnings, but they had lost it to a money-lender for default of debt. After nearly two decades of working in Bombay, apparently fairly regularly and at the same mill,

he thought of returning to his village to do agricultural work. He returned there and purchased a small piece of land and also rented other farms.

But after a further ten years, now in his late thirties, he had returned to Bombay to work as an inter-tenter, leaving his mother, his wife and two children in the village, because 'he could not maintain his family for the whole year on the income of the land. Every year he returns to his village for one or two months'. Similarly, Narayen, a weaver, came to Bombay to repay his family debts. It took him ten years to do so. 'He had no desire to live in Bombay after this. But owing to the irregular monsoons he was required to incur fresh debt.'[166] In both these cases, workers whose object was to return to the land, and indeed to use their wages to invest in it, were being forced back on to the urban labour market. There were others like Krishna Amritya, for instance, who

like city life. He says that in a village landless labourers like him cannot get sufficient to maintain themselves even after working very hard in the fields. Besides this, he says that after living in a city for twenty-five years he finds it difficult to do agricultural work.[167]

For such workers, their savings might be remitted to maintain their village base which helped to support dependents, old and young, and to provide for themselves a basis of material protection against unemployment, illness and infirmity.

To some families, then, cash earnings and urban remittances helped to augment and strengthen their rural base; others received little from those who upon migrating to the city found themselves dawdling irretrievably in the nether regions of the labour market. For most, it was probably the case that remittances helped them simply to hold on to their position in the village. In this respect, Patel's findings for the 1960s, after a century of cash remittances from industry had played upon rural society, are instructive. 'Villages', she observed, 'do not derive any appreciable benefit from urban employment, since migrants are unable to render any substantial financial help to their kinsfolk in the district'. On balance, however, 'those who have relatives working in Bombay are slightly better off than those who do not have any members of the family working in the city'.[168] It is not surprising that after sending several generations of migrants to industrial employment, Ratnagiri, like the Chota Nagpur Plateau, west Bihar and east United Provinces, remained among the poorest districts in India.

From the late nineteenth century onwards, rising demographic pressure upon the land, within the context of an increasingly commercialized economy, appears to have driven a growing number of rural smallholders to seek wage employment in Bombay. This tendency was particularly marked in rural areas which had witnessed little economic diversification. But the forces of industrial development were by no means sufficiently powerful to absorb the slack of the rural economy. The fluctuations of the labour market in Bombay made migrant workers reluctant to sever their rural connections. Indeed, ties of caste, kinship

166 *Ibid.*, XI, ii, 315.
167 *Ibid.*, XI, ii, 313.
168 Patel, *Rural Labour*, pp. 21–2.

and village were vital to the social organization of Bombay's workers. While their rural base served as an important bulwark against the depredations of the urban environment, their cash earnings and their access to credit in Bombay enabled migrant workers to contribute to rural subsistence.

The maintenance by urban workers of their rural connections has often been understood by historians as the persistence of pre-industrial characteristics within the industrial setting. Rural values, it is assumed, were transmitted to the city and decisively influenced the social organization and action of Bombay's workers. But a closer examination of the nature of these rural connections indicates that, far from being ephemeral to the industrial context, they were essential to its constitution. The operation of the family economy enabled Bombay's workers to draw upon their rural resources as they organized to meet their urban needs. Furthermore, the contours of the family economy itself, as it operated across readily perceived boundaries of town and country, were not predetermined; they were shaped by larger patterns of social and economic change.

If Bombay's workers retained their rural ties, they cannot be characterized as peasants temporarily in proletarian grab. Migrant workers, who spent large parts of their adult lives entirely dependent upon industrial and town labour, were not simply rural migrants. If migrant workers had been born in their villages and were to retire there, they spent their adult lives – often after the manner of their fathers and grandfathers before them – in Bombay. They entered thereby into a nexus of social, economic and ideological connections which were specific to the city and autonomous of the countryside. Over a period of several decades by the 1920s, districts like Ratnagiri, whence a large proportion of Bombay's workers came, developed a special relationship with the city and as a consequence, the urban and the industrial had begun to penetrate its society. For this period of their lives, at least, workers remained in the city for ten months in the year and in the case of North Indian workers for several years at a time. Their annual visit to the village was seen in contemporary comment as a pilgrimage to their social roots, yet it also represented an escape and compensation from the rigours of the city, both a physical and a material life-line.

The utility of the rural connections of Bombay's workers varied with their situation, both in the village and in the city. Their use registered differences between them. The nature of these rural connections, observed the Whitley Commission, 'is a variable quantity; with some the contact is close and constant, with others it is slender and spasmodic, and with a few it is more an inspiration than a reality'.[169] The village fulfilled, therefore, not only a material but also at

[169] *Report of the RCLI*, p. 13.

times a utopian function within working-class life. But whatever the depth of their connections with the countryside, Bombay's workers had to organize and act within the social context of the city. Migration brought workers into a social nexus which was autonomous of the countryside even as it was continuously interacting with it, and which was capable of transforming and reformulating 'rural' values, even as it was influenced by them. It is to the social context of the urban neighbourhood that we must now turn.

5   Girangaon: the social organization
of the working-class neighbourhoods

The patterns of capital investment in Bombay, cause and consequence of the constraints within which the economy had developed, shaped business strategies which geared production to the shifting demands of the market. Its effects were registered in fluctuating levels of employment. The overwhelming majority of the labour force in Bombay experienced irregular and uncertain conditions of work. No clear distinction can be sustained between temporary and permanent workers. Those who were regularly employed at one moment could, for a wide range of more or less arbitrary reasons, easily find themselves without a job the next.

The irregular conditions of work and the low wages which accompanied them shaped the social nexus of the working class. This social nexus was composed of several overlapping sets of connections. Although migrant workers came to Bombay to protect their position in the village economy, these conditions perpetuated their need to maintain their rural connections, as an essential base of material provision and social organization. Ties of caste and kinship, based in the village, provided the social framework within which migration occurred. Yet the social organization of Bombay's workers developed beyond their confines. To find and retain employment, and indeed to obtain moral and material support, workers were drawn into networks of patronage based in the urban neighbourhoods. It was, therefore, not only that the rural and urban connections of Bombay's workers were intertwined but the spheres of workplace and neighbourhood also came to be inextricably connected. This chapter will attempt to explore the nature of the linkages between workplace and neighbourhood. In particular, it will investigate the nature of the social organization of Bombay's workers: the power relations which it fostered and the patterns of association which it forged.

The social arena of the neighbourhood

From the later nineteenth century onwards, a distinctly working-class neighbourhood began to form in Bombay. The city's poor began to drift away from the high rents of the native town to the villages of Parel, to Mazagaon and

Table 15. *The Growth of the mill districts of Bombay, 1881–1931*

Section	1881	1891	1901	1911	1921	1931
Mahalaxmi	6,232	17,014	18,092	26,302	37,108	34,880
Byculla	26,842	47,403	57,646	75,348	91,285	89,835
Mazagaon	27,904	33,640	27,933	30,075	32,092	42,992
Parel	18,560	28,740	33,390	45,474	59,534	61,567
Sewri	5,555	6,063	9,294	19,067	27,124	26,556
Sion	17,237	19,601	25,443	30,680	52,913	68,119
Mahim	17,309	8,505	27,386	30,492	47,171	48,502
Worli	14,621	25,493	45,588	89,611	118,045	114,531

Source: Census of India, 1931, IX, ii, 158–9.

Table 16. *Population in districts of the old native town*

Section	1881	1891	1901	1911	1921	1931
Chakla	37,048	32,197	24,384	24,231	22,996	17,322
Mandvi	42,351	37,295	31,402	33,202	38,517	37,719
Umarkhadi	54,656	52,466	48,481	45,679	47,218	40,458
Dongri	33,290	30,317	25,778	27,246	19,966	11,346
Market	49,130	44,751	28,415	30,172	35,080	38,145
Kumbharwada	34,990	32,209	27,544	27,703	32,481	31,743
Khara Talao	28,691	27,035	23,161	22,979	23,925	22,209
Tardeo	20,281	18,980	20,958	27,758	31,933	31,296
Kamathipura	28,455	29,203	26,706	36,751	44,585	37,571

Source: Census of India, 1931, IX, ii, 158–9.

Tarwadi, Sewri and Kamathipura (see tables 15 and 16). Cheaper land values and improved communications encouraged businessmen to locate their cotton mills, workshops and factories beyond the northern boundaries of the native town. Once relatively evenly distributed throughout the old native town, the working classes were now increasingly concentrated in this area. By 1933, three municipal wards contained nearly all the city's cotton mills.[1] Moreover, 90 per cent of the city's millworkers lived within fifteen minutes' walking distance of their place of work.[2] To its inhabitants, this area came to be known as Girangaon, literally the mill village.

[1] Labour Office, Bombay. *Report on an Enquiry into Working Class Family Budgets in Bombay City in 1932–3* (Bombay, 1935), p. 2. Wards E, F and G contained 17, 18 and 39 mills respectively.
[2] *Labour Gazette*, IV, 7 (March 1925), 745–7.

In the public discourse of the inter-war years, the notion that the street and the neighbourhood constituted a distinct arena of social and political action gained increasing strength. As one contemporary observed in 1930, 'thousands of children' in Bombay were

born into homes in which parental control and guidance is almost completely lacking. Their primary education is that of the streets. They get from it a certain superficial sharpness, but little knowledge that is to be of service in the business of life and less than no discipline.[3]

In this view, the street represented the opposite pole to the family. It came to be distinguished from the private sphere of the family and the home, on the one hand, as well as from the public sphere of work and politics on the other. Whatever the perceptions of roughness held by the city's elites, the social connections into which the working class entered to meet their material needs for housing, credit and employment, and the associations which they formed, imparted to the neighbourhood a substantive importance as a social arena.

In the working-class districts, the distinction between the home and the street was eroded by the extent of overcrowding. Housing shortages and high rents combined to ensure that the residents of the working-class neighbourhoods spent a considerable proportion of their lives on the street. Certainly, there was a large and growing army which slept in public places: the verandah of a chawl, the courtyard of a wadi, the street, even in adjoining gymnasiums.[4] One census of housing noted in 1931:

Anyone familiar with Bombay is aware how the streets are used at night as sleeping places. When overcrowding in the houses is considered, there is nothing remarkable in the fact ... Three-fourths of the population of Bombay live in one-roomed tenements and the average floor space available for each occupant cannot be more than what can be covered by a small mat.[5]

The extent of overcrowding meant that the residents of the mill districts spilled out of the chawls and into the streets.

It is not intended to suggest that the street became a social arena simply because people lived on it. The workings of the housing, labour and credit markets helped also to generate loyalties to particular neighbourhoods. For instance, newly arrived migrant workers sought the help of their friends, caste fellows and relatives to find work, housing and credit. Frequently, they lodged

---

[3] J. Mackenzie, 'Education and the City', in C. Manshardt (ed.), *Bombay Today and Tomorrow* (Bombay, 1930), p. 43.

[4] Proceedings of the TLIC, Main Inquiry, Oral Evidence, Examination of Cotton Mill Workers, Bombay, Spinning Side, File 60-A, p. 976, MSA.

[5] *Census, 1931*, IX, i, 88–9.

with them. It was a common occurrence that workers connected in these ways sought to live in proximity to each other.

The context of work also affected people's choice of neighbourhood. The inadequacy and expense of transport underlay the reluctance of the working class to live at 'any distance from their work'.[6] Moreover, the nature and conditions of employment often made proximity of residence essential. The working day, as one official committee reported, 'in many vocations is irregular and inconvenient; early attendance and late dispersal is common'.[7] This was particularly the case in occupations which fell beyond the purview of the factory acts or indeed those trades which worked night shifts.

The mechanisms of the labour market also tied workers to particular neighbourhoods. To find work, most people relied upon their friends and relatives to recommend them to jobbers and supervisors. Casual workers and badlis came to depend upon the jobbers they knew to keep them regularly employed. At the same time, workers who could entrench themselves within the jobber's social web outside the workplace were sometimes also able to moderate his worst exactions.[8]

Irregular earnings and uncertain conditions of work meant that in order to provide for their own subsistence and then to remit money to their families in the rural base, most workers had a continuing need for credit. It was largely through the social ties of the neighbourhood that workers attempted to satisfy these needs. Workers helped to tide their friends and relatives over spells of unemployment by paying their rent or loaning them cash. But it was sometimes necessary to turn to more commercial sources of credit. If workers relied upon the jobbers they knew to keep them employed, they depended upon being known to grain-dealers and money-lenders to obtain loans at cheaper rates and more flexible conditions of repayment than prevailed on the open market. These factors encouraged workers to build up social connections in the neighbourhood and increased their interest in maintaining and perpetuating them. This was why

People insist upon staying in their favourite locality. Proximity of residence to the place of business and the neighbourhood of persons of one's own circle and native place is sought.[9]

The social connections into which they entered served to restrict the mobility of casual labour. The more closely workers relied upon these connections for

[6] Municipal Commissioner, Bombay, to Chairman, Bombay Improvement Trust, no. 14499, 27 August 1903, GOB, General, 1905, vol. 23, p. 205, MSA.
[7] *Report of the Rent Enquiry Committee*, I, i, 20.
[8] Proceedings of the TLIC, Main Inquiry, Oral Evidence, Cotton Mill Workers, Bombay, Spinning Side, File 60-A, p. 992, MSA.
[9] *Report of the Rent Enquiry Committee*, I, i, 20.

their own welfare the less easily they could abandon them and move elsewhere in Bombay. The perception of contemporaries that rootless, migrant workers gravitated towards casual jobs wherever they were offered bore little relation to the conditions in which Bombay's workers lived and laboured.

The material needs of the working class were not the only factor in the constitution of their neighbourhood connections. Leisure and political activities also contributed to the development of the street and the neighbourhood as a social arena. Street entertainers and tamasha players formed the working man's theatre. As Parvatibai Bhor recalled her childhood:

There was an open space in the middle of our four chawls. There the magicians, monkey players or acrobats used to regularly perform their acts. The Nandi bull used to come. I used to be especially afraid of the Kadaklakshmi. To see that they had to beat themselves on their naked bodies in order to fill their stomachs frightened me.[10]

Similarly, the street corner offered a meeting place. Liquor shops as well as gymnasiums drew their membership from particular neighbourhoods. Social investigators continue to be bemused that, when asked to give 'an account of their leisure time activities', the vast majority of workers 'could not be specific and said that they pass time roaming which they consider a mode of relaxation'.[11]

Each neighbourhood organized various forms of communal activities. The toli bands of Mohurram or the melas at Ganpati or Gokulashtami were intrinsic to the social life of the neighbourhood. Large numbers of young males participated in these activities. But these were also communal occasions which the neighbourhood leaders helped to finance and towards which shopkeepers were invited to contribute, sometimes badgered and bullied into paying up. Neighbourhood leaders competed with each other to put on the best celebrations or to invite the city's magnates, trade-union or political leaders to these occasions. Religious festivals and observances constituted important forms of 'leisure': an expression not only of faith but also of community.

Significantly, whole sets of territorial traditions were to develop within the mill districts. The fact that these districts came to be identified as Girangaon suggests a widespread consciousness of its terrain as a social arena. Moreover, within Girangaon, the cotton mills which dominated its landscape came to be known to the working class by names special to the locality, and indeed, to themselves. 'In accordance with a common custom in Bombay', noted the *Gazetteer*, 'mill-hands have names of their own for various mills, which bear no resemblance to their real names'. Thus, the Star of India Mill whose

---

[10] *Eka Rannaraginichi Hakikat*, as told by Parvatibai Bhor to Padmakar Chitale (Bombay, 1977), p. 14.
[11] Patel, *Rural Labour*, p. 150.

machinery was old and noisy was known as Khatara mill; the Union Mill as Bin Chimnichi Giran (chimneyless mill); the Hong Kong and later the Apollo Mill as Tabelyachi Giran, because they were located near the municipal stables; the Jam Mills as Patryachi Giran, since its roof was made of iron sheeting which probably made working conditions extremely hot; the India Mill was known as Mulmulchi Giran after the type of cloth whose production it instituted, the Khatau Mills as Sakli Talayachi Giran, the lock-and-chain mill. Some mills were identified by their location; others by proper names, perhaps of former owners, managers or jobbers, such as Narayan (Meyer Sassoon), Trikamdas (Edward Sassoon), Kapidas (Elphinstone) and Bania Mill (Swan).[12]

These traditions were not shaped by the context of work alone; they were also informed by political and social conflicts. Thus, in the 1930s, Nagu Sayaji's Wadi gained an almost legendary significance as the city's communist stronghold. Moreover, political events and their changing interpretation infused these traditions and provided benchmarks against which present action could be measured: the character of policing, the policies of the state, the leadership and programmes of political parties or trade unions, the generosity and patronage of local magnates.

Since strikes spilled into the neighbourhood, where millowners recruited blacklegs and strikers mobilized pickets, money-lenders extended or withdrew credit and landlords demanded or waived their rents, the momentum of industrial action continuously forged and reconstituted the political traditions of Girangaon.[13] Workers might use their informal social connections to find employment, but they could also deploy these to challenge the jobber's authority and to organize and sustain strikes. Credit was often necessary to tide workers over spells of unemployment, but flexible arrangements with neighbourhood money-lenders were essential in periods of industrial action. The neighbourhood connections of the working class might enable them to organize for work-sharing or for unemployment, but it could also form the basis for industrial action. It was in the chawls and wadis of the working-class districts that factory owners, managers and jobber attempted to recruit strike-breakers and where strike committees and trade unions mounted pickets. Politics was integral to the fabric of social action. But if the neighbourhood formed an autonomous social arena, the experience of living in proximity did not thereby flatten the differences and conflicts within working-class communities into a

---

[12] *Gazetteer*, I, 212–13. Many of these double names were traced where they recurred in handbills issued by trade unions during strikes. The most useful collection of such handbills is to be found in the Exhibits produced by the prosecution for the Meerut Conspiracy Case in the Proceedings of the Meerut Conspiracy Case and Papers relating to the Meerut Conspiracy Case, NAI.

[13] R. Chandavarkar, 'Workers' Politics and the Mill Districts of Bombay Between the Wars', *MAS*, XV, 3 (1981).

smooth uniformity. Indeed, it may have exacerbated these differences. The neighbourhood also formed an arena for the expression of political and social differences within the working class. It was here that strikers fought blacklegs, rival caste groups clashed and Hindus and Muslims cracked open each other's heads.

The social organization of the neighbourhood

As workers organized in the neighbourhood to safeguard their subsistence, the social connections into which they entered created important locations of power and networks of patronage. This section will investigate how the operation of the housing, credit and labour markets influenced the social organization of the neighbourhood. It will also examine the nature of the relationships of power and patronage which developed in its wake.

Historians and sociologists, like contemporary observers, portrayed the social organization of the neighbourhood as a self-regulating mechanism. Colonial officials and social observers sometimes talked about those whom they took to be neighbourhood leaders as 'headmen';[14] later writers have been only too ready to witness the reconstitution of 'villages' in the urban setting and to understand the social institutions of the neighbourhood as its controlling agencies.[15] Here in this view were the neighbourhood leaders, there the mass of its residents; here patrons and magnates, there a body of clients and dependants who might be instigated into riot or cuffed into obedience.

Against the picture of absolute control from above, it is possible to set another: the reciprocity which marked power relations in the neighbourhood. Within the institutions of the neighbourhood and the associations which formed around them, power did not flow in a single direction. The jobber and the landlord, the dada and the money-lender might each exert considerable influence within the neighbourhood but their options were limited by the field within which they operated. Their clients could impose effective pressures, demands and sanctions upon them. The exercise of their dominance was marked by tension and conflict, by competition and rivalry. Their leadership and influence operated within parameters in part governed by the choices exercised by their clients.

---

[14] *RCLI, Evidence, Bombay Presidency*, GOB, 'Conditions of Industrial Workers', I, i, 10.
[15] Newman, *Workers and Unions*; O.M. Lynch, 'Rural Cities in India: Continuities and discontinuities', in P. Mason (ed.), *India and Ceylon: Unity and Diversity* (Oxford, 1967), pp. 142–58; J.C. Masselos, 'Power in the Bombay "Moholla" 1904–15: An Initial Exploration in to the World of the Indian Urban Muslim', *South Asia*, VI (1976) 75–95; S.N. Mukherjee, 'Daladali in Calcutta in the Nineteenth Century', *MAS*, IX, 1 (1975), 59–80. C.A. Bayly, 'Local Control in Indian Towns – the Case of Allahabad 1880–1920', *MAS*, V, 4 (1971), 289–311.

Housing

The supply and control of housing became an important focus of social organization in the neighbourhood. The endemic scarcity of land in Bombay had made
it an invaluable asset since the earliest days of the Company settlement.[16] The
more closely land rights on the island were defined, the more surely did land
values rise. As the rapid growth of the city from the later nineteenth century
was accompanied by rising rents, investment in land and housing became an
increasingly attractive proposition. It brought safe and steady rather than
spectacular returns. Furthermore, it sometimes created opportunities for the
exercise of political influence in the neighbourhood. Anybody who could, but
especially the merchants, bankers and building contractors who profited from
Bombay's commercial and economic development in the later nineteenth
century and the service groups who benefited from its growing importance as
an educational, judicial and administrative centre, invested in land. Thus, Bhai
Jiwanji, managing clerk of a firm of solicitors and a voracious collector of
books, was a major landlord in Girgaum. Anandrao Bhaskar, Judge of the Small
Causes Court, owned large properties in Bhuleshwar. Ganesh Ramji, head
surveyor to the Collector of Bombay, owned 'most of the houses' in 2nd
Bhatwadi, which until 1884 was known as Ganesh Ramji's Wadi.[17] Some
magnates built their own wadis, which contained several houses and chawls,
often their own shops, occasionally a temple, a shrine or a mosque dedicated to
the divine preferences of its inhabitants and endowed by its wealthiest residents.

In the absence of any coherent or sustained urban planning, and sometimes
because of its monumental incompetence,[18] the prodigious growth of the city
in the nineteenth century had been accompanied by the rather haphazard
settlement of the island. Buildings were thus squeezed into every available
space between municipal thoroughfares. Town planners in the early twentieth
century mused upon 'the extraordinary anomaly of rice being cultivated and
buffaloes grazing within a few miles of land selling at Rs. 150 per square yard,
while the bulk of the population is herded together in the south, and centre of
the town'.[19] In Nagpada, a ground area of about 75,000 square yards was

---

[16] 'The Town and Fort in Bombay', *Alexandra's East India and Colonial Magazine*, IX (January–
June 1835), 244; F. Warden, *Report on the Landed Tenures of Bombay, 20 August 1814* (Bombay,
1861), *Selections*, N.S., no. 64.

[17] S.T. Sheppard, *Bombay Place Names and Street Names: An Excursion into the By-Ways of the
History of Bombay City* (Bombay, 1917), pp. 31–4.

[18] See chapter 2 above. For recent studies of housing and urban policies, see Gordon, *Businessmen
and Politics*; Conlon, 'Industrialization and the Housing Problem in Bombay', pp. 153–68; I.
Klein, 'Urban Development and Death in Bombay City, 1870–1914', *MAS*, XX, 4 (1986),
725–54.

[19] Acting Secretary, GOB, General to Chairman, BIT, 9 December 1907, *Annual Administration
Report of the BIT, 1907–8*, Appendix B, pp. xxii–xxiii.

occupied by 168 separate properties 'crowded together without regard to ventilation and served only by very narrow tortuous passages'.[20]

This pattern of building was influenced by tenurial conditions as well as by the high cost of land. Most of the properties in Nagpada, for instance, were held from the freeholder on the condition that on demand the buildings would be removed and the land returned.[21] Similar conditions prevailed under the fazendari tenure. Although 'the Fazindar of today has no interest in the land beyond the annual rent', it was observed, there remained 'a popular idea' that he possessed a reversionary right to the land.[22] The divergence of interest between the landowner and the house-builder fundamentally affected the character and quality of housing in Bombay. Not surprisingly, builders who leased the land constructed, as in Nagpada, 'the most miserable structures at a minimum cost' and covered every possible inch of it in order to recover their initial outlay.[23]

The prevailing tenurial conditions combined with the scarcity and dearness of land to narrow the options before investors in housing in the working-class neighbourhoods and to complicate the mechanisms of the housing market. The fundamental constraint upon the provision of housing for the poor was the existence of a 'noticeable gulf between the rents charged and the capacity of the tenants to pay'. This disparity was created, according to the Rent Enquiry Committee, reporting in the late 1930s, by the workings of an 'uncontrolled property market' and its only solution lay in 'a fundamental change in the attitude towards private ownership in land'.[24] In 1918, A.E. Mirams, the consulting surveyor to the Government of India, estimated that whereas Rs. 2 per month was the maximum rent which an average millworker in Bombay could afford to pay, buildings could not be constructed in the city for an economic rent of less than Rs. 3.[25]

---

[20] *Annual Administration Report of the BIT, 1901–2*, p. 14.

[21] On the history and development of land tenures in Bombay, see Warden, *Landed Tenures, Selections*, N.S., no. 64; *Gazetteer*, III, 308–434.

[22] *Gazetteer*, III, 333–40; R.R. Mody, *Fazendari Tenures and Inami Lands in Bombay City* (Bombay, 1934).

[23] *Annual Administration Report of the BIT, 1901–2*, p. 14.

[24] *Report of the Rent Enquiry Committee*, vol. I, part i, p. 35. 'But', the Committee added prudently, 'we do not propose here to follow this line of thought.'

[25] *IIC*, 1916–18, *Evidence*, Mr A.E. Mirams, Consulting Surveyor to the GOI, IV, 371. This fact acted as a severe constraint upon any extensive state intervention in the provision of housing. Social policy was expensive and if the costs of public housing could not be recovered in rentals, it could only be met through increased taxation. The plague epidemic of the 1890s, which not only disrupted the city's commerce but also brought the threat of disease and death to the doorstep of the rich, injected some sense of urgency into the problem of housing conditions. The City of Bombay Improvement Trust was established in 1898. Despite ambitious beginnings, its efforts were diverted, as the threat of plague receded, into the development of the city's infrastructure for industry and trade. If the Municipal Corporation was 'a wisp of landlords' (Sir George Lloyd to E.S. Montagu, 28 February 1919, Montagu Papers, MSS. EUR. D 523/4, p. 27, IOR), the

Entrepreneurial landlords had several effective responses to the structural limitations of the market in which they operated, but each of these worsened the conditions of working-class life. They could attempt, for instance, to mix the character of the tenements in each chawl, renting the ground floor as 'small shops with narrow frontages and shallow depths, the tenants of which pay high rents',[26] or combining twin-room units which yielded higher rents with single rooms. Thus, 'buildings in Bombay', as the Rent Enquiry Committee discovered, 'have not always uniform types of tenements let at uniform rents'.[27] However, the reluctance of the respectable to live with the rough, the skilled to live with the unskilled, the jobbers to live with ordinary workers and various castes to live with each other limited the range of variations that were possible.

Moreover, even where the tenurial conditions did not so determine, builders often preferred to minimize their initial capital outlay by leasing the land rather than buying it, despite the risk that the landlord would demand its return on the expiry of the lease. Under these conditions, builders were prone to sweat their sites and crowd them with chawls subdivided into a multiplicity of tenements. They could thereby transfer the burden of their ground rent on to their tenants and recover their costs through the collection of rents.

Improvement Trust became increasingly the instrument of the city's businessmen. By 1918, the Trust's schemes for demolition and reconstruction had dishoused 64,000 people and rehoused 14,000. When housing built by private landlords on Trust lands is taken into account, the overall deficit of housing remained in the region of about 17,000 people. See IIC, *Evidence*, A.E. Mirams, IV, 361. According to another estimate, 3,000 fewer tenements had been provided by the Trust or on its lands than had been demolished, affecting between 12,000 and 15,000 people. See Burnett-Hurst, *Labour and Housing*, p. 32. In 1919, Sir George Lloyd, Governor of Bombay, condemning his predecessors for having 'finicked with the question on a scale adequate to a growing village' and for their lack of 'any imagination or real energy at all' (Lloyd to Montagu, 6 June 1919, Montagu Papers, MSS. EUR. D 523/4, p. 73, *IOR*) and the Municipality for being 'responsible and unashamed for a system of housing and insanitation which would have caused the worst of Abdul Hamid's valis to blush crimson' (Lloyd to Montagu, 28 February 1919, *ibid.*, p. 27, IOR), launched his own scheme to construct 50,000 tenements to house 250,000 workers. By 1925, the target was lowered to 16,000 tenements, of which about 12,000 remained unoccupied, partly because at Rs. 8 per month the rentals far exceeded the sums workers could afford to pay. Since the project was being financed by a town duty levied on every bale of cotton imported into Bombay, the scheme, its failure and a famous scandal associated with it caused great resentment among the millowners. See *BMOA, Annual Report*, 1925, pp. 80–5, 86–7, 91–4. The history of housing policies can be traced in the *Annual Administration Reports of the BIT 1898–99 to 1932–33, passim; Report of the Bombay Development Committee (Bombay, 1914); Report of the Committee Appointed by the Government of India to Enquire into the Bombay Back Bay Reclamation Scheme, 1926* (London, 1926) *Back Bay Enquiry Committee, Evidence*, 3 vols. (London, 1926–7); *Annual Administration Report of the Municipal Commissioner for the City of Bombay 1918–19 to 1939–40, passim*. For an account of municipal politics, see Masani, *Local Self Government*; C. Dobbin, 'Competing Elites in Bombay City Politics in the Mid-Nineteenth Century (1852–83)', in Leach and Mukherjee (eds.), *Elites in South Asia*, pp. 79–94; Gordon, *Businessmen and Politics*, pp. 117–54.

[26] IIC, *Evidence*, Mr A.E. Mirams, IV, 354.

[27] *Report of the Rent Enquiry Committee*, I, i, 35.

The most common entrepreneurial response was to economize on the quality of housing, its construction and the amenities provided. 'The commercial spirit of the age', observed the *Gazetteer*, 'which demands a higher return upon investments, the rise in the price of building materials and the high wages of labour have resulted in some sacrifice of durability.'[28] The frequency of newspaper reports every year about houses that collapsed, often resulting in deaths, testifies to the proliferation of 'the ramshackle and jerry-built chawl' from the late nineteenth century onwards. In fact, chawls which boasted the luxury of more than the most sparse bathing facilities were, it was said, subject to 'the speedy dilapidation of timber-frame buildings, as the constant soaking from the washing-places produces rapid rot of pillars and posts'.[29] The Chairman of the Bombay Improvement Trust argued the case more forcefully,

Ordinary chawl-builders generally succeed in making a good profit from the capital spent on their chawls by adopting a very low standard of sanitation and economizing in building materials and supervision ... A private chawl-owner overcrowds his land with chawls, and many rooms consequently get far too little light and air.[30]

The consequence of these responses to the complexities of the lower rental market was invariably the squalor and overcrowding which the working classes had to endure. As A.E. Mirams told the Indian Industrial Commission,

Although I have observed a good deal of poverty in my walk through life and in many countries, and although I had read a great deal about poverty, I confess I did not realize its poignancy and its utter wretchedness until I came to inspect the so-called homes of the poorer working classes of the town of Bombay.[31]

For the most part, the only solution to the problem of high rents and low wages for Bombay's workers was to share their rooms with their friends, relatives and caste-fellows.

The problem of working-class housing was aggravated by the prodigious growth of the city's population from the later nineteenth century onwards. Moreover, it was in the mill districts of the city, roughly comprising the municipal wards E, F and G, that the most rapid expansion occurred. In fact, these wards accounted for almost the whole of the population increase of the city between 1881 and 1931.[32] Furthermore, the rate of growth of the most important mill neighbourhoods was particularly dramatic. In the same period,

---

[28] *Gazetteer*, I, 198–9.
[29] *Ibid.*, I, 199.
[30] Chairman's Notes on Rents of Trust Chawls, *Annual Administration Report of the BIT 1910–11*, Appendix M(4), p. 84.
[31] IIC, *Evidence*, A.E. Mirams, Consulting Surveyor to the GOI, IV, 354.
[32] *Census, 1931*, IX, ii, 158–9. While the population of these wards increased by 371,652, that of the city as a whole increased by 388,187 in the same period.

the number of residents of Worli increased from 14,621 to 114,531, of Parel from 18,560 to 61,567 and of Byculla from 26,842 to 89,835.[33] If the density of population in these districts was not statistically the greatest in the city, this was because their ground area was substantially occupied by cotton mills and workshops and, in their midst, maidans and open spaces. Residential buildings were, however, concentrated on small plots of land crowded with several-storeyed chawls minutely divided into single-roomed tenements.

The extent of overcrowding in the mill districts is easily measured and was indeed frequently described. Between 30 and 40 per cent of its population lived in single rooms inhabited by six or more people.[34] While three-quarters of the population of the city as a whole lived in one-roomed tenements, occupied, with each of them, by at least three other people, their proportion rose to 99 per cent in Byculla, 88 per cent in Parel and Mazagaon and 87 per cent in Second Nagpada.[35] Another investigation conducted in the mid 1930s found that over 35 per cent of untouchable working-class families shared a single room with at least another family, while over 63 per cent lived in a single room.[36] Similarly, Dr Barnes, investigating the conditions of women workers, reported that:

In outside chawls, I have several times verified the overcrowding of rooms. In one room, on the second floor of a chawl, measuring some 15 ft x 12 ft I found six families living. Six separate ovens on the floor proved this statement. On enquiry I ascertained that the actual number of adults and children living in the room was 30. Bamboos hung from the ceiling, over which, at night, clothes and sacking were hung, helped to partition each family allotment. Three out of six of the women who lived in this room, were shortly expecting to be delivered. All three said they would have their deliveries in Bombay. When I questioned the District Nurse, who accompanied me, as to how she would arrange for privacy in this room, I was shown a small space some 3 ft x 4 ft – which was usually screened off for the purpose. The atmosphere at night of that room filled with smoke from the six ovens, and other impurities would certainly physically handicap any woman and infant, both before and after delivery. This was one of many such rooms I saw.[37]

In buildings of several storeys, privies, where they existed, were

placed one above the other and connected by a common shaft. It is through this shaft that

---

[33] *Ibid.* See Table 15, p. 169.
[34] *Census, 1931*, IX, i, 85–8. See also J. Sandilands, 'The Health of the Bombay Workers', *Labour Gazette*, I, 2 (October, 1921), 14–16.
[35] *Census, 1931*, IX, 1, 88–91.
[36] Pradhan, 'Untouchable Workers,' p. 12. Of course, these 63 per cent are not strictly comparable with the 75 per cent of the entire population who lived in one-roomed tenements, for the latter proportion related not to families but to individuals. Moreover, untouchable workers were often excluded from living in the general run of chawls by other castes and thus were forced to live in even worse accommodation of huts and sheds. This also probably tended to depress the proportion who lived in one-roomed tenements. See Burnett-Hurst, *Labour and Housing*, p. 20.
[37] 'Maternity Benefits to Industrial Workers: Final Report of the Lady Doctor', *Labour Gazette*, I (September, 1922), 31.

the excreta of the scores of occupants are discharged and collected in the small basket receptacles on the ground-floor. The sides of the shaft get fouled and the stench which is created is abominable. The tenants complain that the halalkhores shirk their duties and do not remove the receptacles twice daily in accordance with the Health Department regulations. Conditions are aggravated owing to the insufficient supply of conveniences.[38]

'Every sixth person in the city', an official committee modestly estimated in 1939, 'lives in conditions which are prohibited even by the existing antiquated law'.[39] Observers repeatedly described the extreme over-crowding in the working-class chawls: the lack of floor space, ventilation, water, drainage, lavatories and washing facilities. Windows, it was said, had to be kept closed, even in hot and humid weather, 'on account of the close proximity of filthy gutters, privies, buffalo stables etc.' and to prevent 'dirty water from the gutters overflowing into the rooms during the monsoon'.[40] Nonetheless, ethnographers of 'dirty native habits' were often surprised to find against the odds that 'the interior of most of the tenements are wonderfully clean'.[41]

These living conditions, especially the lack of washing and lavatory facilities in the tenements, imposed an enormous strain on the residents, but they were particularly oppressive for women. At any rate, chawls which 'provide "Mori" (washing-place) in the room' were considered 'a very great help to women folk, especially at the time of sickness and delivery ... We know of some cases where a temporary shed was put up in front of the room to wash a newly born baby.'[42] 'Shortage of water and an insufficiency of taps', reported Burnett-Hurst, 'is a constant source of complaint and leads to considerable inconvenience and occasional scuffles during the "rush" hours in the early morning'.[43] The Kamgar Hitwardhak Sabha, a workers' welfare organization, put the point more forcefully: 'The rush near the pipes', it observed, 'invariably results in fighting, which partially accounts for a large percentage of assault cases in our police courts. It will be a great boon, the Sabha submits, if taps are provided on a liberal scale in mill hand chawls'.[44]

Some of the inhabitants of the island lived not in chawls but in huts, put together with dry coconut or date-palm leaves, or sheds 'built of corrugated iron, empty kerosene tins, wood, etc.'.[45] These huts were not evenly distributed throughout the city but were concentrated in particular areas, notably, for

---

[38] Burnett-Hurst, *Labour and Housing*, p. 25.
[39] *Report of the Rent Enquiry Committee*, I, i, 9.
[40] *Labour Gazette*, X, 9 (May 1931), 895 and 875–96.
[41] *Census, 1931*, IX, i, 106.
[42] RCLI, *Evidence, Bombay Presidency*, The Bombay Presidency Women's Council, I, i, 516.
[43] Burnett-Hurst, *Labour and Housing*, pp. 24–5.
[44] *Indian Textile Journal*, XXIX (August, 1919), 209.
[45] Burnett-Hurst, *Labour and Housing*, p. 19.

instance, in 1901, in the outlying districts of Mahim, Worli and Sion.[46] According to the census, their numbers increased until 1921 before declining substantially in the following decade, which, as its compilers observed, was 'a matter for congratulation if enumeration has been satisfactory in this case'.[47] Their location suggests that some of these settlements may have reflected the slow integration of some parts of the island into the town, rather than waves of immigration beyond the capacity of the town to absorb. But to some extent their numbers were a function of the uneven pressure of demand upon housing, created not only by the absolute scarcity of the latter but also by the need of the urban poor to live near their place of work. In addition, it was also an effect of discrimination in the housing market. Untouchables were often excluded from some chawls by its landlord or its residents and many were thus forced to live in these gimcrack sheds. 'Persons of the "depressed" and "backward" classes (i.e. Mahars, Chambhars and Dheds)', wrote Burnett-Hurst,

frequently find great difficulty in obtaining accommodation, as no other community will live near them. When they cannot find room in the chawls set apart for them, they live in huts or sheds.[48]

It should not be assumed that Harijans were consistently and effectively excluded from all chawls or that caste Hindus were able to avoid living near them altogether. Nonetheless, the 'shanties' of the 1920s and 1930s, while fewer in number and often concentrated in enclaves, were largely occupied by 'untouchable' castes. 'The "Zavli" sheds', according to Burnett-Hurst,

are occupied chiefly by Ghati carters, who not infrequently share them with their domestic animals, cows and calves. As sanitary conveniences are absent the ground in the vicinity of these structures is generally defecated.[49]

Tin sheds, 'occupied by the depressed classes', in another description of a slum in Tardeo,

are level with the street and are not high enough for a person to stand erect. The tins are fitted together with stones etc. and men, children, chicken and goats are herded together as one family. Each big shed is divided by cloth drapings into four or six rooms, occupied by four to six families. There is no light, or ventilation, and such huts are absolutely unsuited for any human habitation ... There are no taps, latrines, no water supply, and the habitants have to go a long way for their respective needs ... During the summer the tins are too hot in the afternoons so the inhabitants are found sitting on the roadside in the shade.[50]

---

[46] *Census, 1901*, XIA, vi, Special Table no. 1, 190–203.
[47] *Census, 1931*, IX, i, 80.
[48] Burnett-Hurst, *Labour and Housing*, p. 20.
[49] *Ibid.*, p. 20.
[50] *RCLI, Evidence, Bombay Presidency*, The Bombay Presidency Women's Council, I, i, 516.

The only remedy for them, suggested the Presidency Women's Council sensibly, if somewhat briskly, was to demolish them.[51] In fact, however, they were to become an increasingly important, even characteristic feature of the city's topography in the decades which followed the Second World War.[52]

Many working-class families could not afford to pay the rent for their own rooms and took in lodgers. According to the Indian Seaman's Union,

> The housing accommodation in Bombay is so expensive that seamen who are not born and bred in Bombay very rarely live with their families ... Indian seamen are so poorly paid that they cannot afford to live with their families, and have to live under the most revolting conditions.[53]

In the case of families in which women did not earn, it was said, 'relatives, friends, caste-men or village-men are taken as boarders in order to supplement the earnings of the male members of the family'.[54] While these arrangements provided newly arrived migrants with a foothold in the city, they could also serve to extend the influence of their hosts while enabling the latter to discharge the obligations which custom and expediency imposed upon them within the context of their kinship and caste connections. Moreover, sub-letting could also prove highly profitable, allowing them to do well by doing good. Thus, the Industrial Disputes Committee discovered that some of the lessees of rooms in the Spring Mill chawls were 'making as much as ten rupees a month profit by sub-letting', whereas, in the case of halalkhores who were given accommodation by the Municipality at the especially 'low rent of rupee one and annas three', 'the profit on sub-letting is said to be as high as twenty rupees a month'.[55] For jobbers, better-paid workers or those with access to privileged housing, sub-letting might constitute sound business.

The room-sharing arrangements of Bombay's workers took many forms. Some rented rooms together, others lodged with relatives or friends. Room-sharing did not necessarily mean that each worker paid an equal share of the rent. Indeed, sometimes their rights could vary according to their share of the rent. It was possible for some workers to pay a nominal rent to leave their belongings in the room and then to sleep elsewhere, usually on the verandah outside, in the wadi or on the street. In other cases, the employed might help to bear the costs of those who were out of work. The khanavalis, a characteristic institution of the working-class neighbourhood, were boarding 'houses' to

[51] *Ibid.*, I, i, 517.
[52] A.R. Desai and S.D. Pillai, *A Profile of an Indian Slum* (Bombay, 1972); N. Harris, *Economic Development, Cities and Planning: The Case of Bombay* (Bombay, 1978); Kosambi, *Bombay in Transition.*
[53] *RCLI, Evidence, Bombay Presidency*, Indian Seaman's Union, I, i, 291.
[54] *Ibid.*, Social Service League, I, i, 429–30.
[55] Report of the Industrial Disputes Committee, reprinted in *Labour Gazette*, I, 8 (April, 1922), p. 7.

which people could subscribe and have their meals cooked for them. Again, the keepers of khanavalis sometimes allowed homeless or unemployed workers to use their room as base.[56] They were sometimes organized according to caste, or according to village; some were run by jobbers for the workers whom they hired.

During the 1920s and 1930s, developments in the housing market intensified the problems of tenants at cheaper rentals, with the effect of pulling them more firmly into the social organization of the neighbourhood. The preference of most workers to live near their workplace and their relatives and friends served to exert intense pressure on the housing stock of specific neighbourhoods. Indeed, the strong preference in favour of particular neighbourhoods often meant that 'even unsatisfactory and inadequate accommodation at a higher rent in select areas is welcomed'.[57] Together with the high cost of land and the complexities of tenure, this concentrated demand for housing resulted in rising rents. Moreover, the housing market was generally sensitive to the flows of migration. Periods of high immigration tended to push rents up even further while at the same time intensifying the competition for work.

Rural migration during the First World War rapidly increased the pressure of demand upon rent. At the same time, the last years of the war witnessed growing speculation in land. The property market in any case generally expressed a strong tendency for speculative transactions.[58] Frequent changes in ownership were accompanied by attempts to raise rents. The speculation which accompanied the last years of the war was sharper for its occurrence in boom conditions. Investors paid high prices for land and then attempted to obtain what they considered appropriate returns on their capital by raising rents. As the returns available on alternative sources of investment rose, and the general level of prices followed, landlords raised rents still further. During the war, the state attempted to use the Defence of India rules to check rising rents and in 1918 finally passed a Rent Act. Whereas prices had risen much faster than wages in the war-time inflation, the influx of migrants during the war and especially after the famine and influenza epidemic of 1918–19 generated an excess supply of labour in the city, which brought intermittent spells of unemployment for most workers.[59]

The Rent Act was intended to protect the interests of low-rental tenants. In fact, it had something of the opposite effect. To some extent, landlords withdrew rooms from the market, preferring to leave them vacant and to create scarcities

---

[56] Cholia, *Dock Labourers*, p. 52; Patel, *Rural Labour*, pp. 69–70; RCLI, *Evidence, Bombay Presidency*, I, i, The Bombay Seamen's Union, p. 293; The Indian Seamen's Union, p. 291; Messrs Mackinnon, Mackenzie and Co., p. 545; Mr J.E.P. Curry, Shipping Master, Bombay, p. 180.

[57] *Report of the Rent Enquiry Committee*, I, i, 20.

[58] *Ibid.*, I, i, 31.

[59] *Ibid.*, I, i, 19–20, 24.

which enabled them to levy additional cesses, rather than letting them unprofitably at controlled rents. Alternatively, they tightened their credit, collected rents more vigorously and exercised their powers of eviction with greater regularity. In addition, whereas rent restriction did not inhibit building – indeed there was more construction during the operation of the Rent Act than after its repeal in 1928 – it focussed on the larger tenements which were not liable to rent control.[60] In any case, these were the buildings on which a better return could be obtained during the boom, a consideration which became increasingly important after 1918 as the cost of materials as well as wages continued to rise.[61] During the 1920s, it was in the municipal ward C, outside the mill districts, that the largest increase in the number of newly built chawls was recorded.[62] Housing shortages, already endemic before the Rent Act was passed, were now intensified in the lower reaches of the market. Under these conditions, landlords began to demand pugdee or a large cash payment in advance.[63] This premium helped landlords neutralize tenants' actions against them, especially by using the new legislation to bring down rents, or even simply to abscond without payment. Its effect was to increase the dependence of tenants upon moneylenders, grain-dealers, perhaps even the landlord or the rent collector to whom they might be forced to turn to raise the money for the pugdee.

The collapse of the post-war boom left landlords with falling land values whereas controlled rents limited their returns on capital invested when the prices of land and building materials were high. At the same time, the market in larger tenements was quickly saturated. Consequently, during the 1930s builders turned their attention to single-room chawls.[64] Indeed when the Government of Bombay came to review the effects of its legislation it found that the rents of 'better class dwelling houses and flats [were] lower than they were a couple of years ago. This may not be so with regard to the dwellings of the middle and labouring classes.'[65] Rents appear to have been relatively stable in the mill districts during the 1930s. But the advent of a Congress government in 1937 led landlords to make a determined bid to raise rents in anticipation of measures to control them.[66] Nevertheless, the housing shortage proved intractable and long after the Rent Act was repealed the practice of demanding a sizeable pugdee continued,[67] making tenants yet more dependent upon the patronage and credit networks of the neighbourhood.

[60] *Ibid.*, I, i, 24–7.
[61] IIC, *Evidence*, A.E. Mirams, IV, 356, 358.
[62] *Census, 1931*, IX, i, 81–2.
[63] *Report of the Rent Enquiry Committee*, I, i, 37.
[64] *Ibid.*, I, i, 26.
[65] GOB, General, Departmental Note, 24 May 1924, File 5518-I, p. 23, MSA.
[66] *Report of the Rent Enquiry Committee*, I, i, 32.
[67] Patel, *Rural Labour*, p. 74.

The organization and operation of the housing market brought together within its ambit most of the important institutions and influential figures of the neighbourhood. Some measure of control in the distribution of housing provided an effective base for those who sought to extend their influence within the neighbourhood. At one level, we may place the landlord, the owner of the wadi or the chawls. Investment in the building and rental of cheap single-room tenements was not in itself the most attractive business proposition for private capital. But it brought safe and regular returns and, as the crisis of the textile industry in the 1920s and the slump of the early 1930s increased the risks of alternative forms of investment, a regular income from rentals was not to be spurned. Whereas investors in low-rental tenements often had orthodox business motives, the possibility of recovering political dividends was not lost upon them. A similar complex of commercial and political motives underpinned the organization of the settlements of huts and sheds. One observer described how one such settlement was brought into existence at Tardeo:

A man who owns a piece of land has given a contract for a certain sum to another man who lives in the neighbourhood. This man has again given a contract to the Bhaiya, who charges about Rs. 8 to Rs. 10 per shed to tenants who sublet their rooms to others.[68]

Landlords or rent lords often entered the housing market from an established position of influence in the neighbourhood. Jobbers sometimes rented their own chawls or a number of rooms on their own account and then sub-let them, preferably to workers in their connection. More often, landlords were already successful men of commerce: grain-dealers, shopkeepers and money-lenders. The winder the range of his commercial interests, the greater the concentration of the landlord's power and influence in the neighbourhood was likely to become. Moreover, he could use the influence gained in one sphere of his commercial activities to extend his interests in others. 'Not infrequently', wrote Burnett-Hurst in the 1920s, 'the owner of the chawl maintains his own grain, cloth or toddy (country liquor) shops, which his tenants are expected (and in some cases forced) to patronize.'[69]

Most landlords subcontracted the management of their property to a rent collector, whether at a fixed rental or for a commission calculated as a proportion of the collection. The rent collector often became a figure of considerable influence in his own right. He might arbitrate in disputes between tenants; he could be called upon to lend money, sometimes to help residents pay the tent in periods of unemployment; he had to maintain the property and its facilities, which could necessitate developing connections at the local police station or with the municipal administration. Above all, he possessed the power to evict

[68] *RCLI, Evidence, Bombay Presidency*, The Bombay Presidency Women's Council, I, i, 516.
[69] Burnett-Hurst, *Labour and Housing*, p. 23.

and to fill vacancies which arose in the chawl. Thus, when a police reporter was asked to leave a strikers' meeting during the general strike in July 1929, he refused, 'unless I am told to go by the landlord of the chawl or his rent collector'.[70]

Whereas it was scarcely in the landlord's interest to engage an agent with too much local power, a rent collector who could not develop influential neighbourhood connections was not always able to perform his duties effectively. Often he was forced to deal with jobbers, dadas and grain-dealers; at times, these indeed were the agents who subcontracted to collect rent. For instance, jobbers sometimes rented several rooms and then sub-let them to workers in their connection and organized khanavalis and boarding houses.[71] On the other hand, the configuration of local power determined how far landlords could choose their agents; at times they were simply forced to operate within the local structure of power and come to terms with the bosses of the neighbourhood.

In some cases, chawl or wadi committees were formed by the residents to represent tenants' grievances, to deal with landlords, rent collectors or officials and to settle disputes between neighbours. These chawl committees largely consisted of the most influential and respected inhabitants of the chawl; some might wield power wearing other hats, for instance as jobbers or dadas. The ramifications of the power of these informal neighbourhood councils could extend to the imposition of levies or fines on local residents, whether for the organization of a communal event or as a punitive measure against wrong-doers. In some cases, these committees acted as tribunals and staged public trials. After the Hindu–Muslim riots of 1929, 500 Hindus of Dhaku Parbhu's Wadi at Ghorapdeo met to consider the terms on which the Muslim residents of the wadi would be allowed to return. The terms imposed on their Muslim neighbours are instructive. They had to undertake that assaults on the Hindus of the wadi and in the neighbourhood of Ghorapdeo would not be repeated; that for the murder of Balkrishna Sawant during the riot, they would pay Rs. 500 as compensation to his family and hand over the culprit to the Hindus; that they would compensate for the damage to a room which was set on fire during the riots; that they would apologize for the fact that thirteen Hindus were arrested allegedly on the basis of 'malicious information' provided by the Muslim residents; that they would back their obsequies by petitioning the authorities for their release; and finally that they would no longer sacrifice cows. Five 'responsible' Muslims had to guarantee that these conditions would be fulfilled. 'If all these conditions are accepted', read the agreement, and only then, 'the Mohammedans may come

---

[70] GOB, Home (Sp.) File 543 (10) E Pt D of 1929, pp. 63–73, MSA; see also *Report of the Rent Enquiry Committee*, I, i, 36.
[71] Supplementary Report by Dr (Mrs) Barnes, GOI Industries, 1922, Labour, File L-920 (3), p. 24, NAI.

and live in the wadi'.[72] Whether the conditions were enforced or indeed, in the case of cow killing, sustained over time is not known. What is more clear, however, is that communal sanctions were impressive and the administration of informal justice in the neighbourhood widespread.

Between the landlord and the tenant, between the patrons and their dependents, power and influence were located at several intermediate levels. For instance, migrants who came to the city lodged with their relatives, friends and caste-fellows. In turn, this encouraged the more established workers in the city to help the newly arrived migrants to find work: once they had found a job they could contribute to the rent and the household's income. Whereas most working-class families needed boarders in order to pay the rent, these arrangements served the interests of recently arrived migrants seeking a foothold in the city, created goodwill within the wider kinship structure which not even the most securely established workers could afford to ignore and were in any case integral to the reciprocal obligations which both custom and expediency imposed within the family economy of the working class. A social investigator noted that 'over-crowding in the tenements of the Marathi-speaking depressed classes is in many cases due to the fact that distant relations with a view to finding a job in Bombay come and live with their relatives here'.[73] In addition, the more established workers in the city could, by helping their friends and relatives, develop their own networks of influence both in the workplace and the wadi.

The diffusion of power through the neighbourhood served to limit the influence and control exercised by landlords and rent collectors. Since there were several competing agencies operating in the neighbourhood, their rivalry at certain points and their interdependence at others served to constrain the uninhibited use of the power of each. But there was another instrument available to the residents of a chawl or wadi against the exactions of their patrons. They could quit, leaving behind them accumulated rental debts. In 1939, the landlord's outgoings on the management of his property was estimated at 36 per cent of the gross rent. The major portion of this amount was taken up by municipal taxes, the costs of repair and maintenance, rent collection and general management, insurance charges and sinking funds; but bad debts from rents which could not be recovered and losses from vacancies which could not be filled also contributed to this margin.[74]

---

[72] Commissioner of Police, Bombay to Sec, GOB, Home, no. 2467/A-122, 11 May 1929, GOB, Home (Poll.) File 344 of 1929, pp. 343–5, MSA.

[73] Pradhan, 'Untouchable Workers', p. 12. Middle-class migrants to Bombay followed similar practices. See F.F. Conlon, *A Caste in a Changing World: The Chitrapur Saraswat Brahmans 1700–1935* (Berkeley and Los Angeles, 1977). See also Labour Office, Bombay, *Report on an Enquiry into Middle Class Family Budgets in Bombay City* (Bombay, 1928) and Labour Office, Bombay, *Report on an Enquiry into Middle Class Unemployment in the Bombay Presidency* (Bombay, 1927).

[74] *Report of the Rent Enquiry Committee*, I, i, 34.

The moonlight flit by tenants the night before the rent collector arrived was the landlord's nightmare. But it would be misleading to assume that workers ceaselessly migrated between tenements picking their way between landlords, whose rents they were unwilling or unable to meet. Since the workers' choice of residence was affected by their wider social connections, their mobility between neighbourhoods was effectively restricted. 'Those who remain at a place for some years', as the Social Service League explained in 1929, 'get attached to it owing to friendly relations with the neighbours and are naturally unwilling to change it even for a better one.'[75] At the same time, it was by no means easy to avoid rent debts from one chawl only to seek refuge in the next. Above all, the acute physical shortage of housing stock limited the options before tenants. 'It was true to some extent', declared the Bhadekari Sangh, 'that the risk of bad debts also prevented investors from constructing houses for workmen ... The witness would not, however, say that a great many working class tenants absconded without paying rents.'[76] It may have been easier or more common to evade payments in public housing than in private chawls, and in any case, workers sometimes adopted rather more novel and subtle methods. As one contemporary observed in the mid 1920s:

Not accustomed to paying rent and not desiring to spend any more than they have to in the city, that they may have more to take back with them to the village, the mill operatives take every opportunity to evade the rent collector. They have been known to escape rent by getting into arrears and then going to the superintendent of the chawls and asking for another room under another name. Then they move their belongings secretly to their new room, and the rent collector, suspicious but not sure, contents himself with getting them to pay the rent for the new room.[77]

Credit

The supply of credit, like housing, became a focal point of social organization beyond the workplace. Since one objective of migration to Bombay for most workers was to gain easier access to cash, both in the form of wages and of loans, and since a large proportion of the city's labour force lived perilously near the margins of subsistence, credit constituted a vital resource and a valuable instrument of control in the neighbourhood. Consequently traders, grain-dealers and money-lenders acquired considerable influence. In urban as in rural India, money-lending was not confined to a single class of professional bankers. Anybody with cash reserves might offer credit. Necessarily, substantial lending took place between friends and relatives. At another level, there were numerous formal as well as informal agencies of credit.

[75] *RCLI, Evidence, Bombay Presidency*, Social Service League, I, i, 434.
[76] *Report of the Rent Enquiry Committee*, II, vi, 8.
[77] Rutnagar (ed.), *Bombay Industries*, p. 497.

The most common source of credit, apart from the mutual help which workers afforded each other, was the neighbourhood grain-dealer. The local bania, it was said, gave

abundant credit and the usual supply of provisions is not withheld even if an employee is not of service or unable to attend work owing to illness. Again, the bania is moreover the people's banker and lends them a rupee or two, or even more, as required for petty expenses and holiday making.[78]

Their loans were characterized by their flexibility. They often lent in small amounts, in kind as well as in cash, which was indispensable for workers who often required supplies and credit to tide them over intermittent periods of unemployment and distress. Indeed, what differentiated the banias from other money-lenders was that they were willing to lend in periods of distress when other creditors might be concerned to call back their loans.[79] This was because the demand for their credit was greatest precisely when their customers were unemployed or sick or had suffered bad harvests in their village base. Their profits depended upon their willingness to offer high-risk loans. Indeed, they often lent money without demanding security; frequently, their customers simply could not provide it. Their terms of repayment were accommodating and they were known to extend credit for lengthy periods.[80] Their credit, it was noted, ensured that 'a millhand has got ready money to purchase his daily necessaries'. Indeed, it was their 'promptness in giving petty advances which is a unique feature which makes the worker like the bania most'.[81] Moreover, 'in times of dispute between workers and employers, Bania grain-dealers allow credit to the extent of five or six months'.[82]

The apparent flexibility of his terms sometimes led observers to portray the grain-dealer as a relatively benevolent figure in the credit market. As he had to operate within the community and to some extent was dependent upon it, his power was limited by the pressures imposed upon him by his clients. The fact that he was at least loosely connected with a substantial proportion of his clientele enabled the grain-dealer to operate flexibly, extend credit at times and for periods when others would not and take greater risks than other money-lenders. If this widened the range of options before grain-dealers, it also obliged them to act within the parameters of the expectations and demands of the

---

[78] IIC, *Evidence, Bombay*, A.E. Mirams, IV, 368.

[79] Proceedings of the Bombay Provincial Banking Enquiry Committee, Replies to the Questionnaire ... submitted by the Currimbhoy Ebrahim Workmen's Institute, File 12/C, MSA; IIC, *Evidence*, A.E. Mirams, IV, 368.

[80] IIC, *Evidence*, A.E. Mirams, IV, 368.

[81] Proceedings of the Bombay Provincial Banking Enquiry Committee, Replies to the Questionnaire ... submitted by the Currimbhoy Ebrahim Workmen's Institute, File 12/C, MSA.

[82] *Bombay Chronicle*, 7 February 1940.

neighbourhood. The flexibility of grain-dealers' operations did not derive from philanthropic sentiment, rather they were forced to adapt their business strategies to the economy and politics of the neighbourhood.

Grain-dealers were often willing to lend on demand, without security and in small amounts according to need. They might allow relatively generous terms of repayment. But they might also fix a higher price for the grain they sold on credit or vary their rates of interest to suit each case, charging for the flexible conditions of repayment which they offered.[83] They might also demand the exclusive custom of a debtor as the condition for a loan. Certainly, employers complained that banias would not serve workers who patronized the cheap grain shops, established by some mills once war broke out in 1914. The mill shops and co-operative societies lent limited sums for limited periods and sold grain to each worker only once a week. Few workers could afford to buy their week's supplies in a single transaction. Yet if they ran short of grain in the course of the week, they found that they were boycotted by the local grain-dealer. The result was to force workers to 'buy all the necessaries of life from the bania' and, not surprisingly, mills 'found the grain shops a failure'.[84] Similar methods could be utilized against rival grain-dealers in the neighbourhood. Grain-dealers, who rented shops on the ground floor of a chawl, sometimes entered into rent collection on behalf of the landlord. At times, they even owned and rented the chawl themselves and combining these functions were able to demand the exclusive custom of their tenants as well.[85] Grain-dealers might lend on discriminating terms to regular customers and extend the connections thus developed to a wider commercial field, occasionally into the workplace and sometimes into political organization.[86]

Just as the rent collector was not the only intermediary operating in the housing market, the grain-dealer was scarcely the only money-lender. Apart from the grain-dealer, observers perceived a separate class of professional money-lenders in the credit market. Lacking the close social and commercial ties which characterized the grain-dealer's operations, the professional money-lenders adopted rather different business methods. They offered less flexible terms of credit. They charged a higher rate of interest and often demanded 'the security of a person like a jobber'. Loans guaranteed by trusted agents could be

[83] Proceedings of the BPBEC, Replies to the Questionnaire, Currimbhoy Ebrahim Workmen's Institute, File 12/C, MSA.

[84] IIC, *Evidence*, A.E. Mirams, IV, 368–9.

[85] Burnett-Hurst, *Labour and Housing*, p. 23.

[86] The city's Congress organization in several neighbourhoods was centred upon the influence of the local grain-dealer. Interviews, V.B. Karnik, April 1979, B.T. Ranadive, April 1979. For the example of Ravji Devakram, Dharavi grain-dealer and Congressman, see Proceedings of the BDEC, 1938, GOB, Home (Sp.) File 550 (25) II B, pp. 277–9, MSA.

obtained at cheaper rates of interest.[87] Moreover, the professional money-lenders were commonly feared for their accounting skills: many, it was said, maintained several books and were proverbially adept at making intricate calculations to extort money.[88] Certainly, dealing with a professional money-lender enmeshed workers, dependent upon the protection and security of more influential friends and neighbours, more deeply in the networks of neighbourhood patronage.

The lenders of last resort for the working class were Pathans. This was because they were reputed both to charge double the rate of interest levied by professional money-lenders and to be particularly brutal and violent in the recovery of their loans. They were said to be flexible about repayment as long as the interest charges were met regularly, leaving 'the repayment of capital to the borrower's convenience'.[89] Although the credit they allowed depended to some extent 'on the borrower's employment and sureties',[90] the security which the Pathan relied upon was usually 'the threat of his lathi which was invariably and sufficiently effective for speeding payments of instalments'.[91] When workers failed to meet their dues, the Pathan, it was said, followed his debtor to his home and his workplace and extracted his dues by intimidation and violence. According to the non-Brahmin politician K.S. Gupte, the Pathans

always keep their debtors in mortal fear of them. The Pathan, it appears, never admits that the capital is fully paid up, and he will harass and molest men and women alike. Sometimes their women debtors are kept as mistresses in lieu of interest and they are even known to ask debtors to sell their women's honour to them.[92]

According to Lalji Naranji, they took away not only their debtors' wives but

---

[87] Proceedings of the BPBEC, Replies to the Questionnaire, Currimbhoy Ebrahim Workmen's Institute, File 12/C, MSA.

[88] *Ibid.*

[89] Accompaniment to Letter, Comissioner of Police, Bombay, to Secretary, BPBEC, no. 1496/21-D, 31 January 1930, GOB, Finance, File 48-I of 1929–30, MSA. Their connections extended to the mofussil. In Ratnagiri, for instance, there were reported to be two or three Pathan money-lenders in each of the five talukas. They lived in the taluka headquarters and visited the surrounding villages. It was generally that 'poor persons who have no landed property or ornaments to pawn with village Sowkars borrow money from these Pathans'. Collector of Ratnagiri to Sec, BPBEC, 3 December 1929, no. M.S. c. 71 in *ibid.* Their main centres of operation in the Presidency were Bombay, Poona, Satara and Sholapur. They were also extremely important in Nasik where they facilitated credit to the value of Rs. 70,000. In Satara, the total amount of outstanding credit made available by Pathans was estimated at Rs. 200,000. Everywhere their customers were said to belong to 'those classes of people who have no status'. *Ibid., passim.*

[90] Accompaniment to Letter, Commissioner of Police to Sec, BPBEC, no. 1496/21-D, 31 January 1930, *ibid.*, MSA.

[91] Proceedings of the BPBEC, Replies to the Questionnaire, Currimbhoy Ebrahim Workmen's Institute, File 12-C, MSA.

[92] *TOI*, 9 February 1929.

their children as well.[93] The fact that debt collectors might lie in wait for clients at the factory gates immediately after pay-day no doubt contributed to the high rates of absenteeism at these times.[94]

It is necessarily difficult to ascertain whether Pathan money-lenders were in fact more violent than their counterparts or indeed how far they were simply perceived to be rough and brutal. Many money-lenders, and not Pathans alone, probably relied upon the threat of violence to obtain repayment. On the other hand, the Pathans often lacked the friends and influence in the neighbourhood which for the bania enabled a more painless recovery of loans.

Jobbers also sometimes acted as creditors on their own account. By extending the range of their commercial interests, they could consolidate and advance their position in the neighbourhood. Keeping workers in their debt facilitated their tasks of discipline and supervision in the workplace. But few jobbers commanded sufficient capital to offer credit on an extensive scale. Some pooled their resources to lend money; others acted simply as brokers in the credit market, borrowing from professional creditors to lend to their friends, clients and dependants or otherwise acting as guarantors of loans made by money-lenders. Similarly, the jobber was a useful source of credit when workers needed money to tend to their village base, for it encouraged him to re-employ them on their return. When the jobbers did lend money they usually dealt in relatively small sums and usually within a narrow social circle. Credit was an instrument of domination for jobbers; but they could also be pressured into offering it as a service which the expectations of their clients forced upon them.

These were the most readily identified creditors in the working-class neighbourhood. But there were many others who, with small cash reserves, might be willing to offer short-term loans for modest amounts. Many pedlars, traders and hawkers, who depended upon the quick turnover of cash, participated in the short-term lending of small sums. If grain-dealers came to wield considerable influence in the neighbourhood, these pedlars and hawkers at another level often became brokers in the politics of the street. They were typified in one account, by the itinerant coffee-vendors, 'a characteristic feature of the Mussalman quarters of Bombay':

He is usually an old resident of the city, experienced in the wiles of the urban population and sometimes perhaps a protégé of the local police. He has a perfect acquaintance with the intricacies of the Bombay galis and back-slums, ... and he is not a grasping creditor.[95]

---

[93] See BRIC, 1929, Oral Evidence, Lalji Naranji, File 4, p. 121; see also *ibid.*, P.G. Solanki, File 6, p. 127; and various others who gave evidence before the BRIC. MSA.

[94] Proceedings of the TLIC, Main Inquiry, Oral Evidence, Cotton Mill Workers, Bombay, Spinning Side, File 60-A, p. 1037, MSA.

[95] S.M. Edwardes, *By-Ways of Bombay* (Bombay, 1912), p. 119.

It is understandable that the relationship between creditors and the community within which they operated was characterized by permanent antagonisms, tension and conflict. Their ability to do favours for people in the same chawl or neighbourhood was central to the advancement of their own commercial interests. Indeed, they were expected to perform services for the neighbourhood and they could suffer commercially for their failure to fulfil these expectations. At the same time, the nature of their commerce left them liable to incur the wrath of the neighbourhood and sometimes peculiarly exposed to its consequences. Conversely, those who succeeded in operating within these constraints could develop impressive networks of patronage and influence.

The nature of the demands imposed upon creditors by their clients and the community in general was illustrated by the ways in which grain-dealers, shopkeepers and money-lenders were pressed to finance a variety of social and political activities, from the celebration of religious festivals to industrial action. Thus, Hindu shopkeepers were called upon to finance the Islamic festival of Mohurram.[96] Each street or sometimes whole mohollas spent considerable sums of money to erect a tabut, to organize its procession through the city and to arrange for a maulvi to deliver the waaz up to the tenth day of the month.[97] During Mohurram, it was said, 'youths preceded by drummers and clarionet players, wander through the streets, laying all the shopkeepers under contribution for subscriptions'.[98] The imposition and acceptance of such levies was closely connected with the nature of street commerce. Muslim youths who danced their way around these shops were the customers and debtors of the shopkeeper. The shopkeepers had paid their dues, often no doubt with reluctance, because it was expected that they would. The relationship was more one of obligation than of enforcement. It was only when the arrangements of the ugarani, the collection of funds for the tabut levied by each moholla, broke down that its underlying tensions and antagonisms surfaced. Thus, it appeared to the

[96] The observance of Mohurram over ten days marked the massacre of Hussain and Hasan and their relatives and followers at Kerbala. The Shias regarded it as a period of mourning; for the Sunnis, according to the *Gazetteer*, it was 'an occasion for frolic and mummery, based largely upon spirit-beliefs and ghost-scarings borrowed from Hinduism'. *Gazetteer*, I, 184. Few Shias would have found it necessary to disagree with this interpretation. For a general account of Mohurram, see J.N. Hollister, *The Shia of India* (London, 1953), pp. 164–80. For a recent investigation, see J.C. Masselos, 'Power in the Bombay "Moholla", 1904–15: An Initial Exploration into the World of the Indian Urban Muslim', *South Asia*, VI (1976), 75–95, and J.C. Masselos, 'Change and Custom in the Format of the Bombay Mohurram during the Nineteenth and Twentieth Centuries', *South Asia*, N.S., V, 2 (1982), 47–67.

[97] The tabut, a model of Hussain's tomb, and its procession, cost mohollas between Rs. 100 and Rs. 400. For his description of the martyrdom of Hussain, the maulvi was paid between Rs. 30 and Rs. 100. *Gazetteer*, I, 185. See also Masselos, 'Power in the Bombay "Moholla"', and Masselos, 'Change and Custom'.

[98] *Gazetteer*, I, 185.

Police Commissioner in 1911 that the money was 'extorted – there is no other word for it – from Marwadi and Bania merchants, who are threatened with physical injury unless they subscribe liberally'. At times, it was said,

the collecting party, composed of four or five Muhammadan roughs, would visit the shops of the Jain merchants, carrying a dead rat, and threaten or drop it into the heaps of grain and sugar if the shop-owner did not forthwith hand out a fair sum.[99]

These collections were believed to support not only the festival but also a number of street-corner bosses, dadas and their followers, the youth gangs of the neighbourhood. At such times

some mohollas contrived to raise comparatively large sums, aggregating several hundred rupees, and as only a fractional portion of this money was required to defray the cost of the *tabut* and the paraphernalia of the final procession, the balance was devoted to the support of the hooligans of the *mohollas* during the following few months.[100]

The interplay between popular expectations and local patronage was expressed in 1911 when a group of Marwari merchants lodged a complaint at Pydhonie police station that they were being harassed and assaulted by the Muslims of the Bengalpura moholla. When the police warned the 'leaders' of the moholla not to continue these extortions, 'this was treated as a grievance and Latiff himself had the impertinence to come to the Head Police Office and complain that "the police were not assisting the collection of funds"'.[101]

A similar picture of service, obligation and reciprocity emerges from the role which shopkeepers played in the conduct of strikes. Flexible credit arrangements provide at least a partial explanation for the long general strikes which textile workers were able repeatedly to mount between 1919 and 1940. Not only did grain-dealers sometimes extend credit on flexible, indeed elastic, terms, but trade unions also negotiated with them to supply strikers in periods of industrial conflict. 'In strikes', as S.V. Ghate, a prominent leader of the Girni Kamgar Union, was to recall, 'these shopkeepers played a very good role.'[102] For every 5,000 bags of rice bought by the Joint Mill Strike Committee during the 1928 strike, grain-dealers in the working-class neighbourhoods would give them ten bags of rice free of charge, 'because these fellows thought that feeding the poor

[99] Commissioner of Police, Bombay, to Secretary, GOB, Judicial, No. 545-C dated 20 January 1911, reprinted in S.M. Edwardes, *The Bombay City Police – 1672–1916: A Historical Sketch* (London, 1923), Appendix, p. 198.

[100] Edwardes, *Bombay City Police*, pp. 181–2. Several mohollas could turn out 'several thousand followers' in their tolis. The participation in the street gangs of the neighbourhood even outside the spectacular context of Mohurram was impressive.

[101] Commissioner of Police, Bombay to Secretary, GOB, Judicial, 20 January 1911, in Edwardes, *Bombay City Police*, Appendix, p. 198.

[102] S.V. Ghate, interviewed by Dr A.K. Gupta and Dr Hari Dev Sharma, Oral History Project, Transcript, p. 29, NMML.

was one of the best things',[103] especially no doubt when charity came in the form of bulk orders.

The local grain-dealer or shopkeeper was a figure of considerable importance. It was useful for most workers to cultivate his protection as well as his patronage. At the same time, the relationship between workers and such patrons was imbued with tension which could at times find expression through violence. The wide spectrum of positions occupied by creditors within the neighbourhood was indicated during the one-day textile strike of 7 November 1938. On the one hand, workers sought the protection of some shopkeepers and grain-dealers. Tukaram Laxman, determined to go to work, turned to the bidi shop, when he was threatened by strikers:

I requested the bidi shopkeeper to send me to work. I said, "Mama, anyhow see that I get to work". Then the Bidiwalla asked the [presumably his] motor driver who was nearby to take me to my mill.[104]

On the same day, however, several grain shops were 'looted'. This looting was conducted almost with an air of festivity. Thus, the Police Commissioner described the levity which accompanied these raids:

the shopkeepers were arguing with these people. The crowd seemed to treat the whole affair as a joke. They would just pick up a handful of grain and throw it.[105]

Baijnath Bahadur complained that strikers entered the shop in which he worked, removed the gunny cloth covering the grain, ate the grain and ran away.[106] According to Garib Ganpat, who owned the shop, the police had merely looked on while the mob looted his goods. While he was closing his shop, 'The sergeant advised me to go to the Police Station and report the matter.' 'I said', he added tersely, 'that I would consider the matter.'[107] For Garib Ganpat, as for many others in the working-class neighbourhoods, their suspicion of the police matched their apprehension of the mob. By reporting them to the police, he risked the loss of their custom.

Jobs and jobbers

Of the various locations of power in the neighbourhood, the jobbers' influence in particular was characterized by their penetration of diverse areas of working-

---

103 *Ibid.*, p. 43.
104 Proceedings of the BDEC, Oral Evidence, Tukaram Laxman, GOB, Home (Sp.) File 550 (25), IIIB of 1938, p. 517, MSA.
105 Proceedings of the BDEC, Oral Evidence, W.R.G. Smith, Commissioner of Police, Bombay, GOB Home (Sp.) File 550 (25), IIIB of 1938, p. 1043, MSA.
106 *Ibid.*, Baijnath Bahadur, GOB Home (Sp.) File 550 (25) IIIB of 1938, p. 639, MSA.
107 *Ibid.*, Garib Ganpat, GOB Home (Sp.) File 550 (25) IIIB of 1938, p. 647, MSA.

class life. To perform his functions in the workplace the jobber had to develop and maintain contacts in the wider sphere of the neighbourhood. To recruit and discipline workers 'with success', recorded the *Gazetteer*, the jobber is 'bound to have a following of men and boys who usually live in the same neighbourhood and often in the same chawl as himself'.[108] Burnett-Hurst, in his study of the condition of wage-earners in Bombay in the 1920s, observed that the jobber

> endeavours to acquire an influence over his friends and acquaintances who live in the same or neighbouring chawls. He lends them money, advises them on family affairs and arbitrates in disputes. When labour is required, he uses the influence so gained and is generally successful in procuring hands.[109]

Furthermore, as we have already seen jobbers intervened effectively in various ways and to varying degrees in the provision of housing and credit. In addition, they were prominent in the organization of leisure as well. They organized festivals, ran gymnasiums and liquor shops. They often helped organize khanavalis or boarding houses which catered specially for groups of single workers.

Indeed, what jobbers organized in the neighbourhood was appropriately described as 'an industrial "chummery"'. The ramifications of this 'chummery' cannot easily be mapped; of course, they varied from jobber to jobber, neighbourhood to neighbourhood. Sometimes the jobber found a room for single workers and hired 'an old woman to do the cooking and all other domestic work for them'. But the reach of the jobber's commercial enterprise went even further. One official referring to the extent of 'illegitimacy', reported primly in the early 1920s,

> I have refrained from noting on this so far, but there is a fair amount of this in Bombay ... I found it a very delicate ground upon which to make enquiries. I know of some mills where this is more common than others, but there is no doubt in my mind that there is much of this in Bombay. The conditions of work engender this. Men come from their homes, leaving their families to a strange land, where they find conditions very different to their village lives, and there are so many widows who are willing to cook and take care of an industrial 'chummery' organized by the jobber, and a great deal of unacknowledged illegitimacy results.[110]

Indeed, there was reputedly a higher rate of infant mortality in Bombay than of legitimate births.[111] Historians have often understood the politics of migrant workers as a simple function of their adaptation to the urban environment; it is to be hoped that rural mentalities and urbanization will not suggest an explanation for their sexuality as well.

---

[108] *Gazetteer*, I, 493.
[109] Burnett-Hurst, *Labour and Housing*, p. 46.
[110] Supplementary Report by Dr (Mrs) Barnes, 23 July 1922, GOI, Industries, 1922, Labour, File L-920 (3), NAI.
[111] *Ibid.*

Many jobbers were directly involved in prostitution. Indeed, women jobbers in the cotton mills were, according to Burnett-Hurst, the most deeply involved. 'The naikins as a class', he wrote,

are persons of low morals – some of them keep 'dadas' (hooligan millhands), while others make use of their power over their subordinates to force them into prostitution. Even some of the clerks (especially those attached to the reeling department) and the jobbers take advantage of the helplessness and the poverty of the women.[112]

But there is no reason to suppose, as Burnett-Hurst implies, that the clerks and jobbers were relatively backward in this field of activity. Similarly, 'Raghu, the model mill-hand', as sketched by H.A. Talcherkar, social worker and organizer of the Kamgar Hitwardhak Sabha,

feels disheartened when he thinks of the demoralising life led by some of the female workers in mills. He would not for the life of him allow his wife to enter a cotton mill or in anyway come into contact with the mill fore-women (Naikins) who are known to be notoriously fast and wicked.[113]

In addition, their influence in the neighbourhood and the workplace often made jobbers valuable members of the chawl committee and caste panchayats. This influence at the level of the street and the neighbourhood made jobbers useful allies for politicians at various levels. For instance, Mahadev Naik, who lived at Mahadev Wadi (perhaps his own) was connected with Jinabhai Joshi, member of the Legislative Assembly, and more crucially with S.B. Mahadeshwar, the Vice President of the F Ward District Congress Committee in the 1930s, reputed for his organizational skills and his contacts in the mill district.[114] The most prominent of all dadas in Bombay, Keshav Borkar, was closely associated with the city's Congress boss, S.K. Patil.[115] These high-flying connections, which derived ultimately from their position at work, in turn enhanced their value and their influence within the neighbourhood. Conversely, although jobbers were usually promoted from the shop floor, it was often necessary to exercise some leverage on the existing systems of power and patronage in the neighbourhood in order to obtain the position at the workplace. What Ambalal Sarabhai said for the jobber in Ahmedabad could equally apply to Bombay as well: 'He becomes a jobber if he has friends and relatives in important positions in the mills and is also a favourite of the head of the department; the chances of his becoming a jobber entirely on his own merit are very

112 Burnett-Hurst, *Labour and Housing*, p. 53.
113 *The Indian Social Reformer*, 14 March 1908, p. 328.
114 Proceedings of the BDEC, Oral Evidence, Mahadev Naik, GOB, Home (Sp.) File 550 (25) IIIB of 1938, pp. 53–5, MSA.
115 See below, this chapter. Interview, B. Thorat, millhand in the Digvijay Mills in the late 1930s and later President, Bombay Girni Kamgar Union.

few.'[116] These neighbourhood connections offered the jobber power, prestige and patronage within the mill; the strength derived from his position at work could once again be wielded in the wider community beyond the mill gates. Workplace and neighbourhood were brought into a close and interdependent relationship.

Some contemporary observers and most later historians developed an awesome picture of the power and control invested in the person of the jobber. The jobber's gang was assumed not only to form a social entity, but it was also supposed in one recent account to be 'more than a division of the industrial workforce; it was a unit of urban society with economic, social and political functions'.[117] Although the term was borrowed from the Lancashire cotton mills, the institution of the jobber was often been cast as culturally specific to Indian society. Thus the jobber was frequently likened to the village headman. His practice of charging dasturi or commission to each worker whom he employed is believed to constitute 'one of those customary payments, common in many parts of Indian society, which were symptomatic of a patron–client relationship'.[118] But the jobber, let alone the foreman, was not an Indian invention, and there was nothing unique or culturally specific about the phenomenon of the foreman's bribe in an overstocked labour market.

Many contemporaries believed that the jobber lived in close proximity with his men, marched his gang into the mill and controlled their lives at work through his powers of supervision, recruitment and dismissal. But the jobber's gang did not form a comprehensive social unit encompassing every aspect of the workers' lives. It was by no means common for jobbers to live in the same chawl as the workers they hired,[119] nor for workers from the same mill to live together, nor indeed as was sometimes supposed to enter and leave the mill herded by their jobbers. Dhaku Janu Lad, who claimed to be 'treated as one of the leaders' in the Bombay Cotton Mill, lived in a chawl occupied mainly by millworkers who worked, however, in different mills.[120] Daji Sakharam told the Bombay Disturbances Enquiry Committee that among his co-workers 'no one resides in the same place where I reside'.[121] Mahadev Naik claimed that it was predominantly 'the higher classes' employed in the Kohinoor Mill who lived

---

[116] RCLI, Evidence, Bombay Presidency, Seth Ambalal Sarabhai, Ahmedabad Manufacturing and Calico Printing Company, I, i, 277.

[117] Newman, Workers and Unions, p. 28.

[118] Ibid., p. 31.

[119] Of course, it is easy to understand how this picture emerged from observations of the kind cited above, Gazetteer, I, 493; Burnett-Hurst, Labour and Housing, p. 46.

[120] Proceedings of the BDEC, Oral Evidence, Dhaku Janu Lad, GOB, Home (Sp.) File 550 (25) IIIB of 1938, pp. 103–5, MSA.

[121] Ibid., Oral Evidence, Daji Sakharam, GOB, Home (Sp.) File 550 (25), IIIB of 1938, p. 507, MSA.

in his chawl, but that there were no millworkers among them.[122] Mathura Kuber, a Muslim worker, worked at the Apollo Mill, along with a large contingent of his co-religionists. His evidence is instructive:

Q: When you went to work in the morning were any of the other Muslim workers with you?
A: No.
Q: When you were returning was there any other Muslim worker with you?
A: No; we do not live at the same place. We live at different places.[123]

The assumption that the workers operated within enclosed and self-defining caste and communal groups was so firmly ingrained that workers like Kuber had to assert the contrary repeatedly before the Committee in order to be understood.

The place of the jobber within the web of social and political power in the neighbourhood needs to be qualified further. First, an earlier chapter has already established that there were many kinds of jobbers in the Bombay labour market.[124] Their functions and consequently their power varied considerably. Those jobbers who were responsible for paying their workers were sometimes able to exercise a more direct form of control over them; those who supervised skilled workers might command the ear of their managers but their authority over their subordinates was more limited. The crucial question was the point at which they were lodged in the hierarchies of the workplace, for as intermediaries between managers and men they were liable to be squeezed by the contradictory pressures exerted upon them by both. Second, not all jobbers attempted to establish themselves within the structure of neighbourhood power. Indeed, it cannot be assumed that all jobbers possessed the personal and material resources to enter extensively into commercial and political activities within the neighbourhood. Finally, the jobber was only one among a wide range of influential figures in the neighbourhood. He had to act together with and in relation to the others. Their interaction and rivalries acted sometimes as a constraint upon each.

If the jobber derived his influence from his position within the political and social structure of the neighbourhood, he was also constrained by it. The jobber's power derived from the commercial and social ties he established with his workers. He was forced to respond to the pressures they imposed upon him and could not risk their desertion. His failure to meet their moral and their

---

[122] *Ibid.*, Oral Evidence, Mahadev Naik, GOB, Home (Sp.) File 550 (25), IIIB of 1938, p. 53, MSA.
[123] *Ibid.*, Oral Evidence, Mathura Kuber, GOB, Home (Sp.) File 550 (25), IIIB of 1938, p. 499, MSA.
[124] See above, chapter 3.

material expectations could result in the desertion of his followers, his replacement by rivals outside the mill and even his dismissal from the workplace. Conversely, of course, he could also risk dismissal by responding to the demands of his followers, especially for instance through participation in industrial action.

Moreover, while the jobber's power within the mill rested upon his connections outside, it was when his patronage was extended to the wider organization of credit, housing and recreation that it was exposed to greater competition. Landlords, brothel-keepers, money-lenders and grain-dealers, no less than workers, could choose between jobbers. The more extensive the terrain on which he operated, the greater was the competition to which he was subjected, not only from rival jobbers, but also from other neighbourhood patrons. But if his position within the workplace depended upon his influence outside, it was necessary to expand and diversify the ambit of his control, thus unavoidably weakening his own lines of defence. It was within the neighbourhoods that the reciprocal nature of power relations within the jobber system was most obviously manifested. It was in this arena that the growth of working-class militancy most severely circumscribed the possibilities of jobber power.

Dadas

The 'dada' – essentially a title for a neighbourhood boss – was another influential figure, indeed institution, of the neighbourhood. Who was a dada? The answer is by no means clear. If those who aspired to the status were not always acknowledged as dadas, neighbourhood residents and contemporary observers alike had several, sometimes incompatible notions about who or what he was. To the polite classes, the dada symbolized the roughness of street culture and the violence of the poor. The *Gazetteer*, attaching a page from the ethnographer's manual, described the dada as a 'member of the vagabond and hooligan tribe, who is quite as lazy as the *mowali*, but far more dangerous and troublesome'.[125] Burnett-Hurst described the dada as 'a hooligan, who lives by intimidation. He is both lazy and dangerous and is often in the keep of a Naikin (forewoman)'.[126] Across a wide spectrum of public opinion, to employers and civil servants, policemen and trade-union leaders, and indeed to many residents

---

[125] *Gazetteer*, I, 208. The *Gazetteer* proceeded to list five types of millworkers: first, 'the model hand' who was 'steady, sober and regular in attendance' and 'always ready to perform overtime work'; second 'the substitute or *badliwallah* who fights shy of fixed employment'; third, the '*atawada* or seven-day man', so called because of his habit of working every alternate week; fourth, 'the mowali or Bohemian millhand, who works and rests as the fancy takes him and is prone to vice'. The dada was supposedly the fifth type.

[126] Burnett-Hurst, *Labour and Housing*, p. 49.

of the districts as well, the dada was supposedly given to crime, prone to violence and generally unemployed.[127] Whereas, in times of strife, when the place of the peaceful citizen was at home, it was said, the dada and his hooligans roamed the streets.

In public discourse, neither the employers' nor the workers' organizations cared to be connected with the world of the dada even though they operated within it. Anti-communists used the term to describe the following of communist unions;[128] communists used it to signify strike-breakers.[129] During the investigations which followed the communal riots of 1929, Hindu and Muslim witnesses used the term in connection with the rival rather than their own community.[130] In fact, the term dada, which was also used for an elder brother, signified respect. Although, in public, everybody tried to dissociate themselves from 'dadas', 'I know personally', one trade unionist declared, 'that Dadas like to be called Dadas'.[131]

Despite the taxonomy of working people elaborated by contemporary observers, the dada was not a special kind of working man. Anybody who came to establish himself in a position of influence or leadership in the neighbourhood might be regarded as a dada. Dadas were not always unemployed; but some prided themselves on the fact, or at any rate subscribed fondly, if temporarily, to the myth, that they did not need to work and were admired by their peers for having escaped the toil and uncertainty of the labour market. They were not necessarily criminal or violent. But they were as often respected and feared for their physical strength, their courage and their fighting skills as they were avoided and condemned for their roughness by those among whom they lived and worked. Dadas participated in a wide range of commercial, social and political activities in the neighbourhood. They became jobbers, ran gymnasiums and organized religious festivals. They were valuable members of chawl committees and caste panchayats. They helped landlords collect rent and grain-dealers and creditors to recover debts. They might help politicians acquire votes, trade unionists to organize strikes or millowners to break them. Dada was properly a reputation rather than a status or a profession – a reputation for physical prowess or for getting things done.

The process by which dadas gained their reputations and their positions of leadership cannot easily be tracked down. They might establish their reputation

127 Proceedings of the BRIC, Oral Evidence, R.S. Asavale, File 3, p. 83, MSA: *ibid.*, Syed Munawar, File 3, p. 279; *ibid.*, H.D. Nanavaty, File 6, p. 301, MSA; *Indian Daily Mail*, 7 May 1929; Daily Report of the Commissioner of Police, Bombay, 23 January 1932, in GOB Home (Sp.) File 800 (72), p. 473, MSA.
128 Proceedings of the BRIC, Oral Evidence, S.K. Bole, File 3, pp. 217, 245–7, MSA.
129 *Ibid.*, G.L. Kandalkar and V.H. Joshi, File 16, pp. 69–72, MSA.
130 *Ibid.*, Balubhai T. Desai, File 8; A.R. Dimtimkar and S. Nabiullah, File 7, MSA.
131 *Ibid.*, G.L. Kandalkar and V.H. Joshi, File 16, p. 71, MSA.

in a brawl or by proving themselves particularly effective agents of various neighbourhood patrons, such as landlords or grain-dealers. They gained the respect of their friends and of the neighbourhood by their skill at work, their performance in a mele or a toli during a religious festival, or their athleticism in the gymnasium. Their reputations once established, ostensibly for their skill and proficiency in servicing the local community, had to be maintained through their fulfilment of the expectations of the neighbourhood and by the confirmation of their prowess in relation to rivals. They might be expected to arbitrate justly in disputes, or to help the unemployed find work. Their generosity and kindness, their judiciousness and courage informed the myths that grew around them. They were sometimes also called upon to police the neighbourhood, during communal riots, industrial action or political agitations.

Moreover, dadas operated on varying scales of magnitude. As V.B. Karnik put it, 'there were a large number of dadas – some who were small and some who were big'.[132] Some were motivated by ideological imperatives, others by a sharp business instinct; some dominated an entire neighbourhood, like Keshav Dada Borkar at Ghorapdeo, and others were little men neither respected nor recognized in the next chawl. The dada, said Balubhai Desai,

is a person who has got this reputation by controlling the hooligans by rendering services to the hooligans and protecting them, giving grain to them and really of course controlling them ... some of these Dadas are rich.[133]

Their ability to exert this control depended upon their facility in providing such services. They did not always fight themselves, but they could mobilize men to do their fighting and in any case their leadership depended upon the belief that they were capable of fighting.

In order to protect their followers they had to 'have a fair acquaintance with the lower officials of the police', as well as the means to pay surety for those of their men who were arrested 'and help in any other way they can'. It was only 'in this way [that] they collect the hooligans'.[134] To build up and maintain a following a dada needed influential friends and patrons; but to catch the eye of the great and to achieve a following, he needed to cut an imposing figure on the street corner and in the chawl. In the course of their activities, the dadas became, as V.H. Joshi, an official of the Girni Kamgar Union put it, 'agents dealing in working people'.[135] The metaphor is instructive of the dada's vulnerability to the ultimate sanctions of neighbourhood politics: social and, in reality, commer-

---

[132] Interview, V.B. Karnik, April 1979.
[133] Proceedings of the BRIC, Oral Evidence, Balubhai T. Desai, File 8, pp. 29–31, MSA.
[134] Proceedings of the BRIC, 1929, Oral Evidence, Balubhai T. Desai, File 8, p. 29, MSA.
[135] Ibid., Oral Evidence, G.L. Kandalkar and V.H. Joshi, File 16, p. 69, MSA.

cial boycott. If the dada was 'an agent dealing in working people', he could not alienate his clientele. This was why 'the dadas left to themselves cannot harm a mass of people'.[136] For this reason dadas could be engaged against strikers least easily during periods of solidarity and most readily when workers were the most divided and they, in turn, were in some ways least needed.

The case of Dhaku Janu Lad suggests the nature of the expectations imposed upon dadas by the residents of the neighbourhood. At the same time, it provides an insight into the interplay between the spheres of the workplace and the neighbourhood. Dhaku Janu Lad was a head jobber in the Bombay Cotton Mill. Before the one-day strike of 1938, he was approached by five or six people whom he associated with the communist leaders, Dange and Nimbkar,

They asked me not go to work. They said that if I went to work, I would be assaulted ... [They said] You are a leader; do not go to work and do not allow others to go to work.[137]

Since he was 'likely to be assaulted by these people', he applied for leave from work for the next three days. The alternative before him was to join the strike. Instead, he stayed away but advised his workers to attend to their machines.

His less-prominent brother had, however, managed to enter the mill. Because his brother had not returned when the first shift should have ended, Dhaku Janu walked to the mill to see whether he needed help. Crowds of strikers who had failed to stop some workers entering the mills, now decided to prevent them from leaving instead. The police might escort the workers out of the workplace, but they could not extend this service to their doorsteps. For this reason, it was considered unsafe for the workers to leave the mill. When Dhaku Janu approached the mill gates, 'those who were working in the mill went up to the Manager as soon as they recognized me'. The Manager sought the help of the police to escort the workers out of the mill, and Dhaku Janu Lad took two separate groups of workers to their rooms.[138] The provision of this kind of service was among the most crucial demands made upon dadas and jobbers. They acted as informal guardians of a public order and morality which they interpreted, sometimes arbitrarily, and enforced without an excess of decorum.

Like other dominant figures in the neighbourhood, the dada was often constrained in his activities by the collective action of those who lived there. The threat or use of violence was only the most obvious sanction which residents might wield against a dada. The residents of a wadi sometimes held public

---

[136] *Ibid.*, p. 61.
[137] Proceedings of the BDEC, Oral Evidence, Dhaku Janu Lad, GOB Home (Sp.) File 550 (25), IIIB of 1938, pp. 103–5, MSA.
[138] *Ibid.*, Oral Evidence, Dhaku Janu Lad, GOB, Home (Sp.) File 550 (25), IIIB of 1938, pp. 103–7, MSA.

meetings at which dadas were forced to explain and justify their actions.[139] Blacklegs were brought to strikers' meetings and humiliated.[140] The evidence suggests a widespread use of informal measures of justice in the working-class neighbourhood. Since the status of the dada depended upon his reputation and his public image, he was always subject to the rivalry of others, seeking to test their strength or establish their influence. For the same reason, no dada could afford to lose the confidence of the community upon which he depended.

Whereas the jobber's realm was essentially at the workplace, the domain of the dada is often assumed to lie outside the context of work. However, social organization in the spheres of workplace and neighbourhood was closely interrelated. Workers who acquired extensive influence in the neighbourhood often became jobbers.[141] Moreover, jobbers were often influenced in decisions about the hiring and firing of workers by the dadas of the mill districts.[142] Conversely, it was integral to the leadership of dadas that workers approached them to mediate their differences with their jobbers. In any case, there were several dadas not only among the jobbers but even among the general body of workers as well.[143]

Keshav Dada Borkar

Perhaps the most prominent of all dadas in Bombay in the 1920s and 1930s was Keshav Borkar. The case of Keshav Borkar illustrates many facets of the relationships in which dadas were involved: the nature of their leadership, the place of ideology and commercial interest in their actions, the points at which they could mobilize support and the areas in which they could be isolated. Keshav Borkar began his life as a weaver. By the mid 1920s he combined the roles of shopkeeper, gymnasium owner and neighbourhood boss.[144] In 1933 it appeared that Borkar even had 'some buildings of his own'.[145] In the aftermath of the general strike of 1928, he had been appointed as 'Superintendent of Labour' in the Sassoon Group of mills, where by his own description 'he was doing the work of controlling the labourers in these Mills'.[146] From this

---

[139] Bombay City Police, Individual Files, File 3428/6/62., Office of the Commissioner of Police, Bombay.
[140] GOB, Home (Sp.) File 543 DC Pt IV of 1930, MSA.
[141] RCLI, Evidence, Bombay Presidency, Seth Ambalal Sarabhai, Ahmedabad Manufacturing and Calico Printing Co. Ltd., I, i, 277.
[142] Proceedings of the TLIC, Main Inquiry, Oral Evidence, A.W. Pryde, Government Labour Officer, File 66, 2400, 2452–3, MSA.
[143] Interview, V.B. Karnik, April 1979.
[144] Kamkari, 22 April 1928, Report on the Native Newspapers Published in the Bombay Presidency (henceforth RNNP), 17, 1928.
[145] District Magistrate, Ratnagiri to Secretary, GOB, Home, no. Pol. S.R. 7585, 8 December 1932 in GOB, Home (Sp.) File 800 (14) C-III of 1932, p. 57, MSA.
[146] Petition, K.L. Borkar, to Governor-in-Council, 10 June 1933, ibid., p. 109, MSA.

powerful base in the neighbourhood, Keshav Borkar, now known in Ghorapdeo simply as 'dada', was to launch a long and vigorous campaign against communist activity in Bombay. How he came to occupy this posture of opposition to the communists is uncertain. The catalyst seems to have been his friendship with Mayekar, founder and secretary of the major textile union of the mid 1920s, the Girni Kamgar Mahamandal. When, in early 1928, Mayekar, having already been ousted from his base in Colaba, was displaced within his union by the communist K.N. Joglekar, Borkar's terrain in Ghorapdeo became Mayekar's last refuge.[147]

Throughout 1928, Mayekar, now isolated within the labour movement, dogged the communists with the help of Borkar and attempted on several occasions to break up their meetings. 'For six months and more', reported Horniman's *Indian National Herald*, 'the leaders [the communists of the Girni Kamgar Union] were repeatedly disturbed by his unwelcome presence which at once acted as a disintegrating factor on one section of the workers and an infuriating phenomenon on the other.'[148] The effect of Mayekar's intervention 'through his friend Borkar'[149] at several communist meetings was interpreted very differently by left-wing sympathizers and by the police. While the police commissioner reported that frequent complaints were received that they were 'seeking to stir up trouble at the communist meetings ... but no serious clash occurred',[150] the *Indian National Herald*'s version was that the communist leaders 'went to the length of even dissolving crowded meetings' to avoid a direct confrontation. Indeed, at practically every meeting the leaders exhorted the men to remain restrained in the face of provocation. Mayekar, claimed the paper, only 'masquerades as a labour leader and is, in fact, alleged to be an agent of the Criminal Investigation Department'.[151] If the Mayekar–Borkar alliance had been able to create a riot, the leaders of the Girni Kamgar Union feared, the consequent disorder would have provided the police with the pretext to intervene strongly against them.[152]

On 11 December 1928, Keshav Borkar and a gang of twenty other men attacked the communist leaders, R.S. Nimbkar, P.T. Tamhanekar and Govind

---

[147] Kamkari, 22 April 1928, *RNNP*, Bombay, 17, 1928.
[148] *Indian National Herald*, 7 December 1928.
[149] Commissioner of Police, Bombay to Secretary, GOB, Home no. 5395/L, 13 December 1928, GOB Home (Poll.) File 265 of 1928, p. 41, MSA.
[150] *Ibid.*
[151] *Indian National Herald*, 7 December 1928. Considering how both Mayekar and the CID worked, this was not beyond the realm of possibility.
[152] The vindication of their apprehension is to be found in official discussions of the strategy for dealing with widespread industrial action. See, for instance, in relation to the general strike of 1929, GOB, Home (Sp.) File 543 (10) E, Part D of 1929 and in the case of the 1934 general strike, GOB, Home (Sp.) File 543 (48) of 1934, MSA.

Kasale and some others accompanying them. A message had been received at the Girni Kamgar Union office about labour trouble at the David Sassoon Spinning and Manufacturing Mill at Ghorapdeo, in the heart of Borkar's territory. The message turned out to be false. Nimbkar and his associates were set upon as they left the mill. Complaints lodged at the local police station, however, 'of course failed to trace the assailants'.[153] On the following morning, workers from the David Sassoon, Morarji Gokuldas, Moon and Shapurji Broacha mills did not resume work, in sympathy with their bruised leaders. At a meeting of the Girni Kamgar Union at Poibavdi that morning Kasale, who had taken the brunt of the attack, displayed his wounds. Clearly the temper of the meeting was highly charged. Plain-clothes policemen in the crowd were identified and assaulted.[154] Within minutes, about 500 workers set off towards Borkar's house 'with the intention presumably of settling accounts with him. He got intimation of their advance and left his house.'[155] By the time the crowd reached Borkar's house they were estimated to be more than 3,000 strong. The contents of his house were pulled on to the street and a bonfire was lit. His furniture and cooking utensils were damaged; the house was ransacked, the tiles on his roof were removed and thrown away; his gymnasium was wrecked.[156]

As the morning wore on, mill after mill was brought out on strike by workers who gathered at the gates and stoned the premises until those who had remained inside the mill were locked out by the management. The police were alerted and brought into action: the result was riot. By the time Inspector Klein of Bhoiwada Police Station met the crowd on Suparibagh Road, they were, according to him, armed with sticks, bamboos, iron rods, gymnastic paraphernalia and 'obviously bent on mischief'. With a small force and awaiting reinforcements, the police attempted to stop this crowd by throwing a cordon across the road. The result was that the police were routed. Crowds appeared from every direction and hemmed the police in on all sides, while 'stones were also being thrown from the rooms and windows of the neighbouring houses'. When Klein fired with his revolver, the crowd 'held back slightly but came on with renewed vigour'. The constables began to climb into the police lorry and Klein failed to 'force them to stand fast'.[157]

[153] *Proceedings of the Meerut Conspiracy Case*, statement by S.A. Dange, p. 2522.
[154] Commissioner of Police, Bombay to Secretary, GOB, Home (Sp.), no. 5368 L, 12 December 1928 in GOB Home (Poll.) File 265 of 1928, MSA.
[155] Commissioner of Police, Bombay to Secretary, GOB, Home (Sp.), no. 5395 L, 13 December 1928, GOB Home (Poll.) File 265 of 1928, pp. 41–5, MSA.
[156] Report of H.C. Stokes, Inspector, Byculla Police Station, D Division, GOB Home (Poll.) File 265 of 1928, pp. 13–15, MSA; *TOI*, 21 December 1928.
[157] Report by Inspector Klein, Bhoiwada Police Station to Superintendent of Police, E Division, Bombay, GOB Home (Poll.) File 265 of 1928, pp. 21–5, MSA.

It must be taken as an indication of popular anger and determination that the crowd withstood considerable police firing and returned to counter-attack 'with renewed vigour'. Moreover, the 'mob' on the streets was neither undifferentiated nor exceptional to working-class sentiment. As the Police Commissioner noted, 'I am told by the officers that the stones were being hurled not only by the rioters on the road, but by mill hands who were in the rooms of houses adjoining the road'.[158] The scene of action – Suparibagh Road – was one of the main thoroughfares through the mill district. If we are to believe, with the police, that 'this strike was mainly brought about by those [communist] leaders and was done very secretly and in a well organized way,'[159] we must also believe that this conspiracy involved a substantial proportion of the Bombay working class.

It is important to recognize that this was not simply a festival of freedom for all the roughs of the mill district. On the contrary, it was an expression of protest on an impressive scale against the action of Borkar and his men. The Silk Alliance Mill was Borkar's fortress. With the exception of this mill, and the Indian Manufacturing Mill, which had employed a sizeable contingent of Muslim jobbers and men after the 1928 general strike, all the other mills went out on strike. However, 'the workmen of these two mills refused to stop and were prepared to go to the length of fighting the strikers. As soon as the strikers saw their attitude they stopped troubling them'.[160] But this was, in the context of the whole event, merely a restricted expression of loyalty to Borkar Dada. Indeed, the man who apparently ran Ghorapdeo could not prevent the workers of David Sassoon Mill in the same neighbourhood, and the scene of the attack on the communists, from stopping work; more seriously, he found no sympathizers to defend his home or his gymnasium. Instead, Borkar left home and sought asylum elsewhere. Evidently there were strong limits on what Borkar could persuade his followers to do.

This riot had serious consequences for Borkar, but he soon recovered his position of dominance in Ghorapdeo. He was aided by the revival of the Congress organization in Bombay City from the later 1920s. After the collapse of the non-cooperation campaigns in the early 1920s, its organization had ground to a halt. During the mid 1920s, the communists acquired considerable influence over the party's organization in Bombay.[161] 'Without the active

---

[158] Commissioner of Police, Bombay, to Secretary, GOB, Home (Sp.) no. 5395/L, 13 December 1928, GOB Home (Poll.) File 265 of 1928, p. 45, MSA.
[159] Report, J.W. Power, Superintendent of Police, D Division, GOB Home (Poll.) File 265 of 1928, p. 19, MSA.
[160] *Ibid.*
[161] See B.R. Tomlinson, *The Indian National Congress and the Raj 1929–1942: The Penultimate Phase* (London, 1977); Gordon, *Businessmen and Politics;* R. Kumar, 'From Swaraj to Purna Swaraj: Nationalist Politics in the City of Bombay 1920–32', in D.A. Low (ed.), *Congress and the Raj: Facets of the Indian Struggle* (London, 1977), pp. 77–107.

propaganda of the communists', the Police Commissioner noted in 1929, 'the Congress Party would not have been able to stage any demonstration in Bombay against the Simon Commission.'[162] When the Congress attempted to rehabilitate itself after 1929 there were few better networks of influence upon which to base their revival than this impressively powerful boss of Ghorapdeo. During the 1930s, Borkar had diversified and sophisticated the basis of his local power. He involved himself more widely in the social and welfare organization of the neighbourhood. He established the Ghorapdeo Sarvajanik Karyakari Mandal in 1935 for 'the social and cultural uplift' of the residents of the neighbourhood. In time, he bought a fuel-wood shop, expanded his gymnasium, owned a temple and abandoned the textile industry to become a labour contractor at the Wallace Flour Mills in Ghorapdeo.[163]

At the same time, his influence within Congress had been growing. His presence made Ghorapdeo an important centre of civil disobedience. From 1932 onwards, Borkar became active in the Congress cause. He was arrested, and later released on the condition that he took no further part in the agitation and that he reported every Sunday to the Byculla police.[164] During the civil disobedience campaign, defying the constraints upon him, Borkar became the mainstay of the city's Congress. As the Police Commissioner wrote,

He has been a bully for years together in the mill area. For the last one year or so he has been a Congress hireling and the Congress activities in the mill area and outside it succeeded only on account of his supplying unemployed mill hands to Congress.[165]

For his continued activity, Borkar was arrested and committed to Byculla jail: particularly, because he was 'responsible for organising "raids" on the Secretariat by supplying men from the mill area'.[166] At the insistence of the Police Commissioner, he was transferred to Ratnagiri district prison in September 1932, to keep him away from his political friends.[167]

Following the expiry of his prison sentence, Borkar was confined to Ratnagiri. But Borkar escaped from Varavde, his village in Ratnagiri, and returned to Bombay in November 1932. It was not until March 1933 that he was found and arrested again. 'I was not hiding in Bombay', Borkar declared upon his arrest, but

---

[162] Commissioner of Police, Bombay, to Secretary, GOB, Home (Sp.) no. 5527/A/133, 1 October 1929, GOB, Home (Sp.) File 543 (10) E Pt D of 1929, MSA.

[163] Bombay City Police, File 3221/804/66, Office of the Commissioner of Police, Bombay.

[164] Commissioner of Police, Daily Report, 14 January 1932 in GOB Home (Sp.) File 800 (72) of 1932, p. 345, MSA.

[165] Note by Commissioner of Police, Bombay, U.O.R. no. 1795/H/3905, 10 April 1933, GOB, Home (Sp.) File 800 (14) C-III of 1932, p. 85, MSA.

[166] Commissioner of Police, Bombay to Secretary, GOB, Home (Sp.), Confidential, no. 4862/H, 1 September 1932, GOB Home (Sp.) File 800 (14) C-III of 1932, p. 1, MSA.

[167] Inspector-General, Prisons, Bombay Presidency, to Secretary, GOB, Home (Poll.) No. 925, 15 September 1932, ibid., p. 31, MSA.

living in my usual place of residence. I was all the time in my house because my son was sick. I cannot say why the police did not arrest me … I heard from my aunt that Inspector Bhatkal had asked her how long I was going to stay in hiding and on hearing that I went and reported myself.[168]

The official mind remained sceptical about this rather casual account of Borkar's escape from confinement and his period underground in Bombay. It offered instead an alternative explanation of this course of events. Borkar, the Home Department believed, had 'surrendered himself' for two reasons: first, 'he sees that Congress is losing all round'; and second, 'he is not getting money from the Congress as he thought he would do'.[169] But the Home Department may have failed to take into account Borkar's deep, indeed existential commitment to the Congress cause. For the dada of Ghorapdeo was no simple mercenary.

The Government of Bombay was far more confident about the accuracy of their own explanation of Borkar's behaviour, than about what to do with him once he was arrested. The Police Commissioner declared, 'I do not want him in Bombay at all. He may be transferred to Ratnagiri jail.'[170] But the District Magistrate of Ratnagiri was not too keen to have him either. Nevertheless, he was retuned to the district jail with strict instructions 'to ensure that a careful watch is kept on Borkar so as to prevent his absconding again'.[171]

Borkar was unhappy to be thus returned unceremoniously to his roots and petitioned repeatedly for his release. In June 1933, he pleaded that he had been without work for the past nine months so that his family 'including his wife and children was suffering from want of support and starvation'. He had had nothing to do with the Congress, he said, and nor did he intend to in the future.[172] By January 1934, he emphasized that he had 'no landed property or alternative source of income'. Furthermore, he said that he was willing to give an undertaking that he would not participate in Congress activities and would furnish any terms and conditions deemed fit by the Government.[173]

The Home Department was unmoved. The District Magistrate of Ratnagiri gently suggested in March 1934 that he might be released on parole if he did furnish an undertaking to abjure the Congress cause.[174] But the Police

---

[168] Statement by K.L. Borkar, *ibid.*, p. 79, MSA.
[169] Daily Confidential Report, no. 1529/H/3717, 28 March 1933, *ibid.*, p. 81, MSA.
[170] Note by Commissioner of Police, Bombay, U.O.R. no. 1795/H/3905, 10 April 1933, *ibid.*, p. 85, MSA.
[171] Bombay Special to District Magistrate, Ratnagiri, no. S.D. 2267, 20 April 1933, *ibid.*, p. 95, MSA.
[172] Petition, K.L. Borkar to Governor-in-Council, 10 June 1933, *ibid.*, p. 109, MSA.
[173] Petition, K.L. Borkar to Governor-in-Council, 1 January 1934, *ibid.*, pp. 119–21, MSA.
[174] District Magistrate, Ratnagiri, to Secretary, GOB, Home (Pol.), no. S.R. 7686, 9 March 1934, *ibid.*, p. 129, MSA.

Commissioner in Bombay still 'did not consider his presence here desirable'.[175] In June, when restrictive orders against Congressmen generally were being withdrawn, his case was reconsidered. But it was still considered 'best that Borkar should be kept out of Bombay as long as possible and the order against him may therefore continue in force.'[176] It was not until November, when there were only thirty-four orders outstanding, that the Home Member decided that 'We weed not go out of our way to use the Act in an isolated case of this kind'.[177]

These experiences firmly established Borkar's credentials as a freedom fighter. At the same time, his activities with the Congress had enabled him to establish close connections with S.K. Patil, whose influence with the party was growing rapidly, who had already become and was to remain for over thirty years one of its most important organizers and who by the mid 1960s was one of the most powerful men in the national party. It was to such connections, especially his reputation as 'the right-hand man' of S.K. Patil,[178] that Borkar owed his ascendancy in the city's politics. While they enabled him to establish himself as an effective dada, who was able to get things done, it was Borkar's influence in Ghorapdeo, based on his gymnasium, as well as his social and economic functions, that made him indispensable to the Congress, struggling to snatch mass support from the communists.

Keshav Dada Borkar thereafter rose steadily within the Congress hierarchy, slipping easily between the committee rooms of Jinnah Hall and the street corner. By the mid 1930s, he was elected to the Labour sub-committee of the Bombay Pradesh Congress Committee. In 1937, he presided over the Congress election campaign in the mill district of Bombay.[179] Although his following was to face no serious problems in Ghorapdeo, Borkar and his friends did not have an easy passage elsewhere in the mill districts. For instance, at a meeting in the communist stronghold of Lalbagh in 1937, after Mayekar, Borkar and another associate, Kubal, finished their speeches, a worker, Pandu Shivaji, asked to speak. Having taken the platform, however, he proceeded to give the audience a critical account of Borkar's activities and asked them not to vote for the Congress. As soon as he had finished Borkar's followers 'caught hold of him

---

[175] Note by Commissioner of Police, Bombay, U.O.R. no. 1362/H, 16 March 1934, *ibid.*, p. 131, MSA.
[176] Office Note, Home (Sp.), 19 September 1934, *ibid.*, p. 136, MSA.
[177] Home Member's Minute, 19 November 1934, *ibid.*, p. 149. These thirty-four orders, under the Bombay Special Emergency Powers Act, were distributed as follows: 13 against 'revolutionaries', 5 against 'communists', 15 against residents of provinces outside Bombay, 14 of whom were Indian state subjects, and 1 against 'the "budmush" from Bombay city' confining him to Ratnagiri. Office Note, Home (Sp.) 28 November 1934, *ibid.*, p. 149.
[178] Interview, B. Thorat, April 1979.
[179] Commissioner of Police, Weekly Letter, no. 5, 30 January 1937, pp. 75–6, Office of the Commissioner of Police, Bombay.

and assaulted him.' Sympathizers of Pandu Shivaji began to stone Borkar and his men; a riot ensued as the two rival parties fought it out.[180] For his loyalty, endurance and fighting qualities, Borkar was elected to the managing committee of the Bombay Provincial Congress Committee, as a representative of the E Ward in February 1937.[181] At the same time, he conducted his own private war against communism with the help of men practised in the deft use of the lathi and with strong arms and keen aim when stones had to be thrown. Thus, during the days of the Congress ministry, it was to Borkar that the Congress turned in its attempts to penetrate the trade unions.

Among the organizations established to intervene in labour politics was the Bombay Kamgar Sangh. While communist leaflets described the Sangh as a strike-breaking front sponsored by the Millowners' Association, and claimed that its principal organizer, B.G. Marathe, received money from funds intended by the Congress ministry for welfare work among the labouring classes, the major reason why its formation 'caused considerable perturbation amongst local communists' was their awareness that backed by Borkar's muscle and influence such a trade union could pose awkward problems.[182] Thus, during the one-day strike of 1938, no significant attempt was made either by the communists or the apparently better organized 'volunteers' of Ambedkar's Independent Labour Party to bring out the mills 'in the area which is looked after by Keshav Borkar'.[183] 'It is quite obvious', declared Mr U'ren,

that by virtue of the fact that he holds sway in that area the Red Flag Union did not think that they could get much success there ... The mere fact that he was the headman of that area, I think, was sufficient for the Red Flag volunteers not to bother with that area.[184]

As the Congress acquired greater influence in the city after independence, Borkar's own career advanced more smoothly. He was elected to the All-India Congress Committee; became Municipal Corporator in the city; received the Congress ticket for the State Assembly elections of 1957, but lost the election; and eventually stood down as a municipal corporator in the early 1960s. By then, perhaps, his influence was on the wane. As his local influence declined, perhaps partly due to his own age, his patrons began to desert him. The old boss of Ghorapdeo was now marooned, alone, within it.

[180] Commissioner of Police, Weekly Letter, no. 6, 6 February 1937, p. 164, Office of the Commissioner of Police, Bombay.
[181] Commissioner of Police Weekly Letter, no. 10, 6 March 1937, p. 164, Office of the Commissioner of Police, Bombay.
[182] GOB, Home (Sp.) File 543 (13) B (1) of 1937–8, pp. 227–31, MSA.
[183] Proceedings of the BDEC, Oral Evidence, Mr U'ren, Deputy Commissioner of Police, in GOB Home (Sp.) File 50 (25), III-B of 1938, pp. 681–3, MSA.
[184] Ibid.

Leisure and the patterns of association

The social organization of Bombay's workers was not shaped by material imperatives alone. Social and communal activities beyond the workplace, whether relatively formal, like religious festivals or gymnasiums, or largely informal, forged patterns of association in the neighbourhood. These associations also provided a basis from which the working class could resist the more arbitrary exercise of power by the patrons, magnates and bosses of the neighbourhood. This section will examine some of these social activities and the nature of the collectivities which formed around them.

It would be misleading to construe leisure as an autonomous area of social activity. Leisure activities can scarcely be abstracted from their context in work. The hours and nature of work determined the extent and sometimes influenced the forms of leisure. Thus, dock labourers, it was said, whose earnings were relatively low and whose conditions of work were both dangerous and arduous

are very fond of witnessing wrestling matches. They are generally too tired to participate, but the boys frequently do so, and some form their own gymnasiums.[185]

The interpenetration of work and leisure is illustrated further by the importance attached by workers to the common pastime of visiting friends and relatives. In 1889, a petition from the Bombay millworkers to the Viceroy pleaded for a day's holiday each week and made clear their preference for a Sunday closure because this enabled them to meet 'their relatives or friends, who are otherwise employed, and who enjoy rest on these days'.[186] This activity had important implications for the sphere of work. For it

serves the purpose of gathering news which may be helpful in arranging marriages, finding employment for the members of the family and obtaining information on other relatives and friends who have gone out for gainful employment.[187]

In other words, it lay at the heart of the process by which the social connections of the working class were constituted. Patterns of leisure were vital to obtaining work and to maintaining the social organization of workers in town and country.

If leisure was integral to the context of work, it cannot be neatly distinguished from the sphere of politics. Gymnasiums, for instance, played a vital role in the mechanisms of mobilizations, whether for breaking or enforcing a strike, for political agitation or for the 'protection' of the neighbourhood during Hindu–

---

[185] Burnett-Hurst, *Labour and Housing*, p. 83.
[186] Humble Petition of Bombay Operatives to Viceroy, 24 October 1889, *Report of the IFC*, 1890, Appendix, p. 107.
[187] Patel, *Rural Labour*, p. 148.

Muslim riots.[188] Pleaders' offices and doctors' dispensaries became focal points in the neighbourhood, largely because of the services they offered. Indeed, lawyers and doctors were sometimes able to establish themselves as intermediaries representing industrial as well as political grievances. Their offices were focal points of political organization but they also became social centres. 'There is a constant stream of mill hands to these offices', reported the Police Commissioner in 1914, referring to the proliferation of pleaders in the mill districts, 'which in the evening especially become a regular "rendezvous". Here the millhand gets into touch with the Brahmans or Marathas, who read the vernacular newspapers to them, and not infrequently incite them to strike.'[189] During the 1920s and 1930s, trade-union leaders seeking to enrol new members were liable to adopt the modes of the street entertainer. S.H. Jhabvala, admittedly one of the most 'professional' publicists of labour's cause, and an official of nearly twenty unions in 1929, thus described his own recruiting drive:

I would stand at the end of the street when the factories were whistled off and would cry 'Ye who are fallen and miserable, come ye here and I shall help you out of the slough of distress'. A few letters were scribbled on behalf of the distressed individuals, posted by me to their employers and God helps those who help themselves, strange enough a couple of them were solved, and the poor illiterate flocks thought that I was a good instrument for the redress of their evil lot ... Often I ventured to take a yellow-robed saint with me who attracted a larger crowd. Mr Ginwalla managed to pay him eight annas per day, because he rolled in wealth and had no issue. He (the saint) sang Mahratta songs and I afterwards gave a dose of unionism ... The result was that in a short time flocks of people, man [sic], women and children anxiously waited for me to hear some of their grievances and to get them solved.[190]

Politics and leisure were at these points inseparable.

The associations which formed in the conduct of religious observances became the foci of community sentiment and rivalry. The internal structure and organization of the melas – the companies of dancers at Gokulashtami – provide some insight into the patterns of association in the neighbourhood and the relationship between leaders and their followers. Participation in a mela sometimes depended upon the payment of an entrance fee, a monthly subscription

188 On the role of gymnasiums and dadas in the civil disobedience campaign, see GOB, Home (Sp.), File 800 (4) of 1932, MSA; on Hindu–Muslim riots, see GOB, Home (Poll.), File 344 of 1929, MSA; on strikes, see Proceedings of the BRIC, Oral Evidence, G.L. Kandalkar and V.H. Joshi, File 16, pp. 69–73, MSA.
189 General Department, Order no. 3253/62 – Confidential, 15 May 1917, Bombay Confidential Proceedings, 1917, vol. 25, p. 15, IOR. Similar evidence on the use of tea shops as newspaper libraries is to be found for a later period in Patel, *Rural Labour*, p. 151. For the extent of newspaper reading among workers, see Proceedings of the BDEC, Home (Sp.), File 550 (25) III-B of 1938, MSA.
190 *Proceedings of the Meerut Conspiracy Case*, statement by S.H. Jhabvala, vol. III, Non-Communist Series, pp. 786–7.

and contributions to its general expenses. Before being admitted to the mela, each entrant had to take an oath in which he swore not to divulge its secrets to any other mela and not to join its opposing or rival party even if he severed his connections with his own. Group loyalty was a central feature of these melas. The leader of the mela was afforded considerable respect, usually being a man of some local prominence, and it was expected that the members of the mela would remain strictly obedient to him. But the leader had to manage the mela and protect its interests and was held personally responsible for making all the necessary arrangements of the day. His continued leadership depended upon the satisfaction of his team. The melas came to be known

by their heads, such as Ramji Bawa's mela, Ganuji Patel's mela or simply Bawa Saheb's mela ... All the members of the mela are obedient to their headman or Bawa, and without his orders they do not move an inch. He chastises members in the case of disobedience or mistake committed during the play. It is not that the persons composing the mela are either the relatives or the neighbours of the Bawa. Anyone can join, only he must pay an entrance fee, from 1 to 8 annas.[191]

Similarly, the toli bands of Mohurram, which danced with the tabut procession, symbolically to protect Hussain's tomb from evil spirits by mimic warfare and stick play, were led by the dadas and leaders of the moholla. Some tolis were little more than youth gangs of the neighbourhood. The dynamic of neighbourhood competition during Mohurram lay partly in the reputation which each gang and its leading dadas were seeking to establish or indeed conserve. As one observer put it,

Each street has its own band to parade the various quarters of the city and fight with the bands of rival streets. If the rivalry is good humoured, little harm accrues; but if, as is sometimes the case, feelings of real resentment are cherished, heads are apt to be broken and the leaders find themselves consigned to the care of the police.[192]

No doubt these rivalries led more frequently to broken heads than to imprisonment.

It is not surprising, therefore, that the tolis were perceived as an expression of the roughness of the Muslim mohollas. Whereas the 'badmashes and hooligans' chose 'the sites of the tabuts in the various moholllas as their gathering ground', the respectable Muslim, whether Sunni or Shia, neither 'took part in the annual procession of tabuts, nor would permit his family to visit the *tazias* and *tabuts* during the ten days of the festival'.[193] But it need not be supposed that the respectable, behind their postures of purity, were entirely dissociated from the roughness of the occasion. Indeed, the disturbances and street fighting

[191] K. Raghunathji, *The Hindu Temples of Bombay* (Bombay, 1900), pp. 11–18.
[192] *Gazetteer*, I, 187–8.
[193] Edwardes, *Bombay City Police*, p. 181.

which often occurred at Mohurram, it was said, 'could be used as a lever to secure consideration or concession in other directions' by respectable Sunnis. Nor, indeed, was the role of the police limited to that of the arbiters of neighbourhood conflicts; rather they could profit from them. Thus, 'in times of disturbances', the police

often reaped a fair harvest of tips and presents from timorous townspeople who desired protection from mob-violence, and who also discovered in the aftermath of rioting an easy means of paying off old scores.[194]

At the level of the neighbourhood, the police appear sometimes to have operated as protection racketeers rather like the dadas, whom they branded as rough and criminal, or the groups of Pathans who watched the shops of the bazaar for a price.

Like the great festivals, the gymnasium was an important, albeit less public, focus of working-class culture. The akhada or gymnasium was not necessarily a place which the 'respectable' abjured. Sir Purshottamadas Thakurdas announced proudly that he had trained at one in his youth and that he now sent his grandson to an akhada.[195] Balubhai T. Desai, the Congress politician, claimed in 1929 that he still attended an akhada. It was, however, he added, an akhada only for 'decently behaving gentlemen', and he chose it because it was the only gymnasium in Bombay with machines 'for reducing fat which I am taking advantage of'. A more common feature of gymnasiums, however, was to teach exercises with Indian clubs or lathis. Those who trained in akhadas thus acquired a special skill. Balubhai Desai applauded its use as a form of self-defence. 'A lathi', he said, 'can give you protection if you are surrounded even by 50 people and you can escape unscathed.'[196]

But akhadas were not associated with physical culture or self-defence alone. Young men, brought together at a gymnasium, skilled at fighting and trained in the use of lathis, had considerable potential for political mobilization, and frequently provided a basis for neighbourhood action. As social centres, gymnasiums could also become focal points of political organization. According to the moderate labour leader, Syed Munawar, 'akhadas and teashops were the rendezvous of riff-raffs and hooligans ... those were the best places for them to meet'.[197] The gymnasiums of the mill districts were supposed to be the domain of the unemployed hooligan, the mawali and the badmash. However, those with claims to respectability used gymnasiums as much as those who were labelled as rough and criminal. As one observer put it, 'In the akhadas of course there

---

[194] *Ibid.*, p. 183.
[195] Proceedings of the BRIC, Oral Evidence, Sir P. Thakurdas, File 3, pp. 5–11, MSA.
[196] *Ibid.*, Oral Evidence, Balubhai T. Desai, File 8, pp. 69–71, MSA.
[197] *Ibid.*, Oral Evidence, Syed Munawar, File 3, p. 279, MSA.

are some good workers but some ruffians also join ... also some drunkards and mavalis.'[198] They were frequented, then, not only by the 'hooligans' and the 'riff-raff', but also by 'millworkers', 'dock labourers', 'railway mechanics'. Indeed the Hamuman Vyayam Mandir could report in 1928 that not just ordinary workers but clerks also were becoming enthusiasts for physical culture.[199] It was not merely dadas but jobbers as well who took a leading part in their organization.[200]

There is as yet little available evidence on the organization and working of gymnasiums. Such evidence as exists suggests that the organization of some gymnasiums could be extremely elaborate. For instance, the Hanuman Vyayam Shalla was founded in 1912 by a certain Narayan Rao. By 1928 it claimed branches in parts of the city as dispersed as Vajreshwari, on the outskirts of Bombay in the neighbouring Thana district and Bhoivada in the heart of the mill district, in addition to its headquarters in Prabhadevi. In January 1928 it hosted a contest between fifty other gymnasiums from all over Bombay. This particular occasion involved over 150 wrestling bouts and the collection amounted to over Rs. 2,500. It was likely that sizeable quantities of money would pass through gymnasiums; no doubt competition for their control could be fierce. Elections were held to decide the constitution of the committee. Gymnasiums sometimes even advertised their elections in the Marathi press, notifying their members of the time and place at which they would be held, and announcing how they could establish their qualification to vote. The candidates were sometimes men of considerable importance. In the case of the Shri Samarth Vyayam Mandir, the nationalist campaigner Dr N.D. Savarkar offered himself as a candidate.[201]

It was as much a mark of prestige for gymnasiums as it was for chawl committees and neighbourhood leaders to be able to invite eminent people to their great occasions. When the Hanuman Vyayam Shalla hosted its contest in January 1928 it invited S.K. Bole, founder of the Kamgar Hitvardhak Sabha and, in 1928, Vice President of the Bombay Textile Labour Union, to preside at the function. S.K. Bole, it was reported, gave the gymnasium a handsome donation.[202] Because of their obvious importance in political mobilization, politicians and trade unionists did not treat such connections lightly. Indeed, their political relevance enabled gymnasiums and their dadas to form alliances at exalted levels, which, in turn, then became an important factor in their position within the neighbourhood. According to V.B. Karnik, the prominent trade-union leader of the 1930s,

[198] *Ibid.*, Oral Evidence, Syed Munawar, File 3, p. 281, MSA.
[199] *Nava Kal*, 6 January 1928.
[200] *Gazetteer*, I, 493.
[201] *Nava Kal*, 6 January 1928.
[202] *Ibid.*

Every gymnasium used to have, say, two dozen or three dozen or sometimes even a much bigger number of students and those students were under the control of the gymnasium – that is the dada who taught at the gymnasium. And that dada could utilise his students in any way that he liked ... Every party tried to get the support of one dada or the other.[203]

These associations of young men had considerable potential for political and social organization. As one observer commented, the akhadas 'trained up a regular body of these men to accompany processions such as Hanuman Jayanti or some other Jayanti or some other public occasion.'[204] These collectivities not only provided the basis for street gangs, but they were often pulled into more general political activity: to protect neighbourhoods and attack rivals in communal riots, to mobilize votes and conduct civil disobedience, to smash or safeguard strikers. In the aftermath of the Hindu–Muslim riots of 1929, there were many who lamented the supposed death of the cross-communal akhada and some evoked a golden age of Hindu–Muslim brotherhood which had passed. 'In my childhood', reminisced Nabiullah,

I used to attend a talimkhana. Sometimes there happened to be Hindu Ustads and sometimes Muslim Ustads. There used to be a regular number of pupils, Hindus and Mussalmans, and we used to invoke not only Hanuman but Moula Ali, the strongest man in the world, who were held in great respect by both classes of people ... That very useful and good institution is being destroyed and is being replaced by communal akhadas.

Mirza Ali, a member of the committee, was not to be outdone. He, too, he said, could remember the day when 'both communities were veing [*sic*] in friendly rivalry as we now see on the cricket field'.[205]

Gymnasiums were also pulled into industrial action, on both sides, either by particular workers on strike who by virtue of being dadas themselves were able to utilize them in the conduct of a strike, or by employers who used them as a source of strike-breakers. The role of the gymnasiums in political mobilization is more easily identified than the part they played in industrial action. Political pamphlets and the reported speeches of strike leaders often claimed that gymnasiums were being used in strike-breaking. But it is extremely difficult to document the relationship between gymnasiums and employers. Obviously, strike-breaking could offer gymnasiums a source of income; the greater their income the better equipped they would be in relation to other gymnasiums, the more effective in attracting members and perhaps more successful in the contests arranged between them. It is easy to see that strike-breaking could become an activity essential to the management of some gymnasiums. Employers,

---

[203] Interview, V.B. Karnik, April 1979.
[204] Proceedings of the BRIC, Oral Evidence, A.R. Dimtimkar and S. Nabiullah, File 7, p. 205, MSA.
[205] *Ibid.*, File 7, pp. 205–7, MSA.

on the other hand, relied upon their jobbers and the dadas and gymnasium members among their workforce to contact and deploy gymnasiums. From the point of view of jobbers or employers, importing the hired strength of a gymnasium to settle differences on the shopfloor was neither always advisable nor often necessary. It was only when the employer 'became desperate and wanted to see that the mill started again', when he felt he had exhausted all other options, according to V.B. Karnik,

that he would get hold of a dada and recruit some strike breakers ... it all depended upon the market; if there was demand for cloth then he was anxious to re-open the mill; if there was no demand for cloth then he was not so keen; if the mill remained closed for a week or ten days or even a month it did not matter to him.[206]

These institutions, such as gymnasiums and melas, sprang from informal association within the neighbourhood. Men who boarded at the same khanavali or lived in the same chawl, fraternized at the street-corner, the tea or the toddy shop, came together to celebrate festivals or sometimes to participate in the same gymnasiums. These gangs did not have to be formed; they were embedded within the patterns of everyday life. Rivalries between different gangs were similarly generated. Within each gang, it is possible to see the process by which leadership often came to be forged: individuals came to acquire a reputation for their excellence at wrestling, or their ferocity in street fighting, their shrewdness in dealing with the police or the range of their connections within the neigh-bourhood, their skill at work or their ability to do favours for their fellows or to arbitrate justly in disputes between them. In times of Hindu–Muslim riots, these groups of young men might police their neighbourhood; in strikes, they might help their friends to cross the picket lines or, alternatively, to man them. Some developed political connections, whether through gymnasiums or otherwise, and acted in the roles of, what the Congress, trade unions and political parties came, a trifle euphemistically, to call volunteers. The mainsprings for political action were located within the daily patterns of social life. Furthermore, the processes by which these patterns of association were formed, rivalries gener-ated and leadership forged had some basis in shared values, or more specifically, codes of honour and general conduct, which sometimes acquired an explicit political content.

Caste and community

Caste, kinship and village connections formed the most convenient basis for social organization in Bombay. Migrants to the city sought the help of their caste-fellows, co-villagers and relatives to find work, credit and housing. The

[206] Interview, V.B. Karnik, April 1979.

mutual support which individuals, linked in these ways, could provide each other was indispensable in dealing with the uncertainties of urban life. Through these caste and kinship connections, individuals were able to participate in a system of private security against public risk. Associations based upon these connections were crucial to the social organization of Bombay's workers.

Customarily, the role of caste in the urban context has been discussed largely in terms of an artificial dichotomy of continuity and change. Some anthropologists and historians deduced from the functional role of caste that Indian cities represented an 'urban landscape composed of rural institutions'.[207] The expectation that caste would dissolve under the inexorable pressure of social change suggested that it formed the residual remains of the traditional order which had survived in the modern urban context. The implication was that caste, in the process of dissolution, remained ephemeral to the constitution of the social context in which it operated. Nowhere did the effects of social change appear to be more dramatic in their manifestation than in the development of large-scale industry. In this context, above all, caste distinctions were perceived as 'the institutional carryovers from the rural sector [which] seem to have broken down over time'. They persisted, in this view, only 'because employers found it unnecessary to eliminate them' and 'whenever and wherever industry operations required the disruption of these traditional distinctions, they crumbled'.[208] The fact that caste showed no propensity to crumble appeared to lend credence to the notion that caste was 'the distinctive moral system of India',[209] or in the case of workers, that it 'is the system which forms their preconceptions'.[210]

Both these approaches to the study of caste are profoundly ahistorical. It is scarcely credible to argue that caste is always in the process of dissolution and yet somehow never completely extinct. On the other hand, the notion that caste was the definitive and unchanging cultural system of India suggests that the phenomenon lies beyond mere historical analysis. Caste relationships were neither subject to changeless continuity nor held in some perennial process of dissolution. Within the urban context and industrial setting, they were repeatedly reformulated in numerous ways. This section will, therefore, examine the role of caste in both workplace and neighbourhood.

Furthermore, patterns of association, which emerged not only from caste loyalties but from connections of kinship, village and neighbourhood as well,

---

[207] Lynch, 'Rural Cities', p. 142; see also D.F. Pocock, 'Sociologies: Urban and Rural', *Contributions to Indian Sociology*, IV (1960), pp. 63–81.
[208] Morris, *Industrial Labour Force*, pp. 82–3. See also Morris, 'The Effects of Industrialization', pp. 141–60; and M.D. Morris, 'Caste and the Evolution of the Industrial Workforce in India', *Proceedings of the American Philosophical Society*, CIV, 2 (April 1960), 124–33.
[209] Conlon, *Caste in a Changing World*, p. 4.
[210] Newman, *Workers and Unions*, p. 54.

operated at several levels. But neither caste nor even jati was by any means the sole organizing principle of these connections. The patrons of the neighbour-hood, whether landlords or grain-dealers, jobbers or dadas did not limit their following to endogamous jatis or tightly knit caste structures alone. Thus, we will also have to be concerned with the relationship between these different levels of association and competing social identities in the neighbourhood.

Caste was frequently deployed by workers in restrictive or exclusive practices on the shopfloor, to obtain scarce jobs and command resources, to preserve skill and status and to buttress their bargaining position in relation to their employers. It was a general feature of the city's occupational structure that loose communal clusters – based upon caste and village, language and religion – formed around specific occupations. This was largely the consequence of recruiting practices which centred upon the jobber. Nevertheless, there is as yet little evidence to show any firm connection between specific occupations, let alone particular tasks in particular industries, and jati or caste identities. In general, the evidence relating to caste and factory occupations is extremely scarce and deeply flawed.[211] The best survey of the relationship between caste and occupation in Bombay, which dealt exclusively with the cotton-textile industry, classified some workers according to religion, others according to broad caste categories rather than jati groups and North Indian migrants not according to caste at all, but simply as 'Bhayyas'.[212] Nevertheless, it suggested the tendency for occu-pational clusters to form along the lines of these broad categories (see table 17). Certain patterns of employment are immediately discernible. Marathas and Kunbis were evenly distributed throughout the mill. Muslim women formed an insignificant proportion of the workforce; however, more than half their male co-religionists were employed in the weaving shed. North Indian migrants formed the largest group of workers in the preparatory processes, but they also contributed substantially to 'engineering, mechanic and watch and ward' work-ers. The overwhelming majority of Harijan men were employed in the ring-spinning department and a significant proportion worked in the preparatory

---

[211] As Morris discovered over two decades ago 'the vast official literature' relating to industrial labour 'contains no significant references to the phenomenon' (Morris, 'Caste', 124). This may partly be attributed to the long tradition which expected caste to dissolve in the modern industrial setting. It may also be explained by the extent to which employers locked themselves out of their own systems of labour recruitment and discipline. Employers were primarily concerned not with the caste composition of their workforce so much as with its skill and efficiency, its cheapness and its acquiescence. Problems which arose from caste differences were left largely to the jobber's discretion; when they could not be resolved at these levels, they fundamentally affected the 'efficient utilization' of labour as well as the profits of enterprise. It is significant that, conversely, in contexts in which evidence was collected within such categories, historians and social scientists have often been impressed by the functional importance of caste.
[212] R.G. Gokhale, *The Bombay Cotton Mill Worker* (Bombay, 1957).

Table 17. *Percentage distribution of millworkers by religion and caste*

	Mixing to speed frame	Ring	Winding and reeling	Weaving shed	Engineering, mechanic, watch & ward	Others	Total
Men							
(Hindus)							
Maratha	31.5	41.9	58.2	67.4	40.2	51.9	51.8
Kunbi	4.1	3.4	5.2	4.2	2.4	3.1	3.6
Bhandari	0.9	0.8	6.5	3.1	1.2	4.6	2.4
Bhayya	46.8	4.2	7.4	6.0	14.1	13.2	13.8
Kamati	0.1	3.2	0.3	4.7	1.0	1.0	2.8
Harijan	7.6	39.5	4.3	0.6	10.8	6.5	11.9
Miscellaneous	4.9	3.8	8.0	4.6	7.4	8.1	5.2
Subtotal	95.9	96.8	89.9	90.6	77.1	88.4	91.5
Islam	2.5	2.0	6.5	6.9	11.0	5.6	5.2
Zoroastrian	0.7	0.1	—	0.6	2.5	0.5	0.6
Christian	0.5	0.4	1.2	0.5	4.2	1.8	1.0
Jew	0.1	0.1	1.8	1.1	3.4	2.0	1.0
Jain	—	—	—	—	--	0.1	—
Others	0.3	0.6	0.6	0.3	1.8	1.5	0.7
Total	100.0	100.0	100.0	100.0	100.0	100.0	100.0
Women							
(Hindus)							
Maratha	30.2	15.8	55.9	18.2	17.6	34.7	52.1
Kunbi	4.7	2.8	6.7	—	—	1.6	6.1
Bhandari	—	0.8	4.6	—	—	3.9	4.2
Bhayya	4.7	—	0.1	—	—	0.2	0.2
Kamati	11.6	1.2	2.5	—	—	0.4	2.4
Harijan	31.4	77.8	20.9	18.2	23.5	33.5	24.5
Miscellaneous	11.6	—	7.8	36.3	—	12.2	7.8
Subtotal	94.2	98.4	98.5	72.7	41.1	86.5	97.3
Islam	5.8	1.6	0.6	27.3	—	3.1	1.0
Zoroastrian	—	—	—	—	—	0.2	—
Christian	—	—	0.5	—	11.8	1.0	0.5
Jew	—	—	0.3	—	47.1	9.2	1.1
Jain	—	—	—	—	—	—	—
Others	—	—	0.1	—	—	—	0.1
Total	100.0	100.0	100.0	100.0	100.0	100.0	100.0

Source: Gokhale, *Cotton Mill Worker*, Table A-II, p. 116.

processes as well as in the 'engineering, mechanic and watch and ward' category. More than three-quarters of the Harijan women employed in the industry worked in the winding and reeling departments, where nearly 95 per cent of the labour force was female. But Harijan women made up no more than a fifth of the total workforce engaged in this process, which was dominated by Maratha and Kunbi women. On the other hand, in ring-spinning where fewer women were employed and where jobs were less desirable for them, Harijan women made up nearly 78 per cent of the total female workforce.

Since most millworkers lived in the vicinity of their workplace, the occupational clusters which formed in particular mills often departed considerably from the general tendencies observed for the industry as a whole. For instance, occupational clusters were influenced by the social composition of specific neighbourhoods and the position of various social groups within them. Thus, Marathas from Ratnagiri dominated the weaving shed in the mills of Lalbag, Parel, Dadar, DeLisle Road and Fergusson Road; Muslim weavers were prominent at Jacob Circle and Byculla; Marathas from the Deccan formed the majority of weavers in Ghorapdeo, Kalachowki and Sewri, where their counterparts from the Konkan were pushed into the ring-spinning department.[213] Similarly, Julahi Muslim and Kamati weavers were believed by employers to be the most skilled, and were often assigned to the complicated jacquard and fancy looms. Kamati weavers were employed in small numbers in several mills, but they predominated in the Khatau mills.[214] Moreover, it is probable that the social composition of the workforce, whether in the industry as a whole or in specific mills, was subject to considerable short-term change. The Maratha weavers from Ratnagiri and the Konkan, believed to have been particularly prominent during the general strike of 1928, became the target of the repression which followed it. Millowners and managers tried to reduce their dominance in the weaving shed during the 1930s by engaging a larger number of Marathas from the Deccan, who were perceived as being somewhat more pliable, if rather less skilled.[215] While the Konkani Marathas had by 1940 recovered their position within the industry as a whole, their representation in the prized occupations of the weaving shed continued to decline. Their proportion fell from 41.42 per cent in 1940 to 30.74 per cent in 1955, while over the same period the proportion of 'Ghatis' rose from 47.80 to 51.53 per cent.[216]

As soon as one social group successfully gained a foothold in an industry, and especially in one of its more skilled departments, it attempted to strengthen

[213] Shah, 'Labour Recruitment and Turnover', p. 179.
[214] Ibid., p. 184.
[215] Ibid., pp. 177–9, 182.
[216] Gokhale, Cotton Mill Worker, p. 18.

and even expand its position. The social connections of the working classes injected some dynamism into this process: to retain their command over particular skills or, more generally, specific tasks, they had to continue to import and train a growing number of their own men. At the level of large caste blocks, such as the Marathas of the Deccan or the Konkan, these rivalries were scarcely perceptible and the changes which flowed from them slow to manifest themselves. In general, where these rivalries involved effective social connections based upon jobbers or neighbourhood networks rather than crude caste blocks, they were likely to give rise to more volatile changes and deeper competition. Whereas it would be tempting to conceive of these connections in terms of jati or caste, they formed and fragmented around looser, more diffuse patterns of association.

'Various communities', noted the *Gazetteer*, 'evince a predilection for a particular kind of work and rarely will a member of any one of them be found engaged in any other branch of labour than that in which his caste-people have become specialists.'[217] Yet his occupational distribution reflected neither caste vocation nor the inheritance of special skills. It was produced partly by exclusionary practices by which social groups, once they had obtained a foothold in a particular occupation, 'would not admit an outsider'.[218] How far they succeeded in maintaining their dominance depended upon how indispensable they appeared in terms of skill or loyalty to their employers. Moreover, caste clusters were not always what they first appeared. Observers tended to report not only in terms of crude caste categories but also of large geographical regions, religion and language. Thus, when Burnett-Hurst observed that carpenters in the building trade were Gujaratis, Jews, Konkanis, Mohammedans, Punjabis and Goans, he had probably accounted for the vast majority of the city's labour force.[219] Nevertheless, there was a sufficient tendency in the building trade for castes and particular social groups to cluster around specific occupations to suggest that 'certain classes of work are undertaken by natives of particular districts'.[220] Marathas from the Deccan predominated in the building trade. Carpenters in the trade were mainly drawn from Kathiawar and included a number of Jews resident in the city. Kamatis, also long settled in Bombay, Marwaris and Muslims were the most numerous among bricklayers while most blacksmiths were described as Gujaratis and Marathas. Bohras were reputedly skilled as glaziers, while stonemasons were recruited from Kathiawar and the Deccan and Mahars and Ghatis figured predominantly among 'coolies'.[221]

[217] *Gazetteer*, 1, 207–8.
[218] Cholia, *Dock Labourers*, p. 30.
[219] Burnett-Hurst, *Labour and Housing*, p. 89.
[220] *Ibid.*, p. 86.
[221] *Ibid.*, pp. 86, 89.

Among dock labourers, according to Burnett-Hurst, the Ghatis of Poona and Satara were predominant among matadis or bag carriers, Gujarati Hindus were often employed as baroots, who claimed special skill in stacking case cargo; and low-caste Mahars were engaged 'for handling offensive cargo'. All castes were represented among those hired as 'boy-labour': 'youths, "raw hands" from the village and even elderly men who do not possess the physique to undertake heavier and skilled work'.[222] Lacking sufficient bargaining power, no single group could corner the available work by enforcing caste exclusion. A more detailed survey of dock labourers in the early 1930s revealed a similar pattern of domination of particular jobs by certain ethnic, linguistic, religious and regional groups. Most stevedores were born outside the Presidency and nearly half of them were migrants from the United Provinces, and the majority were Muslims.[223] Almost all shore labourers were recruited from Poona, Satara, Ahmednagar and Sholapur. The majority were Maratha by caste, while the vast majority of Mahars came from Satara and worked as Matadi labourers.[224] They were paid by results, their wages being divided equally between them with a double share for the toliwalla or the labour contractor.[225] To the system of wage payment as well as 'the peculiarly hard nature of the work' was attributed the fact that 'unity among them is so strong that no outsider can come in to share their work'.[226] Almost all the labourers who shifted coal were Mahars and nearly three-quarters of them came from Satara, yet while Mahars from Satara worked on board ship, those from Poona preferred to work on shore and indeed 'do not like to work on colliers in the stream, except on high wages in cases of emergency'.[227] If the shore labourers employed by the Port Trust's 'Hammal-age' department were primarily from the Deccan, the majority of other Port Trust labourers on shore came from Ratnagiri, and significant minorities were drawn from the United Provinces and fewer still from the city and from Satara and Goa.[228] Nearly a third of these workers were Muslims and over 11 per cent were Christians.[229] A smaller though significant minority of Muslims and Christians were employed in the mechanical workshops; about 2 per cent were Chinese and nearly two-thirds were Hindus. While most Marathas were engaged as unskilled labour, Christians, Jews, Parsis and Anglo-Indians were exclusively to be found among the highly paid turners, fitters and carpenters

[222] *Ibid.*, pp. 76–7.
[223] Cholia, *Dock Labourers*, p. 30.
[224] *Ibid.*, p. 44.
[225] *Ibid.*, p. 49.
[226] *Ibid.*, p. 44.
[227] *Ibid.*, p. 61.
[228] *Ibid.*, p. 92.
[229] *Ibid.*, p. 92.

while the Chinese, believed to be 'expert in the art of building wooden boats' were employed mainly as carpenters.[230] The Marathas, Mahars and Muslims were drawn chiefly from Ratnagiri and Satara while the skilled workers were largely resident in Bombay or, especially in the case of some Christians, came from Goa.

The social composition of the railway workshops was extremely diffuse. Parsis were 'generally placed on the most difficult machines' while Punjabi Muslims were 'said by some to be the best workers'. But the vast majority of machinists were Ratnagiri Marathas. Moulders were mainly Kamatis from Hyderabad; tin smiths were largely Bohras; Lohars from Gujarat were preponderant among the smiths in the wheel shop; 'Pardeshis' from the United Provinces accounted for about 'half the unskilled labour'; the majority in the brass foundry were Marathas; the foremen were 'European' while chargemen were recruited from the Goan Christians, Parsis and Anglo-Indians.[231]

Similar caste, linguistic and regional clusters were to be found in the dockyards: Agris and Bhandaris from Ratnagiri, Janjira and Malwan were predominant among the skilled riveters and platers; Gujarati Lohars among the blacksmiths; and Pathans and up-country Muslims 'on heavy work as hammermen'. Carpenters in the joiners' shop came from Surat, Bulsar, Daman and Navsari in Gujarat, while large numbers of Goans were employed as shipwrights. About two-thirds of the unskilled labourers were Kharvas from Kathiawar.[232]

Caste and the social connections built upon it were also used by skilled workers to defend their status and to prevent the encroachments of rivals. Thus Muslims, who belonged to hereditary weavers' castes claimed a higher status than other groups who had merely picked up their skills on the job. They prided themselves on the fact that their womenfolk did not work. Moreover, the bulk of them were employed in the weaving shed. 'As a matter of fact,' the Secretary of the Bombay Millowners' Association observed in 1938, 'such Mohammedan workers do not ordinarily work in mills except in higher-paid occupations'. Furthermore, as one millowner emphasized, 'a Mohammedan worker does not accept a lower wage. There is a higher level for them. I mean the average earnings of a Mohammedan weaver is always more than a Hindu.'[233] Their reputation as skilled weavers was sufficient to enable them to assert a considerable degree of control over their work. They recorded some of the highest rates of absenteeism in the industry and obtained the right to select their own badlis and even to pay them from their own wages. 'In some cases', wrote one

[230] *Ibid.*, pp. 103–4.
[231] Burnett-Hurst, *Labour and Housing*, pp. 97–8.
[232] *Ibid.*, pp. 93–5.
[233] Proceedings of the TLIC, Main Inquiry, Oral Evidence, Representatives of the Bombay Millowners' Association, File 57-A, p. 193, MSA.

observer, 'they have monopolised certain parts of the weaving shed where no one else dare employment'.[234] They were particularly strongly established in the mills located at Jacob's Circle, Madanpura and the general neighbourhood of Byculla. In the mid 1930s when various mills began to introduce night shifts, most workers sought to avoid them if possible, because they were liable to be abandoned at short notice. But in the Jocob Circle mills, Muslim workers simply refused to accept night-shift work and continued to resist effectively the pressure of their employers in this regard to the end of the decade.[235]

Similarly, among the mechanics and artisans employed in the Port Trust workshops, it was reported that 'some of them follow their ancestral occupations and claim to possess some hereditary qualities for their work'.[236] Their claim to skill and status was extended beyond the workplace:

They have their own traditions and mode of living, and are in a position to keep up the same. Consequently, they prefer staying amongst their own people – either coming from the same place or belonging to the same caste or community. This tendency among them is so strong that they would not like to leave the localities and the company to which they are accustomed.[237]

– least of all to move into a port Trust chawl.

Caste was sometimes used in less skilled jobs as well to exercise some leverage over work and to exclude rivals. Matadi labour in the docks, hired to shift bag cargo on the shore, was predominantly of the lowly Mahar caste. Nevertheless, as Cholia put it, 'to carry bags weighing five to six maunds each, easily on the back all day long, requires an experienced labourer'.[238] Although work was spasmodic and the trade seasonal, the need for experienced workers prompted the Port Trust to retain a nucleus of Matadi gangs employed throughout the year, employing additional men when the need arose. The solidarity of the Mahars who were thus employed was sufficient to restrict the employment of 'outsiders'.[239] These exclusive practices were invaluable in an occupation which was liable to arbitrary fluctuations.

The most direct manifestation of caste exclusion practices was the refusal of Maratha weavers to work with untouchable castes. This was because each time a weft bobbin required replacement, the yarn had to be sucked on to the shuttle. Ostensibly, by working with untouchables, caste Hindu weavers risked defile-

[234] Shah, 'Labour Recruitment and Turnover', p. 184
[235] Proceedings to the TLIC, Main Inquiry, Oral Evidence, Representatives of the BMOA, File 57-A, p. 169.
[236] Cholia, Dock Labourers, p. 105.
[237] Ibid., p. 109–10.
[238] Ibid., p. 47.
[239] Ibid., p. 44.

ment and pollution.[240] More crucially, the exclusion of untouchables served to limit the supply of weavers, to preserve their status and to reinforce the barriers of skill. However, this case was marked by several anomalies. If caste Hindus feared defilement by association with untouchables, they were less apprehensive of such contact with Muslim weavers. In addition, Marathas swallowed their fears, shelved their prejudices and worked alongside Mahars in other processes in the cotton mills as well as in other occupations. Furthermore, although Marathas and Kunbis made up the overwhelming majority of weavers in the industry in 1940, there were other significant caste and communal clusters to be found in the weaving shed: Muslims, 'Bhayyas', Kamatis, Bhandaris and sundry smaller groups.[241] Of course, it was unlikely that Maratha weavers could have successfully breached the bargaining position and status which Julahi Muslims acquired in the industry. At the same time, Marathas and other caste Hindus were probably able to resist the entry of untouchable workers only in those occupations, notably weaving, where their skill gave them both organizational as well as bargaining strength. But if, in refusing to work with untouchables, Maratha weavers were simply effecting a closed shop in order to retain their 'monopoly' of the weaving sheds, why did they fail to exclude other social groups, such as North Indian workers and Bhandaris? The exclusion of untouchables from the weaving shed was not simply a function of a scramble for jobs but also an expression of a caste consciousness which extended beyond the workplace.

Research on the role of caste in the urban setting has sometimes suggested that while traditional caste practices might be adapted within the context of work they are reasserted and maintained within the family, the home and the neighbourhood.[242] Yet a closer examination of the evidence from Bombay demonstrates that social organization in the workplace and the neighbourhood were interdependent. They cannot so neatly be separated. It would be misleading to assume that the private sphere was the preserve of a timeless, traditional culture and that the processes of adaptation and modernization arising from the sphere of production and politics worked upon a passive working class. From the role of caste in the workplace, it is necessary to turn to its effect upon social organization in the neighbourhood.

The caste affiliations which contemporary observers identified within the working class were more frequently large caste blocks than endogamous or

[240] Shah, 'Labour Recruitment and Turnover', p. 215; Morris, *Industrial Labour Force*, p. 79.
[241] Gokhale, *The Cotton Mill Worker*, p. 116. See above, p. 221, Table 17.
[242] H.A. Gould, 'Lucknow Rickshawallas: The Social Organisation of an Occupational Category', *International Journal of Comparative Sociology*, VI, 1 (March 1965), 24–47; Newman, *Workers and Unions*, pp. 54–5; H.A. Gould, 'The Adaptive Function of Caste in Contemporary Indian Society', *Asian Survey*, III (1963), 427–38.

inter-marrying and inter-dining jatis, sometimes merely loosely defined regional, religious or even linguistic groupings. In fact, the census commissioners found their efforts at enumerating castes subverted, as late as 1931, because respondents gave 'names of [sic] geographical nature, or names describing occupations or functions' when asked to state their jati. 'Much of the trouble', complained the commissioners, '... arises from the vague connotation of the term "caste". At present, the term "caste" covers distinctions due to racial differences, to topographical origin, to occupation and to social custom.'[243] Caste associations and panchayats which formed beyond the workplace did not operate along the lines of these general categories. Maharashtrian society was characterized by its homogeneity. In particular, the intermediate Maratha caste had become by the late nineteenth and early twentieth century a conglomerate, or a coalition, of numerous intermediate peasant castes.[244] Nevertheless, as Irawati Karve pointed out, 'Each caste has its own area of extent in which there is kinship and marriage, mutual visiting and meeting of caste councils'.[245] Caste organizations in Bombay often consisted of jati and kinship groups belonging to a single and sometimes a collection of neighbouring villages in the district of the workers' origins. Some caste mandalis in Bombay operated across the boundaries of jati. A study of Ratnagiri migrants in Bombay in the 1960s found that 59 per cent of their caste mandalis were organized on the basis of the village from which workers came while only 41 per cent were organized according to jati and, moreover, that no more than 42 per cent of workers were members of their caste organization. Moreover, while some caste mandalis were limited to specific neighbourhoods, others were organized across the city and their jurisdiction sometimes extended to the villages as well.[246]

These caste associations were governed by their more prominent or influential members. They arbitrated disputes, organized the collection of subscriptions and administered their funds. They were also responsible for the welfare of their members. They sometimes even arranged, and certainly approved marriages. Chandri, a resident of Bhaste in Ratnagiri, was tried for bigamy in Bombay in 1917. While her husband was in hospital, it was alleged, she eloped with one Hari Govind and was later found to be working in the Colaba Land Mill. Her defence before the court was that her husband had deserted her for five years and that in any case, her caste had given her permission to re-marry.[247] For caste

---

[243] *Census, 1931*, IX, i, 38–9.
[244] R.E. Enthoven, *The Tribes and Castes of the Bombay Presidency* (Bombay, 1922), vol. III, pp. 3–42; R. O'Hanlon, *Caste, Conflict and Ideology: Mahatma Jotirao Phule and Low Caste Protest in Nineteenth Century Maharashtra* (Cambridge, 1985).
[245] I. Karve, *Hindu Society – An Interpretation* (Poona, 1961), pp. 30–1.
[246] Patel, *Rural Labour*, pp. 151–2, 164.
[247] *Times of India*, 6 July 1917.

councils to establish the legitimacy of their authority, to gain general acceptance for their actions and to win the confidence of their members, it was useful to include in their ranks prominent figures of the neighbourhood: jobbers and dadas, landlords and grain-dealers, policemen and minor functionaries. But it need not be supposed that these associations were formally organized. Frequently, respected residents of the neighbourhood or of a particular caste or community simply came in practice to be invested by their kinsfolk and caste fellows with the status of leadership. Despite the fact that the Pathans in Bombay had a headman for each of their four jamats in the city, it was to a police inspector in the CID, Ubedullakhan, that they brought their disputes in 1917.[248]

In addition, some caste mandalis collected subscriptions from their members and deployed their proceeds on various forms of welfare expenditure. Thus in 1892, the Collector of Bombay observed that whereas workers subscribed willingly to causes which 'their caste or community hold worthy of support ... they hold aloof from similar subscriptions for wage purposes'.[249] Certain castes or 'communities' used the subscriptions they collected to rent rooms and formed what came to be called 'residential clubs'.[250] Sometimes each village had its own club. Every member paid a subscription whether he lived in the room or not. Although every member was allowed to live in the room or leave his belongings there, the unemployed were given preference. 'Each man', it was said, 'had to use his own box containing his belongings as his cot.'[251] Many no doubt slept on the footpaths outside. The rising levels of unemployment increased the strain on these institutions. By the end of the 1920s, it was said, with particular reference to seamen, 'too large a number has to live in houses disproportionately small. In some of the clubs, within an area of 50 square yards not less than twenty men live.'[252] The ubiquitous khanavalis of the mill district operated in a similar fashion. The subscriptions of those who were employed

---

[248] *Ibid.*, 13 July 1917.
[249] *Royal Commission on Labour*, II, Memorandum on the Labour Question in India, Letter from the Collector, Land Revenue, Excise and Opium, Bombay, to Chief Secretary, *PP*, 1892, XXXVI, 128. We need not conclude that a 'caste consciousness' was here operating in conflict with a 'trade union consciousness'. For the Collector also warned that 'any attempt at the widespread lowering of wages' was likely to result in 'a widespread and resolute combination'. Indeed, 'the opposition to any general reduction of wages seems likely to be general and to prove hard to overcome'; *ibid*. At the same time, the distinction between 'caste or community' was vital. It has already been shown that the informal social connections which workers formed in the neighbourhood were deployed not only to find work, to protect their jobs, and to express their grievances but also to provide for periods of unemployment. But these connections did not form along the lines of jati alone.
[250] *RCLI, Evidence, Bombay Presidency*, I, i, the Indian Seamen's Union, 291; The Bombay Seamen's Union, 293; Messrs. Mackinnon and Mackenzie and Co., 545; Patel, *Rural Labour*, p. 31.
[251] *RCLI, Evidence, Bombay Presidency*, The Indian Seamen's Union, I, i, 291.
[252] *Ibid.*, The Bombay Seamen's Union, I, i, 293.

enabled the subsistence of those who were not. Some khanavalis, it was noted, might continue to support unemployed workers for extended periods of six months or even up to a year. But it was expected that once they found work, they would repay their debts. If residents failed to obtain a job, they returned to their villages without settling their debts which were then sometimes considered a charge on their employed co-habitants or simply written off.[253] Similar room-sharing arrangements were developed more informally by workers connected by caste, kinship and village.[254] The collection and deployment of subscriptions became flashpoints of conflict within caste mandalis as members complained about the unsatisfactory use or unequal distribution of their contributions for their welfare needs.[255]

The strength and coherence of caste organization varied widely between different groups of workers in Bombay. In general, the most marginalized groups within the working class, whether as a result of caste and ethnic exclusion or as a consequence of their position in the labour market, tended to develop the most tightly knit and coherent caste connections. Casual, unskilled workers depended more heavily upon their jobbers to keep them in work than those whose experience and skill was valued by their employers. Newly arrived migrants from the United Provinces or Madras, who lacked extensive links in Bombay, or distress migrants who had lost their rural connections had fewer options both within the workplace and the neighbourhood than their better-established counterparts and were, therefore, more heavily dependent upon their patrons.

Caste organization was strong among groups of workers in the small workshops and the casual trades in the city. For example, the cohesion of the informal social connections of these groups was observed in the case of building and dock workers, who experienced casual and uncertain conditions of employment.[256] Similarly, caste organization possessed considerable importance for the Julaha Muslim weavers, employed in the handloom weaving workshops. They were not only employed in a declining trade, but they were social outcasts and often labelled as deviants in the perceptions of contemporaries.[257] Each jamat of the Julaha Muslim weavers was 'more like a caste than a craft guild', with a head and several deputies to execute his orders or to fill his place in his

---

[253] Patel, *Rural Labour*, p. 31.
[254] See above, pp.182–3.
[255] Patel, *Rural Labour*, p. 152.
[256] Burnett-Hurst, *Labour and Housing*, pp. 84, 90.
[257] Commissioner of Police, Bombay to Secretary, GOB, Judicial, 20 January 1911, reprinted in Edwardes, *Bombay City Police*, Appendix, p. 197. For similar perceptions, three decades later, see Note by Commissioner of Police, Bombay, 3 November 1944, GOB, Home (Sp.), File 1002 (1) of 1893–1945, p. 257, MSA. G. Pandey, *The Construction of Communalism in Colonial North India* (Delhi, 1992), pp. 66–108.

absence. Each member paid a 'monthly tax' which varied between 2 and 8 pice per loom. These collections were spent on annual feasts or the purchase of copper pots for public dinners given to mourn deaths and celebrate marriages. The headman of the jamat settled civil and matrimonial disputes and could sanction punishments for offenders against caste discipline. These punishments took the form of fines, according to the means of the offender, or in the case of serious offences, of attempts 'to humiliate and debase the offender in the eyes of his class-men', for instance by making him take off and place the shoes of the jamat on his head as penance or wear a garland of old shoes. The extreme penalty was of course to stop 'huqqah-pani', or, in effect, formal excommunication. In many cases, weavers lived in the house or workshop of their master, which only provided a firmer basis for wider caste solidarity.[258] Weavers who moved into the textile mills used this organization, as we have seen, to strengthen their claim to skilled status and to protect their position at work.

Like the Julaha Muslims, the North Indian migrants were also the victims of the racialist perceptions and social prejudices prevalent in local society. Perhaps, this factor helps to explain why 'bhaiya live with other bhaiya in areas dominated by bhaiya' or why they would 'point out chawls where the "Barbers of Y village live" or "the cowherders of X village reside" '.[259] Thus, one anthropologist was led to conclude, 'Local (Maharashtrian and Gujarati) people have a tendency to look down upon the bhaiya as crude countrymen, an attitude not lost on the bhaiya. Regardless of caste or achieved class position in the city, bhaiya have little meaningful contact with the local population'.[260] This is perhaps to overstate the case. It is doubtful whether within the social nexus of neighbourhood and workplace North Indian workers were able to so thoroughly dissociate themselves from their immediate context. Nevertheless, it suggests the marginalization of North Indian workers in Bombay and the attitude of the local population towards them. As with many other marginalized elements within the working class, it was observed in the 1920s that 'Pardeshi ... "hang together" more than other castes'. As a result, 'when Pardeshis have a grievance, there is generally trouble'.[261] Strong caste organization was also in evidence among the Mochis, Chamars and Dhors in the leather industry.[262]

Conversely, caste organization among Maratha and Kunbi workers,

---

[258] Enthoven, *Cotton Fabrics*, pp. 20–2.
[259] W.L. Rowe, 'Caste, Kinship and Association in Urban India', in A. Southall (ed.), *Urban Anthropology: Cross Cultural Studies of Urbanization* (New York, 1973), pp. 228–9.
[260] *Ibid.*, p. 229.
[261] Burnett-Hurst, *Labour and Housing*, p. 98.
[262] Martin, *Tanning and Working in Leather*, pp. 26–9; see also in connection with the leather workers' strike in the suburb of Dharavi in 1937, GOB, Home (Sp.) File 550 (23) A of 1937, p. 51, MSA.

especially from Ratnagiri, was considerably more diffuse. Migrants from Ratnagiri had sought employment in Bombay before its rapid development in the later nineteenth century. From the earliest days of the textile industry, they had secured jobs within the mills. Because recruitment practices were influenced by caste, village, kinship and neighbourhood connections, they had tightened their grip upon a wide range of jobs within the industry. Institutional factors such as the jobber system of recruitment formed the major impetus to the consolidation and expansion of specific social groups within the workforce and the perpetuation of particular streams of migration. But the more securely established within the workforce they were, the more their social connections both at the workplace and in the neighbourhood were liable to diversify. Consequently, the employment as well as the residential patterns of Ratnagiri Marathas in Bombay were relatively dispersed.[263]

That these social connections did not form exclusively along the lines of jati deserves emphasis. Although they were loosely influenced by kinship ties, they could also take the form of regional, religious or neighbourhood associations cutting across the boundaries of caste. Thus, migrants to the city might congregate around others from the same district who had already established themselves in Bombay.[264] Similarly, a study of North Indian migrants to Bombay observed that:

The ideal of all men of a village being *gaon bhai* or village brothers, has greater meaning in the city than almost anywhere else. Hence in the city relationships among men of different castes but of the same village may be much warmer and closer than in the village.[265]

It should be clear that neither the cultural determinism which understands caste as the force which formed the 'preconceptions' of the working class and thus determined their social action nor the teleology which portrays urban society as if it were passing through a uniform and unilinear process of the 'dissolution of traditional groupings and their submergence in broader ones'[266] are satisfactory. Rather, this chapter has attempted to examine the operation of caste organization, practices and loyalties as they contributed to the creation of their historical setting and were in turn shaped by it. Caste formed one important level of social organization, but there were others. The interaction between the various levels of association which formed among the working classes shaped their perceptions and coloured their political and cultural allegiances.

At one level, of course, social organization was centred upon the family. It

[263] Gokhale, *Cotton Mill Workers;* on residential patterns, see *Census, 1921*, IX, i, 16–17.
[264] *RCLI, Evidence, Bombay Presidency*, Mr J. Ghosal, Commissioner, C.D., Poona, I, i, 205.
[265] Rowe, 'Caste, Kinship and Association', p. 229
[266] Morris, 'The Effects of Industrialisation on "Race" Relations', pp. 158–9.

was the operation of the family economy which both required and facilitated the migration of workers. It shaped the terms on which workers entered the labour market and informed their options as they attempted to deal with its uncertainties. Kinship connections formed the touchstone of patterns of migration, residence and employment in the city for most workers. Kinship provided the basis for the informal welfare systems of the Bombay working class.

Marriage occurred within endogamous jatis, providing a wider level of social organization. The importance of kinship connections to the social organization of Bombay's workers necessarily meant that of all caste-based practices, marriage remained the most resilient to change. Most jatis might begin to live with each other in the same chawl or work together in the same occupation, but inter-marriage was ruled out. Nevertheless through the course of the twentieth century, certain changes are discernible. Marriages continued to be arranged and they were limited by endogamous practices. However, choice, expectations and considerations of status impinged heavily upon the arrangement of marriages. Thus,

Girls brought up in Bombay would never willingly marry an agriculturist in Ratnagiri. Girls dislike to work in the fields and so workers try to find out eligible males for their daughters from among those who work in the same or adjoining mills and reside in the same neighbourhood.[267]

Conversely, a large number of stevedore labourers, it was said, found it difficult to arrange marriages and remained single as a consequence. This has been explained in terms of the weakness of their rural connections: they lacked the village contacts through which to arrange their marriages. On the other hand, endogamy complicated the possibilities of getting married in Bombay.[268] However, a more plausible explanation for their marriage patterns may be based upon the fact that the lack of a rural base was a sign of hopeless distress. In addition, employment as stevedore labour was notoriously liable to interruption. These two factors combined to suggest that the stevedore labourer without a rural base was unlikely to become a major asset to the family economy or to strengthen substantially the kinship connections through which workers acted to modify the uncertainties of the urban and industrial setting.

The neighbourhood clearly provided a third level of social organization. The social connections of the neighbourhood were crucial in helping workers find jobs, credit and housing. These connections were referred back to the village, loosely based upon caste and kinship and could extend into political organization and action. It is significant that even marriage patterns came to be framed

[267] Patel, *Rural Labour*, p. 107.
[268] Cholia, *Dock Labourers*, p. 53.

234 The origins of industrial capitalism in India

by the social connections of the neighbourhood. Within the neighbourhood, gaon bhai and village connections imparted a new meaning to caste identity. Moreover, as we have already noted, workplace and neighbourhood came to be inextricably interconnected. Associations which formed at the workplace also received expression within the neighbourhood.

At another level, caste identities came to be expressed through caste associations which could operate throughout the city. Authority within such associations was diffuse and invariably mediated by locations of power lodged at other levels of social organization. Alongside caste associations, religion, language and even the region from which workers migrated offered a basis for a more general social identity and the expression of wider solidarities.

Finally, their rural connections, the fluctuations and uncertainties of the labour market and the social institutions and power relations of the neighbourhood became integral to the shared social experience of the working class. Of course, since these were experienced in different ways, they did not simply create a homogeneous working class; indeed they often registered differences between workers. Nevertheless, this chapter has suggested that the social identities of the working class were not defined by various ascriptive identities alone. Rather, the urban neighbourhood provided a context within which the working classes, despite their diverse values and expectations, could at times forge wider solidarities.

It has already been noted that the social connections of the neighbourhood did not operate along the lines of caste alone. Although they were based upon and related back to kinship ties, these social connections could also cut across the boundaries of caste. Neither commerce nor patronage nor service could afford to restrict itself to these social limits. Moreover, in the social exchange of the street, ascriptive or acquired status may be repeatedly asserted but was also extremely difficult to maintain. Thus, the heat and the overcrowding and the mosquitoes, it was said, forced

many a respectable householder to shoulder his bedding and join the great army of street-sleepers ... All sorts and conditions of men thus take their night's rest beneath the moon – Rangaris, Kasais, barbers, beggars, wanderers and artisans.[269]

Similarly, leisure too could bring together social groups which might otherwise refuse to inter-marry or to eat with each other. The opium clubs and liquor shops of the city were thus said to be a solvent of social barriers. According to the *Gazetteer*, 'The opium-club of the city draw their patrons from widely differing classes ... for the opium-club destroys all caste prejudices and renders the votaries of "the black smoke" careless of social obligations'.[270]

---

[269] Edwardes, *By-Ways of Bombay*, p. 18.
[270] *Gazetteer*, I, 190.

Similarly, the Islamic festival of Mohurram was in Bombay marked by widespread Hindu participation. It was held to be 'an undeniable fact that Hindus, and particularly the sectional bad characters among them, take a prominent part in the Mohurram tolis and mob'.[271] The spiritual significance of Hindu participation in Mohurram is to be seen in their attraction to the Dula, 'a lean Mussalman, with a green silk skull cap, sitting in a raised recess in front of an urn in which frankincense is burning', who had vowed to become the son-in-law of Hussain:

There he sits craning his neck over the smoke from the urn and swaying from side to side, while at intervals three companions who squat beside him give vent to a cry of 'Bara Imam Ki dosti yaro din (cry din for the friendship of the twelve Imams)'. Then on a sudden [sic] the friends rise and bind on to the Dula's chest a pole surmounted with the holy hand, place in his hand a bunch of peacock's feathers, and lead him thus bound and ornamented on to the highway. Almost on the threshold of his passage, a Panjabi Musalman comes forward to consult him … A little further on the procession, which has now swelled to considerable size, is stopped by a Muhammadan from Ahmednagar who seeks relief … In the Bhendi Bazaar, a Mahar woman comes forward for enlightenment, and the Dula, after repeating the Kalmah, promises that she will become a mother before the year expires; while close to Phul Gali, a Konkani Musalman women who has been possessed for six months by a witch (Dakan) is flicked thrice with the peacock-feather brush and bidden to the Dula's shrine on the following Thursday. So the Dula fares gradually forward, now stopped by a Kunbi with a sick child, now by some Musalman millhands, until he reaches the Bismillah shrine, where he falls forward on his face with frothing mouth and convulsed body. The friends help the spirit which racks him to depart by blowing into his ear a few verses from the Koran, whereat the Dula, after a possession of about four hours, regains consciousness, looks around in surprise and retires to his home, fatigued but at last sane.[272]

Finally, industrial and political action, trade unions and political parties created a wider level of association for the city's workers. For it was often at this political level that the social, economic and ideological differences between workers were negotiated and alliances between them effected on terms of limited advantage and for specific ends. Although, by their very nature, these alliances were necessarily fragile and their goals were effectively limited, this level of political association was integral to the social fabric of the neighbour-hood. 'There is no trade union among the dock workers', wrote Burnett-Hurst in 1925, 'but there is a strong fellow-feeling among them and they are a very united body.'[273] Similarly, despite the fact that there was no organization among the building workers, it was said, 'there exists a close comradeship which on

---

[271] Edwardes, Bombay City Police, p. 209.
[272] Gazetteer, I, 185–6.
[273] Burnett-Hurst, Labour and Housing, p. 84. This was a prescient judgement, looking forward to the dock workers' strike of 1932.

occasions finds expression in joint action'.[274] Moreover, these levels of association were intimately interrelated. It is not surprising, therefore, that some of the first trade unions in Bombay took the form of welfare associations for particular castes, such as Lokhande's Bombay Millhands' Association in the 1890s and the Kamgar Hitwardhak Sabha in the 1910s and early 1920s.[275] During the repeated general strikes of the 1920s and the 1930s, industrial and political action injected considerable dynamism into this level of association, transcending the ascriptive and inherited identities of the working class. In the particularly intense struggles of 1928–9, it is possible to discern what K.F. Nariman called 'a new spirit of organization and class consciousness ... among our labouring classes'.[276]

By the early 1930s, Cholia observed the mutuality which was forged among stevedore labourers in the Bombay cutting across the divisions of caste:

Even though most of the labourers come from different parts of India, their habits and mode of living are not fundamentally different. Living side by side, day in and day out and having little of family traditions because of their emigration from home in childhood, they seem to have adopted a common mode of living, differing from each other in minor details only, on account of religion or individual prejudice.[277]

Although the context of workplace and neighbourhood in Bombay transformed the inherited expectations of the working class, religion and individual prejudice cannot be swept aside as minor details. They testify to the cultural sectionalism of Bombay's working class which was not wholly dissolved by economic development but rather was at times intensified by it. Within their specific historical context, it is more fruitful to examine the interplay, and indeed the contradictions, between these different levels of association among Bombay's workers than the extent to which caste was being progressively dissolved and uniformly submerged into class.

Between the wars, the neighbourhood formed an increasingly important arena for the social organization and political action of Bombay's workers. Migration to Bombay occurred within the matrix of caste, kinship and village connections. To find work, credit and housing, workers entered into a range of social connections and became involved in networks of patronage in the urban neighbourhood. If these social connections enabled them to find work, they often served as the grid for informal systems of mutual support which proved invaluable in periods of unemployment and distress as well. If the nature of the

---

[274] *Ibid.*, p. 90.
[275] *Labour Gazette*, II, 7 (March 1923), 26.
[276] *TOI*, 10 August 1929.
[277] Cholia, *Dock Labourers*, pp. 35–6.

rural connections of Bombay's workers made this pattern of social organization possible, the uncertainties of the labour market made it necessary.

However, it would be false to understand the social organization of the neighbourhood as a simple function of the rural connections of the working class. To many contemporaries, as well as later historians and sociologists, the cohesion of working-class communities in Bombay appeared remarkable. Villages, it seemed, were transplanted to the city. Kinship and caste were assumed to form the indivisible units of social relationships. This chapter has argued that the social institutions of the neighbourhood were not simply the expression of the inherited values of migrant workers. Rather they were moulded by a nexus of social, economic and political forces operating within the urban context. While the maintenance of the village ties of most workers did not necessarily reflect their peasant character, the social connections into which workers entered in the neighbourhood to meet their material needs indicated the depth of their commitment to the urban and industrial setting.

To a large extent, this social nexus was formed by the operation of the labour, credit and housing markets in the working-class neighbourhoods and by the strategies of workers within them. Necessarily, as they organized to meet their urban needs, workers were drawn into various networks of patronage. The material resources commanded by neighbourhood and street bosses, whether landlords or money-lenders, jobbers or dadas, enabled them to develop impressive followings and to wield considerable influence. But it need not be supposed that power flowed in a single direction in the neighbourhood. Far from being concentrated in the hands of the magnates of the neighbourhood, power was diffused and lodged at various levels. Rivalries between influential figures in the neighbourhood impinged upon, indeed limited, the exercise of the power of each. Furthermore, the residents of the neighbourhood sometimes imposed a variety of individual and collective sanctions, ranging from social and commercial boycott to physical assault, upon their leaders. Patrons found themselves humouring their clients. Conversely, local residents were sometimes able to impose their expectations and their will upon the bosses of the neighbourhood.

The social organization of the neighbourhood was not simply determined by the networks of patronage, which developed around workers' strategies to supply their own material needs within an uncertain and unstable economic environment. These strategies for subsistence helped to forge patterns of association within the working class. These associations were most conspicuous in the organization of religious festivals and in the activities of the gymnasiums. But they existed in more permanent forms as well: around the jobber and the dada, in the chawl, the khanavali and in various kinds of room-sharing arrangements, in caste mandalis and in the inchoate fellowship of the street. Historians of labour have generally regarded the workplace as the decisive arena for the development of the political consciousness and political action of the working class. However, as this chapter has shown, the associations forged in the neighbourhood provided an important base for wider social and political organization. Indeed, at many points, politics was integral to the social life of the neighbourhood.

But the experience of living in proximity to each other did not mould Bombay's workers into a single, homogeneous mass. It could also register, indeed exacerbate, differences within the working class. The patterns of association which formed in the neighbourhood took shape at several, sometimes conflicting, levels. The interplay between these levels of association was central to the development of the political consciousness and political action of the working class. Forces which brought workers together also acted to divide them. Within the arena of the neighbourhoods, solidarities within the working class were forged as well as fragmented.

The neighbourhood did not, however, constitute an autonomous arena of social organization. Family, kinship and caste connections provided the touchstone of social organization. At the same time, the public sphere acted continuously upon it. It was in the street and the neighbourhood that workers sometimes confronted the state. The perception of the social life of the working-class neighbourhoods by the ruling elites influenced their attitudes to the lower orders. Similarly, the neighbourhood provided a locus for the common experience of the working class.

Furthermore, the spheres of workplace and neighbourhood were intimately related. In part, this was the consequence of the nature of the city's labour market. The extensive use of casual labour throughout its economy forced workers to maintain close connections beyond the workplace both in order to obtain work as well as to help tide them over periods of unemployment. The jobber system deepened the interconnections between workplace and neighbourhood. To recruit and discipline effectively in the workplace, it was essential for jobbers to intervene and develop networks of influence in the neighbourhood. Finally, if employers brought social forces beyond the workplace to bear upon labour recruitment and discipline, it is not surprising that workers should utilize the social organization of the neighbourhood to protect their jobs and wages. The industrial and political conflicts which affected the working class were often to be witnessed in the street and the neighbourhood. For a better understanding of the interconnections between the workplace and the neighbourhood, and more generally, of the social organization and economy of labour, it is necessary to investigate the former sphere more closely. From the social organization of Girangaon, the focus of this book shifts to the textile mills which dominated the city's working-class neighbourhoods and specifically to the organization of work and the patterns of labour deployment in the city's predominant industry.

6   The development of the cotton-textile industry: a historical context

Cotton textiles, India's most important industry, underpinned the social relations and economy of Bombay City. It was Bombay's staple industry and its only large-scale employer of labour. It was also the foundation of the city's prosperity and growth from the late nineteenth century onwards, and the basis of its claim to be a major industrial metropolis of Asia. Its development influenced the nature of the local labour market, the patterns and rhythms of rural migration and the relationship between workplace and neighbourhood in the city's mill districts. The previous three chapters have analysed the processes of social formation as they affected the city's workers in general. The final three chapters turn specifically to the case of the cotton-textile industry and examine some of the major influences which shaped the relationship between labour and capital. This chapter will examine the origins and development of the cotton-textile industry to delineate a historical context within which business strategies, the organization of work and the deployment of labour took shape.

The Bombay millowners were neither, it would appear, driven by the relentless pursuit of the most advanced and sophisticated techniques nor by the imperative to achieve and maintain ideal standards of labour efficiency. Rather, they sought to maximize profits in the short run within the economic and political conditions in which they found themselves. But this could in its turn militate against the adoption of the best machinery or the implementation of the most efficient methods. The extensive use of casual labour is not generally associated with manufacturing industry. Where a certain minimal level of skill is essential, employers might attempt to train and secure a permanent labour force. Furthermore, to reap the full benefits of machinery, it is necessary to maintain steady levels of production. However, in spite of the high costs of machinery, the millowners, like the entrepreneurs of the small workshops which proliferated in the city, chose to regulate production to the short-term fluctuations of demand. These fluctuations led them to vary their levels of employment and output and intermittently carry the cost of idle capacity. Indeed, it has already been argued that business strategies in the industry bore striking similarities to those which prevailed in the so-called informal sector.

It is conceivable that if the millowners had combined more effectively, at every stage of the production process, from the purchase of raw cotton to the restriction of output and price fixing, they might have disciplined the fluctuations of the market and the intensity of competition between themselves. Individually, they might thus have more successfully specialized in particular lines of production. By taking these steps, the Bombay millowners might have been able to temper the effects of trade fluctuations on their industry, or indeed to have competed more effectively with their foreign rivals. As their fortunes slumped, the millowners responded as they had always done, by cutting operational costs and by seeking to produce whatever might be expected to sell immediately. Despite the apparent concentration of ownership in the industry, the tendency towards combination and collusion remained weak and the response to crisis was short-term and individualistic.

An examination of the development of the cotton-textile industry since the late nineteenth century reveals the changing historical conditions which influenced the business strategies of the millowners. The Bombay millowners have been repeatedly castigated for their apparently short-sighted even speculative management of the industry. Their managerial practice has frequently been explained as a function of their pre-industrial attitudes, which, it is supposed, betrayed the outlook of traders and merchants rather than far-sighted captains of industry, or, alternatively, as a reflection of a culture which was not 'preoccupied in any systematic way with the increase of man's control over his material environment' and in which 'a scientific approach to technology was virtually non-existent'.[1] Although, in this view, colonialism and a greater exposure to the West, occurring through the 'colonial port cities', facilitated the diffusion of novel and scientific methods, it was not until the late 1920s, so this argument goes, that the millowners became fully committed to the application of increasingly efficient, 'rational' and modern methods of production.[2] On the contrary, it will be argued here that the millowners' stewardship of the industry did not reflect an entrepreneurial culture, specific to Indian capitalists, but rather, that managerial practices in the industry reflected the constraints within which it had developed.

The Bombay cotton-textile industry underwent a severe and prolonged crisis in the 1920s and 1930s. Yet at this time Indian industry as a whole appeared to flourish and expand. In the 1930s, rural capital migrated to the towns and came to be invested in a wide range of consumer and processing industries. The sugar industry developed in the United Provinces and the Deccan.[3] The cotton-textile

---

[1] Morris, 'The Growth of Large-Scale Industry', in Kumar (ed.), *CEHI*, II, 562–3.

[2] Morris, *Industrial Labour Force*, pp. 120–1.

[3] Bagchi, *Private Investment*, pp. 359–90; S. Amin, *Sugarcane and Sugar in Gorakhpur: An Inquiry into Peasant Production for Capitalist Enterprise in Colonial India* (Delhi, 1984).

industry expanded in Tamil Nadu and most significantly in Coimbatore.[4] The effects of the international depression were not felt substantially by the Ahmedabad mills until 1933–4.[5] The difficulties encountered by the textile industry were almost exclusively focussed upon Bombay. The specificity of the problems which engulfed the Bombay industry in this period is illuminated by a closer examination of its earlier development. Inevitably, perhaps, the history of the industry and the pattern of its development informed the millowners' understanding of its crises in the 1920s and 1930s and indeed, shaped their responses to them.

Structural constraints

The development of the cotton-textile industry in India, the most important market of Britain's leading industry, has served at times to exemplify what Indian enterprise could achieve when, following the Western example, it introduced the world of modern industry to a traditional economy, despite the absence of the necessary conditions for its growth. Its development sometimes appeared to belie the notion that the colonial power manifested 'an implacable hostility to Indian competition.'[6] But the inception of the cotton-textile industry was neither the result of a structural transformation in the Indian economy nor the outcome of a logical progression from trade to industry. Rather, as we have seen, merchants who had been subordinated in the export trade in raw cotton sought an outlet in spinning and weaving to hedge against its fluctuations.[7] This pattern of diversification to spread their risks and protect their capital was to characterize the subsequent development of the industry. It signified a common response to the structural constraints within which the industry developed.

The imbalanced and uneven nature of industrial development in India created constraints of both supply and demand upon economic growth. On the one hand, the narrow basis of industrial development limited purchasing power in the domestic market and left industries vulnerable to arbitrary fluctuations. On the

[4] C.J. Baker, *An Indian Rural Economy, 1880–1955: The Tamilnad Countryside* (Oxford, 1984), chapter 5.
[5] 'Papers Relating to the Trade Depression, 1933', especially, Note by Textile Labour Association, Ahmedabad, Textile Labour Association Papers, File 40, Microfilm Reel 1, NMML; *Report of the Special Tariff Board on the Enquiry Regarding the Level of Duties Necessary to Afford Adequate Protection to the Indian Cotton Textile Industry Against Imports from the United Kingdom of Cotton Piecegoods and Yarn, Artificial Silk Fabrics and Mixture Fabrics of Cotton and Artificial Silk* (Delhi, 1936), pp. 55–8; Gillion, *Ahmedabad*, pp. 77–104; Mehta, *The Ahmedabad Cotton Textile Industry*; S. Patel, *The Making of Industrial Relations: The Ahmedabad Cotton Textile Industry 1918–1939* (Delhi, 1987), pp. 111–19.
[6] Morris, 'The Growth of Large-Scale Industry', 573.
[7] See above, pp. 63–7

other hand, the cotton-textile industry, like other Indian industries, remained dependent upon relatively expensive imports of capital goods.

Throughout the colonial period, the industry was entirely dependent upon the import of machinery from overseas, primarily from Lancashire. Neither the supply of capital and raw materials nor the extent of domestic demand provided a sufficient basis for the development of a significant capital goods industry, until the state adopted a more positive and interventionist approach in the 1950s and accepted the risks which Indian capitalists refused.[8] The first ring frame was manufactured in India as late as 1946.[9] In 1939, Fred Stones, Director of the Sassoon group of mills, declared that there was an 'enormous field' for the manufacture of textile machinery in India. The existing wire and steel industries could produce the whole requirement of wire healds for the Indian cotton mills 'from a few small machines'. 'It is very annoying to me personally', fulminated Stones, scarcely an inveterate opponent of imperialism, 'to see most excellent equipment for high drafting, manufactured in China, being delivered to India. China has no huge steel industry. The only thing there is cheap labour and capable mechanics ... I wonder why we cannot make them in Bombay. It is criminal.'[10]

At the same time, the fortunes of the cotton-textile industry were to a large extent dependent upon the monsoon, and especially, both directly and indirectly, upon the cotton harvest. Not only did raw cotton constitute the heaviest charge on the total cost of production,[11] but it was widely supposed that the 'the prices of cotton yarn and piecegoods rise or fall in sympathy with the price of raw cotton'.[12] Fluctuations in the price of raw cotton could, therefore, have serious repercussions upon both purchasing power as well as the cost of production. The yield and price of the raw cotton crop could serve as a general guide to the prospects of the industry. However, the price of Indian cotton was determined not by local conditions of supply and demand alone, but also by the

---

[8] Bagchi, *Private Investment*; A. Mukherjee, 'Indian Capitalist Class and Congress on National Planning and Public Sector, 1930–47', in K.N. Panikkar (ed.), *National and Left Movements in India* (Delhi, 1980), pp. 45–79. C. Simmons, H. Clay and R. Kirk, 'Machine Manufacture in a Colonial Economy: the Pioneering Role of George Hattersley in India, 1919–1943', *IESHR*, 20, 3 (1983), 277–315; R. Kirk and C.P. Simmons, 'Lancashire and the Equipping of the Indian Cotton Mills: A Study of Textile Machinery Supply, 1854–1939', in K. Ballhatchet and D. Taylor (eds.), *Changing South Asia: Economy and Society* (London, 1984), pp. 169–81.

[9] Ray, *Industrialization*, p. 192.

[10] Proceedings of the TLIC, Main Inquiry, Oral Evidence, Mr F. Stones, Director, Messrs E.D. Sassoon and Company Limited, File 70, 4388–9, MSA.

[11] *Report of the ITB, 1927*, I, 31. In 1927, it was estimated that raw cotton represented 44 per cent of the production cost of standard grey long cloth when its price was Rs. 290 per candy. But when its price rose to Rs. 450 per candy, it accounted for 56 per cent of the total cost of production. *Report of the ITB, 1932*, p. 88.

[12] *Ibid.*, p. 43.

price and yield of the American crop, with which it was mixed, both in its export and its domestic market.[13] The fluctuations of cotton prices were often determined by factors beyond the control of cultivators, cotton dealers and ginners and millowners. Since they did not necessarily relate to local market conditions, they were extremely difficult to predict.

If the low effective demand in the domestic market was a disincentive to capital investment, the high cost of capital goods meant that industrial development was predicated upon the intensive use of labour. Cheap labour remained the chief competitive advantage of Indian industry. The need to maintain its cheapness provided the structural determinant of industrial relations in India and formed the decisive influence in the structuring of Bombay's labour force.

To attract capital and to overcome its reluctance to step forward for pioneering ventures, which entailed high risks and large outlays, entrepreneurs had to maintain a rapid turnover, show quick profits and pay handsome dividends. In the 1850s when the first mill was built in Bombay, the costs of construction and equipment were said to be two or three times higher than in Lancashire; in the 1880s, they had been pared down to a margin of about 30 to 35 per cent.[14] Moreover, the supposedly inefficient and untrained handling of machinery was thought to make a higher rate of depreciation necessary.[15] Because their capital costs were high, the millowners had both to write off a larger proportion of capital than their competitors and to declare higher dividends. Similarly, since managing agencies took their commission largely on the basis of output, irrespective of profit or sales, it was in their immediate interest to maintain high levels of production even when stocks were mounting. But here lay the rub. For throughout its history, the cotton-textile industry operated within impoverished and precarious markets. In addition, the Indian market for cotton goods remained until the 1920s, primarily in deference to the interests of Lancashire, the most open in the world. The limitations of demand in the domestic market were aggravated by the severity of foreign competition, from Lancashire and later Japan, as well as the development of various up-country centres of production as a major force in the domestic market.

Historically, the flow of investment into the industry had been fitful and spasmodic. Capital was not easily mobilized until the profitability of a particular line of production was proven. Yet once its potential was established, the rush of investment frequently culminated in over-production and saturated markets.

---

[13] *Report of the ITB, 1927*, 1, 31–2; *Report of the ITB, 1932*, p. 43.
[14] Mehta, *Cotton Mills*, p. 49. An estimate made in 1877, however, continued to put the capital outlay of a Bombay mill at three times that of a Lancashire mill. W.W. Hunter, *The Indian Empire* (London, 1892), cited by Morris, 'The Growth of Large-Scale Industry', 579, n. 1.
[15] Rutnagur, *Directory of Indian Manufactories*, p. 10; Rutnagur (ed.), *Bombay Industries*, pp. 322–3.

It was by no means uncommon for the industry, following a spurt of growth, to smash itself against the low and sometimes falling ceiling of demand. Thus, out of ninety-seven mills erected in Bombay between 1855 and 1925, twelve were burnt down or else closed and dismantled, sixteen transferred their agencies voluntarily and forty-five went into liquidation and were reconstructed under other names. Only five mills in 1925 had survived intact from the pioneering days before 1875.[16]

Under these conditions, it is easy to understand why the millowners were less concerned to invest in the newest and best technology than to maximize their profits in the short run within the constraints of the given economic conditions, and to diversify their business interests and spread their risks as swiftly as possible. These strategies of production tended, in turn, to accentuate the differences between millowners. By the 1920s and 1930s, the industry was characterized by diverse interests, and a variety of business methods and objectives.

The founding and early growth of the textile industry

In the late nineteenth century, the Indian textile industry was largely concentrated in Bombay. Even as the industry grew more dispersed in its location, Bombay remained, both in terms of size and, especially, political significance, its most important centre. The early cotton-mill promoters relied heavily upon their caste-fellows, friends and relatives to mobilize capital.[17] But in keeping with an older tradition of commercial enterprise in Bombay, mill flotation did not occur exclusively within the limits of specific communities. The Oriental Mills at Tardeo, one of the earliest mills and the first joint-stock concern in the industry, had 'a mixed and representative Board of Directors' of Bombay's foremost merchant princes: Parsi magnates like Byramjee Jejeebhoy, Ardeshir Dady and Cursetji Cama, as well as the Bhatia merchant Varjivandas Madhavdas and the Baghdadi Jew, Elias David Sassoon, whose family went on 'to control the largest spinning and weaving power in the country'.[18] Finance was also secured by subscription from the city's magnates in exchange for a share in the managing-agency commission. Some notables without a direct interest in the industry and a few like the wealthy lawyer and publicist, Pherozeshah Mehta, invested in particular mills and served on their Boards of Directors. Cotton merchants, coal dealers and store suppliers loaned capital to secure

---

[16] Rutnagur, *Bombay Industries*, p. 37.

[17] *Ibid.*, p. 245.

[18] *Ibid.*, p. 245. For other examples, of the Great Eastern Mill, see *ibid.*, p. 32; the Maneckjee Petit Mill, Mehta, *Cotton Mills*, p. 53; Bombay Dyeing, the Bombay Dyeing and Manufacturing Company, Director's Minute Book, 1879–1907. Office of the Bombay Dyeing Company.

exclusive rights for the supply of necessary commodities to the mill.[19] Selling
agents for the mills also participated in financing its operation.[20] Contracts for
the transport of cotton and machinery were given to those who subscribed the
largest shares, while building contractors were sometimes paid substantial sums
in script rather than cash. Machinery orders were placed with those manufacturers whose agents offered 'tempting commissions to the promoter with a lion's
share for the managing partner'.[21] In fact, the agents of machinery makers tried
to generate trade by successively promoting a number of mills with the profits
of their previous venture.

This was why a number of managing agencies in the textile industry originated as importers of machinery and engineering plant or else diversified into
the trade. Greaves Cotton and Company, who managed the largest group of
mills in the early twentieth century,[22] had diversified into the industry from their
initial activity as suppliers of textile machinery. It was said that they floated the
Connaught Mill primarily 'to demonstrate on a commercial scale the improvement in the Rabbeth Spindle', while the Howard and Bullough Mill, the most
prosperous in the group and named after the Lancashire firm of textile-machinery manufacturers, was appropriately 'projected to demonstrate on a large scale,
the Electric Stop Motion on drawing frames which has proved so successful'.[23]
Although families owning managing agencies often sought to maintain their
control over them, substantial amounts of capital were raised on limited liability
from relatively small investors. They were enumerated in one list as 'bankers,
liquor sellers, contractors, brokers and commission agents, owners of manufactories, ginneries, cotton presses and shops, even salaried and professional
people'.[24]

Moreover, the industry grew only in spurts. After the initial flurry of pioneering activity in the late 1850s, no mills were built in the 1860s. Cotton fetched
higher prices in Lancashire than yarn anywhere else and capital was directed in
Bombay into trade, land reclamation schemes and share speculation. In the
1870s, however, Bombay's exports of yarn to China rose steeply and the city's
mercantile elites were swift to respond.[25] Between July 1873 and December
1874, a further twelve mills were established. Yet by 1877–8 the Bombay mills

[19] Rutnagur, *Bombay Industries*, pp. 46–8.
[20] D.H. Buchanan, *The Development of Capitalist Enterprise in India* (New York, 1934, reprinted
   London 1966), pp. 217–18.
[21] Rutnagur, *Bombay Industries*, pp. 46–8.
[22] In 1915, Greaves Cotton managed eight mills with 283,000 spindles, the largest number under
   any single management. *Ibid.*, p. 61.
[23] *Ibid.*, pp. 27–9.
[24] Guha, 'More about Parsi Seths', 128.
[25] According to Mehta, Bombay's exports of yarn to China increased from 2.4 million pounds in
   1873–4 to 45 million pounds in 1882–3. Mehta, *Cotton Mills*, pp. 47–8.

Table 18. *Proportion of spindles and looms and percentage of total yarn production used to manufacture cloth in Bombay mills, 1875*

Mill	Ratio of spindles per 100 looms	% of yarn used to make cloth
Alexandra Spinning and Weaving Company	7,816	75
Bombay United Spinning and Weaving Company Ltd.	5,983	62.26
Fleming Spinning and Weaving Company Ltd.	4,719	75
New Dhurumsey Poonjabhoy Spinning and Weaving Company Ltd.	8,952	60
New Great Eastern Spinning and Weaving Company Ltd.	5,014	73.33
Morarjee Goculdas Spinning and Weaving Company Ltd.	9,455	50
Oriental Spinning and Weaving Company Ltd.	5,543	82.61
Manockjee Petit Spinning and Weaving Company Ltd.	6,100	57.14
Average for the Bombay textile industry	9,561	45.07

Note: The mills which are listed above had already installed looms. The average for the whole industry is based on all mills, including those which had no weaving capacity at all.
Source: J.M. Maclean, *A Guide to Bombay* (Bombay, 1875), p. 111.

had saturated their markets abroad as well as in India where agrarian scarcity and famine squeezed demand. In perhaps the first of recurrent crises of over-production as many as six mills faced liquidation over two years.[26] It was primarily the export trade in yarn which led the Bombay mills out of this slump. In the 1880s, Indian exports of yarn increased five-fold and the Bombay mills accounted for almost the whole of this expansion.[27] In 1883, the Bombay mills for the first time sold more yarn in China than the Lancashire mills.[28] Until the early 1890s, the Bombay textile industry experienced a relatively stable period of expansion. Between 1875 and 1895, forty-two mills were built in Bombay and of the sixteen which began operations in the following decade, twelve had been floated during this period.[29]

It is frequently assumed that the Bombay textile industry was founded purely as a spinning industry. On the contrary, the earliest mills produced yarn for sale

[26] *Ibid.*, p. 24.
[27] *Ibid.*, pp. 47–8.
[28] Farnie, *The English Cotton Industry*, p. 111. However, the BMOA reported this to be the worst year in their experience. *BMOA, Annual Report, 1883*, p. 1; Mehta, *Cotton Mills*, p. 42. Nevertheless, the trend was clear: the expansion of the Bombay mills undermined Lancashire's position in the Chinese market. For Lancashire's response to the growing competition of Indian mills in the Chinese market, see Manchester Chamber of Commerce, *Bombay and Lancashire Cotton Spinning Inquiry, Minutes of Evidence and Reports* (Manchester, 1888).
[29] Rutnagur, *Bombay Industries*, pp. 16, 20.

to handloom weavers as well as cloth for the domestic market. Indeed, five out of seven mills which began operating between January 1860, and June 1861, were composite units. In 1875, only the smallest mills in terms of paid-up capital and spinning capacity or the most recently established did not install looms, while some among the latter were likely to plough their profits back into diversification.[30] It was, however, the mill-building boom of the 1870s, stimulated by the Chinese demand for yarn, which transformed cotton manufacturing in Bombay into a processing industry, producing yarn for sale to the manufacturer of the finished product. Between 1875 and 1900, the proportion of their own yarn output used by the Bombay mills in the production of cloth declined from 45 per cent to 14 per cent.[31] In 1879–80, nine out of sixteen mills which had begun working after the mid 1870s, as the Chinese market was established, did not install any looms.[32] By 1894, forty-one out of sixty-nine mills in Bombay had no looms at all.[33] The weaving capacity of the industry was utilized largely as a safeguard, to absorb the surplus yarn supplies created when the Chinese demand contracted, just as spinning had been developed in response to the uncertainties of the cotton trade.

The 1870s and 1880s represented, for the Bombay textile industry, a period of steady and relatively stable expansion. From the early 1890s to 1914, however, the industry's performance was subject to considerable short-term fluctuations. Underlying the uncertainties in the Chinese market was the increasing competition which the Bombay mills encountered from the rapid development of the Chinese and, especially, the Japanese spinning industry.[34] Moreover, the later 1890s were years of agrarian scarcity, characterized by a number of famines and a plague epidemic. In this context, the Government of India's monetary policies worsened Bombay's competitive position in its export

---

[30] 'Statement showing the number of Spindles and Looms and the Approximate Total Daily Production of Yarns (say) averaging 20s, by the Local Mills, and the Proportion used in Making Cloth', in J.M. Maclean, *A Guide to Bombay*, (Bombay, 1875), p. 111. See table 18.

[31] *Ibid.*, p. 111; Mehta, *Cotton Mills*, pp. 95–6

[32] 'Statement Showing the Date of Establishment and Progress of Cotton Mills in the Bombay Presidency', Bombay Proceedings, General, 1880, P/1583, IOR.

[33] Rutnagur, *Directory of Indian Manufactories, 1894*, p. 6.

[34] R.H. Myers, 'Cotton Textile Handicraft and the Development of the Cotton Textile Industry in Modern China', *EcHR*, 2nd series, XVIII, 3 (1965), 614–32. A. Feuerwerker, 'Handicraft and Manufactured Cotton Textiles in China', *Journal of Economic History*, XXX, 2 (1970), 338–78; Kang Chao, 'The Growth of a Modern Textile Industry and the Competition with Handicrafts', in D.H. Perkins (ed.), *China's Modern Economy in Historical Perspective* (Stanford, 1975). By 1925, the spinning mills employed 210,000 workers. J. Chesneaux, *The Chinese Labour Movement*, p. 30. See also, A.S. Pearse, *The Cotton Industry of Japan and China: Being the Report of the Journey to Japan and China, February–April 1929* (Manchester, 1929); and A.S. Pearse, *The Cotton Industry of India: Being the Report of the Journey to India* (Manchester, 1930); N. Takamura, 'The Cotton Spinning Industry in Japan During the Pre-World War I Period: Its Growth and Essential Conditions', *Zeitschrift für Unternehmensgeschichte*, Beih. XXII (1982), 207–30. (I am grateful to Dr K. Sugihara for drawing my attention to this article.)

as well as its domestic market. The depreciation of silver in the late nineteenth century had afforded some measure of protection to the industry from Lancashire imports and, in addition, given it a competitive edge in the Chinese market.[35] When the rupee was divorced from the market price of silver in 1893 and the mints closed to coinage, the industry not only lost this element of protection but conceded a substantial advantage to the Japanese and Chinese cotton industry, whose currencies continued to be based on silver. Bombay's exports collapsed and the Millowners' Association was forced to adopt short-time working for significant periods of the year.[36] Although the effects of these adjustments in the rate of exchange were likely to be short term, the Japanese industry was able to gain a foothold in the Chinese market. Between 1895 and 1897, the Japanese yarn exports to China rose from 5,000,000 pounds to 56,000,000 pounds.[37] When the Bombay millowners rushed to take advantage of the first significant sign of recovery in 1895, they accelerated into a glut in the Chinese market. While prices fell and stocks rose in Hong Kong and Shanghai, the domestic market also contracted as a succession of famines and epidemics undermined purchasing power and disrupted trade.

At first the millowners viewed the crisis of the 1890s as a passing phase, a necessary process of adjustment to the new, adverse monetary policy or perhaps a cyclical downswing, rather like the slump they had encountered in 1877–8. Japan had not only to buy its raw materials abroad but also to find foreign markets. Since India figured prominently both as a source of Japan's cotton and as an outlet for its products, the Bombay millowner, as Sir George Cotton, Chairman of the Bombay Millowners' Association, assured its members, 'ought to have a considerable advantage over his friends in the farther East' and in any case, it was well known that 'the Jap does not take kindly to labour in the mills'.[38] But the longer the Chinese market remained depressed the clearer it

---

[35] It is difficult as yet to estimate just how effective was the protection offered by the falling price of silver. Clearly, if it cheapened Indian textile exports to China relative to Lancashire, it also raised the cost to Indian manufacturers of machinery, fuel and stores. Furthermore, 'the instability of the rupee exchange' as Tomlinson has noted, 'had a depressing effect on India's export trade in the 1880s'; Tomlinson, *Political Economy*, p. 17. Presumably this was most marked in primary products exported to gold-based currency areas. For instance, this may have contributed to cotton exporters switching their focus from European markets to Japan in the late 1880s. But together with the rising price of imports, this probably led to declining purchasing power among domestic consumers. The real value of the protection offered by the falling price of silver is, therefore, not easily assessed in the present state of knowledge. For an insight into the impact of the falling price of silver and the monetary policies of the Government of India on the levels of consumption in the internal economy, see Ray, 'Crisis of Bengal Agriculture', 257–8.

[36] BMOA, *Annual Report*, 1893, pp. 12–13. Mehta, *Cotton Mills*, p. 66.

[37] Mehta, *Cotton Mills*, pp. 77–8.

[38] BMOA, *Annual Report, 1893*, pp. i–iii.

The cotton-textile industry 249

became that the future of the industry required the diversification of both output and markets.

Yet several factors impeded such diversification. First, Lancashire was already firmly established in the domestic market. Imports, primarily from Lancashire, supplied two-thirds of the Indian requirements of cloth at the turn of the century.[39] Their position was consolidated in the large Bengal market by locally based British merchants who actively 'resisted a rapid replacement of them [Manchester piecegoods] by Indian piecegoods'.[40] Indeed, Lancashire's strength in the Indian market for cloth helps to explain why the textile industry had concentrated on spinning yarn for export after the initial building of composite mills. The risks of competing with Lancashire in the early twentieth century were magnified by the determination of the colonial state to keep the Indian market open to the metropolitan industry.[41]

Second, the Indian textile industry grew rapidly in this period in its up-country centres, predominantly Ahmedabad. Situated in the cotton tracts, in centres of cheap labour and in proximity to their markets, these up-country centres were able to profit from rising prices and increasing demand in the domestic market. In 1899, there were already 93 mills working outside Bombay; by 1913, their number had increased to 159.[42] At the same time, the outbreak of bubonic plague in the late 1890s affected Bombay with particular severity, led to a massive exodus from the city, creating an acute shortage of labour and necessitating the daily payment of wages at double the rate of 1893, as employers competed fiercely to secure an adequate workforce.[43] High wages granted at the time of the epidemic 'could not be reduced so easily',[44] even as agrarian crisis resulted in shrinking demand.

On the other hand, despite its fluctuations, the Chinese market retained a certain buoyancy. It recovered strongly from crises and each recovery brought profits which exceeded the years before the slump. The resilience of the Chinese

[39] *Report of the ITB, 1927*, I, 12; Farnie, *The English Cotton Industry*, Table 7, pp. 116–18, 96–119; L.G. Sandberg, *Lancashire in Decline: A Study in Entrepreneurship, Technology and International Trade* (Columbus, Ohio, 1974), pp. 165–8.
[40] Bagchi, *Private Investment*, p. 235.
[41] P. Harnetty, *Imperialism and Free Trade: Lancashire and India in the Mid-Nineteenth Century* (Vancouver, 1972); P. Harnetty, 'The Imperialism of Free Trade: Lancashire and the Indian Cotton Duties, 1859–62', *EcHR*, 2nd series, XVIII, 2 (1965), 333–49, P. Harnetty, 'The Indian Cotton Duties Controversy, 1894–96' *English Historical Review*, LXXVII, (October 1962), 684–702; I. Klein, 'English Free Traders and Indian Tariffs, 1874–1896', *MAS*, V, 3 (1971), 251–71; Farnie, *The English Cotton Industry*, pp. 96–119; C.J. Hamilton, *The Trade Relations Between England and India, 1600–1896* (Calcutta, 1919); A. Redford and B.W. Clapp, *Manchester Merchants and Foreign Trade*, vol. II, *1850–1939* (Manchester, 1956).
[42] *Report of the ITB, 1927*, I, 5.
[43] Mehta, *Cotton Mills*, p. 73; Edwardes, *Rise of Bombay*, p. 330; Chandavarkar, 'Plague Panic and Epidemic Politics'.
[44] Mehta, *Cotton Mills*, p. 75.

Table 19. *The growth of the cotton-textile industry in Bombay, 1875–1945*

Year	Mills	Paid-up capital	Spindles	Looms	Workers
1875	28	3,38,58,000	7,52,000	7,780	13,550
1885	49	4,79,62,000	13,47,400	12,010	41,550
1895	70	5,55,46,000	21,24,000	20,220	75,750
1905	82	6,10,35,000	25,61,000	28,100	93,000
1915	86	7,65,98,000	29,94,400	51,900	1,12,000
1925	82	20,40,53,650	34,28,000	71,100	1,48,000
1930	81	13,80,00,000	34,30,733	76,697	1,36,774
1935	74	11,32,00,000	29,90,088	68,385	1,11,147
1940	65	12,71,71,972	27,48,644	65,177	1,04,890
1945	65	10,17,73,700	28,03,406	66,164	1,29,510

Note: The figures in this table are stated in crores and lakhs.
Source: Rutnagur, *Bombay Industries*, pp. 10–23; *BMOA, Annual Reports, passim.* Figures for paid-up capital in 1930 and 1935 are from *Report of the Special Tariff Board*, pp. 53–4, table XL and refer to the calendar years 1931 and 1934.

market encouraged the Bombay mills to reap the handsome profits it offered, albeit intermittently, rather than shoulder the risks and burdens of reorganization. To some extent, of course, the industry did wring some cautious changes. There was an increasing tendency to expand its weaving capacity before 1914, since the trade fluctuations, especially in the Chinese market, affected spinning mills most profoundly. The number of looms installed in Bombay trebled between 1893 and 1914, while the number of spindles increased by less than one-half.[45] The sixteen mills which closed down in 1901 had 242,000 spindles and less than 700 looms between them; similarly, in 1911, the twenty-five mills which shut down were all spinning mills.[46] But the Bombay industry was still dominated by its spinning capacity and sold three-quarters of the yarn it produced.[47] Its idle capacity in spinning oscillated more sharply but it was also, at peak periods, more fully utilized than weaving.[48] Despite the expansion of weaving capacity, the millowners appear to have worked their looms largely to hedge the fluctuations of the yarn trade. The Bombay millowners did not reveal a consistent ambition collectively to transform the character of their industry. Rather, in periods of downswing, they sought individually and separately to vary their lines of production, make whatever could be sold and garner such profits in the short term as the prevailing economic situation permitted.

[45] Calculated from *BMOA, Annual Reports, passim.*
[46] Mehta, *Cotton Mills*, pp. 81, 96.
[47] *Ibid.*, pp. 95–6.
[48] Compare variations in the ratio of spindles and looms installed to spindles and looms working in the Bombay mills, in *Annual Reports of the BMOA, passim.*

The opening years of the twentieth century, once again, witnessed a strong revival of the industry's fortunes, based on the recovery of the Chinese market. Indeed, the first six years of the twentieth century were said to be 'substantially better than some of the best years' of the nineteenth.[49] The Bombay millowners sought to capitalize by working their machines for as long as possible. The introduction of electric lighting into the mills on a large scale enabled them to stretch the working day to thirteen and fourteen hours.[50] But the boom ran into the increasingly familiar problem of saturated markets. Japanese exports to China revived. The Chinese spinning industry was able to produce a higher quality of low-count yarn using longer staple cotton. In 1908, crop failures in India undermined domestic demand. In the next three or four years, several mills returned sheepishly to shorter hours; some closed down for brief periods to clear their stocks; most found that they could not afford to work to capacity.

Boom and bust: from the First World War to the depression

Although the outbreak of war at first induced panic in the cotton and piecegoods markets, within a year its benefits became increasingly apparent. Between 1916 and 1922, the industry experienced its most extensive boom since the 1870s and 1880s. By disrupting international trade, the war protected the Indian textile industry and created fresh opportunities for import substitution. Military needs served up an immediate and substantial market for the industry. Military demand, as well as speculative hoarding by both mills and piecegoods dealers, pushed up prices. The industry in 1917, according to the BMOA, had 'beaten all records in the matter of the prosperity of the Cotton Mill Industry in India'.[51] This buoyancy was not, however, halted by peace. The rise in the price of silver facilitated a dramatic increase in the export of yarn to China from 73 million pounds in 1918–9 to 160 million pounds in 1919–20. At the same time, the dislocation of international trade drastically cut back imports, which in 1919–20 'fell to the lowest level touched for a generation, those of yarn being the smallest recorded since 1866'.[52] The Swadeshi campaign to boycott foreign products 'in favour of Indian-made piecegoods' ensured that imports 'suffered a severe setback' in 1921–2,[53] while the consumption of khadi and coarse cloth, which

---

[49] Mehta, *Cotton Mills*, p. 75.
[50] Collector, Land Revenue, Customs and Opium to General Department, no. F-I 304, 24 January 1905 in GOB, General (Miscellaneous) Proceedings, August 1905, File no. N715/7, serial no. 77, p. 283, MSA; Secretary, GOB, General to Secretary GOI, Commerce and Industry, no. 7154, 23 December 1905, File no. 719/7, serial no. 131, pp. 483–4, MSA; *Report of the IFLC*, I, 7.
[51] *BMOA, Annual Report, 1917*, p. 1.
[52] *Report of the ITB, 1927*, I, 10.
[53] *Ibid*, I, 10–11.

figured prominently in Bombay's output, increased.[54] Furthermore, the international demand for primary products was sufficiently buoyant to enable Indian raw materials 'to find buyers at any price',[55] boosting demand in the domestic market. Once again, in 1920, the Bombay mills enjoyed 'unprecedented and unparalleled prosperity'. The profits of the industry were estimated by the chairman of the Bombay Millowners' Association at Rs. 16 crores,[56] while the official historian of the industry put them modestly at five-fold over their pre-war level.[57]

It was not until June 1922 that it became evident that the post-war boom was spluttering to a standstill and by December the Millowners' Association reported that 'the cycle of prosperity' was at an end.[58] This cycle of prosperity had created the conditions for its own destruction. The nature of its collapse was to leave its imprint firmly on the structure of the industry in the following decades. Several factors combined to worsen the Bombay industry's economic position. If the dislocation of the international economy protected the industry from foreign competition, it also prevented the renewal and replacement of machinery. This was particularly marked in the immediate aftermath of the war.[59] By the time the boom ended, therefore, the machinery of the textile industry had been steadily run down. Between 1914 and 1922, the industry's spindleage stagnated, and the rate of increase in the number of looms installed in Bombay gradually decelerated, even though they were used more intensively after 1918 as cloth production substantially increased (see table 20).[60] In addition, millowners seeking to renew their plant and even expand during the boom freely placed orders for machinery in Britain, and they were further encouraged as the sterling value of the rupee rose in 1919–20. However bottlenecks in supply meant that the machinery arrived after the boom had collapsed and the exchange rate had fallen, ruining importers and raising the costs of the millowners (see table 21).[61]

Moreover, the optimism of the boom came to be expressed not in mill building, restricted by the municipal authorities in 1919, or the extension of machinery, but primarily in the purchase of managing agencies and the conver-

[54] BMOA, Annual Report, 1921, p. 2.
[55] Report of the ITB, 1927, I, 10.
[56] BMOA, Annual Report, 1920, p. vii.
[57] Mehta, Cotton Mills, pp. 152, 155.
[58] BMOA, Annual Report, 1922, p. 1.
[59] R. Kirk and C. Simmons, 'Engineering and the First World War: A Case Study of the Lancashire Cotton Spinning Machine Industry', World Development, IX, 8 (1981), 773–91; Kirk and Simmons, 'Study of Textile Machinery Supply', pp. 169–81; J.D. Tomlinson, 'The First World War and British Cotton Piece Exports to India', EcHR, 2nd series, XXXII, 4 (1979), 494–506.
[60] The number of looms installed in Bombay increased by 70 per cent between 1906 and 1914 and by 34 per cent between 1914 and 1922. Calculated from the BMOA, Annual Reports, passim.
[61] Report of the ITB, 1927, I, 17–18.

Table 20. *Spindles and looms in the Bombay cotton mills, 1914–1922*

Year	Spindles	Looms
1914	3,009,172	48,845
1915	2,994,367	51,846
1916	2,984,575	53,205
1917	2,933,715	57,921
1918	2,822,648	59,162
1919	2,934,476	60,778
1920	2,964,526	60,634
1921	3,025,488	62,763
1922	3,117,284	65,521

Source: BMOA, Annual Report, passim.

Table 21. *Value of machinery imports, 1919–20 to 1925–6*

1919–20	Rs. 1.31 crores
1920–1	Rs. 3.67 crores
1921–2	Rs. 7.64 crores
1922–3	Rs. 8.49 crores
1923–4	Rs. 5.60 crores
1924–5	Rs. 2.68 crores
1925–6	Rs. 2.35 crores

Source: Report of the ITB, 1927, I, 17, 83.

sion of proprietary concerns into joint-stock companies. These sales occurred at the considerably inflated valuations of the post-war boom. At least thirty mills in Bombay were affected by such over-capitalization. By the end of the 1920s, those mills which did not increase their capital during the good years were reported to be 'in the strongest position'.[62]

When the boom ended, therefore, the millowners faced a dual problem. They had to renew their machinery when the falling rate of exchange made it expensive and their markets were depressed, while at the same time, those mills which found themselves over-capitalized had substantially to write down their capital in the midst of the slump. Inadequate allowances for depreciation during the boom only served to intensify the problem of writing down inflated capital during the slump.[63]

[62] *Ibid.*, I, 77–82.
[63] *Ibid.*, I, 83–4.

Fluctuations in the price of raw cotton also added significantly to the burdens of the Bombay mills in the 1920s. During the First World War, the market for Indian cotton was to some extent freed from the effects of fluctuations in the American and Liverpool markets.[64] The price of raw cotton rose spectacularly from Rs. 299 per candy for Broach cotton in 1913 to Rs. 717 in 1917,[65] but it was subsequently subjected to 'violent fluctuations' between 1917 and 1919. A succession of poor American cotton harvests in the early 1920s 'sent the price of Indian cotton in 1924 up to the highest figure ever reached, except in the entirely abnormal conditions of 1918'. Although the prices of raw cotton and yarn and piecegoods were believed to move together and adjust accordingly, cotton prices continued to rise while cloth prices remained stationary. In the mid 1920s, raw-cotton prices fell almost as quickly as they had risen but cloth prices followed the same trend, scarcely allowing the millowners the relief of a significant margin. 'We hold', declared the Tariff Board in 1927, 'that the fluctuations in the price of raw material in recent years must be regarded as one of the most important causes of the condition in which the industry finds itself.'[66]

As the depression set in, portentous shifts began to surface within the industry's markets. First, Bombay was effectively excluded from its Chinese market. In the early twentieth century, China had taken about 90 per cent of Indian yarn exports and this trade was 'practically a monopoly of Bombay'.[67] During the war, shortages of freight combined with the growing demand in the domestic market served to focus the attention of Indian mills on the production of cloth for local and military use.[68] The buoyancy of the domestic market between 1916 and 1922 cushioned the effect of Bombay's declining exports in the Chinese market (see table 22). The neglect of the Chinese market during the war, moreover, made it extremely difficult, indeed eventually impossible, for the Bombay mills to recover their position within it, particularly as Japanese exports rapidly increased. By 1925–6, Bombay had effectively lost the Shanghai and North China markets, almost all its yarn exports being sold in Hong Kong.[69] The Bombay mills switched their yarn increasingly to the manufacture of piecegoods: the proportion of yarn which they marketed fell sharply from 72 per cent in 1907–8 to 38 per cent in 1924–5.[70] By the mid 1920s, however, it was clear to the Bombay millowners that the expansion of weaving had proved insufficient to compensate for the loss of the yarn trade.[71]

[64] BMOA, Annual Report, 1917, p. 1.
[65] Report of the ITB, 1927, I, 9.
[66] Ibid., I, 32.
[67] Ibid., I, 95.
[68] BMOA, Statement Submitted to the Tariff Board (Bombay, 1926), pp. 4–12.
[69] Report of the ITB, 1927, I, 97; Mehta, Cotton Mills, p. 152.
[70] BMOA, Statement … to the Tariff Board, p. 13.
[71] Ibid.

Table 22. *Yarn exports to China from Japan and India (million lbs)*

Year	Japanese exports	Indian exports
1900	74.4	108.6
1901	77.8	260.2
1902	73.8	232.4
1903	118.8	232.4
1904	95.2	236.3
1905	96.0	229.1
1906	99.8	282.0
1907	79.5	223.4
1908	56.3	160.3
1909	95.8	208.0
1910	127.8	200.3
1911	98.9	158.8
1912	133.3	129.3
1913	19.3	183.3
1914	208.4	178.0
1915	211.7	116.7
1916	196.2	140.0
1917	166.0	143.8
1918	177.7	102.2
1919	76.8	48.8
1920	90.0	126.6
1921	92.3	63.4
1922	118.5	62.0
1923	64.7	41.0
1924	63.2	20.7

Source: Report of the ITB, 1927, I, 96, Table LVI.

In the Indian market, the Bombay mills were faced with increasingly severe competition from up-country centres of production. Rising prices of yarn and piecegoods and generally buoyant demand had stimulated the spread of cotton mills across the country. Between 1920–1 and 1924–5, thirty-four new cotton mills started working in various up-country centres, another twenty were reported to be idle and forty-three were in the course of erection. The number of spindles and looms in the up-country centres expanded more than twice as quickly as they did in Bombay.[72] If the Bombay mills were ideally located to exploit the Chinese market, the up-country centres gained from their locational advantages and their access to cheap labour in the domestic market. Moreover, these up-country centres, with the exception of Ahmedabad, produced a similar range of goods to Bombay, primarily low counts of yarn and coarse goods, and thus competed directly with it.[73]

[72] *Report of the ITB, 1927*, I, 13.
[73] *Ibid.*, I, 100–8.

As they turned to the domestic market, the Bombay mills also encountered increasingly severe competition from Japan. Indeed, having been driven out of the Chinese market by the Japanese textile industry, the Bombay mills found that they were being eclipsed in their own hinterland. During the First World War, the import of Japanese yarn and piecegoods increased exponentially.[74] After 1918, Japanese yarn of counts 31s to 40s not only gained steadily at the expense of Lancashire but, by the mid 1920s, equalled the total volume of Indian yarn production in this range. Although 'superior in quality to the comparable Indian product', this Japanese yarn could be sold in India 'at a price which is equal to the cost of manufacture alone of yarn of this count in India without any allowance for profit or depreciation'.[75] Obviously, in these counts, Japanese imports depressed the price of Indian yarn but, in addition, because the price of different counts of yarn were determined in relation to each other, it influenced the whole range of Indian mill production. Since the Bombay mills put a relatively high proportion of their yarn on the market, they were particularly threatened by Japanese competition. At the same time, the dominating presence of Japan in the market for yarn of counts 31s to 40s inhibited the Bombay mills as they tried to diversify into the production of finer counts. Similarly, in the case of piecegoods, Japanese imports competed directly with some of the main lines of Bombay's output: in particular, grey and bleached sheetings and long cloth. As with yarn, these goods could be sold in the Indian market more cheaply than local mills were able to manufacture them, and, further, it was noted, 'their quality is distinctly superior'.[76] Thus, Japanese imports also depressed the prices of Bombay's main lines of cloth production. It was estimated in the mid 1920s that about 40 per cent of the volume of Japanese cloth imports competed directly with staple products of Indian mills, and in piecegoods woven from yarn of counts between 31s and 40s Indian mill production barely exceeded the total quantity of Japanese imports. Their impact was even more devastating because the bulk of Japanese imports – touching a peak of nearly three-quarters in 1923–4 – were taken by the Bombay piecegoods market.[77] It was the Bombay mills, therefore, which felt the fiercest blast of Japanese competition.

The Bombay industry entered the slump of the early 1920s with the composition of its output concentrated in those lines of production, low counts of yarn and coarser varieties of piecegoods which were not only the most congested in the Indian market but also formed the staple of the expanding up-country mills. As they attempted to diversify into higher counts of yarn, they entered markets which were deeply influenced by Japanese goods, and within which their

[74] *Ibid.*, I, 8.
[75] *Ibid.*, I, 39.
[76] *Ibid.*, I, 49–50.
[77] *Ibid.*, I, 46–7.

Ahmedabad rivals had already established a significant lead. British imports continued to dominate the Indian market for the very high counts and finest varieties of piecegoods. The more the Bombay mills diversified their output, the wider was the range of competition that they faced. Underlying this structural problem of the Bombay industry lay a central fact: it had increasingly and decisively lost its initial advantage of cheap labour to its rivals.

During the First World War, high profits and spiralling inflation prompted a demand for higher wages and led in 1917 to a series of sporadic strikes. Concerned to keep their machines running in a period of high profits, millowners began to make concessions. Following general strikes in 1919 and 1920, these increases, given in the form of an allowance for the dearness of food prices, had risen as a percentage of the basic wage to 70 and 80 per cent for time- and piece-rated workers respectively. When the boom collapsed, the Bombay millowners tried to discontinue bonus payments instituted in more prosperous times, but succeeded only after they endured a month-long stoppage in January 1924. Further attempts to cut wages by 11.5 per cent, calculated to be the additional cost imposed by the excise duty, culminated in another general strike in July 1925, which continued for three months. The millowners withdrew the wage cut when the Government of India abolished the excise duty in 1925.[78] It was becoming increasingly clear to the millowners that wage reductions could only be effected in the face of determined labour resistance. More crucially, such stoppages could reduce their share of the markets and threaten their weak financial structure.

By contrast, wage cuts were most easily enforced in centres which already paid lower wages. In the Indian states, where wages were much lower, cotton mills enjoyed freedom from factory legislation, high taxes and trade unions. Labour in Coimbatore was reputed to be the lowest paid in the country.[79] Where Bombay failed in 1925, Ahmedabad had already succeeded. In 1923, the Ahmedabad millowners effected wage reductions of 15.5 per cent, despite a ten-week strike, and proceeded to consolidate, from their standpoint, a more effective system of industrial relations over the next couple of decades.[80] 'I do

---

[78] Chandavarkar, 'Workers' Politics and the Mill Districts in Bombay'; Newman, *Workers and Unions*, pp. 120–67: BMOA, *Annual Report, 1924*, pp. 70–8; *ibid.*, pp. 40–55 and Appendix 15; B. Chatterji, 'The Political Economy of "Discriminating Protection": The Case of Textiles in the 1920s', *IESHR*, XX, 3 (1983), 239–75.

[79] Pearse, *The Cotton Industry of India*, pp. 105–13; Shiva Rao, *The Industrial Workers in India*, p. 121; Ramaswamy, *The Worker and His Union*, pp. 17–32; Baker, *An Indian Rural Economy*, p. 361ff.; E.D. Murphy, *Unions in Conflict: A Comparative Study of Four South Indian Textile Centres, 1918–39* (Delhi, 1981); E. Perlin, 'Eyes Without Sight: Education and Millworkers in South India, 1939–1976', *IESHR*, XVIII, 3 & 4 (1981), 263–86.

[80] Patel, *The Making of Industrial Relations*; M. Desai, *A Righteous Struggle* (Ahmedabad, 1951); Mehta, *Cotton Mills*, pp. 277–86; Gillion, *Ahmedabad*, pp. 77–104.

not think you would have got a trades union in Ahmedabad', Fred Stones, Director of the E.D. Sassoon group of mills, explained to the Textile Labour Inquiry Committee in 1939, 'but for the personality of Gandhiji. Had we Gandhiji in Bombay, I say our firm would have saved lakhs and lakhs of rupees.'[81] In addition, many up-country centres, located in proximity to their raw materials and markets, were able to economize on their initial capital costs by buying second-hand machinery, scrapped by mills in Bombay, sometimes, ironically, due to their own difficulties.[82]

The success of the Bombay industry had allowed it to concentrate upon spinning yarn for export and to turn its back on the Indian market. The combination of the depression of the early 1920s and the loss of the Chinese trade, therefore, forced important structural adjustments upon the Bombay industry precisely when its markets had slumped. In particular, the Bombay mills had to redirect their attention to the domestic market when demand had contracted and the competition to serve it intensified. But its traditions, its trading practices and the composition of its output scarcely prepared the Bombay industry for an assault on the home market.[83] The composition of its output was symptomatic of its neglect of 'the tastes and requirements of the upcountry consumer'. In this respect, the industry's response to the slump appeared to be slow and somewhat inflexible. Thus, it seemed that in the mid 1920s the Bombay mills were 'content to go on producing the same counts of yarn and the same varieties of cloth without regard to whether these find a ready market or not'. They concentrated upon the spinning of low-count yarn, in which it met 'the greatest competition from mills in upcountry centres', and since weaving had developed in an auxiliary role to spinning, they continued to place a relatively large proportion of this yarn on the market. This neglect of the domestic market was also reflected by 'the small extent to which Bombay participates in the trade in dhotis'. Although Bombay made 'nearly half the total Indian production of cloth in 1925–6', it wove only 22 per cent of the total output of dhotis. Moreover, it was said, Bombay lacked the wide looms necessary to weave the dhotis of forty-four inch width which were 'the staple of the very large Bengal market'.

Similarly, the Bombay industry's trading practices were badly suited to the needs of the domestic market. Ahmedabad millowners were believed to be 'far more ready to meet the wishes of possible customers in regard to such matters as the acceptance of small orders, the manufacture of counter-samples in small

[81] Proceedings of the TLIC, Main Inquiry, Oral Evidence, Mr F. Stones, Director, Messrs. E.D. Sassoon and Co., File 72, p. 3624, MSA.

[82] *Ibid.*, Mr F. Stones, Director, Messrs. E.D. Sassoon and Co., File 70, p. 3466, MSA.

[83] All quotations, and other material, in this and the following paragraph are drawn from *Report of the ITB, 1927*, I, 102–8.

quantities, packing of different varieties in a bale, and stamping the stamp, name and number of the merchant purchasing the cloth' than their counterparts in Bombay. The Madras market, which received frequent visits from representatives of the Ahmedabad mills and in which that centre had made marked progress, 'had been neglected by Bombay on account of its comparative smallness'. It was doubted 'whether the Bombay millowners had sufficiently exploited the possibilities of the large market for bleached and coloured goods in the Punjab'. Because the manufacture of cloth in Bombay had been historically a means of safeguarding against the fluctuations of the yarn trade, the Bombay mills had tended to produce staple coarse goods, and in view of the volume of their output and their share of the market, they had required little aggressive marketing.

Until the mid 1920s, the slump appeared 'to have grown in intensity with each succeeding year whilst signs of a revival are still not visible'.[84] The mills found it difficult to liquidate their stocks even at extremely low prices and several mills faced serious financial problems. Their flow of credit dried up while a substantial proportion of their assets remained locked up in unsold stocks bearing high interest and storage charges.[85] There was, however, a fleeting promise of recovery in 1927. Several millowners were able to make large purchases of abnormally cheap American cotton, only to find that cotton prices began to rise in the following months and with them, the demand for mill-made goods began to recover.[86] The favourable movement and timing of cotton prices allowed many mills to return profits. This buoyancy continued into the early months of 1928 until it was interrupted by the general strike which began in April.[87] Fettered by industrial action, over the next two years, the Bombay mills lost a substantial share of their market to their rivals, which they were never again to recover fully.[88]

The effects of the trade depression fell differentially upon the Bombay mills. Some mills did better than others. In 1925, out of fifty-nine mills whose balance sheets were examined, sixteen had made a profit and thirteen declared dividends, mostly varying between 5 and 20 per cent, but rising in two cases to 34 and 130 per cent respectively.[89] Two years later, while seventeen mills had

---

[84] *BMOA, Annual Report, 1926*, p. 1.

[85] *Ibid., 1925*, p. 1–3; *ibid., 1926*, pp. 1–4.

[86] *BMOA, Annual Report, 1927*, pp. 1–3.

[87] *Investors' India Year Book, 1928–29* (Calcutta, 1929), p. 130; Proceedings of the BRIC, 1929, Oral Evidence, Sir M.M. Ramji, File 2, pp. 365–7, MSA.

[88] *Ibid.*, File 2, p. 367, MSA. Bombay's share of Indian yarn production fell from 43 per cent in 1926–7 to less than 24 per cent in 1928–9 and had recovered to only 33 per cent in 1931–2. Similarly, its share of the piecegoods market fell from 50 per cent in 1926–7 to 28 per cent in 1928–9 and recovered slowly to 41 per cent in 1931–2. *Report of the ITB, 1932*, Table V, p. 13; Table XIII, pp. 22–3; see also the discussion on pp. 12–13, 20–3, 118.

[89] *Report of the ITB, 1927*, I, 24–5.

suffered losses, another fifty had returned handsome profits.[90] Even in the midst of the depression of the early 1930s, the Tariff Board observed that in the case of about 10 per cent of the Bombay mills, 'a few are even now in a position to dispense with protection', while the majority of these 'first class mills' could soon 'dispense with any assistance'. Among the 'good second class mills', it continued, there were 'a certain number ... whose costs are considerably lower than the estimated average'.[91] Conversely, 'none of the mills which has so far gone into liquidation', it reported in 1927, 'had the smallest chances of surviving except in boom conditions'.[92] If the crisis of the Indian textile industry came to be focussed largely upon its oldest and largest centre, there were variations in the performance of individual mills within it throughout the extended period of depression.

The depression and the Bombay mills

By 1930, when commodity prices collapsed, the Bombay textile industry had already endured depressed markets for several years. 'It is felt in many quarters', the *Indian Investors' Yearbook* reported optimistically, 'that the trade cycle has at last begun to move upwards though there are still difficulties ahead.' If commodity prices were to rise, it tried to assure its readers, demand would recover and help to dispel 'the depression which has overhung the textile industry for the last seven or eight years'.[93] But commodity prices did not rise. From 1928 onwards, raw-cotton prices had shown a tendency to fall, but it was in February 1930 that the market collapsed. Traders who held stocks suffered losses. As prices continued to decline, dealers began to liquidate their stocks and by June 1930 the cotton market was in a 'state of panic'. Since the prices of all other agricultural products were similarly affected, cotton growers did not switch to alternative crops and despite the poor returns continued to place their commodity on a nervous market. Between 1928 and 1931, the average price of Broach cotton per candy had halved.[94] The effects were swiftly and dramatically imprinted on the prices of yarn and piecegoods. The price of yarn, which had tended to rise between 1926 and 1928, fell by about one-third between 1929 and 1931, while in the case of piecegoods the effect of the import duties imposed in 1930 was 'outweighed by the influence of the world collapse

[90] Proceedings of the BSEC, I, 585, MSA.
[91] *Report of the ITB, 1932*, p. 121.
[92] *Report of the ITB, 1927*, I, p. 18–19.
[93] *The Investors' India Yearbook, 1929–30* (Calcutta, 1930), p. 141. It is estimated that 53 out of 74 mills in Bombay had made a profit in 1929, although once allowance was made for depreciation, their numbers dwindled to three. *Ibid.*, p. 136.
[94] *Report of the ITB, 1932*, pp. 43–7.

Table 23. *Bombay's share of capacity and output of the Indian textile industry (percentages)*

Year	No. of mills	No. of spindles	No. of looms	Yarn produced	Cloth produced
1898–9	44.3	51.4	58.2	—	—
1903–4	41.5	49.4	53.6	57.6	58.5
1907–8	36.2	46.8	52.1	54.4	55.8
1912–3	32.6	44.4	48.4	52.0	50.3
1917–8	34.5	43.9	51.0	49.7	50.7
1920–1	33.8	44.1	50.7	50.3	51.3
1923–4	28.8	42.3	47.0	45.5	47.9
1930–1	23.3	35.8	41.1	31.0	36.0
1934–5	19.6	29.7	33.3	26.0	30.0

Note: The figures for capacity relate to the year ending 31 August 1899 and for output for the year ending 31 March 1900, and on the same basis for each year to 1934–5.
Sources: Report of the ITB, 1927, I, 5–14, tables I–V; *Report of the Special Tariff Board,* tables III–IV, pp. 16–18.

in prices'.[95] The Government of India's deflationary budgetary policies, its contraction of money supply and the high exchange rate aggravated the situation and further depressed consumption. Official short-term borrowing necessitated by the Government's difficulties in meeting its sterling obligations pushed up interest rates and further dislocated the credit market.[96] The Government of India's economic policies, Sir Homi Mody, Chairman of the Bombay Millowners' Association, thundered, reflected their 'utter irresponsibility', and would 'leave them without a friend in the country'.[97] If its tariff policies had long proved inadequate, its currency and exchange policies served to negate the meagre benefits of protection. Increased taxation and deflationary budgetary policies were, Mody said, 'the very last straw on the unfortunate camel's back'.[98] But this was neither the last nor the least of the burdens which were to fall on the unfortunate camel as it lumbered through the 1930s in an increasingly ungainly fashion.

In its early stages, the renewal of the swadeshi campaign to boycott foreign cloth acted to mitigate the worst effects of the depression. It helped to stem the flow of imports, increased the consumption of Indian cloth and boosted the demand for the finer varieties of cloth produced by the Indian mills. 'It is

[95] *Report of the Ibid.,* p. 49, and table XLIII, p. 48.
[96] B.R. Tomlinson, 'Britain and the Indian Currency Crisis, 1930–32', *EcHR,* 2nd series, XXXII, 1 (1979), 88–99; Tomlinson, *Political Economy of the Raj,* chs. 3 and 4, but especially pp. 82ff; Bagchi, *Private Investment,* pp. 34–67.
[97] *BMOA, Annual Report, 1931,* Proceedings of the AGM, Chairman's Speech, pp. ii–iii.
[98] *Ibid., 1931,* Proceedings of the AGM, Chairman's Speech, p. iv.

doubtful', reported the Millowners' Association in 1930, 'whether, but for the intense Swadeshi movement which prevailed during the period, several Bombay mills could have continued their operations during the year.'[99] By no means either loyal or natural allies of the Congress, the Bombay millowners now discovered a modest taste for swadeshi. But they could not entirely overcome their ambivalence towards the campaign. Its economic consequences were double edged. The swadeshi boycott which reduced the import of cloth also impeded the import of fine yarn and artificial silks.[100] Civil disobedience led to 'frequent hartals', as piecegoods dealers closed their markets, 'dislocated trade and industry and created a feeling of considerable uncertainty'.[101] Finally, there was always the danger that it might unleash rough and disorderly beasts to wreak revenge on those who pretended to control them. 'I have all along felt from the very start that this sort of civil disobedience may be suitable to us at the moment', Sir Purshottamdas Thakurdas, a leading Bombay businessman, wrote to the Ahmedabad millowner and Gandhian, Ambalal Sarabhai, in November 1930, 'but it might teach the people an extremely dangerous lesson, which may greatly inconvenience even a Swaraj Government.'[102] It was therefore 'with unbounded satisfaction', or at any rate bottomless relief, that the Millowners' Association welcomed the truce negotiated in the Gandhi–Irwin Pact in 1931.[103]

The worst effects of the depression were mitigated by the dramatic decline of imports in 1930 and 1931. Although they recovered some ground in 1932–3, they declined once more and were never to return, as a proportion of total production, to the levels of the previous decade. Lancashire's imports fell more quickly than Japan's, which, despite their absolute decline from the peak of 1929–30, rose as a share of total imports.[104] The magnitude of the decline of imports suggests that it cannot be satisfactorily explained in terms of a single factor, such as the swadeshi campaign. Other developments within the Indian market – the collapse of domestic demand, even the raising of the tariff duties – must have contributed to checking the flow of imports. But structural problems internal to the Lancashire cotton industry were perhaps the most important

---

[99] *Ibid., 1930*, p. xiv.

[100] *Report of the ITB, 1932*, p. 37.

[101] *BMOA, Annual Report, 1930*, Proceedings of the AGM, Chairman's Speech, p. iii.

[102] Thakurdas to Sarabhai, 18 November 1930, Thakurdas Papers File 42 (VI), NMML.

[103] *BMOA, Annual Report, 1931*, Proceedings of the AGM, Chairman's Speech, p. ii. S. Sarkar, 'The Logic of Gandhian Nationalism: Civil Disobedience and the Gandhi–Irwin Pact (1930–31), *Indian Historical Review*, 3, 1 (1976), 114–46; Gordon, *Businessmen and Politics*, especially ch. 6; C. Markovits, *Indian Business and Nationalist Politics, 1931–39: The Indigenous Capitalist Class and the Rise of the Congress Party* (Cambridge, 1985), pp. 68–82; Bipan Chandra, 'The Indian Capitalist Class and Imperialism before 1947', *Journal of Contemporary Asia*, V, 3 (1974), 309–26.

[104] Calculated from *Report of TLIC*, I, 14, Table V; *Report of the ITB, 1932*, pp. 28–9, Table XIX; *Report of Special Tariff Board, 1936*, p. 24, Table X; Bagchi, *Private Investment*, p. 238, table 7.5.

reason for its continuous decline in the Indian market after the First World War, and its steady surrender of its market share to Japan. In a market where prices were falling, purchasing power weakening, and per capita consumption of cloth stagnant or in decline, Lancashire's costs of production precluded its effective competition in most lines of production, except the finer varieties.

The decline of Lancashire imports did something to temper the worst consequences of the depression. But the help afforded by changing tariff policies is more difficult to evaluate.[105] The suspension of the excise duty in 1925, and its abolition in the following year, probably reduced Bombay's costs of production slightly at a crucial time. In 1924, the BMOA had estimated that their labour costs rose from 40 per cent of the total cost of manufacture (excluding raw materials) to slightly less than 45 per cent, when the excise duty was omitted from the calculation,[106] and in the following year, they argued that its burden would be neutralized by a wage cut of 11.5 per cent. Similarly, the duty on the import of yarn, introduced in 1927, particularly affected the range between 30s and 40s counts in which the competition between Japan and Bombay was at its sharpest.[107] It was not until 1930 and 1931, when 'the adverse effects upon the Indian revenues of this depression'[108] and the fear of the political consequences of the collapse of the Bombay industry prompted the Government of India to raise the duties on cotton piecegoods, that Indian mills were afforded a significant measure of protection. The Millowners' Association appreciated its benefits immediately. As early as 1930, its Chairman reported that protection 'has undoubtedly helped the industry in its struggle against foreign competition'.[109] Its effects were most palpable in particular lines of production, notably the import of grey piecegoods, which fell sharply.[110] Certainly, the Tariff Board believed the 'severe fall in the imports of Japanese woven goods ... to be chiefly a result of the specific duty imposed on this class of goods in 1930'.[111]

However, tariffs were scarcely the panacea for which the Bombay millowners had hoped. Their beneficial effects were offset by the collapse of prices in the domestic market.[112] The high exchange rate maintained at 1s. 6d. from the

---

[105] For a convenient chronology of the various duties affecting cotton textiles, see *Report of the Special Tariff Board*, pp. 6–12 and table 1; and Bagchi, *Private Investment*, pp. 237–47. On the making of tariff policy and its wider implications, see Dewey, 'The End of the Imperialism of Free Trade' and Chatterji, 'Business and Politics'.

[106] *Report of the ITB, 1927*, I, 113.

[107] Bagchi, *Private Investment*, p. 240.

[108] *Report of the ITB, 1932*, p. 5

[109] *BMOA, Annual Report, 1930*, Proceedings of the Annual General Meeting, Chairman's Speech, p. ii.

[110] *Report of the ITB, 1932*, Tables XIX–XXI, pp. 28–31; *Report of the Special Tariff Board*, Table X, p. 24.

[111] *Report of the ITB, 1932*, pp. 34–5.

[112] *Ibid.*, p. 49.

1920s, probably offset the protective influence of the tariff, although the depreciation of the gold value of the rupee shored up primary product prices and helped to limit the decline of purchasing power. The Japanese textile industry demonstrated that it could compete in the Indian market in 'a sufficiently flexible manner to meet effectively the adverse influence of both higher duties and higher exchange rate'. The rapid depreciation of the yen against the rupee facilitated a sudden and substantial increase of Japanese imports into Bombay in 1931–2 and threatened 'the home industry with the most serious menace'.[113] In the early 1930s, 'large arrivals from Japan of cheap textile goods had a depressing effect on all markets'.[114] In 1932, though not for this reason alone, eleven mills in Bombay had temporarily closed down, nineteen had been liquidated and the remainder were operating at between two-thirds and three-quarters of their total capacity.[115] The increased duty on non-British imports had proved insufficient to stem the Japanese advance in the domestic market, and it was raised further to 75 per cent in June 1933. The Indo-Japanese Trade Agreement, negotiated in 1934, restricted Japanese imports of piecegoods to a specified quota.[116] But in 1936, it was found, the competition from Japanese piecegoods of an intermediate class 'undoubtedly exercises a depressing influence on the selling prices, not only of Indian goods but also of imports from the United Kingdom'.[117]

Moreover, if tariff duties were originally intended to save the Bombay mills from destruction in the crisis of the early 1930s, the more healthy and expanding up-country centres were probably able to take far greater advantage of the protection they offered. In any case, the depression witnessed 'everywhere an expanding [textile] industry' and 'an all-round increase in the industry's productive capacity, except at Bombay'.[118] Indeed, the total number of mills in India increased from 274 in 1925 to 312 in 1931 and 336 in 1935.[119] When demand collapsed under the initial shock of the depression, Indian mill production continued to increase and, as the market began to recover, Indian mills raised their output and rushed to off load their goods. Mills in Bombay and Ahmedabad increasingly worked two shifts. The effect of keen internal competition in some lines periodically saturated the market and drove down prices, frequently depressing all varieties. For, the 'persistently low level of values ruling in India for the lower grades of both yarn and cloth … react on better

---

[113] *Report of the Indian Tariff Board Regarding the Grant of Additional Protection in the Cotton Textile Industry* (Calcutta 1932), pp. 5–8.
[114] *Report of the Special Tariff Board*, p. 46.
[115] Mehta, *Cotton Mills*, p. 180
[116] Bagchi, *Private Investment*, p. 241; Chatterji, 'Business and Politics'.
[117] *Report of the Special Tariff Board*, p. 84.
[118] *Ibid.*, pp. 19, 17.
[119] *Report of the ITB, 1932*, pp. 9–12; *Report of the Special Tariff Board*, p. 13.

qualities to the advantage of the consumer and the disadvantage of the manufacturer'.[120] In the 1920s, colonial officials had argued that tariffs might simply
allow the Bombay millowners to raise their output prices and perpetuate their
inefficiency. By 1936, it was clear that internal competition had effectively
prevented 'the manufacturer from passing on to the consumer the full effect of
the higher duties'.[121]

Despite the initial enthusiasm of the Bombay millowners for tariffs, several
factors acted to neutralize their protective effect. In the context of the depression,
perhaps the most that can be said about the impact of the tariff was that it enabled
large sections of the Bombay textile industry to survive and limited the long-term
damage of the crisis. Thus, the Tariff Board found in 1932 that

in the case of every important class of piecegoods manufacture in India, the majority of
the mills will find it impossible without the aid of protection to realise any return on
capital or to find adequate sums for depreciation and in several cases even to meet the
whole of their out-of-pocket expenses.[122]

Tariffs may have also enabled some mills to diversify into the production of
higher counts of yarn and finer varieties of piecegoods. But in the finer reaches
of the market, where alone Lancashire could hope to compete in the 1930s, the
element of protection remained minimal, and by the end of the decade the duties
on British goods were being reduced and their preferences in the Indian market
more carefully safeguarded.[123]

As the Bombay mills strove to retrieve their declining share of the domestic
market, the depression struck and important shifts in demand began to occur.
Of course, the collapse of commodity prices in 1930 led to the sudden contraction of demand. The per capita consumption of cloth did not recover its pre-war
level until the late 1930s.[124] Nonetheless, falling prices of yarn and piecegoods
meant, according to Sir Joseph Kay, the Chairman of the Millowners' Association, speaking in 1936, that 'the total amount being spent on cotton piecegoods
today is very much less than what it was ten years ago'.[125] While the prices
index of all commodities fell faster than the fall in the manufactured goods, the
prices of agricultural commodities exceeded the decline of both.[126] It is likely,
therefore, that overall purchasing power for manufactured goods was considerably weakened.

---

[120] *Report of the Special Tariff Board*, 1936, p. 46.
[121] *Ibid.*, p. 51.
[122] *Report of the ITB, 1932*, p. 116.
[123] *Report of the Special Tariff Board, 1936*; Chatterji, 'Business and Politics', 564–73.
[124] Bagchi, *Private Investment*, pp. 245–6.
[125] *BMOA, Annual Report, 1935*, Proceedings of the Annual General Meeting, Chairman's Speech,
   p. iii.
[126] Bagchi, *Private Investment*, pp. 245–7, especially Tables 7.8 and 7.9.

In the 1930s, however, there were two discernible, if opposing, trends in the movement of demand. First, the evidence suggests that there may have been some increase in the consumption of finer varieties and better qualities of piecegoods. The relative price movements could imply a growing inequality of income distribution. At the same time, falling prices made available cheaper food as well as cheaper manufactures. While some urban groups and perhaps a wealthy rural stratum experienced rising real incomes, they may have sought out better qualities and finer varieties of piecegoods.

The increasing production of yarn of over 30s counts and finer varieties of piecegoods in Bombay and especially Ahmedabad might serve to confirm this hypothesis. The production of yarn of counts higher than 30s increased from less than 4 per cent to over 13 per cent in Bombay between 1926–7 and 1931–2 and further to 17 per cent in 1934–5.[127] It was only in these higher counts that Bombay's share of the total output increased over this period.[128] Similarly, the Bombay mills made spectacular increases in the production of cambrics and lawns which were woven exclusively from higher counts. The Tariff Board estimated that the percentage of cloth woven from finer counts increased from below 10 per cent of the total weight of Bombay's output in 1926–7 to 21 per cent in 1931–2.[129] These trends were continued in the early 1930s, but the rate of increase slowed. If the average length per pound of piecegoods is taken as an index, there was only a slight increase in the production of finer varieties in grey and bleached as well as coloured cloth in Bombay.[130]

On the other hand, the significance of this shift in demand and output needs to be qualified. To some extent, the expansion of higher count yarn and finer piecegoods in Bombay and Ahmedabad was facilitated not simply by the pull of fresh demand but by the substitution of declining imports. Second, although income distribution became more skewed in the depression, it is unlikely that those making gains were numerous enough or their purchasing power strong enough to transform the structure of demand. Elsewhere, wages were more easily reduced in the 1930s. Moreover, in Bombay, large numbers of millworkers were thrown out of work in the early 1930s. While real wages may have risen for those who remained in work, albeit more slowly in the early 1930s, this was less likely for those who had to chance their luck in the casual labour market.[131] Indeed, one of the major attractions of urban investment for rural

---

[127] *Report of the ITB, 1932*, p. 15, especially, Table VII; *Report of the Special Tariff Board*, p. 20, Table VI.

[128] *Report of the ITB, 1932*, p. 17 and Table VIII, p. 16.

[129] *Ibid.*, pp. 24–5.

[130] *Report of the Special Tariff Board*, Table IX, p. 22.

[131] Labour Office, Bombay, *Wages and Unemployment in the Bombay Cotton Textile Industry* (Bombay, 1934), pp. 56–7; *Report of the TLIC*, I, 22; K. Mukherji, 'Trend in Real Wages in Cotton Textile Mills in Bombay City and Island, from 1900 to 1951', *Artha Vijnana*, I, 1 (1959), 82–96.

capital, during the depression, was the growing number of migrants who, fleeing the countryside, swelled the supply of labour to the towns and reduced its cost.[132] Nonetheless, some portion of the growing output of finer varieties does reflect an increased consumption of higher-quality goods.

The structure of demand was also being pulled in another and opposite direction, and perhaps more strongly, at the same time. Significantly, if the demand for piecegoods as a whole declined between 1929–30 and 1931–2, the output of Indian mills increased by 23 per cent. This fact reflected deeper trends. While the imports of piecegoods fell by 30 per cent between 1918–9 and 1936–7, the output of Indian mills, which predominantly produced coarser goods, increased by 146 per cent. In the 1930s, demand stagnated, and its impact fell almost exclusively on imports. Imports which had increased substantially in the 1920s registered an equally impressive contraction in the 1930s. Indian mill production increased steadily throughout this period, although its growth was somewhat faster in the 1920s, and its share of the total quantity of mill-made piecegoods available in India rose from 57 per cent in 1918–19 to 82 per cent by 1936–7.[133] That this trend was sustained and even accelerated in the 1930s is perhaps best explained 'by the fact that the general fall in purchasing power naturally led to a diversion of demand from high priced to low priced goods, thus favouring the Indian industry'.[134] This is borne out by the rapid growth in this period of up-country mills: most notably in Coimbatore and Tamil Nadu,[135] but also in Bengal,[136] which in the context of falling prices and shrinking demand were the most likely to prosper. 'To all except those mills which are geographically well-placed for raw materials and markets', the *Indian Investors' Yearbook* observed in 1935–6, 'margins have been negligible.'[137] Conversely, it was also reflected in the difficulties which engulfed the highly efficient, fine-goods-producing Ahmedabad mills in the mid 1930s, after they had emerged from the slump of the early 1920s largely unscathed and weathered the crisis of 1930–1 with relative ease. Even in the early 1920s, they had begun increasingly to diversify their output into higher counts of yarn and finer piecegoods. That the Coimbatore mills prospered while the highly efficient Ahmedabad industry floundered in the mid 1930s can to some extent be taken as an indication of the direction in which domestic demand was moving.

132 Baker, *An Indian Rural Economy*, especially ch. 5.
133 Calculated from *Report of the TLIC*, I, 14, Table V.
134 *Report of the ITB, 1932*, p. 120.
135 *Report of the Special Tariff Board*, p. 15; *Report of the ITB, 1932*, pp. 10–11 and Table I; Baker, *An Indian Rural Economy*, pp. 339–72.
136 The number of cotton mills in Bengal increased from thirteen in 1932 to nineteen in 1936 while, in addition, three mills were idle and twenty-four were in the course of erection or only recently registered. See *Report of the Special Tariff Board*, p. 15.
137 *Investors' India Yearbook, 1935–36* (Calcutta, 1936), p. 135.

The expansion of the up-country mills fed the prevailing tendency towards over-production and helped to check the recovery of prices. It contributed to the declining share of Bombay's output, capacity and employment. The intensity of internal competition, especially in the cheaper and coarser varieties, encouraged competitive price-cutting and forced down their level. But depressed prices at the lower end of the market also dragged down the prices of the better qualities. In these lines of production, British imports were already forcing down the price of Indian manufactures while Japanese imports exerted a depressive influence upon both. Thus, as the Bombay mills sought to diversify in the 1930s out of the highly congested lines of production into higher counts and finer varieties, they entered markets which are not only fiercely competitive but were also stagnant and depressed. As domestic cloth production increased and purchasing power collapsed, sales had to be effected at prices 'consistently below the cost of production'.[138]

From the mid 1930s, trading conditions improved once more for the Bombay mills. The prices of primary products began to recover, demand appeared to improve and the Bombay mills were able to clear some of their unsold stocks.[139] In 1934, idle capacity was halved and the proportion of looms employed on the night shift had been increased from 11 to 30 per cent.[140] The growth of Japanese imports was checked by the Indo-Japanese Trade Agreement while the Sino-Japanese War not only further restricted their inflow but also created fresh opportunities for Bombay in its export markets.[141] British imports, which had been as badly affected by Japanese competition as the Bombay mills, showed little sign of recovery. The reduction of import duties, recommended by the Special Tariff Board, 'failed to rally them' and it became increasingly clear that British imports 'are not likely in the near future to rise above the low level to which they declined during the depression'.[142] The Spanish Civil War generated additional orders for the Bombay mills and the disruption of Japanese imports helped to maintain yarn and cloth prices while the steep fall in the prices of American cotton reduced the industry's raw material costs in 1937.[143] At the

[138] Mehta, *Cotton Mills*, p. 179.
[139] BMOA, *Annual Report, 1934*, p. 3; *ibid., 1936*, Proceedings of the AGM, Chairman's Speech, p. ii; *Investor's India Yearbook, 1934–35* (Calcutta, 1935), p. 142; *ibid., 1936–7* (Calcutta, 1937), p. 137; Mehta, *Cotton Mills*, pp. 182–4.
[140] BMOA, *Annual Report, 1934*, Proceedings of Annual General Meeting, Chairman's Speech, p. ii.
[141] BMOA, *Annual Report, 1937*, Proceedings of the AGM, Chairman's Speech, p. iii; *ibid.*, p. 6; *Investors' India Yearbook, 1934–35*, p. 142., *ibid., 1936–37*, p. 137; *Report of the TLIC*, I, 15–16, 43; Mehta, *Cotton Mills*, pp. 187–8.
[142] *Report of the TLIC*, I, 14.
[143] *Ibid.*, I, *passim; BMOA, Annual Report, 1937*, Proceedings of the AGM, Chairman's Speech, p. iii.

same time, a succession of good harvests strengthened purchasing power and commodity prices continued to improve.

Following a long period of depression, it was both inevitable and understandable that piecegoods dealers and millowners should have responded more enthusiastically to the changed conditions than the extent of the recovery warranted. The first signs of a revival in demand were accompanied by saturated markets. If they failed to control output successfully, Sir Homi Mody, Chairman of the Bombay Millowners' Association, warned his fellow-members in 1935, they would almost inevitably be faced with 'an indiscriminate resort to double shift working, resulting in sudden spurts of production, followed by an equally erratic abandonment of that process as soon as the inexorable laws of supply and demand assert themselves'.[144] The markets frequently anticipated a crisis of over-production and were often proved right.

The revivals of 1934 and 1936–7 did, indeed, prove to be fleeting. They had been created by fortuitous circumstances which could just as easily be reversed. Commodity prices fell once more so that 'the purchasing power of the farmer has declined considerably'.[145] As the Sino-Japanese war ended, the return of Japanese goods, both in their domestic and their export markets, increased the competitive pressures on the Bombay mills. 'Our future', as one millowner put it in 1937, 'is in the laps of the Gods and the Japanese'.[146] The end of the decade was characterized once more by over-production and increased labour costs, the growth of idle capacity especially in spinning and the intermittent reduction of night-shift working. In 1939, cotton prices rose but such was the pessimism in the trade that yarn and cloth prices did not follow, forward orders stagnated and stocks continued to accumulate. The various centres of industry could no more easily agree to a restriction of output. Under the circumstances, Bombay could scarcely 'take action independently of the rest of India without serious detriment to the future of the local industry'.[147] The old familiar problem of 'accommodating production to demand' simply would not go away. By early 1939, the Bombay millowners were grimly anticipating serious difficulties 'probably for some years to come'.[148]

Once again the war rescued the Bombay millowners. International catastrophe had always provided the conditions for the Bombay industry to flourish. The 1940s represented a decade of massive and rising profits for the industry.

144 BMOA, Annual Report, 1934, Proceedings of Annual General Meeting, Chairman's Speech, p. ii.
145 BMOA, Annual Report, 1937, p. 6.
146 Proceedings of the TLIC, Interim Inquiry, Oral Evidence, BMOA, File 42, p. 32, MSA.
147 BMOA, Annual Report, 1938, Proceedings of the Annual General Meeting, Chairman's Speech, p. iii.
148 Ibid., Proceedings of the Annual General Meeting, Chairman's Speech, p. v.

Imports were dramatically curtailed while the large demand from the armed forces for the coarser lines of production offered a guaranteed outlet, while it also created scarcities at home and raised prices throughout the market. Speculative hoarding as well as more widespread inflationary pressures pushed up the price of mill-made goods. The official historian of the industry found it 'hard to deny that the actions of large sections of the industry were anti-social in character, even if they were not positively illegal'. In fact, Mehta added,

the millowner frequently held back stocks in the hope of realising higher prices. He shifted production schedules according to his estimates of the profitability of producing different items ... The shifts in production implied much greater magnification of shortages in individual varieties of cloth.[149]

While Japanese military successes generated panic in the Indian market in 1941–2, confidence returned quickly as the Japanese advance slowed down. The Quit India movement disrupted the trade briefly but, as the Ahmedabad mills virtually stopped working for three and a half months, it also accentuated the shortfall of supply and enabled the Bombay mills to get rid of their stocks and boost their sales. Moreover, the millowners enjoyed a period of industrial peace after the general strike of 1940. The communist Girni Kamgar Union appeared in a conciliatory mood; the people's war received a higher priority than the people's wage. In any case, the Defence of India Rules fettered the freedom to strike while some of the provisions of the Industrial Disputes Act, which purported to protect labour, especially the requirement that employers give notice before altering the character of production and therefore the conditions of work, were relaxed.[150]

The end of the war slackened demand which had been created by army requirements but inflationary pressures and the disruption of international trade delayed the crisis which might otherwise have beckoned. The removal of wartime price and production controls, which led to an immediate and massive price hike, had to be brought back within four months. The atomic bomb removed the industry's major foreign competitor in the domestic market and created fresh opportunities abroad. The Bombay mills did encounter intermittent difficulties. Wages had been increasing with the addition of a dearness allowance, narrowing the margin between the cost of production and output prices. Moreover, the last year of British rule was characterized by widespread labour unrest, intense competition between trade unions seeking to win representative status under the new Bombay Industrial Disputes Act and, partly as a consequence, the intensification of industrial violence often directed at

[149] Mehta, *Cotton Mills*, pp. 196–7.
[150] *Ibid.*, pp. 192–8.

'managers, departmental heads, supervisors and jobbers'.[151] Similarly, the upheavals of partition brought large waves of migrants to Bombay, unsettling prevailing alliances in the neighbourhood as well as their relationship to systems of discipline and control at the workplace. It was not, however, until 1952 that these buoyant and profitable conditions petered out. Underlying the post-war prosperity had been Bombay's success in export markets in the East. The re-emergence of Japan as a significant factor in world textile markets fundamentally transformed the basic conditions of Bombay's success. By the early 1950s, therefore, the official historian of the industry could write soberly that 'the textile mills have substantially returned to normal conditions'.[152] There had been, however, one significant change: between 1940 and 1952, the Bombay mills had effected a marked shift, initiated in the late 1920s, towards the production of finer counts and varieties of yarn and cloth, had extended their bleaching and dyeing operations and diversified into mercerizing and calico printing.[153]

The history of the Bombay cotton-textile industry is often written in terms of its gradual and inexorable decline from the 1890s onwards. Although the Bombay mills encountered numerous crises, these were often followed by periods of strong recovery. Moreover, not all mills or managing agencies were affected by the periods of slump in the same way. Some mills continued to prosper. Even in the 1920s and 1930s, when the industry appeared to endure almost chronically depressed conditions, it also experienced revivals and intermittent prosperity. Finally, it was perhaps precisely because the Indian textile industry had been dominated by Bombay that the erosion of its share of capacity and output mattered less to its millowners than the capture of an increasing proportion or specific areas of the domestic market mattered to Ahmedabad and the up-country centres. At any rate, there was little reason for the decline of its share, until it quickened in the 1920s and early 1930s, to precipitate a sense of crisis or a consciousness of impending doom generally among the Bombay millowners. The neglect of the domestic market could, therefore, be seen as a rational response to their general situation rather than a function of a peculiar managerial culture. It was the loss of the Chinese market in the early 1920s which made this neglect critical.

Between 1923 and 1939, the Bombay textile industry was confronted by a complex set of structural problems. Having lost their Chinese market by the mid 1920s, the Bombay mills were forced to penetrate the domestic market. Yet the

---

[151] *Ibid.*, p. 198; *Interim Report by the Industrial Conditions Enquiry Committee on the Cotton Textile Industry in Bombay City and Bombay Suburban District* (Bombay, 1948), pp. 17–19, 22, 25–6, 42.
[152] Mehta, *Cotton Mills*, pp. 202, 198–209.
[153] *Ibid.*, p. 200.

domestic market, kept open by the colonial state in the interests of Lancashire, was an arena of intense competition, generated by British and Japanese exports as well as by the expansion of up-country centres of production. Furthermore, domestic demand was stagnant in the late 1920s and 1930s. As per capita income and cloth consumption stagnated or even declined, and domestic textile production continued to increase, the home market was frequently saturated. The effect of the import trade as well as the intensity of internal competition was to depress the price of yarn and cloth. In the 1920s and especially the 1930s, it was imperative for the industry, as a whole, to reduce its cost of production if it were to survive and compete in the domestic market.

The diversity of the industry and the variations in the performance of the mills impeded combined action in this direction by the millowners. The response of most millowners to the slump of 1923, therefore, was to maximize their profits in the short run within the constraints of the prevailing economic situation. They could ride the crisis by using their machinery as fully as possible to produce such varieties of yarn and piecegoods which they knew would find buyers, or cut their losses and wait for times to improve. They might hope or even anticipate that the depression would have a cathartic effect upon the industry, breaking the weaker mills and so leave the markets to a smaller number of more efficient producers as trade picked up again. Their hopes, it turned out, were not entirely misplaced. But at the time, when conditions varied enormously between mills and the effects of the depression fell unevenly upon the industry, this individualistic and short-term response was not only the most likely course to follow, but was also perhaps inevitable.

It also became clear by the mid 1920s that Bombay millowners would have to diversify their output into higher counts of yarn and finer varieties of cloth. Yet, in this range, the market was dominated by the imports of Lancashire and especially Japan, as well as the growing threat of Ahmedabad. To the Bombay millowners, therefore, tariff protection against foreign and especially Japanese competition seemed a matter of some considerable urgency. In addition, it was clear that to compete with Japanese imports or the proliferating Indian cotton mills, Bombay would have to reduce its labour costs. Yet this was always liable to provoke fierce and disruptive labour resistance. These two strands came to be inextricably linked.

In the 1920s, therefore, the Bombay Millowners' Association argued that the root of their difficulties lay not in the organization and efficiency of their industry but in the baneful effects of government policy and the harsh political and economic environment created by the colonial state.[154] Their contention was that the industry possessed sufficient vigour to handle its competitors so

---

[154] BMOA, *Statement Submitted to the Tariff Board* (Bombay, 1926).

long as the excise duty was abolished, a favourable exchange policy instituted and, above all, effective protection offered against imports, especially from Japan. But the colonial state, concerned as far as possible to keep the Indian market open to Lancashire, preferred to lay the blame upon the inefficiency of the Bombay industry and, in particular, its high labour costs. Thus, the Tariff Board observed in 1927,

By far the greatest disability from which Bombay suffers is its high costs of labour ... So far as costs of production are concerned, it is in labour costs that is to be found the main reason why the depression in the industry has been felt so much more acutely in Bombay than it has elsewhere.[155]

Recommending 'internal economies', the Tariff Board suggested that 'in a time of depression, the most obvious method of effecting an economy in the cost of production is by reducing the wages of labour.' However, it recognized that Bombay was 'at a marked disadvantage in this respect'. Following their failure to cut wages in 1925, the Bombay millowners were wary of repeating the attempt and 'every month which elapses makes it more difficult to effect a reduction in wages'. Since the millowners were 'anxious to avoid another strike', the Tariff Board concluded, 'The only alternative to a reduction in wages is increased efficiency and it is in this direction that, in our view, the true line of advance lies'.[156] Indeed, 'the problem before the Bombay mill industry' was identified as 'the maintenance of its labour efficiency relative to that of other centres'.[157] To this end, it suggested the extension of piece rates to spinners and increased workloads all round, which would 'tend to economy and give increased earnings ... even when accompanied by a slight reduction in rate'.[158] Fewer workers would be employed, but their workloads would be increased; they would be paid less, but they would earn more. The 'true line of advance', therefore, lay in internal reform: especially through the adoption of efficiency measures and rationalization schemes. Tariffs, it was argued, would simply protect the industry at the expense of the consumer and promote and perpetuate inefficiency. On the other hand, as the millowners often pointed out,[159] it was unrealistic to expect them to risk their capital in effecting structural change or even diversifying their output and rationalizing their deployment of labour, when faced with severe competition in an open market. In the absence of adequate protection, the industry was likely to respond to falling profits and shrinking markets simply by cutting wages and retrenching labour.

---

155 *Report of the ITB, 1927*, I, 123.
156 *Ibid.*, I, 133.
157 *Ibid.*, I, 136.
158 *Ibid.*, I, 137.
159 For instance, *BMOA, Annual Report, 1929*, Proceedings of the Annual General Meeting, Chairman's Speech, p. v.

It was in this context that the methods of labour management in the cotton-textile industry in Bombay entered public discourse from the late 1920s onwards. At least nine committees of inquiry discussed and commented upon rationalization and standardization schemes, scrutinized the organization and performance of the industry and made recommendations for the more efficient management of the workforce.[160] Some even attempted to monitor the implementation of rationalization. The progress made by the millowners to improve their efficiency by these methods was an important criterion by which the state, fellow capitalists and publicists assessed how far the millowners had brought their labour troubles on themselves by their own intemperate and ill-considered methods of management and judged accordingly whether they deserved state assistance. On the other hand, attempts to effect rationalization schemes culminated in three major general strikes in the industry between 1928 and 1934, and caused numerous mill and departmental closures throughout the late 1920s and 1930s.[161]

In view of the tasks facing the industry and the emergence of a fresh discourse for its consideration in the 1920s, it is tempting to regard the end of this decade as a watershed. Indeed, historians have perceived portentous changes flowing from the recommendations of the Tariff Board: 'technological change that led to consequential changes in the structure of the workforce',[162] the adoption by managers of increasingly effective modes of discipline and modern methods of management[163] and even a greater degree of unity among both employers and workers.[164]

But the continuities of production strategies and labour deployment are more striking than the changes. Of course, the output of the industry was diversified (see table 24) and its productivity increased. Thus, between 1925–6 and 1931–2, the average number of hands daily employed in Bombay fell by 13.5 per cent, but the industry's output of yarn increased by 23.4 per cent and of woven goods

---

[160] The Indian Tariff Board in 1927; the Bombay Strike Enquiry Committee in 1928; the Committee of Enquiry into the 1929 strike; more ephemerally, the Bombay Riots Inquiry Committee in 1929; the Royal Commission on Labour in India in 1931; the Indian Tariff Board in 1932; the Special Tariff Board in 1936; the Textile Labour Inquiry Committee's Interim Report in 1937 and its Final Report concluded in 1940 but published in 1953. The proceedings of some of these committees, especially those into the strikes and riots of 1928–9, were reported in detail by the newspapers.

[161] Chandavarkar, 'Workers' Politics and the Mill Districts in Bombay'; Newman, *Workers and Unions*, pp. 168–250; S. Bhattacharya, 'Capital and Labour in Bombay City, 1928–29', *Economic and Political Weekly*, Review of Political Economy, XVI, 42 and 43 (17–24 October 1981), PE36–PE44; G.K. Leiten, *Colonialism, Class and Nation: the Confrontation in Bombay Around 1930* (Calcutta, 1984).

[162] Newman, *Workers and Unions*, p. 253.

[163] Morris, *Industrial Labour Force*, pp. 33–4, 107–28 and more generally, pp. 101–77.

[164] See especially, Newman, *Workers and Unions*, p. 84; Bhattacharya, 'Capital and Labour'.

Table 24. *Diversification of production in the Bombay cotton-textile industry, 1921–22 to 1938–39*

| Year | Yarns of over 30s counts (million lbs) | Piecegoods made from yarn of over 30s counts (million lbs) | |
		Dhotis	Cambrics and lawns
1921–2	6.9	121.8	4.5
1924–5	11.1	111.0	2.4
1925–6	8.4	115.4	1.4
1926–7	13.5	150.1	0.4
1927–8	17.3	168.8	2.4
1928–9	11.7	86.5	1.8
1929–30	17.7	170.8	0.8
1930–1	33.2	229.4	7.5
1931–2	42.4	287.6	14.5
1932–3	44.5	343.1	14.6
1933–4	32.2	239.6	14.6
1934–5	43.9	268.1	31.7
1935–6	56.8	407.1	41.1
1936–7	58.6	317.3	44.0
1937–8	84.6	357.2	79.5
1938–9	88.3	457.4	64.3

Sources: Report of the ITB, 1927, I, table LXIII, 102, table LXIV, 104–6; Report of the TLIC, vol. II, Final Report (Bombay, 1953), tables XLIX and L, 217–19.

by 32 per cent.[165] Between 1931 and 1935, eight mills in Bombay stopped working. The number of spindles installed in working mills fell by 15.4 per cent and of looms by 13.4 per cent and the average number of workers fell by nearly 14 per cent. Nevertheless, the consumption of raw cotton increased by 5.4 per cent.[166] Although these figures do not allow for changes in the composition of output which could inflate the length and weight of yarn and cloth, 'the increased consumption of raw material in spite of strikes and of the reduction in machinery and labour employed points to a more efficient working now than four years ago'.[167] To some extent, it probably reflected the collapse of the least efficient mills in the industry. But increased efficiency was achieved by various expedients. Night shifts were adopted from 1930 (see table 25). Workloads were steadily increased. Attempts were made to cheapen labour costs by attacking the position of relatively privileged, skilled and better-paid groups of

[165] *Report of the ITB, 1932*, pp. 11–12.
[166] *Report of the Special Tariff Board*, Table III, p. 16.
[167] *Ibid.*, p. 17.

Table 25. *Number of textile mills working night shifts and the number of workers employed in Bombay City, 1930–9*

Period	Number of mills	Number of operatives
December 1930	16	3,592
January 1931	17	5,951
July 1931	33	14,347
January 1932	30	17,118
July 1932	18	10,017
January 1933	19	9,734
July 1933	13	4,854
January 1934	14	10,021
July 1934	21	12,691
January 1935	33	27,500
July 1935	34	27,680
January 1936	35	29,386
July 1936	33	22,013
January 1937	38	26,362
July 1937	48	39,568
January 1938	48	47,524
July 1938	52	53,059
January 1939	51	46,894
July 1939	39	34,591

Source: Report of the TLIC, II, 162–3.

workers, such as weavers. On the other hand, there was scarcely any uniform or orchestrated attempt to introduce new technology, more modern methods of discipline or a more consistently rational deployment of labour. Certainly, there was little unity or even uniformity of interest on either side, whether among employers or workers, and the Millowners' Association failed to effect any coherent policy towards labour.

The standardization of wages across the industry was more intensively discussed than ever before. Yet apart from a minimum-wage schedule introduced by the Millowners' Association in 1934 to bring to a halt competitive wage-cutting by its members, which had disruptive effects on the labour market, no standardization scheme was implemented. If, following the Tariff Board recommendations, rationalization and efficiency schemes obtruded increasingly upon public discourse, their implementation remained extremely limited in scope. The tendencies towards mergers or combinations remained weak and, indeed, grew weaker in the 1930s. Less than 10,000 workers were employed in 'efficiency schemes' in 1939, which in any case meant little more than the allocation of a larger number of machines to each of them in certain specific processes (see table 26). 'Because we have not gone so far with the efficiency schemes', said Fred Stones, in many ways their pioneer and architect, the outlay

Table 26. *Number of workers employed on efficiency systems, 1934–9*

	Number of men					
Occupation	August 1934	August 1935	December 1936	July 1937	March 1938	March 1939
2 hopper feeders per man	32	39	42	44	4 7	46
2 scutchers per man	106	134	168	157	178	183
2 men per 3 drawing heads	415	638	624	758	787	787
2 roving frames per man	323	596	590	760	797	759
2 ring spinning sides per man	2,035	2,986	3,147	3,795	3,892	3,857
3 looms per weaver	261	574	545	636	574	556
4 looms per weaver	2,111	2,192	2,754	2,735	3,079	2,716
6 looms per weaver	368	496	472	509	504	501

Source: Report of TLIC, II, table XLIV, 187.

on them was 'very little compared to the total capital invested.'[168] Far from any coherent or sustained attempt to reorganize the industry, the millowners responded to the slump largely by perpetuating business strategies which had long characterized the industry. They tailored production to the fluctuations of the market and accordingly varied their levels of employment. They also retrenched labour, increased workloads and when it was possible, reduced wages. It is necessary to examine the nature of the textile industry more closely in order to understand why the millowners responded to new problems in accustomed ways. The structural characteristics of the industry which limited their options in response to slump also conditioned their policies towards the deployment of labour and the organization of work.

[168] Proceedings of the TLIC, Main Inquiry, Oral Evidence, BMOA, File 57–A, pp. 96–7, MSA.

7 The workplace: labour and the organization of production in the cotton-textile industry

The cotton mills of Bombay not only dominated the landscape of Girangaon, influenced its social organization and informed its political traditions, but they also determined the structure of the city's economy. The organization of work in the industry conditioned the social organization of workers in the neighbourhood. The extensive use of casual labour forced workers to maintain social connections beyond the workplace, whether in the village or the urban neighbourhood. Furthermore, employers depended upon jobbers to maintain a regular supply of labour in the face of fluctuating demand. In their turn, as we have seen, jobbers had to develop contacts within the neighbourhood to enable them to hire additional workers at short notice or lay them off when they were no longer needed. Thus, the operation of the jobber system also integrated the social spheres of workplace and neighbourhood.

The trend of investment in the textile industry was characteristically labour-using, which gave rise to substantial differences between mills and led to divergent and conflicting interests among the employers. By impeding combined action, these differences in turn limited the options before the employers. Moreover, it was a common tendency among the millowners to regulate production according to the short-term fluctuations of demand. Their labour-intensive strategies may be understood in terms of the high costs of machinery and the scarcity of capital. However, by regulating production to demand, the millowners appeared to sacrifice the optimal use of machinery. In addition, the demand for labour varied with changing patterns of production encouraging the extensive use of casual labour within the industry. This pattern of labour use shaped the structure of the workforce and conditioned the social relationships of the workplace.

This chapter will investigate how the economics of the textile industry shaped the structure of the workforce, the distribution of power at the workplace, differentials of skill and wages and the patterns of labour deployment. Social relationships of the workplace were not simply determined by neutral technological forces, but were also shaped by pressures exerted by workers themselves. The interplay of production conditions and working-class action influenced the structure of authority or the diffusion of power at work, defined the nature and social meaning of skill, informed the structure of wages and occupational hierarchies and shaped the patterns of labour deployment. The organization of work in the cotton-textile industry was not only affected by social organization beyond the workplace but it also contributed to the constitution of the social nexus of the working class in Bombay.

Business strategies and the organization of production in the textile industry

The development of the cotton-textile industry was predicated upon the more intensive use of labour rather than the progressive introduction of labour-saving technology. Since textile machinery had to be imported and was, therefore, relatively expensive, and finance to meet its costs was not easily secured, employers used old machinery as long as possible. Entrepreneurs often simply inherited the plant with the mill they bought and sometimes purchased equipment which had already been scrapped. In some cases, it was said, the machinery had not been renewed in sixty years. Even the Sassoon group, one of the most efficient in Bombay, worked equipment which was forty years old. 'If I had the money', Fred Stones, its director, said about these machines, 'I would not replace them.' When old machinery required renewal or replacement, many mills changed only certain parts, such as gears, spindles or the rollers on the speed frames.[1] Over these extended periods the plant had sometimes been fully depreciated, so that its subsequent use was in effect free of cost.

Moreover, the utilization of machinery was also labour intensive. 'I find', said Fred Stones, with a touch of disingenuity, 'that modern machinery gives higher production than makers guarantee. We are running it with higher speeds in India than Great Britain.'[2] The practice of running machines above the prescribed speeds generally required a larger number of workers to mind them. But in India, as the representative of the Eastern Bedaux Company put it, 'it is cheaper to run [spindles at] higher speeds and use more labour than to run lower speeds and use less labour as practiced in America'.[3] In addition, the quality of the raw material and its preparation also influenced the deployment of labour and the utilization of machinery. The effects of the economics of the textile industry upon the patterns of labour deployment and the organization of work may be clarified by a closer investigation of the process of production.

The margin in the cotton-textile industry between the cost of the raw material and the price of varieties of yarn and cloth largely determined the profits of the

---

[1] Proceedings of the TLIC, Main Inquiry, Oral Evidence, BMOA, File 57-A, p. 115, MSA.
[2] Ibid., Main Inquiry, Oral Evidence, BMOA, File 57-A, pp. 194–5, MSA.
[3] Ibid., Main Inquiry, Oral Evidence, Representatives of the Eastern Bedaux Co., File 77-C, p. 4978, MSA.

enterprise. The quality of the final product depended upon the quality of its preparation in the preceding processes. The types and mixings of raw cotton, their purification, carding and spinning, sizing and winding, each affected the results which a weaver might obtain. But many of these preparatory processes could be manipulated according to market fluctuations so as to maximize the margin of profit.

There was, for instance, a wide range of raw-cotton mixings in infinitely varying proportions which could be employed to spin yarn of a particular count. Of course, a mixing which employed superior varieties of cotton and a low proportion of waste was likely to yield a higher outturn, whereas inferior mixings resulted in a larger number of breakages and more modest output. However, as one mill manager put it, 'A mixing that may really be good for outturn may not necessarily be a paying one, and one that may be a paying one may not necessarily yield a good outturn.'[4] Preparing a mixing of yarn of 20s count 'at an extra superior quality of higher cost with the intention of getting an extra good outturn per spindle' could easily exceed 'a reasonable working limit' and thus prove 'wasteful of good fibre'. The small proportion of value added in the spinning of low-count yarn made the optimal purchase and mixing of raw cotton of 'the right sort consistent with the quality and quantity of yarn'[5] extremely important. For this reason, 'under certain conditions of the cotton market ... a mill might very advisedly restrict itself and be satisfied' with a lower output based upon a cheaper, albeit inferior, mixing.[6]

Since most mills, in order to minimize their overheads, bought their cotton according to need at the jaitha in Mazagaon, its purchase became a highly skilled and hazardous exercise. The buyer had not only to anticipate the price movements of raw cotton but of yarn and cloth as well. Moreover, employers also had to accept orders and set their production targets according to their predictions of the relative movements of different varieties in the cotton, yarn and cloth markets.

Most mills produced a wide range of yarn and cloth and often varying qualities of each count of yarn or type of cloth. Before 1914, it was not unusual to find that 'half a dozen counts varying from 6s up to 20s and even up to 24s and 30s are attempted to be spun in a small mill' or that millowners made 'contracts of yarn deliveries ... of half a dozen sorts to be delivered at one and the same time'.[7] In the 1920s and 1930s, as the industry's output was diversified so the range of goods produced by the Bombay mills widened. The causes,

---

[4] A Retired Mill Manager, *The Bombay Cotton Mills: The Spinning of 10's, 20's and 30's Counts* (Bombay, 1907), p. 7.
[5] *Ibid.*, p. 8.
[6] *Ibid.*, p. 7.
[7] *Ibid.*, p. 11.

largely financial, of these practices, and their consequences for the nature of competition in the industry will be examined later. Here it is necessary to investigate its effects on the utilization of machinery and men.

Most mills in Bombay were laid out and equipped to spin yarn of 10s and 20s counts and to weave coarse grey cloth on one or two looms. In some of the larger mills, it was sometimes possible to separate the machines adjusted specifically for particular mixings, counts and qualities; but even in these cases, this degree of organization depended upon the range and consistency of orders which had been received and, therefore, the extent to which the flow of production might be maintained. In smaller mills, the attempt to spin several counts of yarn and manufacture different varieties of cloth demanded a large measure of improvisation and could result in the sacrifice of quality. Cotton of different staple and varying proportions of impurity had to be put through the same machines in the blow room. Mixings for higher counts, passed through the same scutcher on which low counts had been worked, could damage the long staple of the former and prevent it from yielding its maximum outturn and quality. Cards, better suited to counts of 20s and 30s, might sometimes be switched to mixings suitable to counts of 10s in order 'to meet certain urgent deliveries under some contract arrangement, or a financial stress', thus sacrificing quality and reducing the efficiency of the cards themselves.[8] In the drawing frame and speed frames when the sliver of cotton was elongated, evened out and given some twist, 'the proportion of supply from one machine to another is greatly disturbed when an extra preparation, or two, have to be changed from 20s to 10s to meet certain demands of the market' and 'a variety of makeshifts has to be adopted by the tactful carder, or manager'.[9]

The cotton which emerged from the mixing and blow rooms and the carding process was passed through two or three sets of drawing frames. The task was to give the sliver of cotton taken from the carding machine a uniform thickness and, as it was drawn, gradually to give it twist. Lower counts or yarn or inferior mixings necessitated more twist. Adjustments could be required in the weight of the drafting rollers through which the sliver of cotton was drawn or the distance between them or in the speed of the machine. At times, it became necessary to pass the sliver of cotton through two, rather than three, sets of speed frames, passing the roving (as a sliver of cotton which had acquired twist was known) from the slubber directly to the roving frame and missing the intermediate frame. Yet the nature of this 'roller-drafting' system and the drawing frames made it essential that the sliver be passed through several processes because too much drafting done at any one stage gave rise to an irregular thickness of roving.

[8] *Ibid.*, p. 13.
[9] *Ibid.*, p. 16.

The range of options before an employer was greater in the lower counts and coarser varieties. In the mixings for yarn of counts of 10s, spun on the mule – a more pliable machine than the more widely used ring frame – it was possible for employers 'to convert all the waste of the mill into yarn which, however poor in quality, will leave them a reasonable margin of profit'.[10] On the other hand, it was said,

> The spinning of 30s ceases to pay as soon as any attempt is made to lessen its first cost. The higher the count the greater is the room for improvement in the strength of the blend to ensure as good an output per spindle as may be possible within the working conditions of the machinery ... There is a good margin of elasticity in the rates realised between a poor, medium and good quality of this count in the market ... In the spinning of higher counts, it is the best only that pays, there being a very indifferent demand of lower qualities, unlike what we see in the case of 20s and more so in the case of 10s.[11]

The manipulation of mixings and the changing of lines of production necessarily registered an effect throughout the weaving process. Winding for the warp beam or the weft shuttle for dyeing and mercerizing, affected the supply to the subsequent processes. The amount and nature of sizing required depended upon the quality of the yarn. By passing the yarn evenly through the sizing mixture, it was given the strength and resilience to withstand the friction to which it would be subjected on the loom. The propensity of the yarn to break on the loom depended to a large extent on the quality of sizing. The occupation was skilled and valued, but it was also extremely unhealthy. Drawing-in was another vital process for weavers when sized yarn was passed through the healds and reeds before the warping beam was sent to the loom. It demanded enormous manual dexterity and was strenuous on the eyes as each thread had to be passed 'through the eyes of a heald according to the order of drafting and through the dent of the reed'.[12] When patterns had to be woven, drawing-in could be an extremely complicated process. Moreover, the quality and accuracy of the work was vital to the weaving process, for errors at this stage often resulted in the weaving of defective cloth.

In weaving, the type of cloth being produced affected the nature and pattern of the weave, the setting of the healds, the number of picks per inch and the reed space. Dobby and jacquard looms were employed for the weaving of patterns and borders. Cloth had to be woven not only according to style but also according to width so that changes in patterns of production and the flow of orders could necessitate the use of wide looms for narrower widths of cloth.[13]

[10] *Ibid.*, p. 5.
[11] *Ibid.*, p. 10.
[12] Shah, 'Labour Recruitment and Turnover', p. 43.
[13] Proceedings of the TLIC, Interim Inquiry, Oral Evidence, Mr A.W. Pryde, Labour Officer to the Government of Bombay, File 42, pp. 457–58, MSA.

The number of picks per inch had to be increased for the heavier construction of cloth and usually signified a better quality. Finer counts of yarn had a lesser breaking strength and required a higher number of picks per inch which, in turn, meant that the loom was worked more slowly. In the weaving shed, fluctuations of the market and the composition of orders affected the allocation of looms and governed the organization of production. Inferior or unsuitable mixings, foreshortened processes, maladjusted machine speeds and disruptions in production flows affected outturn as well as the quality of the product. Attempts to increase productivity through speeding up the machines or driving the workforce were likely to undermine quality further and promote discontent. As one mill manager observed:

The impression created on looking at a frame spinning well with all ends up, producing the least amount of waste with full well shaped yarn bobbins is certainly better than that of a frame with many a broken end and the floor underneath covered with fluff and bondas, and piecers sweating and struggling to piece up the broken ends to the best of their ability.[14]

The consequence of improvisation in the use of machinery and raw materials to achieve changing production targets heightened the dependence of employers on the skill and resourcefulness of their workforce. This is illustrated by an incident which occurred in the 1870s when the Maneckjee Petit Mill attempted to fulfil an order for dhotis with red borders. Unaccountably small white specks began to appear on the border through the warp thread. 'Each jobber', it was said,

tried out a different method of handling the difficulty: some utilized bags containing soap water; others had rags dipped in coconut oil with the result that black spots instead of white appeared on the border; some others inserted paraffin rags between the warp kegs, while others applied rags dipped in water or oil to the vibrating shafts.[15]

Jobbers and supervisors with a talent for obtaining exceptional levels of production, deft weavers and dexterous piecers were often bought out by rival millowners. The official historian of the industry observed the existence of 'a spy system' as employers attempted to ferret out the trade secrets not only of their rivals but also of their own spinning and weaving masters. Indeed, spinning and weaving masters frequently kept trade secrets from their own men. According to Mehta,

A spinning master would not show to his junior colleagues, as a matter of normal practice, the composition of roller varnish. He would place obstacles as a trainee started to grasp the essentials of setting up a card. The cooking of the correct mixture of sizing materials was one of the most frequent and important items in the 'confidential' file.[16]

[14] A Retired Mill Manager, *Bombay Cotton Mills*, p. 5.
[15] Mehta, *Cotton Mills*, p. 108.
[16] *Ibid.*

It was precisely their dependence upon their workers' skills which led the millowners to complain frequently and vociferously about the inefficiency of their labour force. 'If a Lancashire girl could manage six looms', S.D. Saklatvala asked rhetorically in 1939 – and 'you know what type of girls you have in Lancashire' – and a Japanese girl, 'perhaps with a weaker physical condition manages 8 plain looms', how could 'a hefty strong Indian ... claim that he cannot manage more than two looms?'[17]

But by running their machines above the normal speeds, using equipment and inferior materials and employing makeshifts in the process of production, millowners increased the intensity of effort demanded of their workforce. According to Mr J.M. Moore of the Eastern Bedaux Company, consultants on scientific management, a ring sider in India had to deal with nine times as many breakages per 100 spindle hours as his counterpart in the United States, 'so that it shows', he argued, 'that whereas in India we are only tending two sides, still they may be doing in India almost as much work as they would be doing in America if they watched 8 or 10 sides'.[18] In other cases, employers preferred to employ a larger number of men to mind expensive equipment rather than risk damage. Thus, it was said, whereas one man watched six boilers in America, he managed only two in India. 'This is not because the man could not watch the water in six boilers, but rather because management is afraid to entrust the watching of six expensive boilers to one man.'[19]

The labour-intensive strategies of the millowners gave rise to widely varying conditions of work in the industry. In an industry characterized, since the mid nineteenth century, by spurts of mill construction and intermittent liquidations, the age and nature of the machinery varied widely.[20] These variations were accentuated by the millowners' practice of adapting or effecting minor adjustments to their machinery rather than replacing it altogether.[21] There were also considerable differences in the layout of mill buildings, which in turn affected the nature and arrangement of machinery and the patterns of labour deployment which could be adopted. Since the problems of raising capital were most serious in the initial stages of mill flotation, many employers economized on their building costs and subsequently found themselves extending new processes inside unsuitable spaces.[22] There were further variations, as we have seen, in

---

[17] Proceedings of the TLIC, Main Inquiry, Oral Evidence, BMOA, File 57-A, p. 225, MSA.

[18] *Ibid.*, Main Inquiry, Oral Evidence, Representatives of the Eastern Bedaux Company, File 77-C, pp. 4983–4, MSA.

[19] *Ibid.*, Main Inquiry, Oral Evidence, Representatives of the Eastern Bedaux Company, File 77-C, p. 4961, MSA.

[20] *Ibid.*, Main Inquiry, Oral Evidence, Mr F. Stones, Director of Messrs E.D. Sassoon and Company, File 72, p. 3613, MSA.

[21] *Ibid.*, Main Inquiry, Oral Evidence, Mr F. Stones, File 70, pp. 3469–70, MSA.

[22] Proceedings of the BSEC, Examination of Sir Joseph Kay, Managing Director, W.H. Brady and Company Ltd., I, 620–21, MSA.

the choice of the appropriate speed for their machines or the most suitable mixings of raw cotton for a particular count and quality of yarn or indeed of the mix of weft and warp yarn to be used in the manufacture of specific varieties of cloth. Numerous factors affected such decisions: the financial position of the mill, its stocks, its flow of orders, the custom and conventions of its workforce, and the range and composition of its output. They could not, as one millowner vehemently argued, simply be standardized for the entire industry. Thus,

The selection of cotton is special work, and different people have different views as to what is good cotton and what is bad and how it mixes. It is an extraordinary thing to suggest a standardization of mixings in an industry which produces such a great variety of goods.[23]

The diversity of conditions and working practices in the industry exacerbated by the labour-using trend of investment made it virtually impossible for the Millowners' Association to formulate general policies acceptable to its members. Although the Millowners' Association was founded in 1875, it remained a cockpit of rivalries, a loose coalition of diverse and conflicting interests. According to the Government Labour Officer in 1939, the Association's 'instructions are never read or understood by those persons who are connected with the mill administration'. Should the Association try 'to enforce their authority on any individual mill', it was likely that the millowner would consider his subscription not worth paying and resign his membership.[24] Indeed, the millowners were often embarrassed by the state of their organization. They were only too aware that their association was laid open to the same charge which they so frequently levelled against the trade unions: that it was unrepresentative and unable to obtain the acceptance of its members for the agreements which it might negotiate. Thus Fred Stones tried to argue before the Textile Labour Inquiry Committee that competitive wage-cutting by individual mills in the early 1930s, 'definitely was a concerted action ... It was a concerted decision that each mill should tackle it [wage cuts] separately' and then, when pressed harder that, perhaps, 'it may not have been concerted action, but it was a concerted agreement that concerted action did not pay'.[25]

Underlying the failure of the millowers to combine lay not only the diversity of conditions in the industry, but also the widespread practice of regulating production according to short-term fluctuations of demand.[26] 'There are many

[23] *Ibid.*, I, 639, MSA.
[24] Proceedings of the TLIC, Main Inquiry, Oral Evidence, Mr A.W. Pryde, Government Labour Officer, File 66, pp. 2479, 2483, MSA.
[25] *Ibid.*, Main Inquiry, Oral Evidence, Mr F. Stones, File 72, pp. 3624–5, MSA.
[26] The wider context of this strategy and its effects on the labour market as a whole are set out above, see chapters 2 and 3.

mills', declared the Chairman of the Millowners' Association in 1939, 'which either through their financial position or for reasons of general policy do not make heavily to stock. They do not subordinate their selling to their production. They make what they sell.'[27] This pattern of production arose in part from seasonal fluctuations, both in the supply and price of various types of raw cotton, and the demand for varieties of yarn and piecegoods.[28] But it was also subjected to numerous refinements according to the varieties of yarn and cloth manufactured.

For instance, in the case of fancy goods, printed cloth and varieties which required special processing, it was uneconomical to adjust output to the short-term fluctuations of the market. 'It is very difficult', explained one millowner, 'to swing off printed goods as you can swing off coarse grade cloth. If you swing off prints you have no use for that plant.'[29] Output was, therefore, geared to forward sales which enabled millowners to maintain relatively longer or at least more predictable runs of production.

Stockpiling was made easier in coarse goods, according to one millowner, by the fact that 'the only factor for sales is price and that the goods will sooner or later sell'.[30] But this was not always a viable option for all millowners. For various reasons, most millowners preferred to maintain a rapid turnover rather than produce to stock. For one thing, the amount of value added in coarse goods was relatively small. In the 1890s, it was estimated that dyeing and printing processes would increase the value of cotton piecegoods by between 30 and 70 per cent.[31] The rising price of particular varieties of cotton often 'prevented the spinners of ring 20s from making any margin of profit on their output'.[32] If prices fell, producers with large stocks on their hands found themselves undersold and were sometimes forced to liquidate them at ruinous prices.[33]

Before 1914, the industry was in this respect particularly vulnerable to trade fluctuations because it sold about 75 per cent of its yarn, exporting substantial quantities to the increasingly unstable Chinese market. Later, in the 1920s, when it attempted to consume its output of yarn in the production of cloth, for the

[27] Proceedings of the TLIC, Main Inquiry, Oral Evidence, Confidential Examination of the BMOA, File 78-C, p. 5338, MSA.
[28] Ibid., Main Inquiry, Oral Evidence, BMOA, File 57-A, p. 203, MSA.
[29] Ibid., Main Inquiry, Oral Evidence, BMOA, File 57-A, p. 101, MSA.
[30] Ibid., Main Inquiry, Oral Evidence, Confidential Examination of the BMOA, File 78-C, p. 5338, MSA.
[31] Papers Relating to the Indian Tariff Act, 1896, Parliamentary Papers LX (1896), 110–11; Bagchi, Private Investment, p. 230.
[32] A Retired Mill Manager, Bombay Cotton Mills, p. 6.
[33] Proceedings of the TLIC, Main Inquiry, Oral Evidence, Confidential Examination of the BMOA, File 78-C, p. 5359, MSA.

domestic market, it encountered a situation of over-supply.[34] 'My personal impression', Dharamsey Khatau told the Textile Labour Inquiry Committee in 1939, 'is that mills at the present time do not manufacture unless they have got orders, because prices have been falling.'[35] Moreover, as the industry diversified its production to finer counts of yarn and varieties of piecegoods in the 1930s, the composition of its output leaned increasingly towards goods which millowners preferred to produce to order. By 1939, grey cloth woven from yarn of counts under 20s was still considered 'a stable sort' but it did not 'by any means constitute the bulk of our production'.[36] Diversification into the production of higher counts had been the traditional response of the millowners to situations of falling prices and rising stocks before 1914. Rather than accumulate stocks when demand declined, mills concentrated on the spinning of counts of 30s. Indeed, the production of yarn of 30s counts was in the early twentieth century a 'makeshift ... only undertaken in the depressed periods of the yarn trade'. This had the advantage of reducing outturn, labour and raw-cotton requirements while avoiding the overhead costs of a partial or complete stoppage.[37]

It was integral to the strategy of regulating production to demand that the mills produced and sold a wide range of goods. Indeed, 'the range of piecegoods which enters India', it was observed in the 1920s, 'is probably greater than that imported by any other country in the world'.[38] Moreover, the quality of yarn of the same count or a particular type of cloth often varied widely.[39] During the 1930s, the industry diversified its output still further. In addition, the improvisation in machinery and materials which resulted from the continuous adjustment of production to fit the changing patterns of demand probably accentuated the variability of the quality of its products. Under these circumstances, it is not surprising that prices were affected by 'the reputation of the firm which makes the cloth or the merchant who sells it'.[40]

---

[34] Between 1918–19 and 1925–26, up-country mills increased their production of yarn by 115 million pounds and of cloth by almost 400 million pounds. At the very moment when domestic supply had increased so rapidly, the Bombay mills, switching their yarn to the manufacture of cloth, 'had to find an outlet in the home market for the equivalent of an extra 300 million yards of cloth'. The effect of this competition was accentuated by the fact that 'the up country mills manufacture goods which are mostly of the same qualities as those made in Bombay'. *Report of the ITB, 1927*, I, 101.

[35] Proceedings of the TLIC, Main Inquiry, Oral Evidence, Confidential Examination of the BMOA, File 78-C, pp. 5353–4, MSA.

[36] *Ibid.*, Main Inquiry, Oral Evidence, Confidential Examination of the BMOA, File 78-C, p. 5368, MSA.

[37] A Retired Mill Manager, *Bombay Cotton Mills*, p. 3.

[38] *Report of the ITB, 1927*, I, 48.

[39] *Ibid.*, I, 37, 48.

[40] *Ibid.*, I, 48.

The differentiation in the quality of their products and the fragmentation of demand might suggest that employers would specialize in particular lines of production and even combine to dominate sections of the market. However, the wide spectrum of goods produced by the industry actually militated against collusion and specialization. According to one millowner, the industry 'is dealing with the individual person's tastes which necessitates the production of different styles of cloth'. Its consequence was that 'the individual employer still thinks he can serve his customers better and more efficaciously than by working in combination'.[41]

This paradox is best explained in terms of the fact that individual segments of the market were often too small and the risks of adaptation and investment too great to support any substantial degree of specialization. Seasonal fluctuations, competitive influences and the changeability of taste meant that when the demand for certain varieties fell, others rose and when one line of production proved profitable, others failed. It was misleading

to regard the cotton textile industry as being composed of entirely separate branches according to the class and kind of cloth woven ... The immense variety of piecegoods required in the Indian market renders specialised production by Indian mills a matter of considerable difficulty.[42]

Rather than specializing in producing for particular segments of the market, therefore, most mills turned out a large number of counts of yarn and a wide range and variety of cloth. In the early twentieth century, the manager of a spinning mill argued that the best results in terms of quality and outturn

would be obtained by equipping three separate classes of spinning respectively 1's to 8's, 10's to 16's and 20's to 40's ... But commercially such arrangements do not appear to pay from the standpoint of a millowner or agent. He would try to spin from the coarsest 1's up to 30's or 40's from one mill on the same machinery.[43]

In the late 1920s, the Toyo Podar Mills spun counts of yarn ranging from 9s to 36s, and, on eleven different types of looms, produced between 30 and 37 varieties of cloth.[44] Many mills produced a wider range of varieties. As output was diversified in the 1930s, this range widened still further.[45] By 1934, it was observed, the mills 'produce the lowest as well as the highest [qualities] and

[41] Proceedings of the TLIC, Main Inquiry, Oral Evidence, BMOA, File 57-A, p. 103, MSA.
[42] Report of the ITB, 1932, p. 109.
[43] A Retired Mill Manager, Bombay Cotton Mills, pp. 1–2.
[44] Proceedings of the BSEC, Mr T. Sasakura, Managing Director, Toyo Podar Cotton Mills Ltd, I, 507–8, MSA.
[45] In 1928, S.A. Dange, the leader of the Girni Kamgar Union cited the case of one mill which produced 500 or 600 varieties of cloth. Proceedings of the BSEC, I, 287, MSA. Similarly, S.D. Saklatvala, a partner of Tata Sons, enumerating the difficulties which the Millowners' Association faced in regulating trade marks and quality numbers explained, 'it is extremely

weave a bewildering variety of cloth'.[46] As late as 1953, the Bombay mills still showed the greatest variation in the minimum and maximum counts of yarn spun in India.[47]

Most mills, therefore, competed, across the whole spectrum of the market. 'If a certain line is moving profitably', admitted one millowner, 'I am afraid we all pounce down on it. People will sell only these profitable styles, there is over-production, the price comes down, and there is a setback.'[48] The fact that a large number of producers competed in the same range of goods only served to intensify trade fluctuations.

The variable quality of output, the personalized character of demand, the extensive range of production and the attempts to regulate production to constantly changing market conditions intensified the degree of competition between mills. Nothing illustrated the intensity of competition better than the attempts by millowners to poach the trade marks of their rivals.[49] Each mill stamped its label on every piece which it manufactured, and usually added a trade number to indicate the quality of the cloth. In some cases, the trade numbers 'got very famous in certain markets, and these goods were identified with the goods of a particular make'. In their turn, piecegoods dealers began to place their order according to trade numbers, by which they 'meant the number as used by that particular mill'. Rival millowners, their commission agents and dealers, copied these numbers in the hope of replacing the established products in particular markets with their own goods. The poaching of trade marks resulted in acrimonious conflicts and even legal battles between the millowners.[50]

Apart from copying numbers and trade marks, mills attempted to increase their profit margins or indeed undercut their rivals by reducing the quality of the cloth while maintaining its original number.[51] Underlying this tendency to

difficult to use five or six digits on a cloth of small width'. Some mills required a thousand numbers not because they produced a thousand varieties, but because each variety could have different widths and would therefore need different numbers. *Ibid.*, I, 605, MSA.

[46] Labour Office, Bombay, *Report on Wages and Unemployment in the Bombay Cotton Textile Industry* (Bombay, 1934), pp. 43–4.

[47] Mehta, *Cotton Mills*, Tables E (I)–(XII), pp. 250–63. See table 27.

[48] Proceedings of the TLIC, Main Inquiry, Oral Evidence, BMOA, File 57-A, p. 101, MSA.

[49] Secretary, BMOA to Secretary, GOI, Commerce, no. 1446/131, 21 August 1928, Proceedings of the BSEC, I, 158, MSA.

[50] Proceedings of the BSEC, I, 601–6, MSA. The regulation of trade marks and labels remained one of the most complex and persistent problems which the BMOA encountered between the wars, as their annual reports and minute books testify.

[51] 'Our investigation showed', reported the Tariff Board in 1927, 'that goods bearing the same number and trade mark have in some cases showed a marked reduction in quality from year to year even when made by the same mill. This reduction is sometimes secured by a reduction in the number of ends or picks per inch, sometimes by an alteration in the counts of yarn used and sometimes by an alteration in either width or length, but as a general rule, the reduction in weight has been brought about by a combination of two or more of these methods.' *Report of the ITB, 1927*, I, 151.

Table 27. *Correlation between Bombay mills grouped according to the range of minimum and maximum counts spun in 1953*

Maximum / Minimum	26s–30s	31s–40s	41s–50s	51s–60s	61s–70s	71s–80s	81s–100s	101s and over	Total	Percentage	Cumulative percentage
1s– 5s	1	2	2	5	1	2	1	2	16	30.2	–
6s–10s	–	6	1	4	–	3	–	–	14	26.4	56.6
11s–15s	1	3	1	3	–	3	–	–	11	20.7	77.3
16s–20s	–	3	–	–	–	3	–	–	6	11.3	88.6
21s–25s	–	–	–	–	–	–	–	–	–	–	88.6
26s–30s	–	1	1	–	–	–	–	–	2	3.8	92.4
31s–40s	–	–	–	–	–	1	1	–	2	3.8	96.2
41s and over	–	–	–	–	–	1	1	–	2	3.7	99.9
Total	2	15	5	12	1	13	3	2	53		
Percentage	3.8	28.3	9.4	22.6	1.9	24.5	5.7	3.7			
Cumulative percentage	..	32.1	41.5	64.1	66.0	90.5	96.2	99.9			

Source: Mehta, *Cotton Mills*, Table E (IV), p. 254.

manipulate the numbers and reduce the quality of cloth lay a sharp competitive edge:

Commission agents, in order to compete with goods already established in the market, have obtained from the mills for which they act similar goods but of slightly lower quality which they have placed on the market at a lower rate. The mill which was first to manufacture the particular quality lowers its quality to enable it to hold its own and so the process goes on.[52]

These practices necessarily served to increase the importance of the mill's reputation to the consumer.

Moreover, the methods, and indeed the limitations of industrial finance meant that mills were often under pressure to sell their goods and maintain a rapid rate of turnover rather than lock up their capital in unsold stocks. In the late 1930s, the cost of 1,000 bales of cloth in stock was estimated at Rs. 3 lakhs. Only a very large, successful or especially efficiently managed mill could carry such large quantities of stocks.[53] Whereas capital was scarce and difficult to mobilize, machinery was expensive and required a high rate of amortization. Few mills were able to raise enough paid-up capital to meet the costs of their block investments. Thus, a part of their fixed costs and the whole of their working expenditure had to be met through the fluctuating supply of capital in the money-market. As a result, the Bombay mills were invariably saddled with high interest charges. Conversely, it was essential to return high dividends in order to gain public confidence and attract investment. 'You can only attract capital into the industry', one millowner observed, 'by giving investors a chance of realising high dividends. By restricting dividends, you won't achieve the rapid industrial development India wants and needs'.[54] The contradictory pressures of writing down capital in large amounts and paying high dividends, while, in addition, bearing heavy interest charges, accentuated the need to maintain a rapid turnover.

The financial practices of the industry, determined by the inadequacy of banking services, served to encourage business strategies predicated upon the regulation of production to the short-term fluctuations of demand. The need to rely upon the money-market and upon short-term credit for a proportion of their fixed capital and the whole of their working costs rendered the financial structure of most mills extremely precarious. To meet these costs, mills depended upon short-term deposits for a period of six months or a year and advances from banks in the form of cash credits or loans.[55] But banking practices

---

[52] *Ibid.*, I, 151. See also Proceedings of the BSEC, I, 606, MSA.
[53] Proceedings of the TLIC, Main Inquiry, Oral Evidence, Confidential Examination of the BMOA, File 78-C, p. 5354, MSA.
[54] *Ibid.*, Main Inquiry, Oral Evidence, BMOA, File 57-A, p. 111, MSA.
[55] *Report of the ITB, 1927*, I, 90–2; *Report of the ITB, 1932*, pp. 82–4.

were inadequately geared to industrial need. For instance, mills had no access to bills of exchange which might enable them to cover their supplies of cotton or stores for a period of time and thus to keep control over necessary supplies without having to lock up capital. On the contrary, Indian mills had to provide ready cash for their purchases.

Most mills were able to raise a substantial proportion of their needs in the form of advances from the commercial banks. But since banks were reluctant to lend in excess of the liquid assets of a mill, millowners had to turn to other informal sources of credit for about 25 to 30 per cent of their requirements.[56] On the other hand, such facilities as were offered by the commercial banks could not be fully exploited by the mills,

owing to their objection to hypothecate goods to the banks on the grounds that this involves visible control by the banks which would lower their standing in the eyes of their creditor and of the investing public and thus increase the difficulty of obtaining fixed deposits.[57]

These structural problems of industrial finance were brought sharply into focus when prices fell and markets slumped. In times of depression, most mills struggled to obtain short-term deposits. Yet it was precisely at such times when stocks mounted, that additional finance was required to service them and the millowners' need for short-term deposits became most urgent.[58] Similarly, when prices fell commercial banks called on the mills to reduce their credit or increase their securities, at the very point at which their value had deteriorated. The demand for the immediate repayment of bank loans, like the withdrawal of short-term deposits, often resulted in forced sales. The 'weaker mills' in particular 'had perforce to liquidate their stocks at prices which contribute to force down the level of the whole industry'.[59] The working costs of a mill could be substantially reduced by regulating production to demand, for this facilitated the maintenance of a rapid turnover, which in turn enabled employers to meet their financial obligations.

[56] Report of the ITB, 1927, I, 91.
[57] Ibid., I, 92.
[58] The onset of the depression was marked by a large-scale withdrawal of public deposits from the mills. Between 1930 and 1937, the volume of deposits invested in the mills fell by 55 per cent. See Mehta, Cotton Mills, p. 178. These had to be made up by loans provided by the managing agents. The specialist function of the managing agent was to arrange finance for the mills. Already in 1931, they provided 21 per cent of the total capital of the Bombay mills. In addition, they guaranteed bank loans, mobilized capital through the sale of shares on the strength of their reputation and influence and attracted public deposits which depended 'partly on the earning capacity of the company and partly on the standing and reputation of the managing agent'. In addition, the managing agent held 'a considerable part of the share capital, in several cases the greater part of it'. Report of the ITB, 1932, pp. 82–3.
[59] Report of the ITB, 1927, I, 91–2.

It is possible that many of the structural weaknesses of the industry could have been overcome by combined action. Ostensibly, collusion may have enabled millowners to iron out the fluctuations of demand or to shore up falling prices. Yet despite the apparent concentration of ownership,[60] the tendencies towards combination or collusion were weak. Early in 1930, an attempt was made to amalgamate thirty-four mills which operated at the time under seven managing agencies. Among its objectives was the standardization of output, the specialization of production and co-ordination in the purchase of cotton, machinery and stores, and the sale of yarn and cloth. Factors which had historically served to intensify the competition among the mills in Bombay ultimately destroyed this scheme. The extent of their debts meant that some agents could not hand over their mills to the merger corporation at the valuations fixed. The now-familiar problems of financing their working expenses as well as the burden of the costs of merger itself served as further obstacles to amalgamation.[61]

Underlying the failure of the scheme lay the fact that 'the Bombay cotton textile industry is imbued with the spirit of individualism' and that 'in any scheme of amalgamation the initiative which the management of an independent unit of production enjoys is liable to be impaired and the flexibility of operations which is valuable for successful working is often lost'.[62] The following year the largest group of mills in Bombay, managed by Currimbhoy Ebrahim and Sons, was taken into liquidation, after it had for several years grappled with the legacy of its over-capitalization in the post-war boom.[63] The concentration of ownership in the industry was progressively diluted in the 1930s. The failure of the largest group of mills in Bombay induced doubts about the viability and virtues of large-scale organization. 'Better results are likely to be attained', the Tariff Board declared in 1932, 'by economies resulting from close personal attention than from large-scale production or management.'[64]

---

[60] In 1927, the two largest managing agents, E.D. Sassoon and Co. and Currimbhoy Ebrahim, between them, accounted for twenty-three out of eighty-three mills in Bombay, roughly a third of the industry's capacity in spindles and looms and about half of its total paid-up capital. Calculated from *Report of the ITB, 1927*, I, Appendix XII, 258; *BMOA, Annual Reports*, 'Statement of Cotton Spinning and Weaving Mills in India'.

[61] *Report of the ITB, 1932*, p. 75.

[62] *Report of the TLIC*, II, 213.

[63] The details of its over-capitalization may be found in *BMOA, Annual Reports*, 'Statement of Cotton Spinning and Weaving Mills in India'. More concisely, see the figures provided for the Bradbury, Madhorao Scindhia, Kasturchand and Mathuradas Mills in *Report of the ITB, 1927*, I, 77–84, especially Table XLIII, 77. The financial condition of the group was the underlying factor in the position which Sir Fazulbhoy Currimbhoy adopted during the mid 1920s. In brief, he opposed the adoption of either short time or wage cuts as both these courses carried the risk of stoppage through industrial action. BMOA, Minute Books, Proceedings of the Fortnightly Meeting of the Committee of the BMOA, 18 May 1925, and General Meeting of the Members of the BMOA, 27 July 1925, Office of the BMOA.

[64] *Report of the ITB, 1932*, p. 89.

It is not intended to suggest the millowners abjured combination altogether.[65] But the nature and conditions of the industry made combined action even of a more limited kind extremely difficult. The variations in the conditions, types and servicing needs of machinery rendered the combined purchase of stores and spare parts useless. Since they produced to order, the millowners' requirements of raw cotton varied and in any case few millowners agreed about the best varieties of raw cotton or their optimum mixings. The personalized character of demand reduced the incentive to combine in the matter of sales. Finally, 'the heterogeneous character of the demand for cotton piecegoods in India' complicated the possibilities of specialization.[66]

The difficulties of price fixing and combined action arose also in part from causes larger than the internal structure and organization of the industry. Falling prices, as the Secretary of the Millowners' Association argued in 1939, 'cannot be checked by reducing production in Bombay alone ... and it might not be checked even if the whole of India reduced production'.[67] The uneven performance and regional diversity of the industry posed a major problem. In the early 1920s, it was said that the fact that 'the depression has not been felt so acutely in up country centres as it has been in Bombay ... rendered combined or even general action in regard to curtailment of production impossible'.[68] Indeed, any initiative taken in Bombay alone 'would only have accentuated the competition of up-country mills'.[69] It has already been shown, moreover, that these up-country centres of the industry continued to expand during the depression of the 1930s.

What ultimately devastated attempts at collusion was the intensity of foreign, and especially Japanese, competition in the absence of effective tariff policies. The force of foreign competition was felt most keenly in the medium to fine counts of yarn and varieties of piecegoods. Finer goods were in India almost exclusively produced in Bombay and Ahmedabad. Mills in these two centres failed to effect limited combinations to fix prices and dominate the market in these lines of production largely because it was in medium and fine qualities that foreign competition was most intensely felt. The Japanese mills, as we have seen, could place these goods on the Indian market at prices lower than their manufacturing cost in an efficient Indian mill.[70] Tariff duties after 1930 did not

[65] The most notable cases of combined action were taken in order to reduce the cost of power, supplied by the Tata Hydro-Electric Agencies, and to establish an insurance scheme to deal with workmen's compensation for accident and injury. *Report of the TLIC*, II, 214.
[66] *Report of the ITB, 1932*, p. 89.
[67] Proceedings of the TLIC, Main Inquiry, Oral Evidence, Confidential Examination of the BMOA, File 78-C, p. 5345, MSA.
[68] *Report of the ITB, 1927*, I, 18, 100–2.
[69] *Ibid.*, I, 109.
[70] *Ibid.*, I, 39, 50.

provide a lasting solution. 'The competitive power of Japan', it was reported in the early 1930s, 'has been exerted in a sufficiently flexible manner to meet effectively the adverse influence of both higher duties and a higher exchange rate.'[71] The 'adaptability' of Japanese industry had already been demonstrated when, following the curtailment of Bombay's output during the general strikes of 1928–9, Japanese imports increased by 42 per cent, while the remaining centres of Indian industry were only able to increase their production by a mere 18 per cent to supply the deficiency created by Bombay's withdrawal. There was little doubt, during the 1930s, that

if a serious decline in the production of Bombay mills occurs ... the immediate result will be a substantial increase in imports, especially from Japan. Indian mills are not in a position to adapt the scale of their production to the varying requirements of the market with the flexibility and quickness which characterise the Japanese industry.[72]

The capricious exigencies of finance required the Bombay millowners to maintain a delicate balance between several sets of contradictory pressures. They had to reconcile the difficulties of mobilizing working capital with the expense of fixed capital. By producing to stock, they could economize on their fixed costs. But high interest charges and the problems of obtaining short-term credit especially when their market slumped forced them to maintain a rapid turnover. If the latter strategy was fostered by the lack of working capital, the consequence of varying production levels to fit fluctuations in demand could result in the under-utilization of machinery and, therefore, increased working costs. To reap the full benefit of machinery, it was preferable to set up long runs of standardized output. Yet under the existing market conditions, this was effectively impossible. Although the high costs of capital suggested the value of the more intensive use of machinery, the Bombay millowners were also faced in the slump of the 1920s with rising wage costs. It was precisely because capital was expensive that their response to the slump lay in attempts to cheapen the cost of labour, by cutting wages, varying levels of employment and increasing workloads. It was in this context that the labour force in the textile industry was formed.

The structure of authority

The strategy of regulating production to demand gave rise to fluctuating levels of employment. It also shaped the deployment of labour, the structure of authority and the organization of work. The jobber was a pivotal figure in the

[71] *Report of the Indian Tariff Board Regarding the Grant of Additional Protection to the Cotton Textile Industry* (Calcutta, 1932), p. 7.
[72] *Report of the ITB, 1932*, p. 118.

organization of work and in particular, the enforcement of labour discipline in the cotton mills. The specificities of the jobber system were shaped by the organization of the cotton-textile industry. First, fluctuations in the demand for labour, which were in turn determined by the short-term fluctuations of the market, gave rise to systems of recruitment which enabled mills to lay workers off or hire extra hands according to need. Second, since cheap labour was the chief comparative advantage of the industry, the jobber's role as an agent of discipline acquired considerable importance. As the Bombay mills lost this advantage in the inter-war period and were forced to squeeze their operational costs, the jobbers were subjected to several contradictory pressures. They were increasingly called upon to prevent wages rising and yet attract workers, to enforce wage cuts in the face of growing industrial action and to maintain the efficiency and discipline of the labour force despite the fluctuations of employment.

The demand for labour did not simply vary with the rates of absenteeism. Rather, it was determined by the short-term fluctuations of raw cotton, the prices and the pattern of demand for yarn and cloth, the accumulation of stocks and the changing supply of credit. Consequently, the industry employed a significant proportion of casual labour. By the mid 1930s, it was estimated, the number of badlis used amounted to about 28 per cent of the average daily employment of the industry.[73] The Secretary of the Millowners' Association estimated in 1938 that the industry required about 20,000 casual workers each day or about one-sixth of the average number employed daily in that year.[74] Another survey, made in the late 1930s, based upon the musters and attendance records of various mills, estimated that two badlis had to be kept ready for every worker employed over a period of a month and eight over a whole year.[75]

The importance of the jobber's recruiting function derived from the extensive use of casual labour in the industry. However, as the reserve supplies of labour expanded and became more readily available at the mill gates, the importance of the jobber's recruiting function declined. 'As the supply of labour has been greater than the demand for a considerable time past', reported the Labour Office in 1934, 'the agency of the jobbers is not much in requisition today.'[76] But if their role in the recruitment of labour became less crucial, the pressure upon jobbers as agents of discipline and control increased. In addition, some jobbers also fulfilled various technical functions. As the jobber was vital to the

---

[73] Labour Office, Bombay, *Report on Wages ... in the Textile Industries, General Wage Census, Part I – Perennial Factories, Third Report*, p. 20.
[74] Proceedings of the TLIC, Main Inquiry, Oral Evidence, BMOA, File File 57-A, p. 208, MSA.
[75] Shah, 'Labour Recruitment and Turnover', p. 111.
[76] Labour Office, Bombay, *Report on Wages ... the Textile Industries, General Wage Census, Part I, Third Report*, p. 16.

maintenance of discipline, it was logical to make him responsible for the care of the machinery as well. To extract the maximum production from both men and machines constituted the crux of the problem of labour discipline.

Furthermore, the recruiting, technical and disciplinary functions of the jobber came to be intimately interconnected. It was in order to enable him to control labour effectively that extensive powers for hiring and firing workers were delegated to the jobber, allowing him the authority to decide whom he would choose to control. The jobber played an important role in the allotment of work, the distribution of raw materials and machinery and the administration of fines.[77] His discretion could determine which men worked with the most efficient machinery and the best raw materials. He influenced the distribution of workloads, the calculation of wages and the levying of fines.

The fulcrum of the jobber's power lay in the use of casual labour. Through their orchestration of labour supply, jobbers inflated and reduced the size of the casual labour force and contributed to the creation of a permanent army of workers in possession of some skill and experience of work in the industry.[78] But the jobbers, like the millowners, were not simply free to manipulate labour at will. Casual hiring may have permitted firms considerable flexibility in choosing their production targets, but it was also expected of the jobber, and sometimes directly in his interests, to maintain optimum levels of attendance. It was, therefore, essential for him to maintain connections beyond the workplace to recruit badlis of whose skill and ability he was aware, and over whom he possessed some measure of influence. As the pressure of the millowners to increase productivity grew, jobbers had to be mindful of the quality of the badlis they employed. The demands of efficiency, the need to maintain the unity of the workforce and a variety of social pressures exercised by their clients exerted important controls upon the jobbers' arbitrary manipulation of the casual workforce.

Recruitment through the jobber had several further advantages for the employer. It reinforced social identities which had little to do with the workplace by creating vertical loyalties which millowners could utilize to their own advantage. Vertical loyalties thus generated proved a basis for the organization of strike-breaking by the millowners. While it took time to build up a safe jobber network, and managers did not relish the frequent reshuffling of their jobbers, the system itself made it possible to replace sizeable sections of their workforce. Workers who went on strike without their jobber could be dismissed. Jobbers who stopped work along with their men could be replaced by a rival jobber and

---

[77] Labour Office, Bombay, *Report on an Enquiry into the Deductions from Wages or Payments in Respect of Fines* (Bombay, 1928).
[78] *RCLI, Evidence, Bombay Presidency*, M.S. Bhumgara, I, i, 501.

the loss of their position at work could seriously diminish their influence outside. Furthermore, through the jobber system, the cultural diversity of the workers was brought into the workplace. These factors made the jobber system an impressive bulwark against combination and a useful mechanism for strike-breaking. 'In times of strikes', the Bombay Textile Labour Union complained, 'these men are seen running about from locality to locality in the city to find out labour to break the strikes ... In times of strikes, they play the role of strike breakers by dividing the ranks of the workers.'[79]

The authority of the jobber in the cotton-textile industry was neither undifferentiated nor uncontested. Above all, it was not monolithic. There were, in other words, several kinds of jobbers and the extent and nature of their power varied. It was the head jobber who commanded the most decisive authority in the workplace – indeed over assistant and line jobbers as well – and who was often able to develop impressive networks of influence in the neighbourhood.

Moreover, it has already been suggested that the jobber's influence in the textile industry varied according to the department which he supervised. In many of the preparatory processes, jobbers recruited and supervised unskilled labour. Their powers of hiring and firing gave them considerable power over the team of workers in their charge, but their supervision was sometimes less crucial to the profits of the mill than jobbers in the spinning and weaving sections. Even among the preparatory processes there were important differences in the status and authority of the jobber. Good carding was essential to the quality of spinning. Frequent changes in production often called for resourcefulness and improvisation from the jobber and his men in the card room, whereas the workers in the mixing and blow rooms performed tasks more clearly directed by the managers and departmental heads.[80] Jobbers in the preparatory departments might wield greater power over the unskilled workers they supervised but commanded less influence in the mill, whether in the structure of its management or among the workers.

Under the head jobber came the line jobber who supervised particular production processes. They were responsible for a certain series or combination of machines in each department. For instance, in the blow room, it consisted of a line of exhaust, intermediate and finisher scutchers; in the card room, a given number of cards and preparations; in spinning, a series of spindles or sometimes a set of frames; and in weaving between thirty-six and forty-four looms.[81] Line

[79] Ibid., BTLU, I, i, 296–7; for examples of strikes led by the BTLU being broken by the action of the jobbers, see ibid., I, i, 298–9.
[80] Proceedings of the BSEC, I, 670, 678–9 and, ibid., II, 695, MSA; A Retired Mill Manager, Bombay Cotton Mills, pp. 13–6.
[81] Proceedings of the BSEC, I, 675; II, 695, 731–3, 797–8, 814–7, 819–28, MSA; Report of the TLIC, II, 44.

jobbers were expected to direct and supervise the workers under their charge, to effect minor repairs to the machinery, to oversee its maintenance, and to ensure that the flows of production were maintained. Their function was primarily 'to drive men'.[82] In the weaving shed, where piece rates predominated, they were paid according to the output of their team in order to ensure that they both maintained their looms properly and extracted maximum efficiency from their workers.[83]

There were other jobbers who supervised specific occupational groups, such as the flat grinders and strippers in the card room, the doffers and tarwallas in spinning and the creel boys of the warping department.[84] Similarly, fancy jobbers supervised the work of weavers who operated high shaft dobby or jacquard looms. Unlike the line jobbers in the weaving shed, the fancy jobbers were paid according to time while the weavers they supervised were remunerated by results.[85] The nature of the jobbers' influence also varied with the tasks they performed. Line jobbers exerted their authority over a small team of workers whom they supervised directly. Fancy jobbers who supervised weavers operating dobby looms dispersed through the mill were thought to have the opportunity to develop more extensive contacts and a wider network of influence within the workforce. G.L. Kandalkar, the President of the Girni Kamgar Union in the early 1930s, had been, for instance, a fancy jobber in the Simplex Mills.

But it is not intended to suggest that the jobbers' influence derived simply from the nature of their work. It has sometimes been argued that line jobbers and their teams of workers had a greater identity of interest with each other since they were paid on the same basis, whereas jobbers on fixed wages were 'less responsive to the feelings of the ordinary worker and correspondingly closer to the managerial staff'.[86] But the interdependence of the line jobber and his team could also provoke antagonism between them. Since the jobber was responsible for repairs, the maintenance of machinery and the distribution of raw materials, dissatisfaction with his mechanical skill, his ability to procure the best yarn or the most paying orders formed important sources of tension within jobber gangs. Since it was in the interests of the line jobbers to keep the machines running for as long as possible, they might stop the looms for repairs or other necessary adjustments as rarely as possible, or else speed up the looms unduly. If cloth was damaged as a consequence, they could attempt to recover lost wages by levying fines on the weavers they

---

[82] Proceedings of the BSEC, II, 732–3, MSA.
[83] Report of the TLIC, II, 44.
[84] Report of the BSEC, I, 130–4.
[85] Report of the TLIC, II, 44, 37–40.
[86] Newman, Workers and Unions, p. 29.

supervised.[87] The cause of damaged cloth remained a perennial bone of contention. Thus, the Government Labour Officer said in 1939 that the age of the machinery was a less frequent grievance among pieceworkers than 'complaints that the jobbers do not attend to the machinery properly when it requires attention and that therefore they are losing their earnings, that the cloth is damaged, etc.'.[88] Conversely, absenteeism, spoiling cloth and the slowing down of production by weavers could also act as effective checks on the arbitrary exercise of the jobber's power.[89]

The jobber's influence also varied according to the skill and bargaining position of the group of workers which he supervised. Weavers, for instance, were relatively more independent of his control than spinners or carders. Since the cloth trade became increasingly the dynamic sector of the industry, there was usually a steady demand for good weavers. As a result they were better placed than most other occupational groups to demand and sometimes to obtain the necessary quality of raw materials and working conditions. 'The weavers who sustain loss owing to defective machinery and bad yarn', it was observed, 'are always on the look-out for better jobs.'[90]

Most groups of workers recognized that the departure or the dismissal of their jobber unsettled their conditions of employment. The new jobber might bring in his own friends and dependants. He could favour them with promotion, the best raw materials and machinery, the most paying varieties or the least arduous tasks. Indeed, jobbers wary of the problems of disciplining workers they did not know were sometimes equally anxious to employ men with whom they were directly connected. But weavers remained an exception. According to the manager of the Khatau Makanji Mills, they were often 'very reluctant to leave a mill where they may have worked for a number of years in spite of a change of their jobbers'.[91] Similarly, nearly a decade later, Fred Stones observed that weavers after being laid off sought to return to the same loom with which they had worked before. 'An Indian worker', declared Mr Stones,

is a conservative. Suppose we stop a shift. The worker will go away leaving a post card

---

[87] Clearly, there were controls on the system of fines; in some cases they had to be accounted for or sanctioned by the supervisory staff. But these were precisely the areas of labour management in which millowners and managers intervened as little as possible. Labour Office, Bombay, *Report on … Deductions from Wages … in Respect of Fines.*

[88] Proceedings of the TLIC, Main Inquiry, Oral Evidence, Mr A.W. Pryde, Government Labour Officer, File 66, p. 2334, MSA.

[89] Proceedings of the BSEC, I, 494, MSA; *Report of the IFLC*, I, 61; *RCLI, Evidence, Bombay Presidency*, Seth Ambalal Sarabhai, I, ii, 114; *BMOA, Annual Report 1938*, p. 53.

[90] *RCLI, Evidence, Bombay Presidency*, Mrs K. Wagh, Senior Lady Investigator, Labour Office, Bombay, I, i, 193.

[91] *Ibid.*, Mr M.S. Bhumgara, I, i, 502.

with his address. But when he comes back, he does not go to a jobber or a weaver. He wants a particular loom. He does not roam about for work.[92]

Behind this apparent conservatism lay sound material calculation, for as one mill manager explained,

The man who, by dint of his steady application to his machine for a number of years, has thoroughly mastered it, knows it and understands it perfectly well. In a way, he has learnt to understand his machine's many and odd eccentricities and know how to get the most and the best work out of it.[93]

Put on to a new machine, the weaver was also liable to find his earnings reduced. The fact that weavers preferred to stay with their looms rather than move with their jobber suggests not only that they were able to appropriate a measure of control over their own working conditions but also that they were confident of their ability to defend it against new jobbers. Furthermore, unlike any other occupational group, weavers were able to appropriate some control in the most crucial domain of the jobber's power: the appointment of casual workers. Weavers nominated their own badlis. Even when they stayed away from the mill, they were regarded as having attended so long as their badlis worked their looms in their absence. Moreover, despite their absence, they were paid 'the full earnings due on the actual production of the looms' allotted to them, and in turn, they were expected to pay their badlis out of their own wages.[94] Consequently, weavers were able to construct on these foundations their own systems of patronage within the mill. With many strategic areas of their control pared down and challenged, weaving jobbers had to remain responsive to the needs of the workers they supervised or else risk their desertion to rivals. If their domination was thus checked and modified by the resistance of the weavers, jobbers who nonetheless could hold the workforce together, maintain discipline and efficiency and obtain high levels of production commanded the respect and the ear of mill managers. Successful head jobbers in the weaving shed often cut impressive figures in the mill as well as the neighbourhood.

The nature and extent of the jobbers' power varied not only according to their role in the process of production but also from mill to mill. In an industry characterized by the diversity of its working conditions and wages, workers tried to move into neighbouring mills which either paid higher wages, or were known to have better working conditions. Thus, it was said, workers preferred to be employed in mills where they could 'earn higher wages at the end of the

---

[92] Proceedings of the TLIC, Main Inquiry, Oral Evidence, Mr F. Stones, Director, Messrs. E.D. Sassoon and Co. Ltd., File 70, p. 3534, MSA.

[93] *RCLI, Evidence, Bombay Presidency*, Mr M.S. Bhumgara, I, i, 501.

[94] Labour Office, Bombay, *Report on Wages … in the Textile Industries. General Wage Census. Part I, Third Report*, p. 19.

month with the same exertion'. On the other hand, mills known for their 'used-up machinery and bad material ... do not get a supply of steady workmen'. In the less desirable mills,

the jobbers resort to various methods to have a sufficient number of workmen at their beck and call e.g. by advancing them money or standing surety for them at the moneylender's. This enables them to gain a hold over the men who in their turn prefer to have such relations with the jobbers, knowing that the latter being interested in their employment for the recovery of the loans advanced by or through them would connive at irregularities and never sack them.[95]

Thus, jobbers who found their position undermined by poor working conditions or by the skill and bargaining strength of their subordinates sought to bring in the social connections of the neighbourhood to reassert their control in the workplace.

It should be clear that the jobbers were not a homogeneous body. Their functions and their power were differentiated. All jobbers did not wield the same degree of influence within the managerial structure of the industry; some were more vulnerable than others to the pressures exerted by the workforce. Historians have exaggerated the uniformity of the jobbers' role and have tended to assume that the structure of authority at work was effectively concentrated in their hands. But the differences in the nature and extent of the jobbers' power throughout the industry, between mills and according to their function in the process of production, suggests rather that authority was diffused and lodged at various levels within the workforce and among the supervisory and managerial ranks. This is clarified by a closer examination of alternative locations of power and influence with the workplace.

Managing agents delegated large powers in the daily organization of production to the mill manager and his staff. It was the manager's responsibility to co-ordinate the operations of the various departments of a mill, and changing market conditions often called for numerous daily adjustments in the organization of production. The manager often made decisions about the mixings to be employed and the allocation of sets of machines to particular lines of production. It was not simply that numerous adjustments might have to be made in the processes of production but also that a considerable degree of improvisation was required to adapt machines, their speed and quality and the aptitudes of the workforce to the changing production targets. Obviously, these signified crucial areas of decision-making which could affect the profitability as well as the working conditions of a mill.[96]

The manager was assisted in these functions by the heads of particular

[95] RCLI, Evidence, Bombay Presidency, The Social Service League, I, i, 432.
[96] A Retired Mill Manager, Bombay Cotton Mills.

departments: for instance, the carding, spinning and weaving masters. Like the manager, these officials were accountable to the agent for the organization of work and the performance of their departments. In turn, they were required to supervise the activities of the jobbers who worked under them. They impinged in various ways directly upon what historians have often identified as the exclusive domain of the jobber. While mill managers selected the staff who worked under them, these departmental heads were often responsible for the recruitment or promotion of jobbers.[97] The Millowners' Association claimed in 1929 that 'operatives as a rule are not finally engaged by the jobber' and that 'the final selection and appointments are made by the heads of the department concerned'.[98] It is doubtful whether this was generally the case. The bulk of the evidence suggests that jobbers continued throughout the period to exercise the predominant influence over the recruitment of labour.[99] However, the carding, spinning and weaving masters, in overseeing the jobber's activities, checked his freedom and at least acted as an alternative source of authority and patronage. As the competitive position of the industry weakened and its labour costs rose in relation to those of its rivals, the jobber probably came under increasing pressure from his superior officers.

Moreover, the carding, spinning and weaving masters sometimes intervened directly in the recruitment of workers and even developed social and commercial interests in the neighbourhood. The Social Service League described the ways in which recruitment and dismissals orchestrated by mill officials encouraged bribery and corruption:

In times of severe unemployment the petty officials who have the power to appoint and dismiss workmen have the temptation to use it unjustly and arbitrarily. Vacancies caused through dismissals offer them opportunities to obtain fresh bribes from persons in need of employment … It is often complained in respect of certain departments of several mills and factories that the spoils are divided among all the officers of the department, and that the jobbers act as intermediaries between the officer who has the power to give employment and the persons who are willing to offer bribes for securing it.[100]

Furthermore, it was essential for jobbers to establish close connections with the supervisory and managerial ranks simply to safeguard their own positions in relation to the workforce. The efficacy of the jobber in his contradictory functions, of disciplining the workforce and yet coaxing them into higher levels of productivity, depended upon his ability to bargain for better conditions for

---

[97] *RCLI, Evidence, Bombay Presidency*, BMOA, I, i, 387; *ibid.*, M.S. Bhumgara, I, i, 503.

[98] *Ibid.*, BMOA, I, i, 386.

[99] Labour Office, Bombay, *Report on Wages … in the Textile Industries, General Wage Census, Part I, Third Report*, pp. 15–7; *Report of the TLIC*, II, 337–8; *RCLI, Evidence, Bombay Presidency*, Mr M.S. Bhumgara, I, i, 500.

[100] *Ibid.*, The Social Service League, I, i, 432.

his men. Heads of department were also interested in developing close connections with effective jobbers. When they changed mills, they sometimes took their jobbers away with them. It was said, for instance, that weaving masters, particularly concerned about the quality of sizing, often took the most able sizers with them from mill to mill.[101] Indeed, the cooking and mixture of sizing materials was said to be one of the most closely guarded secrets in the industry.[102] This was because the strength of the yarn and its ability to withstand the vibrations of the loom was largely determined by the quality of the sizing. Occasionally, it was even reported that the resignation or dismissal of a manager resulted in a complete change of staff, including department heads and jobbers.[103]

But it should not be supposed that the relationship between these levels of authority may be understood simply according to their position in the administrative hierarchy. It was not unknown for managing agents and proprietors to develop special relationships with jobbers and the lesser supervisory ranks in order to keep themselves informed about happenings on the shop floor. Indeed 'the thorough-going, regular spy system' which was developed in 'many leading companies' was intended not only to secure technical secrets but also to inform the agents about the daily problems and politics of the workplace.[104] No managing agent could afford to be the captive of his mill manager.

Furthermore, in so far as the managers and their subordinate staff were responsible for the organization of production, as well as the output and the performance of particular departments, there were important conflicts of interest between various levels of this managerial hierarchy. 'Many a time', one mill manager complained, 'managers, carders and spinners are taken to task by the millowners by a mere comparison of the production of such and such a mill with their own. No heed is paid to the peculiar circumstances in which each may be working.'[105]

Within the industry, many people had a vision of the independent manager or supervisor who would stand up to the agent and prevent the undue manipulation of men, machines and materials. 'Experienced and firm minded carders and managers would not consent', one manager declared, 'to work any drafts or hanks in the preparatory processes of rovings, as would a less independent man to gain a temporary good record from the millowners and agents.'[106] But

[101] Shah, 'Labour Recruitment and Turnover', p. 76.
[102] Mehta, Cotton Mills, p. 108.
[103] Report of the ITB, 1927, Evidence of Local Governments, Official Witnesses, Chambers of Commerce, Labour Organizations and Other Associations, Girni Kamgar Mahamandal, III, 570.
[104] Mehta, Cotton Mills, p. 110.
[105] A Retired Mill Manager, Bombay Cotton Mills, p. 7.
[106] Ibid., p. 18.

the independent manager was an elusive figure. As another manager observed,[107] managers and departmental heads believed that if they attempted to place the workpeople's case before the agents they themselves would incur the latter's displeasure. Faced with the pressure to match the productivity and profits of rival mills under difficult and changing conditions, managers imposed considerable demands upon their subordinates who in turn attempted to drive the workforce harder. The technical and disciplinary problems of mill management were intensified at every level. The failure to meet production targets or make adequate profits could send recriminations and blame through the entire structure. At such times, one manger said, 'Some mangers like to give the agents the idea that the mills are in a helpless state due to the workpeople's vagaries.'[108]

In addition to the jobbers and the supervisory staff, there were others who could develop their own networks of influence in the mills. For instance, the functions of timekeepers who maintained the attendance registers and musters, drew up lists of absentees and calculated the checked wages at the end of the month, impinged directly upon the hiring of badlis and, in the granting of leave and discharge passes, upon dismissal and absenteeism as well. Similarly, departmental clerks, who weighed or measured the output, checked its quality and calculated wages, could use the leverage so gained upon piece workers.[109]

This diffusion of power and influence in the mill occurred not only above the jobber within the hierarchy of the mill administration but within the ranks of the workforce as well. It has already been noted that semi-skilled and skilled groups of workers were able to wrest a measure of control over their own work from their supervisors. In addition, principal operatives in each process of production were assisted by a number of subordinate helpers. Thus, in the mixing and waste rooms, lattice feeders who put cotton on to machines which opened out the cotton fibre were helped by machine tenters or bale breakers; at times, frequently depending upon the layout of the mill, the former operative performed the latter function as well.[110] Similarly in the blow room, there were bardan pickers who 'sit down and pick up cotton stuck up on the wrappers of cotton bales',[111] or dropping carriers who carried waste, droppings and fly from the blow room to the willow which cleaned the droppings and separated the dirt from the cotton.[112] The role of helpers was yet more obvious in the spinning and weaving sections. Thus doffer boys and tarwallas worked under jobbers but directly as helpers for the ring sider.[113] Coolies were employed in the winding

[107] RCLI, Evidence, Bombay Presidency, Mr M.S. Bhumgara, I, i, 503.
[108] Ibid., Mr M.S. Bhumgara, I, i, 504.
[109] Ibid., BMOA, I, i, 388; ibid., Girni Kamgar Mahamandal, I, i, 456.
[110] Report of the BSEC (Bombay, 1929), I, 129; Proceedings of the BSEC, I, 673–4, MSA.
[111] Proceedings of the BSEC, II, 684, MSA.
[112] Ibid., II, 686–93, MSA.
[113] Ibid., II, 731, MSA.

department to carry baskets full of pirns to the weft and the warping machines.[114] Creel boys, like the doffers in spinning, removed and replaced bobbins on the warp machines.[115] In sizing and weaving there were numerous kinds of helpers, such as beam carriers, who had to move the heavy beams from the warping department and lift them into the creel of the sizing machine – or in the later process into the loom – and gaiters who arranged the beams and prepared them for sizing and weaving.[116] The number of helpers supplied was sometimes an issue of contention and source of dissatisfaction between operatives, jobbers and the spinning or weaving master. Moreover, in piece-work occupations, the efficiency of the helpers could affect the earnings of the operative. Although many of these helpers worked under a jobber, their work was necessarily supervised by the principal operative whom they assisted, creating for them a double structure of command and an alternative source of patronage.

Finally, the diffusion of power and patronage within the workforce was also manifested in the patterns of recruitment. Although the jobber exercised the predominant influence over recruitment, his selections were often determined by workers in his connection. In practice, a variety of factors influenced the recruitment of labour: 'personal acquaintance, introduction through one or another source, past obligations, friendship' being the 'questions which are generally considered'.[117] It has already been argued that workers migrated within the framework of their social ties.[118] Migrants sought the help of their relatives and friends in the city to find work. Thus, Dattaram found work as a warping boy in the Mathradas Mill through his father, who had worked as a weaver in the industry for thirty years, and 'with the assistance of a neighbour, a clerk'.[119] In the years which followed, he moved with the assistance of various friends, through a number of jobs both within and outside the industry. Govind Sanoo found work as a doffer in 1891 at the age of eleven through a relative who was a jobber in Bombay.[120] Dagdoo Hari found work in a mill through his brother-in-law who was a mukadam in an oil mill.[121] Anaji Shinde found work as a doffer boy through 'his brother-in-law's friend'.[122] The examples may be multiplied. They serve to show the numerous pressure points which modified the exercise of power within the jobber system. In a functionalist model of the

---

[114] *Ibid.*, II, 796, MSA.
[115] *Ibid.*, II, 799, MSA.
[116] *Ibid.*, II, 802–32, MSA.
[117] *RCLI, Evidence, Bombay Presidency*, Mr M.S. Bhumgara, I, i, 503.
[118] See chapter 4.
[119] *RCLI*, 'Life histories of 12 typical immigrant workers', XI, ii, 313.
[120] *Ibid.*, XI, ii, 316–17.
[121] *Ibid.*, XI, ii, 317–18.
[122] *Ibid.*, XI, ii, 317.

jobber system, most commonly adopted by historians, power was supposed to be concentrated in the jobber's hands. In practice, however, the structure of authority at work, shaped by the patterns of labour deployment, was characterized by internal tensions and conflicts and by the diffusion rather than the concentration of power.

The wage structure and the labour market

The labour-intensive strategies of the millowners influenced the structure of authority at work. It also shaped the changing relationships between different groups of workers. Indeed, the character and organization of the textile industry structured the sectionalism of industrial workers and fragmented what is frequently assumed to be their homogeneous interests and their apparently natural solidarities.

It is often suggested that industrial workers in the so-called 'organized sector' formed a relatively privileged group within the working class. Certainly, the millowners in the 1920s and 1930s were prone to complain that their workers were the highest paid in the city.[123] Recently, one historian has argued that wages in the textile industry were 'maintained at a level substantially higher than the alternative earnings of labour in the rural sector', by a margin of up to 150 per cent.[124] The maintenance of these wage disparities in an overstocked labour market is explained by the existence of 'two basic types' of labour supply to the industry: 'the stable and the unstable from the point of view of commitment to industrial work'.[125] The millowners, in this view, were forced to buy out of the countryside the kind of labour supply they sought. Far from labour costs being cheap, it is implied that industrial wages were high.[126]

It has already been argued in an earlier chapter that the so-called formal and informal sectors were closely inter-related.[127] It would be false to assume that industrial workers in the formal sector formed a single, homogeneous class, neatly distinguished from casual labour in the informal sector, whether by the stable conditions of work or by their attitudes to employment. Permanent industrial workers could easily, and often arbitrarily, lose their jobs and thus be thrown on to the casual labour market. Furthermore, wage differentials, gradations of skill and differences in their bargaining power divided industrial workers.[128]

---

[123] Proceedings of the TLIC, Main Inquiry, Oral Evidence, BMOA, File 57-A, p. 3, MSA.
[124] Mazumdar, 'Labour Supply', 480.
[125] *Ibid.*, 487.
[126] The implications of Mazumdar's argument are drawn out by Washbrook, 'Law, State and Agrarian Society', pp. 700–6.
[127] See chapter 3.
[128] Nor can it be assumed, as Mazumdar does, that rural migrants were unstable workers, single

It is easy to be misled by the complaints of the millowners about the burden of their wage costs. In fact, as we shall see, the wage structure was not characterized by a wide and consistent differential, whether between formal, industrial employment and casual labour in the urban labour market, or indeed between rural and urban labour in general. Rather, it was characterized by numerous smaller gradations between the lowest- and the highest-paid occupations which shaded into each other. Wages were not determined by the dual character of labour supply or within rigidly segregated markets.

The development of the cotton-textile industry in Bombay had been predicated upon low wages. As they lost the competitive advantage of cheap labour between the wars, the millowners struggled to suppress wage costs. As a rule, millowners attempted to buy labour in the cheapest market. But the cheapest cost of labour to the industrial employer not only required the payment of a subsistence wage for the worker and his family but, in addition, its price had to cover the costs of migration, the additional expenses of city life and a margin to attract smallholders and field labourers in the city.[129] It is in this light that we should examine the evidence of wage disparities to investigate how far employers had to exceed what might reasonably be considered the subsistence and reproduction costs of labour.

The available evidence suggests that wage levels in urban, industrial occupations, on the one hand, and rural field labour, on the other, were more closely related than has often been supposed. Most available wage surveys of textile labour were based upon the average earnings of the main occupations in particular mills.[130] Yet these statistical averages are riddled with difficulties of interpretation.

males who sought temporary and casual work wherever it may be found. See Mazumdar, 'Labour Supply'. On the contrary, family migration was often the result of hopeless rural distress while the most stable and committed workers retained their rural connections and retired to their village base in old age. See chapter 4.

[129] For theoretical and comparative insights on these questions, see E.J. Hobsbawm, 'Custom, Wages and Work-Loads in the Nineteenth Century', in his *Labouring Men: Studies in the History of Labour* (London, 1964), pp. 344–70.

[130] Mazumdar, 'Labour Supply'. For instance, Mazumdar relies upon the figures employed by Mukherji, 'Trend in Real Wages', 82–96. See also K. Mukherji, 'Trend in Textile Mill Wages in Western India: 1900 to 1951', *Artha Vijnana*, IV, 2 (1962), 156–66. These were in turn based largely upon the official publication *Prices and Wages in India*, which collected wage data for particular occupations in a single cotton mill in Bombay and took it to be representative for the entire industry. For comments on this wage data, see Bagchi, *Private Investment*, pp. 121–4. The subsequent data collected by the Labour Office were more comprehensive, but they were not always comparable and focussed largely upon the mainline occupations in the industry. The Labour Office, Bombay, *Wages and Hours... in the Cotton Mill Industry* conducted its survey in May 1921. See Labour Office, Bombay, *Report on an Enquiry into Wages and Hours of Labour in the Cotton Mill Industry in August 1923* (Bombay, 1925), especially pp. 1–5, for a discussion of changes in method from the earlier survey. Labour Office, Bombay, *Report on an Enquiry into Wages and Hours of Labour in the Cotton Mill Industry, 1926* (Bombay, 1930), made direct use of musters in nineteen selected mills rather than basing itself, as its predecessors did, upon schedules; see especially pp. 1–6. The most comprehensive wage survey is to be found

In conducting wage surveys the Labour Office was repeatedly bewildered
by the range of different occupations returned by each mill and by the variety
of terms used for them in the industry. In 1926, when the Labour Office
appealed to the Millowners' Association for help, the latter simply 'suggested ... that it would be sufficient if the statistics of the more important
occupations in each department' were collected.[131] Thus, one official later
recalled, the mills returned sixty-one occupations for ring spinning alone
'but the Millowners' Association thought it would be all right if all these
occupations were grouped under 9 different heads'.[132] These methods of
calculation were liable to inflate the level of average wages. For instance, 'the
process operatives ... were the only persons considered for the purposes of the
departmental inquiry' in 1937 while 'a very large number of low paid workers'
were excluded.[133]

In 1934, the Millowners' Association drew up their own 'minimum wage
schedule' to cover time-rated workers. Yet, even then it excluded, according to
A.W. Pryde, the Government Labour Officer, 'a large number of what I call
unscheduled occupations'. There were, he continued 'many occupations where
they are drawing even less' than the lowest-paid workers in the schedule and as
far as these occupations were concerned, 'it is very difficult to find out what
they do earn'.[134] Sizeable sections of the labour force earned considerably less
than the statistical averages which the Labour Office calculated for the occupational categories of their own making.

Whatever its limitations, the available evidence does not support the notion
that a wide wage differential separated workers in Bombay from rural field
labour in the major areas of migration to the city. In the early 1920s, wages of
unskilled labour in Alibag taluka, Kolaba and Kalyan taluka, Thana, neighbouring districts of Bombay, stood at about 10 annas per day, and skilled labour
earned up to 24 annas.[135] At the same time, the Labour Office calculated that
40 per cent of adult male textile workers in 1921 earned less than eighteen annas

in Labour Office, Bombay, *Report on Wages...in the Textile Industries, May 1934, General
Wage Census, Part I – Perennial Factories, Third Report.*

[131] Labour Office, Bombay, *Report on an Enquiry into Wages ...in the Cotton Mill Industry, 1926,*
pp. 10–11.

[132] Proceedings of the BSEC, I, 667, MSA.

[133] Proceedings of the TLIC, Interim Inquiry, Oral Evidence, Mr J.F. Gennings, Commissioner of
Labour and Chief Conciliator, Bombay, and N.A. Mehrban, Assistant Commissioner of Labour,
File 42, p. 413, MSA.

[134] *Ibid.,* Interim Inquiry, Oral Evidence, Mr A.W. Pryde, Labour Officer to Government, File 42,
p. 461, MSA.

[135] *Settlement Report on Alibag Taluka, Kolaba District,* by J.R. Hood, no. S.R.V.A. 28, 30 April
1924, para. 21, *Selections,* N.S. no. 632; *Settlement Report on Kalyan Taluka, Thana District,*
by M.J. Dikshit, no. 555, 5 September 1923, para. 48, *Selections,* N.S. no. 613. These figures
are also matched by Labour Office, Bombay, *Report on an Enquiry into Agricultural Wages in
the Bombay Presidency,* by G. Findlay Shirras (Bombay, 1924) and Mazumdar's wage data in
'Labour Supply', 495–6.

per day and about 5 per cent earned less than 12 annas. Moreover, 64 per cent earned less than 24 annas, the rate for 'skilled' rural labour. In addition, about 40 per cent of the women and more than 44 per cent of adolescents and children earned less than the unskilled rural wage.[136] Of course, these figures cannot be taken as a precise statement of the extent of wage differentials. They need to be adjusted for the number of days for which rural labourers found employment, for payment in kind and for subsistence provided by their smallholdings or crop shares. They also need to be qualified by the irregularity of work in the textile industry. But they are sufficient to suggest that rural and urban wages in Bombay and its hinterland were not determined in completely segregated and independent labour markets.

Moreover, wages in the textile industry were not in every case 'significantly higher than those of other urban labourers' (see table 28).[137] Even in the case of the mainline occupations in the textile industry, excluding the 'unscheduled occupations' or the low-paid workers who were often sacrificed in the calculations of average earnings, their wages did not uniformly exceed the levels of other industrial occupations in the city. Similarly, in 1929, millworkers on strike reported that they could earn between 6 annas and a rupee from casual labour in the city.[138] But the average daily wage for field labour in the Konkan in 1929 was, according to Mazumdar, 9 annas and 6 pice.[139] Furthermore, the wage differential between casual and permanent workers, Mazumdar himself admitted, was 'accounted for largely in terms of the under-employment of the former rather than of a differential wage structure within the industry'.[140]

If the framework of wage determination was established by the subsistence costs of the worker and his family, these did not by any means constitute an absolute or objective standard. Rather, subsistence was a relative category determined by custom, negotiation and struggle. Moral imperatives, not simply the principles of political economy, formed the underpinnings for the perception of what constituted a living wage. The Government Labour Officer declared that he did not believe that 'all minimum wages in the schedule [the minimum wage schedule of 1934 drawn up by the Millowners' Association] are living wages for Bombay.'[141] The scheduled wage for a doffer – 16 rupees and 4 annas per month or roughly 10 annas per day – was not, he considered, 'an adequate wage ... but I do believe that there are many occupations where they are drawing

---

[136] Labour Office, Bombay, *Report on Wages and Hours of Labour*, May 1921, pp. 6–7.
[137] Mazumdar, 'Labour Supply', 490.
[138] Proceedings of the Court of Enquiry, 1929, Examination of Ramchandra Balaji, File 6, p. 37 and Babu Sakharam, File 6, p. 53, MSA.
[139] Mazumdar, 'Labour Supply', 495.
[140] *Ibid.*, 490.
[141] Proceedings of the TLIC, Interim Inquiry, Oral Evidence, Mr A.W. Pryde, Labour Officer to Government, File 42, p. 476, MSA.

Table 28. *Average monthly earnings of certain industrial workers in Bombay City, 1934–5*

Cotton-mill industry		Engineering industry		Printing industry		Unregulated factories	
Occupation	Earnings	Occupation	Earnings	Occupation	Earnings	Occupation	Earnings
Doffers – men	14 12 1	Oilmen	27 4 7	Ballers	21 2 4	*Motor repairing, etc.*	
Single side-spinners – men	18 14 0	Ordinary Moulders	29 2 2	Proof readers	62 9 7	Fitters	35 14 2
Tarwallas	18 1 9	Rivet heaters and holders	21 2 1	Copy holders	30 6 5	Turners	44 3 0
Reelers – women	14 10 8	Hammermen and strikers	27 12 0	Hand pressmen	26 1 1	Carpenters	46 2 8
Grey Winders – women	14 9 7	Ordinary fitters	35 12 10	Paging men	27 8 6	Painters	25 9 1
Two-loom weavers	33 1 1	Ordinary carpenters	31 5 6	Binders	30 0 1	Polishers	29 4 6
Folders	20 0 0	Ordinary motor mechanics	27 8 1	Wire and hand stitchers	23 13 10	*Printing Press*	
Ticket Boys	28 0 10	Motor cleaners	25 13 11			Compositors	37 5 9
Coolies – men	18 13 5	Motor polishers	22 4 1			Pressmen	34 8 2
Coolies – women	13 7 2	Ordinary painters	32 4 3			Coolie – motor repairing	16 14 9
		Call boys	18 8 5			Coolie – metal foundries	16 8 0
		Ordinary tailors	38 7 1			Coolie – metal works	16 7 2
		Packers, wrappers and labellers – men	21 2 5				
		– women	16 0 5			*Furniture manufacturing*	
		Mechanics' assistants	23 9 3			Carpenters – boys	19 15 0
		Warehousemen	27 15 7			Polishers – boys	10 0 0

Note: The figures are expressed in rupees, annas and pice.
Source: Labour Office, Bombay, *Report on ... Wages, Hours of Work and Conditions of Employment in the Retail Trade*, p. 92.

even less', especially in the 'large number' of occupations which were omitted from the schedule.[142] Furthermore, he observed, 'there is a tendency ... to go below even that scheduled minimum wage which the millowners themselves have laid down'.[143] It would appear, therefore, that sizeable sections of the textile workforce did not even earn bare subsistence wages in Bombay.

Wage determination in the Bombay labour market occurred not simply according to the supply price of different kinds of labour but within the framework of wage competition for various occupations within each industry as well as across the urban economy as a whole. In devising their minimum wage schedules, the millowners said they fixed a 'fair' wage by taking the lowest-paid and the lowest-skilled jobs as their base and making further allowances for skill and the nature of work in other occupations. 'We found what a coolie or a sweeper gets', said Fred Stones, 'and fixed the rates accordingly.'[144] In the process, they explained, 'we have borne in mind the amount of wages paid by competing industries'.[145] This was necessary not only for unskilled but for skilled labour as well. Thus, the Commissioner of Labour explained in 1937:

In the Bombay mills, the wages of fitters, turners, mechanics – people who generally attend to the mechanical side of the industry – have got to remain on the same level as obtain in most of the bigger engineering concerns such as railway workshops, Royal Indian Marine Dockyard, etc. If wages are not maintained at the same level there would be a drift of good mechanical labour away from the mills.[146]

The level of wages in the cotton-textile industry was determined in direct relation to the tendencies which informed the Bombay labour market at a whole.

Although wages in the textile industry were broadly determined within the framework of comparable occupations, there were wide disparities in methods of wage calculation as well as earnings in the industry. As the Millowners' Association reported in 1892, 'Rates of wages are very various, depending on the situation of the mills, the class of material operated upon and the general

[142] Ibid., Interim Inquiry, Oral Evidence, Mr A.W. Pryde, Labour Officer to Government, File 42, p. 461, MSA.
[143] Ibid., Main Inquiry, Oral Evidence, Mr A.W. Pryde, Government Labour Officer, File 66, p. 2308, MSA.
[144] Ibid., Main Inquiry, Oral Evidence, BMOA, File 57-A, pp. 27–9, MSA.
[145] Ibid., Main Inquiry, Oral Evidence, BMOA, File 58-A, p. 326, MSA.
[146] Ibid., Interim Inquiry, Oral Evidence, J.F. Gennings, Commissioner of Labour and Chief Conciliator, and N.A. Mehrban, Assistant Commissioner of Labour, File 42, p. 415, MSA. On the railways, see GIP Railway, Report for the Royal Commission on Labour (Bombay, 1929), pp. 41–5, Appendix 2, p. 157 (for comparative statistics on wages paid by railway workshops and leading engineering firms in Bombay) and Appendix AA, pp. 159–60 (for wages of low-paid staff in Engineering Department and similar occupations in other undertakings in the same locality). See also Labour Office, Bombay, General Wage Census, Part I – Perennial Factories, First, Second, Third and Fourth Reports (Bombay, 1936–9).

regulations under which the mills are worked.'[147] Four decades later, little had changed. According to the Labour Office in 1934, 'Wage rates – both time and piece – not only vary widely between centre and centre and unit and unit in the same centre but also between different individuals in the same occupation in one unit.'[148] The range of variation between mills in Bombay, as table 29 shows, was indeed considerable.

To some extent, these variations may be explained in terms of the wage policies of particular employers. Thus, most of the mills which had made no reduction when wages were slashed across the industry in 1935 were already paying their two-loom weavers and single-ring siders above the average earnings for these occupations in the industry, 'whereas in mills which have cut down the allowances the most the earnings were much below the average'.[149] Similarly, in 1939, five years after the Millowners' Association had drawn up its minimum wage schedule, the Government Labour Officer was able to identify three classes of mills: those which paid above the minimum rates to attract more skilled workers; those which when 'faced with any difficulties are always prepared to go slightly above the minimum'; and about half the mills in the city which 'stick to the bare minimum'.[150] But the industry cannot simply be divided between high-paying mills and low-paying mills. The same mill could yield relatively low average earnings in certain occupations but rank among the highest in others.[151] Moreover, mills which ranked among the highest-paying units in certain occupations did not necessarily retain this position over time.

Another possible explanation of wage variations would lie in the fragmentation of the labour market. Certainly, wage bargaining was influenced by rates and conditions in neighbouring mills.[152] Whereas millowners justified wage cuts or changes in work practices on the basis of the policies of their rivals, workers' demands were often grounded on precedents already established in other local mills. Despite this, wage variations between mills located in the same municipal ward exceeded those between different wards.[153] If the market for

[147] *Royal Commission on Labour, 1892*, vol. II, 'The Labour Question in India', BMOA, *PP*, XXXVI, 130.
[148] Labour Office, Bombay, *Report on Wages … in the Textile Industries, General Wage Census, Part I, Third Report*, p. 71.
[149] Labour Office, Bombay, *Wages and Unemployment*, p. 33.
[150] Proceedings of the TLIC, Main Inquiry, Oral Evidence, Mr A.W. Pryde, Government Labour Officer, File 66, p. 2311, MSA.
[151] Labour Office, Bombay, *Wages and Hours of Labour, 1926*, p. 35; Morris, *Industrial Labour Force*, p. 157.
[152] Proceedings of the BSEC, I, 66–7, MSA; Labour Office, Bombay, *Wages and Unemployment*, pp. 25–8; Proceedings of the TLIC, Interim Inquiry, Oral Evidence, Mr A.W. Pryde, Labour Officer to Government, File 42, p. 459, MSA.
[153] Labour Office, Bombay, *Wages and Unemployment*, pp. 34–6; Morris, *Industrial Labour Force*, pp. 154–61. Of course, municipal divisions could lump together mills which were not necessarily in the same neighbourhood and separate others which were.

Table 29. *Frequency distribution of wage variations in the textile industry, 1934*

Limits of daily earnings (annas)	2-loom weavers	3-loom weavers	4-loom weavers	Ring siders (single side)	Ring siders (two sides)	Women reelers	Women winders Grey	Women winders Colour
Below 8	—	—	—	—	—	9	5	5
8 and below 9	—	—	—	—	—	5	4	5
9/10	—	—	—	—	—	3	6	2
10/11	—	—	—	—	—	6	12	7
11/12	—	—	—	1	—	8	8	3
12/13	—	—	—	3	—	4	3	4
13/14	—	—	—	7	—	—	3	4
14/15	—	—	—	16	1	4	4	2
15/16	3	—	—	8	1	—	1	—
16/17	3	—	—	4	1	—	—	1
17/18	1	—	—	2	3	1	—	—
18/19	1	—	—	—	1	—	—	3
19/20	—	—	—	—	1	—	—	1
20/21	5	1	—	—	—	—	—	—
21/22	—	—	—	—	1	—	—	1
22/23	3	1	—	—	1	—	—	—
23/24	3	1	1	—	—	—	—	—
24/25	6	—	—	—	—	—	—	1
25/26	4	—	—	—	2	—	—	—
26/27	5	—	1	—	—	—	—	—
27/28	—	—	1	—	—	—	—	1
28/29	1	—	—	—	—	—	—	—
29/30	1	—	—	—	—	—	—	—
30/31	3	2	1	—	—	—	—	—
31/32	2	—	1	—	—	—	—	—
32 and over	2	1	4	—	—	—	—	—

Source: Labour Office, Bombay, *Wages and Unemployment,* p. 36.

textile labour was geographically fragmented, it would be reasonable to suppose that as transport facilities improved and, as trade unions, the Millowners' Association and the state intervened increasingly in wage bargaining, the labour market would be more closely integrated. On the contrary, wage variations not only continued to exist but may even have widened in the 1930s.[154]

---

[154] Labour Office, Bombay, *Wages and Unemployment,* pp. 34–6; Morris, *Industrial Labour Force,* pp. 154–61.

The most convincing explanation for this eclectic wage structure may be found in the diversity of conditions which prevailed in the industry. Necessarily, the wage policies of the employers were governed by the composition of output, the quality of materials and machines and the financial conditions of particular mills. The industry was characterized by a plurality of occupations ambiguously defined. Workers employed in the same occupation in different mills did not always perform the same tasks and were thus paid differently. Moreover, the diversity of working conditions in the industry meant that even when two operatives performed the same function, their earnings would vary according to the character of production, the age and efficiency of the plant, and the skill and resourcefulness of workers as well as managers.[155] As the industry diversified the range of its output in the 1920s and 1930s, so the wage variations between mills for the same piece-rated occupation were likely to increase.

Similar factors also affected the wage rates of workers paid according to time. Since the estimation of labour costs was essential to the acceptance, planning and delivery of an order, millowners expected their jobbers and departmental heads to ensure that these costs were not exceeded and that certain minimum levels of speed, workloads and productivity were maintained. In establishing acceptable time wages, as much as in fixing piece rates, millowners and workers took into account conditions of work, the nature and quality of machinery and material and the character of production.[156] The variations of wages for the same occupation in different mills suggests less that the labour market was minutely fragmented than that the conditions of production and work practices were widely divergent.

This situation was further complicated by the 'very wide variations' which existed 'both in the methods of payment and the manner in which they were fixed'.[157] The wages of time workers were calculated either at a daily or a monthly rate, and the definition of the month varied from mill to mill. At times, some mills worked a short Saturday but made up the lost time by working longer hours, within the statutory limits of the Factory Act, later in the week. This complicated the problem of calculating the earnings of daily-rated workers. On the other hand, whereas daily-rated workers received wages for the number of days worked, there was no uniform practice in the calculation of the monthly rate. In principle, monthly-rated workers were paid only for days worked. The majority of mills calculated earnings for the number of days actually worked as a fraction of the number of working days in a month: in some cases, this was twenty-seven, in others twenty-six; while a few based the monthly rate on the

---

[155] Labour Office, Bombay, *Wages and Unemployment*, pp. 34–5.
[156] For a useful discussion of the piece basis of time wages and time basis of piece rates, see D. Schloss, *Methods of Industrial Remuneration* (London 1892), pp. 11–47.
[157] Labour Office, Bombay, *Wages and Hours of Labour, 1926*, p. 29.

number of days in the particular month but attached various conditions to 'the earning of a hypothetical pay for Sundays and holidays'.[158]

If the absence of 'universally fixed periods of time for which time rates are reckoned'[159] complicated the calculation of earnings for time workers, piece prices presented even more intricate problems. For weavers, these could be calculated by the piece, by the yard or by weight and varied according to the counts of warp and weft yarn, reed space, the number of picks to the inch and, sometimes, the width of the loom. The weaving of borders and designs required the payment of special allowances. There were not only 'very wide variations' in method from mill to mill, but also a 'vast number of different qualities for which varying rates are fixed'.[160] The variety of methods of wage calculation resulted, to some extent, in the wage variations which characterized the industry. But changes effected in the rates were liable to exacerbate them. 'In view of the wide disparity in rates and the manner in which they are calculated' reported the Labour Office, 'different individual operatives working in individual units are variously affected' by wage increases and reductions effected for the industry as a whole between the wars.[161] It cannot be taken for granted, therefore, that the responses of the workforce to the initiatives of the millowners would be uniform.

Wage differentials, hierarchies and skill

If the wage structure was influenced by general tendencies operating within the labour market as a whole, it was also shaped by differentials which came to be established between occupational groups. When they devised their standardization schemes in 1929 and 1939 and their minimum wage schedule in 1934, the Secretary of the Millowners' Association explained,

We tabulated every occupation in the mill and placed it in its true order with relationship to every other occupation. And then we fixed the wages to suit the degree of skill involved in each occupation over and above the minimum.[162]

But there were 'no objective tests which can determine the differences that should obtain in wage payments between any two occupations and current

[158] Labour Office, Bombay, *Report on Wages ... in the Textile Industries, General Wage Census, Part I, Third Report*, pp. 43–5.

[159] *Ibid.*, p. 71.

[160] *Ibid.*, p. 75.

[161] *Ibid.*, p. 71; on the variety of ways in which the wage increases of 1917–20 and the wage cuts of 1933–4 were calculated, and implemented, see Labour Office, Bombay, *Report on Wages ... in the Textile Industries, General Wage Census, Part I, Third Report*, p. 24; Labour Office, Bombay, *Wages and Unemployment*, pp. 25–39.

[162] Proceedings of the TLIC, Main Inquiry, Oral Evidence, BMOA, File 58-A, p. 339, MSA.

practice must largely guide decisions in this matter'.[163] Moreover, whereas 'the labour and skill involved in work in the different occupations is undoubtedly the main criterion to be adopted in determining differentials ... the evaluation of this criterion may differ from centre to centre'.[164] Skill was, therefore, a relative and socially determined category. And 'current practice' varied from mill to mill, from one centre of industry to another.

However, it is possible to identify hierarchies which came to be established between specific occupations within the workforce. Thus, fly gatherers and lap carriers in the card room were sometimes promoted to the grade of strippers and grinders, who undertook to maintain the cards, set their parts, clean the cylinders and grind the flats.[165] Doffers were promoted as tarwallas and subsequently to ring siders. The tarwallas, also known in the industry as gaiters or followers, were required to connect the yarn to the bobbins and prepare the ring frame for operation when the doffers had put the empty bobbins on the spindles. In Ahmedabad, gaiting was done by the siders themselves. But in Bombay, 'this occupation of gaiting was specially introduced as an intermediary stage of promotion between the doffers and ring siders'.[166] According to the millowners, workers 'go from doffer to tarwalla and from tarwalla to side-boy and from side-boy to line jobber and head jobber'.[167] Yet even in Bombay there were variations. In Tata's Swadeshi mills, doffers did the work of tarwallas and were paid higher wages than the latter received in other Bombay mills; in the Finlay groups of mills, however, it was the sider who was expected to perform the tarwalla's function.[168] Similarly, plain weavers who worked one or two looms considered it a matter of prestige and promotion to be put on to a fancy or jacquard loom.[169]

There were various differentials which came to be established as customary in the industry. For instance, in the frame department, differentials existed between slubbing, intermediate and roving tenters (see table 30). Slubbing tenters who performed the initial drafting were paid more than the intermediate and roving tenters. Too much drafting in the early stages could give the slivers of cotton an irregular thickness. At certain times, depending upon the rush of work and the quality of production, the intermediate process was dispensed with, requiring a greater degree of improvisation and skill from the slubbing tenter.

Similarly, differentials existed between weft and warp frames. 'In Bombay,

[163] *Report of the TLIC*, II, 122.
[164] *Ibid.*, II, 104.
[165] Proceedings of the BSEC, II, 695–700, MSA; *RCLI, Evidence, Bombay Presidency*, The Bombay Textile Labour Union, I, i, 307.
[166] Labour Office, Bombay, *Report on Wages ... in the Textile Industries, General Wage Census, Part I, Third Report*, p. 11.
[167] Proceedings of the BSEC, II, 731, MSA.
[168] *Ibid.*, II, 731–2, MSA.
[169] *RCLI, Evidence, Bombay Presidency*, The Bombay Textile Labour Union, I, i, 307.

Table 30. *Wage differentials between speed frame tenters (wages in rupees–annas–pice)*

	1921	1934	1937
Slubbing tenters	1–6–2	1–2– 1	1– 1–0
Intermediate tenters	1–5–1	1–0–10	0–15–6
Roving tenters	1–3–4	1–0– 1	0–14–0

Sources: Labour Office, *Wages and Hours, May 1921*; Labour Office, *Report on Wages ... in the Textile Industries, General Wage Census, Part I, Third Report; Report of the TLIC*, II.

it has been a tradition', said S.A. Dange, the Girni Kamgar Union leader, about this differential, and added rather vaguely, 'but at the same time, I think there is some technical justification for it.'[170] On the other hand, the Millowners' Association which favoured the abolition of this differential argued 'that there should be no additional strain involved in minding weft frames as compared with minding warp frames, but they were not able to show that the additional strain did not exist in practice'.[171]

These differentials were scarcely maintained in any uniform manner over time or between industrial centres. In 1929, the Bombay Strike Enquiry Committee, for instance, recommended, largely on the basis of the millowners' evidence, that warping creelers be paid a higher rate than doffers because the work of the former 'is a little superior as they have to arrange the bobbins on the creels with a little more attention, especially if there are yarns of different colours in the warp'.[172] A decade later, the representatives of the Bombay Millowners' Association were arguing that 'the work of a creeler was neither more strenuous nor more skilled than that of a doffer', while their counterparts of the Khandesh, Berar and Burhanpur Millowners' Association favoured a differential on the grounds that it was both.[173] Similarly, in Bombay in the

[170] Proceedings of the TLIC, Main Inquiry, Oral Evidence, Bombay Provincial Trades Union Congress, File 80-A, p. 5691, MSA.
[171] *Report of the TLIC*, II, 124.
[172] *Report of the BSEC*, I, 143.
[173] *Report of the TLIC*, II, 103–4. The extent of these differentials also varied. In the standardization schemes presented to the TLIC by various millowners' associations, the differentials on monthly earnings (in rupees-annas-pice) varied thus:

	Bombay	Sholapur	Khandesh
Doffer (ring and frame)	17–0–0	13–8–0	9–0–0
Creeler (warping)	17–0–0	15–0–0	12–8–0

Source: Report of the TLIC, II, 104.

1930s, especially after the wage cuts of 1933–4, the wages of back sizers came to be fixed at half those of front sizers and those of reachers in the same proportion to the wages of drawers-in, whereas reachers in most other centres got 'more than half the wages of the drawers-in'.[174] In Bombay, in any case, drawing-in was considered 'merely an avenue for employment in the weaving department'.[175]

It is extremely difficult to trace the evolution of these differentials and hierarchies within the industry. Until the Millowners' Association formulated a standardization scheme for the Fawcett Committee in 1928–9, no concerted action had been taken by millowners with regard to wages or working conditions. There were wide variations, therefore, in wages and working conditions, in the layout, machinery and output of mills, and in the definition of occupations in the industry. Moreover, the tasks performed by workers in the same occupational category differed from mill to mill. Wage rates varied widely even 'between different individuals in the same occupation' in a single mill while the 'grading of occupations into classes' across the entire industry remained one of the most difficult problems encountered by investigators who attempted to compile wage surveys for the industry.[176] It is reasonable to suppose under these circumstances that wage differentials and the hierarchies of the workforce evolved largely 'in a haphazard fashion over a series of years'.[177]

This haphazard pattern of development, however, was conditioned by the changing character of the industry. This process is best illustrated by the differential which came to be established between spinners and weavers. During the 1920s and 1930s, the millowners were particularly concerned about the extent of wage disparities between spinners and weavers. In the late nineteenth century, the cotton-textile industry had acquired the character of a primarily spinning industry. Since it competed against Lancashire, particularly in unpredictable foreign markets, and produced low value or coarse goods, spinners were made to work, as Fred Stones put it, for 'phenomenally low wages and phenomenally long hours'.[178]

In the early years of the twentieth century, however, cloth production became an increasingly important means by which the millowners hedged against the fluctuations of the export trade in yarn. 'With the loss of the trade with China', S.D. Saklatvala was to say, 'we had to organize the industry as a weaving

[174] *Ibid.*, II, 128.
[175] Proceedings of the BSEC, II, 812, MSA.
[176] Labour Office, *Report on Wages … in the Textile Industries, General Wage Census, Part I, Third Report*, p. 71.
[177] *Report of the TLIC*, II, 93.
[178] Proceedings of the TLIC, Main Inquiry, Oral Evidence, Mr F. Stones, Director, Messrs. E.D. Sassoon and Co. Ltd., File 72, p. 3883, MSA.

industry.'[179] Higher wages had to be paid to attract skilled weavers to the city.[180] Moreover, 'to induce the spinners to turn into weavers, we had to keep a margin of Rs. 8 to Rs. 10 over the spinners' wage.'[181] With the further expansion of weaving capacity, 'there was such a huge number of looms in Bombay that the weavers were definitely at a premium and bigger wages were offered by every mill to draw in labour'.[182] Finally, during the post-war boom, wage increases were given in the form of percentages based upon existing wages, which tended to widen the disparity between the low-paid and the highly paid workers, and, in addition, weavers received a larger allowance, by a margin of 10 per cent, than spinners.

Underlying these disparities lay the fact that hereditary weaving castes, especially the Julaha Muslims, laid claims to a skilled status. It was widely observed that the weaver considered himself superior to almost any other occupational group in the industry. Increasingly, weavers appropriated important areas of control over their own labour. Muslim weavers of Jacob Circle, the millowners repeatedly complained, refused to work on night shifts.[183] Their average earnings were reputed to exceed those of their Hindu counterparts. Indeed, as Maloney, Secretary of the Millowners' Association, put it, 'Mahomedan workers do not ordinarily work in mills except in higher paid occupations'.[184] Weavers in general and Julahas in particular, who sometimes appeared to 'have a lien on their post',[185] registered the highest rates of absenteeism.[186] Whereas Maratha weavers from Ratnagiri maintained close connections with their villages, Muslim weavers were among the most urbanized in the workforce. Clearly, no simple connection between labour turnover, stability and commitment on the one hand, and the migrant character of the workforce on the other, is easily sustained. Finally, weavers, especially Marathas from Ratnagiri, were known to be the most prominent in industrial disputes and in the vanguard of political action. Between 1918 and 1929, 52 per cent of the disputes in the Bombay mills, excluding those whose departmental origins were unknown, and those which affected the whole mill, occurred in the weaving department.[187]

---

[179] Proceedings of the BSEC, I, 14, MSA.
[180] Proceedings of the TLIC, Special Memorandum submitted by Mr F. Stones, Director, Messrs. E.D. Sassoon and Co. Ltd., File XLV, question 49, MSA.
[181] Proceedings of the BSEC, I, 14, MSA.
[182] Proceedings of the TLIC, Main Inquiry, Oral Evidence, Mr F. Stones, Director, Messrs. E.D. Sassoon and Co. Ltd., File 72, p. 3883, MSA.
[183] Ibid., Main Inquiry, Oral Evidence, BMOA, File 57-A, p. 169, MSA.
[184] Ibid., Main Inquiry, Oral Evidence, BMOA, File 57-A, p. 193, MSA.
[185] Ibid., Main Inquiry, Oral Evidence, BMOA, File 58-A, p. 358, MSA.
[186] Shah, 'Labour Recruitment and Turnover', p. 143.
[187] Calculated from Newman, Workers and Unions, Table III, p. 63. Out of 474 industrial disputes in the 1920s, 152 affected weaving. The next largest category was 'unknown' which

It was precisely because weavers had been able to appropriate key areas of control over their own labour in the first two decades of the twentieth century that the millowners began step by disjointed step to attack their privileged wage and bargaining position from the mid 1920s onwards. Following the general strike of 1925, when the millowners' attempt to reduce wages by $11\frac{1}{2}$ per cent was thwarted, trade union spokesmen began to complain that employers effected hidden cuts in the earnings of piece workers. To cheapen their wage costs, it was alleged, employers altered the character of production without making corresponding adjustments in the piece rates.[188]

In the standardization scheme which the millowners brought to the Fawcett Committee after the general strike of 1928, the only wage cut to which they admitted was a reduction of $7\frac{1}{2}$ per cent which applied to weavers alone. This was justified on the grounds that 'the weaver has been getting far more than the spinner in relation to the work he performs' and indeed 'a cut ... at least of 30 per cent would be fully justifiable in the weaving section'.[189] The standardization scheme was never implemented and the millowners failed to enforce a uniform reduction in the wage rates of the weavers. But the argument that 'the average wage of the weaver is very much higher than it should be compared to the amount of work he has to do'[190] remained the employers' constant refrain in the 1930s about the most militant section of their workforce.

Between 1926 and 1937, the earnings of two-loom weavers fell more steeply than those of any other occupational group in the industry (see table 31). Increasingly, in the 1930s, the disparities between weavers and spinners were pared down. While the earnings of two-loom weavers were reduced by more than a quarter, a new category of spinner was created who minded two sides of a spinning frame, usually worked finer counts of yarn and was paid considerably higher wages than the traditional single-sider who spun coarse yarn.[191] At the same time wider differentials began to open up between the two-loom weavers and the four- and six-loom weavers (see table 32).

The changing relative positions of different occupational groups in the industry were shaped by two factors. First, obviously, the millowners were

accounted for 133 disputes and 49 which affected the whole mill. Of particular departments 30 disputes affected workers on the drawing and speed frames.

[188] Proceedings of the BSEC, I, 66–8, MSA.

[189] Proceedings of the BSEC, I, 12, 15–16, MSA.

[190] Proceedings of the TLIC, Main Inquiry, Oral Evidence, BMOA, File 57-A, p. 156, MSA.

[191] The wage census of 1934 revealed that while the average earnings of 8,062 single-siders in the industry was Rs. 0–13–7 per day or Rs. 18–14–0 per month, that of 3,257 double-siders was Rs. 1–2–6 per day and Rs. 25–9–8 per month. Furthermore, only 216 spinners were employed at piece rates, all of whom worked as double-siders. Their average earnings were calculated at Rs. 31–8–8 per month or Rs. 1–6–7 per day. Labour Office, Bombay, *Report on Wages ... in the Textile Industry, General Wage Census, Part I, Third Report,* Table II, pp. 149–55.

Table 31. *Earnings of mill workers (in rupees–annas–pice) in selected occupations, 1926–37*

Occupations	Average daily earnings July 1926	Average daily earnings December 1933	Percentage change since July 1926	Average daily earnings October 1934	Percentage change since July 1926	Average daily earnings July 1937	Percentage change since July 1926
Drawing tenters[a]	1– 4– 8	1– 2– 8	– 9.68	1– 0– 6	– 20.16	0–15–11	– 2.98
Slubbing tenters[a]	1– 6– 3	1– 3–10	– 10.86	1– 2– 0	– 19.10	1– 1– 0	– 23.60
Intermediate tenters[a]	1– 4– 6	1– 3– 2	– 6.50	1– 0–10	– 17.89	0–15– 6	– 4.39
Roving tenters[a]	1– 3– 8	1– 2– 4	– 6.78	1– 0– 2	– 17.80	0–14–10	– 24.58
Ring siders							
Men[a]	1– 0– 3	0–14–10	– 8.25	0–13– 7	– 16.41	0–13– 8	– 15.46
Women	0–15– 2			0–13– 2	– 13.19		
Tarwallas							
Men	0–15– 5	0–13– 2	– 12.22	0–12–10	– 16.76	0–12–11	– 13.89
Women	0–14– 3			0–11–11	– 16.37		
Doffers – men and women	0–12– 1	0–10–10	– 10.34	0–10– 2	– 15.86	0–10– 5	– 13.79
Weavers, 2-loom[a]	1–13– 4	1– 8–10	– 15.34	1– 6– 1	– 24.72	1– 5– 8	– 26.14
Winders, grey – women[a]	0–11– 9	0–11– 9	– 7.84	0– 9–11	– 15.60	0– 9–11	– 15.60
Winders, colour – women[a]	0–14–11			0–13– 5	– 10.06	0–12– 8	– 15.08
Reelers – women[a]	0–10–11	0–11– 0	+ 0.76	0–10– 2	– 6.87	0– 8–11	– 18.32

[a] Includes piece-rated wages
Source: Report of the TLIC, I, Table VII, 24–5.

Table 32. *Wage differential among weavers in Bombay, 1934 (in rupees–annas–pice)*

Occupation	Number of weavers	Average daily wage	Average monthly wage
Two-loom weavers	24,623	1– 6– 1	33– 3– 5
Three-loom weavers	589	1– 8– 2	36–12– 1
Four-loom weavers	3,384	2– 1– 1	46–15–10
Six-loom weavers	1,445	1–15– 4	45–10– 5
Automatic-loom weavers [a]	34	2– 8–11	65– 0– 4

[a] Paid according to time.
Source: *Report on Wages . . . in the Textile Industry, General Wage Census, Part I, Third Report*, Table II, pp. 149–55.

seeking to reduce the supposedly inflated position of the two-loom weavers. To achieve this, they attempted to flatten the gradient of existing differentials between two-loom weavers and single-side spinners, by creating an intermediate category of double-siders. Second, it also became clear that widening the differential between single and double-siders, and between two-loom, four-loom and automatic-loom weavers was integral to their attempts to encourage workers to accept increased workloads, or what the millowners called rationalization schemes. Rationalized occupations had to be paid higher wages. Moreover, workers who accepted and stuck to rationalized jobs were favoured when chances of promotion arose.[192] Although they wanted to narrow the existing differentials, the millowners admitted, 'we know the practical difficulty'. This was why they had 'tried to encourage a degree of rationalization in the spinning side of the mill, which was itself calculated to remove a lot of this difference'.[193]

Clearly, skill was not the only criterion by which wage differentials were determined. 'Suppose a coolie gets Rs. 20/-', one millowner pointed out, 'we consider that a doffer boy should get less than him as he undergoes a training and is given that job as a learner.'[194] The doffer, argued Maloney, 'is not entitled to a full adult skilled worker's wage because he is unskilled. He comes as a raw hand'.[195] Moreover, since the doffer was expected to be promoted to higher

---

[192] Proceedings of the TLIC, Main Inquiry, Oral Evidence, Cotton Mill Workers, Spinning Side, File 60-A, p. 990, MSA.
[193] *Ibid.*, Main Inquiry, Oral Evidence, Confidential Examination of the BMOA, File 78-C, pp. 5410–11, MSA.
[194] *Ibid.*, Main Inquiry, Oral Evidence, BMOA, File 57-A, pp. 28–9, MSA.
[195] *Ibid.*, Main Inquiry, Oral Evidence, BMOA, File 78-C, p. 5388, MSA.

grades, this justified his being paid a lower wage during his apprenticeship.[196] But many doffers found themselves languishing in low-wage apprenticeships for extended periods. 'I am afraid', the Government Labour Officer said in 1939, 'the doffer boy is no longer an adolescent in Bombay ... Today we find people doing the work of doffer boys are men of middle age'.[197] When the millowners' reasoning was challenged on the grounds that 'most of these doffers are no longer really learners or apprentices' and that 'they stick to the jobs because there are not enough vacancies' in the higher grades, Baddeley, the chairman of the Millowners' Association, declared that they remained doffers only 'because they have not got the intelligence'.[198] In the early days of the industry, doffing had been a child's occupation; the decline of child labour left it in the ranks of the lowest paid.

There were other low-paid jobs in the industry, however, which carried no prospects of promotion. Their status was not always justified on the basis of skill. Thus, S.A. Brelvi, a member of the Textile Labour Inquiry Committee, questioned the millowners about these low-paid grades:

BRELVI: What about pickers?
STONES [BMOA]: These are women.
BRELVI: What about stamp boys?
STONES: These are adolescents.
BRELVI: Then you have carriers, etc.?
STONES: They are coolies and unskilled.[199]

Low-paid jobs which had no prospects of promotion, explained Fred Stones, were generally 'petty jobs given to ordinary men who are usually elderly and have come down to that job', to those workers, in other words, who were unable 'to do a better job'.[200] Similarly, T. Maloney, the Secretary of the Millowners' Association, declared, 'bardan picking ... is a job for somebody whom you do not want to throw out.'[201]

But these jobs, readily identified with boys, women or the elderly, were not simply free of skill requirements. Although labellers and bundle boys did 'more or less a boy's job', as Maloney admitted, 'they have to have a certain amount of skill and a certain amount of responsibility ... they have got to be intelligent and to be able to read and make careful records of tickets. We have to recognise that they are educated.' Nevertheless, theirs was not an adult job: 'as far as I am

[196] *Ibid.*, Main Inquiry, Oral Evidence, BMOA, File 57-A, p. 163, File 79-A, p. 5503, MSA.
[197] *Ibid.*, Main Inquiry, Oral Evidence, Mr A.W. Pryde, Government Labour Officer, File 66, pp. 2383–4, MSA.
[198] *Ibid.*, Main Inquiry, Oral Evidence, BMOA, File 81-A, p. 5822, MSA.
[199] *Ibid.*, Main Inquiry, Oral Evidence, BMOA, File 57-A, pp. 190–1, MSA.
[200] *Ibid.*, Main Inquiry, Oral Evidence, BMOA, File 57-A, p. 191, MSA.
[201] *Ibid.*, Main Inquiry, Oral Evidence, BMOA, File 79-A, p. 5522, MSA.

concerned, they are boys'.[202] Similarly, it was observed in 1929 that the coolies in the winding department who carried baskets filled with pirn to the weft and warping machines were paid more than the winder who did 'a skilled job'. The reason, explained Stones, was that 'the one is a man and the other is a woman'.[203] As long as a particular occupation could be classified as boys' or women's work, its wages could be related to the rates which unskilled adolescent and female labour found in the city. Certain occupations were also converted into specifically women's work in order to enable and justify wage reductions. 'We are not encouraging the employment of male sweepers', announced one millowner in 1939, '... because it is not an occupation in which a reasonable wage may be given.'[204]

This interplay between the perceptions of the employers, an integral part of a wider public discourse, in which some workers also sometimes shared, and the bargaining strength of labour extended beyond categories of age and sex to caste and community as well. Groups of workers whose social organization in the working-class neighbourhoods was weak found it difficult to enter the more skilled and prized sections of the textile workforce. Marginalized within the city, and its working class, they were crowded into the lowest-paid jobs and frequently failed to defend even this position. Their concentration in these occupations was then interpreted by the millowners as a reflection of their meagre needs and humble expectations, an indication of their lack of skill and aptitude and therefore, a justification for their low wages. 'The Pardeshis', said Stones, about North Indian Hindu workers, 'still stick to the card room, a very dirty job and by no means a healthy job ... The Julhai Mahommedans and Marathas ... understood their job and went for good posts.'[205] 'The better skilled worker', he continued, had to be remunerated for 'his intelligence and skill' in relation to the lower paid. The carder, generally, according to Stones, 'a Pardeshi', had 'the lowest standard'. This was, he explained, because 'there is a variation in the needs of the workers due to their caste, creed etc.' But asked whether, in the event of all North Indian workers being replaced by Marathas, he would raise their wages, Stones protested 'that would not be possible'.[206]

The most familiar case of caste exclusion was that which kept Mahars and the untouchable castes out of the weaving sheds. The millowners favoured the breaking of caste-exclusive practices in this instance because it would help to breach the skilled status and undermine the bargaining strength of the weavers.

202 *Ibid.*, Main Inquiry, Oral Evidence, BMOA, File 79-A, pp. 5522–3, MSA.
203 Proceedings of the BSEC, II, 796, MSA.
204 Proceedings of the TLIC, Main Inquiry, Oral Evidence, BMOA, File 57-A, p. 162, MSA.
205 *Ibid.*, Main Inquiry, Oral Evidence, Mr F. Stones, Director, Messrs. E.D. Sassoon and Co., Ltd., File 70, p. 3386, MSA.
206 *Ibid.*, Main Inquiry, Oral Evidence, Mr F. Stones, File 70, p. 3422, MSA.

The objection of caste Hindus to the employment of untouchable workers as weavers was ostensibly that the yarn sometimes had to be sucked on to the shuttle from the bobbins. 'We tried to get over it', in the Sassoon groups, said Stones, 'by stopping shuttle sucking. Many of our mills have self-threading shuttles.' Despite this, it was impossible to employ untouchable workers 'because the others won't work with them'. Nevertheless, the fact remained that when the Sassoon group attempted to employ untouchable workers in the weaving shed by setting aside one shed in which 'none but depressed classes' worked, the results were not promising. 'Out of the numbers that I tried', said Stones, 'I found 2 men who could run 2 looms. The others were not fit for one loom.'[207] This was not surprising since few of these workers had handled a loom before. Such simple facts did not, however, intrude upon the association by employers of this social group, marginalized within the working class, with low skill and status at the workplace.

Patterns of labour deployment

The patterns of labour deployment in the industry, like the variations in wages and work practices, were symptomatic of the labour-intensive strategies of the millowners. The fluctuations of employment gave rise to varying labour needs, called for considerable flexibility in the deployment of labour and resulted in the ambiguous definition of occupations. In 1923, the Labour Office, according to one of its officials, experienced 'very great trouble in finding out exactly what each occupation was doing'.[208] In its next attempt at a wage census in 1926, the Labour Office found that 'all the mills used an aggregate of over 1,000 terms for specifying different occupations'.[209]

The diversity of conditions within the industry meant that the number of workers required for particular operations, and indeed the nature of the job itself, varied widely from mill to mill. The quality of mixings determined the number of piecers which each mill required. Cheap or inferior mixings resulted in a larger number of breakages, especially when they were stretched to the production of higher counts. The age and efficiency of the plant also influenced labour deployment. Old spinning frames required more oilers and fitters to make adjustments to the machinery as well as closer attention from siders and tarwallas because it was likely to give rise to a greater number of breakages and larger quantities of waste. The layout of the mill determined the number of bobbin carriers, coolies and helpers required as well as the number of jobbers

---

[207] *Ibid.*, Main Inquiry, Oral Evidence, Mr F. Stones, File 70, p. 3550, MSA.
[208] Proceedings of the BSEC, I, 667, MSA.
[209] Labour Office, Bombay, *Report … Wages and the Hours of Labour in the Cotton Mill Industry, 1926*, pp. 10–11.

and supervisors. Labour requirements and tasks varied according to the number of machines, the conditions of production and the composition of output.[210] But these conditions, as one millowner pointed out, varied not only between mills but also within the same mill. Patterns of labour deployment had to be adjusted if 'you go on coarser counts, or finer counts, stop some looms or change the speed, or deliberately stop certain ring frames or go on working your mill day and night'.[211] Labour needs thus varied not only from mill to mill or from day to day but within the same mill on a single day, tending at times during a shift, to create a surplus labour force within the mill. The nature of industrial production in cotton textiles called for flexibility in the deployment of labour and the organization of work.

From the earliest days of the industry, observers commented on the fact that workers appeared to spend a considerable proportion of their time away from their machines. 'We have ourselves seen them', one factory commission reported, 'engaged in drinking water, washing, smoking and looking about.'[212] The Indian worker, another factory commission explained, was 'naturally disposed to take work easily'[213] and 'to a great extent counteracts the evil effects of an increase of working hours by idling more while at work'.[214] These 'habits', it was generally believed, were the consequence of the fact that they were 'agriculturists at heart'.

Such evidence has led historians to argue that 'discipline at the workplace was fundamentally lax and ramshackle'. Until 1927, according to Morris 'all evidence points to the fact that ... the mills had no serious interest in eliminating irregular work behaviour and made little effort to do so'. After 1927, spurred on by the Tariff Board, they began 'to move in the direction of more effective discipline'.[215] Indeed, historians have frequently assumed that just as in the early stages of industrialization workers were irregular and wayward in their approach to work, so employers did not fully appreciate the value of tighter discipline.

However, the apparent laxity of discipline and the elasticity evident in the organization of production were not simply the direct consequence of the attitudes of workers, 'agriculturists at heart' and maladjusted to the industrial setting. Rather in the case of cotton textiles it arose from the nature of industrial production. For if labour needs varied not only from day to day, but within a single shift, it is not surprising that observers might find, at times during the day, a certain number of workers away from their machines – apparently unoccupied within the mill.

210 Proceedings of the BSEC, I, 287–90, MSA.
211 Proceedings of the TLIC, Main Inquiry, Oral Evidence, BMOA, File 81-A, p. 5853, MSA.
212 Report of the IFC, 1890, p. 14.
213 Report of the IFLC, I, 21.
214 Ibid., I, 27.
215 Morris, Industrial Labour Force, pp. 117, 120, 121.

Furthermore, it was scarcely as if the millowners tolerated indiscipline simply because they knew no better or that they allowed such laxity when it did not suit the conditions of production, even in the late nineteenth century. Thus a woman winder in the New Great Eastern Mill told the Factory Commission in 1890 that 'there is no great difficulty in getting leave if there is sufficient yarn in the factory. But if there is a press of work, even if anyone died in her family, she cannot get leave.'[216] Similarly, as Shaikh Mahomed, a weaver in the same mill, complained:

Piece-work is not voluntary as regards the operatives, inasmuch as a man cannot leave off work when he likes. He must remain and work until the mill stops. But it is optional for the owner to stop the working of the machinery whenever he likes, and he pays no compensation to the hands for sending them away in the middle of the day.[217]

Indeed, employers adopted various expedients precisely to accommodate the variations in the demand for labour which could arise in the course of the working day. This was most evident in the employment of children and adolescents. There was a widespread falsification of age, following the passing of factory legislation, to enable children under nine years to work as half-timers and those under fourteen to work fulltime. In Bombay, 14 per cent of half-timers in 1908 were estimated to be below nine years of age although they had been passed as being older by the certifying surgeon.[218] Frequently, half-timers were employed with the intention of making labour available throughout the day. In some mills, half-timers worked in two shifts, separated by a long recess. But the children were required to remain in the mill during rest periods so that jobbers could utilize them if the working of certain mixings, counts of yarn and varieties of cloth created a temporary shortage of labour. Other mills ran fictional schools for half-timers which were 'used solely for the purpose of retaining the children at the mill during the whole working day, in order that this additional supply of labour might be utilized either as a regular measure or temporarily when occasion demanded'. In fact:

The "schools" were in many cases held in most unsuitable buildings; frequently no building at all was provided; the children who were supposed to be under instruction were often unable to read or write even the simplest words; no arrangements were made to secure their attendance, though half-timers are in general not permitted to leave the mill compound; and the teachers were, as a rule, hopelessly incompetent. In one case, for example, a teacher entirely ignorant of English was supposed to be giving instruction in that language.[219]

---

[216] *Report of the IFC, 1890, Evidence*, Awdi, female winder, New Great Eastern Mill, p. 23.
[217] *Ibid., Evidence*, Shaikh Mahomed, weaver, New Great Eastern Mill, p. 25.
[218] *Report of the IFLC*, I, 16.
[219] *Ibid.*, I, 15.

The apparent laxity of discipline in the late nineteenth and early twentieth centuries need not be construed either in terms of traditional and dysfunctional methods of management or in terms of the rural mentalities of labour.

Significantly, the laxity of discipline which was so frequently observed before the 1920s was scarcely eradicated in the subsequent decades. The late 1920s did not constitute, as some historians have supposed, a watershed in the development of efficient management and effective discipline. In the aftermath of the 1928 strike, the millowners appeared to accept the need to frame standardized rules and regulations for the industry as a whole. 'The standing orders which emerged from the negotiations', declared Morris, 'involved a rather significant break from the industry's traditions.'[220] In fact, it constituted nothing of the kind. The old set of predominantly informal and diverse disciplinary practices continued. Although the Fawcett Committee which investigated the 1928 strike made its recommendations on the standing orders the following year,[221] the Millowners' Association did not even formalize its own set of regulations until 1931.[222] As late as 1934, the Labour Office still found that most mills followed their own individual rules and disciplinary practices.[223]

The loose organization of work built various inequities into the contract of employment. Although employers often penalized late attendance, there were no corresponding allowances made for the late starting of the machinery or the failure to maintain the flow of production and thus to provide work at the right time and in sufficient quantity, which vitally affected the earnings of workers paid according to results.[224] Such established, even customary, practices in the industry could be enshrined in the standing orders when the millowners came to standardize them. Thus the Fawcett Committee judged that the custom of 'playing-off', whereby mills could, according to the draft standing orders presented to it, stop their machines 'when it is necessary to do so because of the state of trade' and the workers affected were 'considered ... as temporarily unemployed and will not be entitled to wages', was 'obviously a practice of a one-sided kind'.[225] Yet the only alternative for the employers, under the prevailing conditions of production, was to employ a surplus labour force. To a large extent, millowners followed both practices to varying degrees. There is no reason to suppose that 'playing-off' ceased during the slump of the 1930s. On the other hand, several mills often found themselves with a larger labour force than they strictly required.

---

[220] Morris, *Industrial Labour Force*, p. 122.
[221] *Report of the BSEC*, I, 12–55.
[222] *BMOA, Annual Report, 1931*, pp. 82–8.
[223] Labour Office, Bombay, *Report on Wages ...Textile Industries, General Wage Census, Part I, Third Report*, pp. 45–51.
[224] *Report of the BSEC*, I, 13.
[225] *Ibid.*, I, 33–6.

In 1928, Saklatvala told the Fawcett Committee, 'In our industry a good deal of casual labour is employed over and above the usual workers ... My submission is that it is this casual labour which is going to be affected most' by the proposed schemes of the millowners for retrenchment and standardization.[226] But five years later it was still found that 'some cotton mills maintain certain percentages of spare hands on their permanent musters'.[227] At the end of the decade, employers continued to comment on the number of 'super-numerary' occupations in the mills.[228] 'There are a tremendous number of people', commented Fred Stones in 1939, 'who are somewhat redundant in the mills.'[229] A.W. Pryde, the Government Labour Officer, estimated in the same year that 25 per cent of the workforce could be found 'sitting outside the mill' at any one time.[230]

The nature of factory discipline should not be understood merely as the reflex of the early stages of industrialization. On the contrary, the continuities which characterized methods of management and forms of behaviour at work, in spite of further industrial development, were remarkable. The contours of factory discipline necessarily had to be fitted to the rhythms of production and the patterns of labour deployment. Since there were no fundamental changes in the business strategies of the millowners, directed primarily at the adjustment of production to short-term market fluctuations, it is not surprising that there was no transformation in the organization of work. The nature of discipline in the Bombay mills was in part the consequence of their varying labour needs fostered by prevailing strategies of production.

However, factory discipline was not simply determined by the pattern of production. The enforcement of discipline was negotiated, albeit on unequal terms, between employers and the workforce, between jobbers and their teams of workers and between the various elements which operated within the structure of authority at work. In this light, forms of behaviour such as loitering at the workplace or the slowing down of production need not be construed as negative responses of migrant workers to the industrial setting but also as positive forms of working-class action. 'The workers in Bombay', said Fred Stones, 'seem to favour the idea of half work for everybody rather than full work for a few.'[231] Workers who experienced fluctuating and uncertain conditions of

[226] Proceedings of the BSEC, I, 11–12, MSA.
[227] Labour Office, Bombay, Report on Wages ...Textile Industries, General Wage Census, Part I, Third Report, pp. 19–20.
[228] Proceedings of the TLIC, Main Inquiry, Oral Evidence, Mr F. Stones, Director, Messrs. E.D. Sassoon and Co. Ltd., File 70, p. 3424, MSA.
[229] Ibid., Main Inquiry, Oral Evidence, Mr F. Stones, File 73, p. 4097, MSA.
[230] Ibid., Main Inquiry, Oral Evidence, Mr A.W. Pryde, Government Labour Officer, File 66, p. 2365, MSA.
[231] Proceedings of the TLIC, Main Inquiry, Oral Evidence, Mr F. Stones, File 70, p. 3426, MSA.

employment sought to slow down production and to control the intensity of effort which employers demanded of them. Yet, if work-sharing practices forced millowners at times to employ additional workers, they could also provide them with arguments to justify wage cuts and the retrenchment of labour.

If the prevailing patterns of labour deployment, and more generally the labour-using trend of investment, narrowed the millowners' freedom of action, they also contributed to the tensions and conflicts within the workforce. The flexibility which employers sought in the deployment of labour arose to a large extent from their business strategies, while the ambiguous definition of occupations was a natural corollary to these patterns of labour deployment. As long as employers did not specify the duties of each worker, they gained a certain flexibility in the use of his labour. Thus Maloney, the Secretary of the Millowners' Association, declared,

I would say it is practically impossible to set out a definition of the duties which each particular workman in a mill should perform. In fact, today they will vary considerably from mill to mill, and the danger of putting down the duties, which you think cover the general case, is that they do not cover a particular case. Then you have labour troubles, because some fellow reads a definition of duties, and if he has got to do a little bit of unspecified work, he will say 'I will not do this unless I get more money.'[232]

This was believed to be a common occurrence. However, the failure to define duties or standardize musters made it difficult for the workers or their trade unions to defend their positions at work and indeed made them vulnerable to attack. Employers could, for instance, increase workloads or the intensity of effort demanded of the workers without discussion or negotiation. Without the stipulation of numbers and occupations, it was difficult to effect any wage agreement.

Furthermore, the ambiguous definition of duties intensified rivalries and promoted conflicts between workers, as they attempted to stake out and protect their own occupational territories. When employers attempted to increase workloads by requiring siders to clean their machines or by reducing the number of helpers for weavers, the ambiguities in the definition of duties were liable to result in industrial disputes.[233] Citing the case of recent strikes in the Spring and Textile Mills, the trade-union leader, S.A. Dange, told the millowners in 1938:

When a certain task was forced on them, the operatives said it was not their duty and there was a strike. It is in fact in your interests that the duties are defined.[234]

But the millowner, S.D. Saklatvala, insisted that 'it is the defining of the duties

232 Proceedings of the TLIC, Main Inquiry, Oral Evidence, BMOA, File 79-A, pp. 5506–7, MSA.
233 Ibid., Main Inquiry, Oral Evidence, BPTUC, File 80-A, p. 5641, MSA.
234 Ibid., Main Inquiry, Oral Evidence, BPTUC, File 80-A, p. 5683, MSA.

that sometimes causes trouble. I can give you examples where strikes have taken place because the duties are defined.'[235] However, rivalries within the workforce did not always result in strikes. They were often conducted or resolved at the level of the jobber or the weaving or spinning master. Disputes of this kind might result in the desertion of a jobber by his team of workers, or their departure along with their jobbers, or most simply in their dismissal and replacement by less recalcitrant workers.

The labour-intensive strategies of the millowners served to encourage rivalries within the workforce in other ways as well. The diversity of conditions within the industry, accentuated by these strategies of production, informed competition and conflicts within the workforce. The quality of machinery, the layout of the mill, the policies and attitudes of managers and the composition of output varied throughout the industry and influenced the wages which could be earned and the working conditions which prevailed in particular mills. These differences in conditions induced labour mobility between mills as well as wage competition among millowners. Furthermore, on the basis of these discrepancies, millworkers demanded improved conditions and better wages from their managers or put pressure on their jobbers to obtain them. The competition between millworkers occurred not only as they faced each other across the labour market, but could also be expressed at the level of the jobber. As millowners attempted to regulate production to the patterns of demand, they effected continuous changes in the composition of output, altering the counts of yarn to be spun or the varieties of cloth manufactured. Necessarily, this entailed slowing down certain machines and speeding up others, reducing the output of certain departments and employing additional men to swiftly expand production elsewhere. Changes effected in the mixings of cotton, the counts and quality of yarn to be spun and the type and construction of cloth could disturb the flow of work from one process to the next.

Adjustments in the composition of output, therefore, fundamentally affected the patterns of labour deployment. When a mill switched a proportion of its spindles to higher counts, it could render a corresponding proportion of its preparatory machines idle, while requiring fewer doffers, gaiters and even siders since the machines were run at slower speeds. 'Last year, and the year before that', wrote one mill manager in 1907,

the abnormal production of 10's which was found the most remunerative count to spin, compelled many to use most of their machinery suited for 20's to 10's, notwithstanding that a large number of spinning spindles had to be stopped for want of a sufficient supply of rovings ... The card rooms were worked longer than the spinning rooms ... Most of the mills had to go from three heads of drawing frames to two, and some of them had to

---

[235] *Ibid.*

take their slubbing bobbins direct to roving frames … The speed of machines had necessarily to be lowered to keep things going under such conditions.[236]

Similar factors affected most processes throughout the cotton mill. The amount of reeling and winding required varied widely according to the proportion of yarn to be placed on the market or consumed in the production of cloth. Weaving was liable to sharper fluctuations of output and employment in the 1920s and 1930s than spinning, for yarn could either be sold or else unsold stocks be deployed in the weaving shed as market conditions allowed.

Thus, the impact of changing market conditions fell differentially upon the workforce. Even in periods when mills could make profits, labour might have to be laid off in certain processes. In periods of depression, it was rarely the case that the entire workforce was affected in the same way. The labour-intensive strategies of the millowners which gave rise to diverse interests within the industry also served to exacerbate the sectionalism of the workforce.

It cannot be taken for granted, in the development of industrial relations, that the interests of capital or labour were monolithic. This rivalries and conflicts between the millowners in Bombay were deepened by their reliance upon labour-intensive strategies. Their differences limited their options in dealing with the long-term crisis of the 1920s and 1930s and prevented them from formulating and implementing coherent policies towards labour. The larger constraints within which the industry developed determined the adoption of labour-intensive strategies; they also accounted for the peculiar intensity and prolonged character of the economic crisis which the Bombay textile industry experienced in the 1920s and 1930s.

The shape of the workforce and the patterns of labour deployment may be best understood in terms of the production strategies of the employers. The nature of the jobber system of recruitment and discipline was conditioned by the varying demand for labour in the textile industry, which was in turn a consequence of the widespread tendency to regulate production according to the fluctuations of the market. The structure of authority at work, often assumed to be concentrated in the person of the jobber, was on the contrary diffuse. As a result, there were several discernible points through which power was exercised and challenged, and around which the tensions within the workforce came to be expressed.

The production strategies of the employers in the textile industry cast some doubt on social and economic theories which have emphasized the dual character of the urban economy in Third World cities. In this case, the formal sector represented by the textile industry followed strategies prevalent in the so-called informal sector and indeed relied upon the extensive use of casual labour. An

---

[236] A Retired Mill Manager, *Bombay Cotton Mills*, p. 18.

examination of the wage structure of the industry further suggests that wage levels were determined by tendencies operating within the labour market as a whole, rather than its 'primary' or formal sector alone.

The extensive use of casual labour may at first lend credence to another common assumption in the literature: that the level of skill was uniformly low. Of course, it is not intended to suggest that the barriers of skill were insuperable. But it would be misleading to assume that skill was an absolute category. Rather it was often socially rather than technologically determined. Wage differentials were not always an accurate reflection of the level of skill. Moreover, the workforce cannot be neatly segregated into skilled and unskilled occupations. A wide range and varying levels of skills were demanded in different occupations. The production strategies of the employers often called for improvisation and their successful execution frequently depended upon the resourcefulness of the operatives.

The patterns of labour deployment have often been understood as a reflex of the attitudes of employers and, more crucially, workers in the early stages of industrialization. Methods of management in the Bombay industry, it is supposed, were dysfunctional to the long-term interests of industry. In fact, the patterns of labour deployment admirably dovetailed with the business strategies of the employers. Thus, even when methods of management were supposedly modernized in the 1930s, they failed to transform existing modes of labour discipline and control. Yet the patterns of labour deployment were not simply determined by technological imperatives but were also influenced by working-class action. Indeed, labour resistance sometimes halted the forward march of technology.

It is frequently assumed that industrialization tends to increase the homogeneity of the working class, that as workers are concentrated into larger masses, their interests become monolithic and their struggles find a common base. On the other hand, in the conventional view, the neighbourhood was portrayed as the arena in which working-class sectionalism flourished: caste and kinship appeared to form the organizing principle of social relationships; villages, it seemed, were recreated in the city; neighbourhood leaders were styled as headmen. It has already been argued that the solidarities of class were not simply fragmented but could also be forged in the neighbourhood. Conversely, the development and organization of the textile industry served to structure the sectionalism of the working class. Industrialization did not always reduce, sometimes it intensified, the competition between workers and exacerbated the diversity of their interests. Workers in the industry were involved not simply in a single relationship of exploitation with capital but also in relationships of competition with each other.

8 Rationalizing work, standardizing labour: the limits of reform in the cotton-textile industry

From the late 1920s onwards, the problems of the Bombay textile industry focussed in public discourse upon its allegedly inefficient and intractable labour force. For what came to be perceived as its 'labour problem', the colonial state prescribed rationalization. This official panacea for the industry's problems was conceived in a highly charged political context. In the 1920s, as chapter 6 has shown, the Bombay industry was forced to adapt to the imperatives of the domestic market, in which demand was stagnant and contracting, and which was in addition saturated with the cheap coarse goods produced by the expanding up-country mills. In the finer varieties, however, the Ahmedabad mills and the imports of Lancashire and, especially, Japan, had established a powerful, indeed daunting presence. Moreover, the Bombay mills were trying to adjust to an internal market which was reported to be the most open in the world. The Bombay millowners urgently sought tariff protection. But for the colonial state, keeping the Indian market open for British manufactures was one of its most important imperial commitments. Rationalization thus became the official alternative to tariffs and indeed, the progress made by the millowners to implement the former became, at least rhetorically, the yardstick by which the colonial state measured how much they deserved protection.

It has been readily assumed that the late 1920s, when the Tariff Board first directed attention to rationalization, constituted the turning point when old habits were cast aside and the Bombay millowners took a decisive step in their progression from traditional pre-industrial practices to modern methods of management.[1] The prominence which rationalization acquired in public discourse, in the innumerable inquiries conducted in the following dozen years into the state of the industry and in the three general strikes fought over its consequences, has facilitated the assumption that fundamental changes flowed from

---

[1] Newman, *Workers and Unions*, pp. 253, 34–35, 69–84; Morris, *Industrial Labour Force*, pp. 107–53; Bhattacharya, 'Capital and Labour', PE36–PE44. For Morris, this transformation flowed from the report and recommendations of the Tariff Board (Morris, *Industrial Labour Force*, p. 121).

their formulation. In fact, rationalization appears to have been as widely discussed as it was weakly implemented.

According to the ideal types of entrepreneurial behaviour, rationalization could be seen as the necessary response of entrepreneurs, when pressed by their rivals, to raise their levels of efficiency, increase labour productivity and adopt the newest and best technology. Alternatively, for Marxists, rationalization signified the attempt by capitalists to appropriate an increasing share of surplus value by developing the labour process and sophisticating the division of labour. The progressive introduction of new technology in this view did not simply raise 'efficiency' but reduced skill, undermined the worker's control over his own labour process and contributed to the continuing degradation of work.[2] Consequently, it would appear, the workforce was moulded into a single homogeneous whole and the lines of class conflict were more clearly and starkly drawn.

In both sets of arguments, it is assumed that rationalization reflected the tendency for the millowners, on the one side, and the workers, on the other, increasingly to combine, develop uniform interests and discover solidarities.[3] Yet, as this chapter will argue, rationalization and standardization not only exposed the diversity of interests and conditions within the industry, but their implementation exacerbated its internal differences. Similarly, it is often taken for granted that the Bombay millowners, once awakened to the imperatives of rationalization, were able consistently to realize their intentions. But in view of their diverse interests and their failure to combine, it would appear rash to expect that they might share and sustain such wide aims in common or put them into practice at their own choosing. The pervasiveness of the discourse of rationalization as well as these models for its interpretation have made it easier to assume the common intent of the millowners to transform their methods of management than to assess the extent and depth of the changes which they effected.

This chapter will examine the discourse of rationalization in Bombay, particularly as it took shape around the schemes formulated in its name. These schemes were devised first under the stimulus of the Fawcett Committee, set up to arbitrate over the causes of the general strike of 1928, and then, later, the Textile Labour Inquiry Committee appointed by the Congress ministry in the late 1930s. By investigating their formulation and the failure to implement them, it seeks to illuminate the nature and development of capital–labour relations in early-twentieth-century Bombay.

[2] H. Braverman, *Labour and Monopoly Capital: The Degradation of Work in the Twentieth Century* (New York, 1974); Bhattacharya, 'Capital and Labour'.
[3] According to Newman: 'Economic crisis introduced a new sense of unity on both sides of the industry. The Millowners' Association began to speak and act for all its members instead of being an arena of factionalism. The millhands discovered a sense of common interest as prices soared and then began to evolve a broader and more elaborate form of leadership; Newman, *Workers and Unions*, p. 84. See also Bhattacharya, 'Capital and Labour'.

Faced with intense competition in contracting markets, and lacking the protection of tariffs, the Bombay millowners were reluctant to risk their capital in a major programme of reorganization. Under these circumstances, their immediate response to their difficulties was to manipulate their labour force, cutting wages, retrenching workers and increasing workloads. Consequently, they often provoked thereby fierce labour resistance. Yet, paradoxically, it was the anticipation of sustained and disruptive industrial action which had in part deterred the millowners from attempting the fundamental reorganization of their industry. While rationalization presupposed, and promised, a greater degree of combination and collusion among the millowners, the formulation and discussion of the schemes only served to expose their internal schisms and lay bare their mutual jealousies and antagonisms. For the millowners, the diversity of interests within the industry clouded any simple, collective view of their future. On the other hand, workers' resistance to rationalization did not necessarily reflect their increasing homogeneity or the entrenchment of a permanent sense of common interests. Changing market conditions or shifts in employer politicies affected the workforce in diverse ways. Solidarities negotiated between diverse groups of workers for limited objectives within specific political conjunctures remained for this reason fragile and highly vulnerable. Nonetheless, their resistance, however divided and enfeebled, often thwarted the initiatives of the millowners and opened up and exposed divisions within their ranks.

Defining rationalization: objectives and constraints

When the Tariff Board prescribed rationalization as the cure for the industry's problems, it was not, of course, advancing an original concept, but simply drawing upon the spreading fashion of scientific management associated with the American writer, Frederick Winslow Taylor. Its objective was to obtain the maximum effort from the workforce, eliminate waste and simplify and standardize production processes. By the 1920s, its significance in the West began to shift to a broader and more radical vision, inspired by Ford, of the fundamental reorganization of production, not only in relation to labour but also in its wider commercial and financial aspects.[4]

At the centre of the discourse about rationalization in Bombay lay an abiding

---

[4] Indeed, its significance extended beyond the factory and became enmeshed with wider intellectual and political trends. See, for instance, C.S. Maier, *In Search of Stability: Explorations in Historical Political Economy* (Cambridge, 1987), pp. 19–69; R. Brady, *The Rationalization Movement in German Industry: A Study in the Evolution of Economic Planning,* (Berkeley, 1933); J.A. Merkle, *Management and Ideology: The Legacy of the International Scientific Management Movement* (Berkeley and Los Angeles, 1980); Braverman, *Labour and Monopoly Capital.*

ambiguity about the meaning of the term. It was sometimes used to signify the financial and technological reorganization of the industry, and sometimes, primarily, to describe changes in the pattern of labour deployment; and, indeed, the nature of the relationship between the two has not perhaps been fully explored. Moreover, since rationalization altered working conditions and thereby increased the diversity within the industry, the millowners often sought, and indeed were at times called upon, to combine their efficiency measures with schemes for the standardization of wages and conditions. Contemporaries sometimes used the terms rationalization and standardization interchangeably and subsequent discussion has not always differentiated between them or elaborated their relationship. Indeed, just what was being rationalized or standardized was at times left unclear. In its final report, compiled in 1940, the Textile Labour Inquiry Committee was led to observe plaintively that the term rationalization 'is used in such a variety of meanings that a discussion about it tends to result in confusion'.[5] We may sympathize with the Committee's sentiment.

The scientific pretensions of rationalization have also helped to obfuscate its real nature. Asked by the Textile Labour Inquiry Committee to explain the scientific basis of their methods, the representative of the scientific management consultants, the Eastern Bedaux Company, confessed: 'We have gradually brought up the efficiency more by guess work than by any other method.'[6] Invited to explain the secret of the Bedaux system, their representative, J.M. Moore, dilated on how they had sophisticated Taylor's method:

Taylor said, 'It takes ten seconds for a man to walk from A to B'. Bedaux said, 'All right, put a hundred pound sack on that man's back and he will still walk from A to B in ten seconds, but he has done four times as much work.'[7]

It may be that Bedaux's representative did not do his guru's genius justice; but his briskness suggests something of the spirit in which rationalization was applied in Bombay.

The objectives envisaged in the abstract by the advocates of rationalization were in practice riddled with difficulties and, indeed, beset with internal contradictions. 'The aim of the industrialist', the Committee opined, 'is to produce goods with as much profit as can be obtained in the prevalent circumstances, and from this standpoint his success would be measured by his efficiency in that direction.' But, it added, this success would depend upon the 'efficiency of machines' in producing 'with minimum cost and maximum of

---

[5] *Report of the TLIC*, II, 180.
[6] Proceedings of the TLIC, Main Inquiry, Oral Evidence, Representatives of the Eastern Bedaux Company: Messrs. J.M. Moore, M.K. Rao, M.R. Leach, D.D. Fouche, 2 April 1939, File 77-C, p. 4955, MSA.
[7] *Ibid.*, p. 4957.

output', the 'efficiency of men' in 'turning out the largest quantity of products' and 'the efficiency of management in preventing waste and eliminating unnecessary costs'.[8] Yet, as Bombay's millowners were only too aware, maximizing profits within the constraints of the prevailing circumstances was not always compatible with maximizing efficiency. The quest for optimum efficiency demanded a considerable outlay and it could encounter fierce and disruptive opposition from the workforce.

To the extent that rationalization signified the progressive adoption of the most sophisticated technology, it raised another fundamental problem for the millowners and their putative advisors. The Textile Labour Inquiry Committee stumbled upon it almost accidentally in 1940:

The growth in productive capacity has apparently outstripped the increase in consumption, notwithstanding efforts to bring down the price level. The demand for cotton fabrics is not likely to expand appreciably in the near future, while with the introduction of rationalization and as a consequence of steady technical advance, the productive capacity may grow continuously.[9]

The Committee was led to the conclusion that the industry should, therefore, combine to restrict output. This had scarcely appeared even remotely possible in the decades between the two world wars. More significantly, it was unrealistic to expect the millowners to invest relentlessly and progressively in the most sophisticated technology, while at the same time seeking defensively within saturated markets to restrict output, which in turn could commit them to intermittently rendering some of their machinery idle.

Moreover, rationalization could either be conceived in a wider sense or else it could be interpreted narrowly. As the Textile Labour Inquiry Committee observed,

Rationalization in its widest sense comprehends all measures that can, on grounds of systematic reasoning, be recommended for adoption by an industry for improving its technique, its management and its finances.[10]

In this sense, rationalization might involve 'financial and industrial reorganization' and could be extended to matters pertaining to the workers' welfare. But the more generously it was defined, the more limited were the achievements of the Bombay millowners. Indeed, rationalization in its 'widest sense' demanded a considerable financial outlay and the fundamental reorganization of the industry's machinery as well as its methods. Faced with tight markets, severe foreign and growing internal competition and the unfavourable exchange, financial and especially tariff policies of the colonial state, most millowners

[8] *Report of the TLIC*, II, 180.
[9] *Ibid.*, II, 224.
[10] *Ibid.*, II, 211.

were either unable or unwilling to entertain ambitions of these heroic proportions. 'We have not been sitting idle whining over foreign competition', Homi
Mody, the Chairman of the BMOA asserted in 1930.[11] But,

It should also be made perfectly plain that the problems of this magnitude cannot be
tackled while the industry is subject to fierce competition which cripples its resources
and seriously impairs its competitive ability.

Similarly, T.V. Baddeley, Vice Chairman of the Millowners' Association,
explained in 1931, 'progress towards the adoption of many of the recommendations [of the Tariff Board and the Whitley Commission] must be slow'.[12]
Although tariffs were raised in the early 1930s, they did not provide the
necessary shelter from competition to steel the entrepreneurs' nerve.

The quest for optimum efficiency was in these circumstances likely to be as
elusive as the Holy Grail; its pursuit also demanded a similarly unshakeable
faith. The enormous range of interests within the industry militated against
sustained and effective combination to eliminate waste, reduce competition and
pare down costs. Indeed, the millowners' failure to combine was so comprehensive that the attempt itself appears retrospectively to have been unrealistic.
If combination was often difficult to effect, it was not always desirable or greatly
advantageous. The diversity of conditions in the industry meant that the requirements of each mill with regard to stores, machinery and plant varied considerably. Similarly, buying cotton, selling cloth and yarn and securing credit and
finance hinged upon highly personalized arrangements which each millowner
guarded jealously and which none was willing to surrender to collective
regulation. Combined action brought limited gains: cheaper power through the
Tata Hydro-Electric Power scheme; the sharing of market information in the
export trade, where nonetheless buying and selling remained highly individualized;[13] and mutual insurance against workmen's compensation.[14]

Nor did the Bombay millowners reveal a marked preference for the progressive introduction of the latest and best technology. In the late nineteenth century,
it has been argued, they were slow to replace their mule spindles with ring
frames. This persistence with the mule has been portrayed as an 'irrational
choice of technique', a function both of their myopic entrepreneurship, which
failed to allow adequately for depreciation and which sought immediate gain at
the expense of the long-term interests of the industry, and also of the technical

---

[11] *BMOA, Annual Report, 1929*, Proceedings of the Annual General Meeting, Chairman's Speech,
    p. v.
[12] *Ibid., 1931*, Proceedings of the Annual General Meeting, Vice-Chairman's Speech, p. vi.
[13] Proceedings of the TLIC, Main Inquiry, Oral Evidence, BMOA, File 57A, pp. 102–3, MSA.
[14] The Millowners' Mutual Insurance Company proved to be a highly profitable enterprise, largely
    because of the reluctance of industrial tribunals to grant compensation to injured workers. Their
    hearings were reported regularly in the *Labour Gazette*.

incompetence which left them at the mercy of British machinery manufacturers for market information as well as supplies.[15] There is some force in these arguments, but the millowners' response to technological change was far more nuanced than this portrayal allows. The choices made by the millowners cannot be dismissed simply as irrational within the wider economic context in which they were made. As the case of the mule spindle shows, the depreciation policies of the Bombay millowners can only be fairly judged in the context of the constraints which operated on the mobilization of capital as well as the high cost of imported machinery.

The mule possessed a number of advantages which were highly compatible with business strategies commonly adopted by the Bombay millowners. Not only did it require a smaller initial outlay, but it was considered a far more flexible machine which could spin a wider range of counts and which allowed the product to be more easily switched than the ring frame.[16] The mule was considered more 'pliable' and 'less rigid and exacting in its operations than a ring frame'. Some of its flexibility derived from its ability to convert waste into profit in the lowest counts. Although it is sometimes assumed – and the weight of contemporary trade and technical opinion in India supported this view – that the ring frame yielded better results in quality, output and costs than mule spinning in coarse counts, mill managers in Bombay believed that 'if handled well', the mule could produce in counts of 10s 'as much outturn per spindle as that from an ordinary ring mixing and perhaps leave a better margin of profit'.[17] The malleability of the mule and its facility for switching counts of yarn may explain why the Punjab and North Indian mills continued to buy them until 1920.[18] Kiyokawa has argued that the slow diffusion of ring spinning and therefore the technological backwardness and conservatism of the Bombay millowners explains why they were displaced by the Japanese spinning industry in the Chinese market. But another comparative study of ring diffusion has attributed the persistence of the mule in India partly to the fact that the industry 'quickly developed major yarn markets at home and abroad which could not be

[15] Y. Kiyokawa, 'Technical Adaptations and Managerial Resources in India: A Study of the Experience of the Cotton Textile Industry From a Comparative Standpoint', *The Developing Economies*, XXI, 2 (1983), 97–133. See also G. Saxonhouse and G. Wright, 'Rings and Mules Around the World: A Comparative Study in Technological Choice', *Research in Economic History*, supplement 3 (1984), *Technique, Spirit and Form in the Making of the Modern Economies: Essays in Honor of William N. Parker*, ed. G. Saxonhouse and G. Wright (Greenwich, Conn., 1984), pp. 271–300; K. Otsuka, G. Ranis and G. Saxonhouse, *Comparative Technology Choice in Development: The Indian and Japanese Cotton Textile Industries* (London, 1988).

[16] Mehta, *Cotton Mills*, pp. 43–4; Kiyokawa, 'Technical Adaptations and Managerial Resources', 108–9.

[17] A Retired Mill Manager, *The Bombay Cotton Mills*, p. 6.

[18] Kiyokawa, 'Technical Adaptations and Managerial Resources', pp. 114–15.

cheaply serviced by wooden bobbin-using rings'. It was only after it lost its Chinese market for yarn and began to develop its weaving capacity, that the Bombay industry's 'interest in the ring greatly increased'.[19] In fact, it is salutory to recall that the major casualty of the falling trade in yarn exports was Greaves Cotton and Company, the largest group of spinning mills in Bombay, which had introduced the ring frame and pioneered its development on a large scale.[20]

So the stubbornness of the mule was not as irrational as it appeared at first glance. In fact, the Bombay mills had, on the back of the mule, prospered in the Chinese market in the late 1870s and 1880s, eclipsed Lancashire and, as late as 1908, still been able to sell three times as much yarn as the Japanese. They had few reasons to embark upon major technological transformation. When market conditions changed from the late 1890s onwards, they were in a far weaker position to renovate their machinery and when prosperity returned their invest- ment focussed on the expansion of their weaving capacity.[21] In spite of these immediate advantages of mule spindles, they accounted for only 57 per cent of the industry's spinning capacity in 1894.[22] In this light, the diffusion of ring- spinning technology appears to have occurred relatively swiftly. New mills in Bombay, and especially in up-country centres, which expanded rapidly in the 1890s, were equipped more extensively with ring spindles. Older mills were slower to replace their mules, some of which were expected to last for sixty years, but they added ring spindles to their stock, for most mills had some of each in the early 1890s. This pattern of development contrasted sufficiently with that of Lancashire, which continued to renew its mules in the 1920s and favoured them particularly for their utility in higher counts, to cast doubt upon the notion that the Bombay millowners were blinded by the technical knowledge of the British machinery manufacturers and victims of their own incompetence and ignorance. Indeed, the pattern of ring diffusion across the world, its extent and timing, was determined by a wide range of factors in each case, and 'is not easily subject to a single variate explanation'.[23]

In the 1920s, the Bombay millowners showed no radical transformation in their attitude towards technological progress. Indeed, in their experience, the blessings of technology had always been mixed. A broadly similar combination of factors impinged upon their entrepreneurial choices in the 1920s and 1930s. The permanent constraints of both capital and demand were now felt yet more forcefully. The benefits of the most advanced technology were in general most likely to be realized with long runs of production. The cost-reducing effects of

---

[19] Saxonhouse and Wright, 'Rings and Mules Around the World', p. 291.
[20] Mehta, *Cotton Mills*, p. 44; Rutnagur, *Bombay Industries*, pp. 19, 27–9, 61.
[21] See chapter 6 above.
[22] Calculated from Rutnagur, *Directory of Indian Manufactories*, p. 6.
[23] Saxonhouse and Wright, 'Rings and Mules Around the World', pp. 286–8.

machinery could only be fully realized if the flow and consistency of orders in particular styles and qualities of cloth were maintained. But the Indian market was too fragmented to permit such simple organization or guarantee long runs of production. The need to switch their machines from one line of production to another according to the fluctuations of demand further constrained millowners from investing in new technology or indeed implementing rationalization schemes. Moreover, the advantages of new technology were most clearly manifested in the higher counts of yarn and finer varieties of piecegoods. High draft spinning or automatic looms would not yield their best results in the coarser lines of production. Yet in the depressed conditions of the 1930s, demand was perceptibly shifting away from high priced and high quality goods. These factors began to interact with each other. The introduction of new technology often required changes in the organization of production, from the buying and mixing of cotton to the final stages of the process, and necessarily in work practices. The response of textile workers to altered conditions also informed the decisions of millowners.

How these factors – the entrenched business strategies of the millowners and the force of labour resistance – worked upon the attitude of entrepreneurs towards the introduction of new technology is illustrated by the case of the automatic loom. From at least the late 1920s, some millowners had considered importing automatic looms. Certainly the question had been pressed upon them by the numerous committees which inquired into the affairs of the textile industry in the following decade. The Northrop loom required a greater capital

Most Bombay mills, especially those which were constructed in the 1870s and 1880s, had been equipped primarily to spin coarse yarn. In the late 1920s, it was found, as in the case of the Swadeshi Mills, that the old frames continued to produce 'good results in spinning but in weaving it is at a disadvantage, because the bobbin runs off the shuttle in a shorter period'.[24] The Swadeshi Mill introduced universal pirn winders which would increase the quantity of weft yarn in the shuttle and expected in return that it was 'up to labour to improve also their efficiency'.[25] Despite his reformist zeal and his determination to break labour resistance to the introduction of fresh methods and novel techniques in the industry, Mr T. Sasakura, the Managing Director of the newly taken over Toyo Podar Mills, had to abandon the use of the universal winding machine because wages proved to be too high.[26] The returns of introducing universal winding machines could not justify their expense unless weavers agreed to mind three or four looms and this proved impossible to secure.

How these factors – the entrenched business strategies of the millowners and the force of labour resistance – worked upon the attitude of entrepreneurs towards the introduction of new technology is illustrated by the case of the automatic loom. From at least the late 1920s, some millowners had considered importing automatic looms. Certainly the question had been pressed upon them by the numerous committees which inquired into the affairs of the textile industry in the following decade. The Northrop loom required a greater capital

---

[24] Proceedings of the BSEC, I, 255, MSA.
[25] *Ibid.*
[26] Proceedings of the BSEC, I, 224–8, 493–525, MSA.

outlay and higher rate of depreciation than the ordinary Lancashire loom. Moreover, stores and spare parts for the automatic loom were both relatively more expensive and less readily obtainable. This additional cost had to be made up, as the Tariff Board noted, by 'higher production, higher prices or a reduction in labour costs'. For most of the 1920s and 1930s, there was little prospect of rising prices. Trial runs conducted in Bombay revealed that the automatic loom did not yield an appreciably higher output. Furthermore, the automatic loom required weft yarn of a higher quality and greater strength. In turn, this called for a better quality of raw cotton, improved mixings and preparation as well as the adoption of different techniques of winding, for the weft yarn had to be put on to special pirns. In 1927, these adjustments alone were estimated to increase the costs of production by seven pies per pound, at a time when certain lines of Bombay's output were being undersold at the cost of production by Japanese mills in the domestic market. In any case, raising the quality of yarn and cloth would have repercussions for the organization of the entire mill: for the production patterns and output of every preparatory process and thus for the pattern of labour deployment in every department. It was scarcely economic to 'swing off' automatic looms as most mills did with regard to the ordinary loom. To supply the Northrop loom adequately, each process of production would have to be suitably adapted. Its adoption would require the lengthening and standardization of production runs throughout the mills from the preparatory processes to the weaving shed. Under these conditions, it would be more difficult for mills to remain alert to market fluctuations and to the varieties and specificities of taste. Given their financial structure and their volatile market conditions, the millowners could scarcely transform their production patterns so thoroughly.

The viability of the automatic loom, therefore, came to turn increasingly upon whether labour costs could be reduced. The millowners were reluctant to promulgate direct wage cuts which they realistically expected would provoke strikes. The possibility of reducing labour costs would depend upon whether the number of looms allocated to each weaver could be increased. It was very apparent at the time, however, that 'it would be difficult to get weavers in Bombay to look after more than four looms'. Yet, even if the number of automatic looms per weaver was raised to six, the ordinary loom would still be more economical.[27] In one of its nicer formulations, the Tariff Board concluded that 'in present conditions no solution of the problem presented by labour costs in Bombay lies in the introduction of the Northrop loom'.[28] Five years later, another Tariff Board was to find conditions unchanged:

The general conclusion is that the adoption of automatic looms will not reduce costs

[27] The preceding paragraphs are based upon *Report of the ITB, 1927*, I, 143–5.
[28] *Ibid.*, I, 144.

unless a weaver will agree to work a larger number of looms than he does now ... The opinion is widely held that the kinds of cloth required for the Indian market are not sufficiently standardised to justify the installation on a large scale of automatic looms. The advantage secured by automatic looms on wage costs is more than off-set by additional charges, mainly the much greater interest and depreciation charges.[29]

Despite the recovery of the mid 1930s, a greater measure of protection and the extent of unemployment which created a reserve supply of labour, the millowners remained reluctant to invest in the Northrop loom. Although 'you want less skilled workers for it and fewer looms', the innovative Fred Stones declared in 1938,

I personally would not import an automatic loom. The net result in view of the increased capital expenditure does not warrant it. Here the automatic loom cannot compete with the six-loom system.[30]

The future, as the millowners perceived it, lay with the Lancashire loom; and the line of advance was the traditional response of the industry: to increase the number of old looms tended by each weaver.

Although changing production patterns were an important factor in the millowners' reluctance to implement rationalization or introduce more advanced technology, it is not intended to suggest that it was the most important. In the manipulation of mixings and the counts and the quality of the yarn or in the constant adjustments and changes of production patterns millowners were liable to provoke labour discontent and encounter resistance. The case of the automatic loom shows that while capital costs, low prices and foreign competition as well as fluctuations of quality and composition of output contributed to the lack of enthusiasm with which the Northrop was received in Bombay, the most significant factor was the difficulty of getting weavers to work a larger number of looms. In 1939, it was clear, as Maloney, the Secretary of the Millowners' Association, put it, that 'lack of capital' was not so much 'the main cause of slow progress' in the implementation of rationalization as the 'opposition of the workers'. And as Stones added, 'progress is hampered very much by the fact that there are so many strikes, and it would be inadvisable to invest money in machinery in the circumstances'.[31]

The intense competition within the industry did not always promote technological diffusion; it could also inhibit and restrict innovation. The development of printing had been limited by the fact that engraved copper rollers had to be imported and then, after use, shipped back to England for new designs to be engraved.[32] In the mid 1930s, printing began to develop and proved very

[29] *Report of the ITB, 1932*, pp. 65–7.
[30] Proceedings of the TLIC, Main Inquiry, Oral Evidence, BMOA, File 57-A, p. 52, MSA.
[31] *Ibid.*, Main Inquiry, Oral Evidence, BMOA, File 57-A, p. 63, MSA.
[32] *Ibid.*, Main Inquiry, Oral Evidence, BMOA, File 57-A, pp. 99–101, MSA.

remunerative until Japanese importers, needing sterling, began to undersell Bombay. By 1939, printed cloth was sold at a smaller margin than ordinary coarse goods. Moreover, printing plant was expensive and could not easily be switched between designs. To operate at high efficiency, a finishing plant needed to be supplied with a large volume of goods beyond the ability of an average mill working on its own.[33] But the millowners were reluctant to pool their resources in a joint venture, partly because the financial condition of the industry precluded any substantially increased investment and the resources available were needed for the 'replacement of old machinery on a larger scale than had hitherto been possible'.[34] The millowners who may have been in a position to invest had, a few years previously, when the Sassoon group introduced five printing machines, swiftly followed the leader.[35] It was by the end of the decade beyond consideration that they would scrap their machines and invest in a more modern plant for a combined operation.

The 1920s, according to one historian, 'marked the dawn of a new era for textile technology'.[36] The new era did not entirely pass the industry by, despite its own financial and trading difficulties. The Textile Labour Inquiry Committee listed 'some of the innovations which had added to the efficiency of several mills': 'continuous process machinery in the blow room, vacuum stripping in the card room, high drafting of the Casablanca or other types, lengthening of frames, high speed winding and warping, improved machinery for dyeing and finishing'.[37] But it is difficult to estimate how widely they were applied. T. Maloney, the Secretary of the Millowners' Association, had said somewhat airily before the Textile Labour Inquiry Committee that such changes 'have become very general in Bombay as sound efficiency schemes',[38] but their representatives had at other times testified that their outlay for rationalization schemes had been small and their efforts to revamp their machinery rather modest.[39] Moreover, they complained that textile machinery prices had risen dramatically, almost doubling the cost of a ring-spinning frame,[40] due to the cartelization of the suppliers. Fred Stones told the Committee that no agent would put money forward for the reconstruction of a spinning department; Dharmsey Khatau explained that the first priority for industry and its 'only hope'

---

[33] *Ibid.*, Main Inquiry, Oral Evidence, II, 222–3, MSA.
[34] *Report of the TLIC*, II, 222.
[35] Proceedings of the TLIC, Main Inquiry, Oral Evidence, BMOA, File 57-A, p. 99, MSA; *Report of the TLIC*, II, 222–3.
[36] Kiyokawa, 'Technical Adaptations and Managerial Resources', 103.
[37] *Report of the TLIC*, II, 224.
[38] Proceedings of the TLIC, Main Inquiry, Oral Evidence, BMOA, File 57-A, p. 98, MSA.
[39] *Ibid.*, p. 96, MSA.
[40] *Ibid.*, p. 179, MSA.

was 'to earn enough to take care of its arrears of depreciation' before it set out 'to buy new machines ... or to do anything possible to become efficient'; and Maloney declared that new capital to extend efficiency schemes would be 'very shy'.[41] Moreover, textile-machinery imports declined steadily from the peak of the early 1920s until the end of the 1930s.[42]

In 1937, as trading conditions improved, much still remained to be done in the renewal and replacement of machinery, 'finance for which could not be found in the very lean years through which we have been passing'.[43] In their evidence before the Textile Labour Inquiry Committee, the Bombay millowners reiterated that 'additions to capacity, unfortunately, we have hardly known in Bombay for a number of years'.[44] Since the average size of the Bombay mills was large, the capital required to renovate them was considerable. 'No one would have the courage', as Sir Chunilal Mehta explained,

to put that money up in unfavourable circumstances. It becomes a sort of vicious circle ... There is no money in running mills in Bombay on account of the competition of up country mills which have the benefit of the cotton on the spot and the local cloth market. You must, therefore, turn to finer counts and the machinery for that purpose requires very large sums of money.[45]

In any case, the shift of demand towards low-priced goods meant that coarse-cloth production by the mid 1930s was the more profitable. Several mills which had taken to the production of fancy goods encountered difficulties and some were taken into liquidation.[46] It is likely, therefore, that the adoption of these technological innovations was slow, halting and uneven within the industry. Some mills may have been able to innovate on a substantial scale; but most probably struggled to survive on the strength of manipulating their ageing plant.

Rationalization and standardization in the 1920s: setting the agenda

The 'rationalization' which was effected in Bombay in the 1920s and 1930s did not, therefore, amount to the financial and industrial reorganization of the cotton-textile industry, a relentless attempt to maximize efficiency or, indeed, the progressive adoption of the most recent and most sophisticated technology.

---

[41] *Ibid.*, p. 180, MSA.
[42] Bagchi, *Private Investment*, pp. 258–61; Kirk and Simmons, 'Lancashire and the Equipping of the Indian Cotton Mills,' table, p. 171.
[43] *BMOA, Annual Report, 1936*, Proceedings of the Annual General Meeting, Chairman's Speech, p. iii.
[44] Proceedings of the TLIC, Interim Inquiry, Oral Evidence, BMOA, File 42, p. 16, MSA.
[45] *Ibid., pp. 35–6, MSA.*
[46] Proceedings of the TLIC, Main Inquiry, Oral Evidence, BMOA, File 57A, p. 284; *ibid.*, Interim Inquiry, Oral Evidence, BMOA, File 42, p. 319, MSA.

In the late 1920s and 1930s, rationalization largely implied the increased production of finer varieties of yarn and cloth and increased workloads. These objectives were closely related. The production of higher counts of yarn and finer varieties of piecegoods required fewer workers and enabled them to operate more machines. This was rationalization in its narrow sense. If, as the Textile Labour Inquiry Committee had observed, rationalization 'has a wider and a narrower meaning', 'improvements in labour productivity and efficiency' constitute 'one aspect of the latter sense'.[47] The Bombay millowners did not proceed far beyond this partial aspect of the narrow construction of its scope: the implementation of 'efficiency schemes' by which workloads were increased and labour retrenched. Weavers who worked two looms were now to be put in charge of three or four while ring spinners would have to mind both sides of the frame. Yet even these efficiency schemes were neither comprehensive nor far-reaching. In the late 1930s, less than a fifth of the weavers in the Bombay mills worked more than two looms and less than one half of the siders worked two sides.[48] The increasing emphasis upon the production of higher counts of yarn and piecegoods facilitated this deployment of labour. But it involved little technological change or innovation, the introduction of new machines or the replacement of old plant. Across the industry as a whole, it entailed only as much or as little adaptation, reorganization and investment as the individual millowner desired. The Bombay millowners, as a body, did not respond to their competitive situation or to official exhortations by consistently rationalizing the structure and organization of their industry or effecting technological change.

However, rationalization in its narrow meaning fitted admirably with the needs of industry in the mid 1920s. It is difficult to know what else, other than diversifying output and cheapening their labour costs, the millowners might have done when faced with the slump. By producing larger quantities of fine yarn and cloth, the Bombay mills sought to escape the most congested areas of the domestic market. In any case, the production of finer yarn and cloth had been a common and recurrent response to falling demand since the late nineteenth century. By spinning finer yarn, millowners could curtail their output, cut their losses on overheads – which a stoppage would otherwise have entailed – and reduce their consumption of cotton.[49] The spinning of finer yarn also reduced the labour requirements of the mill in the preparatory processes while allowing it to work those processes most fully in which the most value was added to the raw material.[50] Weaving cloth of finer quality or heavier

[47] Report of the TLIC, II, 183.
[48] Report of the TLIC, II, 187, table no. 44.
[49] A Retired Mill Manager, Bombay Cotton Mills, p. 3.
[50] Note by J. Westland, in Indian Tariff and Cotton Duties: Papers Relating to the Indian Tariff Act, PP, 1895, LXXII, 7–8.

construction could also fulfil the same function. Since the amount of value added in manufacturing rose as the processing of cotton became more elaborate and the quality of output improved, the production of finer varieties could be looked upon as a means of reducing labour costs as a proportion of the margin between the price of raw material and the price of the finished product.

In the long run, the production of higher counts and finer varieties could not be sustained simply by manipulating the mixings of cotton. Since this manipulation could only be effected at the expense of quality, these products were unlikely to be competitive or indeed remunerative. To compete effectively in the market for higher counts of yarn and finer piecegoods, the industry would have to revamp its methods. It would have to buy more suitable cotton, adapt the preparatory processes for spinning and effect necessary adjustments to its machinery. These measures were bound to require changes in the industry's pattern of labour deployment.

The second desideratum was for the millowners to cheapen their labour costs.[51] Indeed, the initial response of the millowners was to make varying use of their capacity and especially to cut wages. Short-time working in any case could only be a temporary measure and it would increase their overhead charges. It would leave the field open to their rivals without necessarily or substantially relieving the pressure of supply in their markets. Fearing that individual wage cuts effected by their members would engender chaos in their labour market, the Millowners' Association resolved to take the initiative. But wage cuts promulgated by the Millowners' Association would in all probability commit the industry to facing a general strike and, as a consequence, inflict considerable losses without, as they learnt in 1925, necessarily obtaining a reduction in wages. By producing higher counts of yarn and finer piecegoods, mills could reduce their labour costs, not only because these lines of output required fewer workers but also because they could then increase the number of machines assigned to each worker, an arrangement which might later be continued, even as they switched back to coarser goods. Although there were many ways of reducing labour costs, it became increasingly clear that this was most easily achieved along the narrow front of wages. Increased efficiency was an obvious alternative: but it was more easily projected than effected. 'I do not want wages to come down', declared Fred Stones, 'but I do want that the cost should come down.'[52] Many mills could not afford the outlay which increased efficiency demanded; the first step towards lower costs lay in reduced wages. The changing composition of output created the opportunity to reduce piece rates when a new variety was introduced or to maintain workloads, increased for a particular line of production.

---

[51] Proceedings of the BSEC, I, 171, 615, MSA.
[52] Proceedings of the TLIC, Main Inquiry, Oral Evidence, Mr F. Stones, File 72, p. 3610, MSA.

Indeed, the industry's response to the crisis of the early 1920s was, as we have seen, largely individual. Mills which switched their lines of production or tried to manufacture finer varieties, reduced their labour costs, without necessarily increasing efficiency. Since the changing character and composition of production had varying requirements of both machinery and labour, they often left some of their capacity idle and retrenched parts of their labour force. Not only did this induce a sense of uncertainty among the workforce, but it also increased the workloads of those who were employed. Wage reductions were also effected indirectly when the character of production was changed but piece rates were not: thus, where payment was by weight and rates were unchanged, weaving cloth from higher counts of yarn yielded lower earnings. But, spinning higher counts without parallel improvements in the raw material, its mixing or its preparation, led to more breakages and thus increased the sider's workloads; but this weakness could be carried over to the loom where it affected the weaver's wage. The use of artificial silk in the mixing or the speeding up of machinery beyond its capacity was also liable to increase the number of breakages. Moreover, switching production between different varieties of cloth, according to short-term fluctuations of demand, could require the weaving of narrow widths of cloth on wider looms and thus this too could slow down the pace of work.[53]

In 1928, the millowners had argued before the Fawcett Committee that the wage reductions alleged by the Joint Mill Strike Committee and cited as a cause of the general strike in 1928, were not wage cuts at all but 'mere adjustments in weaving rates which had always been taking place',[54] whenever new varieties or qualities of cloth were introduced.

That is not a practice which is followed now. It had been followed for years past. The thing is that Mr Joshi is now trying to organize unions and complaints are now received by him. It is for the first time perhaps that he comes to know of such adjustments. He thinks (erroneously though) that they are reductions in wages.[55]

It is possible, however, that these adjustments became more frequent and more consistently exerted a downward push on wages as the mills began to feel more acutely the pressure of saturated markets and intensifying competition after 1922–3.[56]

In the later 1920s, as conditions began to improve, more mills sought to diversify their output into higher counts of yarn and finer piecegoods. Once the

---

[53] *Ibid.*, Interim Inquiry, Oral Evidence, A.W. Pryde, Government Labour Officer, Bombay, File 42, pp. 457–8, MSA.
[54] Proceedings of BSEC, I, 9, MSA.
[55] *Ibid.*, I, 118, MSA.
[56] *Report of the ITB, 1927, Evidence of Local Government, Official Witnesses...*, Bombay Textile Labour Union, III, 446–7.

Tariff Board had reported, these 'adjustments' in wages and the character of production acquired a name and were legitimized as integral to the necessary programme of rationalization. As their introduction sharpened the competitive edge between mills, they also became more widespread. 'My experience of the last two years as an officer of a trade union', N.M. Joshi said in 1928,

was that various employers in the city began to change their conditions on the ground that other employers had other conditions of service and in this way an employer cut down the rates saying that the rates in other mills were low. He similarly changed the conditions in other mills also.[57]

Some groups of mills, notably the Sassoons, which pioneered efficiency schemes as early as 1923, the Bombay Dyeing, Finlay and Kohinoor mills, began to produce finer varieties and adjusted their pattern of labour deployment accordingly. The failure of the millowners' attempt to cut wages across the industry as in 1925 and the legitimacy given to the so-called rationalization schemes by the Tariff Board quickened the movement of other mills in this direction. They reduced workers without the necessary changes in the organization of production, using the opportunity of changes in the composition of output to reduce rates and, to effect what Fred Stones called 'the surreptitious cutting of wages'.[58]

Rationalization introduced in a piecemeal fashion was bound to exacerbate the already staggering diversity of conditions within the industry. It was likely to intensify wage competition between mills. 'Amongst ourselves there is also a rivalry', Saklatvala had confided to the Fawcett Committee: 'every mill wants to have the best labourers.'[59] Moreover, as attempts to introduce efficiency schemes encountered resistance, there were some millowners who grew concerned to restore some semblance of order to their industry. Indeed, the race to extend efficiency schemes indiscriminately, to cut costs and wages competitively or to increase workloads to match the standards of the neighbouring mill was likely to imperil the attempt by some to expand their output of higher counts and finer varieties and increase their productivity, especially in these lines. Resistance to the piecemeal introduction of efficiency schemes also dissuaded millowners from bringing upon themselves individually the threat of closure which could force them to sacrifice their competitive position to their rivals. Faced with labour resistance, as Sir Joseph Kay explained, the managing agents W.H. Brady and Company, decided to 'stop our personal efforts to introduce a standardisation scheme, and put our case in along with that of Millowners'

---

[57] Proceedings of BSEC, I, 272, MSA.
[58] Proceedings of the TLIC, Main Inquiry, Oral Evidence, Mr F. Stones, Managing Director, Messrs. E.D. Sassoon and Co. Ltd, File 72, p. 3903; see also *ibid.*, File 70, p. 3454, MSA.
[59] Proceedings of BSEC, I, 257, MSA.

Association'.[60] All these factors focussed the minds of the millowners on the formulation of a standardization scheme for their whole industry, largely as a framework for the introduction of efficiency measures and as a means of ironing out the discrepancies between mills.

In 1928, standardization was scarcely a novel idea. It had been one of the more traditional, perhaps pious, aims of the Millowners' Association and some of its leading members. Since at least the 1890s, the Millowners' Association had grappled with the diversity of conditions and interests within the industry and their often baneful consequences. Periods of sharp contraction or rapid expansion had always intensified the competition between mills and, in particular, complicated the task of recruiting and disciplining labour. Changes in working conditions as well as wages quickened labour mobility between mills and unleashed chaos in the labour market. It also prompted resistance from workers, either when they refused to accept worse terms than their neighbours or they demanded that their employers match conditions offered elsewhere. In these periods, the whole structure of labour management was subjected to intense pressure but perhaps especially at its most vulnerable point: the jobber system. Squeezed between the employers and the workforce, jobbers found it increasingly difficult to satisfy either and found themselves exposed to the rivalry of others seeking to usurp their influence or cut down their pretensions.

The question of standardization had been first raised within the Millowners' Association as early as the 1890s, when competitive wage-cutting in the face of the slump provided a spur to industrial action. Thus, in September 1893, the *Indian Textile Journal* reported that

strikes of workpeople continue in irregular fashion to interrupt work at several mills, due largely to the diversity of rates of pay at various factories, arising from the absence of any definitely accepted scale of wages among the millhands.[61]

Attempts to standardize wages failed because some mills found the standard impossible to attain, while others, in a position to purchase at a premium, if necessary, the kind of labour force they wanted, were reluctant to surrender this option. Thus, some millowners complained that workers on strike found employment in other mills and prevented 'their cases being adequately dealt with by their employers'.[62]

Similarly, disparities in wages and conditions undermined the stability of the workplace in the prosperous years between 1904 and 1908 when mills began to lengthen their working day with the introduction of electric lighting. Mills which worked the usual daylight hours 'found in some cases that their best

---

[60] *Ibid.*, I, 617, MSA.
[61] *Indian Textile Journal*, III, no. 36 (22 September 1893), p. 237.
[62] *BMOA, Annual Report, 1893*, p. 11.

workers were leaving in order to take advantage of the longer working day in other mills'. Attempts were made by the Bombay Millowners' Association to restrict its members to a twelve-hour day, and control the chaos which uneven conditions created for labour management. But it remained 'powerless to enforce its resolution'.[63] Wage competition resulted in chaos, strikes and, in October 1905, in widespread riots, and even led the Police Commissioner to inform the Millowners' Association that the situation was beyond his control.[64]

These problems recurred yet again during the inflationary period at the end of the First World War and in its immediate aftermath. In a period of high profits, millowners had preferred to make concessions and keep production going rather than risk stoppages when faced with wage demands. Between 1917 and 1920, the industry witnessed 189 strikes in individual mills[65] in addition to the two long, bitterly fought general strikes of 1919 and 1920.[66] The Millowners' Association was anxious to avoid a repetition of the wage competition of 1904–8, but the highly speculative climate of the boom limited the possibilities of wage regulation. From August 1917, the Millowners' Association stipulated wage increases for the industry as a whole to offset the consequences of sporadic increases by individual mills. These increases, which took the form of an allowance for the dearness of the cost of living, paid as a percentage of the basic wage, did little to reduce disparities between mills. Each mill chose different base years for the calculation of the dearness allowance and defined the basic rates according to its own lights. In any case, wage increases granted as percentages of current wages were bound to perpetuate the existing disparities.

The wage competition of this period was further intensified by the prospect of double shift working. The Millowners' Association was divided on the issue: Sir Dorab Tata proposed that it should impose a ten-hour day on the industry as a whole;[67] N.N. Wadia of the Bombay Dyeing group opposed this resolutely and threatened to operate two shifts regardless of its rulings. The most serious consequences of the controversy were spelt out by the Governor of Bombay:

If the two-shift system extends there is bound to be trouble, because many of the mills, on account of technical difficulties cannot follow suit, will in consequence lose their

[63] *Report of the IFLC, 1908*, I, 6–8.
[64] *BMOA, Annual Report, 1905*, p. 8; see also *BMOA, Annual Report, 1906*, Annual General Meeting, pp. ii–xv, *BMOA, Annual Report, 1907*, Annual General Meeting, pp. xiv–xvi; *Report of IFLC, Evidence*, II, 85, 109, 182; L. Fraser, *India Under Curzon and After* (London, 1911), pp. 34–5; Morris, *Industrial Labour Force*, pp. 164–5.
[65] Burnett-Hurst, *Labour and Housing*, Appendix IV, pp. 146–7; Newman, *Workers and Unions*, tables II and III, pp. 62–3.
[66] R. Kumar, 'The Bombay Textile Strike, 1919', *IESHR*, VIII, 1 (1971), 1–29; Newman, *Workers and Unions*, pp. 120–37.
[67] *BMOA, Annual Report, 1921*, pp. 39–43; Lloyd to Montagu, July 24, 1919, Montagu Papers, MSS. EUR. D 523/24, pp. 97–9, IOR.

labour to those who can and in self-defence and in the vain hope of keeping their labour will independently bid for that labour by giving higher wages and then comes the inevitable strike due to unequal conditions.[68]

The controversy dominated the affairs of the Millowners' Association until the downturn of 1922 made two shifts far less attractive. By then, Wadia had resigned from the Association, a few mills had been expelled and a number reported by their rivals for transgressing the rule and invited to explain their activities to its committee. It was not surprising, therefore, that the Industrial Disputes Committee which reported in 1922 was to press upon the millowners

the importance of a common practice on the scale of wages which if it is not reached by agreement from amongst the employers will eventually be arrived at by pressure from amongst the men at a greater sacrifice of industrial peace,

for, as it pointed out, the

uncorrelated raising of wages in one factory is almost invariably seized upon as a grievance in other factories of the same class, and instances of strikes caused in this way are within the memory of all.[69]

Indeed, the chain of events which had culminated in the general strike of 1919 had begun with the demand from the Century Mill workers that they receive one day's pay for two days of enforced armistice holidays in the same way as the workers in the neighbouring Textile Mill.[70]

Since the 1890s, repeated attempts by the millowners to standardize wages in the industry had thus consistently failed. They were only too aware that the standardization of wages and conditions would facilitate combined action on their own part. Yet it was precisely this staggering diversity of conditions within the industry which made standardization appear such an unrealistic, even utopian, objective. To lay down a standard for the whole industry was to deprive individual millowners of the flexibility which was so crucial to their style of management and to encroach upon their highly personalized arrangements, in relation to their markets, supplies, finance and methods of labour recruitment and control. Most millowners zealously defended and preserved these freedoms. Standardization amounted, therefore, to the violation of the entrenched traditions and conventions of the industry. The Millowners' Association's claim to embody the interests of its members rested on its willingness to let them interpret those interests variously, representing them only when their mutuality was unshakeably established. The energetic enforcement of a uniform standard upon the industry, however, threatened to draw the opposition of its fractious

[68] Lloyd to Montagu, 20 October, 1919, Montagu Papers, MSS. EUR. D 523/24, pp. 140–1, IOR.
[69] *Report of the Industrial Disputes Committee* (Bombay, 1922), p. 2.
[70] Bombay Confidential Proceedings, Judicial, February 1919, vol. 46, pp. 19–36, IOR.

members, divide its ranks and even destroy its organization. On the other hand, by the late 1920s, the Tariff Board had inextricably linked rationalization and standardization with the millowners' quest for protection. To press their claim for the latter, they would have to show progress with the former. In addition, wage disparities and competition injected instability into the labour market and undermined their own systems of labour discipline and control centred on the jobber. It was, therefore, with some ambivalence that the millowners approached the question anew in 1928.

The general strike of 1928: formulating a scheme

By the late 1920s, the diversification of output and individualistic responses to the slump, especially attempts to reduce earnings and increase workloads, had exacerbated differences within the industry. The piecemeal introduction of rationalization or 'efficiency schemes' only heightened the urgency for mill-owners to try to standardize conditions. In January 1928, the Millowners' Association appointed a standardization sub-committee 'to report on measures which might reasonably be taken for the standardization of muster rolls and wage rates'.[71] By then, strikes in the Sassoon Group as well as the Spring Mill, in response to the introduction of efficiency measures, such as assigning two sides of a ring frame to each spinner, were already under way. The standardization sub-committee of the Millowners' Association was expanded in March 1928. It reported in the following month after the textile workers had effected a general strike across the industry. The scheme was now being formulated neither in the abstract nor on the basis of pure and systematic reasoning nor according to the canons of scientific management. It amounted, in fact, to a statement of the terms and conditions, in particular, the level of wages and workloads, upon which the millowners were prepared to settle the strike and re-open their mills. Significantly, the strike, involving about eighty-five mills and more than 150,000 workers, which had begun in April and ended in October 1928, brought the millowners to the negotiating table on terms which were more nearly equal than ever before or ever again in the colonial period. The millown-ers' scheme, as it evolved during the strike, was placed before the Fawcett Committee and discussed in detail with the representatives of the Joint Strike Committee. This scheme represented the first attempt to formulate a programme of rationalization and to reconcile it with the existing structure and organization of work. It provided the basis for the further attempt, a decade later, to draw up

---

[71] BMOA, Minute Books, Proceedings of the Special Meeting of the Committee of the BMOA, 6 January 1928, Office of the BMOA. The Standardization Sub-Committee consisted of the Chairman, the Vice Chairman, Sir Ness Wadia, and Messrs. C.N. Wadia, S.D. Saklatvala and T. Watts.

a scheme for rationalization and standardization. The process by which the
standardization scheme was formulated in 1928, its basis, method and logic,
should therefore help to illuminate the nature and scope of the programme of
reform which was projected and discussed in such grandiose terms in the late
1920s and 1930s.

The Millowners' Association had to build its standardization scheme on the
base of the widely divergent conditions in the industry. The scheme had to
incorporate within its framework the efficiency measures which were randomly
and intermittently introduced by individual millowners. It would have to allow
for the most poorly organized and equipped as well as the most efficient mills,
some of which it was said could compete on an equal basis with their rivals in
Japan and Lancashire.[72] Finally, the standardization scheme, at a time when
economies were essential, would also have to leave room for the possibility of
wage cuts. These requirements jostled with each other and fundamentally
contradicted the objectives of standardization. How were these contradictions
to be resolved? At the same time, if every mill was adjusting in its own way to
the industry's difficulties and altering conditions of work in different directions,
at different times, how could this diversity, indeed anarchy, be standardized?
And if a standardization scheme was devised, what was the likelihood that the
Millowners' Association would be able to enforce it or even gain the acquiescence, let alone the assent, of its members? Since the quality and speed of
machinery, the layout of the mill, the nature of the material supplied and the
types of goods produced determined the optimal number of workers required,
and changes in any one of these variables called for substantial adjustments in
every other, 'one difficulty raised by the millowners' in formulating a standardization scheme at all in 1928 was 'the impossibility of fixing an absolute
standard for every mill'.[73]

These complexities ensured that the method and logic of the Millowners'
Association's schemes remained simple or, from a different viewpoint, arbitrary. The standardization sub-committee which reported in April 1928, primarily considered the 'double frame system' which had been introduced by the
Sassoons and the Finlay mills and incorporated suggestions made by Watts,
Superintendent of the Currimbhoy group, for the reorganization of the industry.[74] Clearly, their report could not be based on a comprehensive survey of
conditions in the industry, but only on the most accessible information from
the most progressive mills. Two days later, Homi Mody, Chairman of the

[72] *Report of the ITB, 1932*, p. 121.
[73] Proceedings of the BSEC, I, 669, MSA.
[74] BMOA, Minute Books, Proceedings of the Fortnightly Meeting of the Committee, 16 April 1928;
see also 20 March 1928. Office of the BMOA.

Association, asked for detailed information to be obtained from all mills on steps taken to reduce manufacturing costs and increase efficiency.[75] On 8 May, the Standardization of Wages sub-committee reported that they had failed to come to any definite conclusions but 'felt that the rational system was not possible of adoption on a large scale in Bombay mills'. The best way to proceed, they advised, was to persevere with 'the present system' but on a standardized basis.[76] It was not until June that a scheme was formulated, rejected, revised and adopted with a ceiling of Rs. 42 on the earning of weavers and incorporating a wage cut which the Joint Mill Strike Committee estimated at $12\frac{1}{2}$ per cent.[77] This scheme was discussed by the Millowners' Association and the labour leaders of the Joint Mill Strike Committee before the Fawcett Committee, which, where agreement could not be reached, arbitrated over the differences.

The Millowners' Association proposed a uniform wage applicable to all mills for workers paid according to time. It was no simple matter, however, to establish whether the workers designated under the same occupation did the same kind of work in different mills.[78] The standardization scheme would have also effected a reduction in the number of workers, estimated by the Joint Strike Committee at 10,000 or 12,000[79] and later, more modestly by the millowners at 2,000 or 3,000.[80]

The real effects of the scheme on workloads and the total volume of employment depended upon too many variables, some of which even the scheme could not adequately cover, to be estimated with any degree of accuracy. Clearly, however, the consequences of introducing 'efficiency measures', such as assigning both sides of a frame to one operative, would depend upon the extent to which the mill concerned adapted its other working conditions to them. The representatives of the Joint Strike Committee insisted before the Fawcett Committee that the fixed wage workers would suffer wage reductions both in the form of direct cuts as well as increased workloads at the old rate of remuneration.[81]

In the case of piece workers, their rates were based upon an efficiency standard. To arrive at this standard, they estimated the maximum production possible over a ten-hour day and then made allowances for stoppages, accidents,

[75] Ibid., Proceedings of a Special Meeting of the Committee, 18 April 1928. Office of the BMOA.
[76] Ibid., Proceedings of an Urgent Meeting, 8 May 1928. Office of the BMOA.
[77] Ibid., Proceedings of a Special Meeting of the Committee, 14 May 1928. Office of the BMOA; Proceedings of the Meerut Conspiracy Case, Statement by S.A. Dange, p. 2436; Report of the BSEC, I, 2–11.
[78] Proceedings of the BSEC, I, 666, MSA. Labour Office, Bombay, Wages and Unemployment, pp. 3, 35.
[79] Proceedings of the BSEC, I, 293, MSA.
[80] Ibid., I, 304 and II, 760, MSA.
[81] Ibid., I, 281–2, MSA.

changes of shuttle, breakages in the warp and the style and design of the cloth. The efficiency standard for a particular line of output was then expressed as a percentage of the maximum production. The efficiency standard, explained S.D. Saklatvala, also took into consideration the fact that 'the weaver also requires some time ... although we maintain that he wastes a little more time than he ought to'.[82] So if their consideration was brisk, their criteria were severe. Furthermore, they even allowed, Saklatvala claimed, a sizeable margin in arriving at their efficiency standard so that even 'if some mills are inefficient, still the weaver will at least get the wages we say he ought to get'.[83] These wages were found by the Fawcett Committee to entail a reduction of $7\frac{1}{2}$ per cent but their advice to millowners was that, to gain the goodwill and co-operation of their workers for the implementation of the scheme, it should not be enforced.[84] Since a weaver's earnings were directly affected by the conditions under which he worked and the type of cloth he wove, this could only be a notional figure, of no more than rhetorical interest at the time, which, in addition, probably concealed, as the labour leaders suspected, much larger reductions.[85]

It was precisely because conditions varied so enormously that the uniform rates and general efficiency standards acquired an inherently arbitrary basis. The standardization scheme was devised with insufficient evidence. The Millowners' Association, alleged Dange, would find it impossible to collect the necessary information for putting together a comprehensive standardization scheme. 'Most of the millowners are in competition with one another', he said, 'and they would not like to have their secrets made open to a committee of the Association on which sits two formidable members.'[86] Although discomfited by the charge, the millowners found it difficult to deny altogether. An official of the Millowners' Association, B.K. Mantri, admitted that 'jealousy' between millowners existed 'as far as our trade secrets go, as far as manufacturing processes go, but as regards power charges etc. they are not at all secret'.[87] Similarly, Saklatvala argued vehemently that 'costing is the private property of the firm, which it has every right not to give out'.[88] Nor were any detailed surveys made or reports assembled about the prevailing conditions in each mill and their effect upon standardization. 'A report was not necessary', he declared happily, 'because the Bombay millowner knows exactly the condition of the mills.'[89] This created a moment's alarm. For the Fawcett Committee had been

[82] *Ibid.*, I, 262, MSA.
[83] *Ibid.*, I, 267, MSA.
[84] *Report of the BSEC*, I, 126–7.
[85] Proceedings of BSEC, I, 281–4, MSA.
[86] *Ibid.*, I, 278, MSA.
[87] *Ibid.*, I, 551, MSA.
[88] *Ibid.*, I, 642–3, MSA.
[89] *Ibid.*, I, 645–6, MSA.

'told that certain tests were made on a very wide basis to show what production would be obtained under the present scheme'.[90] But as Saklatvala further explained:

These tests were not taken for the simple reason that each man was familiar with his own conditions. At a meeting of the main committee [of the Millowners' Association], we asked members to bring their own technical men ... We did not ask each technical expert to give us figures of his tests but we got each one's opinion and then arrived at a fair standard.[91]

In these circumstances, standardization had to be based upon the average mill. Yet in Bombay this was a notion which defied the most active imagination. Since the standardized list was devised with the intention of being applied to every mill, Fred Stones explained,

We took no notice whether the wages were high or low; but what we considered was whether it was a fair wage consistent with a fair day's work.[92]

However gimcrack their hastily assembled scheme may have been, the matter was scarcely so simple or convenient. The millowners' notions of 'a fair wage' and 'a fair day's work' were likely to differ as substantially as their financial position, their labour relations and their methods and conditions of production. The introduction of a standardization scheme was likely to increase the wage bill of some mills and reduce that of others. To be acceptable to its members and indeed enforceable at all, the scheme would have to be grounded on the lowest common denominator of wages. Standardization, in Sir Joseph Kay's reasoning,

implies that you are trying to bring to one common level the varying rates being paid in the various mills. As I pointed out, there is a tremendous difference so that the standardization would have to be on the lower rates rather than the higher.

Standardization on the higher rates, he declared, was 'no standard list at all' but simply 'levelling up'.[93]

The consequences of a standard rate or an efficiency standard for both employers and workers would necessarily vary with the conditions and methods of production in each mill. Since these conditions were so diverse, the practicability of a standardization scheme for the millowners largely depended upon its flexibility. Every attempt to define for the industry as a whole the terms on which production might be organized inevitably narrowed the individual millowner's freedom of manoeuvre. Yet the pursuit of this freedom had frequently

[90] *Ibid.*, I, 650–1, MSA.
[91] *Ibid.*, I, 651–2, MSA.
[92] *Ibid.*, I, 637, MSA.
[93] *Ibid.*, I, 623, MSA.

resulted in fierce and corrosive internal competition and provided a spur to industrial action. Moreover, the Millowners' Association could scarcely deal effectively with industry-wide strikes or put pressure on the colonial state, if it was beholden to diverse interpretations of the industry's problems or conflicting visions of its own future. Standardization by definition undermined this flexibility, but the greater degree of flexibility the scheme permitted, the less it was likely to overcome the problem of disparities within the industry or indeed to standardize anything at all.

For the workers, prevailing conditions of production would determine the effect of a standard rate on their earnings and workloads. If efficiency measures were to be introduced, much would depend upon how far the basic pre-conditions for them had been met. While the introduction of these efficiency schemes was a piecemeal process, the preparation for them was extremely uneven. After the Sassoons initiated them in the early 1920s,

One or two millowners thought we were getting the benefit they ought to get and they without making any preparations began to reduce the number of workers. The result was that a man was asked to do something it was impossible to do.[94]

The communist leader, S.A. Dange, described this competitive dynamic at work in the introduction of rationalization. The Sassoon group of mills introduced some efficiency measures in August, 1927, and was immediately faced with a strike. The employers then agreed to make the scheme voluntary for their spinners and weavers. To assign weavers two or three looms and spinners both sides of a ring frame, it was essential to reorganize production, to alter the mixing and preparation of cotton and increase the counts of yarn spun, to make adjustments in the reeling and winding as well as the sizing processes, to adapt the layout of the mill, the speeds of machinery and the number of helpers assigned to particular operatives. The introduction of efficiency measures in a manner which realized their full benefits called for extensive surveys, trials and preparations. Finding their rivals were trying to imitate their own managerial system, and fearing that 'the other mills would get a march over them', the Sassoon group introduced their efficiency measures before they had completed their preparations. This was why, claimed Dange,

they wanted to introduce it bit by bit, and that is exactly what they mean by saying that they made it voluntary. That means, where conditions are ready and the workers were convinced that the employers had made the conditions ready, they might be persuaded to accept the new system.[95]

Then they discovered that other millowners, having prepared even less for the

[94] Proceedings of the TLIC, Main Inquiry, Oral Evidence, Mr. F. Stones, File 70, p. 3456, MSA.
[95] Proceedings of BSEC, I, 204, 203–6, MSA.

new system, introduced it competitively. This forced the hand of the Sassoon group and they introduced their scheme as a whole, irrespective of their state of readiness. The Sassoons were thereby 'deliberately putting the workers into a bad position by giving them bad machines, unsuitable situations and conditions, and to [sic] force them to work the new system.' Meanwhile, although they were not ready for it, weaker mills extended their own schemes.[96] Consequently, a growing number of workers were exposed to increasingly adverse conditions of work, in which their workloads continued to rise and their wages fell.

Efficiency measures which increased workloads without necessarily improving the quality of the raw material and the machinery or providing adequate supplementary labour, simply meant harder work, fewer jobs and sometimes less wages. By hitching standardization to efficiency schemes, the millowners were, S.A. Dange argued, creating the opportunity for cutting wages. 'The method of reducing the rate', he explained, 'is either by putting an efficiency so high that the worker cannot get it, or putting a speed so high that the machine cannot get it.' Thus, in his view, standardization was nothing more than a scheme 'for hiding from the public the big cut in wages that it represents'.[97] The standardization of wages was meaningless, therefore, unless the condition of machines and materials passing through them as well as the number of workers employed at various stages of the production process were also standardized. 'We also made standardization as our demand', N.M. Joshi told the Fawcett Committee on behalf of the Joint Strike Committee in 1928,

but we did not say that standardization should be reduction of wages and reduction of workers. We asked for standardization of wages, conditions of work and employment, and we wanted scientific standardization, not the standardization which the millowners have done.[98]

But the diversity of conditions, business strategies and the good custom of the industry were likely to make 'scientific' standardization impossible to implement. The Millowners' Association could scarcely enforce the standardization of conditions upon its members, most of whom in any case would not risk the capital outlay for such comprehensive renovation and restructuring of the industry. Since the lines of production and volume of output in each mill were subject to considerable fluctuation, 'scientific' standardization would limit their ability to manipulate their material and its processing and to vary their levels of employment accordingly. Individual millowners would have found this unacceptable and indeed, in the light of the current practice, unworkable.

---

[96] *Ibid.*, I, 205, MSA.
[97] *Ibid.*, I, 283–5, MSA
[98] *Ibid.*, I, 107, MSA.

By laying down a general, if apparently arbitrary, standard, the Millowners' Association sought to leave the organization of production in each mill intact. Within the moveable parameters of their standardization scheme, individual millowners had to be given the freedom to alter working conditions when necessary, to reduce wages, increase workloads, effect retrenchment and most crucially, switch their lines of production according to demand.

The standardization scheme as amended by the Fawcett Committee was completed by January 1929, and was due to be put into effect by the following October. But it was swiftly overtaken by events. Between October 1928 and April 1929, there had been seventy-one lightning strikes in the industry. The momentum of industrial action and intensity of class conflict which developed during the general strike of the previous six months were not easily dissipated. The communist-led Girni Kamgar Union had emerged from the general strike with 54,000 members and a sophisticated organizational structure which extended to active mill and neighbourhood committees. It had acquired for the first, indeed perhaps the only, time in the history of the industry in the colonial period, the recognizable characteristics of an effective trade union. Their success generated panic both within the colonial state and among the millowners. Many of the city's inhabitants, from mill managers to magistrates, rival labour leaders and merchants to policemen and civil servants, sensed an air of menace and violence and perceived the threat of insurrection in the mill districts.[99] It was against this background that the Government of India launched its plan to arrest the Bombay communist leaders along with a few communist activists in the provinces, and to prosecute them for conspiracy to overthrow the King-Emperor.[100] In early April, all the leading communists of the Girni Kamgar Union were arrested and taken to jail in Meerut, awaiting trial. They did not return until the mid 1930s.

At the same time, further developments at the workplace were creating conditions which militated against the implementation of the reform schemes formulated and elaborated before the Fawcett Committee. Although the Millowners' Association was willing to abandon the wage cut of $7\frac{1}{2}$ per cent embodied in their standardization scheme, individual millowners continued to alter conditions of work, workloads and wages. The changing composition of a mill's output invariably necessitated adjustments to wage rates. In some cases, mills took the opportunity to increase the number of spindles or looms assigned

---

[99] Chandavarkar, 'Workers' Politics', 631–47.
[100] The plot to prosecute the communists can be examined in GOB, Home (Sp.) Files 543 (18) A of 1928, 543 (18) C of 1928, 543 (18) G of 1928, 543 (18) I of 1929, 543 (18) K of 1929, 543 (10) E–BB of 1929, 543 (10) E Part H of 1929, MSA; and GOI, Home (Pol.), File nos. F 18/VII/28 and Keep Withs I–IX, and 18/VII/1928, and Home (Pol.), 303/1929 and Keep Withs I and II, NAI.

to each worker. Of course, the greater the changes effected in the organization of work, before the scheme was instituted formally across the industry, the less resemblance it would bear to the terms and conditions negotiated before and settled by the Fawcett Committee.

Moreover, a number of millworkers had taken a very prominent role in the organization of the general strike, particularly through the mill and neighbourhood committees. After the strike ended, this organization had remained largely intact. It had enabled workers to observe changes in rates and conditions introduced by individual millowners across the industry, to resist retrenchment and victimization and to exchange information swiftly between mills. It provided an effective means of channelling the grievances and protests of the workforce, and created obvious bargaining agents to deal with the jobbers, supervisors and managers at the workplace. Above all, it offered an alternative source of authority, power and patronage to the jobber, both in the workplace and in the neighbourhood. In the early months of 1929, millowners, their managers and jobbers took advantage of the prevailing state of flux in the workplace to dismiss irreconcilable and recalcitrant workers, in particular the activists who had acquired some prominence during the strike and in its aftermath. The changing conditions of work and the victimization of trade-union activists and prominent strikers provoked the lightning strikes at the level of the individual mill which proliferated in this period and contributed to another general strike in April 1929.[101] The Bombay Riots Inquiry Committee found soon afterwards that the communists had been primarily responsible for the communal riots which occurred in February and May 1929. Subsequently, the Pearson Committee, appointed under the terms of the Trades Disputes Act, to investigate the occurrence of the second general strike once more pinned the blame firmly on the backs of the communists and their vehicle, the Girni Kamgar Union.[102]

Subject to severe repression at every level of their organization and to the deprivation and division which accompanied the second general strike, the Girni Kamgar Union crumbled when the strike collapsed in September 1929. In the following year, the Millowners' Association took advantage of this combination of circumstances to withdraw their recognition of the union as a responsible bargaining agent in the industry. For the rest of the decade, it entertained no further dealings with the Girni Kamgar Union except when forced to do so by the momentum and scale of industrial action. The millowners were subsequently to argue that this industrial action and its disruptive consequences

[101] Chandavarkar, 'Workers' Politics'.
[102] *Report of the Bombay Riots Inquiry Committee, 1929* (Bombay, 1929); *Report of the Court of Inquiry into a Trade Dispute Between Several Textile Mills and their Workmen* (Bombay, 1929).

prevented the implementation of the standardization scheme.[103] To be workable, they argued, such a scheme required the co-operation of an effective trade union and by the end of 1929, partly as a consequence of their repression, no such institution could be said to exist. The Girni Kamgar Union, which had in its pomp driven the millowners to the wall, could now scarcely expect an even break as it lay bruised and battered in the scrap yard of industrial politics in 1930.

However, the Bombay millowners had reasons of their own for postponing the implementation of standardization schemes. If the industry had suffered severe disruption due to the general strikes of 1928 and 1929, the following year saw prices and demand collapse while civil disobedience intermittently closed their piecegoods markets and disrupted trade. In the grip of severe trade depression, the industry would not bear the strain of fundamental changes in the structure of work and organization of production. These were not conditions conducive to the stipulation and imposition of uniform standards upon the industry as a whole. Indeed, the attempt to impose uniformity was most likely to be honoured only in the breach. It was probably with some relief that the millowners were able to conceal their own difficulties behind the public discourse which readily cast the Girni Kamgar Union as the universal villain at the root of all the problems encountered by the cotton-textile industry.

The depression and the minimum wage schedule

The anxieties expressed by the representatives of the Joint Strike Committee in 1928 about the likely manner and probable consequences of the piecemeal introduction of the efficiency schemes were, in many cases, borne out in the 1930s. During the early 1930s, as prices fell and demand slumped, most mills began to nibble at piece rates, retrench their workforce and increase workloads. The Labour Office inquiry into wages and unemployment in 1934 discovered that wages tended to vary significantly between mills as well as between municipal wards in the city.[104] Wage reductions had done very little to standardize their level. Twenty-six out of forty-nine mills admitted to having cut their basic rates, but four of these claimed to have restored them. A further eight mills reported having increased their rates due to changes in the character of production, but this did not necessarily mean that earnings would have risen as well.[105] The overwhelming majority of mills made several and substantial cuts in their dearness-of-food allowances, and they varied widely in extent. But in the case

---

[103] *Report of the ITB, 1932*, pp. 60–2; *Report of the TLIC*, II, 100.
[104] Labour Office, Bombay, *Wages and Unemployment*, pp. 35–6.
[105] *Ibid.*, p. 25.

of nearly half the mills, they were reduced from the original level of 80 per cent of the basic wage for piece workers and 70 per cent for fixed wage workers to below 35 per cent.[106] The Millowners' Association had apparently taken the view that wage cuts were 'the most important factor in the reduction of costs, and the cost of living having fallen, it was argued that the position of the workers would not be worsened as the result of the cuts as compared with the years before prices fell'.[107] Mills which had advanced furthest with the adoption of efficiency schemes, and thus paid the highest wages, had either made no cuts or in some cases, even increased their basic rates.[108] It was indeed likely that wage disparities widened during the early 1930s, and that they were accentuated by the piecemeal extension of efficiency schemes. Clearly, the sporadic and competitive wage cuts effected at the time were not motivated by a concern to make the structure of wages uniform. Some mills, the Labour Office observed, 'have not reduced wages and yet are paying good dividends'. Conversely, nine mills claimed that they would have had to close down if they had not reduced wages while a further twenty-two gave the trade depression as their reason for cutting wages.[109]

Moreover, the implementation of rationalization was very uneven and often served to accentuate disparities. Less than a third of the mills which were covered by the inquiry even attempted rationalization and many of these had done so only partially. The overwhelming majority of mills which did not adopt rationalization gave technical reasons for avoiding it: either it was simply not feasible or economical to implement or their stock of machinery, often old plant, made it preferable to work with coarser counts. Moreover, increased efficiency through changes in the plant or the character of production or the use of better mixings was not always or necessarily reflected in earnings. Indeed, the effect of rationalization on earnings in different mills varied enormously. There were 'striking differences' in the earnings of weavers 'as between different mills working on a rationalized basis'. In one extreme case, the wages of a six-loom weaver working a seven-hour shift were less than an ordinary two-loom weaver. Similarly, in some mills operating efficiency schemes, spinners were receiving the same wage for working two sides as those who worked a single side on the old system in other mills. It was also suggested that, in some cases, efficiency measures were adopted as 'a thin end of the wedge' to accustom more workers to the idea of increased workloads by employing badlis on them.[110] The Labour Office cited the case of four mills which had increased their basic rates by

[106] Ibid., pp. 25–9.
[107] Ibid., p. 44.
[108] Ibid., pp. 26–7.
[109] Ibid., p. 43.
[110] Ibid., pp. 45–55.

between 35 and 50 per cent because they asked operatives to tend more machines; but those 'who still insist on working on a non-rationalized basis' found their whole dearness allowance taken away and basic rates pitched at pre-war levels.[111] Efficiency schemes facilitated not only the reduction of wages and numbers employed, but they continued to be used to weed out truculent and undesirable workers. Indeed, workers who were willing to operate efficiency schemes were rewarded, it was said, with quicker promotion.[112] Moreover, as unemployment increased rapidly between 1930 and 1934, it was highly probable that workloads were more consistently and effectively increased, as efficiency schemes were introduced without necessarily a corresponding improvement in the quality of material or machines, or, indeed, wages. The average extent of the wage reductions effected in this period was estimated at 21 per cent between July 1926 and April 1934 and further cuts were made between April and October.[113]

This competitive wage-cutting by individual mills provoked strikes and quickened the momentum of industrial action until, by July 1934, it culminated in another general strike which lasted for three months. It was immediately after the collapse of the strike that the Millowners' Association devised and implemented a minimum-wage schedule. As R.S. Nimbkar, the labour leader, described it,

The workers' strength was completely exhausted by a long and protracted struggle and taking advantage of their position the millowners imposed this schedule on us effecting a wage cut.[114]

For the Millowners' Association, however, the effects of individual and competitive wage reductions focussed their minds once more on the problem of standardization. The effects of these wage cuts upon the organization of work and, indeed, the disruption which followed in the form of a general strike, were preferably to be avoided, especially when markets were depressed. Maloney, the Secretary of the Millowners' Association described the view from Churchgate Street:

Unfortunately, wage cuts had to be made to save the industry. These cuts should have taken place in 1926 or 1927 ... We did not succeed [then] in effecting any wage cuts ... Therefore, when the mills closed down, the position of the workers became very bad and when the mills, one after another, began to close down there was a lot of labour seeking employment under any conditions and we allowed the mills to take individual action,

[111] Ibid., p. 27.
[112] Proceedings of the TLIC, Main Inquiry, Oral Evidence, Cotton Mill Workers, Spinning Side, File 60A, p. 990; ibid., A.W. Pryde, Labour Officer, Bombay, File 66, p. 2430, MSA.
[113] Labour Office, Bombay, Wages and Unemployment, p. 39; Report of TLIC, I, 22.
[114] Proceedings of the TLIC, Main Inquiry, Oral Evidence, BPTUC, File 58A, p. 567, MSA.

whatever they thought was reasonable and just. It was then that we stepped in and said: 'So far you may go, but no further.' That was what happened and the minimum wage was fixed according to the standards ruling then.[115]

The minimum-wage schedule, the millowners claimed, was introduced 'to regulate the extent to which cuts in pay could be effected'.[116] In fact, it laid the floor, after wages had collapsed on to it, beneath which they should not be allowed to fall. It froze into the wage structure the reductions, which the mills had effected in competition with each other, at their lowest point reached after the collapse of the general strike.

It is difficult to assess how far the minimum-wage schedule protected the lowest paid. It had, after all, always been problematic in the industry to enumerate occupations or to relate a designated occupation to the particular task performed within mills as well as between them. The Government Labour Officer, A.W. Pryde, observed that there were 'a large number of what I call unscheduled occupations' and their wages varied enormously from mill to mill. In fact, 'it was very difficult to find out what they do pay [workers in unscheduled occupations]. It is only when a wage dispute crops up that it comes to our notice.'[117] There had been several instances in the last eighteen months, reported Pryde in 1937, 'when standard rates were not being paid'.[118] Since no facilities for inspection or machinery of investigation existed, he could only have discovered these discrepancies from 'such complaints as came before the Labour Officer' or else 'when by chance I happen to notice them while looking through the pay muster in connection with some dispute'.[119] The minimum-wage schedule only covered time-rated workers. In the case of weavers, Sir Homi Mody had assured the Government of Bombay in 1935 that the aim of the Millowners' Association was to establish Rs. 35 per month as the minimum standard earning, whatever their output and piece rate. Yet in 1937 at least fourteen mills were believed to pay their weavers less than Rs. 35.[120]

The minimum-wage schedule undoubtedly served as a convenient standard by which to assess demands for higher wages or settle claims of underpayment brought before the Labour Officer for conciliation under the Trade Disputes Act of 1934.[121] Yet as the representatives of the Bombay Provincial Trade Union Congress pointed out before the Textile Labour Inquiry Committee, conciliation

---

[115] Proceedings of the TLIC, Main Inquiry, Oral Evidence, BMOA, File 57A, p. 149, MSA.

[116] Ibid., p. 148.

[117] Proceedings of the TLIC, Interim Inquiry, Oral Evidence, A.W. Pryde, Labour Officer to the Government, File 42, p. 461, MSA.

[118] Ibid., p. 446, MSA.

[119] Ibid., p. 470, MSA.

[120] Ibid., pp. 465, 473, MSA.

[121] Ibid., pp. 466–7, 471, 476–8, 482–3; ibid., J.F. Gennings, Commissioner of Labour and Chief Conciliator, File 42, pp. 420, 422–3, MSA.

based on the minimum-wage schedule allowed mills which yielded higher earnings to effect and justify reductions in piece rates or even fixed wages. It also acted as a hedge against increases. It tended, therefore, to turn the minimum wage into a maximum wage.[122] The *Indian Textile Journal*, neither the most unremitting defender nor the most passionate advocate of workers' interests, observed in 1937 that the minimum-wage schedule had aggravated the situation created by the competitive wage-cutting spiral of 1933–4 'by offering an inducement to the better paying mills to make further wage cuts'. Indeed, it added,

When the minimum schedule was laid down it was affirmed that it was devised to meet the needs of the weakest mills and that the better paying mills would continue to pay at the higher rates. This affirmation soon melted into thin air.[123]

Nonetheless, some groups of workers probably benefited from the minimum-wage schedule. Workers who were covered by the schedule but whose earnings fell below the average may have gained. The wage schedule facilitated the closer intervention by the Millowners' Association and the state in the affairs of individual mills. In particular, mills which paid low wages were under growing pressure to improve conditions. In fact, the schedule was accompanied by the injunction upon low-paying mills to raise their wage levels.[124] The Association advised its members to put up notices about rates and allowances in every department in the following year[125] and two years later this advice received the sanction of law under the Payment of Wages Act.[126] In 1936, the Association called upon its members to notify them about their plans to change wage rates and sought to regulate the fixing of piece rates when machines, supplies, the composition of output or the complement of workers were altered.[127] The Government Labour Officer believed his exertions, along with the activities of his counterpart in the Millowners' Association, had been effective in raising wage levels in mills which fell below the standard.[128]

In principle, the use of the minimum-wage schedule as a point of reference

---

[122] Proceedings of the TLIC, Main Inquiry, Oral Evidence, BPTUC, File 58A, pp. 469–70, MSA; *Report of the TLIC*, II, 81–99, especially 98–9.
[123] *Indian Textile Journal*, XLVIII (September, 1937), 438.
[124] BMOA, *Annual Report, 1934*, pp. 36–8; Morris, *Industrial Labour Force*, pp. 172–4.
[125] BMOA, *Annual Report 1935*, p. 28.
[126] *Labour Gazette*, XVI, 10 (1937), 760.
[127] BMOA, *Annual Report, 1936*, pp. 39–40.
[128] Proceedings of the TLIC, Interim Inquiry, Oral Evidence, A.W. Pryde, Labour Officer to the Government of Bombay, File 42, pp. 466–7; and *ibid.*, Main Inquiry, Oral Evidence, A.W. Pryde, Labour Officer to the Government of Bombay, File 66, pp. 2456–60. MSA; *Report of the TLIC*, II, 83–5. See also A.W. Pryde, 'The Work of the Labour Officer', in C. Manshardt (ed.), *Some Social Services of the Government of Bombay* (Bombay, 1937), pp. 85–7; Morris, *Industrial Labour Force*, pp. 172–4.

for conciliation and as a ceiling on earnings should have tended towards standardization. But to conclude that 'the net effect' of Government action 'was to move the industry inexorably in [the direction] of standardization'[129] is perhaps also to overestimate the efficacy of the measures adopted by the Labour Officer and even the Millowners' Association. In fact, it is improbable that standardization was the objective of the Association when it drew up the minimum-wage schedule. By the late 1930s, the Millowners' Association was taking pains to reject the notion that the minimum-wage schedule amounted to a standard wage and to reiterate that it constituted nothing more than an attempt to draw the parameters within which wage reductions or wage competition might occur. Their schedule was 'commonly known as a minimum wage schedule,' the Textile Labour Inquiry Committee observed in 1940, 'but the [Millowners'] Association prefers to describe it as a schedule of fair occupational wages'.[130] Indeed, by the end of the decade, the minimum wage had increasingly entered the discourse of industrial relations as a fresh principle for the determination of wages. This only made it more crucial for the millowners to ensure that there was no confusion over the distinction between a minimum or living wage and a standard wage. While they might reject the principle of the former concept, they accepted the latter but simply could not realize it.

Standardization revived, 1937–39

Towards the end of the decade, the question of standardization was revived again when it was listed among the terms of reference of the Textile Labour Inquiry Committee. Wage disparities were still considered the most significant cause of labour disputes, so it followed that wage standardization was the necessary remedy. When the Textile Labour Inquiry Committee called upon the millowners to draft a fresh standardization scheme in the late 1930s, the problems which had riddled its previous incarnation remained largely unresolved. The broad structure of the millowners' scheme was based upon the proposals they had presented to the Fawcett Committee, and it was no less gimcrack than their previous effort.

In 1928, their scheme was formulated in the context of a general strike and with the stimulation of class conflict. In the late 1930s, the question had been raised in the abstract. In fact, in 1939, the millowners had been reluctant to discuss the question at all and when their hand was forced, the arithmetical and conceptual frailties of their hurriedly sketched proposals became only too clear. Under some fierce cross-examination from D.R. Gadgil, a member of the

---

[129] Morris, *Industrial Labour Force*, p. 173.
[130] *Report of the TLIC*, II, 83.

Textile Labour Inquiry Committee, Maloney admitted that their scheme had been prepared in six hours and that their figures for average earnings, including those based on piece rates, were based on 'impression', or as Gadgil put it more forcefully, 'a hypothetical figure which is at the back of your mind'.[131] To prepare a wage bill 'which should be treated seriously', Maloney had added, 'it would take months to get the returns from each individual mill'.[132] Moreover, the scheme they put forward in 1939 had not received the assent of the millowners. It was not even 'known to all members of the Association', let alone 'endorsed by them'.[133]

Once again, the millowners' suspicion of each other, and indeed, on this occasion, of their Ahmedabad rivals, too, limited the detailed information available to the authors of the scheme.[134] Asked for a list of essential changes to machinery necessary to implement a satisfactory rationalization scheme, Fred Stones flatly refused. He had invested capital in pioneering these schemes, employed an expert 'to see whether we over-work or under-work a man' and run experiments to test changes about to be introduced. 'To pass them on to the industry', he said simply, 'is not possible.'[135] Subsequently, he complained that the Bombay Millowners' Association had poached not only his Labour Officer, C.A. Dalal, after he had trained him, but also 'the man I trained to replace him' and borrowed and extended the badli control system which had originally been instituted by the Sassoon group.[136]

The scheme drawn up in 1939 made no effort to standardize 'musters' or stipulate the number of workers to be assigned to a particular line of production. Yet the number of workers assigned to a particular process or the number of helpers made available for the working of efficiency schemes could have a significant effect on earnings. Conversely, the refusal to standardize musters would necessarily mean that workloads would vary in each mill. 'That we shall not be able to deal with,' Baddeley declared, on behalf of the Millowners' Association, referring to the standardization of musters, 'because to be perfectly candid, we are not in agreement within ourselves. We feel that in Bombay at least the industry at present is not ready for the standardization of musters.'[137] Underlying their refusal was the recurrent problem of the bewildering diversity of conditions and the range of goods produced.[138] Not only did the conditions within the industry vary between mills but the labour needs of a single mill

---

[131] Proceedings of the TLIC, Main Inquiry, Oral Evidence, BMOA, File 79A, pp. 5512–15, MSA.
[132] Ibid., Main Inquiry, Oral Evidence, BMOA, File 79A, pp. 5337–8, MSA.
[133] Ibid., Main Inquiry, Oral Evidence, BMOA, File 79A, p. 5541, MSA.
[134] Ibid., Main Inquiry, Oral Evidence, BMOA, File 78C, p. 5426, MSA.
[135] Ibid., Main Inquiry, Oral Evidence, Mr F. Stones, File 70, pp. 3461–2, MSA.
[136] Ibid., Main Inquiry, Oral Evidence, Mr F. Stones, File 70, p. 3458, MSA.
[137] Ibid., Main Inquiry, Oral Evidence, BMOA, File 77B, p. 5021, MSA.
[138] Ibid., Main Inquiry, Oral Evidence, BMOA, File 78C, p. 5415, MSA.

fluctuated considerably.[139] To formulate a scheme for standardizing musters for the industry as a whole was, in their view, not simply 'undesirable'; it was 'not even feasible'.[140] Moreover, to standardize musters, the Millowners' Association argued, would serve as a constraint upon the further extension of rationalization schemes by which mills could alter the character of production, adapt their patterns of labour deployment and increase workloads. In their first session in camera with the Textile Labour Inquiry Committee, Baddeley had protested,

It will be a very serious thing indeed for us to be tied down to the standardization of musters at present, because so many Bombay mills are working on very coarse counts and have not been able to rationalize at all, and on them the incidence of this wage increase [granted by the interim report of the TLIC] is very high.[141]

A month later, their argument had become at once more sophisticated and more sanctimonious. 'We must not be hampered in any way', they insisted, 'from moving along towards higher wages by means of efficiency schemes.'[142] Indeed, 'any definite standardization of musters of a permanent character', it was argued, would prevent the mills from freely varying the size of their labour force according to the changing composition of output or trade fluctuations. The resistance of the millowners to the standardization of musters highlighted a fundamental problem inherent in any standardization scheme in Bombay. The imposition of a standard necessarily narrowed the millowner's freedom of manoeuvre, whereas his business strategies demanded that he remain alert and adaptable to constantly changing market conditions and political circumstances. Yet unless workloads were specified, duties defined and musters standardized, the standardization of wages alone became a rather pointless exercise. The Millowners' Association's solution to this riddle was rather disingenuously to allow the question to resolve itself. Having repressed workers' combinations and excluded trade unions from the workplace, its representatives argued that the standardization of musters 'will come through ordinary negotiations between trade union leaders and millowners over a period of years'.[143]

The millowners' scheme also set out to standardize earnings rather than rates. The relative merits of these methods of procedure had received attention in 1928 and the problem arose once more in the late 1930s as the Textile Labour Inquiry Committee contemplated the question. To achieve standard earnings under diverse conditions, it would be necessary for each mill to fix different rates for the same product. In other words, standardized earnings would have to assume that the conditions of production throughout the industry were uniform. But it

[139] *Ibid.*, Main Inquiry, Oral Evidence, BMOA, File 81A, p. 5853, MSA.
[140] *Ibid.*, Main Inquiry, Oral Evidence, BMOA, File 81A, p. 5802, MSA.
[141] *Ibid.*, Main Inquiry, Oral Evidence, BMOA, Fille 77C, p. 5022, MSA.
[142] *Ibid.*, Main Inquiry, Oral Evidence, BMOA, File 79A, pp. 5510–11, MSA.
[143] *Ibid.*, Main Inquiry, Oral Evidence, BMOA, File 81A, p. 5863, MSA.

was precisely the variations in conditions between mills which made standard rates extremely difficult to devise. To draw up a list of standardized rates which covered all varieties of cloth produced in Bombay was necessarily a task of enormous complexity. It posed a number of logistical problems. It would, for instance, have to be based on a detailed census of machinery, their speeds and efficiency, the layout and design of the buildings, the number and distribution of workers between different processes and a schedule of the content, quality and volume of production covering every mill. But, as we have seen, millowners were rarely forthcoming with such information. Yet even if the millowners were able to cover sufficiently wide circumstances to make the list meaningful, its effects on the cost of production of a particular mill could not be easily reckoned with any accuracy. 'About the standard list for weaving', Fred Stones told the Fawcett Committee, 'in our meetings we broke up always on what the reduction should be'.[144] To base this scheme on actual rates was even more difficult. As Maloney confessed ten years later, 'Technical experts have been working on this scheme for years together and still they are unable to evolve any completely satisfactory rates standardization scheme'.[145]

Fixing weavers' wage rates had always been a fractious process. The most common method was simply trial and error. When a new variety of cloth was introduced, the rate fixed was tested against output and if it vastly increased the wage bill or provided unacceptably low earnings for the weaver, they were adjusted in the appropriate direction.[146] 'In the beginning', Saklatvala explained,

it is very difficult to fix up a rate ... the weaver himself adopts an indifferent attitude and does not turn out the production which later on he does. Sometimes we fix the rate and find that the rate is too high but we find that out after about a month is over. In the first month, the weaver does not work to his fullest efficiency but later on, when the rate is fixed, we find that where we thought a weaver would draw Rs. 48/- he actually draws Rs. 54/-. Then during the next month or as soon as this is brought to our notice we reduce that rate.[147]

Conversely, inferior mixings of cotton, machinery in poor repair or otherwise inadequately maintained, changes in the character of production or a rush of orders which required the cloth to be woven on a wider loom, could each reduce the weaver's wage, whereas good machines, high quality material and efficient supervision yielded higher earnings at the same rate. Since the weavers' wages were 'based on a very complicated system of working out rates for different kinds of work', the Commissioner of Labour, who also served as a court of

[144] Proceedings of BSEC, II, 819, MSA.
[145] Proceedings of the TLIC, Main Inquiry, Oral Evidence, BMOA, File 57A, p. 65, MSA.
[146] Proceedings of the BSEC, I, 113, MSA.
[147] *Ibid.*, I, 118, MSA.

appeal in the conciliation and arbitration of wage disputes, observed, it was always 'liable to give rise to a certain amount of suspicion in the minds of workers that ... he has been wrongly paid'.[148] But its complexities also enabled employers to manipulate the rates, for when a bewildering variety of cloth was woven, 'workers sometimes do not notice these cuts'.[149] Most disputes over wage rates occurred 'on the weaving side ... where you arrive at wages by intricate calculations of perhaps 200 different sorts in the course of a month'.[150]

Since conditions as well as the character of production varied significantly between mills, standardized rates could perpetuate disparities in earnings, force reductions upon some workers in some mills and increase the wage bill arbitrarily in others. The millowner, Dharamsey Khatau, warned the Textile Labour Inquiry Committee that the standardization of rates would 'lead to the diversity of wages earned by different workers' and would consequently heighten the dissatisfaction and unrest among them.[151] If disparities in earnings were likely to cause discontent and instigate wage competition and labour mobility, variations in rates would also lead to 'odious comparisons'.[152] The Labour Officer elaborated this argument:

There are always cases cited in which one mill is said to be paying say 12 pies per pound for a particular kind of cloth as against 13 $\frac{1}{2}$ pies paid by a certain other mill for the same kind of cloth because weavers get together in their chawls and they discuss rates etc ... Therefore, I think the pieceworkers do feel that they are not quite satisfied with existing state of affairs.[153]

Conversely, however, the standardization of earnings did not prevent 'odious comparisons' about the quality of machinery and materials and the conditions of work in different mills. Indeed, unless conditions of work were more comprehensively standardized, the problem of wage disparities could not be resolved. Thus,

If you do get a dispute when wages [i.e. earnings] are standardized you will have rates varying from mill to mill as they do today and there will be odious comparisons ... Of course, if you have standardized rates, you will have varying wages.[154]

[148] Proceedings of the TLIC, Interim Inquiry, Oral Evidence, J.F. Gennings, Commissioner of Labour, File 42, p. 419, MSA.

[149] Ibid., Interim Inquiry, Oral Evidence, National Trade Union Federation and All-India Trades Union Congress, p. 109, MSA.

[150] Ibid., Interim Inquiry, Oral Evidence, J.F. Gennings, Commissioner of Labour, File 42, p. 433, MSA.

[151] Ibid., Main Inquiry, Oral Evidence, BMOA, File 57A, pp. 65–67, MSA.

[152] Ibid., Main Inquiry, Oral Evidence, A.W. Pryde, Labour Officer to the Government of Bombay, File 66, p. 2337, MSA.

[153] Ibid., Interim Inquiry, Oral Evidence, A.W. Pryde, Labour Officer to the Government of Bombay, File 42, p. 459, MSA.

[154] Ibid., Main Inquiry, Oral Evidence, A.W. Pryde, Labour Officer to the Government of Bombay, File 66, p. 2337, MSA.

As long as disparities remained, some degree of wage competition and its resulting conflicts were unavoidable. The factors which suggested the need for a standardization scheme also served to limit its scope. The standardization of wages could scarcely be effective so long as every other factor which had a bearing on the organization of production remained untouched in its diversity.

Yet there was another consideration which to the millowners made the standardization of earnings preferable to the standardization of rates. Indeed, it demonstrated the firm limits within which the millowners conceived their schemes for radical change. The standardization of rates imposed a more rigid framework upon individual millowners than the standardization of earnings. The effect of standardized rates on the wage bill of particular mills was impossible to predict. In fact, their effect could be sufficiently random to destroy any semblance of consensus among the millowners. Standardized rates could make particular lines of production too expensive to maintain in some mills. If musters and conditions were also specified, millowners would lose the option of persevering with a particular type of cloth, despite its wage costs under the standard, by using, for instance, inferior cotton and manipulating its mixings and preparation, machine speeds and the deployment of labour.

When Fred Stones submitted a scheme of standard wage rates for winding, based on the experience of the Sassoon mills, another leading millowner, Krishnaraj Thackersey, observed that, 'if we adopt Mr Stone's scheme, we will have to dismiss about two-thirds of the winders who are working in each mill'.[155] More crucially, most millowners would have rejected or, if implemented, simply have ignored a rate standardization scheme and it would in turn have proven impossible to enforce. In fact, such a scheme was liable to exacerbate rivalries and antagonisms between the millowners while the attempt to enforce it would irrevocably break up the fragile coalition which the Millowners' Association rather precariously embodied.

On the other hand, the standardization of earnings afforded millowners a far greater degree of flexibility in managing their affairs. Its consequences for their cost of production and wage bill were more easily predicted. Moreover, to the extent that it served as a standard, it could place a ceiling on wages. If earnings tended to increase, due to changes in the composition of output, millowners could still pare down their wage rates, distribute their reductions across the whole spectrum of their products and justify their reductions as an attempt to conform to the general standard of earnings. 'The standardization of earnings', as Maloney told the Textile Labour Inquiry Committee, was in fact 'the standardization of nothing but a minimum wage.'[156] Used as a benchmark in

---

[155] *Ibid.*, Main Inquiry, Oral Evidence, BMOA, File 78C, p. 5405, MSA.
[156] *Ibid.*, Main Inquiry, Oral Evidence, BMOA, File 57A, p. 65, MSA.

the conciliation of wage disputes, this minimum wage could, like the 1934 schedule, turn into a maximum wage. The standardization of earnings, therefore, left employers a wider range of options than the standardization of rates or musters. In particular, each millowner could choose more freely the means by which he might reach the standard. Of course, this choice was not unrestricted and indeed, the standard would not be attainable in every mill. But in devising the standard the Millowners' Association was only too aware of the difficulties of reducing wages which once fixed could become burdensome, when trade conditions deteriorated. In addition, they also recognized the futility of setting standards beyond the reach of the weaker mills.

The standardization scheme was, indeed, based upon a minimum wage. This minimum, however, measured the 'wants of labour' strictly 'by what other people are paying'.[157] Thus, as Khandubhai Desai, another member of the Textile Labour Inquiry Committee observed, the millowners simply took what 'an unskilled worker in the city of Bombay might be had for' and then added a small margin.[158] The Textile Labour Inquiry Committee meditated extensively in its report upon the 'minimum', the 'living' and the family wage, and necessarily their relationship to each other, as an essential guide to wage determination. Their deliberations with the millowners over these questions rapidly covered vast abstract spaces. Indeed, their report has been sometimes interpreted as an expression of an emergent ideology which sought to re-define the working-class family.[159] In fact, the millowners were guided by rather more mundane considerations:

We have not taken into account the living wage standard, whether it is adequate for a man, wife and two children etc. We have taken what we consider fair, judged by the position of the industry and given the man a standard compared with the rest of the working-class population of the city.[160]

Inevitably, the definition of a standard for the industry as a whole would mean that some millowners would have to increase their wages while others would be able to lower theirs. 'It is alright for mills whose wages are higher than the standard wages', Sir Homi Mody warned the Textile Labour Inquiry Committee, 'but mills whose wages are lower than this will suffer.'[161] As the Labour Office had discovered in 1934, mills which paid the lowest wages were often, though not necessarily, also those which operated on very narrow margins.[162]

---

[157] *Ibid.*, Main Inquiry, Oral Evidence, BMOA, File 78C, p. 5400, MSA.
[158] *Ibid.*, Main Inquiry, Oral Evidence, BPTUC, File 58A, p. 570, MSA.
[159] Radha Kumar, 'Family and Factory: Women in the Bombay Cotton Textile Industry, 1919–1939', *IESHR*, 20, 1 (1983), 81–110.
[160] Proceedings of the TLIC, Main Inquiry, Oral Evidence, BMOA, File 79A, p. 5527, MSA.
[161] *Ibid.*, Main Inquiry, Oral Evidence, BMOA, File 78C, p. 5380, MSA.
[162] Labour Office, Bombay, *Wages and Unemployment*, pp. 43–4, 26–8.

For them, a sudden increase in their wage bill could quickly raise their costs beyond the capacity of the market to bear and severely damage their competitive position. It was partly for this reason that the Millowners' Association repeatedly expressed doubts about their scheme being accepted by their members.[163] In addition, most millowners were anxious that a standard wage would deprive them of the flexibility which had conventionally characterized their business strategies. They feared not only that wages once fixed could not be painlessly reduced, but also that a deterioration of trade conditions or changes in taxation or social welfare obligations could leave them with a hopelessly inflated cost structure.[164]

Conversely, as Maloney argued, 'We will also find difficulty in reducing wages in those mills which are already paying wages higher than the standard wage.'[165] Indeed, in 1928, some millowners had opposed the Association's standardization scheme 'not because we were giving too much in any case but because we were paying too little.'[166] The lower standard would be difficult to achieve without provoking the opposition of workers. Some feared they would be stranded with higher wage bills than their rivals. Others resented the fact that conforming to the lower standard, rigidly applied, could deprive them of the choice of employing the most skilled workers, while preserving their current wage levels would simply perpetuate wage disparities and their disruptive consequences. 'I do not think the millowners of these highly paid mills would agree to accept the standardization of rates', observed the Labour Officer, 'because they do not want their workers to earn less.' Instead, they preferred to retain the right to buy the best and most skilled workers. Finlay Mills, in particular, produced a large volume of fine-count and fancy goods. Their weavers earned more on a single loom than many two-loom weavers employed on a rationalized basis in other mills. It was 'because they were working very fine qualities', as the Labour Officer explained, 'they expect a high standard of workmanship, and their rates are based on very low efficiency in fact'.[167] Subsequently, Pryde was able to confirm the reluctance of the Finlay Mills to participate in the millowners' scheme:

I had a conversation with Mr Burns of Finlays and he told me that if there was a standardization of rates, he would not be prepared to accept it.[168]

[163] Proceedings of the TLIC, Main Inquiry, Oral Evidence, BMOA, File 78C, pp. 5361, 5438; File 81, pp. 5801, 5839, MSA.
[164] Proceedings of the TLIC, Main Inquiry, Oral Evidence, BMOA, File 77B, p. 5026, MSA.
[165] Ibid., Main Inquiry, Oral Evidence, BMOA, File 78C, p. 5380, MSA.
[166] Proceedings of the BSEC, I, 257, MSA.
[167] Proceedings of the TLIC, Main Inquiry, Oral Evidence, A.W. Pryde, Labour Officer to the Government of Bombay, File 66, pp. 2341, 2338, MSA.
[168] Ibid., Main Inquiry, Oral Evidence, A.W. Pryde, Labour Officer to the Government of Bombay, File 66, p. 2368, MSA.

The Millowners' Association could, therefore, expect resistance to their standardization scheme from every quarter and indeed, all their members, with the exception of the Association's spokesman at the meeting of the Textile Labour Inquiry Committee, appeared pessimistic about the reception of the scheme. For this reason, too, they steadfastly pursued a minimalist strategy in drawing up their scheme. They set out guidelines but left the individual millowner to organize production according to his lights and more critically his means. Above all, they aimed to disturb as little as possible. After several hours of discussion with and cross-examination of the representatives of the Millowners' Association, D.R. Gadgil concluded, 'It boils down to this. The standardization scheme as presented to us is taking more or less average conditions to-day and standardizing it.'[169] This method of procedure, based on a notional average which could be conjured up in six hours, was allied with objectives which were highly circumscribed in scope and intent.

In April 1939, the Bombay Millowners' Association had argued that their standard list was based on what the industry could afford to pay six months earlier.[170] But the subsequent deterioration of trade conditions meant that 'we are not even sure whether our own members would feel that they could work on such a list'.[171] By September, they were willing to admit that their interpretation of average conditions in the standardization scheme had reduced wages by 8 per cent and that some of their members had approached the Committee of the Association to effect a cut of between 10 and 20 per cent, irrespective of the fate of the scheme.[172] For the most part their aim had been to offset the wage increases granted on the basis of the findings of the Textile Labour Inquiry Committee in their interim report in 1937. 'I think the effect of the standardization scheme', Maloney said, 'would be to reduce wages as compared with the wages paid to today including the interim increases.'[173] The Committee itself took a rather more trenchant view of the situation.

Even a cursory examination of the proposals put forward by the Millowners' Association shows that they constituted an attempt to standardize wages at the level reached during the depression. The minimum wage schedule of the Association adopted in 1934 represented a level below which on the evidence of the Association itself, it would be unfair to pay a worker even in bad times. Yet a comparison of the rates paid by the Association in its scheme of standardization for workers covered by the minimum schedule showed little difference between the two sets of wage rates. In some cases

---

[169] *Ibid.*, Main Inquiry, Oral Evidence, BMOA, File 79A, p. 5521, MSA.

[170] *Ibid.*, Main Inquiry, Oral Evidence, BMOA, File 78C, p. 5361, MSA.

[171] *Ibid.*, Main Inquiry, Oral Evidence, BMOA, File 77C, p. 5000, MSA.

[172] *Ibid.*, Main Inquiry, Oral Evidence, BMOA, File 79A, pp. 5844–7, MSA.

[173] *Ibid.*, Main Inquiry, Oral Evidence, BMOA, File 79A, p. 5545, MSA.

the standardization scheme attempted actually to reduce the level accepted by the Association as the minimum in 1934 ... We could not possibly believe that a level for normal times could be almost the same as that laid down by the millowners themselves as the minimum in times of acute depression after the complete collapse of a general strike.[174]

Renewing the quest for efficiency

The framing of a standardization scheme was complicated by the introduction and extension of efficiency measures. How far workloads could be usefully increased, or what the consequences of producing finer varieties of yarn and cloth would be for wages and employment, were conditioned by a wide range of factors. The varieties of goods produced, the quality of machinery and the material passing through it, the number of helpers provided, each affected not only the number of spindles and looms which could be managed by a single worker but also his or her earnings. The real effect of the standardization of earnings would depend to a large extent on how far these conditions were realized. In some mills, operatives could not achieve the standard wage; in others, the prevailing conditions enabled workers to exceed it and employers perhaps to reduce the rates to bring their earnings into line. The standardization of earnings in the midst of variations in production conditions would not level the wage disparities or eliminate competition for workers in the industry. In the event, the adoption of efficiency schemes was only likely to exacerbate these differences.

If production were shifted to higher counts of spinning, this would reduce the complement of workers required in every process, alter their distribution and sometimes change the intensity of effort demanded. Higher counts of yarn required fewer bales of cotton.[175] The cotton, provided it was of an appropriate quality, required less twist in roving, although it had sometimes to be passed through additional processes, like the sliver and ribbon-lap machine or the combing machine, to ensure the uniformity of thickness.[176] Higher counts of yarn required fewer spindles on the ring frame and therefore fewer siders to operate them;[177] while the bobbins needed to be doffed less frequently.[178] The quality of cotton and its mixing itself determined the nature and extent of preparation required. Clearly, long-staple cotton which yielded the best results

---

[174] *Report of the TLIC*, II, 116.
[175] Proceedings of the BSEC, II, 669, MSA.
[176] *Ibid.*, II, 649, 730, MSA.
[177] Labour office, Bombay, *Report on Wages and Unemployment*, p. 18; Proceedings of the TLIC, Interim Inquiry, Oral Evidence, BMOA, File 42, p. 9, MSA.
[178] Proceedings of the BSEC, II, 734–5, MSA; Proceedings of the TLIC, Main Inquiry, Oral Evidence, Mr F. Stones, File 72, p. 3607, MSA.

in high-count spinning often dispensed with some of these initial processes. If the cotton yielded less waste and fewer impurities, the carding machines needed to be stripped and their teeth ground less frequently. The amount of yarn which was sold determined the extent of reeling which might be required. Winding and sizing machines could be run more quickly with higher counts. In the case of sizing, the fewer ends and lesser weight of finer yarn enabled the machine to be speeded up.[179] Similarly, coarse counts required more frequent changes of the shuttle on the loom than the finer yarn; and the shuttle was most quickly expended in the case of khadi.[180] Changes in the character of yarn or cloth could thus affect the deployment of labour as well as the use of machinery throughout the production process. Their effect on any one process was transmitted to the next. In the weaving shed, therefore, the factors which affected the deployment of labour were considerably complicated.

Of course, it was not simply the count of yarn spun or the type of cloth woven which determined the number of workers or the nature of the machines required and the possible earnings in different parts of the process. What was often far more important was the quality of the material passing through the machines. Fred Stones, who was perhaps more than anyone else in the industry involved in and responsible for the development and application of efficiency measures, said plainly,

I lay more stress on the material going through the machine than on the machine itself. The machine may only increase the production by a very small amount but the basis of rationalization is how much work a man has to do.[181]

It was often considered difficult, even inadvisable, to put siders on to both sides of a ring frame while spinning coarse counts. Pryde, the Labour Officer, believed that there was only one mill in Bombay which worked coarse counts on two sides of the frame.[182] 'Though there is no agreement on the exact point', the Textile Labour Committee observed,

it is admitted in all quarters that below a given count a sider cannot mind two sides under existing conditions. The majority of the single siders in Bombay today mind only one side not because they are incapable of minding or unwilling to mind two sides but because the frames on which they work spin counts so coarse that double side working becomes impossible.[183]

In general, the coarser the count the fewer spindles that a sider could reasonably

---

[179] Proceedings of the BSEC, II, 805, MSA; Shah, 'Labour Recruitment and Turnover', pp. 21, 43.
[180] Proceedings of the BSEC, I, 262–3, MSA.
[181] Proceedings of the TLIC, Main Inquiry, Oral Evidence, Mr F. Stones, File 70, p. 3,469, MSA.
[182] Ibid., Interim Inquiry, Oral Evidence, A.W. Pryde, Labour Officer to the Government of Bombay, File 42, p. 478, MSA.
[183] Report of the TLIC, II, 125.

or usefully be asked to manage. Yet to a large extent, the number of spindles which a sider could manage was determined by the number of breakages in the yarn which had to be pieced. In counts below 30s, it was still possible to minimize the number of breakages if the quality of cotton, its mixing and preparation were improved and the frame itself regularly oiled and adequately repaired. If mixing and preparation were standardized in a mill at a high level of quality, and enough doffers employed to remove the bobbins, it became possible for one man to work both sides.[184] Since mills switched their lines of production and the quality of cotton mixings and counts of yarn were varied, these pre-conditions were difficult to achieve consistently and not always economical to sustain. This is perhaps why the mills predominantly worked coarse counts on a single-side system throughout the 1930s. This problem of organization was further compounded by the variety of ring frames used in the industry. The number of spindles per ring frame varied between 120 and 270 on each side so that a double-sider could in effect be asked to mind between 240 and 540 spindles. These variations in the length of ring frame occurred within mills as well as between them. 'Double side working', the Textile Labour Inquiry Committee sagely observed, 'does not, therefore, involve the same amount of work in every unit.'[185]

The nature and quality of the work done in the preparatory and spinning processes was directly reflected in efficiency, output and quality in the weaving shed. Coarse weft required more frequent changes of the shuttle and slowed down production. The quality of sizing determined the frequency of breakages in the warp. The speed of the loom was affected by the width of cloth; and the wider the loom the slower it worked.[186] Wage rates were usually based on the width of the cloth rather than the width of the loom. Sometimes, a rush of orders necessitated narrower widths of cloth to be woven on looms which were unduly wide, slowing down production and reducing, thereby, the earnings of the weaver.[187] Since mills wove several hundred varieties of cloth based on numerous counts and qualities of yarn, the number of workers required in each process fluctuated, while conversely, to maintain the flow of production and, therefore, to supply the weaving shed adequately could require that machines in the preceding processes be speeded up or higher counts be spun than warranted by the quality and mixing of cotton.[188] Similarly, the layout of the mill determined

[184] Proceedings of the TLIC, Main Inquiry, Oral Evidence, Mr F. Stones, File 72, pp. 3607–8, MSA.
[185] Report of the TLIC, II, 201.
[186] Proceedings of the BSEC, I, 263–6, MSA.
[187] Proceedings of the TLIC, Interim Inquiry, Oral Evidence, A.W. Pryde, Labour Officer, File 42, pp. 457–8, MSA.
[188] Proceedings of BSEC, I, 285–7, MSA.

the number of workers required at every stage of the production process: from nowghanies and coolies to bobbin carriers and doffers to jobbers and supervisors.[189] Not only did the deployment of labour in the spinning processes affect the outcome of weaving, but the layout of the mill could also influence the number of looms which a weaver might operate and the results he might obtain. 'The weaving shed', commented one observer,

is usually close and hot with much moisture and air. The looms are often so closely packed that it is difficult to walk between rows and the noise is deafening.[190]

If the weaver were to work more than two looms, it was necessary to improve the layout of the shed as well as the ventilation within it.[191]

Indeed, a number of conditions had to be fulfilled for a weaver to work a larger number of looms. Of course, a better quality of raw material and mixing of cotton yielded a higher outturn and superior yarn.[192] Moreover, the use of high-draft machinery had the advantage that in some cases 'you can get the same result in your finished yarn from an inferior mixing – you can either get increased production from the same mixing or you can get a lower mixing with the same texture or you can get half-way between the two'.[193] Similarly, the quality of winding and warping had to be maintained. It was necessary to ensure that the looms were regularly oiled and cleaned and labour deputed specifically to this task.[194] It was also an advantage to maintain the same type of production. The Sassoon Group, according to the Labour Officer, only wove long cloth on their six-loom system.[195] In their Manchester Mill, according to Fred Stones, they used only one count of weft when a weaver looked after six looms. This meant that the weaver was subjected to fewer interruptions and he could be more regularly supplied with requisite yarn, while the cloth he produced tended in turn to have a more regular and even quality. In some of their other mills, they used two or three counts of weft yarn and in general, he thought, up to six counts were manageable. While working four looms, however, it was possible to use different counts of weft yarn on all the looms. But, in either case, it was essential that a weaver should be supplied with adequate help, to carry bobbins to the weaving shed, to change the shuttle, to gait the beam, and to take the finished cloth off the loom and to carry it to the

[189] *Ibid.*, I, 286–9 and *ibid.*, II, 665, MSA.
[190] J.H. Kelman, *Labour in India: A Study of the Conditions of Indian Women in Modern Industry* (London, 1923), p. 73.
[191] Proceedings of the TLIC, Interim Inquiry, Oral Evidence, A.W. Pryde, File 42, p. 478, MSA.
[192] Proceedings of the TLIC, Main Inquiry, Oral Evidence, Mr F. Stones, File 74, pp. 4444–6. MSA.
[193] *Ibid.*, Main Inquiry, Oral Evidence, Mr F. Stones, File 73, p. 3960, MSA.
[194] *Ibid.*, Main Inquiry, Oral Evidence, Mr F. Stones, File 73, p. 3973, MSA.
[195] *Ibid.*, Main Inquiry, Oral Evidence, A.W. Pryde, File 66, p. 2327, MSA.

warehouse.[196] Moreover, it was necessary to maintain some consistency in the width and type of cloth produced and it had to be matched with the dimensions of the loom. 'It is very difficult to introduce rationalization in weaving', as the Textile Labour Inquiry Committee had observed, 'where there are a number of looms of different widths producing different styles and designs of cloth.'[197]

The Sassoon mills had been the earliest to introduce efficiency measures and had, along with a few others, carried them furthest. Few mills were, however, similarly equipped to fulfil these conditions. Indeed, the Bombay mills were characterized by their diversity in mill construction and equipment as well as the quality and type of goods produced.[198] In 1928, Sir Joseph Kay had dwelt on this diversity within the four mills of the Brady group, especially in their weaving shed.[199] Moreover, the millowners' representatives readily admitted that 'all mills were not constructed to take modern machinery' and their introduction could in many cases require the reconstruction of their buildings.[200] At the end of the 1930s, a decade of apparent improvement, reform and rationalization had not altered the fact that for most mills 'one of the great drawbacks [to rationalization] is that the weaving sheds are not properly laid out for working four looms'.[201]

Moreover, in conditions where the nature of occupations and the definition of duties were often vague, increased workloads were not always accompanied by an adequate complement of helpers for the weaver. Thus in 1928, Dange told the Fawcett Committee that if the shuttle broke, in some mills, the weaver had to take it to the 'smithy shop' to be repaired and 'in this manner most of the weavers lose in efficiency and ... they lose in earnings'.[202] This was not, of course, the universal practice and S.D. Saklatvala expressed his surprise at Dange's statement:

The practice is that we employ special men and even where special men are not employed it is the duty of the jobbers to fetch these articles. It may be that the jobber asks the weaver in some cases but the jobber ordinarily would not do it because his earnings depend on the production that the weaver turns out.[203]

However, Saklatvala's argument was perhaps a trifle disingenuous. It is doubtful whether jobbers would have taken kindly to fetching and carrying and it was

[196] Ibid., Main Inquiry, Oral Evidence, Mr F. Stones, File 74, pp. 4446–9 and File 73, pp. 3973–4, MSA.
[197] Report of the TLIC, II, 201.
[198] Proceedings of the BSEC, I, 286, MSA.
[199] Ibid., I, 619–24, MSA.
[200] Ibid., I, 643, MSA.
[201] Proceedings of the TLIC, Interim Inquiry, Oral Evidence, A.W. Pryde, Labour Officer to the Government of Bombay, File 42, p. 478, MSA.
[202] Proceedings of the BSEC, I, 292.
[203] Ibid., I, 304, MSA.

probably not beyond them to make weavers compensate them for a shortfall or defects in production. Nonetheless, it is also likely that different practices obtained in different mills at different times. Such tensions between jobbers and weavers were probably heightened in the 1930s as managers attempted to increase workloads, alter the character of production and manipulate wage rates. The whole weight of their dissatisfaction with working conditions would therefore be thrust upon the jobber.[204]

From 1928 onwards, every scheme to standardize wages had formally to incorporate rationalization measures. In this context, rationalization signified the production of finer goods and the steady increase of workloads. The effect of these efficiency measures upon work and wages would depend to a large extent on how adequately mills had prepared for their introduction, whether in terms of the quality of raw material and the maintenance of the machinery, the standardization and even specialization, however partial, of output and the provision and deployment of a team of supporting workers. By 1939, however, A.W. Pryde, the Labour Officer, expressed the view that with the exception of the Sassoon group, and to a lesser extent, Bombay Dyeing, no mills had taken the preparatory measures necessary to make the efficiency schemes an unqualified success.[205] No doubt a few more names may have been added in a less exacting and stringent assessment. From Pryde's own account, the Finlay Mill had clearly made considerable preparations for their high-count varieties.[206] Similarly, the Toyo Podar Mill, now having lost its Japanese stake, was said to be the only mill which spun yarn of 8's counts on a double-side efficiency system and which still paid its siders a basic wage of Rs. 35, excluding the interim increment recommended by the Textile Labour Inquiry Committee in 1937.[207] The Kohinoor Mill was also frequently mentioned for its pioneering efforts and progress in the introduction of rationalization schemes.[208] But the overwhelming majority adopted efficiency schemes intermittently, produced higher counts of yarn and finer varieties of cloth as orders were placed for them and varied their workloads and levels of employment accordingly. Managing agencies, which, like the Sassoons, prepared extensively for the production of finer goods and increased workloads resented

---

[204] Proceedings of the TLIC, Main Inquiry, Oral Evidence, A.W. Pryde, Labour Officer to the Government of Bombay, File 66, p. 2334, MSA.

[205] *Ibid.*, Main Inquiry, Oral Evidence, A.W. Pryde, Labour Officer to the Government of Bombay, File 66, p. 2327, MSA.

[206] *Ibid.*, Main Inquiry, Oral Evidence, A.W. Pryde, Labour Officer to the Government of Bombay, File 66, pp. 2338 ff., MSA.

[207] *Ibid.*, Main Inquiry, Oral Evidence, A.W. Pryde, Labour Officer to the Government of Bombay, File 66, p. 2345, MSA.

[208] *Ibid.*, Main Inquiry, Oral Evidence, BMOA, File 58A, pp. 308–9 and Mr F. Stones, File 72, p. 3605, MSA.

the copy-cat rationalization of their rivals. In the later 1920s, Fred Stones told the Textile Labour Inquiry Committee,

a very large group of mills decided that they could save money by cutting wages surreptitiously ... There was also the introduction of rationalization by some mills in haste, alongside the cutting of wages ... If there had been no surreptitious cutting of wages, our programme would have gone according to schedule.[209]

Yet a decade later, the old practice continued: 'I know certain mills introduce rationalization without making sure that the conditions were right.'[210] For these reasons, Stones argued that rationalization needed to be more closely regulated and that millowners should have been required to give notice before it was introduced. He suggested that the standard list for wages should be separated from a rationalization list. Mills, in his scheme, would have to apply to a standing committee or a wage board if they wished 'to claim for rationalization' and prove to its satisfaction that 'they have satisfied those conditions'.[211] The standing committee would be empowered to stipulate the changes a given mill would have to make before it could introduce rationalization and to fix the suitable rates when new machines were introduced.[212] Stones also argued, in contrast to the Millowners' Association delegation, that the standardization of musters was essential and should be closely supervised to ensure that they 'are adhered to strictly'.[213] In fact, every mill should be required to guarantee its working conditions and the quality of its machinery before it started functioning 'in the same way as a guarantee is to be given by the owner of a building that the sanitary arrangements have been provided for properly'.[214] These were rather radical demands from the Managing Director of E.D. Sassoon and Company, by no means a champion of state regulation and fully aware of its impractibility in an industry whose owners were to be irreconcilably hostile to regulation of any except the most unambiguously favourable kind. Moreover, it was highly improbable that either the colonial state or the Millowners' Association would accept the burdens and responsibility of regulation in this fractious domain. Fred Stones' trenchant view on the regulation of rationalization demonstrated the depth of the hostility of some millowners to those whom they felt introduced efficiency schemes competitively, as a short-term expedient rather than a systematic reform.

In practice, wage rates, musters and conditions were regulated within each individual mill in an informal and unequal process of bargaining between the

---

[209] *Ibid.*, Main Inquiry, Oral Evidence, Mr F. Stones, File 72, p. 3903, MSA.
[210] *Ibid.*, Main Inquiry, Oral Evidence, Mr F. Stones, File 72, p. 3604, MSA.
[211] *Ibid.*, Main Inquiry, Oral Evidence, Mr F. Stones, File 70, p. 3456, MSA.
[212] *Ibid.*, Main Inquiry, Oral Evidence, Mr F. Stones, File 70, p. 3465, MSA.
[213] *Ibid.*, Main Inquiry, Oral Evidence, Mr F. Stones, File 72, p. 3615.
[214] *Ibid.*, Main Inquiry, Oral Evidence, Mr F. Stones, File 70, pp. 3465–6, MSA.

managers, jobbers and workers. The wage rates in the Sassoon mills, according to Stones, were fixed in relation to prevailing conditions 'by agreement between the section of the workers and myself',[215] and in a patrician moment, he described how workers came to see him as 'the final court of appeal' if they had any complaints.[216] But these arrangements were inadequate to serve the industry as a whole. When the common problems of millowners had to be resolved or their common interests advocated, it was sometimes necessary to act on a larger scale than the individual mill. Wage disparities and the uneven adoption of efficiency schemes across the industry had a direct bearing upon the recruitment and control of labour in the individual mill. If millowners were to negotiate systematically with their workforce across the industry over wage rates, changes in production and the observance of the essential pre-conditions for rationalization, they would necessarily have to accept workers' combinations and indeed integrate trade unions within the managerial structure of the industry. This they were scarcely prepared to do.

Collective bargaining once it was institutionalized would close their options even more swiftly than an effective standardization scheme. It might, after all, foster the development of trade unions. For individual millowners, it could mean that the wider interests and institutions of the working classes could be called in to bolster the bargaining position of labour in their mill. Dange saw the potential in these circumstances for the development of trade unions. 'I think standardization is going to put us in power', he told the Textile Labour Inquiry Committee. This was a rather optimistic assessment. Nonetheless, as he pointed out, even if the Millowners' Association stipulated the pre-conditions necessary for the introduction of rationalization, only the workers could ensure that they were obtained. Unless the representatives of the workers were allowed to oversee whether these conditions were indeed observed in a particular mill, 'a simple statement that the Committee of the Millowners' Association have made such and such change cannot suffice'.[217] In the 1930s, the acceptance of trade unions would have meant that the millowners would have had to accredit the communist Girni Kamgar Union as the bargaining agent of the working classes. But on this point there was no ambiguity in the millowners' position. Thus, T.V. Baddeley declared on behalf of the Millowners' Association:

We have never welcomed the representatives of the Girni Kamgar Union inside our mills, and we could certainly not wish to have any roving commission wandering inside our mills to check rates.[218]

215 *Ibid.*, Main Inquiry, Oral Evidence, Mr F. Stones, File 70, p. 3454, MSA.
216 *Ibid.*, Main Inquiry, Oral Evidence, Mr F. Stones, File 70, p. 3569, MSA.
217 *Ibid.*, Main Inquiry, Oral Evidence, BPTUC, File 58A, p. 477, MSA.
218 *Ibid.*, Main Inquiry, Oral Evidence, BMOA, File 81A, p. 5817, MSA.

In the 1930s, therefore, there was a neither a formal system of collective bargaining nor a method for regulating the introduction of rationalization, outside the developing machinery for the conciliation and arbitration of disputes. Mills tried to produce finer varieties as they received orders for them and to increase workloads steadily wherever they could. For most workers, therefore, efficiency schemes increased their workloads, though not necessarily or consistently their earnings, and most mills extended them without preparing what were generally considered to be the necessary conditions for their introduction.

The sporadic use of efficiency methods in the 1930s meant that the effects of rationalization and the manner of its implementation described by the Labour Office inquiry in 1934 continued to prevail at the end of the decade and is unlikely to have changed in the 1940s. While a few mills had adopted new technology, most mills had effected little more than repairs on their machines or replaced parts, altered the character of production and introduced better mixings. Such gains in efficiency which resulted were not necessarily reflected in higher earnings. While the effect of rationalization on earnings in different mills was extremely varied, the most consistent result of its introduction was the increase of workloads.[219] In 1939, S.D. Saklatvala of the Tata Group stated that the reduction of employment in the industry in the 1930s had been due less to the replacement of machinery and adoption of new technology than the change in the character of production from coarse to fine-count production.[220] The Labour Officer agreed that the introduction of machinery was not the main cause of unemployment.[221] Spinning machinery was gradually being replaced, he reported, but far less change was effected in weaving, except in the use of automatic looms on a modest scale. The two-loom system was the most widespread in Bombay. 'The Jacquard loom', he said, 'is such a complicated thing that I do not think many are going in for it.'[222]

The Sassoon group was generally believed to have been one of the most advanced in the implementation of rationalization schemes and efficiency systems. Yet it was by no means single-minded in its commitment to technological change. Rationalization for Fred Stones meant simply that 'the work should run smoothly. This is a question of organization.'[223] It was far more

[219] Labour Office, Bombay, *Wages and Unemployment*, pp. 45–6.
[220] Proceedings of the TLIC, Main Inquiry, Oral Evidence, A.W. Pryde, Labour Officer to the Government of Bombay, File 66, p. 2411, MSA.
[221] *Ibid.*, Main Inquiry, Oral Evidence, A.W. Pryde, Labour Officer to the Government of Bombay, File 66, p. 2333, MSA.
[222] *Ibid.*, Main Inquiry, Oral Evidence, A.W. Pryde, Labour Officer to the Government of Bombay, File 66, p. 2331.
[223] *Ibid.*, Main Inquiry, Oral Evidence, Mr F.Stones, File 72, p. 3874, MSA.

important, in his opinion, to improve the quality of cotton, its mixings and preparation, the condition of the machinery and the deployment of labour, than necessarily to buy the best machines.[224] There were clearly some instances in which machinery did serve to displace labour: bale-stacking machines could reduce the number of coolies; beam carriers could be replaced with overhead cranes;[225] self-stripping devices and other mechanical advancements had made it possible to reduce the frequency of stripping from four and five times a day to once every one and a half days.[226] For the most part, however, changes in the character of production allowed mills to hire fewer workers with relatively little change in plant, as in sizing[227] or in warping where increased productivity was not the result of the renovation of machinery 'but a little adjustment'.[228] In the case of winding, the problem was rather more complicated. Where it was achieved, a greater uniformity in the varieties of cloth produced, and improvements in the quality of cotton and yarn, and in the speed and condition of the machinery had increased productivity as well as wages. The effect, claimed Stones, was that 'I can get more work out of the existing machines on account of rationalization without displacing anybody.'[229]

Since women could not be employed on night shifts, the mills were faced with the option of hiring male winders at night or completing all the necessary work for the night shift during the day. Rationalization, Stones appeared to argue, preserved winding as women's work. 'We have bought new machinery and brought them upto date', claimed Stones, 'to permit our women to work in the ordinary hours.'[230] But in grey winding, the Sassoons had found their existing machines with certain adaptations to yield better results than expensive modern machinery.[231] Yet elsewhere he admitted that the number of winders employed in one of their mills had been halved, although their earnings had increased by 50 per cent.[232] Winding and reeling, where women predominated, were also believed by most millowners to be particularly over-(wo)manned. Increased productivity and wage rates were likely to heighten the pressure to reduce their numbers. It has been suggested that women workers were particularly affected by technological change.[233] To some extent, new processes in winding, some arising from the diversification of output and the expansion of

224 *Ibid.*, Main Inquiry, Oral Evidence, Mr F. Stones, File 70, p. 3469, MSA.
225 *Ibid.*, Main Inquiry, Oral Evidence, Mr F. Stones, File 70, p. 3424, MSA.
226 *Ibid.*, Main Inquiry, Oral Evidence, Mr F. Stones, File 70, p. 3515, MSA.
227 *Ibid.*, Main Inquiry, Oral Evidence, Mr F. Stones, File 70, p. 3517, MSA.
228 *Ibid.*, Main Inquiry, Oral Evidence, Mr F. Stones, File 70, p. 3443, MSA.
229 *Ibid.*, Main Inquiry, Oral Evidence, Mr F. Stones, File 70, p. 3446, MSA.
230 *Ibid.*, Main Inquiry, Oral Evidence, Mr F. Stones, File 70, p. 3506, MSA.
231 *Ibid.*, Main Inquiry, Oral Evidence, Mr F. Stones, File 70, p. 3469, MSA.
232 *Ibid.*, Main Inquiry, Oral Evidence, Mr F. Stones, File 70, p. 3506–7, MSA.
233 Kumar, 'Family and Factory'.

bleaching, dyeing and finishing processes, did reduce the numbers of women employed in the industry. The available figures suggest both an absolute decline in their numbers as well as in their share of the workforce as a whole. The latter was perhaps in the 1930s more significantly the result of the increased employment of men on night shifts. But the decline in the volume of female employment was the result of a number of factors, only some of which can be directly related to technological change. It was seriously affected by the reduction of reeling, as mills sold less of their yarn and required more of it to be wound for weaving. The increasing protection of women by legislation, however limited, gave rise to the apprehension among millowners that female employment would reduce their flexibility in the deployment of labour and increase their transactional costs. During the 1940s more men were employed in this traditional domain of women's work and the pressure to eliminate surplus labour and work sharing from the reeling and winding departments increased. In particular, the apprehension that the government would introduce mandatory minimum wages led millowners to reduce the strength and increase the productivity of their workforce in these departments to match the level of payment to which they might be nailed.

Although attempts had been made before 1928 to standardize wages, these had been even more desultory and less systematic than schemes which were formulated in the following decade. Moreover, the schemes drawn up after 1928 not only had to standardize wages but to incorporate within their framework the effects of rationalization. In fact, the efficiency systems which were introduced in Bombay may be considered only a partial fulfilment of the Textile Labour Inquiry Committee's definition of the narrow construction of rationalization. Frequently, they were introduced simply as short-term expedients to meet changing patterns of demand or as a temporary response to overstocked markets, and in the longer run as an instrument for increasing workloads and establishing a high intensity of effort as customary within the workforce. In most cases, working conditions, materials and machinery in the mills were rarely adequately prepared to facilitate increased workloads or to extend to the workers a substantial share of the benefits of rationalization.

If the Fawcett Committee's scheme was overtaken by a general strike, the Textile Labour Inquiry Committee's findings were engulfed by the Second World War. The committee submitted its scheme to the Government of Bombay on 23 December 1939.[234] Before the wheels of bureaucracy had begun to turn, the textile workers demanded an increase in their dearness-of-food allowance to match rising prices. The standardization scheme had not anticipated the question of a dear-food allowance.[235] While the workers' demands were under

[234] *Bombay Chronicle*, 2 February 1940.
[235] *TOI*, 2 February 1940.

negotiation, it was 'considered unlikely that any early decision in the matter will be taken.'[236] On 4 March, the 'mahagai' agitation became a general strike which was not called off until 13 April.[237] It occurred in the context of the Congress campaign of individual civil disobedience and was followed by the Quit India movement. At the same time, during the war India's strategic and economic value appeared indispensable to the colonial state and its resources had to be mobilized on an unprecedented scale. This was scarcely an opportune moment at which to introduce a standardization scheme, whose implementation would necessarily dislocate prevailing wage structures, work practices and patterns of labour deployment. The process of adjustment to these fundamental changes would have led to the proliferation of labour disputes. It was only in 1947, on the eve of independence, and significantly in a period of rising wages and general buoyancy, that a standardization scheme based on the proposals of the Millowners' Association and the Textile Labour Inquiry Committee in 1938–9 was given effect.[238]

Explaining failure: 'the labour problem'

The failure of these successive attempts to standardize wages after 1928 has been explained by contemporary officials as well as later historians in terms of the weakness, sometimes the irresponsibility, of labour organizations. Once the general strikes of 1928–9 had devoured every semblance of trade-union organization in Bombay, the Tariff Board asserted in 1932,

the absence of any organized representation of labour has prevented further discussion of the schemes for standardization of wages and muster rolls or the extension of 'Efficiency Schemes' to more mills ... the Fawcett Committee's report represents a substantial measure of agreement achieved between the representatives of millowners and labour in 1928–9 which could probably be adopted with little or no modification as soon as proper representation of labour can be organised to discuss it.[239]

While in 1938 the Millowners' Association retrospectively laid the blame on the 'unwillingness of labour to cooperate', the representatives of the Bombay Provincial Trade Union Congress attributed its failure to 'the arrest and imprisonment of all the organizers of the Bombay Girni Kamgar Union who had knowledge of the scheme and had participated in the negotiations'.[240] This

---

236 *Bombay Chronicle*, 3 February 1940.
237 GOB, Home (Sp.) File 543 (13) 13 (3) of 1940, pp. 57–105; File 550 (23) C (2) of 1940; File 550 (23) C-I of 1940, File 550 (23) C-I (a) of 1940, MSA.
238 Mehta, *Indian Cotton Textile Industry*, p. 34; Morris, *Industrial Labour Force*, pp. 175–6; Mehta, *Cotton Mills*.
239 *Report of the ITB, 1932*, p. 62.
240 *Report of the TLIC*, II, 100.

was a preening and self-regarding view: the leading spokesmen for the Bombay Provincial Trade Union Congress in 1939, Dange, Mirajkar and Nimbkar, had been the very organizers to be arrested ten years earlier and imprisoned at Meerut. While the communist trade-union leaders exaggerated their own importance retrospectively, they neglected the role of the resistance of workers themselves to the rationalization and standardization schemes. On the other hand, for the employers to attribute the failure of their scheme to the obstruction of the workforce was to adopt the happy, if convenient, formula that all their troubles came from outside. Their explanation, said the Labour Officer, 'struck me as a very poor excuse'.[241] It certainly could not account for their failure to standardize wages in the 1980s or early 1920s or to mask their continuing differences in the 1930s.

The limited scope of reform in the industry cannot simply be attributed, on the one hand, to the jealousies of the millowners, their lack of discipline or authority and their speculative and myopic approach to the affairs of their industry, and, on the other hand, to the workers' immaturity in the 'early stages of industrialization' and their inability to organize for the sustained collective bargaining which a standardization scheme demanded. The millowners' claim that labour's refusal to co-operate undermined their modernizing intentions is belied by their own reluctance to discuss their schemes with their workers. The standardization sub-committee of the Millowners' Association had not consulted labour in drawing up their scheme in 1928. Asked to explain this before the Fawcett Committee, Sir Joseph Kay offered several but conflicting explanations. 'The difficulty of the Millowners' Association', he said at first, 'was to know from whom they would get the labour point of view';[242] then, that they had concluded that 'there was no object to serve in consulting anybody [i.e. trade-union leaders] about labour questions that did not know anything about labour questions';[243] later still that, although there were three trade unions, albeit of a rather limited membership and uncertain provenance, there was 'no responsible body of labour to meet us to discuss matters in dispute';[244] and finally, that 'we could not consult them because we had not met local labour leaders in those days at all'.[245]

Until 1929, Fred Stones claimed on behalf of the Millowners' Association, 'our attitude definitely was, if the workers changed these men we would meet them. Unfortunately they did not do so and on the findings of the Pearson

---

[241] Proceedings of the TLIC, Main Inquiry, Oral Evidence, A.W. Pryde, Labour Officer to the Government of Bombay, File 66, p. 2498, MSA.
[242] Proceedings of the BSEC, I, 625, MSA.
[243] Ibid., I, 626.
[244] Ibid., I, 627.
[245] Ibid., I, 628.

Committee we had to refuse recognition to these unions.'[246] By 1939, he said, 'with one possible exception, I do not think there is a trade union leader in Bombay to-day who can understand a standardised weaving list'. This was not surprising, since the millowners did not give the leaders, as Stones admitted, an opportunity to visit the mills and get acquainted with the actual working conditions. 'The dangers of doing that', he told the Committee, perhaps recalling the activities of the mill committees of the Girni Kamgar Union in 1928–9, 'you will understand if you read the Pearson report. We prefer to keep them outside.'[247] Yet, left outside, they could scarcely become the effective bargaining agent which the millowners claimed so loudly and longingly to desire.

Required to present a standardization scheme to the Textile Labour Inquiry Committee in 1939, the millowners sought to give evidence in camera, and showed that their intentions with regard to consulting labour had become both simpler and clearer. 'I am really trying to make the point clear', T.V. Baddeley told the Committee in April 1939:

that in putting forward any scheme, we shall be putting it forward to the Committee, and I am afraid we shall not be prepared thereafter to make it a basis of a series of meetings and discussions with other people.[248]

Subsequently, their standardization scheme was presented in camera and discussed in confidence. Indeed, at their very first round of discussions, Baddeley reiterated the point that theirs was a scheme of 'absolutely maximum wages. It is not before us as a bargaining point.' They would only proceed on condition that 'we shall not be expected to enter in direct negotiations either with labour … or anybody else'. They insisted that their standardization scheme should not be shown to labour representatives until it had been fully considered and decisions taken. In return, they received the assurance of the Chairman of the Inquiry Committee:

One thing is certain that we shall first discuss the scheme with you and then we shall consider it among ourselves and if we at all wish to consult labour we shall do so.[249]

So while the millowners entertained a public dissatisfaction about 'the unwillingness of labour to cooperate', they were stricken by a private alarm at the prospect of such offers of assistance.

The representatives of the Bombay Provincial Trade Union Congress presented a rather similar, or at least matching, interpretation of events. They

246 Proceedings of the TLIC, Main Inquiry, Oral Evidence, BMOA, File 57A, p. 214, MSA.
247 Ibid., Main Inquiry, Oral Evidence, BMOA, File 57A, p. 216, MSA.
248 Ibid., Main Inquiry, Oral Evidence, Confidential Examination, BMOA, File 77B, pp. 5026–7, MSA.
249 Ibid., Main Inquiry, Oral Evidence, Confidential Examination, BMOA, File 78C, pp. 5361–3, MSA.

recognized the importance of some form of collective bargaining to the implementation and development of rationalization and standardization. Yet, as Dange said, his knowledge of the working conditions in the mills was at least ten years old.[250] Now he said, he was refused permission to enter a mill, 'because they say one does not know what will happen if I go into a mill'.[251] The Girni Kamgar Union, the only effective labour organization in the industry, could have no knowledge of the 'day to day working of the processes in the mills'. On the other hand, its communist leaders believed, the workers are 'not so well-equipped that they can explain the working conditions properly'. This view served conveniently to privilege the role of their leaders. As Nimbkar added, the working of the mills 'could be understood only by an intelligent member' of the Union, yet 'facilities are not given to us ... For instance, to calculate wages in weaving, the ordinary worker does not know how to do it.' Thus, as Dange asserted, however many members a union boasted and whatever the proportion of millworkers on its executive committee, 'the collective agreement has to be made by the Union as a whole and in the absence of recognition, the presence of Mr. Bhise [President of the Girni Kamgar Union and a textile worker] does not help'.[252] But in place of recognition, the Girni Kamgar Union and its representatives experienced only repression and exclusion from the workplace. It was not only the communist leaders but the union itself which was refused access to the mill. The problems faced by the Girni Kamgar Union were elaborated by Nimbkar:

We visit the localities of the workers, consider their grievances. As our union is not recognised it becomes impossible for us to get their grievances redressed. If the grievance is of a major character we write letters to the mill concerned and to the Millowners' Association. We do not get any reply from them. Then there are the major issues on which we have to carry on propaganda. As however our union is not recognised we are not able to settle any dispute or get any grievance redressed ... Now not a single pie can be collected within the mills. If we try to collect the dues at the mill gates, police arrest our men. So we have to go to the workers' chawls and collect dues. In a big city like Bombay this would require a large machinery which we cannot maintain.[253]

At the same time, the Labour Officer, appointed under the Trade Disputes Act, which in turn had been explicitly formulated to extirpate communism from the textile industry,[254] appeared to possess all these advantages:

The labour officer has got an access to the mill. So when the worker finds that his union

[250] Ibid., Main Inquiry, Oral Evidence, BPTUC, File 58A, p. 447, MSA.
[251] Ibid., Main Inquiry, Oral Evidence, BPTUC, File 58A, p. 505, MSA.
[252] Ibid., Main Inquiry, Oral Evidence, BPTUC, File 58A, pp. 503–5, MSA.
[253] Ibid., Interim Inquiry, Representatives of the National Trade Union Federation and the All-India Trade Union Congress, File 42, pp. 129–30, MSA.
[254] GOB, Home (Sp.) File 543 (48) L of 1934, MSA; Indian Textile Journal, 44 (August 1934), 379; BMOA, Annual Report, 1934, pp. 24, 22–31.

cannot redress his grievance he goes to the labour officer and the labour officer goes to the mill concerned and works in collaboration with the mill. The result is that the worker finds that his union is not in a position to redress his grievances while ordinarily that must be his natural expectation. So the union is deprived of its legitimate function of redressing the day to day grievances of the worker. Therefore the appointment of the labour officer is a hindrance to the growth of the trade union movement in the city of Bombay.[255]

Five years later, following the logic of his own argument perhaps, Nimbkar took up employment as the Labour Officer for the Government of the United Provinces. His was a rather gloomy view. The Labour Officer in Bombay was never entirely able to displace trade unions. Barely three years after he had thus spoken, Nimbkar was able to lead the Girni Kamgar Union into another five-week-long general strike in Bombay. Nonetheless, the machinery of conciliation established by the Act, the refusal of the millowners to recognize the union, the victimization of workers who stepped forward as spokesmen and the creation of the Labour Officer combined to choke the most obvious means by which a trade union might establish itself within the industry. Without some measure of tolerance from the millowners and the state, it was unlikely that trade unions could sustain their presence or their organization in the workplace. In the face of their repression, or what one leader of the Girni Kamgar Union had described as 'the cold-blooded, planned-out war policy of the millowners',[256] it was scarcely possible for them to function at all in any conventional sense.

So having destroyed trade unions and ensured that they could not develop in the industry unless the unions satisfied their own rather narrow, even unrealistic definitions, millowners and colonial officials complained that, without them, it was impossible to effect extensive rationalization and standardization. On the other hand, there was some force in the argument made by the Bombay Textile Labour Union (BTLU) in 1927 that standardization called for 'an organization among the millowners themselves'.[257] Yet the diverse and fractious interests among the millowners, on the one hand, and the reluctance, even refusal of labour to co-operate, on the other, were largely the symptoms of the problems which obstructed and limited the implementation of rationalization and standardization. These problems lay within the workplace, and stemmed from the organization of production and the nature and conditions of its development. They were the result neither of a specific managerial culture nor of 'pre-industrial' attitudes to work.

255 Proceedings of the TLIC, Interim Inquiry, Oral Evidence, Representatives of the National Trade Union Federation and the All India Trade Union Congress, File 42, p. 130, MSA.
256 Proceedings of the Bombay Riots Inquiry Committee, Oral Evidence, G.L. Kandalkar and V.H. Joshi, File 17, p. 89, MSA.
257 Report of the ITB, 1927, Evidence of Local Governments, Bombay Textile Labour Union, III, 539.

In this context, it became for more difficult to implement rationalization, let alone the accompanying standardization of wages, in periods when millowners were seeking to reduce their cost of production. Both the millowners and the labour leaders were agreed that wage standardization would be more easily achieved when earnings could be increased. For labour, standardization would not necessarily imply falling wages and rising workloads. Workers would, therefore, as the labour leaders argued, submit to it more willingly. On the other hand, the millowners would also more readily arrive at a consensus among themselves. Mills which paid below the standard rate would feel more prepared to raise their levels in prosperous times while mills whose wages exceeded it would not necessarily feel impelled to reduce them.[258] In fact, when wages were rising, the standard could act as a ceiling upon their upward movement. For while high-paying mills could justify by the standardization scheme holding the line of their wages, low-paying mills could better afford to reach its level. Moreover, when the markets were buoyant, it was also probable that the demand for finer varieties would increase, making it easier to implement the efficiency systems by which employment was reduced and workloads increased. These factors help to explain, at least partially, why standardization was effected in 1947, even if it was initiated within the courtroom rather than the weaving shed.[259]

Throughout the 1920s and 1930s, however, the mill workers perceived rationalization and standardization as schemes for cutting wages and increasing unemployment. 'Standardization', as Dange told the Textile Labour Inquiry Committee in 1939,

has come every time before the worker in the garb of standardization, but really has been a scheme of wage cuts and that is why a sort of prejudice has been developed in the mind of Bombay workers that it is a ruse to cut wages.[260]

Nimbkar himself told the Textile Labour Inquiry Committee that 'as a man who knows the modern world', he was, indeed, in favour of rationalization, but he represented 'the viewpoint of the manual worker' and 'in the mind of the textile worker in Bombay, there is a prejudice against rationalization'.[261] Yet in the light of the previous decade's experience, this was not a prejudice but a realistic appreciation of the facts. On the other hand, the millowners remained deeply divided. In 1928, Dange was to recall, 'a block of nearly 22 mills or so were

---

[258] Proceedings of the TLIC, Main Inquiry, Oral Evidence, BPTUC, File 58A, p. 443, and BMOA, File 78C, p. 5380, MSA.

[259] Morris, *Industrial Labour Force*, pp. 175–6.

[260] Proceedings of the TLIC, Main Inquiry, Oral Evidence, BPTUC, File 80A, p. 5337, MSA.

[261] *Ibid.*, Main Inquiry, Oral Evidence, BPTUC, File 58A, p. 405, MSA. See also Dange's comments in *ibid.*, p. 476 and File 80A, p. 5637, MSA.

opposed to the standard scheme' and wanted to make an independent deal with the Joint Strike Committee outside its framework:

Of course, when the proposal was put before us, and we inquired why it was so, we found that those mills were such as would have to pay a bit higher wage according to the standard scheme than the one they were paying. So the standard scheme was such a one that even the millowners were not agreed upon it.[262]

By 1939, however, little had discernibly changed. 'Even today', Dange told the Textile Labour Inquiry Committee,

they are divided, because standardization would mean guaranteeing certain working conditions, which some of the millowners, who cannot improve conditions, would object to. Therefore they would not like the standardization scheme.[263]

The notion of a uniform standard, even in its minimal form, whether of wages, musters or conditions, was the individual millowner's nightmare. To surrender their options in their mill for the rigidities of a definition of an average for the whole industry violated their traditions, methods and business practices. The spectre of combined action and increasing homogeneity exacerbated their differences, intensified their antagonisms and jealousies, heightened their conflicts and tensions and threatened to rend them apart. This was not surprising. Throughout the 1920s and 1930s, the millowners had relied upon the manipulation of their labour force as a means of alleviating the problems of their industry. Labour, it appeared to them, was the only significant factor in the affairs of the textile industry which seemingly lay within the ambit of their control. They could scarcely collude with other centres of the Indian textile industry to restrict output and fix prices. They could not compete effectively with Japanese or Lancashire imports, especially in the higher counts and finer varieties. They could not conjure up the banking facilities or financial services they wanted. Their influence over the colonial state in matters of financial, fiscal and monetary policies, and increasingly over questions of social-welfare legislation, appeared palpably, indeed, frustratingly, weak. Cotton prices in India were often determined by the state of the crop and the volume of its supply from America. Not only were their markets governed by the customs of the piece-goods trade, but the demand for their products continued to be vitally influenced by the monsoon and the harvest.

Yet even in relation to labour, their strengths were often more apparent than real. They could not consistently realize their aims and objectives. Their attempts to manipulate labour frequently had consequences which they neither intended nor desired. If the exploitation of labour in the pursuit of short-term

262 *Ibid.*, Main Inquiry, Oral Evidence, BPTUC, File 58A, p. 444, MSA.
263 *Ibid.*, Main Inquiry, Oral Evidence, BPTUC, File 58A, pp. 443–4, MSA.

expedients to postpone their moment of truth, was their last resort, they also encountered resistance on a dramatic scale and consistently experienced numerous widespread strikes for varying, often damaging, lengths of time. The passive Indian workers were difficult to manage, not simply because they dragged their feet, spread rumours, whispered in dark corners or erupted spasmodically into violence, but because they combined and acted in concert and opposition. There was little that was 'customary' about their subordination.[264] Rather, they appropriated and exerted an impressive degree of control over their own labour. They did not avoid confrontation; instead they launched and sustained repeated general strikes across the industry. In so doing, they often brought the mills and even, at times, the city to a standstill. Their last throw in 1982, when the textile workers sustained a general strike for over a year, built the headstone and inscribed the epitaph for the Bombay cotton-textile industry.[265]

[264] Arnold, 'Industrial Violence'; D. Chakrabarty, 'On Deifying and Defying Authority: Managers and Workers in the Jute Mills of Bengal, circa 1890–1940', *Past and Present*, C (1983), 124–46.

[265] For an account of the 1982 strike, see D. Bhattacherjee, 'Unions State and Capital in Western India: Structural Determinants of the 1982 Bombay Textile Strike', in R. Southall (ed.), *Labour and Unions in Asian and Africa: Contemporary Issues* (London, 1988), pp. 211–37.

9   Epilogue: workers' politics – class, caste and nation

This book has attempted to examine the social processes underlying the formation of the working classes in Bombay in the early twentieth century and their interaction with the strategies of capital: how the processes of social formation were shaped by the nature and forms of industrial capitalism and how they were constrained and conditioned by its pattern of development. The economy of Bombay's workers has been analysed in terms of a nexus of social connections, which operated across the boundaries of city and village, workplace and neighbourhood, the 'formal' and 'informal' sector. The extensive use of casual labour in the textile industry, and its preponderance outside, the operations of the jobber system and the pattern of industrial action, as the repression of combinations at work drove workers to organize in the street, integrated the spheres of workplace and neighbourhood. The social relations of the workplace cannot, therefore, be abstracted from the wider social context of the neighbourhood. Moreover, the casual and uncertain conditions of employment forced most workers to maintain their links with their villages. It also shaped the social organization of the neighbourhood. Since jobs were easy to lose but difficult to obtain, most workers sought to develop connections with jobbers, who might keep them in employment. Similarly, grain-dealers and shopkeepers known to them might extend credit without guarantees and help to tide them over periods of unemployment. Landlords or rent collectors might offer discriminating terms to or exercise patience in receiving rents from men in their connection. Friends and relatives, co-villagers and cohabitants, neighbours and caste-fellows might be called upon for small loans, for help with the payment of rents or for assistance in the quest for work. The rural base sometimes provided for the subsistence of a worker's family and a retreat from the city in times of distress. But it also constituted the hub of wider connections in Bombay through which migrants might find work, credit and housing. The social organization of Bombay's workers stemmed from these informal systems of mutual assistance. But the connections developed in this way could also be deployed to protect their position at work or to orchestrate political action.

The social action and organization of workers limited the options and influenced the strategies of capital. In view of the high risks of industrial investment, capital was characteristically mobilized in small pools for enterprises whose profitability was proven and whose risks were known and its uses were always liable to be swiftly diversified. Entrepreneurs both in the cotton-textile industry and in the so-called 'informal sector' hoped that they might attract capital by adopting strategies which enabled them to minimize stocks, maintain a rapid turnover and show quick profits and, accordingly, they attempted largely to regulate production to the short-term fluctuations of demand. In this way, industrial production flourished upon, and indeed perpetuated, an excess supply of labour. But this did not mean, as some historians have assumed, that employers were simply free to choose their own modes of labour control. Indeed, when swiftly changing production targets inflated their needs, employers sometimes experienced acute shortages of labour. The mechanisms of the labour market encouraged workers to develop and maintain their village and neighbourhood connections, upon whose strength they drew to resist more effectively the demands and defy the pressures of their employers.

The nature of the cotton-textile industry's problems, certainly its responses to them, were shaped by the labour-intensive strategies of employers. These strategies exacerbated the diversity of conditions in the industry and limited the possibilities of combination among the millowners. They also influenced the structure and the organization of the workforce. The labour-intensive strategies of the millowners increased their dependence upon the skill and resourcefulness of the workers, and thereby increased the latter's bargaining power. In the 1920s and 1930s, the millowners attempted to transfer the weight of the industry's problems on to the labour force and not surprisingly, they encountered fierce resistance. From the late 1920s, rationalization schemes were formulated partly with the objective of undermining workers' resistance. But they represented for the most part attempts by the millowners to manipulate the use and deployment of labour rather than a concerted or coherent assault upon the industry's structural problems. As their effect was to nibble wage rates, increase workloads and disturb the conditions of employment, they served largely to intensify workers' resistance.

Far from increasing the homogeneity of the workforce, industralization acted to intensify its sectionalism. The sectionalism of the working class did not simply derive from traditional social organization, but was integral to the social process itself. Of course, it is possible to sketch a social experience which the working class shared in common. Yet the very features which they shared in common served to divide them. Workers faced each other as antagonists across the labour market as they competed for scarce jobs. Similarly, workers competed within the workplace, for the best raw materials or the most efficient machines, and divided along the lines of jobber, neighbourhood or trade-union organization. The social experience of migration, which was common to the vast majority of the city's workers, also registered differences between them.

They emigrated from a variety of social contexts. The particular circumstances of their family economies differed. The extent to which they could draw upon rural resources varied. Their ability to contribute effectively to their replenishment was scarcely uniform. In many ways, the social experience of the neighbourhood brought workers together, and sometimes created a sense of mutuality among them. But the patronage networks which formed within the neighbourhood frequently found themselves competing ferociously with each other. Solidarities were sometimes forged within the neighbourhood during general strikes or other moments of collective action; but the neighbourhood could also become the arena for bitter antagonisms and conflicts.

Just as the social formation of the working classes is often conceptualized in terms of its evolution from 'pre-industrial' characteristics, through 'early industrialization' to full-blown proletarian maturity, so the social consciousness of the working class is still often analysed in stages of development from 'prepolitical' consciousness through 'trade-union' and 'reformist' consciousness to its apotheosis in 'revolutionary' and 'socialist' consciousness. Against these models, historians have attempted to measure the level or specify the depth of political consciousness attained by workers in particular cases. Within the terms of this theoretical discourse, however, it would be difficult to make sense of the industrial and political action of the Bombay working class.

Conditions for the development of working-class politics

In the last decades of colonial rule, Bombay became the scene of massive political unrest. In the 1920s and 1930s, Bombay City, whose politics had once appeared unerringly loyal, now ranked among the most important centres of nationalist agitations and anti-imperial politics. At the same time, the city's labour force effected eight general strikes between 1919 and 1940 as well as thousands of smaller ones, under communist leadership from the late 1920s onwards, so that at times it came to be regarded anxiously by colonial rulers as an insurrectionary centre. In addition, the city was engulfed by communal riots between Hindus and Muslims with growing frequency, which not only affected industrial action and trade-union politics and nationalist agitations, but was sometimes stimulated by them. Yet this industrial and political action was effected by a workforce, consisting largely of rural migrants, casually employed, operating in an overstocked labour market and fragmented by caste and religion as well as by skill and the division of labour. Furthermore, no trade unions achieved any level of stable organization, disintegrating as rapidly and numerously as they appeared. On any conventional expectations of workers' politics, industrial action on this scale should never have happened.

The casual poor and rural migrants, it is often supposed, are characterized by their rootless volatility, their aversion to routine and their inability to organize.

In any case, the conditions of an overstocked labour market are always likely to provide employers with the opportunity to undermine workers' combination and break strikes. Similarly, rural migrants are often believed to lack a commitment to the urban and industrial setting. As peasants on a temporary sojourn in the factories, their interests are supposed to lie in the village and their will to defend their rights or transform their social and political situation in the city considered correspondingly weak. Urban neighbourhoods composed of rural migrants or the casual poor, deeply marked by their peasant origins, have been thus perceived as rural cities and urban villages. Their social organization has frequently been portrayed in terms of its 'primordial' or traditional characteristics. Conventionally, these have appeared to offer poor materials from which working-class movements might be constructed.

However, on closer scrutiny, each of these elements might be sighted in a different perspective. Once the assumption is set aside that the informal sector was constituted by workers who sought out casual employment wherever it might be found and manifested values, attitudes and behavioural styles specific to their occupational domain, it becomes far more difficult to postulate that there were socially or culturally innate reasons for their failure to organize or sustain concerted political action. Village connections did not simply infuse workers with bucolic sentiments or fill them with a longing to return to the land. On the contrary, the more defined the purpose of their migration – to facilitate the maintenance of their stake in the village – the greater was the 'commitment' to their urban interests which workers were likely to display. If the millowners attempted to transfer the costs of the reproduction of the labour force to the rural economy, textile workers sometimes deployed their village connections in defence of their urban interests and in particular to sustain strikes for extensive periods.

The ties of caste, kinship and village through which they migrated to the city were brought together within the social arena of the neighbourhood. Although it reminded numerous observers of the village and repeatedly invited description in rural metaphors, the social organization of the neighbourhood was, in fact, shaped by its continuous interaction with the workplace. Just as the management and deployment of labour called upon jobbers and managers to straddle the divide between workplace and neighbourhood, so workers had to act within both spheres to obtain work, to tide them over periods of unemployment and to orchestrate collective action to defend their jobs, earnings or status within the workplace. Workers' combinations, often repressed in the workplace, sometimes reconstituted themselves in the neighbourhood. In times of industrial action, the issues of the workplace were placed before the working-class neighbourhoods as a whole. Strikes which began on the shopfloor sometimes, not necessarily in violence or riot, spilled over into the street. It was in the neighbourhood, in the political theatre and trenches of the street, that workers most consistently experienced the nature of the state; and it was in relation to this experience, rather than that of production alone, that their political consciousness was shaped. At the same time, the operation of their neighbourhood connections – for instance, changes in the generosity and utility of their patrons – informed their political perceptions. The fragile and shifting coherence which these connections imparted to social groups may have informed the tensions underlying political action, but they also injected solidarities into the labour movement. Similarly, the patterns of association or sociability which formed around or emerged from this social nexus not only influenced the social organization of the neighbourhood but also facilitated political mobilization and political action.

On the other hand, the momentum and scale of industrial action in the 1920s and 1930s cannot be explained simply as a consequence of the aggregation of large groups of workers within the mills. The history of the Bombay textile workers is frequently interpreted in two conflicting ways and sometimes in both senses at the same time. When they are perceived as workers in the 'early stages of industrialization', the organization of work and politics is portrayed accordingly and the sectionalism of the workforce can be attributed to its stage of development. When historians observe the intensity of class conflict, they seek to explain it as a special case, arising out of Bombay's role as an advanced centre of Indian industrial development. Yet as the preceding chapters have shown, industrialization often exacerbated the divisions within the workforce. Workers competed for jobs, the best raw materials, the most paying orders and the most productive machines. Rivalries which arose out of the division of labour and the divergence of workers' interests at the point of production sometimes involved and engulfed the whole structure of mill management, from jobbers and head jobbers to departmental heads and managers, and shaped factions competing for neighbourhood domination. Trade-union rivalries need to be comprehended in terms of this competition both between workers and jobbers and, in addition, at the level of politics, between publicists, spokesmen and union leaders. What are often perceived as the 'pre-industrial' characteristics of the workforce did not in themselves offer a sufficient explanation for working-class sectionalism and trade-union rivalry. Rather, it would appear that rivalry and competition were integral to the formation of the labour force and endemic to labour politics. The assumption that the concentration of workers into larger masses, with the development of factory industry, made their interests uniform has led historians to seek to explain why nonetheless tensions and rivalries persisted within the workforce and why they failed to perceive their common interests. This study has tried to suggest that it would be more fruitful to proceed in the opposite direction. Since Bombay's workers were so deeply divided in so many different ways, we need rather to explain why and how they came together at all, often at specific moments for specific ends.

Workers, trade unions and the state

The notion that the pattern of trade-union growth, and especially its weaknesses, may be explained in terms of the pre-industrial characteristics of the workforce or the 'early stages of industrialization' in the Indian economy need not detain us unduly. Nor is there a compelling reason to read the level of social conscious-ness from or measure the political maturity of the workforce by the nature and extent of trade-union organization, at any stage of industrial development. Even in the most 'advanced' centres of industrial capitalism, a recurring theme of labour history has been the small minority of the working classes who were organized into trade unions. Before 1914, less than a tenth of the working class in France and only about a quarter in Germany and Britain belonged to economic or political organizations.[1] Like other social groups and institutions, trade unions formed within specific social and political conjunctures. Contro-versy in the British case has raged around the issue of whether industrial relations were shaped more 'by informal groups or spontaneous social and economic processes than by institutional forces'.[2] But this polarity between the spontaneous and the organized appears particularly meaningless in contexts where the institutions of trade unionism have no more than an ephemeral and evanescent existence and where their absence has not precluded negotiation and bargaining between workers and employers. Trade unions and collective bar-gaining procedures need not necessarily be perceived as inherently conciliatory and they may well serve the interest of the workforce in significant ways. But, in either case, to take the role of institutional forces in collective bargaining as given and, indeed, primary and determining in its effects, is to beg questions about why employers and the state accepted workers' combinations in the first place. In India, employers and, to varying degrees, the state refused to counte-nance their existence or, alternatively, sought to define their scope closely. The vagaries and weaknesses of trade-union growth are perhaps more consistently explained in terms of the hostility of employers and the state than as a direct consequence of the values, aspirations and consciousness of the workers them-selves. Indeed, the willingness of employers to tolerate and negotiate with workers' combinations was sometimes a preference for dealing with repre-sentatives when their resistance proved too strong, disorderly and disruptive. But concessions forced upon employers by industrial or political militancy were always liable to be reversed when the opportunity presented itself.

The nature of trade-union organization in Bombay should be considered in relation to the formidable obstacles to workers' combination. In this context,

---

[1] R. Geary, *European Labour Protest, 1848–1918* (Cambridge, 1981), p. 15.
[2] J. Zeitlin, 'From Labour History of the History to Industrial Relations', *EcHR*, 2nd series, XL, 2 (1987), 159–84.

the colonial state did not offer the most consistent or the most resolute opposition to the growth of trade unions.[3] At its different levels, the colonial state was vulnerable to a wide range of pressures and a coherent or sustained attempt to destroy the labour movement would have opened up irreconcilable differences within its structure.[4] There was, indeed, an important contradiction in the official attitude of the colonial state to trade-union development. While the colonial state was often apprehensive of the threat which the development of working-class politics might pose to the social order, they also understood the value of promoting what they called genuine and healthy trade unions.[5] The state did not set out to prevent trade unions from organizing at all costs. Indeed, the intervention of the state, at certain points, promoted trade-union growth – even of the wrong kind. The Trade Unions Act of 1926, which required them to register, stimulated their formation.[6] Similarly, the industrial disputes legislation of the 1930s created a space within which trade unions could play an important role in regulating the relationship between workers, employers and the state. On the other hand, it is doubtful whether the struggle to form trade unions was waged solely around the state. The constellation of forces which disciplined workers at the point of production devastated their attempts at combination more consistently, if less visibly, than police action or the persecution of trade-union activists.[7]

The daily social relations of the workplace equipped employers, managers and jobbers with numerous sanctions by which to cajole, threaten or dismiss recalcitrant workers.[8] They could simply dismiss workers who were prominent in effecting combinations or too vociferous in representing their grievances. But there were more subtle and more chronic pressures which mill officers could apply to their workforce. They held wages in arrears and imposed fines and

---

[3] See, for instance, Arnold, 'Industrial Violence'.

[4] This was illustrated during the discussions between the city police, the Government of Bombay and the Government of India about policies to contain the 'communist menace'. See GOB, Home (Sp.) File 543 (18) of 1928, MSA; GOI, Home (Pol.), File nos. F/18/VII/28 and Keep Withs (KWs), F/18/VII/28, 303/1929 and KWs 1 and 2, NAI.

[5] Bombay Confidential Proceedings, Judicial, November 1920, vol. 53, pp. 467–84, IOR.

[6] RCLI, Evidence, Bombay Presidency, GOB, 'Conditions of Industrial Labour in the Bombay Presidency', I, i, 104. The proliferation of unions, once they could be registered, can be observed in the Labour Gazette's statements of trade unions in Bombay Presidency and their membership.

[7] For a different view, see Chakrabarty, Rethinking Working Class History, p. 170, who, leaning upon Foucault, writes 'In the jute mills of Bengal, then, managerial power worked more by making a spectacle of itself and less the quiet mechanism of "discipline" that acts through the labour market, technology and the organization of work.'

[8] BMOA, Annual Report, 1893, p. 16; RCLI, Evidence, Bombay Presidency, The Social Service League, 1, i, 445; Proceedings of the TLIC, Main Inquiry, Oral Evidence, Mr A.W. Pryde, Labour Officer, Government of Bombay, File 66, pp. 2371–2, MSA.

deductions for poor work, insubordination or absenteeism.[9] They could also discriminate between workers in distribution of raw materials, the allocation of machinery and the assignment of the most paying orders. Since the rules governing conditions of work were often rather vaguely stipulated and erratically observed, and since records pertaining to leave, absenteeism and employment were often poorly kept, managers and jobbers could enforce them selectively and indeed choose the circumstances and the form of their implementation. But it would be misleading simply to juxtapose the employers and the workforce as two monolithic structures facing each other in positions which were entrenched and adversarial. From managing agent to jobber, every level and rank of supervisory and managerial personnel were involved in networks of patronage and interest which extended into the workforce. The workers' grievances were often expressed through jobbers or departmental heads; employers who disregarded them could open up differences within the structure of supervision and management.[10]

When disputes could not be settled within the framework of the jobber system or the managerial structure of the mill, employers could sometimes resolve them with an adroit mixture of concession and dismissal. But these sanctions against workers often made it preferable to seek the assistance of pleaders, publicists and trade-union leaders to represent their grievances. Yet trade unions which formed in this way could readily be isolated by the same means. Employers would normally refuse to negotiate with them unless the trade union commanded the support of a significant proportion of their workforce and when they did, the employers might concede in the short term while gradually replacing their employees. From the standpoint of labour, the best means of forcing their grievances upon the employers was simply to stop work. But strikes necessarily jeopardized workers' jobs. As the veteran labour leader V.B. Karnik observed, in the view of officials and employers, 'a strike was regarded as an act of insubordination and indiscipline, an illegal breach of contract'.[11] Incomplete strikes were, therefore, extremely difficult to defend and often resulted in the victimization of the most active workers.[12]

Trade unions often formed during strikes. Some were never more than hastily assembled strike committees, and many of these collapsed with the strikes

[9] 'Report by Chief Inspector of Factories on the Working of the Factories Act in the Town and Island of Bombay' in *Provincial Report on the Working of the Indian Factories Act in the Bombay Presidency for the Year 1892* (Bombay, 1893), pp. 14–15; *RCLI, Evidence, Bombay Presidency*, Government of Bombay, I, i, 89–91, BMOA, I, i, 401; Labour Office, Bombay, *Report on Wages ...the Textile Industries, General Wage Census, Part I, Third Report*, pp. 35–52; *Labour Office, Bombay, Report of an Enquiry into Deductions of Wages*.
[10] See chapter 7 above.
[11] Karnik, *Strikes in India*, pp. 24–5.
[12] For instance, see *RCLI, Evidence, Bombay, Presidency*, I, i, 445.

which gave rise to them. Several trade unions were swept away during moments of industrial action when the militancy of rival organizations drew away and undermined the basis of their following. The general strikes of 1919 and 1920 were directed by what were essentially strike committees. The Girni Kamgar Mahamandal formed in the course of a bonus dispute in 1924 and the Bombay Textile Labour Union emerged out of the general strike of the following year, when workers resisted the wage cuts imposed by the Millowners' Association. The communist-led Girni Kamgar Union formed similarly as a nucleus within the Joint Strike Committee in 1928. The militancy of its rhetoric and its political activity in the context of the general strike enabled it to burrow beneath the foundations of its apparently dominant partner, the BTLU. In the 1930s, the repressive policies of the state dismembered and nearly destroyed the Girni Kamgar Union. But in 1934, 1938 and 1940, the Union was still able to renovate its linkages and adopt the leading role in the general strikes of those years.[13]

In the 1920s, the colonial state as well as, intermittently, some employers recognized more readily the utility of trade unions. If they developed along the right lines, they could hold out the possibility that workers' grievances could be represented and indeed, mediated before relations had broken down completely. The institutionalization of workers' combinations might serve to constrain lightning strikes and develop proper channels for negotiation. At the same time, the extension of the principle of elections to representative bodies at various levels of the state made working-class votes increasingly difficult to ignore. Labour representatives, now nominated to provincial and central legislatures, discovered fresh political opportunities. For trade-union leaders and their organization to be accredited at these levels, they had to establish their legitimacy as spokesmen and representatives of the labour interest. But the labour interest eluded definition and its interpretation was invariably disputed. Those who developed a following in the workplace did not always appear to the employers and the state as responsible or desirable spokesmen for their workers. Conversely, those who were accredited as the proper representatives of the working classes could not always inspire their confidence.

In practice, therefore, to gain acceptance by the employers or the respect of colonial officials, it was more important for trade-union leaders to prove that they were 'responsible' to civil society than to demonstrate that they were representatives of working-class opinions, aspirations and sentiments. For trade unionists who also operated as vakils and pleaders in the mill district, writing notices, pursuing wage arrears and filing claims in the small-causes courts on behalf of the workers, their acceptance by employers and the state was good for

---

[13] Chandavarkar, 'Workers' Politics'; Newman, *Workers and Unions*, pp. 120–210.

business.[14] For publicists, championing the workers' cause, it could also advance political careers. Workers, too, sometimes found that they could secure their needs or resolve minor grievances through their offices. But the blessings of tolerance from employers did not disguise the limits within which such trade unions could operate. By intervening too zealously in the daily problems of the workplace, trade unions could upset the delicate alliances upon which the discipline and control of labour rested and since these extended into the upper reaches of mill management, the disruptive consequences of their action rapidly drew the hostility of the employers upon themselves. But if they abstained too scrupulously from such intervention, trade-union leaders found themselves swiftly disengaged from their political base. By leading strikes, they incurred the displeasure of the employers and the state; when they remained aloof, they were jostled aside by more adventurous and militant rivals.

In the 1920s and 1930s, there were few trade unions which consistently adopted a mediatory role or wholly secured the confidence of employers. The Bombay Textile Labour Union was never fully accredited by the millowners until their membership dwindled into insignificance in the early 1930s.[15] Some trade-union leaders aspired to be recognized as responsible spokesmen for labour in their own right but among those who achieved such recognition, few were able to sustain it. S.H. Jhabvala who intermittently displayed this ambition was arrested, imprisoned at Meerut and tried for conspiring to overthrow the King Emperor. R.R. Bakhale always commanded more influence among colonial officials than among either the employers or the workers. N.M. Joshi uniquely both gained the confidence of officials and, in view of his following in the mill districts, could not entirely be ignored by the millowners; but after the 1928 strike, he became less an active participant, and more an observer and adviser to those who listened, in trade-union politics.[16]

The Girni Kamgar Union experienced nothing but sustained hostility from the employers and the state. It was afforded no privileged bargaining status, its members and supporters suffered 'victimization' at work and, after the success of the 1928 general strike, colonial officials grew increasingly concerned to extirpate the red peril. Throughout the 1930s, the millowners excluded its leaders from their mills and refused to recognize or negotiate with them. The Union's only defence was to escalate out of the repressive structure of industrial relations by intervening energetically in every dispute, building up extensive connections throughout the industry and sometimes generating the momentum

---

[14] Bombay Confidential Proceedings, General Department, May 1917, vol. 25, pp. 15–19.
[15] The workings of this union can be studied in the extensive N.M. Joshi Papers, NMML. For the union's lament, see *RCLI, Evidence, Bombay Presidency*, I, i, 353.
[16] *Proceedings of the Meerut Conspiracy Case, Statement by S.H. Jhabvala*, vol. II, *Non-Communist Series*; Karnik, *N.M. Joshi*.

for general strikes. Since they were excluded from the workplace, they sought assiduously to develop connections in the neighbourhood. Their ability to survive in the face of state repression and to sustain their following among millworkers was largely due to the linkages they forged in the neighbourhood. In 1928–9, their union centres and mill committees provided an effective structure within which they could develop and sustain the alliances of workplace and neighbourhood. In 1933–4, this decaying structure provided the Girni Kamgar Union with the basis and opportunity for revival. If trade unions which adopted strategies of conciliation often operated at a level removed from the daily social relations of the workplace, those which espoused strategies of confrontation found few opportunities to consolidate the linkages of direct action within it.[17]

The strategy of confrontation necessarily entailed extremely high risks for trade unions and especially for the strikers. To be at all effective, strikes had necessarily to be complete. In view of the diversity of interests within the textile industry and especially its workforce, this was extremely difficult to ensure. However, several factors operated in the 1920s and 1930s to generalize disputes and to facilitate concerted action. Some of these have already been mentioned. The strategy of confrontation adopted by the Girni Kamgar Union during this period necessarily created a propensity for large-scale industrial action. But general strikes had occurred in the early 1920s before the establishment of the Union. Moreover, confrontational strategies might foster widespread industrial action but they cannot explain why workers combined on an extensive scale.

After the First World War, the Millowners' Association began to take a centralizing initiative in some matters of labour policy. Individual millowners jealously guarded their independence from central regulation, even when its source was their own committee and not colonial officials. But wage disparities engendered intense competition for labour between mills, raised demands from workers that their wages and conditions should match their colleagues in neighbouring mills and often disrupted the workings of the labour market as well as the organization of production. The Millowners' Association was allowed to assume responsibility for stipulating wage increases in 1917 largely to set rough limits upon disparities. Similarly, in the mid 1920s, millowners tried, through their Association, to dispense with bonus payments and reduce wages to compensate for the maintenance of excise duties. The introduction of rationalization schemes in 1928–9, once more entailing lower wages, retrenchment and increased workloads, and the sporadic wage cutting of the early 1930s, laid bare the limits of the efficacy of workers' resistance at the level of the

---

[17] Chandavarkar, 'Workers' Politics', and above, pp. 385–6, 388–93.

individual mill.[18] To some extent, the tendency for millowners to take concerted action for limited purposes also stemmed from their need to put pressure on the colonial state for the abolition of the excise duty, the raising of tariffs, the lowering of the rupee–sterling ratio and favourable financial policies.

Second, the obstacles to combination at the workplace often meant that the disputes of particular occupational groups or individual mills had to be organized and were indeed conducted in the neighbourhood. Workers in a line or a department wanting to register their complaints about the erosion of piece rates, the quality of the raw material or the machinery, or the treatment of jobbers and supervisors might stop work and assemble in the mill compound to force the attention of the manager. Strikes launched on a larger scale or lasting longer than a few days were marked by daily processions and open-air meetings in the mill districts. During general strikes, such activity, intended to maintain morale and proclaim the importance of their cause, became yet more vigorous. Most strikes witnessed considerable action at the mill gates: workers gathered to observe how strongly industrial action was supported and to assess the risks of staying out or alternatively of resuming work; here managers and jobbers sometimes tried to escort blacklegs into the mill and pickets attempted to prevent workers from returning to their jobs.[19] Moreover, in an overstocked labour market, where employers sought to dismiss strikers and replace them with new recruits, it was often necessary for workers to bring pressure to bear within the neighbourhoods to protect their jobs. At times, they were forced to picket more vigorously in the workers' chawls than at the mill gates. In any event, to conduct strikes, indeed even to put sufficient pressure on jobbers and mill officials to persuade them to negotiate, it was often necessary to mobilize their caste and kinship connections, patronage networks and social associations in the neighbourhood. These conditions sometimes worked to the advantage of the Girni Kamgar Union who, having been excluded from the workplace, had necessarily relied upon their connections outside. The importance of organization and action in the neighbourhood propelled the particular disputes of the workplace into a wider and public arena and placed them before the working class as a whole.[20]

The third factor which often generalized the specific issues and conflicts at work was the role of the state. Of course, by acting in the public arena workers

---

[18] See chapter 8 above. The trend towards centralized initiatives from the BMOA, and the resistance which it encountered from its members, can be observed in the *BMOA, Annual Reports*, and the Minute Books of the Committee of the BMOA, Office of the BMOA.

[19] These recurring patterns of industrial action are revealed by the extensive reports of strikes, especially the general strikes, in the daily newspapers and in the *Labour Gazette*'s monthly reports on industrial disputes.

[20] Chandavarkar, 'Workers' Politics'.

sometimes hoped that the state would intervene to redress the injustices perpe-
trated by their employers, managers and supervisors. But the consequences of
official action were not always perceived as benevolent by the workers. The
most immediate experience of the state for most workers lay in the policing of
the working-class neighbourhoods, notably during strikes. In general, the colonial state was anxious not to meddle in the disputes of the street corner or the
workplace. To a large extent, the statecraft of colonialism relied upon their
resolution, accommodaticn or settlement within local structures of power. Yet
beyond a certain threshold, an industrial dispute could rapidly take the shape of
public disorder, the conflicts of the workplace could spill into the streets and
the antagonisms of the neighbourhood could flicker into riot. The colonial state
could not satisfactorily or easily enforce the principle of salutary neglect. Thus,
the police had frequently found themselves intervening, even arbitrating, in
particular and localized disputes. The Police Commissioner played a prominent
role in the settlement of the general strike of 1919.[21] But as the momentum of
industrial action quickened and joined up in the official mind with perceptions
of the threat of nationalist agitation, as negotiations were conducted at more
elevated and centralized levels and as millowners and local elites gained
increasing control over the local structures of the state, the police appeared more
prominently and singularly to play a repressive role. They acted to protect
blacklegs and even escorted them into work; they regulated pickets and weakened them; they supervised their processions and public meetings more closely,
monitored the language of their speakers and prosecuted some for incitement
and sedition.[22] From 1929 onwards, the state often proclaimed their hostile
intentions towards the communists of the Girni Kamgar Union, and more
frequently realized them in practice.[23] At another level, the state was more
readily identified with economic policies which were formulated, it was often
argued, in the imperial interest to the detriment of the textile industry and its
workforce.

    It would be misleading, however, to suppose that the purposes and intentions
of state intervention were to antagonize the working classes. In its earliest

---

[21] See, for instance, Edwardes, *Bombay City Police*, Appendix, p. 197; Commissioner of Police,
Bombay to Secretary, GOB, Judicial, 29 January 1919, Bombay Confidential Proceedings,
Judicial, February 1919, vol. 46, 26–30, IOR.

[22] See GOB, Home (Sp.) Files 543 (18) G of 1928, 543 (18) D part II of 1928, 543 (10) E-(BB) of
1929, 543 (10) E part G of 1929, 543 (18) K of 1929, 543 (10) E part G of 1929, 543 (18) I of
1929, 543 (10) E part F of 1930, MSA; GOI, Home (Poll.) Files F/18/VII/28 and KWs I and II,
F/18/VII/1928, 10/10/1930 and KW, 303/1929 and KWs I and II, NAI.

[23] *Report of the Court of Inquiry Into a Trade Dispute; Report of the Bombay Riots Inquiry
Committee*; and their proceedings in the MSA. The most dramatic manifestation of these
intentions was the mass arrest and prosecution of the communists for conspiracy to overthrow
the King Emperor in the Meerut Conspiracy Case.

phases, colonial expansion appears to have facilitated an increasing subordination and more intensive exploitation of labour by capital. But in the later nineteenth century, the colonial state showed a growing reluctance to accept the full consequences of capital accumulation and a growing concern to shore up the fragile small-holding base of the agrarian economy.[24] The Bombay millowners ranked among the most favoured collaborators of the colonial state. Nonetheless, the colonial state was willing at times to safeguard the interests of the workforce at their expense. Sometimes, it could thereby also serve the interests of metropolitan capital. Factory legislation in the late nineteenth and early twentieth century was intended to protect the workforce and negate the advantages of cheap labour secured by local capitalists in their competition with metropolitan industry.[25] In the 1920s and 1930s, the colonial state enacted a number of measures concerned to secure the welfare of factory workers: from maternity benefits and workmen's compensation in the event of accidents to regulations governing the payment of wages. The Labour Office collected statistics and information about the working classes, inquired into their wages, conditions of work and standards of living, and the effects of its intervention were not always simply to exert tighter control to their disadvantage. The Labour Officer sought vigilantly to protect the workers' interests, wages and conditions, and attempted with uneven success to win their confidence and dig out their grievances.[26] Indeed, in the 1930s, as Congress appeared rather less threatening as the champion of mass nationalism and Indian business interests appeared to hold radicalism in check, the colonial state was willing to countenance the collaboration of the urban working classes.

However nuanced the relationship of the working classes to the colonial state may have been, they encountered it most immediately and prominently in the form of police actions which appeared often to contribute to undermining their demands, dividing their ranks and destroying their organization. The political consciousness of the working classes was constituted and developed in relation to the state. Perceptions of the repressive, unjust or arbitrary character of the

---

[24] See Stokes, *The Peasant and the Raj*, pp. 205–27, 243–89; Washbrook, 'Law, State and Agrarian Society'.

[25] Manchester Chamber of Commerce, *Bombay and Lancashire Cotton Spinning Enquiry; Report by W.O. Meade King on the Working of the Indian Factories Act in Bombay together with Certain Suggestions and Proposals* (Bombay, 1982); *Report of the Indian Factory Commission, 1890; Report of the IFLC*, vol. I; L. Fraser, *India Under Curzon and After* (London, 1911), pp. 131–6. See especially the incisive account in Mehta, Cotton Mills, pp. 124–32.

[26] See GOB, General, Files 5773-D, Part I, of 1924–8, 5773-D Part II of 1927 and 5773-D Part III of 1927; *Annual Reports on the Working of the Workmens' Compensation Act in the Bombay Presidency*; A.W. Pryde, 'The Work of the Labour Officer', in C. Manshardt (ed.), *Some Social Services of the City of Bombay* (Bombay, 1937); the *Labour Gazette* from the mid 1930s carried monthly reports on the work of the Labour Officer and on welfare measures adopted for industrial labour.

state, in every sphere of their lives, from the incidence of land revenue and its consequences in the village to police activity on the picket lines and the effects of fiscal and monetary policies on their conditions of employment, fostered, at particular moments, a sense of shared interests and informed a political understanding of their situation and the possibility for change. It was at this point that the communists, who seemed resolutely to refuse to collaborate with the employers and the state, to display a concrete concern with the daily issues of the workplace and to show a greater willingness in moments of conflicts to give workers' militancy its head, emerged as the one political group in the labour movement which appeared to act consistently in the interests of the working class.

Working-class support for the communists did not, however, arise simply from a fusion of shared antagonisms towards the capitalist class and the state. Nor was this support unquestioningly loyal: once committed never withdrawn. The communists' stance of continued opposition to employers and the state may have attracted public sympathy among the working classes. But what was perceived as their adventurism after the general strike of 1928 and their misjudged refusal to associate with Congress in the early 1930s cost them a considerable following at the time. Similarly, their social and political vision was tied rather narrowly to the city and the urban working classes. They made few attempts to engage with the problems of the countryside or to develop a theoretical perspective and rhetoric which could find some resonance in a working-class experience which straddled town and country and was shaped by the strength and persistence of their rural connections. Thus, in the late 1930s, Ambedkar's Mahar movement showed precisely the promise of a political rhetoric which was able to register and encompass the rural as well as the urban nexus of working-class lives.[27] The communists of the Girni Kamgar Union remained moored within an increasingly rigid and arcane theoretical discourse of class, which mystified and eluded, as often as it described or explained, the conditions of working-class existence.

Nationalism and the working classes

The political perceptions and actions of the working classes were not simply formed within the workplace or the sphere of production relations alone. They were also fashioned by the tensions and conflicts, the debates and arguments conducted within wider political arenas. Political conflicts which occurred along the lines of caste, religious and national identity registered their effects

[27] GOB, Home (Sp.) Files 927 A of 1938; 927 A Part I of 1939; D. Keer, *Dr Ambedkar: Life and Mission* (Bombay, 1954, 2nd edn, 1962), pp. 292–315.

on workers, not only in trade-union rivalries or wider political affinities, but sometimes at the point of production as well.

The Indian National Congress had always maintained a highly ambivalent attitude to the working classes. This ambivalence reflected deeper contradictions. The effectiveness of the Congress as a bargaining agent with the colonial state and, therefore, its ability to attach significant local interests rested on its claim to represent the nation as a whole. To fortify this claim, the party would have to speak with one voice. Yet to demonstrate its representative character, it was essential for the Congress to expand and diversify its social base. As the composition of its allies grew more diverse, the task of welding these disparate elements into a single coalition grew increasingly complex. Since its inception, therefore, the Congress had been forced to gloss over issues which might divide and concentrate resolutely upon those which might unite their constituents.[28] Just as the colonial state had to avoid becoming the prisoner of its own collaborators, so the Congress could not afford to become the champion of a particular social group.

In the late nineteenth century, the more prominent nationalist spokesmen had been 'indifferent or hostile to the efforts being made to ameliorate the conditions of work' and even the 'radicals' among them, including Tilak, were 'insensitive and even opposed to the cause of labour'.[29] By 1918, however, it was becoming impossible for the Congress and its leading publicists consistently to ignore labour's cause and indeed the contradictions implicit in their relationship with the working classes were brought more prominently to the surface.[30] As strikes became more frequent and occurred on a larger scale than ever before, and labour established an increasingly prominent presence in the political arena, the Congress developed increasingly intimate connections with big business and derived both power and resources from these connections.[31] Following the

---

[28] Seal, *Indian Nationalism*, pp. 194–297; Johnson, *Provincial Politics*, pp. 5–52; J.R. McLane, *Indian Nationalism and the Early Congress* (Princeton, 1977).

[29] B. Chandra, *The Rise and Growth of Economic Nationalism in India: Economic Policies of Indian National Leadership 1880–1905* (Delhi, 1966), p. 330.

[30] For recent attempts to examine Congress attitudes to labour, see S. Bhattacharya, 'Swaraj and the Kamgar: The Indian National Congress and the Bombay Working Class, 1919–1931', in R. Sisson and S. Wolpert (eds.), *Congress and Indian Nationalism: The Pre-Independence Phase* (Berkeley and Los Angeles, 1988), pp. 223–49; S. Bhattacharya, 'The Colonial State, Capital and Labour: Bombay, 1919–31', in S. Bhattacharya and R. Thapar (eds.), *Situating Indian History* (Delhi, 1986), pp. 171–93; R. Kumar, 'From Swaraj to Purna Swaraj: Nationalist Politics in the City of Bombay, 1920–32', in D.A. Low (ed.), *Congress and the Raj: Facets of the Indian Struggle* (London, 1977), pp. 77–107; Kapil Kumar (ed.) *Congress and Classes: Nationalism, Workers and Peasants* (Delhi, 1988).

[31] A.P. Kannangara, 'Indian Millowners and Indian Nationalism before 1914', *Past and Present*, XL (1968), 147–74; Gordon, *Businessmen and Politics*; C. Markovits, *Indian Business and Nationalist Politics, 1931–39: The Indigenous Capitalist Class and the Rise of the Congress Party* (Cambridge, 1985); B. Chandra, 'The Indian Capitalist Class and Imperialism before

Assam tea coolies' strike, Gandhi had declared in 1921, 'We seek not to destroy capital or capitalists but to regulate the relations between capital and labour. We want to harness capital to our side.'[32] But programmes designed to 'harness capital to our side' were unlikely to yoke the working classes.

The relationship between the Congress and the working classes in Bombay City was further complicated by its antecedents. Until 1918, the city Congress was embodied in the Bombay Presidency Association. One of the three founding political associations of the Congress, it was primarily the club of the city's mercantile, millowning and professional elite.[33] Firmly entrenched in local government since the 1830s, and frequently consulted by colonial governors and officials, these elites had little cause to cultivate the city's working classes. From this secure and powerful base, they extended their influence over provincial affairs and, by the 1890s, came to exercise the determining influence within the Indian National Congress.[34] The intimate connections between the Bombay Presidency Association and the millowners, on the one hand, and the role of the city's elites as some of the most favoured and influential collaborators of the British on the other, coloured working-class perceptions of their politics.

In the early twentieth century, however, changes in India's political structure forced the Congress to entertain a closer relationship with the working classes. The gradual expansion of the political system at municipal and provincial levels created opportunities for lesser politicians to challenge the dominance of entrenched elites and power brokers by developing a wider social following among the newly enfranchised. More workers now had the vote and while special labour constituencies were created at the lesser levels of the political structure, the government began to nominate labour representatives to the provincial and central legislatures. With the growing importance of the working classes within the formal institutions of the state and their increasing militancy on the streets, a number of publicists sought to represent labour in the councils of the state or to mediate their disputes with employers.

In the 1920s and 1930s, most Congress politicians had to act broadly within the framework of the colonial political system. Few could afford to abjure it

---

1947'; B. Chandra, 'Jawaharlal Nehru and the Indian Capitalist Class in 1936', *Economic and Political Weekly*, X, 33–5 (1975), 1307–24; S. Bhattacharya, 'Cotton Mills and Spinning Wheels: Swadeshi and the Indian Capitalist Class, 1920–22', *Economic and Political Weekly*, XI, 47 (1976), 1828–34; Sarkar, 'The Logic of Gandhian Nationalism', 114–46; A. Mukherjee, 'The Indian Capitalist Class and Foreign Capital, 1927–47', *Studies in History*, I, 1 (1979), 105–48.

[32] *Young India*, 15 July 1921, 'Lessons of Assam', *Collected Works of Mahatma Gandhi*, vol. XX (Ahmedabad, 1966), p. 228.

[33] Dobbin, *Urban Leadership*; Seal, *Indian Nationalism*, pp. 231–4.

[34] Johnson, *Provincial Politics*, chs. 1 and 2; R. Cashman, *The Myth of the Lokamanya, Tilak and Mass Politics in Maharashtra* (Berkeley and Los Angeles, 1975) pp. 151–71; Kannangara, 'Indian Millowners and Indian Nationalism before 1914'.

altogether. For linkages which they forged during agitations could easily be broken and reclaimed by rivals more willing to enter the councils and exercise the patronage of office. Conversely, alliances made and constituencies fashioned by politicians working within the legislatures and municipalities could sometimes be pressed into service during movements of protest. Yet operating within the framework of the state necessarily constrained them as spokesmen for workers and mediators in industrial disputes. While leading labour against their employers, they had to remain mindful of their own need to nurture and develop connections, indispensable to their other political interests, with magnates, merchants and industrialists. The Congress as a whole did not, indeed it could not, set out to lead a specifically working-class movement and the terms on which it attempted to pull workers into a nationalist alliance were unlikely always to encourage them. As President of the All-India Trade Union Congress in 1929, Jawaharlal Nehru had declared, 'Of course, everyone knows that the Congress is not a labour organization ... To expect it to act as a pure labour organization is a mistake. The National Congress is a large body comprising all manner of people.'[35] To identify itself too closely with a working-class interest jeopardized for the Congress other, sometimes more powerful, groups which coalesced within it and called upon it to surrender its claim solely to represent the nation as a whole.

Congressmen, who participated in the organization of trade unions and the conduct of strikes, were expected to act not as agents of the party but emphatically in their individual capacities. Political parties operating within the Congress, like the Home Rule Leagues in the late 1910s or the Congress Socialists in the mid 1930s, intervened in workers' politics strictly as only one element in the 'large body comprising all manner of people' and not as its organic representative. When individual Congress politicians sought to represent workers' grievances, they could not escape the constraints which bound the movement as a whole. Significantly, politicians who stepped forward as advocates of labour's cause often came from the ranks of out-factions in local politics or indeed marginal groups within the Congress. It would seem that only those politicians operating on the margins of the Congress could afford the flexibility to manoeuvre within the tight constraints which industrial relations imposed upon labour leaders.

Subject to these constraints, arising as they did from the conditions of local politics and from a national and colonial discourse, the rhetoric of the Congress remained ambiguous, reflecting perhaps the ambivalence which characterized its relationship with labour. Since the interventions of the Congress in workers'

---

[35] J. Nehru to D.B. Kulkarni, 10 September 1929, AICC Papers, File 16 of 1929, pp. 111–13, NMML.

politics were so individualized, it is difficult to attribute to the Congress a single, uniform or univocal rhetoric. Certainly, Congressmen spoke in many tongues to the working classes, as they did to other social groups, and their rhetoric was inflected by particular circumstances and local contingencies. Despite these variations, however, it is possible to identify the recurring theme of class harmony in the nationalist discourse on labour. Thus, nationalist leaders emphasized the shared interests between labour and capital, espoused 'the higher idea of partnership'[36] and advised workers to sink their differences with their employers and combine with them against the British.[37] In Ahmedabad, Gandhi asserted the workers' inalienable right to their basic needs and then qualified it according to the financial condition of the industry.[38] The balance between these needs and obligations was to be found through the good sense and self-restraint of both workers and capitalists and, if this was not enough, the arbitration of an 'umpire'. Although employers were never entirely at ease with the meddling of outsiders in matters of labour discipline, this portrayal of industrial relations did not alarm or offend them. They had repeatedly used the notion of 'what the industry will bear' to reduce wages or resist demands for an increase. In addition, arbitration proceedings were more alarming in prospect than in practice. For it was unlikely that an award which did not meet with the approval of the employers could be enforced or realized in practice. Moreover, as workers sought to fulfil the necessary conditions of instituting arbitration proceedings, employers could act to undermine their fragile unities.

A corollary to the nationalist conception of regulating relations between labour and capital was to invite workers to sacrifice their current needs for the future of the nation. Grievances which could not be resolved under British rule would be redressed by a future Swaraj. In the meantime, strikes which could damage the interests of Indian capitalists only served to exacerbate foreign domination. If, in this view, it was imperative for labour to refrain from industrial action, it was also necessary for Indian capitalists to fulfil their own obligation by satisfying the basic needs of the workforce. In this way, the Indian people should bury their social and economic differences and march behind the Congress banner to freedom.

Nationalist rhetoric along these lines did not readily find a resonance in the

---

[36] Joseph Baptista, President of the All-India Trade Union Congress, quoted in S. Sarkar, *Modern India, 1885–1947* (Delhi, 1983), p. 200.

[37] Tilak preached this sermon to the Bombay millworkers during the general strike of 1919. See Cashman, *The Myth of the Lokamanya*, p. 185.

[38] Patel, *The Making of Industrial Relations*, especially ch. 3; Desai, *Righteous Struggle*; *The Collected Works of Mahatma Gandhi*, vols. XIV–XX (Ahmedabad, 1965–6), especially, vol. XIV, 214–75; P.P. Lakshman, *Congress and the Labour Movement in India* (Congress Economic and Political Studies no. 3, Economic and Political Research Department, AICC, Allahabad, 1947); Bhattacharya, 'Swaraj and the Kamgar'.

daily struggles of the workplace and neighbourhood. Higher ideals of partnership, the measurement of basic needs according to communal obligations,
theories of class harmony or a counsel for the postponement of grievances did
not offer a framework which might plausibly clarify their situation for workers
or suggest possible means by which it might be alleviated or transformed. The
ambiguity and contradictions of the nationalist discourse and the limited interventions of the Congress in workers' politics suggest why its working-class
support was halting, uneven and sporadic.

There was no single, homogeneous working-class constituency for nationalism. Nor was its response uniform and consistent. Throughout the 1920s and
1930s, the Congress was able to draw repeatedly upon the support of the
employees of the cloth, cotton and grain markets in the city, whose merchants
were also among their most loyal supporters. But the response of other occupational groups was varied. Millworkers, who had taken action against Tilak's
conviction in 1908, supported the moderates of the Bombay Presidency Association at the Willingdon Memorial meeting in 1918 and appear largely to have
held aloof from the Rowlatt Satyagraha in the following year.[39] The Home Rule
Leagues developed some working-class following but their intervention in the
general strike of 1919 exposed the limitations of their strategy in the face of
workers' militancy.[40] Millworkers were at best erratic in their response to the
non-cooperation movement. They refused to work on the day Tilak died and
were prominent during the riots which followed the Prince of Wales' visit to
Bombay on 17 November 1921.[41] But for substantial periods they were inactive,
even somnolent. Indeed, the dominant feature of the working-class participation
in the non-cooperation movement was their selective involvement in particular
forms of agitations. The picketing of liquor shops registered the most general
plebeian enthusiasm in the early 1920s.[42] Similarly, a decade later, it was the
boycott of foreign cloth which evoked the most passionate response during civil
disobedience.[43]

In the early 1930s, the Governor of Bombay was in no doubt that the civil

[39] J. Masselos, 'Some Aspects of Bombay City Politics in 1919', in R. Kumar (ed.), *Essays on
Gandhian Politics: The Rowlatt Satyagraha* (Oxford, 1971), pp. 145–88.
[40] 'A Report from the Commissioner of Police, Bombay, to Government of Bombay, Concerning
Political Developments before and during 1919', Curry Papers, Box IV, nos. 54 and 55, Centre
of South Asian Studies, Cambridge.
[41] Bombay Confidential Proceedings, Home, December 1921, vol. 62, pp. 771–81, IOR.
[42] GOB, Home (Sp.) File 355 (21) F of 1921, MSA; see also *Source Material for a History of the
Freedom Movement in India*, vol. VI, *Non-Co-operation Movement, Bombay City, 1920–1925*,
edited by B.G. Kunte (Bombay, 1978).
[43] GOB, Home (Sp.) File 750 (26) of 1930, 750 (92) of 1930, 750 (76) of 1930, 750 (39) I–VI of
1930; 800 (72) Parts 1–6 of 1932, MSA. See also J. Masselos, 'Audiences, Actors and Congress
Dramas: Crowd Events in Bombay City in 1930', in J. Masselos (ed.), *Struggling and Ruling:
The Indian National Congress, 1885–1985* (Delhi, 1987), pp. 71–86.

disobedience campaign in the city had assumed the proportions of 'practically a mass movement'.[44] According to Brigadier Giles, 'the general situation' in Bombay City in June 1930 seemed 'far worse than I had imagined could be possible; to the outward eye and the man in the street, the Congress Raj is on top'.[45] But it is as well to inquire further into the identity of the man in the street. Indeed, a closer examination revealed that the civil disobedience had 'the support of practically the whole of the very large Gujarathi population of Bombay, the great majority of whom are engaged in business, trade or as clerks and are consequently suffering severely from trade depression and unemployment'. But it seemed that 'for the present other elements in Bombay, Deccanis, Mill-hands, Muhammadans, Parsis are taking practically no part in movement'.[46]

Railway workers, especially from the Great Indian Peninsular workshop, were prominent in the early stages of the civil disobedience movement in 1930.[47] The Great Indian Peninsular Railway workers had been engaged in a long and bitterly fought strike in Bombay, as well as along the line, which had appeared to be on the verge of disintegration when the civil disobedience movement began to gather momentum. By attaching themselves to the Congress campaign, the railway workers were to find a wider legitimacy for their industrial action. They adopted the methods of satyagraha to shore up the strike, against blacklegs, on the picket lines and with their landlords, money-lenders and grain-merchants. The Congress campaign provided the workers with a wider focus for their grievances and helped them to prolong their strike for a while. In the dock workers' strike of 1932, the leading role played by publicists closely associated with the Congress enabled the latter to link these proletarian struggles with their own campaign and to give it an apparently deeper and wider base.

The qualified and conditional support which the Congress obtained from the working classes should not lead to the conclusion that their main preoccupation was with subsistence, not politics, class struggle rather than nationalism. Nor should it be assumed that the working classes represented a natural, if latent, resource for nationalism, merely waiting to be tapped by suitable leaders. The nationalism of the working classes flowed neither from their commitment to a territorial principle nor from the perception of a single, homogeneous national interest. Rather the political response of the working classes to nationalism might

[44] Sykes to Irwin, 20 June 1930. Sykes Papers, MSS. EUR. F 150 (2a), p. 130, IOR.
[45] Memorandum by Director, Intelligence Bureau, 2 June 1930, Home (Pol.), 1930, KW 3 to F/257/3, NAI.
[46] Express Letter, Bombay Special to Home Simla, Secret, 4 June 1930, in GOB, Home (Sp.) File 750 (26) of 1930, p. 27, MSA.
[47] GOB, Home (Sp.) Files 543 (10) DC of 1930, 543 (10) DC Pt. A of 1930, 543 (10) DC, Pts. II – IV of 1930; 543 (10) DC Pt. C of 1930, MSA.

be explained in terms of how its wider social and political implications could be given meaning within the context of their everyday lives.

For the cotton-mill workers, for instance, a wide range of connections could easily be made between their relationship with their employers, the role of the state and their political experience of the city's elites. The higher supervisory and lower managerial grades in the cotton-textile industry were dominated by 'Europeans', largely Lancashire men, and Parsis who were, in public perception, closely associated with the British and with the millowners.[48] The relationship between European supervisors and managers and their Indian colleagues, on the one hand, and the workforce, on the other, was riven with conflict. In the late nineteenth century, millowners complained that their Lancashire recruits 'often failed to give satisfaction': they were often found to be inexperienced, sometimes barely literate and often wholly dependent on the assistance of their Parsi subordinates, who were paid much less.[49] Their relationship with Indian technical and managerial cadres was often characterized by suspicion, jealousy and antagonism.[50] But for the workers, it was often a short step to extend their immediate experience of European and Parsi supervisors and managers, and their employers – often Parsi, more occasionally European millowners – to a more general understanding of the distribution of power and privilege in the wider society. Their supervisors and managers could readily be identified with the colonial regime. The apparently close relationship between European and Parsi officers in the mills could appear as a refraction of their collaboration in local and national politics. Indian elites who dominated the Bombay Presidency Association and maintained an aloof, even unsympathetic attitude towards the working classes were readily perceived as an inseparable part of this ruling nexus. These strands were sometimes combined in a single political moment. Their coming together might help to explain why Tilak evoked such a vigorous and sympathetic response from the millworkers in 1908. Although he appeared to have little interest in their cause, his rhetoric directed at the bigwigs of the Bombay Presidency Association and their Congress allies and his apparent defiance of the colonial state clarified the lines of their own antagonism against the structures of authority within and outside the mill. A similar set of connections effected during the non-cooperation movement contributed to the Prince of Wales riot in 1921 when millworkers manifested, it was said,

a hostile attitude against the European mill staff ... Englishmen had to face single-handed the brutal and cowardly assaults from hundreds of mill hands, whom they had never injured or offended.[51]

[48] Rutnagur, *Bombay Industries*, p. 294.
[49] *Ibid.*, p. 289.
[50] Mehta, *Cotton Mills*, pp. 100–13.
[51] Rutnagur, *Bombay Industries*, pp. 292–3.

In the 1920s and early 1930s, millworkers were able to identify the prolonged crisis of the textile industry, which the millowners claimed necessitated retrenchment and wage cuts, directly with foreign competition and colonial policies. Indeed, millowners, merchants and publicists had frequently explained the industry's crisis in these terms. Significantly, nationalist spokesmen had long argued that colonial policies had been determined by Britain's imperial interests rather than India's social and economic needs. In 1925, the millowners cut wages by $11\frac{1}{2}$ per cent and explained the figure as the margin by which the excise duty on Indian mill-made production inflated their costs. Following a three-month general strike, the Government of India suspended and then abolished the excise duty, lending credence to the millowners' argument, and the latter accordingly withdrew their wage cut. The policies of the state appeared to lie at the core of workers' struggles.[52] In the late 1920s, workers readily drew connections between the rationalization schemes, which led to wage cuts, increased workloads, retrenchment and deteriorating conditions of employment, and the Tariff Board's determination to keep the Indian market open for the declining Lancashire industry.

Similarly, during the controversy over the rupee ratio in the 1920s, the government's case for a higher exchange rate rested upon the contention that a lower ratio would depreciate wages and lead to serious strikes, while the capitalists argued that an over-valued rupee would force wage cuts upon them simply in order to withstand foreign competition. As the colonial state and the capitalists sought to justify their own particular interests in terms of the welfare of the working classes, they were viewed within an increasingly assertive labour movement with considerable scepticism. While posing as the guardians of labour, both appeared resolutely to advance their own selfish interests.[53]

In the 1920s and 1930s, the colonial state was subject to increasingly stringent political criticism. The rhetoric of the Congress became more explicitly anti-colonial. It no longer spoke of the un-Britishness of British rule in India, but questioned the morality of the colonial state. It challenged the justice of its laws; it withheld its co-operation from the government; it elevated civil disobedience into an act of heroism. Although some Congressmen entered the councils in 1923, council entry could only be justified by the objective of wrecking the legislatures from within. Of course, this had greater symbolic or rhetorical value than any consistent practical effect. The effects of this anti-colonial rhetoric were unintended and unforeseen, but their implications for the development of

---

[52] For an account of the 1925 strike, see Newman, *Workers and Unions*, pp. 153–67; on the abolition of the excise duty, see B. Chatterji, 'The Political Economy of "Discriminating Protection": The Case of Textiles in the 1920s', *IESHR*, XX, 3 (1983), 239–75.

[53] *Proceedings of the Meerut Conspiracy Case, Statement by S.A. Dange, Made in the Court of R.L. Yorke, I.C.S., Additional Sessions Judge, Meerut, 26 October 1931*, pp. 2428–9.

working-class politics were considerable. Its benefits accrued to political groups who, seeking to represent labour, had been marginalized by employers as well as the state rather than those, like the Congress trade-union organizers, who, seeking to balance their diverse interests, often proceeded in a conciliatory manner. The former type of publicist, like the communists of the Girni Kamgar Union, excluded from the workplace and sometimes subject to severe repression, were not only forced to adopt a stance of continuous opposition to the employers and the state but also through their repeated interventions in the disputes of workplace and neighbourhood to realize this rhetoric in political action. In the 1920s and 1930s, one of the most significant factors in working-class politics was the growing presence of the state. Attempts to recruit workers for a distant and irrelevant war caused considerable disquiet in 1917. The economic dislocations of the war and its immediate aftermath were widely perceived as a failure of government. The tariff, excise and monetary policies of the state impinged directly upon working conditions, employment and wages, and sharpened the lines of antagonism between workers and the state. Large-scale, sometimes industry-wide, strikes, frequently prolonged and bitter disputes, stoked official anxieties about public order. Strikes were more closely policed. The intervention of the state to settle disputes served more often to defeat workers' objectives and to negate their demands than to secure them. In the 1930s, the effect of trade-union legislation was largely to narrow the already limited freedom of manoeuvre which workers and their representatives had previously possessed.

The political experience of the working classes was constituted in relation to the state. In the late 1920s and 1930s, in Bombay and Sholapur, and later in the decade in Coimbatore, Kanpur and Calcutta, communist trade unions gained considerably from their stance of consistent opposition to the state. The anti-colonial rhetoric of the Congress, by challenging the legitimacy of the state, paid handsome dividends to trade unions and political groups which pursued an active strategy of confrontation. Opposition to the state provided a focus around which a fragmented and sectionalized working class could at times coalesce, though not necessarily behind the banner of the Congress.

Communalism, caste and class

Just as languages of class and nation interacted with each other, so caste and religious identities, in turn, played upon, indeed interrogated, their definition. The rapid growth of Bombay City in the nineteenth century had ensured that no single caste, religious or even linguistic community dominated its politics. The city's politics had been characterized by cross-communal alliances. The political dominance of this cross-communal elite had encouraged the development of a secular political language. It was only in the 1910s and 1920s, with wider electorates and the expansion of the political system, that the hegemony of this cross-communal elite was breached by the entry of new mercantile groups. As the old supra-communal coalition broke down, so from the late 1920s communal conflicts began to proliferate.

It would be facile to assume, however, that Hindu–Muslim riots occurred for the first time in the late 1920s.[54] It is more likely that incidents of violence between Hindus and Muslims acquired a new social meaning in the twentieth century. While they were registered in the late nineteenth century as neighbourhood conflicts and local rivalries, reflecting competition over trade, employment, housing or local power, they had by the 1920s come to be perceived and explained in explicitly communal terms. They were no longer confined to the neighbourhood, but swiftly engulfed and consumed the city and were readily linked to larger conflicts in provincial and national politics.

If political discourse acquired a sectarian inflection, partly as a consequence of shifts in the patterns of political dominance in the city and of changes in political rhetoric, it was also stimulated by the sharper definition of communal interest in national politics. As social competition and political conflict within provincial and national arenas were increasingly described and mediated in communal terms, so local conflicts came to be perceived and understood in the same categories. Skirmishes over the appropriation or control of territory in the neighbourhood could be more readily identified with struggles over political space offered by special electorates and communal safeguards. Rivalries between neighbourhood or jobber gangs over jobs or strikes could swiftly, though not necessarily permanently, solidify into 'communal' conflicts. The communalization of many social conflicts which may have occurred in the 1880s in the United Provinces or even in the neighbouring districts of the Deccan[55] did not take root in Bombay until the 1920s.

Three factors in particular shaped the communal conflicts which recurred

---

[54] The cow-protection riots of 1893 remain a large exception to the general rule that Hindu–Muslim riots in Bombay were rare before the 1920s. See *The Bombay Riots of 1893: Reprinted from the Times of India* (Bombay, 1893); GOB, Judicial, 1893, vol. 194, Compilation no. 948 Part I; and GOB Home (Sp.) File 1002 of 1893, MSA; Cashman, *Myth of the Lokamanya*, pp. 67–72; McLane, *Indian Nationalism and the Early Congress*, pp. 309–31; S. Krishnaswamy, 'A Riot in Bombay, August 11 1893: A Study in Hindu–Muslim Relations in Western India During the Late Nineteenth Century', unpublished PhD thesis, University of Chicago, 1966. For an attempt to quantify incidents of violence in the 1870s, showing some evidence of Hindu–Muslim conflict, see J. Masselos, 'Social Segregation and Crowd Cohesion: Reflections around some Preliminary Data from 19th Century Bombay City', *Contributions to Indian Sociology*, N.S., XIII, 2 (1979), 145–67.

[55] C.A. Bayly, 'The Pre-History of "Communalism"? Religious Conflict in India, 1700–1860', *MSA*, XIX, 2 (1985), 177–203; G. Pandey, 'Rallying Round the Cow: Sectarian Strife in the Bhojpuri Region, *c*. 1888–1917', in R. Guha (ed.), *Subaltern Studies* (Delhi, 1983), vol. II, pp. 60–129; Cashman, *Myth of the Lokamanya*.

with alarming frequency after the ferocious riots of February and May 1929: competition for and disputes related to work; struggles associated with the assertion of territorial and political rights by rival communities; and the unintended consequences of nationalism. In the late 1920s and early 1930s, jobs became increasingly scarce. Mills were shut down, either partially or fully, for varying lengths of time. The effects of the contraction of the city's leading industry were felt in a wide range of trades and occupations. Since workers often organized around ties of caste, kinship and village to secure jobs and to protect them, competition in the labour market could acquire a communal edge. This edge was sharpened particularly when employers brought the social and religious diversity of the working classes into the workplace, to thwart attempts at combination and to break strikes.

The riots of February 1929 were the product of precisely such circumstances. Pathans, who served as moneylenders of last resort and had been employed to break a strike at the Sewri oil refinery, became the initial target of working-class violence in the mill districts. During the 1928 strike, millworkers had borrowed from whoever was willing to lend. As workers returned intermittently to the mills in the strife-ridden months which followed its end, they resented the efforts of the Pathans to recover their loans and feared the consequences of default. For Pathans were not only reputed to charge exorbitant rates of interest, but also to be particularly brutal and violent in their methods of debt collection.[56]

A few months later, as another general strike was effected, the millowners attempted to undermine it by recruiting Muslim workers. Similar attempts to recruit blacklegs had often contributed to violence at the mill gates and in the chawls. Now it exploded into a communal riot which quickly spread through the city.[57] 'One likes to see the strike ended', G.D. Birla, the shrewdest political tactician among the Indian capitalists, wrote to Sir Purshottamdas Thakurdas in Bombay, 'but I am a bit upset by the way in which the communal tension has been utilized by the Millowners for ending the strike.'[58] Recalling 'the excesses committed by the Mohammedan mobs on the innocent Hindus in the last riots in Bombay', he warned Thakurdas gravely:

And God help the Hindus if the peaceful Hindu labour were kicked out of Bombay and replaced by Mohammedan hooligans.[59]

No such sense of impending doom hindered the use of Pathans to break the dock workers' strike of 1932 which contributed to the occurrence of yet another major

[56] This paragraph is based on the *Report of the Bombay Riot Inquiry Committee* (Bombay, 1929) and the oral evidence taken in the Proceedings of the Bombay Riots Inquiry Committee, 1929, 18 vols, MSA.
[57] GOB, Home (Sp.) File 348, Part II of 1929; GOB Home (Poll.), File 344 of 1929, MSA.
[58] G.D. Birla to P. Thakurdas, 9 May 1929, Thakurdas Papers File 42 (II), 1923–34, NMML.
[59] Birla to Thakurdas, 4 May 1929, Thakurdas Papers File 81 (II) of 1929, pp. 287–85, NMML.

riot.[60] In each of these cases, what might have passed for a confrontation between rival groups of workers or neighbourhood gangs acquired a larger communal provenance in the prevailing political context.

Second, there was also a territorial element to communal conflicts. Many of its recurring causes – music before the mosque, the routes of festival and funeral processions, cow-slaughter and its site – were related to conflicts over physical and, more fundamentally, social space. Muslim fears that they would be swamped by a Hindu majority in a future Congress Raj linked up with debates about separate representation, special electorates and communal safeguards both within the bureaucracy and the electoral system. Negotiations over these questions reflected the nature of the rights which they might be allowed in the independent nation of the future. The attitudes of local governments towards the use of public space could also be interpreted in terms of the distribution of social entitlements which a Hindu majority or a Congress Ramrajya might tolerate. In this way, the question of territory and social space could be raised metaphorically in the context of larger political and constitutional debates. Thus, the *Muslim Herald* observed in 1932 that Hindus had recently became increasingly belligerent about:

playing music before mosques ... This clearly shows that the Hindus want to overawe the Musalmans and that they are proud of their majority ... and want to compel Government to yield to their demands. The Musalmans do not want to be left at the mercy of the Hindus, because they have been deceived quite often.[61]

In addition, some neighbourhoods had a concentration of particular caste or religious groups. When communal riots occurred, Muslims or Hindus who lived in streets and neighbourhoods mainly inhabited by the rival religion sometimes fled to safer districts. Chawls and neighbourhoods sometimes actively organized to defend themselves and to this end, they called upon the melas or tolis, dadas and gymnasiums. Local youths borrowing a phrase from the non-violent campaigns of the Congress formed themselves into 'volunteer corps'. After the riot, as people returned to their homes, majority communities at times placed conditions on the return of those who had fled, for instance levying collective fines, demanding compensation for the injured or simply requiring public apology.[62]

Significantly, communal riots did not take the form of pitched battles between Hindus and Muslims. Violence was characteristically confined to assaults upon

---

[60] *TOI*, 30 March 1932; GOB Home (Sp.) Files 792 of 1932, 793 (1) of 1932, 793 (1) Parts I–III of 1932, MSA.
[61] *Muslim Herald*, 20 April 1932 in GOB Home (Sp.) File 792 of 1932, MSA.
[62] GOB Home (Poll.) File 344 of 1929, MSA; see also GOB Home (Sp.) File 793 (1) of 1932, p. 109, MSA.

individuals who had strayed into hostile territory,[63] either because the presence of strangers was viewed with suspicion, fear and even panic by its residents or because it allowed dadas to show their prowess and gave the neighbourhood 'volunteers' a chance to flex their muscles. The term 'communal riots', therefore, primarily described a period during which the authorities could expect that most 'inter-personal violence' would be directed against those who could be identified as members of a different religion or caste.

A further territorial element in communal conflict derived from the consequences of municipal and government agencies in Bombay to improve and develop the city. In practice, the efforts of the Improvement Trust and the Development Department schemes were to demolish more houses than they built and to widen roads or construct new highways to facilitate trade rather than improve the living conditions of the majority of its inhabitants. Nonetheless, these schemes disturbed existing neighbourhoods. Their formulation and implementation could generate anxieties and resentments among local residents, landlords and traders, and they frequently fed communal tensions and antagonisms. Thus, the Byculla temple–mosque dispute arose largely as a consequence of one such 'improvement' scheme. Municipal appropriations of some temple lands to widen a road necessitated the relocation of the temple's layout. While this was being carried out, local Muslims began to fear that the reconstruction of the temple would bring unwanted music even closer to the mosque. In fact, it emerged that there had apparently been no previous complaints about music and there was no particular reason to expect that it would become a problem in the future. Anxieties, fostered by municipal policies which disrupted existing patterns of neighbourhood life, fed into wider suspicions about how far the rights and immunities of the rival communities would be respected by the state and then developed into communal antagonisms expressed in terms of rival encroachments upon each other's physical and social space.[64]

Finally, the nationalist movement at times had the unintended consequence of exacerbating communal tensions. Congress rhetoric, it has often been noted, sometimes acquired a Hindu tone.[65] Certainly, the Congress campaigns led Muslims to ask themselves about the rights they might enjoy in a Ramrajya. By its very nature, the Congress had to resist pressures to define the terms on which different social groups might be incorporated within the nation. Congress agitations could aggravate local conflicts and give them a communal colouring.

[63] Based on the discussions and reports in GOB Home (Sp.) Files dealing with the various communal riots of the 1920s and 1930s as well as newspaper accounts and police reports.
[64] GOB Home (Sp.) Files 870 of 1935–36, 870 (2) of 1936, 870 (2) Part I of 1936, 870 (1) of 1936, 870 (10) of 1936, 870 (8) of 1936, MSA.
[65] Cashman, Myth of the Lokamanya; G. Pandey, The Ascendancy of the Congress in Uttar Pradesh, 1926–1934: A Study in Imperfect Mobilization (Delhi, 1978), pp. 74–153.

Thus, the picketing of liquor shops deepened antagonisms between Muslims and Parsi retailers.[66] The boycott of foreign cloth during the civil disobedience movement opened up rifts in the trade between those who controlled the import trade and those who concentrated on internal markets. Since many of the large import traders were Muslims, the boycott and the picketing of their shops and markets were infused with and generated communal antagonisms and sometimes provoked violence. In fact, the communal riots of May 1932 developed, in part, from commercial rivalries arising out of the boycott campaign.[67] Similar market disputes led to further Hindu–Muslim violence in Lal Baug in the following year.[68]

At the same time, constitutional negotiations about special electorates and communal safeguards, which brought in their train issues about rights and immunities, increasingly informed the ways in which Hindus and Muslims perceived each other. The suspension of non-cooperation after Chauri Chaura was regarded by many Muslims as a betrayal of, indeed treachery against, the Khilafat. The refusal of the Congress to countenance communal electorates and constitutional safeguards, for instance in the Nehru Report, was sometimes perceived as a signal that it intended to assert a Hindu hegemony and marginalize Muslim interests.[69] Such suspicions and anxieties were, of course, deepened and consolidated by the recurrent outbreaks of communal violence in the late 1920s and 1930s. By the 1940s, prosperous Muslim merchants and traders, especially of a middling sort, marginalized from the commercial elites in the city, hoped that Pakistan would create a political structure more favourable to their interests than a strong unitary Indian centre in which they would have to scramble for the crumbs thrown to them by the 'big' predominantly Hindu capitalists.[70]

Just as a specifically Muslim politics was slow to manifest itself in Bombay, so non-Brahminism gathered little momentum in the city. Unlike Poona, Bombay was not dominated by a Brahmin elite, nor even primarily by Hindus. Its

---

[66] GOB, Home (Sp.), File 355 (21) F of 1921, MSA; Bombay Confidential Proceedings, Home, December 1921, vol. 62, 771–81, IOR.

[67] *Times of India*, 5 April 1932; Report by B.N. Karanjia, 22 May 1932 in GOB Home (Sp.) File 793 (1) of 1932, pp. 199–207, MSA.

[68] GOB Home (Sp.) File 793 B of 1933, MSA.

[69] These views were expressed before the Bombay Riots Inquiry Committee in 1929. See Proceedings of the BRIC, Oral Evidence, Maulana Shaukat Ali Files 8 and 11; S. Nabiullah and A.R. Dimtimkar, Files 7 and 15, MSA. See also G. Minault, *The Khilafat Movement: Religious Symbolism and Political Mobilization in India* (Delhi, 1982), ch. 4; Mushirul Hasan, '"Congress Muslims" and Indian Nationalism: Dilemma and Decline, 1928–1934', *South Asia*, VIII, 1 and 2 (1985), 102–20.

[70] R. Coupland, *The Indian Problem*, 3 vols. (London, 1944), vol. III, *The Future of India*, pp. 78–9; H. Alavi, 'Class and State', in H. Gardezi and J. Rashid (eds.), *Pakistan: The Roots of Dictatorship: The Political Economy of a Praetorian State* (London, 1983), pp. 46–54.

business, political and intellectual elites included Parsis, Muslims, Jews, Jains, Bhatias and Pathare Prabhus as well as Brahmins. Their diversity and their interconnections enabled them to transcend and traverse barriers of caste and religion. Not surprisingly, these dominant cross-communal elites were particularly responsive to the rhetoric of social reform. This necessarily implied, in particular, the reform of the caste system. Through the Social Service League and the Depressed Classes Mission, some of the leading figures of the Bombay Presidency Association had established close connections with the working classes, and in the case of the latter, untouchables, which they drew upon during the Willingdon Memorial controversy and enabled some, like Narayan Chandavarkar, to intervene in the general strike of 1920.[71] In a city by no means dominated by Brahmins alone, it was scarcely clear why large numbers should be mobilized against them rather than against capitalist exploiters or foreign imperialists. Certainly, the arguments of non-Brahminsm appeared far less persuasive in Bombay than they did among the upwardly mobile, independent peasants of the Deccan or the literate burghers of Poona, confronted by a more pristine, orthodox Brahmin elite.[72]

Since caste and kinship ties, village and neighbourhood connections were so vital to their social organization, it should not be surprising that workers' combinations were sometimes shaped by them. This was particularly the case before 1920. In the 1890s, the Collector of Bombay had observed that while workers subscribed willingly to causes which 'their caste or community hold worthy of support', they appeared to 'hold aloof from similar subscriptions for wage purposes'.[73] Muslim weavers appeared throughout the period to act as a craft union and even as late as the 1930s seemed able collectively to influence the terms on which they worked.[74] The most prominent millhands' association in the late nineteenth century was formed by Narayan Meghaji Lokhande, the non-Brahmin publicist and editor of *Din Bandhu*.[75] Lokhande achieved this prominence largely by his attempts to secure factory legislation to regulate the laws and conditions of work in the cotton mills. But his influence derived more from the Government of Bombay's willingness to seek his advice and accredit his status as a spokesman for labour than from the strength of his popular

---

[71] Masselos, 'Bombay City Politics in 1919'; G.L. Chandavarkar, *The Wrestling Soul: Story of the Life of Sir Narayan Chandavarkar* (Bombay, 1955). E. Zelliot, 'Congress and the Untouchables', in Sisson and Wolpert (eds.), *Congress and Indian Nationalism*, pp. 182–84.

[72] GOB, Home (Sp.) File 363 (5) of 1928, MSA; O'Hanlon, *Caste, Conflict and Ideology*; G. Omvedt, *Cultural Revolt in a Colonial Society: The Non-Brahman Movement in Western India, 1873 to 1930* (Bombay, 1976).

[73] RCL, 1892, Evidence, Mr J.M. Campbell, Collector, Land Revenue, Excise and Opium, Bombay, p. 128, *PP*, 1892, vol. XXXVI.

[74] See above, pp. 225–6, 230–1, 299–302, 320–1, 343–5.

[75] Omvedt, *Cultural Revolt*, pp. 249–53; O'Hanlon, *Caste, Conflict and Ideology*, pp. 288–95.

following. Thus, in 1892, the Inspector of Factories had observed that although Lokhande rather grandly

describes himself as President of the Bombay Mill-hands Association, that Association has no existence as an organized body, having no roll of membership, no funds and no rules. I understand that Mr. Lokhanday simply acts as Volunteer Advisor to any mill-hand who may come to him.[76]

Lokhande and his Millhands' Association were neither the first nor the last of the labour organizers to find themselves in this rather desolate position.

Similarly, the Kamgar Hitwardhak Sabha, founded in 1909, operated as a welfare organization for non-Brahmin workers, which was intermittently drawn into the mediation, or conduct, of industrial disputes.[77] S.K. Bole, its moving spirit, was to remain one of the leading non-Brahmin spokesmen in Bombay until the 1930s.[78] The Social Service League was another organization for social work whose attempts to improve the lot of the working classes and the poor in Bombay turned it increasingly into a prominent spokesman on labour's behalf. Its connections and following formed the basis of the Bombay Textile Labour Union which formed during the general strike of 1925 and exercised some influence in the industry until it was eclipsed during the general strike of 1928.[79] In the 1920s and 1930s, trade unions took greater care to distinguish themselves from caste organizations. Nonetheless, they sometimes derived their support from particular caste groups. The Girni Kamgar Union submerged any analysis of caste within its rhetoric of class. But its most loyal constituency could be identified among Marathas from Ratnagiri. It is likely that their caste connections contributed to the cohesion and solidarities of class.[80]

Just as employers attempted to use communal tensions within the workforce to destroy combinations and break strikes, so they tried to diversify its caste composition. After the general strike of 1928, the Bombay Millowners' Association encouraged attempts to recruit untouchables into the weaving sheds, to divide their most militant workers and to break their carefully constructed barriers of skill.[81] This initiative met with limited success, partly because workers resisted its implementation and partly because the managers themselves lost

[76] Report by the Chief Inspector of Factories on the Working of Factory Act in the Town and Island of Bombay, 1892 in *Provincial Report on the Working of the Indian Factories Act in the Bombay Presidency for the Year 1892* (Bombay, 1893), p. 15.
[77] 'The Kamgar Hitwardhak Sabha: A Brief Sketch', *Indian Textile Journal*, XXIX (July 1919), 177–9 and *ibid*, XXIX (August 1919), 209–10.
[78] Omvedt, *Cultural Revolt*, pp. 250, 253–5; Newman, *Workers and Unions*, pp. 111–13.
[79] Newman, *Workers and Unions*, pp. 113–9; Omvedt, *Cultural Revolt*, p. 254; V.B. Karnik, *N.M. Joshi*, pp. 36–99.
[80] *Meerut Conspiracy Case, Statements Made by the Accused, Non-Communist Series*. Examination of S.H. Jhabvala, p. 756.
[81] *BMOA, Annual Report*, 1928, p. 71; see above, chapters 5 and 7.

interest. As their more experienced employers began to return to work, they began to complain that Harijan workers lacked the necessary skill and aptitude for weaving.[82] Caste tensions and competition in the workplace were sometimes extended into the higher reaches of trade union and political rivalries. In 1929, when the Meerut arrests had removed most of the leading communists of the Girni Kamgar Union, Bhasakarrao Jadhav, the Local Self-Government Minister, sought to promote Arjun Alwe and G.R. Kasle against the communist rump which remained on the Girni Kamgar Union's managing committee.[83] At the same time, the Congress had attempted to gain a foothold within the union through an alliance with G.L. Kandalkar.[84] In the 1930s, Alwe and Kandalkar were to act together as a dissident faction within the union. Towards the end of the decade, caste tensions within the workforce once more found emphatic political expression when Ambedkar's Independent Labour Party obtained considerable support from Mahar millworkers. By linking his opposition to the Trade Disputes legislation of 1938 with an anti-khot agitation in Ratnagiri, he brought together issues bearing upon both the rural and urban interests of the working class and showed how narrowly conceived the communist strategy had been.[85]

Although publicists were able to marshall a significant following behind the banner of non-Brahminism and the Depressed Classes at specific moments, this support was not easily sustained. Not only was it difficult to sustain a movement against Brahmins in a city which they did not obviously dominate, but the assertion of the mutuality of non-Brahmins frequently served to expose the tensions and antagonisms between them. The Mahar movement often exacerbated conflicts between rural, often untouchable, labour and more substantial Maratha peasants who employed them and in any case aspired to a purer Kshatriya status. The Brahmins and non-Brahmins, it was reported in 1928, 'see eye to eye in keeping the Depressed Classes in their place'.[86] Non-Brahminism was not synonymous with radicalism. It drew its greatest strength from among the few 'rich peasants' to be found in the arid Deccan plateau, who sought social mobility through education and government employment to match and, indeed, to perpetuate their rising agrarian prosperity. Their apparent hostility to Brahmins was 'due not so much to their being members of particular castes as to the privileged position enjoyed by them in common with other advanced

[82] Proceedings of the TLIC, Main Inquiry, Oral Evidence, Mr F. Stones, File 70, p. 3,550, MSA.
[83] Omvedt, *Cultural Revolt*, pp. 259–61.
[84] GOB Home (Sp.) File 750 (39)–II of 1930, pp. 39, 43, MSA.
[85] GOB, Home (Sp.) File 927-A of 1938, File 927-A Part I of 1939, File 550 (25)–B of 1938; File 550 (25)–III of 1938. File 550 (25)-III B of 1938, MSA. See also Keer, *Dr Ambedkar*, pp. 293–315.
[86] Commissioner, Southern Division, to Secretary, GOB Home (Poll.), 12 January 1928 in GOB Home (Sp.) File no. 363 (5) of 1928, p. 34, MSA.

communities in all other spheres of public activity'.[87] By the early 1930s, dominant peasants in the Deccan who had discovered in non-Brahminism a means of expressing their social aspirations now began to drift into the Congress. Some were inspired by the civil disobedience movement; others were driven into opposition by the depression. For many dominant groups in the Deccan countryside, even erstwhile seekers after truth, entry into the provincial legislatures or control over the local Congress provided the most promising method of perpetuating their social dominance in the face of a changing political structure.[88]

Neither the non-Brahmin nor the Depressed Classes movement consistently offered a realizable social charter for the working classes. As social categories, they were shaped by the framework and the statecraft of the colonial state. Their focus rested most firmly upon education, government employment and political representation. These matters were not simply the concern of clerks, scribes and aspiring bureaucrats. However small the literate elites of a caste or kinship group might be, they could, once lodged within the administrative structure, do favours, perform services and create opportunities for their kinsmen, co-villagers and caste-fellows.[89] Nonetheless, a political programme composed in this fashion suffered serious limitations in expressing the specific and diverse interests of the working classes or consistently finding a resonance in the daily struggles of workplace and neighbourhood. Its weakness was that workers could not easily forge fresh political strategies from within its programmatic framework to alter, alleviate or transform their immediate situation.

In the maelstrom of popular politics, various competing and often uneasily co-existing identities played upon each other. The question of social identity and its relationship to political action has often been misleadingly posed as a choice between exclusive choices, loyalties and allegiances. In fact, the working classes combined a wide range of identities, from family to class, from caste to religion, from neighbourhood to nation, and their expression depended upon the social and political context in which they were articulated. Class consciousness should no more be regarded as inherent to or immanent within the working classes than affinities derived from caste or tribe, religion or nation, family

---

[87] *Ibid.*, p. 33, MSA.

[88] J. Lele, *Elite Pluralism and Class Rule: Political Development in Maharashtra* (Toronto, 1981), pp. 46–55; R. O'Hanlon, 'Acts of Appropriation: Non-Brahmin Radicals and the Congress in Early Twentieth Century Maharashtra', in M. Shepperdson and C. Simmons (eds.), *The Indian National Congress and the Political Economy of India* (Aldershot, 1988), pp. 102–46.

[89] Keer, *Ambedkar*; E. Zelliot, 'Learning the Use of Political Means: The Mahars of Maharashtra', in R. Kothari (ed.), *Caste in Indian Politics* (Delhi, 1970), pp. 29–69. For a general interpretation along these lines, see H. Alavi, 'Politics of Ethnicity in India and Pakistan', in H. Alavi and J. Harriss (eds.), *South Asia* (London, 1989), pp. 222–46.

or neighbourhood. The interaction between them took complex and often unexpected forms. The communist leaders of the Girni Kamgar Union expected that class consciousness was a function of industrial development and proletarian maturity. In fact, the rural connections of workers were often as significant in shaping their perception of class interests in the urban context. Moreover, what facilitated the political solidarity of Bombay's workers was not the homogeneity apparently fostered by the large-scale industry, and the 'real subsumption of labour to capital', but their experience of the state as a repressive, antagonistic force in moments of industrial action. Indeed, the success of the Girni Kamgar Union owed something to their own agitational interventionist style in the daily affairs of the workplace and something to their marginalization and repression by employers and the state. They were unencumbered by their connections within the state or the patronage of their employers. They were free to be seen, and indeed at liberty to present themselves, as the true champions of working-class interests.

As the rhetoric of the Congress became explicitly anti-colonial, so it helped to identify the state as the focus of workers' resistance. Indeed, the slump in the fortunes of the textile industry and the city was sometimes attributed, most vociferously by the millowners, to the policies of the state. This did not, however, appear to prevent both employers and the state joining together to blame labour for its incorrigible inefficiency, its inflated wage demands and its innate lack of discipline. Working-class nationalism did not necessarily signify a commitment to a territorial principle or the perception that the interests of all-India were uniform. But it was a short step, sometimes easily taken, for workers to extend their immediate experience of European and Parsi supervisors and managers and their employers, who associated so closely with the British, to an understanding of the nature of colonial power and authority in the city as a whole, and beyond. Moreover, the city's political elites, whether in the Bombay Presidency Association, or later in the Congress, sometimes appeared aloof from working-class politics and associated closely with the state. This set of connections might readily give social antagonisms a nationalist colouring. If working-class consciousness was constituted in relation to the state, nationalism served to clarify its perception and advance its programme, rather than to dissolve or postpone class differences. Nationalism also sharpened communal differences. As Congress attempted to define the nation and assert and fortify its claim to represent it, others interrogated and challenged their credibility, whether, for instance, in the form of the 'two-nations theory' or in Ambedkar's delineation of what Gandhi and the Congress had done to the untouchables. Congress rhetoric sometimes acquired a Hindu idiom and a revivalist tone. It could not always satisfactorily indicate how justly and equally rights in the nation might be distributed. For many Muslims, their experience of the Congress only served to heighten their suspicion of what the Ramrajya might bring.

Communal antagonism, even the ferocious riots of 1929, 1932 and 1936, did not make it impossible for workers to forge class solidarities in the general strikes of 1934 and 1940. Although caste and religious differences could be exploited to open up differences within unions, to break strikes and undermine neighbourhood and political alliances, they did not capture, contain or comprehensively describe the political networks, perceptions and action of the working classes. If workers' politics were often constituted in relation to the state, caste and communal movements operated within its framework. Their focus rested on questions of education and government employment. They offered little which could be translated into a programme of immediate relevance in the realm of the daily politics of workplace and neighbourhood. Nor did they provide a critical perspective upon the state, beyond the complaint that it failed to comply with their special and particular demands.

The interplay of these various identities, sometimes competing, sometimes co-existing, within the working classes meant that political unities which appeared to have been forged and flourished at one moment could disappear or be submerged at the next. Political action has often been most securely grasped in terms of given social categories. It is perhaps more important to recognize that these social categories were not given in the first place but politically constructed, and that the process of the social formation of the working class was shaped by an essentially political dimension at its core.

Bibliography

Note: The bibliography is arranged under the following headings:

Government records

Official publications

1. Parliamentary papers
2. His Majesty's Stationery Office (HMSO)
3. Government of India
4. Government of Bombay
5. Labour Office, Bombay
6. Census
7. Imperial Gazetteers
8. Bombay Presidency Gazetteers
9. Other Gazetteers
10. Annual reports

Unpublished proceedings of committees of enquiry

Private papers

Papers of organizations

Non-official reports

Newspapers

Interviews

Books, pamphlets and articles

Unpublished dissertations

GOVERNMENT RECORDS

Records of the Secretary of State for India, India Office Library and Records, London
    Public and Judicial Department
    Economic and Overseas Department
Proceedings of the Government of India, India Office Library and Records
    Judicial, Revenue, Commerce and Industries, Home Departments
Records of the Government of India, National Archives of India, New Delhi
    Home, Commerce and Industries, Industries and Labour Departments
Proceedings of the Government of Bombay, India Office Library and Records
    General, Judicial, Home, Revenue (Commerce and Industry), and Revenue (Land)
Proceedings of the Government of Bombay, Confidential, India Office Library and
    Records
    Judicial, Home, General, Revenue (Commerce and Industries)
Records of the Government of Bombay, Maharashtra State Archives, Bombay
    Home (Poll.), Home (Sp.), Finance, Revenue, Development, General, Public Works
    Departments
Records of the Commissioner of Police, Bombay, Office of the Commissioner of Police,
    Bombay
Records of the Deputy Inspector-General of Police, Criminal Investigation Department,
    Bombay, Maharashtra; Secret Abstracts of Intelligence, Bombay Presidency Police,
    Office of the Deputy Inspector General of Police, Criminal Investigation Depart-
    ment, Maharashtra, Bombay

OFFICIAL PUBLICATIONS

1. PARLIAMENTARY PAPERS

Indian Tariff and Cotton Duties: Papers Relating to the Indian Tariff Act and the Cotton Duties, 1894, vol. LXXII, 1895. Cmd 7602
Papers Relating to the Indian Tariff Act, 1896 and the Cotton Duties Act 1896, vol. LX, Cmd 8078
Royal Commission on Labour, Foreign Reports, vol. II, The Colonies and the Indian Empire with an Appendix on the Migration of Labour, 1892, vol. XXXVI, Cmd 6795–XI

2. HIS MAJESTY'S STATIONERY OFFICE (HMSO)

Royal Commission on Indian Currency and Finance, vol. IV, *Minutes of Evidence taken in India*. London, 1926
Report of the Royal Commission on Agriculture in India. London, 1928
Royal Commission on Agriculture in India, Appendix to the Report, vol. XIV, London, 1928
Royal Commission on Agriculture in India, vol. II, *Evidence taken in the Bombay Presidency*. London, 1928
Report of the Royal Commission on Labour in India. London, 1931
Royal Commission on Labour in India, vol. I, *Evidence taken in the Bombay Presidency (including Sind)*. London, 1931
Royal Commission on Labour in India, vol. XI, *Supplementary Evidence*. London, 1931

3. GOVERNMENT OF INDIA

Report of the Indian Factory Commission, Appointed in September 1890, under the Orders of His Excellency, the Governor-General-in-Council, with Proceedings and Appendices. Calcutta, 1890

Report of the Indian Factory Labour Commission 1908, 2 vols. Simla, 1908

Indian Industrial Commission, vol. I – Report 1916–18, vols. II – V – Evidence. Calcutta, 1918

A.G. Clow, *Report on the Recruitment of Indian Seamen.* Calcutta, 1922

Report of the Indian Tariff Board Regarding the Grant of Protection to the Magnesium Chloride Industry (Including the Evidence Recorded During the Enquiry). Calcutta, 1925

Report of the Committee Appointed by the Government of India to Inquire into the Bombay Back Bay Reclamation Scheme, 1926. London, 1926

Report of the Back Bay Inquiry Committee, Evidence, 3 vols., London, 1926–7

The Indian Tariff Board (Cotton Textile Industry Enquiry), 1927, vol. I – Report, vols. II–IV – Evidence. Calcutta, 1927

Indian Central Banking Enquiry Committee, vol. I – *Reports*, vols. II–III – Evidence. Calcutta, 1930–2

Report of the Indian Tariff Board Regarding the Grant of Protection to the Cotton Textile Industry. Calcutta, 1932

Report of the Indian Tariff Board Regarding the Grant of Additional Protection to the Cotton Textile Industry. Calcutta, 1932

Report of the Special Tariff Board on the Enquiry Regarding the Level of Duties Necessary to Afford Adequate Protection to the Indian Cotton Textile Industry Against Imports from the United Kingdom of Cotton Piecegoods and Yarn, Artificial Silk Fabrics and Mixture Fabrics of Cotton and Artificial Silk. Delhi, 1936

Main Report of the Labour Investigation Committee. Delhi, 1946

4. GOVERNMENT OF BOMBAY

Conybeare, H. *Report on the Sanitary State and Requirements of Bombay, Selections from the Records of the Bombay Government*, N.S., no. 11. Bombay, 1855

Correspondence Relating to the Prohibition of Burials in the Back Bay Sands, and to Dr Leith's Mortuary Report for 1854. Bombay, 1855

Warden, F. *Report on the Landed Tenures of Bombay, dated 20 August 1814. Selections from the Records of the Bombay Governmnet*, N.S., no. 64. Bombay, 1861

Report of the Bombay Health Officer, for the 3rd Quarter of 1871. Bombay, 1871

Candy, E.T. *Selections with Notes from the Records of Government Regarding the Khoti Tenure, Selections from the Records of the Bombay Government*, N.S., no. 134. Bombay, 1873

Report by W.O. Meade King on the Working of the Indian Factories Act in Bombay together with Certain Suggestions and Proposals. Bombay, 1882

Report of the Commission Appointed to Consider the Working of Factories in the Bombay Presidency, 1888. Bombay, 1888

Snow, P.C.H. *Report on the Outbreak of Bubonic Plague in Bombay, 1896–97.* Bombay, 1897

Condon, Capt. J.K. *The Bombay Plague, Being A History of the Progress of Plague in the Bombay Presidency from September 1896 to June 1899.* Bombay, 1900

Lawrence, H.S. *Statistical Atlas of the Bombay Presidency.* Bombay, 1906

Report on the Leather Industries of the Bombay Presidency. Bombay, 1910
Report of the Bombay Development Committee. Bombay, 1914
Papers Relating to the Second Revision Settlement of the Ratnagiri Taluka of the Ratnagiri Collectorate, by J.A. Madan, 11 September 1914. *Selections from the Records of the Bombay Government*, N.S. no. 574. Bombay, 1920
Report of the Prostitution Committee. Bombay, 1921
Report of the Industrial Disputes Committee. Bombay, 1922
Mann, H.H. *The Economic Progress of the Rural Areas of the Bombay Presidency*. Bombay, 1924
Report of the Bombay Stock Exchange Inquiry Committee, 1923–24. Bombay, 1924
Mann, H.H. *Statistical Atlas of the Bombay Presidency*. Bombay, 1925
Papers Relating to the Second Revision Settlement of the Panvel Taluka, including Uran Mahal, of the Kolaba District, by J.R. Hood, 31 July 1922. *Selections from the Records of the Bombay Government*, N.S., no. 609. Bombay, 1925
Papers Relating to the Second Revision Settlement of the Kalyan Taluka of the Thana District, by M.J. Dikshit, 5 September 1923, *Selections from the Records of the Bombay Government*, N.S., no. 613. Bombay, 1927
Papers Relating to the Second Revision Settlement of the Patan Taluka of the Satara District, by C.H. Bristow, 27 February 1925. *Selections from the Records of the Bombay Government*, N.S., no. 623. Bombay, 1928
Papers Relating to the Second Revision Settlement of the Madangad Petha of the Ratnagiri District, by R.G. Gordon, 4 July 1924. *Selections from the Records of the Bombay Government*, N.S., no. 619. Bombay, 1928
Papers Relating to the Second Revision Settlement of the Khed Taluka of the Ratnagiri District, by R.G. Gordon, 4 July 1924. *Selections from the Records of the Bombay Government*, N.S., no. 627. Bombay, 1929
Papers Relating to the Second Revision Settlement of the Alibag Taluka of the Kolaba District, by J.R. Hood, 30 April 1924. *Selections from the Records of the Bombay Government*, N.S., no. 632. Bombay, 1929
Papers Relating to the Second Revision Settlement of the Satara Taluka of the Satara District, by H.D. Baskerville, 30 July 1923. *Selections from the Records of the Bombay Government*, N.S., no. 635. Bombay, 1929
Papers Relating to the Second Revision Settlement of the Man Taluka of the Satara District, by M. Webb, 2 March 1923. *Selections from the Records of the Bombay Government*, N.S., no. 634. Bombay, 1929
Report of the Bombay Strike Enquiry Committee, vol. I. Bombay, 1929
Report of the Bombay Riots Inquiry Committee, 1929. Bombay, 1929
Report of the Court of Inquiry into a Trade Dispute Between Several Textile Mills and Their Workmen. Bombay, 1929
Report of the Bombay Provincial Banking Enquiry Committee, vol. I – Report, vols. II–IV – Evidence. Bombay, 1930
Telang, S.V. *Report on the Handloom Weaving Industry in the Bombay Presidency*. Bombay, 1936
Report of the Bombay Stock Exchange Enquiry Committee, 1936–37. Bombay, 1937
Report of the Textile Labour Inquiry Committee 1937–38, vol. I – *Interim Report*. Bombay, 1938
Report of the Rent Enquiry Committee, with Evidence. Bombay, 1939

Interim Report by the Industrial Conditions Enquiry Committee on the Cotton Textile Industry in Bombay City and Bombay Suburban District. Bombay, 1948

Report of the Textile Labour Inquiry Committee, vol. II, *Final Report.* Bombay, 1953

Source Material for a History of the Freedom Movement in India, vol. VI, *Non-Co-operation Movement, Bombay City, 1920–25*, edited by B.G. Kunte. Bombay, 1978

5. LABOUR OFFICE, BOMBAY

Labour Gazette (monthly)

Report on an Enquiry into the Wages and Hours of Labour in the Cotton Mill Industry, May, 1921, by G. Findlay Shirras. Bombay, 1923

Report on an Enquiry into Working Class Family Budgets in Bombay, by G. Findlay Shirras. Bombay, 1923

Report on an Enquiry into Agricultural Wages in Bombay Presidency, by G. Findlay Shirras. Bombay, 1924

Report on an Enquiry into Wages and Hours of Labour in the Cotton Mill Industry in August 1923. Bombay, 1925

Report on an Enquiry into Middle Class Unemployment in the Bombay Presidency. Bombay, 1927

Report on an Enquiry into Middle Class Family Budgets in Bombay City. Bombay, 1928

Report on an Enquiry into the Deductions from Wages or Payment in Respect of Fines. Bombay, 1928

Report on an Enquiry into Wages and Hours of Labour in the Cotton Mill Industry, 1926. Bombay, 1930

Wages and Unemployment in the Bombay Cotton Textile Industry. Bombay, 1934

Report on an Enquiry into Working Class Family Budgets in Bombay City. Bombay, 1935

Report on an Enquiry into Wages, Hours of Work and Conditions of Employment in the Retail Trade of Some Towns in the Bombay Presidency. Bombay, 1936

Report on an Enquiry into Wages, Hours of Work and Conditions of Employment in the Engineering Industry in the Bombay Presidency (excluding Sind), May 1934. General Wage Census, Part I – Perennial Factories. First Report. Bombay, 1936

Report on an Enquiry into Wages, Hours of Work and Conditions of Employment in the Printing Industry in the Bombay Presidency (excluding Sind), May 1934. General Wage Census, Part I – Perennial Factories. Second Report. Bombay, 1936

Report on an Enquiry into Wages, Hours of Work and Conditions of Employment in the Textile Industries (Cotton, Silk, Wool and Hosiery) in the Bombay Presidency (excluding Sind), May 1934. General Wage Census, Part I – Perennial Factories. Third Report. Bombay, 1937

Report on an Enquiry into Wages, Hours of Work and Conditions of Employment in the Oils, Paints and Soap, Match Manufacturing and Other Miscelleneous Industries in the Province of Bombay, May 1934. General Wages Census, Part I – Perennial Factories. Fourth Report. Bombay, 1939

Report on an Enquiry into Wages, Hours of Work and Conditions of Employment in Seasonal Factories of the Bombay Province, 1936. General Wage Census, Part II – Seasonal Factories. Bombay, 1939

6. CENSUS

Census of the Island of Bombay taken on 2nd February 1864. Bombay, 1864

Census of the City of Bombay taken on 21st February 1872. Bombay, 1872
Census of the Bombay Presidency, 1872. Bombay, 1875
Census of the City and Island of Bombay taken on 17th of February 1881 by T.S. Weir, Surgeon-Major, Health Officer, Acting Municipal Commissioner. Bombay, 1883
Census of India, 1891, vols. VII & VIII. 1892
Census of India, 1901, vol. XI. Bombay, 1901
Census of India, 1911, vol. VIII. Bombay, 1912
Census of India, 1921, vol. IX. Bombay, 1922
Census of India, 1931, vol. VIII. Bombay, 1933
Census of India, 1931, vol. IX. Bombay, 1933

7. IMPERIAL GAZETTEERS
Imperial Gazetteer of India, Provincial Series, Bombay Presidency, 3 vols. Calcutta, 1908

8. BOMBAY PRESIDENCY GAZETTEERS
Gazetteer of the Bombay Presidency, vol. I, part 2, *History of the Konkan, Dakhan and Southern Maratha Country.* Bombay, 1896
Gazetteer of the Bombay Presidency, vol. II, *Surat and Broach.* Bombay, 1877
Gazetteer of the Bombay Presidency, vol. IV, *Ahmedabad.* Bombay, 1879
Gazetteer of the Bombay Presidency, vol. X, *Ratnagiri and Savantwadi.* Bombay, 1880
Gazetteer of the Bombay Presidency, vol. XII, *Khandesh.* Bombay, 1880
Gazetteer of the Bombay Presidency, vol. XVIII, parts 1–2, *Poona.* Bombay, 1885
Gazetteer of the Bombay Presidency, vol. XIX, *Satara.* Bombay, 1885

9. OTHER GAZETTEERS
Gazetteer of Bombay City and Island, 3 vols. Bombay, 1909

10. ANNUAL REPORTS
Administration Report of the City of Bombay Improvement Trust
Administration Report of the Government of Bombay
Administration Report of the Municipal Commissioner for the City of Bombay
Annual Statement of the Sea-Borne Trade and Navigation of British India
Factory Report for the Bombay Presidency
Prices and Wages in India. Calcutta
Report of the Department of Industries in the Bombay Presidency
Report on the Native Newspapers Published in the Bombay Presidency
Report on the Working of the Development Department in Bombay
Report on the Working of the Indian Factories Act

UNPUBLISHED PROCEEDINGS OF COMMITTEES OF INQUIRY

Bombay Strike Enquiry Committee, 1928. Maharashtra State Archives
Bombay Riots Inquiry Committee, 1929. Maharashtra State Archives
Court of Enquiry, 1929. Maharashtra State Archives
Bombay Provincial Banking Enquiry Committee, 1929. Maharashtra State Archives
Meerut Conspiracy Case, Statements and Exhibits, 1929–33. National Archives of India

Textile Labour Inquiry Committee, Interim and Main Inquiry, 1937–40. Maharashtra
    State Archives
Bombay Disturbances Enquiry Committee, 1938. Government of Bombay, Home (Sp.)
    Files. Maharashtra State Archives

PRIVATE PAPERS

Papers of J.C. Curry, Centre of South Asian Studies, Cambridge
Montagu Papers, MSS. Eur. D 523, India Office Library and Records
Papers of N.M. Joshi, Nehru Memorial Museum and Library, New Delhi
Papers of Sir Frederick Sykes, India Office Library and Records
Papers of Sir P. Thakurdas, Nehru Memorial Museum and Library

PAPERS OF ORGANIZATIONS

Minute Books of the Committee of the Bombay Millowners' Association, Office of the
    Bombay Millowners' Association, Bombay
All-India Trade Union Congress, Nehru Memorial Museum and Library
Ahmedabad Textile Labour Association, Microfilm copy. Nehru Memorial Museum and
    Library

NON-OFFICIAL REPORTS

Annual Reports of the Bombay Millowners' Association
The Investor's India Yearbook, annual. Calcutta
The Bombay Riots of February 1874: Reprinted from the Times of India. Bombay, 1874
The Bombay Riots (reprinted from the Bombay Gazette). Bombay, 1874
Manchester Chamber of Commerce, *Bombay and Lancashire: Cotton Spinning Inquiry:
    Minutes and Evidence.* Manchester, 1888
The Bombay Riots of 1893: Reprinted from the Times of India. Bombay, 1893
Great Indian Peninsular Railway, *Report for the Royal Commission on Labour in India.*
    Bombay, 1929
All-India Manufactures' Organization, *Industries in Bombay City.* Bombay, 1944

NEWSPAPERS

Bombay Chronicle
Bombay Sentinel
Indian National Herald
The Indian Social Reformer
Kranti (Marathi)
Nava Kal (Marathi)
Times of India

INTERVIEWS

S.V. Ghate, Interviewed by Dr A.K. Gupta and Dr Hari Dev Sharma, Nehru Memorial
    Museum and Library Oral History Project, Transcript, Nehru Memorial Museum
    and Library
V.B. Karnik. April 1979
B.T. Ranadive. April 1979
P.G. Sawant. March – April 1979
B. Thorat. April 1979
Other interviews which were most useful, but are not cited in the footnotes were with
    S.A. Dange, Maniben Kara and S.G. Sardesai

BOOKS, PAMPHLETS AND ARTICLES

Adams, J. 'A Statistical Test of the Impact of Suez Canal on the Growth of India's Trade',
    IESHR, VIII, 3 (1971), 229–40
Alavi, H. 'Class and State', in H. Gardezi and J. Rashid (eds.), *Pakistan: The Roots of
    Dictatorship: The Political Economy of a Praetorian State*. London, 1983, pp.
    40–93.
    'Politics of Ethnicity in India and Pakistan', in H. Alavi and J. Harriss (eds.), *South
    Asia*. London, 1989
Amin, S. *Sugarcane and Sugar in Gorakhpur: An Inquiry into Peasant Production for
    Capitalist Enterprise in Colonial India*. Delhi, 1984
Anon, *The Bombay High Court, 1862–1962*. Bombay, 1962
Anon. 'The Town and Fort of Bombay', *Alexandra's East India and Colonial Magazine*,
    IX (Jan.–June 1835), 243–45
A Retired Mill Manager. *The Bombay Cotton Mills: The Spinning of 10's, 20's and 30's
    Counts*. Bombay, 1907
Arnold, D. 'Industrial Violence in Colonial India', *Comparative Studies in Society and
    History*, XIII, 2 (1980), 234–55
    'Touching the Body: Perspectives on the Indian Plague, 1896–1900', in R. Guha (ed.),
    Subaltern Studies, vol. V, Delhi, 1987, pp. 55–90
Bagchi, A.K. *Private Investment in India 1900–1939*. Cambridge, 1972
    'De-Industrialization in Gangetic Bihar 1809–1901', in B. De (ed.), *Essays in Honour
    of Professor S.C. Sarkar*. Delhi, 1976, pp. 499–522
    'De-Industrialization in India in the Nineteenth Century: Some Theoretical Implica-
    tions', *Journal of Development Studies*, XII, 2 (1976), 135–64
    'Reflections on Patterns of Regional Growth in India During the Period of British
    Rule', *Bengal Past and Present*, XCV, 1 (1976), 247–89
    'A Reply', *IESHR* XVI, 2 (1979), 147–61
Bagchi, A.K. and N. Banerjee (eds.). *Change and Choice in Indian Industry*. Calcutta,
    1984
Bahl, J.C. *The Oilseeds Trade of India*. Bombay, 1938
Bairoch, P. 'International Industrialization Levels from 1750 to 1980', *Journal of
    European Economic History*, XI, 2 (1982), 269–333
Baker, C.J. *The Politics of South India 1920–37*. Cambridge, 1976
    'Economic Reorganization and the Slump in South and South-East Asia', *Compara-
    tive Studies in Society and History*, XXIII, 3 (1981), 325–49

An Indian Rural Economy 1880–1955: The Tamilnad Countryside. Oxford, 1984
Baker, C.J., G. Johnson and A. Seal. *Power, Profit and Politics: Essays on Imperialism, Nationalism and Change in Twentieth Century India*, Special Issue, *Modern Asian Studies*, XV, 3 (1981), 355–721
Ballhatchet, K. *Social Policy and Social Change in Western India 1817–1830.* Oxford, 1957
Banaji, D.R. *Bombay and the Sidis.* Bombay, 1932
Banaji, J. 'Capitalist Domination and the Small Peasantry: Deccan Districts in the Late Nineteenth Century', *Economic and Political Weekly*, XII, 33–4, Special Number, 1977, 1375 – 1404
Banaji, K.N. *Memoirs of the Late Framji Cowasji Banaji.* Bombay, 1892
Banerji, A.K. *India's Balance of Payments, 1921–22 to 1938–39.* London, 1963
Basu, D.K. (ed.). *The Rise and Growth of the Colonial Port Cities in Asia.* Santa Cruz, 1979
Bates, C.N. 'The Nature of Social Change in Rural Gujarat: The Kheda District, 1818–1918', *MAS*, XV, 4 (1981), 771–821
Bayly, C.A. 'The Age of Hiatus: The North Indian Economy and Society, 1830–50', in C.H. Philips and M.D. Wainwright (eds.), *Indian Society and the Beginnings of Modernization.* London, 1976
   Rulers, Townsmen and Bazaars: North Indian Society in the Age of Expansion. Cambridge, 1982
   'The Pre-History of "Communalism"? Religious conflict in India, 1700–1860', *MAS* XIX, 2 (1985), 177–203
Bellwinkel, M. 'Rajasthani Contract Labour in Delhi: A case Study of the Relationship between Company, Middleman and Worker', *Sociological Bulletin*, XXII, 1 (March 1973), 78–97
Benjamin, N. 'Bombay's "Country Trade" with China (1765–1865)', *Indian Historical Review*, I, 2 (1974), 295–303
Bharadwaj, Krishna. 'Towards a Macro-Economic Framework for a Developing Economy: The Indian Case', *Manchester School of Economic and Social Studies*, III (September 1979), 270–302
Bhattacharya, S. 'Cotton Mills and Spinning Wheels: Swadeshi and the Indian Capitalist Class, 1920–22', *Economic and Political Weekly*, XI, 47 (1976), 1828–34
   'Capital and Labour in Bombay City, 1928–29' *Economic and Political Weekly, Review of Political Economy*, XVI, 42 and 43 (17–24 October 1981), pp. PE36 – PE44
   'The Colonial State, Capital and Labour: Bombay, 1919–31', in S. Bhattacharya and R. Thapar (eds.), *Situating Indian History.* Delhi, 1986, pp. 171–93
   'Swaraj and the Kamgar: The Indian National Congress and the Bombay Working Class, 1919–1931', in R. Sisson and S. Wolpert (eds.), *Congress and Indian Nationalism: The Pre-Independence Phase.* Berkeley and Los Angeles, 1988, pp. 223–49
Bhattacherjee, D., 'Unions, State and Capital in Western India: Structural Determinants of the 1982 Bombay Textile Strike' in R. Southall, (ed.), *Labour and Unions in Asia and Africa: Contemporary Issues*, London, 1988, pp. 211–37
Blyn, G. *Agricultural Trends in India 1891–1947: Output, Availablility and Productivity.* Philadelphia, 1966
Bose, A. 'Six Decades of Urbanization in India', *IESHR*, II, 1 (1965), 23–41

Urbanization in India: An Inventory of Source Materials. Delhi, 1970

Brady, R. *The Rationalization Movement in German Industry: A Study in the Evolution of Economic Planning.* Berkeley, 1933

Brahma Nand. 'Agricultural Labourers in Western India: A Study of the Central Division Districts of the Bombay Presidency During the Late Nineteenth and Early Twentieth Century', *Studies in History*, N.S., I, 2 (1985), 221–46

Braverman, H. *Labour and Monopoly Capital: The Degradation of Work in the Twentieth Century.* New York, 1974

Breman, J. *Patronage and Exploitation: Changing Agrarian Relations in South Gujarat, India.* Berkeley and Los Angeles, 1974

'A Dualistic Labour System: A Critique of the "Informal Sector" Concept', *Economic and Political Weekly*, XI, 48 (27 November 1976) 1870–76; XI, 49 (4 December 1976) 1905–8; XI, 50 (11 December 1976) 1939–44

Briggs, A. 'The Language of "Class" in Early Nineteenth Century England', in A. Briggs and J. Saville (eds.), *Essays in Labour History.* London, 1960, pp. 43–73

Broeze, F.J.A. 'The Muscles of Empire: Indian Seamen and the Raj, 1919–1929', *IESHR*, XIII, 1 (1981), 43–67

Bromley, R. *The Urban Informal Sector: Critical Perspectives, World Development*, Special Issue, VI, 9 and 10 (1978)

Bromley, R. and C. Gerry (eds.), *Casual Work and Poverty in Third World Cities.* Chichester, 1979

Buchanan, D.H. *The Development of Capitalist Enterprise in India.* New York, 1934. Reprinted, London, 1966

Burnell, J. *Bombay in the Days of Queen Anne*, edited by S.T. Sheppard. London, 1933

Burnett-Hurst, A.R., *Labour and Housing in Bombay: A Study in the Economic Condition of the Wage-Earning Classes of Bombay.* London, 1925

Burns, Cecil L. *A Monograph on Gold and Silver Work in the Bombay Presidency.* Bombay, 1904

Cannadine, D. 'The Present and the Past in the English Industrial Revolution, 1880–1980', *Past and Present*, CIII (1984), 131–71

Cashman, R.I. *The Myth of the Lokamanya: Tilak and Mass Politics in Maharashtra.* Berkeley and Los Angeles, 1975

Catanach, I.J. 'Plague and the Tensions of Empire, 1896–1918', in D. Arnold (ed.), *Imperial Medicine and Indigenous Societies.* Manchester, 1988, pp. 149–71

Chakrabarty, D. 'On Deifying and Defying Authority: Managers and Workers in the Jute Mills of Bengal, circa 1890–1940', *Past and Present*, C (1983), 124–46

Rethinking Working-Class History: Bengal, 1890–1940. Delhi, 1989

Chakravarthy, L. 'Emergence of an Industrial Labour Force in a Dual Economy – British India 1880–1920', *IESHR*, XV, 3 (1978), 249–327

Chandavarkar, G.L. *The Wrestling Soul: Story of the Life of Sir Narayan Chandavarkar.* Bombay, 1955

Chandavarkar, R. 'Workers' Politics and the Mill Districts in Bombay between the Wars', *MAS*, XV, 3 (1981), Special Issue, *Power, Profit and Politics: Essays on Imperialism, Nationalism and Change in the Twentieth Century*, edited by C.J. Baker, G. Johnson and A. Seal, pp. 603–47

'Industrialization in India before 1947: Conventional Approaches and Alternative Perspectives', *MAS*, XIX, 3 (1985), 623–68

'Plague Panic and Epidemic Politics in India, 1896–1914' in P. Slack and T. Ranger (eds.), *Epidemics and Ideas: Essays on the Historical Perceptions of Pestilence.* Cambridge, 1992, pp. 203–40

Chandra, B. *The Rise and Growth of Economic Nationalism in India: Economic Policies of Indian National Leadership 1880–1905.* Delhi, 1966

'The Indian Capitalist Class and Imperialism before 1947', *Journal of Contemporary Asia,* V, 3 (1974), 309–26

'Jawaharlal Nehru and the Indian Capitalist Class in 1936', *Economic and Political Weekly,* X, 33–5 (1975), 1307–24

Charlesworth, N. 'Rich Peasants and Poor Peasants in Late Nineteenth Century Maharashtra', in C.J. Dewey and A.G. Hopkins (eds.), *The Imperial Impact: Studies in the Economic History of Africa and India,* London, 1978, pp. 97–114

'Trends in Agricultural Performance in an Indian Province: The Bombay Presidency 1900–1920', in K.N. Chaudhuri and C.J. Dewey (eds.), *Economy and Society: Essays in Indian Economic and Social History.* Delhi, 1979, pp. 113–40

Peasants and Imperial Rule: Agriculture and Agrarian Society in the Bombay Presidency, 1850–1935. Cambridge, 1985

Chartier, R. *Cultural History: Between Practices and Representation.* Cambridge, 1988

Chatterji, B. 'Business and Politics in the 1930s: Lancashire and the Making of the Indo-British Trade Agreement', *MAS,* XV, 3 (1981), Special Issue, *Power, Profit and Politics: Essays on Imperialism, Nationalism and Change in the Twentieth Century,* edited by C.J. Baker, G. Johnson and A. Seal, pp. 527–73

'The Political Economy of "Discriminating Protection": The Case of Textiles in the 1920s', *IESHR,* XX, 3 (1983), 239–75

Chaudhuri, B.B. 'The Land Market in Eastern India (1793–1940)', in two parts, *IESHR,* XII, 1 (1975), 1–42 and XII, 1 (1975), 133–68

'Agrarian Relations: Eastern India', in D. Kumar (ed.), *The Cambridge Economic History of India,* vol. II, *c.* 1757–*c.* 1970. Cambridge, 1982

Chaudhuri, K.N. 'The Structure of the Indian Textile Industry in the Seventeenth and Eighteenth Centuries', *IESHR,* XI, 2–3 (1974), 127–82

Chaudhuri, K.N. and C.J. Dewey (eds.), *Economy and Society: Essays in Indian Economic and Social History.* Delhi, 1979

Chesneaux, J. *The Chinese Labour Movement, 1919–1927.* Stanford, 1974

Choksey, R.D. *Economic Life in the Bombay Karnataka 1818–1939.* Bombay, 1963

Economic Life in the Bombay Konkan. Bombay, 1960

Cholia, R.P. *Dock Labourers in Bombay.* Bombay, 1941

Coats, T. 'Account of the Present State of the Township of Lony', *Transactions of the Literary Society of Bombay,* III (1823), 183–250

Cohn, B.S. 'From Indian Status to British Contract', *Journal of Economic History,* XXI, 4 (1961), 613–28

Conlon, F.F. *A Caste in a Changing World: The Chitrapur Saraswat Brahmans, 1700–1935.* Berkeley and Los Angeles, 1977

'Industrialization and the Housing Problem in Bombay, 1850–1940', in K. Ballhatchet and D. Taylor (eds.), *Changing South Asia: Economy and Society,* School of Oriental and African Studies, London, 1984, pp. 153–68

'Caste, Community and Colonialism: Elements of Population Recruitment and Urban Rule in British Bombay, 1665–1830', *Journal of Urban History,* XI, 2 (1985), 181–208

Connell, J., B. Dasgupta, R. Laishley and M. Lipton. *Migration from Rural Areas: The Evidence from Village Studies*. Delhi, 1979

Coupland, R. *The Indian Problem*, 3 vols. London, 1944

Dandekar, H.C. *Men to Bombay, Women at Home: Urban Influence on Sugao Village, Deccan Maharashtra, India, 1942–1982*. Ann Arbor, Michigan, 1986

Dantwalla, M.L. *A Hundred Years of Indian Cotton*. Bombay, 1948

Darukhanawalla, H.D. *Parsi Lustre on Indian Soil*. Bombay, 1939

Das, R.K. *History of Indian Labour Legislation*. Calcutta, 1941

Das Gupta, A. *Indian Merchants and the Decline of Surat, c. 1700–1750*. Weisbaden, 1979

Das Gupta, R. 'Factory Labour in Eastern India: Sources of Supply 1855–1946: Some Preliminary Findings', *IESHR*, XIII, 3 (1976), 277–328

David, M.D. *History of Bombay, 1661–1708*. Bombay, 1973

Davis, J. 'Jennings' Buildings and the Royal Borough: The Construction of an Underclass in Mid-Victorian England', in D. Feldman and G. Stedman Jones (eds.), *Metropolis London: Histories and Representations since 1800*. London, 1989

Davis, K. *The Population of India and Pakistan*. Princeton, 1951

Desai, A.R. and S.D. Pillai. *A Profile of an Indian Slum*. Bombay, 1972

Desai, A.V. 'The Origins of Parsi Enterprise', *IESHR*, V, 4 (1968), 307–17

  'Revenue Administration and Agricultural Statistics in Bombay Presidency', *IESHR*, XV, 2 (1978), 173–86

Desai, D. *Maritime Labour in India*. Bombay, 1940

Desai, M. *A Righteous Struggle*. Ahmedabad, 1951

Desai, M.B. *The Rural Economy of Gujarat*. Oxford, 1948

Dewey, C. 'The End of the Imperialism of Free Trade: The Eclipse of the Lancashire Lobby and the Concession of Fiscal Autonomy to India', in C. Dewey and A.G. Hopkins (eds.), *The Imperial Impact: Studies in the Economic History of Africa and India*. London, 1978, pp. 35–68

  '*Patwari and Chaukidar*. Subordinate Officials and the Reliability of India's Agricultural Statistics', in C. Dewey and A.G. Hopkins (eds.), *The Imperial Impact: Studies in the Economic History of Africa and India*. London, 1978, pp. 280–315

Dewey, C.J. and A.G. Hopkins (eds.). *The Imperial Impact: Studies in the Economic History of Africa and Asia*. London, 1978

Divekar, V. 'Pune', in J.S. Grewal and I. Banga (eds.), *Indian Urban History* (n.d., n.p.), pp. 91–106

Dobbin, C. 'Competing Elites in Bombay City Politics in the Mid-Nineteenth Century (1852–83)', in E.R. Leach and S.N. Mukherjee (eds.), *Elites in South Asia*. Cambridge, 1970, pp. 79–94

  'The Parsi Panchayat in Bombay City in the Nineteenth Century', *MAS*, IV, 2 (1970), 149–64

  Urban Leadership in Western India: Politics and Communities in Bombay City, 1840–85. London, 1972

Dongerkery, S.R. *A History of the University of Bombay, 1857–1957*. Bombay, 1957

Drummond, I.M. *British Economic Policy and the Empire, 1919–1939*. London, 1972

Dwarkadas, Kanji, *Forty Five Years with Labour*. Bombay, 1962

Edwardes, S.M. *A Monograph upon the Silk Fabrics of the Bombay Presidency*. Bombay, 1900

  The Rise of Bombay – A Retrospect. Bombay, 1902

By-Ways of Bombay. Bombay, 1912

The Bombay City Police: A Historical Sketch, 1672–1916. Bombay, 1923

Eka Rannaraginichi Hakikat, as told by Parvatibai Bhor to Padmakar Chitale. Bombay, 1977

Enthoven, R.E. *The Cotton Fabrics of the Bombay Presidency.* Bombay, 1897

The Tribes and Castes of Bombay, 3 vols., Bombay, 1920–2

Farnie, D.A. *East and West of Suez.* Oxford, 1969

The English Cotton Industry and the World Market, 1815–96. Oxford, 1979

Fawcett, C.G.H. *A Monograph on Dyes and Dyeing in the Bombay Presidency.* Bombay, 1896

Feuerwerker, A. 'Handicraft and Manufactured Cotton Textiles in China', *Journal of Economic History,* XXX, 2 (1970), 338–78

Fraser, L. *India Under Curzon and After.* London, 1911

Fukuzawa, H. 'Land and Peasants in the Eighteenth Century Maratha Kingdom', *HJE,* VI, 2 (1965), 32–61

'Rural Servants in the Eighteenth Century Maharashtrian Village – Demiurgic or Jajmani System', *HJE,* XII, 2 (1972), 14–40

'Agrarian Relations and Land Revenue: The Medieval Deccan and Maharashtra', in T. Raychaudhuri and I. Habib (eds.), *The Cambridge Economic History of India,* vol. 1, *c. 1250–1700,* Cambridge, 1982, pp. 249–60

Furber, H. *Bombay Presidency in the Mid Eighteenth Century.* London, 1965

Gadgil, D.R. *Regulation of Wages and other Problems of Industrial Labour in India.* Gokhale Institute of Politics and Economics, publication no. 9. Poona, 1954

Gandhi, M.K. *The Collected Works of Mahatma Gandhi,* 90 vols. Delhi, 1958–84

Geary, R. *European Labour Protest, 1848–1918.* Cambridge, 1981

Genovese, E.F. and E.D. 'The Political Crisis of Social History', *Journal of Social History,* X, 2 (1976), 205–21

Gillion, K. *Ahmedabad: A Study of Indian Urban History.* Berkeley and Los Angeles, 1968

Gokhale, B.G. 'Ahmedabad in the XVIIth Century', *Journal of the Economic and Social History of the Orient,* XII, 2 (1969), 187–97

Surat in the Seventeenth Century: A Study in Urban History of Pre-Modern India. London, 1978

'Some Urban Commercial Centres of the Western Deccan in the XVIIth Century', in N.K. Wagle (ed.), *Images of Maharashtra: A Regional Profile of India.* London, 1980, pp. 57–67

Gokhale, R.G. *The Bombay Cotton Mill Worker.* Bombay, 1957

Gopal, S. *Commerce and Crafts in Gujarat in the Seventeenth Century: A Study in the Impact of European Expansion in a Pre-Capitalist Economy.* Delhi, 1975

Gordon, A.D. 'Businessmen and Politics in a Developing Colonial Economy: Bombay City, 1918–1933', in C.J. Dewey and A.G. Hopkins (eds.), *The Imperial Impact: Studies in the Economic History of Africa and India.* London, 1978, pp. 194–215

Businessmen and Politics: Rising Nationalism and a Modernising Economy 1918–1933. Delhi, 1979

Gordon, D.M. *Theories of Poverty and Underemployment: Orthodox, Radical and Dual Labour Market Perspectives.* Lexington, Mass., 1972

Gordon, S. 'The Slow Conquest: Administrative Integration of Malwa into the Maratha Empire, 1720–1760', *MAS*, XI, 1 (1977), 1–40
'Bhils and the Idea of a Criminal Tribe in Nineteenth Century India' in A. Yang (ed.), *Crime and Criminality in British India*. Tucson, Arizona, 1985, pp. 128–39
Gould, H.A. 'The Adaptive Function of Caste in Contemporary Indian Society', *Asian Survey*, III (1963), 427–38
'Lucknow Rikshawallas: The Social Organisation of an Occupational Category', *International Journal of Comparative Sociology*, VI, 1 (March 1965), 24–47
Gray, R. *The Aristocracy of Labour in Nineteenth Century Britain, c. 1850–1900*. London, 1981
Greenberg, M. *British Trade and the Opening of China, 1800–1842*. Cambridge, 1951
Griffiths, Sir P. *The History of the Indian Tea Industry*. London, 1967
Guha, A. 'Parsi Seths as Entrepreneurs, 1750–1850', *Economic and Political Weekly*, V, 35 (29 August 1970) *Review of Management*, pp. M-105 to M-115
'The Comprador Role of Parsi Seths, 1750–1830', *Economic and Political Weekly*, V, 48 (28 November 1970)
'More About the Parsi Seths: Their Roots, Entrepreneurship and Comprador Role, 1650–1918', *Economic and Political Weekly*, XIX, 3, 21 Jan. 1984, 117–32
Guha, Ramchandra, 'Forestry and Social Protest in British Kumaun, c. 1893–1921', in R. Guha (ed.), *Subaltern Studies* (Delhi, 1985), vol. IV, pp. 54–100
Guha, R. (ed.). *Subaltern Studies*, 6 vols. Delhi, 1982–9
Guha, S. *The Agrarian Economy of the Deccan, 1818–1941*. Delhi, 1986
Habib, I. 'The Potentialities of Capitalist Development in Mughal India', *Journal of Economic History*, XXXIX, 1 (1969), 32–78
Hamilton, C.J. *The Trade Relations Between England and India, 1600–1896*. Calcutta, 1919
Hardiman, D. 'From Custom to Crime: The Politics of Drinking in Colonial South Gujarat', in R. Guha (ed.), *Subaltern Studies* vol. IV, Delhi, 1985 pp. 165–228
Harlow, V. *The Founding of the Second British Empire, 1763–93*, vol. II, *New Continents and Changing Values* London, 1964
Harnetty, P. 'The Indian Cotton Duties Controversy, 1894–96', *English Historical Review*, LXXVII (1962), 684–702
'The Imperialism of Free Trade: Lancashire and the Indian Cotton Duties, 1859–1862' *EcHR*, 2nd series, XVIII, 2 (1965), 333–49
'Cotton Exports and Indian Agriculture, 1861–70', *EcHR*, 2nd Series, XXIV, 3 (1971), 414–29
Imperialism and Free Trade: Lancashire and India in the Mid-Nineteenth Century. Vancouver, 1972
Harris, F. *Jamsetji Nusserwanji Tata: A Chronicle of His Life*. London, 1925, 2nd edn, Bombay, 1958
Harris, N., *Economic Development, Cities and Planning: The Case of Bombay*. Bombay, 1978
Harriss, J. 'The Working Poor and the Labour Aristocracy in a South Indian City: A Descriptive and Analytical Account', *MAS*, XX, 2 (1986), 231–83
Hasan, M. '"Congress Muslims" and Indian Nationalism: Dilemma and Decline, 1928–1934' *South Asia*, VIII, 1 and 2 (1985), 102–20
Heston, A. 'Official Yields per Acre in India 1886–1947', *IESHR*, X, 4 (1973), 303–32

'A Further Critique of Historical Yields per Acre in India', *IESHR* XV, 2 (1978), 187–210

'National Income', in D. Kumar (ed.), *The Cambridge Economic History of India*, vol. II, *c. 1757–c. 1970*. Cambridge, 1982, pp. 376–462

Hobsbawm, E.J. *Labouring Men: Studies in the History of Labour*. London, 1964

'From Social History to the History of Society', in M.W. Flinn and T.C. Smout (eds.), *Essays in Social History*. Oxford, 1974, pp. 1–22

'Artisan or Labour Aristocrat?' *EcHR*, 2nd series, XXXVII, 3 (1984), 355–72

Hoey, W. *A Monograph on Trade and Manufactures in Northern India*. Lucknow, 1880

Hollister, J.N. *The Shia of India*. London, 1953

Holmström, M. *Industry and Inequality: Towards a Social Anthropology of Indian Labour*. Cambridge, 1984

Hunter, Sir W.W. *Bombay, 1885 to 1890: A Study In Indian Administration*. London, n.d. (1892?)

Hurd, J.M. 'Railways', in D. Kumar (ed.), *The Cambridge Economic History of India*, 2 vols., vol. II, *c. 1757–c. 1970*, Cambridge, 1982, pp.737–61

Jackson, S. *The Sassoons*. London, 1968

Jagalpure, L.B. and K.D. Kale. *Sarola Kasar: Study of a Deccan Village in the Famine Zone*. Amednagar, 1938

Jain, L.C. *Indigenous Banking in India*. London, 1929

James, R.C. 'Labour Mobility, Unemployment and Political Change: An Indian Case', *Journal of Political Economy*, LXVII, 6 (December 1959), 545–57

'The Casual Labour Problem in Indian Manufacturing', *The Quarterly Journal of Economics*, LXXIV, 1 (February 1960), 100–16

Jevons, H.S. *Money, Banking and Exchange in India*. Simla, 1922

Johnson, G. 'Chitpavan Brahmins and Politics in Western India in the Late Nineteenth and Twentieth Centuries', in E.R. Leach and S.N. Mukherjee (eds.), *Elites in South Asia*. Cambridge, 1970, pp. 95–118

Provincial Politics and Indian Nationalism: Bombay and the Indian National Congress, 1880–1915. Cambridge, 1973

Joshi, C. 'Kanpur Textile Labour: Some Structural Features of Formative Years', *Economic and Political Weekly*, XVI, 44–6, Special Number (November 1981), 1823–38

'Bonds of Community, Ties of Religion: Kanpur Textile Workers in the Early Twentieth Century' *IESHR*, XXII, 3 (1985), 251–80

Joshi, H. and V. Joshi. *Surplus Labour and the City: A Study of Bombay*. Delhi, 1976

Joshi, P.C. 'The Decline of Indigenous Handicrafts in Uttar Pradesh', *IESHR*, I, 1 (1963), 24–35

Joyce, P. *Work, Society and Politics: The Culture of the Factory in Late Victorian England*. London, 1980

Judt, T. 'A Clown in Regal Purple: Social History and the Historians', *History Workshop Journal*, VII (1979), 66–94

Kang Chao. 'The Growth of a Modern Textile Industry and the Competition with Handicrafts', in D.H. Perkin (ed.), *China's Modern Economy in Historical Perspective*. Stanford, 1975, pp. 167–201

Kannangara, A.P. 'Indian Millowners and Indian Nationalism before 1914', *Past and Present*, XL (1968), 147–74

Kaplan, S. (ed.), *Understanding Popular Culture: Europe from the Middle Ages to the Nineteenth Century*. Berlin and New York, 1984

Kaplan, S. and C. Koepp (eds.), *Work in France: Representations, Meaning, Organization and Practice*. Ithaca, 1986

Karaka, D.F. *A History of the Parsis, Including Their Manners, Customs, Religion and Present Position*. 2 vols. London, 1884

Karnik, V.B. *Indian Trade Unions: A Survey*. Bombay, 1966
Strikes in India. Bombay, 1967
N.M. Joshi. – Servant of India. Bombay, 1972

Karve, I. *Hindu Society – An Interpretation*. Poona, 1961

Katzellenbogen, C. 'Labour Recruitment in Central Africa: The Case of Katanga', in C. Dewey and A.G. Hopkins (eds.), *The Imperial Impact: Studies in the Economic History of Africa and Asia*. London, 1978, pp. 270–9

Keatinge, G. *Agricultural Progress in Western India*. London, 1921

Keer, D. *Dr Ambedkar: Life and Mission*. Bombay, 1954; 2nd edn, 1962

Kelman, J.H. *Labour in India: A Study of Conditions of Indian Women in Modern Industry*. London, 1923

Kennedy, R.E. 'The Protestant Ethic and Parsis', *American Journal of Sociology*, LXVIII, 1 (1962), 11–20

Kirk, R. and C.P. Simmons, 'Engineering and the First World War: A Case Study of the Lancashire Cotton Spinning Machine Industry', *World Development*, IX, 8 (1981), 773–91
'Lancashire and the Equipping of the Indian Cotton Mills: A Study of Textile Machinery Supply, 1854–1939', in K. Ballhatchet and D. Taylor (eds.), *Changing South Asia: Economy and Society*, SOAS. London, 1984, pp. 169–81

Kiyokawa, Y. 'Technical Adaptations and Managerial Resources in India: A Study of the Experience of the Cotton Textile Industry from a Comparative Standpoint', *The Developing Economies*, XXI, 2 (1983), 97–133

Klein, I. 'English Free Traders and Indian Tariffs, 1874–96', *MAS*, V, 3 (1971), 251–71
'Urban Development and Death: Bombay City, 1870–1914', *MAS*, XX, 4 (1986), 725–54
'Plague, Policy and Popular Unrest in British India', *MAS*, XXII, 4 (1988), 723–55

Kling, B. 'The Origin of the Managing Agency System', *JAS*, XXVI, 1 (1966), 37–48

Kooiman, D. 'Jobbers and the Emergence of Trade Unions in Bombay City', *International Review of Social History*, XXII, 3 (1977), 313–28
'Bombay Communists and the 1924 Textile Strike', *Economic and Political Weekly, Review of Political Economy*, XV, 29 (19 July 1980), 1223–36
'Bombay from Fishing Village to Colonial Port City (1661–1947)', in R. Ross and G. Telkamp (eds.), *Colonial Cities: Essays on Urbanism in a Colonial Context*. Dordrecht, 1985, pp. 207–30.

Kosambi, M. 'Commerce, Conquest and the Colonial City: The Role of Locational Factors and the Rise of Bombay', *Economic and Political Weekly*, XX, 1 (5 January, 1985), 32–7
Bombay in Transition: The Growth and Ecology of a Colonial City, 1880–1980. Stockholm, 1986

Kotovsky, G.G. 'Agrarian Relations in Maharashtra in Late 19th and Early 20th Centuries', in I.M. Reisner and N.M. Goldberg (eds.), *Tilak and the Struggle for Indian Freedom*, New Delhi, 1966, pp. 99–119

Krishnamurty, J. 'Secular Changes in Occupational Structure of the Indian Union, 1901–61', *IESHR*, II, 1 (January 1965), 42–51

'The Growth of Agricultural Labour in India – A Note', *IESHR*, IX, 3 (1973), 327–32

'The Distribution of the Indian Working Force 1901–1951', in K.N. Chaudhuri and C.J. Dewey (eds.), *Economy and Society: Essays in Indian Economic and Social History*. Delhi, 1979, pp. 258–76

'The Occupational Structure', in D. Kumar (ed.), *The Cambridge Economic History of India*, vol. II, *c. 1757–c. 1970*, Cambridge, 1982, pp. 533–50

'De-industrialization in Gangetic Bihar during the Nineteenth Century: Another Look at the Evidence', *IESHR*, XXII, 4 (1985), 399–416

Krishnamurty, S. 'Agriculture in the Bombay Deccan, 1880–1922: Trends in Area and Output', in *Oxford University Papers on India*, edited by N.J. Allen, R.F. Gombrich, T. Raychaudhuri, and G. Rizvi, vol. I, part 2, pp. 126–51. Delhi, 1987

'Real Wages of Agricultural Labourers in the Bombay Deccan, 1874–1922', *IESHR*, XXIV, 1 (1987), 81–98

Kulke, E. *The Parsees in India: A Minority as Agent of Social Change*. Delhi, 1978

Kumar, D. *Land and Caste in South India*, Cambridge, 1969

Kumar, D. (ed.). *The Cambridge Economic History of India*, vol. II, *c. 1757–c. 1970*. Cambridge, 1982

Kumar, K. (ed.). *Congress and Classess: Nationalism, Workers and Peasants*. New Delhi, 1988

Kumar, Radha. 'Family and Factory: Women in the Bombay Cotton Textile Industry, 1919–1939', *IESHR*, XX, 1 (1983), 81–110

Kumar, R. *Western India in the Nineteenth Century: A Study in the Social History of Maharashtra*. London, 1968

'The Bombay Textile Strike, 1919', *IESHR*, VIII, 1 (1971), 1–29

'From Swaraj to Purna Swaraj: Nationalist Politics in the City of Bombay, 1920–32', in D.A. Low (ed.), *Congress and the Raj: Facets of the Indian Struggle*. London, 1977, pp. 77–107

Lakshman, P.P. *Congress and the Labour Movement in India*. Congress Economic and Political Studies, no.3, Economic and Political Research Department, All-India Congress Committee, Allahabad, 1947

Leach, E.R. and S.N. Mukherjee (eds.). *Elites in South Asia*. Cambridge, 1970

Lee, C.H. 'The Effects of the Depression on Primary Producing Countries', *Journal of Contemporary History*, IV, 4 (1969), 139–55

Leiten, G.K. *Colonialism, Class and Nation: The Confrontation in Bombay Around 1930*. Calcutta, 1984

Lele, J. *Elite Pluralism and Class Rule: Political Development in Maharashtra*. Toronto, 1981

Lewandowski, S. 'Changing Form and Function in the Ceremonial and the Colonial Port City in India: An Historical Analysis of Madurai and Madras', in K.N. Chaudhuri and C.J. Dewey (eds.), *Economy and Society: Essays in Indian Economic and Social History*. Delhi, 1979, pp. 299–329

Lokanathan, P.S. *Industrial Organization in India*. London, 1935

Lokhandawalla, S.T. 'Islamic Law and Ismaili Communities (Khojas and Bohras)', *IESHR*, IV, 2 (1967), 155–76

Low, D.A. (ed.). *Congress and the Raj: Facets of the Indian Struggle*. London, 1977

Lynch, O.M. 'Rural Cities in India: Continuities and Discontinuities', in P. Mason (ed.), *India and Ceylon: Unity and Diversity*, Oxford, 1967, pp. 142–58

McAlpin, M.B. 'Railroads, Cultivation Patterns and Food Availability: India 1860–1900', *IESHR*, XII, 1 (1975), 43–60

'The Effects of Expansion of Markets on Rural Income Distribution in Nineteenth Century India', *Explorations in Economic History*, XII (1975), 289–302

'Death, Famine and Risk: The Changing Impact of Crop Failures in Western India, 1870–1920', *Journal of Economic History*, XXIX, 1 (1979), 143–57

'The Impact of Trade on Agricultural Development: Bombay Presidency 1855–1920', *Explorations in Economic History*, XVII (1980), 26–47

Subject to Famine: Food Crises and Economic Change in Western India, 1860–1920. Princeton, 1983

Mackay, A. *Western India: Reports Addressed to the Chambers of Commerce of Manchester, Liverpool, Blackburn and Glasgow.* London, 1853

McLane, J.R. *Indian Nationalism and the Early Congress.* Princeton, 1977

Maclean, J.M. *A Guide to Bombay.* Bombay, 1875

Maier, C.S. *In Search of Stability: Explorations in Historical Political Economy.* Cambridge, 1987

Malabari, P.B.M. *Bombay in the Making.* London, 1910

Mandlik, N.V. *Writings and Speeches of the Late Honourable Rao Saheb Vishvanath Narayan Mandilik.* Bombay, 1896

Mann, H.H. *Land and Labour in a Deccan Village, no. 1.* London, 1917

The Social Framework of Agriculture: India, Middle East, England, ed. D. Thorner. Bombay, 1967

Mann, H.H. and N.V. Kanitkar. *Land and Labour in a Deccan Village: Study No. 2.* Bombay, 1921

Manshardt, C. (ed.). *Bombay Today and Tomorrow.* Bombay, 1930

Markovits, C. *Indian Business and Nationalist Politics, 1931–39: The Indigenous Capitalist Class and the Rise of the Congress Party.* Cambridge, 1985

Marks, S. and R. Rathbone (eds.). *Industrialization and Social Conflict in South Africa: African Class Formation, Culture and Consciousness, 1870–1930.* London, 1982

Marshall, P.J. *Problems of Empire: Britain and India, 1757–1813.* London, 1968

Martin, J.R. *A Monograph on Tanning and Working in Leather in the Bombay Presidency.* Bombay, 1903

Masani, R.P. *Evolution of Local Self-Government in Bombay.* Oxford, 1929

Dadabhai Naoroji: The Grand Old Man of India. London, 1939

N.M. Wadia and His Foundation. Bombay, 1961

Mason, P. (ed.). *India and Ceylon: Unity and Diversity.* Oxford, 1967

Masselos, J.C. 'Some Aspects of Bombay City Politics in 1919', in R. Kumar (ed.), *Essays on Gandhian Politics: The Rowlatt Satyagraha.* Oxford, 1971, pp. 145–88

'The Khojas of Bombay: The Defining of Formal Membership Criteria During the Nineteenth Century', in I. Ahmad (eds.), *Caste and Social Stratification Among the Muslims.* Delhi, 1973, pp. 1–20

Toward Nationalism: Group Affiliations and the Politics of Public Associations in Nineteenth Century Western India. Bombay, 1974

'Power in the Bombay "Moholla", 1904–15: An Initial Exploration into the World of the Indian Urban Muslim', *South Asia*, VI (1976), 75–95

'Social Segregation and Crowd Cohesion: Reflections around some Preliminary Data from 19th Century Bombay City', *Contributions to Indian Sociology*, N.S., XIII, 2 (1979), 145–67

'Jobs and Jobbery: The Sweeper in Bombay under the Raj', *IESHR*, XIX, 2 (1982), 101–39

'Change and Custom in the Format of the Bombay Mohurram During the Nineteenth and Twentieth Centuries', *South Asia*, N.S., V, 2 (1982), 47–67

'Audiences, Actors and Congress Dramas: Crowd Events in Bombay City in 1930', in J. Masselos (ed.) *Struggling and Ruling: The Indian National Congress, 1885–1985*. Delhi, 1987, pp. 71–86

Mazumdar, D. 'Labour Supply in Early Industrialization: The Case of the Bombay Textile Industry', *EcHR*, second series, XXVI, 3 (1973), 477–96

Mehta, M.J. *The Ahmedabad Cotton Textile Industry: Genesis and Growth*. Ahmedabad, 1982

Mehta, S.D. *The Indian Cotton Textile Industry: An Economic Analysis*. Bombay, 1953

The Cotton Mills of India, 1854–1954. Bombay, 1954

'Professor Morris on Textile Labour Supply', *Indian Economic Journal*, I, 3 (January 1954), 333–40

Melling, J. 'Non-Commissioned Officers: British Employers and their Supervisory Workers, 1880–1920', *Social History*, V, 2 (1980), 183–221

Merkle, J.A. *Management and Ideology: The Legacy of the International Scientific Management Movement*. Berkeley and Los Angeles, 1980

Minault, G. *The Khilafat Movement: Religious Symbolism and Political Mobilization in India*. Delhi, 1982

Mishra, S.C. 'Commercialization, Peasant Differentiation and Merchant Capital in Late Nineteenth Century Bombay and Punjab', *Journal of Peasant Studies*, X, 1 (1982), 3–51

'Agricultural Trends in the Bombay Presidency, 1900–1920: The Illusion of Growth', *MAS*, XIX, 4 (1985), 733–59

Misra, B. 'Factory Labour During the Early Years of Industrialization: An Appraisal in the Light of the Indian Factory Labour Commission', *IESHR*, XII, 3 (1975), 203–28

Mody, J.R.P. *The First Parsee Baronet*. Bombay, 1966

Mody, R.R. *Fazendari Tenures and Inami Lands in Bombay City*. Bombay, 1934

Morris, M.D. 'Some Comments on the Supply of Labour to the Bombay Cotton Textile Industry, 1854–1951', *Indian Economic Journal*, I, 2 (October 1953), 138–52

'Caste and the Evolution of the Industrial Workforce in India', *Proceedings of the American Philosophical Society*, CIV, 2 (April 1960), 124–33

'The Labour Market in India', in W.E. Moore and A.S. Feldman (eds.), *Labour Commitment and Social Change in Developing Areas*. New York, 1960, pp. 173–200

'The Recruitment of an Industrial Labour Force in India with British and American Comparisons', *Comparative Studies in Society and History*, II, 3 (1960), 305–28

'The Effects of Industrialization on "Race" Relations in India', in G. Hunter (ed.), *Industrialization and Race Relations: A Symposium*. London, 1965, pp. 141–60

The Emergence of an Industrial Labour Force in India: A Study of the Bombay Cotton Mills, 1854–1947. Berkeley and Los Angeles, 1965

'Private Industrial Investment in the Indian Sub-Continent 1900–1939: Some Methodological Considerations', *MAS*, VIII, 4 (1974), 535–55

'The Growth of Large-Scale Industry to 1947', in Dharma Kumar (ed.), *The Cambridge Economic History of India*, vol. II, c. *1757–1970*, Cambridge, 1983, pp. 553–676

Mowat, J.L. *Seafarers' Conditions in India and Pakistan*. ILO, Geneva, 1949

Mukherjee, A. 'The Indian Capitalist Class and Foreign Capital, 1927–47', *Studies in History*, I, 1 (1979), 105–48

'Indian Capitalist Class and Congress on National Planning and Public Sector, 1930–47', in K.N. Panikkar (ed.), *National and Left Movements in India*. Delhi, 1980, pp. 45–79

Mukherjee, R.K. *The Indian Working Class*. Bombay, 1945

Mukherjee, S.N. 'Daladali in Calcutta in the Nineteenth Century', *MAS*, IX, 1 (1975), 59–80

Mukherji, K. 'Trend in Real Wages in Cotton Textile Mills in Bombay City and Island, from 1900 to 1951', *Artha Vijnana*, I, 1 (1959), 82–96

'Trend in Textile Mill Wages in Western India: 1900 to 1951', *Artha Vijnana*, IV, 2 (1962), 156–66

Murphey, Rhoads. 'Traditionalism and Colonialism: Changing Urban Roles in Asia', *JAS*, XXIX, 1 (1969), 67–84

Murphy, E.D. *Unions in Conflict: A Comparative Study of Four South Indian Textile Centres, 1918–1939*. Delhi, 1981

Myers, C.A. *Labour Problems in the Industrialization of India*. Cambridge, Mass., 1958

Myers, R.H. 'Cotton Textile Handicraft and the Development of the Cotton Textile Industry in Modern China', *EcHR*, 2nd series, XVIII, 3 (1965), 614–32

Newman, R. 'Social Factors in the Recruitment of the Bombay Millhands', in K.N. Chaudhuri and C.J. Dewey (eds.), *Economy and Society: Essays in Indian Economic and Social History*. Delhi, 1979, pp. 277–95

Workers and Unions in Bombay, 1918–29: A Study of Organisation in the Cotton Mills. Canberra, 1981

'India and the Anglo-Chinese Opium Agreements, 1907–1914', *MAS*, XXIII, 3 (1989), 525–60

Nightingale, P. *Trade and Empire in Western India, 1784–1806*. Cambridge, 1970

Nissim, J. *Wire and Tinsel in the Bombay Presidency*. Bombay, 1909

O'Hanlon, R. *Caste, Conflict and Ideology: Mahatma Jotirao Phule and Low Caste Protest in Nineteenth Century Maharashtra*. Cambridge, 1985

'Acts of Appropriation: Non-Brahmin Radicals and the Congress in Early Twentieth Century Maharashtra', in M. Shepperdson and C. Simmons (eds.), *The Indian National Congress and the Political Economy of India*, Aldershot, 1988, pp. 102–46

Omvedt, G. *Cultural Revolt in a Colonial Society: The Non-Brahman Movement in Western India, 1873 to 1930*. Bombay, 1976

'Migration in Colonial India: The Articulation of Feudalism and Capitalism by the Colonial State', *Journal of Peasant Studies*, VII, 2 (1980), 185–212

Orr, J.P. *Density of Population in Bombay: Lecture Delivered to the Bombay Cooperative Housing Association*. Bombay, 1914

Otsuka, K., G. Ranis and G. Saxonhouse, *Comparative Technology – Choice in Development: The Indian and Japanese Cotton Textile Industries*, London, 1988

Ovington, J. *A Voyage to the East*, ed. by H.G. Rawlinson. London, 1928

Pandey, G. *The Ascendancy of the Congress in Uttar Pradesh, 1926–1934: A Study in Imperfect Mobilization*. Delhi, 1978

'Economic Dislocation in Nineteenth-Century Eastern Uttar Pradesh: Some Implications of the Decline of Artisanal Industry in Colonial India', in P. Robb (ed.), *Rural South Asia: Linkages, Change and Development*. London, 1983, pp. 89–129

'Rallying Round the Cow: Sectarian Strife in the Bhojpuri Region, c. 1888–1917', in R. Guha (ed.). *Subaltern Studies*, vol. II. Delhi, 1983, pp. 60–129

The Construction of Communalism in Colonial North India, Delhi, 1992

Pandey, S.M. *As Labour Organises: A Study of Unionism in the Kanpur Cotton Textile Industry*. New Delhi, 1970

Pandit, D. 'The Myths around Subdivision and Fragmentation of Holdings: A Few Case Histories', *IESHR*, VI, 2 (June 1969), 151–63

Panikkar, K.N. (ed.). *National and Left Movements in India*. Delhi, 1980

Patel, K. *Rural Labour in Industrial Bombay*. Bombay, 1963

Patel, S. *The Making of Industrial Relations: The Ahmedabad Textile Industry, 1918–1939*. Delhi, 1987

Patel, S.J. *Agricultural Labourers in Modern India and Pakistan*. Bombay, 1952

Patterson, M.L.P. 'Changing Patterns of Occupation among Chitpavan Brahmins', *IESHR*, VII, 3 (1970), 375–96

Pearse, A.S. *The Cotton Industry of Japan and China: Being the Report of the Journey to Japan and China, February–April 1929*. Manchester, 1929

The Cotton Industry of India, Being the Report of the Journey to India. Manchester, 1930

Pearson, M.N. *Merchants and Rulers in Gujarat: The Response to the Portuguese in the Sixteenth Century*. Berkeley and Los Angeles, 1976

Perlin, E. 'Eyes Without Sight: Education and Millworkers in South India, 1939–1976', *IESHR*, XVIII, 3 and 4 (1981), 263–86

Perlin, F. 'Proto-Industrialization and Pre-Colonial South Asia', *Past and Present*, XCVII, (1983), 30–95

Perlman, J. *The Myth of Marginality: Urban Politics and Poverty in Rio de Janeiro*. Berkeley, 1977

Pillai, P.P. *Economic Conditions in India*. London, 1928

Playne, S., assisted by J.W. Bond, ed. A. Wright, *The Bombay Presidency, the United Provinces, the Punjab, etc.: Their History, People, Commerce and Natural Resources*. London, 1917–20

Pletsch, Carl E. 'The Three Worlds, or the Division of Social Scientific Labour, circa 1950–1975', *Comparative Studies in Society and History*, XXIII, 4 (1981), 519–38

Pocock, D.F. "Sociologies: Urban and Rural', *Contributions to Indian Sociology*, 4 (1960), 63–81

Prakash, G. *Bonded Histories: Genealogies of Labour Servitude in Colonial India*. Cambridge, 1990

Pryde, A.W. 'The Work of the Labour Officer', in C. Manshardt (ed.), *Some Social Services of the Government of Bombay*. Bombay, 1937

Punekar, S.D. *Trade Unionism in India*. Bombay, 1948

Rabitoy, N. 'Administrative Modernization and the Bhats of British Gujarat, 1800–1820', *IESHR*, IX, 1 (1974), 46–73

'System vs. Expediency: the Reality of Land Revenue Administration in Bombay Presidency, 1812–1820', *MAS*, IX, 4 (1975), 529–46

Raghunathji, K. *The Hindu Temples of Bombay*. Bombay, 1900
Bombay Beggars and Criers (n.d., n.p.)
Ramaswamy, E.A. *The Worker and His Union: A Study in South India*. New Delhi, 1977
Ray, R.K. 'The Crisis of Bengal Agriculture, 1870–1927 – The Dynamics of Immobility', *IESHR*, X, 3 (1973), 244–79
Industrialization in India: Growth and Conflict in the Private Corporate Sector, 1914–47. Delhi, 1979
'Pedhis and Mills: The Historical Integration of the Formal and Informal Sectors in the Economy of Ahmedabad', *IESHR*, XIX, 3 and 4 (1982), 387–96
'The Bazaar: Changing Structural Characteristics in the Indigenous Section of the Indian Economy Before and After the Great Depression', *IESHR*, XXV, 3 (1988), 263–318
Redford, A. and B.W. Clapp. *Manchester Merchants and Foreign Trade*, vol. II, *1850–1939*. Manchester, 1956
Revri, C. *The Indian Trade Union Movement*. New Delhi, 1972
Rowe, W.D. 'Caste, Kinship and Association in Urban India', in A. Southall (ed.), *Urban Anthropology: Cross Cultural Studies of Urbanization*. New York, 1973, pp. 211–49
Rungta, R.S. *The Rise of Business Corporations in India 1851–1900*. Cambridge, 1970
Rutnagur, M.C. *The Indian Textile Journal Directory of Indian Manufactories, 1894*. Bombay, 1894
Rutnagur, S.M. (ed.). *Bombay Industries: The Cotton Mills – A Review of the Progress of the Textile Industry in Bombay from 1850 to 1926 and the Present Constitution, Management and Financial Position of Spinning and Weaving Factories*. Bombay, 1927
Sabel, C. and J. Zeitlin. 'Historical Alternatives to Mass Production: Politics, Markets and Technology in Nineteenth Century Industrialization', *Past and Present*, CVIII, (1985), 133–76
Saha, P. *History of the Working Class Movement in Bengal*. New Delhi, 1978
Samant, D.R. and M.A. Mulky. *Organisation and Finance of Industries in India*. Bombay, 1937
Sandberg, L.G. *Lancashire in Decline: A Study in Entrepreneurship, Technology and International Trade*. Columbus, Ohio, 1974
Sandbrook, R. and R. Cohen (eds.). *The Development of an African Working Class: Studies in Class Formation and Action*. London, 1975
Sandilands, Dr J. 'The Health of the Bombay Worker', *Labour Gazette*, I, 2 (October 1921), 14–16
Santos, M. *The Shared Space: The Two Circuits of the Urban Economy in Developing Countries*. London, 1979
Sarkar, S. 'The Logic of Gandhian Nationalism: Civil Disobedience and the Gandhi–Irwin Pact (1930–31)', *Indian Historical Review*, III, 1, 1976, 114–46
Modern India, 1885–1947. Delhi, 1983
Saul, S.B. *Studies in British Overseas Trade 1870–1914*. Liverpool, 1960
Saxonhouse, G. and G. Wright. 'Rings and Mules Around the World: A Comparative Study in Technological Choice', *Research in Economic History*, supplement 3 (1984), *Technique, Spirit and Form in the Making of the Modern Economies: Essays in Honor of William N. Parker*, edited by G. Saxonhouse and G. Wright, Greenwich, Conn., 1984, pp. 271–300

Schloss, D. *Methods of Industrial Remuneration*. London, 1892
Scott, J.C. *Weapons of the Weak: Everyday Forms of Peasant Resistance*. New Haven, 1985
'Everyday Forms of Peasant Resistance', in J.C. Scott and B.J.T. Kerkvliet (eds.), *Everyday Forms of Peasant Resistance in South-East Asia*. London, 1986
Seal, A. *The Emergence of Indian Nationalism: Competition and Collaboration in the Later Nineteenth Century*. Cambridge, 1968
Sedgwick, L.S. 'The Composition of Bombay City Population in Relation to Birth Place', *Labour Gazette*, I, 7 (March 1922), 15–19
Sen, S.K. *The House of Tata 1839–1939*. Calcutta, 1975
Sewell, W.H., Jr. *Work and Revolution in France: The Language of Labour from the Old Regime to 1848*. Cambridge, 1980
Shah, A.M. 'The Political System of Gujarat', *Enquiry*, N.S., I, 1 (1964), 83–95
Shah, K.T. and G.J. Bahadurji. *Constitution, Functions and Finance of Indian Municipalities*. Bombay, 1925
Sheppard, S.T. *Bombay Place Names and Street Names: An Excursion into the By-Ways of the History of Bombay City*. Bombay, 1917
Shiva Rao, B. *The Industrial Worker in India*, London, 1939
Shukla, J.B. *Life and Labour in a South Gujarat Village*. Calcutta, 1937
Siddiqi, A. 'The Business World of Jamsetjee Jejeebhoy', *IESHR*, XIX, 3 and 4 (1982), 301–24
Silberrad, C.A. *A Monograph on Cotton Fabrics Produced in the North Western Provinces and Oudh*. Allahabad, 1898
Simmons, C.P. 'Recruiting and Organizing an Industrial Labour Force in Colonial India: The Case of the Coal Mining Industry, *c*. 1880–1939', *IESHR*, XIII, 4 (1976), 455–85
Simmons, C.P., H. Clay and R. Kirk, 'Machine Manufacture in a Colonial Economy: The Pioneering Role of George Hattersley in India, 1919–1943', *IESHR*, XX, 3 (1983), 277–315
Sivasubramoniam, S. 'Income from the Secondary Sector in India 1900–1947', *IESHR*, XIV, 4 (1977), 427–92
Smith, T.C. 'Peasant Time and Factory Time in Japan', *Past and Present*, CXI, (1987), 165–97
Spear, T.G.P. *The Nabobs: A Study in the Social Life of the English in Eighteenth Century India*. Oxford, 1963
Spodek, H. 'Studying the History of Urbanization in India', *Journal of Urban History*, VI, 3 (1980), 251–95
Staples, A.C. 'Indian Maritime Transport in 1840', *IESHR*, VII, 1 (1970), 61–90
Stedman Jones, G. *Outcast London: A Study in the Relationship Between Classes in Victorian Society*. Oxford, 1971
'From Historical Sociology to Theoretical History', *British Journal of Sociology*, XXVII, 3 (1976), 295–306
Languages of Class: Studies in English Working Class History, 1832–1982. Cambridge, 1983
Stichter, S. *Migrant Labour in Kenya: Capitalism and African Response, 1895–1975*. London, 1982
Stokes, E. *The English Utilitarians and India*. Cambridge, 1965
'Dynamism and Enervation in North Indian Agriculture: The Historical Dimension',

in E. Stokes, *The Peasant and the Raj: Studies in Agrarian Society and Peasant Rebellion in Colonial India*, Cambridge, 1978, pp. 228–42

'Privileged Land Tenure in Village India in the Early Nineteenth Century', in E. Stokes, *The Peasant and the Raj: Studies in Agrarian Society and Peasant Rebellion in Colonial India*. Cambridge, 1978, pp. 46–62

'The Return of the Peasant to South Asian History', in E. Stokes, *The Peasant and the Raj: Studies in Agrarian Society and Peasant Rebellion in Colonial India*. Cambridge, 1978, pp. 265–89

'The Structure of Landholding in Uttar Pradesh', in E. Stokes, *The Peasant and the Raj: Studies in Agrarian Society and Peasant Rebellion in Colonial India*. Cambridge, 1978, pp. 205–27

Subramaniam, L. 'Bombay and the West Coast in the 1740s', *IESHR*, XVIII, 2 (1981), 189–216

'Capital and Crowd in a Declining Asian Port City: The Anglo-Bania Order and the Surat Riots of 1795', *MAS*, XIX, 2 (1985), 205–37

'Banias and the British: The Role of Indigenous Credit in the Process of Imperial Expansion in Western India in the Second Half of the Eighteenth Century', *MAS*, XXI, 3 (1987), 473–510

Sullivan, R.J.F. *One Hundred Years of Bombay: History of the Bombay Chamber of Commerce*. Bombay, 1937

Taira, K. *Economic Development and the Labour Market in Japan*. New York, 1970

'Factory Labour and the Industrial Revolution in Japan', in P. Mathias and M.M. Postans (eds.), *The Cambridge Economic History of Europe*, vol. VII, *The Industrial Economies: Capital, Labour and Enterprise*. Part 2. Cambridge, 1978, pp. 134–214

Takamura, N. 'The Cotton Spinning Industry in Japan during the Pre-World War I Period: Its Growth and Essential Conditions', *Zeitschrift für Unternehmensgeschichte*, Beih. 22, (1982), 207–30

Talcherkar, H.A. 'Raghu: The Model Millhand. A Sketch', *Indian Social Reformer*, VII March 1908

Thacker's Directory of the Chief Industries of India, Burma and Ceylon. 1926 n.d., n.p.

Thomas, P.J. 'India in the World Depression', *Economic Journal*, XLV, (1935), 469–83

Thorner, Alice and Daniel. *Land and Labour in India*. London, 1962

Tinker, H. *A New System of Slavery: The Export of Indian Labour Overseas 1830–1920*. London, 1974

Tomlinson, B.R. 'India and the British Empire, 1880–1935', *IESHR*, XII, 4 (1975), 339–80

The Indian National Congress and the Raj 1929–1942: The Penultimate Phase. London, 1977

'Britain and the Indian Currency Crisis, 1930–32', *EcHR*, 2nd series, XXXII, 1 (1979), 88–99

The Political Economy of the Raj: The Economics of Decolonization in India, London, 1979

Tomlinson, J.D. 'The First World War and British Cotton Piece Exports to India', *EcHR*, 2nd series, XXXII, 4 (1979), 494–506

Torri, M. 'In the Deep Blue Sea: Surat and the Merchant Class during the Dyarchic Era, 1759–1800', *IESHR*, XIX, 3 & 4 (1982), 267–99

'Surat During the Second Half of the Eighteenth Century: What Kind of Social Order? – A Rejoinder to Lakshmi Subramaniam', *MAS*, XXI, 4 (1987), 679–710

Tsurimi, E.P. 'Female Textile Workers and the Failure of Early Trade Unionsm in Japan', *History Workshop Journal*, XVIII (Autumn 1984), 3–27

Twomey, M. 'Employment in Nineteenth Century Indian Textiles', *Explorations in Economic History* 20, 1 (1983), 37–57

Van Onselen, C. *Chibaro: African Mine Labour in Southern Rhodesia*. London, 1976

Venkatasubbiah, H. *The Foreign Trade of India, 1900–1940: A Statistical Analysis*. New Delhi, 1946

Vicziany, A.M. 'The De-Industrialization of India in the Nineteenth Century: A Methodological Critique of Amiya Kumar Bagchi', *IESHR*, XVI, 2 (1979), 105–46

'Bombay Merchants and Structural Changes in the Export Community, 1850 to 1880', in K.N. Chaudhuri and C.J. Dewey (eds.), *Economy and Society: Essays in Indian Economic and Social History*. Delhi, 1976, pp. 163–96

Wacha, D.E. *The Life and Life Work of J. N. Tata*. Madras, 1915

Wadia, P.A. and G.N. Joshi. *Money and the Money Market in India*. London, 1926

Wadia, R.A. *The Bombay Dockyard and the Wadia Master Builders*. Bombay, 1955

Scions of Lowjee Wadia. Bombay, 1964

Walter, W. *History of the Culture and Manufacture of Cotton in Dharwar District*. London, 1877

Washbrook, D.A. 'Country Politics: Madras, 1870–1930', in J. Gallagher, G. Johnson and A. Seal (eds.), *Locality, Province and Nation: Essays on Imperialism and Nationalism in India, 1870–1940*. Cambridge, 1973

The Emergence of Provincial Politics: The Madras Presidency, 1880–1920. Cambridge, 1976

'Law, State and Agrarian Society in Colonial India', *Modern Asian Studies*, XV, 3 (1981), Special Issue, *Profit, Power and Politics: Essays on Imperialism, Nationalism and Change in Twentieth Century India*, edited by C. Baker, G. Johnson and A. Seal, pp. 649–721

'Progress and Problems: South Asian Economic and Social History, 1720–1860', *MAS*, XXI, 1 (1988), 57–96

White, D.L. 'Parsis in the Commercial World of Western India, 1700–1750', *IESHR*, XXIV, 2 (1987), 183–203

Yang, Anand A. 'Peasants on the Move: a Study of Internal Migration in India', *Journal of Interdisciplinary History*, X, 1 (Summer 1979), 37–58

Zachariah, K.C. *A Historical Study of Internal Migration in the Indian Sub-Continent*. New York, 1964

Migrants in Greater Bombay. Bombay, 1968

Zeitlin, J. 'From Labour History to the History of Industrial Relations', *EcHR*, 2nd series, XL, 2 (1987), 159–84

Zelliot, E. 'Learning the Use of Political Means: The Mahars of Maharashtra', in R. Kothari (ed.), *Caste in Indian Politics*. Delhi, 1970, pp. 26–69

'Congress and the Untouchables', in R. Sisson and S. Wolpert (eds.), *Congress and Indian Nationalism. The Pre-Independence Phase*. Berkeley and Los Angeles, 1988, pp. 182–97

UNPUBLISHED DISSERTATIONS

Krishnaswamy, S. 'A Riot in Bombay, 11 August 1893: A Study in Hindu – Muslim Relations in Western India During the Late Nineteenth Century', Ph.D. thesis. University of Chicago, 1966

Mishra, S.C. 'Patterns of Long Run Agrarian Change in Bombay and Punjab 1881–1972', PhD thesis, University of Cambridge, 1981

Newman, R. 'Bombay and the China Trade', Seminar paper. Centre of South Asian Studies, Cambridge, 1987

Newman, R.K. 'Labour Organization in the Bombay Cotton Mills, 1918–1929', DPhil thesis, University of Sussex, 1970

Pradhan, G.R. 'The Untouchable Workers of Bombay City', MA thesis, University of Bombay, 1936

Prakash, S. 'The Evolution of the Agrarian Economy in Gujarat (India), 1850–1930', PhD thesis, University of Cambridge, 1983

Shah, M.M. 'Labour Recruitment and Turnover in the Textile Industry of Bombay Presidency', PhD thesis, University of Bombay, 1941

Vicziany, A.M. 'The Cotton Trade and the Commercial Development of Bombay, 1853–1875' PhD thesis, University of London, 1975

Index

458

Hanuman Vyayam Shalla 216
Hari, Dagdoo 164, 306
Harijans, in the cotton-textile industry 220–2,
    428
hawkers 92–3, 192
Hindi language 33
Hindu vania merchants 56–7
Hindu–Muslim riots 174, 186–7, 212–13, 217,
    218, 399, 421, 422, 423, 425
Hindus
    in Bombay 31
    and communal conflicts 423
    in the cotton mills 221, 325–6
    and Muslims 32
    occupations 224
    railway workers 103, 104
    weavers 226–7
Home Rule Leagues 414, 416
housing, see also chawls; rents
    in Bombay 36, 43–4, 170–1, 175–88
    demolition of 44
    huts 36
    overcrowding 170, 178–9, 180, 187
Hunter, Sir William 27

illegitimate births 196
Indian Factory Labour Commission 125
Indian Industrial Commission 178
Indian National Congress 412–18, 419–21,
    429, 430
    and Keshav Dada Borkar 207–8, 209–11
Indo–Japanese Trade Agreement 264, 268
industrial development, in India 11–12
industrial disputes see strikes
Industrial Disputes Committee 182, 354
industrial economy 3–4
    in Bombay 4–6
infant mortality 196
intermediate goods industries 87
Ismaili communities 56
itinerant traders 92–3

Jains
    bankers 56–7
    in Bombay 32
    in the cotton-textile industry 221
Japan, trade with 44
Japanese textile industry 243, 247, 248, 254,
    255, 256, 262, 263, 264, 268, 271, 272,
    294–5, 335
    and technological progress 341, 342, 344
Jardine and Mathieson 58, 60–1
jatis 220, 223, 228, 233
Jejeebhoy, Byramjee 244
Jejeebhoy, Jamsetjee 57, 58, 60–1
Jewish traders 61–2

Jews
    in Bombay 31, 32, 223
    in the cotton-textile industry 221
    occupations 224–5
Jhabvala, S.H. 213, 406
Jiwanji, Bhai 175
jobbers 10, 12, 93, 148, 190, 237, 238, 297,
    see also foremen
    and the badli control scheme 156, 157
    and casual labour 108, 109, 171, 230, 297,
        301
    in the cotton mills 101, 278, 283, 295–307,
        315, 333;
        fancy 298–9;
        line 298–9;
        sanctions against workers 403–4;
        and standardization 352, 355;
        and weavers 299–301, 382–3
    and dadas 201, 203, 204
    and factory discipline 296–7, 330
    gangs 10, 198, 299
    and labour supply 112, 121, 199
    as landlords 182, 185, 186
    and mill managers/supervisors 302–5
    as money-lenders 192
    and neighbourhood organization 101, 171,
        173, 174, 195–200, 218
    and the recruitment of labour 100–2, 104,
        105, 107–9, 122, 220, 232, 296, 297–
        8, 306
    and strikes 105, 297–8, 332, 363
Joglekar, K.N. 205
Joint Mill Strike Committee 350, 355, 357,
    361, 364
Joshi, Jinabhai 197
Joshi, N.M. 83, 361, 406
Joshi, V.H. 202
Julaha Muslims 230–1, 320

Kamgar Hitwardhak Sabha 180, 236, 427
Kandalkar, G.L. 299, 428
Karnik, V.B. 202, 216–17, 218, 404
Karve, Irawati 228
Kasle, G.R. 428
Kay, Sir Joseph 265, 351, 359, 382, 390
khanavalis (boarding houses) 182–3, 186,
    196, 218, 229–30
Khandesh, money-lending 54
Khatau, Dharamsey 287, 346–7, 373
Khoja traders 56, 57, 58, 61–2
khoti landlords, in Ratnagiri 133–9
Khoti Settlement Act (1904) 53
kinship 10, 11, see also families
    and Gujarati migrants 145
    and the jobber 108
    and the labour market 122, 123, 306

Cambridge South Asian Studies

These monographs are published by the Syndics of Cambridge University Press in association with the Cambridge University Centre for South Asian Studies. The following books have been published in this series:

Cambridge South Asian Studies

Printed in the United States
23938LVS00003B/30

9 780521 525954